TRAVEL GEOGRAPHY HANDBOOK

TRAVEL
GEOGRAPHY
HANDBOOK

QUENTIN GILLARD, Ph.D.
President, TravelSearch, Bend, Oregon

VNR TOURISM AND COMMERCIAL RECREATION SERIES

VNR VAN NOSTRAND REINHOLD
New York

Copyright © 1991 by Van Nostrand Reinhold

Library of Congress Catalog Card Number 90-12483
ISBN 0-442-00158-4

Printed in the United States of America

Van Nostrand Reinhold
115 Fifth Avenue
New York, New York 10003

Chapman and Hall
2-6 Boundary Row
London, SE 1 8HN, England

Thomas Nelson Australia
102 Dodds Street
South Melbourne 3205, Victoria, Australia

Nelson Canada
1120 Birchmount Road
Scarborough, Ontario M1K 5G4, Canada

16 15 14 13 12 11 10 9 8 7 6 5 4 3 2 1

Library of Congress Cataloging-in-Publication Data

Gillard, Quentin, 1947-
    Travel geography handbook / Quentin Gillard.
       p.   cm. — (VNR tourism and commercial recreation series)
    ISBN 0-442-00158-4
    1. Tourist trade. 2. Geography. 3. Travel. I. Title.
II. Series.
G155.A1G48   1990   90-12483
910'.3 — dc20   CIP

**This book is dedicated to
Linda, Lauren, Tyson, Ruth, Gwyn, Hazel, and Helen.**

Contents

Foreword

Geographic literacy is now emerging as a national priority for formal education. The appalling level of misunderstanding and ignorance of the world's geograpic features has been cited in recent test results for elementary, secondary and college students, particularly in the U.S. and more recently in the U.S.S.R.

One would expect that travel professionals would be at the vanguard of world geographic literacy. Unfortunately, this is not the case. Recent studies of tourism students and travel professionals have cited basic deficits in geographic awareness and a lack of vital travel destination information. It is encouraging to find that the American Society of Travel Agents and the National Tour Foundation are now establishing cooperative programs with the National Geographic Society and other concerned groups to remedy this situation.

Tourism involves an interraction between people of two unique places. People travel from one region with distinctive characteristics to another region with another set of distinctive characteristics. This book provides basic geographic knowledge of tourist destinations and their accessibility. It places appropriate emphasis on the cultural dimensions of geography, which is essential to a travel professional's understanding of the complex interractions between the world's physical features and the human elements of our common environment.

The search for current information on geographic characteristics and destination features relevant to tourism is a never-ending process. The chapter on information sources provides a comprehensive listing of important resources, with explanatory notes and annotations.

Finally, this book includes current information on specific destinations by region of the world. The information presented is essential to travel specialists who assist tourists in making intelligent decisions of where and when to travel to a particular destination and identifying how to get there and what to do after arrival. This is the type of information now provided to travel agents and tour operators by TravelSearch in Bend, Oregon, a destination information service published by the author.

It is appropriate and fitting that one of the first books in the travel and tourism series focuses on the geography of tourism. This text should contribute to improving geographic and tourism destination knowledge and literacy levels for students and professionals, enabling them to serve as counselors and mentors for travelers seeking knowledge of the world through travel.

Donald E. Hawkins
Professor of Travel and Tourism
The George Washington University
Washington, D.C.

General Editor
Tourism and Commercial Recreation Series
Van Nostrand Reinhold

Preface

This book is intended to provide a basic geographical background to the study of travel destinations for the reader who has no special training in geography and who is starting out on a career as a travel agent-destination consultant. It can also be profitably used by professionals already in the travel industry who want to brush up on their knowledge of basic geography and/or destinations in a particular country or part of the world with which they are not familiar.

Chapter 1 covers some real basics or fundamentals of planet earth and its physical features. Chapter 2 covers the essentials for understanding and appreciating climate and weather, two crucial influences on travel and tourism. Chapter 3 provides a brief overview of the cultural geography of the world, so that you can better understand and appreciate differences in human characteristics and the human condition. Chapter 4 presents the principal tourist destinations of the world, by continent or region (in the case of the Caribbean Islands) and by country. Chapter 5 highlights the characteristics and attractions of individual cities or resorts around the world, ordered by continent-region and country or island. Lastly, a resources section includes the many sources of destination information that are available to the travel agent-destination consultant.

The information presented in this handbook, particularly the all-too-brief coverage of basic physical and cultural geography and the destination highlights, is not intended to replace or compete with the many travel information sources, such as travel books/guides, travel magazines, good Sunday newspaper supplements, trade publications, newsletters, and even good geography texts or magazines referred to in the appendix. The good travel agent-destination consultant will have to stay on top of them all to be an effective professional. Nor is it intended to be a substitute for actual first-hand travel experience, the best teacher of all.

The information is, however, intended to introduce you to the fascinating variety of travel destinations and will, it is hoped, whet your appetite for more information and encourage you to do more reading, to discuss and argue the merits and demerits of different destinations among friends and fellow travel professionals, and to visit as many places as you can. You will gain, professionally and personally, and your clients will definitely be able to tell the difference and will come back for more advice.

Acknowledgments

For my early academic training, I would like to thank Brian Greenwood, John Cole, Ronald Beazley, and Brian Berry—all of whom instilled in me a profound respect for learning and a love of geography. To all of the loyal travel agents who have supported TravelSearch and offered many valuable suggestions, I would like to say thanks. All of the research for TravelSearch's destination sheets made the city/resort details in this book possible. Lastly, I would like to thank my wife, Linda, for her continual support and sage counsel and, not least, for drawing the country maps in this book. All of the above have enabled me to pursue two passions: travel and geography. Finally, I would like to express my appreciation to Pamela Chirls and the staff at Van Nostrand Reinhold and Barbara Russiello of Spectrum Publisher Services for their fine editing.

Physical Geography

Planet Earth

Earth, our home, is the third planet, 93 million miles from the sun. It is traveling through space at 18.5 miles per second, on an annual 584-million-mile trip around the sun. About 4.5 billion years old, some 24,901 miles in circumference, and with a surface area of roughly 197 million square miles, earth is a small planet—less than one-millionth the size of our sun, which itself is a relatively small star among others in the universe. Earth is made effectively smaller still by the fact that the oceans comprise 71 percent of the surface area, or 140 million square miles, and land only 29 percent, or 57 million square miles. As we shall see later on, even these 57 million square miles (about 7 acres for every man, woman, and child alive today), are not all available for our habitation or exploitation.

As we said, the earth is hurtling through space at 18.5 miles a second. At the same time, the whole solar system travels at some 170 miles a second within the Milky Way Galaxy, of which it is a part, and the Milky Way itself zips along in an empty vastness. Earth's orbit around the sun takes 365 days, 6 hours, 9 minutes, and 10 seconds. Once a day (every 23 hours, 56 minutes, and 4 seconds) it turns on its own axis.

Our Spherical Earth

Earth is not, in fact, a perfect sphere, rather it is an ellipsoid, flattened at the poles and with a lopsided bulge below the equator (the earth's diameter is 26 miles larger through its bulge at the equator than through the poles). This fact complicates accurate mapping in many cases but is really of concern only to cartographers, not to us.

The earth spins like a top on an axis, eastward at the equator, or counterclockwise at the north pole. One earth-turn, or rotation, with respect to the sun defines the solar day, to which we have arbitrarily assigned a value of 24 hours. The axis of spin determines the north pole and south pole, which are fixed points of reference.

Locations on this spherical form can be determined with reference to a geographic grid of meridians and parallels. Meridians are imaginary half-circles around the earth that pass through a given location and terminate at the north and south poles. Parallels are imaginary lines on the earth that are parallel to the equator and pass through all places the same distance to the north or south of it. Figure 1.

Coordinate positions on the meridian-parallel grid are measured in terms of longitude and latitude. The longitude of a place is its distance east or west from a prime meridian, usually the one that passes through the old location of the Royal Observatory at Greenwich, England (near London), measured in degrees. The longitude of any given point on the globe is measured eastward or westward from this meridian, whichever is the shorter arc. Longitude may thus range from 0 degrees to 180 degrees, either east or west.

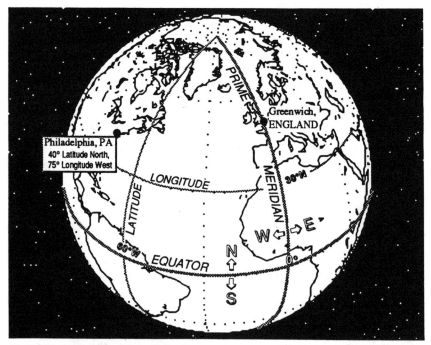

Figure 1. *Latitude and Longitude.*

The latitude of a place is its distance north or south of the equator. Latitude is measured in degrees of arc from the equator (0 degrees) toward either pole, where the value reaches 90 degrees. All points north of the equator (in the northern hemisphere) are designated as north latitude; all points south of the equator (in the southern hemisphere) are designated as south latitude. The location of Philadelphia, PA, thus is approximately 40 degrees north latitude and 75 degrees west longitude (Figure 1).

It is important to remember that statements of latitude and longitude tell nothing about distance in miles, although rough conversions can be made. One degree of latitude is approximately 69 miles (111 km) of surface distance north-south (Table 1). For example, New York at approximately 41 degrees north, and Lima at approximately 12 degrees south along the 75th meridian, are roughly 3,657 miles apart (41 + 12 = 53 × 69 = 3,657).

East-west distances cannot be converted so readily, because of the convergence of meridians poleward (see Figure 1). At the equator, a degree of longitude is 69 miles, but at 60 degrees north (or south), a degree of longitude is only about 35 miles (56 km), as is seen in Table 1. Thus, New York, at 41 degrees north and 74 degrees west is about 2,650 miles from Eureka, California, which is located at 41 degrees north and 124 degrees west. (124 − 74 × 53 = 2,650).

Meridians have another function: They help to determine what time it is around the globe.

Global Time

Besides generating the geographic grid, the rotation of a spherical earth has a cultural impact through the phenomenon of global time. Where the sun's rays strike the earth most directly, solar noon is occurring. A single meridian, called the *noon meridian,* marks the north-south line on which it is noon, and sweeps westward around the globe, always staying directly beneath the sun. Directly

Table 1. LENGTHS OF DEGREES

Of the Meridian		Of the Parallel	
Latitude	Statute Miles	Latitude	Statute Miles
0	68.703	0	69.172
10	68.722	10	68.129
20	68.781	20	65.026
30	68.873	30	59.956
40	68.986	40	53.063
50	69.108	50	44.552
60	69.224	60	34.674
70	69.320	70	23.729
80	69.383	80	12.051
90	69.407	90	0.0

opposite on the globe is an imaginary midnight meridian, also sweeping westward, and maintaining a separation of 180 degrees of longitude from the noon meridian. The noon meridian separates the morning from the afternoon of the same calendar day, and the midnight meridian is the dividing line between one calendar day and the next.

Because the noon meridian sweeps over 360 degrees of longitude every 24 hours, it covers 15 degrees of longitude every hour. This forms the basis for all calculations concerning time belts of the globe. Global standard time is based on standard meridians spaced 15 degrees apart around the globe. With reference to the Greenwich meridian, which is the world standard for reckoning time, twelve time zones lie in the eastern hemisphere, and twelve in the western hemisphere. The twelfth zone is shared by the two hemispheres. That half of the zone lying on the Asiatic side of the 180th meridian is exactly one full calendar day later than, or behind, the half on the American side. For this reason, the 180th meridian defines the position of the International Date Line (check a good atlas or globe).

The major cities on the east coast of the United States are all fairly close to the 75-degree-west meridian, and they are all in the Eastern Standard Time zone. Since meridians are located 15 degrees apart, the Eastern Standard Time zone straddling the 75th meridian is 5 hours (75 divided by 15) behind Greenwich, London. Or there is 5 hours "difference" between London and New York City. Thus, a 5-hour flight departing New York at noon EST, will arrive in London at 10 P.M. Greenwich Mean Time (GMT). Just to make sure that you understand this sometimes confusing concept: What time will a 5-hour flight leaving London at noon GMT arrive in New York?

Notice that along meridians there are no time differences. Thus, travelers flying from New York City to Lima, Peru, will not have to reset their watches because both places are in the same time zone. Check a good globe. Many people do not realize that almost all of South America lies southeast of North America and not due south.

The United States encompasses six time zones (Eastern, Central, Mountain, Pacific, Alaska-Hawaii, Bering). While the Soviet Union, for example, encompasses eleven time zones—the most of any country—some time zones have several different countries within them. Indeed, many countries can be flown over in a matter of minutes. We shall explore the comparative sizes of countries later.

Note that the time zones are not equally distributed on both sides of the standard meridians (check a good atlas or globe). Frequently, natural physiographic boundaries have been used to demarcate time zones, or political boundaries may be used so that all locations under the same political jurisdiction share the same time zone—the most extreme case being China (about the same size as the United States) where the entire country is on Beijing time! The sun, of course, does not recognize such accomodations, and the sun sets one hour later for every 15 degrees of longitude no matter what arbitrary time zone we have demarcated.

A complication in calculating time difference between places on the globe occurs when one place adopts the *daylight saving time* adjusted time system during the summer, and another place does not, or does but over a different time period. Such nuances are important not only in determining local arrival and departure times, but also in determining appropriate times for placing international phone calls, calculating the times of connecting flights, or the probabilities of being on time for a meeting, and so on. Travelers crossing several time zones can experience "jet lag."

Map Projections

As mentioned earlier, most maps tend to distort reality in some respect or another. That is why the use of a good globe is highly recommended. Clearly, when a three-dimensional sphere is represented as a two-dimensional map, there must be some surface distortion to make it fit. The systems or ways of showing the earth on a map are called projections.

The four basic aspects of the earth's surface that cartographers try to represent are: distance, direction, shape, and area. One map, or projection, can never show all these aspects correctly at the same time. Different projections are suited to different purposes, depending on which feature or characteristic is most important for the purpose at hand. Check a good atlas for examples of the following projections.

Projections Showing True Direction

Projections showing true direction are clearly superior for navigational purposes, where the shortest possible air route between two points is needed. One such projection is the gnomonic projection. On this, any great circle on the globe is shown as a straight line on the map (a great circle is any circle that cuts the globe into two equal parts). Notice that somebody flying from New York to Moscow would actually fly over Labrador, Iceland, and Scandinavia, rather than farther south over the North Atlantic and the British Isles as might be inferred from looking at a Mercator, or even Mollweide, projection map. Similarly a flight from Seattle to Athens would cross over Canada, Baffin Island, Greenland, Scandinavia, and eastern Europe, rather than across the United States, the Atlantic, and Spain, as the rhumb line would depict. However, areal exaggeration, especially toward the edges of the map, is a problem.

Projections Showing Correct Shape

Although no projection shows shapes correctly over large areas, nearly correct shapes of small areas can be shown on conformal projections, a good example of which is the Mercator projection. On a Mercator projection, both parallels and meridians are straight lines, crossing at right angles. Thus directions can be easily plotted and read. The Mercator is a good projection for depicting winds and ocean currents or time zones. However, since the meridians do not converge at the poles (as they do on a globe) and the parallels of latitude are spaced further and further apart toward the poles, this grid causes increasing distortion of size moving poleward from the equator. Land areas near the poles look much larger than they really are. For example, Greenland looks about the same size as South America, yet in reality it is only about a tenth as large. Similarly, Great Britain looks about the same size as Madacascar, but is only about a third as large.

Projections Showing Equality of Area

Equal-area projections are good for depicting information on the distribution on the earth of such things as population, rainfall, languages, religions, agricultural practices, and types of vegetation.

The Mollweide projection is a good example of an equal-area projection. While the area of one part of the earth is in correct proportion to the area of another part of the earth, shapes are distorted, particularly toward the edges of the map. The homolosine projection is another equal-area projection, but in order to minimize the distortion in the shape of the continents, maps using this projection cut, or interrupt, the picture of the earth in the ocean areas.

The point to remember is that every map projection has its strengths and weaknesses, and that each can generate misconceptions. Just be sure which one you are using before making inferences about distance, shape, or area.

Distances

We have already mentioned that the circumference of the globe is approximately 24,900 miles around, and that the earth covers some 197 million square miles, the land area of which covers some 57 million square miles, or nearly 16 times the size of the United States.

Although small in planetary terms, earth is still a large place. From New York to Athens is 4,920 miles; New York to Tokyo is 6,740 miles via the great circle; New York to Vladivostock is 6,420 miles. In practise, of course, it is rarely feasible to travel directly between two places on the earth's surface. Flights by air rarely go directly along the shortest (great circle) route from airport to airport. They tend to fly in "straight" sections from one control point to another, and there are usually very different courses over which it is possible to travel on a scheduled flight between two places.

Time Distance

Of interest, too, is the fact that time distance may be a more useful measure of distance between a pair of places than space distance. For the client who only has a four-day weekend, or furlough, for his or her vacation, accessibility in terms of elapsed time may be much more critical than actual distance. For example, due to the nature of airline hubs and airline schedules, Puerto Rico is more accessible than the Turks and Caicos, and Honolulu is more accessible than Hilo, even though the Turks and Caicos and Hilo are closer to the continental United States.

Cost Distance

Moreover, cost distance may be an even better reflection of accessibility. Los Angeles is much more accessible from New York, in these terms, than is Kansas City, even though Kansas City is only half as far away. Similarly, London, Frankfurt, and Amsterdam are much more accessible from New York than are Lisbon, Madrid, and Dublin, largely as a function of traffic volume and competition, which help keep air fares lower.

Cultural Distance

Social, economic, ideological, and cultural distances also may play a role in a client's decisions. England and Ireland are much closer to North Americans (WASPs at least), than Mexico, Venezuela, or even Quebec. Such distances may be incorrectly perceived, but they reflect a kind of proximity that should not be ignored in counseling clients.

Physical Features of the Earth

Ranging from 29,028 ft. above sea level (Mt. Everest), to 1,286 ft. below (the Dead Sea), the land area of our planet is incredibly diverse. Encompassing impressive, rugged mountain ranges like the Himalayas, the Andes, and older, more subdued mountains like the Appalachians; vast plains like the pampas of Argentina, the Russian steppes, the African veldt, and the Canadian prairies; and low lying areas like the polders of the Netherlands, and the Gulf coastal plain of North America, earth's topographical variety is astonishing.

From the dry Sahara and Gobi deserts of Africa and Asia, to the lush tropical Amazon and Congo basins of South America and Africa; from the huge, frigid subarctic and arctic wastelands of northern Canada and Siberia, to the hot, dry Sonoran desert of the southwestern United States and the Australian interior, the climatic variation is equally impressive.

As we shall see, this tremendous variation plays a significant role in tourism. Those places that are blessed with spectacular natural attractions, both in physical scenery (Grand Teton National Park, the Alps), and in natural biotic attractions (the Everglades, the Amazon), are sought out by the traveler.

Oceans and Continents

Oceans cover 71 percent of the world's area, or some 139 million square miles (38 times the size of the United States). The *Pacific Ocean* alone covers one third of the planet (63.8 million square miles), more than all the continents combined (Figure 2). Although dotted with islands (the Polynesian group between Hawaii, New Zealand, and Easter Island; the Micronesian group to the west and north of the equator; and the Melanesian group NE of Australia), the Pacific Ocean is vast and distances large. From Los Angeles to Sydney, Australia, is approximately

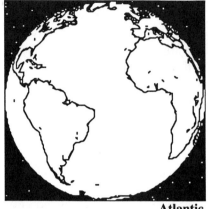
Atlantic

Pacific

Arctic

Antarctic

Indian

Figure 2. *Comparative Sizes of the World's Oceans.*

7,644 miles, or a third of the way around the globe. The major islands of the Pacific include the Bismarck Archipelago (New Britain, New Ireland) and the Solomon Islands, New Caledonia, Guam, Samoa, Fiji, Tahiti, the Hawaiian Islands, and New Zealand.

The *Atlantic Ocean,* about half the size of the Pacific, is still large (31.8 million square miles). It is 3,154 nautical miles from New York to Southampton, while its length stretches from the Arctic Ocean southward to Antarctica. Unlike the Pacific, however, it does not have large numbers of islands dotting its surface (Figure 2).

The principal islands in the North Atlantic are Greenland, Iceland, the British Isles, the Azores, and the Canary Islands. In the South Atlantic they are Acension, St. Helena, the Tristan da Cunha group, and Falklands and South Georgia.

The *Indian Ocean* covers 28 million square miles, a little less than the Atlantic, and stretches some 4,900 miles from Africa to Australia. Its principal islands are Madagascar, off the coast of Mozambique; the Mascarene Islands further east; the Maldive and Laccadive island groups off the SW coast of India; Sri Lanka, off the SE tip of India; the Seychelles north of Madagascar; the Chagos Archipelago, further south of the Maldive islands; and the Prince Edward, Crozet, and Kerguelen islands in the southern Indian Ocean (Figure 2).

The *Arctic and Antarctic oceans* were once considered separate oceans, but today most geographers agree that they are really extensions of the Atlantic, Pacific, and Indian oceans (Figure 2).

Apart from the oceans, there are other major bodies of salt water, the *seas,* that are important and you should know their location and something about them. The largest, at over one million square miles, is the *Caribbean,* which is really an extension of the Atlantic Ocean into the North and South American land masses. The second largest sea is the *Mediterranean,* dividing Europe from Africa and covering almost one million square miles (the Aegean and Adriatic seas are considered part of the Mediterranean). It is connected to the *Black Sea* (178,000 square miles). The *Caspian Sea,* although a saltwater body, is really a lake. The third largest sea (875,000 square miles) is the *Bering Sea,* between Alaska and Siberia, north of the Aleutian Islands. Along the eastern Pacific coastline of Asia, from north to south, are the *Sea of Okhotsk,* the *Sea of Japan,* and the *East China Sea* (589, 389, and 482,000 square miles).

The *Andaman Sea* (307,954 square miles), between India and Thailand; the *North Sea* (222,000 square miles), between the United Kingdom and Norway; the *Red Sea* (169,000 square miles), separating Africa from the Arabian Peninsula; and, the *Baltic Sea* (163,000 square miles), between Sweden and Finland and the Soviet Union, round out the major seas. Figure 3.

Because of their relative compactness, the numbers and diversity of the islands that dot their surface, and the cultural richness of the shorelines that surround them, some of these seas—particularly the Caribbean and Mediterranean—have become major cruising grounds.

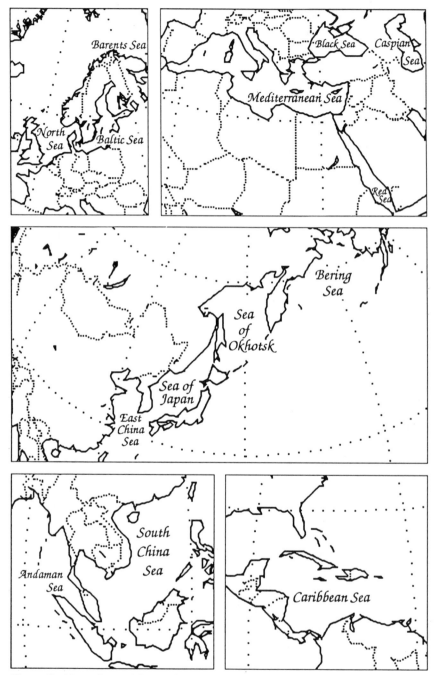

Figure 3. *Major Seas of the World.*

Gulfs and Bays

There are a number of gulfs and bays, which are indentations of shoreline that should be recognized. The main ones are the *Hudson Bay* in the Canadian north, the Gulf of Mexico south of the United States, the *Bay of Bengal* south of East Pakistan, the *Gulf of California* between Baja California and the Mexican mainland, the *Persian Gulf* between Saudi Arabia and Iran, and the *Gulf of Carpentaria* off northern Australia (Figure 4).

The Seven Continents

A continent is understood by geographers to be a sizable landmass that stands more or less separate from other landmasses. The world's seven continents are identified in Figure 5. The largest is *Asia,* covering nearly 17 million square miles, with the Soviet Union, China, and India comprising 80 percent of its total land area. *Africa,* with 11.5 million square miles, is the second largest continent, occupied by some 35-odd countries, the largest of which is the Sudan (967,500 square miles). Algeria and Zambia are both over 900,000 square miles in area.

With an area of 8.4 million square miles, *North America* is the third largest continent, occupied by ten countries, with two (Canada and the United States) each well over 3.5 million square miles in area. At 6.8 million square miles, *South America* is the fourth largest continent, comprised of 13 countries. Brazil and Argentina occupy some 64 percent of its land area. *Antarctica's* 5.5 million square miles makes it the fifth largest continent. Largely uninhabited, and with several countries claiming portions of its land mass, it has only recently figured as a tourist destination.

Europe is the sixth largest continent, at 3.75 million square miles. Although not strictly a separate physical entity, it is a distinctive cultural area, and the convention of including it as a separate continent has persisted for a long time. Other than the western part of the Soviet Union, its countries range in size from France's 213,000 square miles to tiny San Marino with 24 square miles and the Vatican City's 109 acres!

With 2.9 million square miles, *Australia* is the smallest continent. Apart from Antarctica, it is the least populated of the seven continents, and is also comprised of one nation. The comparative sizes of the world's continents, oceans, and seas are shown in Table 2.

A thorough exploration of each continent's principal tourist destinations will be made in later chapters. Here, a brief discussion of the major physiographic regions of each continent will introduce you to their major physical features. The destination consultant should not be in a position of having to scramble when a client states that he or she wants to take a trip to Mt. Cook or wants to see the Victoria Falls.

Therefore you should know not only where the Andes and Himalayas are, but where the Pyrenees, and Blue Mountains are; not only where the Amazon, Rhine, and Nile rivers run, but where the Danube, Thames, and Yangtze run; where the Angel, Yosemite, and Victoria waterfalls are and also where Niagara and Dunn's falls are; where the Great Lakes are, and where Lake Geneva, Lake

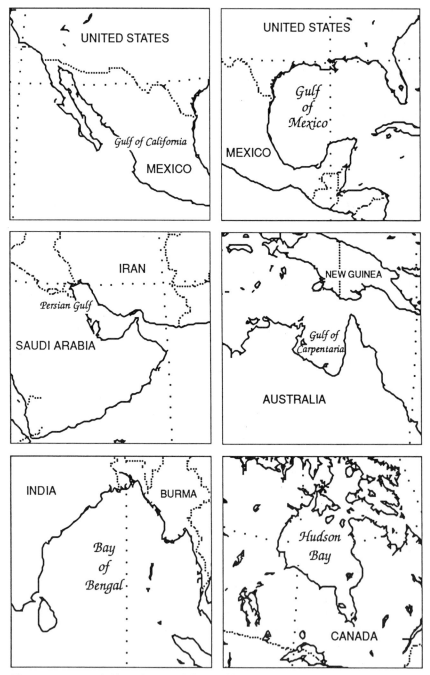

Figure 4. *Major Gulfs and Bays of the World.*

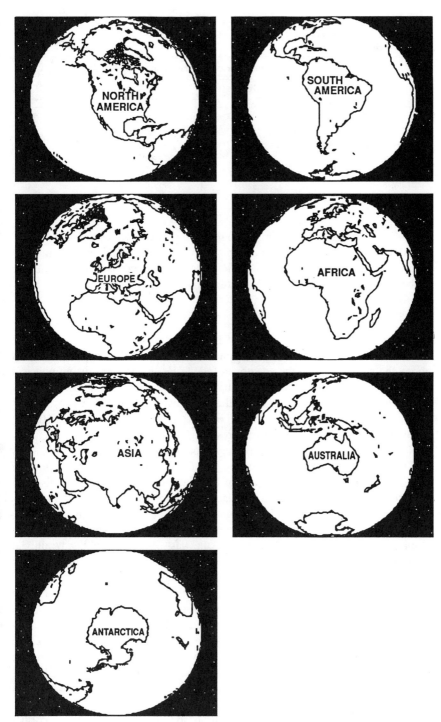

Figure 5. *Comparative Sizes of the World's Continents.*

Table 2. COMPARATIVE SIZES OF THE WORLD'S CONTINENTS, OCEANS, AND SEAS

Continents		Area (millions of square miles) Oceans		Seas	
Asia	16.9	Pacific	63.8	Caribbean	1.06
Africa	11.5	Atlantic	31.8	Mediterranean	.97
N. America	8.4	Indian	28.4	Bering	.88
S. America	6.8			Sea of Okhotsk	.59
Europe	3.8			East China	.48
Australasia	2.9			Hudson Bay	.47
Antarctica	5.5				

Como, and the Lake District are; not only where Mount Everest, Mount Kenya, the Matterhorn, and Mt. Shasta are, but also where Mt. Cook and Mauna Loa are. When reviewing the following brief descriptions do consult a good atlas or globe that highlights the physical features of each continent.

Asia

Covering almost a third of the earth's land area, Asia (Figure 5) stretches some 6,000 miles from the eastern Mediterranean to Korea on the Pacific, from well above the arctic circle to the equator in Indonesia. Its most prominent physical feature is the Himalayan mountain chain, stretching north of the Indian subcontinent from Pakistan through Nepal and Bhutan to China. Between 100 and 200 miles wide, the Himalayas contain over 40 peaks higher than 24,000 ft. and the earth's highest point: Mount Everest, at 29,028 ft.

North of the Himalayas lie the sparsely populated high plateaus and mountains of Tibet, the desert basins of Sinkiang, the Gobi Desert of Mongolia, and the vast, flat permafrost-afflicted plains of Siberia, stretching from the Urals eastward to the mountainous Eastern Highlands. East and northeast of the Himalayas lie the heavily populated river basins and highlands of east China and Manchuria, drained by the Changjiang (Yangtze) and Huang (Yellow) rivers. South of the Himalayas lie the Himalayan foothills, the vast, heavily populated, alluvial plains of the Ganges and Indus rivers, and, further south, the hilly upland area of the Deccan Plateau, which occupies most of central and southern India.

Southeastern Asia is shaped like a fan, with its apex near the eastern end of the Himalayas. From this apex several ranges of rugged mountains stretch out across the mainland of Southeast Asia, the southeast ends of which are partly submerged in the ocean, forming chains of islands. Between the mountain ranges are some of the world's largest rivers: the Irrawaddy in Burma, the Salween, the Chao Phraya in Thailand, the Mekong in Vietnam, and the Hong in China.

The islands of Southeast Asia are arranged in great arcs extending south and east from the mainland. Sumatra, Java, the Celebes, the Philippines, and then Taiwan and Japan. Along the crest of the island arcs are some of the world's most active volcanoes.

West of the Himalayas lies arid, hot southwestern Asia, stretching from the rugged Hindu Kush mountains of Afghanistan to the barren, desolate Empty Quarter of the Arabian Peninsula.

Africa

Second largest of the seven continents, covering over 11.5 million square miles, Africa (Figure 5) is huge, extending some 5,000 miles north to south, and 4,600 miles east to west. Straddling the equator, over 75 percent of its area lies within the tropics, although two thirds of Africa lies north of the equator.

Northern Africa is dominated by the world's largest desert, the vast Sahara, largely comprised of hamadas (rocky plateaus) interrupted by wadis (dry valleys). In contrast to popular opinion, sand dunes (ergs) comprise only some 10 percent of the surface of the Sahara. Stretching from south of Casablanca in Morocco, through northern Algeria, into Tunisia, are the rugged, often snow-capped, Atlas mountains. To the east, the Nile River, the world's longest, pierces through the Sahara desert, bringing life to the Sudan and Egypt.

In western Africa, south of the Sahara, is the Sahel, extending from Senegal into southern Chad. A semiarid plain, it occupies the transition zone between the dry desert and the rolling plains of savanna and grass woodland that extend southward to the Atlantic coast of West Africa, between Liberia and Nigeria, and eastward across the Central African Republic into Uganda, around Lake Victoria. The Zaire (Congo) Basin lies south of the rolling savanna plains; to its east is the East African plateau, dissected by the rift valleys, running north-south and extending northward from Lake Malawi in Mozambique. The western belt runs north of Lake Malawi through Lake Tanganyika and Lake Albert in Uganda; the eastern belt runs north of Lake Malawi, through Tanzania, on across Kenya to Lake Turkana, and on to the Red Sea. This high plateau country is punctuated by isolated volcanic peaks such as Kilimanjaro (19,340 ft.) and Mount Kenya (17,058 ft.).

South of the Zaire Basin lies the Bihe Plateau, which extends eastward to the East African plateau. The Kalahari Basin lies to the south of this and is in turn fringed by the Great Escarpment and highveldt of South Africa.

North America

Extending from the Pacific Ocean in the west to the Atlantic Ocean in the east, and from the Arctic to the Gulf of Mexico, North America (Figure 5), is the third largest continent, covering some 8.4 million square miles, with Canada and the United States covering most of the land area. It is almost 4,000 miles across at its widest point (Alaska to Newfoundland, Canada), and some 5,000 miles from Ellesmere Island, in its far northern reaches above the arctic circle, to the Panama Canal.

The dominant physiographic feature of North America is the Rocky Mountain chain, extending from the Yukon down through Mexico and Central America. Not as tall as the Himalayas, the Rockies nevertheless constitute a formidable backbone of the continent. To the west of the Rockies lie the plateaus and intermountain basins of Utah and Nevada. Along the Pacific coast, the small Pacific Coastal ranges separate the Valley of California from the ocean; inland a line of mountains—including the Sierra Nevada, the Cascades, the Coast Mountains of British Columbia, and the Alaska Range containing the continent's highest point, Mount McKinley (20,320 ft.)—stretches northward from the Mojave Desert.

To the east of the Rocky Mountains are the Great Plains, stretching from Texas northward all the way into Saskatchewan and Alberta. Further east, these plains feed into the interior and coastal plains of the United States, and the Hudson Bay in Canada. Still further east, the interior plains give way to the Appalachian mountains, stretching from Georgia to New England, and the Laurentian Shield plateau of Ontario and Quebec. Lastly, the Atlantic seaboard of the United States is bordered by a coastal plain south of New Jersey.

South America

Extending some 4,600 miles from Punta Gallinas, Colombia, to Cape Horn, Tierra del Fuego, and some 3,200 miles across at its widest, South America (Figure 5) is the fourth largest continent, with some 6.8 million square miles, 64 percent of which is occupied by two countries, Brazil and Argentina. Physiographically it is dominated by the great chain of the Andes (the world's longest and second highest mountain chain), running like a backbone down the western edge of the continent, and occupying almost a quarter of South America. The Andes almost literally drop off into the Pacific Ocean, although there is a narrow coastal strip between the two. East of the Andes, north of Bolivia, lies the vast South American jungle, stretching eastward from eastern Ecuador, Peru, and Colombia to the Atlantic Ocean at the mouth of the Amazon.

North of Amazonia are the Guiana Highlands of eastern Venezuela, Guyana, Surinam, and French Guiana. South of Amazonia lies the Mato Grosso, a high flat savannah, and the wide, endless plains and pampas of Paraguay, Uruguay, and northern Argentina. Further south lies barren, desolate, Patagonia, south of the Rio Colorado. On the continent's eastern side, south of the Amazon in northeast Brazil, is the Brazilian Highlands plateau.

Antarctica

Often described as the most remote, inaccessible, and inhospitable place on earth Antarctica (Figure 5) is the fifth-largest continent, with over 5.5 million square miles. Not "owned" by any nation, the continent basically serves as a scientific research post for the United States, the Soviet Union, Australia, and several other countries. Lying almost entirely within the antarctic cirle, it is indeed a formidable place. With ice covering virtually its entire surface (up to 10,000 ft. thick in places), it holds 90 percent of the world's ice. Its major physiographic feature is the Transantarctica Mountains, between the Ross Ice Shelf and the polar plateau surrounding the South Pole.

Europe

Europe (Figure 5), the second smallest of the seven continents, is not really a continent at all, but rather an extension of the great Eurasian landmass. However, its unique cultural, religious, political, and economic history have combined in perpetuating the convention of treating it as a continent. Covering 3.8 million square miles, it stretches from the Atlantic and Arctic in the west some 2,800 miles to the Ural Mountains and the Caspian Sea in the Soviet Union. Its southern edge is marked by the Mediterranean and Black seas, its northern limits by the Arctic and Barents Sea, some 2,400 miles further north.

Its major physiographic feature is the series of mountains that starts in the Pyrenees, continues through the Alps, and ends in the Carpathian mountains of southern Poland and Romania. South of this interrupted chain lie the Iberian, Italian, and Balkan peninsulas, which jut southward into the Mediterranean. North of the chain is the great North European plain, stretching eastward from Paris to Moscow, and on into the Soviet Union. The Scandinavian peninsula lies north of the Baltic Sea.

Although they are large islands lying offshore, the British Isles and Iceland are conventionally included in Europe.

Australia

Australia, like Africa one of the oldest of the earth's land masses, is bounded by the Timor and Arafura seas to the north, the Indian Ocean to the west and south, and the Coral and Tasman seas to the east (Figure 5). At 2.9 million square miles it is the smallest of the seven continents, but at some 2,500 miles from east to west, and some 2,300 miles from north to south at its longest, it is still large—and is occupied by just one nation.

Mainly because of its age, it is the flattest of the continents, and thus does not have some of the dominant physiographic features of the others. A huge, arid plateau occupies three quarters of Australia, covering practically all of Western Australia, most of the Northern Territory, and parts of South Australia and Queensland. Eastern Queensland and New South Wales are dominated by the Great Dividing Range, parts of which reach 7,000 ft. in altitude. Off the northeastern Queensland coast lies the Great Barrier Reef, which extends over 1,200 miles from the tropic of capricorn to the island of New Guinea.

Climate and Weather

Earth's Orbit Around the Sun

As it rotates on an axis, the earth simultaneously revolves around the sun in a counterclockwise direction, completing one revolution in about $365\frac{1}{4}$ days, or one *tropical year*. This sets the timing for climatic seasons. But to fully understand how seasons are generated, two other facts must be recognized.

First, the earth's axis is not perpendicular to its plane of ecliptic (the plane containing the earth's orbit). The earth's axis has a substantial tilt, in fact exactly $23\frac{1}{2}$ degrees from the perpendicular (Figure 1).

Second, the earth's axis, while always holding the angle $66\frac{1}{2}$ degrees with the plane of the ecliptic, maintains a fixed orientation with respect to the stars. The north end of the earth's axis points constantly toward Polaris, the North Star.

Solstice and Equinox

The consequence of these two facts is that at one point in its orbit, the earth's axis leans toward the sun, and at an opposite point in the orbit the axis leans away from the sun. At the two intermediate points, the axis leans neither toward nor away from the sun (Figure 1).

On June 21 or 22, the earth's north polar axis leans at the maximum angle of $23\frac{1}{2}$ degrees toward the sun, and the northern hemisphere is tipped toward the sun. This is the *summer solstice*. Six months later, on December 21 or 22, the earth is in an equivalent position on the opposite point in its orbit (i.e., the *winter*

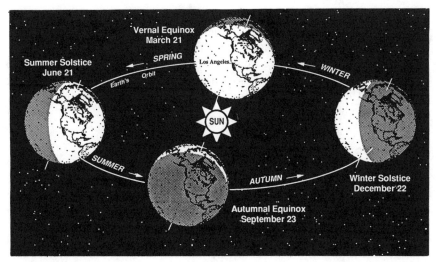

Figure 1. *Tilt of the Earth's Axis and Rotation of the Earth Around the Sun, with Shaded Portion Representing Night.*

solstice). At this time the earth's axis is at a maximum inclination toward the sun, but now it is the southern hemisphere that is tipped toward the sun.

Midway between the solstices occur the *equinoxes,* when the earth's axis makes a 90-degree angle with a line drawn to the sun, and neither the north pole nor the south pole has any inclination toward the sun. Conditions are identical in terms of earth–sun relationships. The *vernal equinox* occurs on March 20 or 21; the *autumnal equinox* occurs on September 22 or 23 (Figure 1).

Let us look at conditions at the equinoxes. Figure 1 shows that the earth is at all times divided into two hemispheres with respect to the sun's rays. One hemisphere is lighted by the sun; the other lies in darkness. Separating the hemispheres is a circle of illumination, dividing day from night. At either equinox the circle of illumination cuts precisely through the north and south poles. The point at which the sun's rays are perpendicular to the earth, or the subsolar point, is located exactly at the equator. At both poles, the sun's rays graze the surface. As the earth turns, the equator receives the maximum intensity of solar energy; the poles receive none. Look at the winter solstice conditions, as shown in the right side of Figure 1. Because the maximum inclination of the axis is away from the sun, the entire area lying inside the *arctic circle,* latitude $66\frac{1}{2}$ degrees north, is on the dark side of the circle of illumination for the entire day. All of the area lying south of the antarctic circle, latitude $66\frac{1}{2}$ degrees south, is under the sun's rays and enjoys 24 hours of day. The subsolar point has shifted to a point on the *tropic of capricorn,* latitude $23\frac{1}{2}$ degrees south.

At the summer solstice, conditions are exactly reversed from those of winter solstice. As the left side of Figure 1 shows, the subsolar point is now on the *tropic of cancer,* latitude $23\frac{1}{2}$ degrees north. Now the region poleward (north) of the arctic circle experiences a 24-hour day; that poleward (south) of the antarctic circle experiences a 24-hour night. From one solstice to another, the subsolar point has migrated over a latitude range of 47 degrees.

This progression of changes from equinox to solstice to equinox and back to solstice initiates the astronomical seasons: spring, summer, autumn, and winter (Figure 1). The inflow of energy from the sun is thus varied in an annual cycle, and climatic changes are generated.

Latitude Zones

We have seen that as a consequence of the tilt of the earth's axis and its consistent orientation with respect to the stars, the tilted earth assumes a different position with respect to the sun's rays. The intensity of insolation on the ground is a function of the angle at which the sun's rays strike the earth, and the length of time of exposure to the rays. These factors vary by latitude and by the seasonal changes in the path of the sun in the sky. Indeed, the globe can be divided into latitude zones.

The *equatorial zone* straddles the equator and covers roughly 10 degrees north and south. Within this zone, the sun provides intense isolation throughout the year, and day and night are of roughly equal duration. Quito, Ecuador; Bogota, Colombia; Manaus and Belem, Brazil; Lagos, Nigeria; Nairobi, Kenya; Kuala Lumpur, Malaysia; Jakarta and Bali, Indonesia; and Darwin, Australia, are all in this zone.

Astride the tropics of cancer and capricorn are the *tropical zones,* spanning the latitudes 10 to 25 degrees north and south. In these zones, the sun takes a path close to the zenith at one solstice, and is much lower at the opposite solstice. The total annual insolation is large, but there are seasonal cycles. Mexico City and Acupulco, Mexico; the Caribbean Islands; Lima, Peru; Rio de Janeiro, Brazil; Khartoum, Sudan; Madras, India; Harere, Zimbabwe; Manila, Philippines; and Cairns, Australia, are all in these tropical zones.

Poleward of the tropical zones, between 25 and 35 degrees north and south, are the transitional *subtropical zones.* Florida; Baja California; Santiago, Chile; the Canary Islands; Cairo, Egypt; Israel; South Africa; Shanghai, China; Osaka, Japan—all are in the subtropical zone.

The *midlatitude zones,* lying between 35 and 55 degrees north and south, are belts in which the sun's angle shifts through a relatively large range, so that seasonal contrasts in insolation are strong. Strong seasonal differences in lengths of day and night exist as compared with the tropical zones. San Francisco, Seattle, Chicago, Oklahoma City, Raleigh, and Boston, in the United States; Buenos Aires, Argentina; much of western Europe, excluding Scotland and Scandinavia; most of Honshu and Hokkaido, Japan; Victoria and Tasmania, Australia—all lie in this zone.

Poleward of the midlatitude zones are the *subarctic and subantarctic zones,* 55 to 60 degrees north and south. Juneau, Alaska; much of northern British Columbia, Alberta, Saskatchewan, Manitoba, Ontario, and Quebec, Canada; Scotland;

Oslo, Norway; Stockholm, Sweden; and Leningrad and Kamchatka, U.S.S.R. are in the subarctic zone.

Astride the arctic and antarctic circles, 66.5 degrees north and south, lie the *arctic and antarctic zones*. The arctic and antarctic zones have an extremely large yearly variation in lengths of day and night, resulting in enormous contrasts in insolation from solstice to solstice. Anchorage and Fairbanks, Alaska; Canada's Northwest Territories; Iceland; much of Scandinavia; and Siberia are all in the arctic zone; while the edges of Antarctica are in the antarctic zone.

The *polar zones,* north and south, are circular areas between about 75 degrees latitude and the poles. Here the polar regime of a six-month day and six-month night is predominant, with a resultant extreme contrast in seasonal insolation.

Major Climates

Many factors other than the insolation budget—such as the global circulation of the atmosphere and oceans, and atmospheric moisture and precipitation—have an impact on the world's climate and weather. Anyone who is involved in getting clients to warm, sunny spots in January, or to skiing areas in May; or who is thinking of developing resort properties in the Caribbean, Mexico, South America, or anywhere else, should know something about seasons, climates, and weather. You should know what to expect of a given season, in terms of climate and weather, in a given destination.

Remember that *climate* is the characteristic condition of the atmosphere near the earth's surface at a given place or over a given region. It is a generalization of *weather*. Weather information deals with specific events (cloud cover, humidity, rainfall amounts, temperature, and so on), while climate is described through weather observations accumulated over many years' time.

Geographers and climatologists have spent a great deal of time classifying climates. All classification systems use essentially the same categories of information, but with different degrees of emphasis. These are: air temperature and thermal regimes, precipitation, and air masses and frontal zones.

An adaptation of one of the most widely accepted and used classification systems, which gives a brief description of each climate along with its significance for tourism is the following:

Tropical Humid Climate

Characteristics Moderately high temperatures and high humidity year-round. Uniform temperatures year-round. No real dry season.
Examples Amazon and Congo River basins, Indonesia and the Philippines, coastal Central America, Caribbean, South Pacific islands.
Tourism Significance Beach tourism important in coastal areas due to warm water temperatures and "cooling" effect of sea breezes. Inland, high temperatures and high humidity have tended to discourage tourism.

Arid and Semi-arid Climate

Characteristics Very high maximum temperatures, low humidity, moderate annual range, but high diurnal range of temperatures. Little or no rainfall. Nights much cooler, and midlatitude interior locations can get very cold in winter. Intense sunshine.

Examples Southwestern United States, coastal northern Chile and Peru, northern Africa, Arabian peninsula and Middle East, southwestern Africa, southwestern Asia, and western and interior Australia.

Tourism Significance Dry, sunny areas with warm to hot temperatures are ideal for outdoors-oriented recreation, particularly where such facilities have been developed. Some clients may have trouble coping with the hot, dry heat.

Mediterranean Climate

Characteristics Warm to hot and dry summers, mild wet winters with moderate annual temperature range. Abundant sunshine.

Examples Southern California, central Chile, Mediterranean Sea rim of southern Europe, Morocco, Algeria, and Tunisia, extreme southwestern tip of Africa, southwestern and southern coastal Australia.

Tourism Significance Ideal climate for tourism, particularly beach tourism.

Humid Severe Winter Climate

Characteristics Pronounced seasonal changes. Warm, humid summers with moderate rainfall, cold winters. Weather is highly variable.

Examples Northeastern and north central United States and southern, eastern Canada, central and eastern Europe, northern China.

Tourism Significance Only summers suitable for tourism.

Humid Mild Winter Climate

Characteristics Warm to hot humid summers, cool winters, abundant rainfall, variable weather.

Examples Southeastern United States, southern Brazil and northeastern Argentina, western Europe, southern Africa, eastern Australia, northern South Asia, southern China.

Tourism Significance Summer tourism more favorable than winter, especially for beach-oriented tourism.

Subarctic Climate

Characteristics Short, cool summers and long, cold winters; long hours of darkness; low precipitation.

Examples Much of Canada, interior Alaska, Tierra del Fuego, central and northern Scandinavia, much of the Soviet Union, northern Japan.

Tourism Significance Tourism opportunities limited to short summer months only.

Polar Climate

Characteristics Very brief, cool summers, very cold winters, low annual average temperatures.
Examples Northern Canada and Alaska, Greenland, Antarctica, extreme northern Scandinavia, the Soviet Union.
Tourism Significance Tourism opportunities extremely limited, unless of "adventure tourism" nature.

Mountain Climate

Characteristics Cool to cold, usually moist climates, very dependent on altitude and slope orientation.
Examples Higher reaches of the Rocky Mountain, Sierra Nevada, and Cascade ranges in North America, the Andes, Ethiopian Highlands, European Alps, and Himalayas.
Tourism Significance Midlatitude mountainous areas are frequently outdoor recreation meccas, with skiing, hiking, and other outdoor activities. Closer to the equator, high-altitude mountain resorts offer relief from the tropical heat and humidity.

Far more detailed and complex classification systems exist, but this system represents a perfectly adequate generalization. More detailed information can be obtained from any of the weather sources identified later.

In any case, you should have an idea of the basic characteristics of, say, wet equatorial, trade-wind and monsoon coastal, tropical wet dry, and Mediterranean climates, *and* where these types are to be found. For example, where are the Mediterranean climates of the world?

Weather Extremes and Hazards

In addition to knowing something about the major climate types, you should also be aware of the potential for weather extremes or hazards. Temperature and precipitation averages are useful, but so are humidity and wind speed averages. Most people can stand dry heat much better than damp heat (which makes most people listless and weak). Going to Hong Kong between May and September is probably not the best idea, since the humidity is high (relative humidity is around 87 percent in the morning, 77 percent in the afternoon) and the weather is often very sultry and oppressive.

Exactly how hot or cold we feel often is also a function of wind speed. On hot days a brisk wind helps most people keep cool. Thus, many equatorial and tropical destinations located on the coast are made less uncomfortable by daily sea breezes. Conversely, on days with very cold temperatures, a strong wind makes one feel even colder. In such countries as Canada, the United States, and the Soviet Union, where very low temperatures and strong winds are normal during the winter, somebody from western Europe or the Caribbean is likely to get a shock! The difference between daytime and nighttime temperatures varies greatly from country to country. This is particularly true for places with sunny, dry desert climates (North Africa, the American Southwest), where the daily range is quite high and nights can be surprisingly cold. Similar conditions exist in mountain areas. As a general rule, the diurnal range is greatest inland and least on the coast.

In addition to temperature, humidity, wind, and diurnal range, another factor that affects our degree of comfort is the type of precipitation. The weather information sources identified later generally give data on the amount and frequency of rainfall, from which it is possible to deduce the probability of wet days (one in two in London from November though January, for example, or only one in thirty in July in Nice, France). From both temperature and precipitation data one can infer whether snow or rain is likely to fall.

Weather can also be highly variable, both from year to year and from day to day. Consequently, average temperature and precipitation figures can be misleading. Many of the midlatitude climates experience variable weather.

Altitude is another factor that influences our degree of comfort. As a general rule temperatures fall one degree Fahrenheit for every 330-foot gain in altitude. Thus, a 12,000-foot mountain-top retreat in Switzerland can be expected to be 27 degrees cooler than the lodge in the valley below at 3,000 feet. Diurnal temperature ranges tend to be exaggerated with altitude, and the atmosphere becomes much thinner at altitudes over 6,000 feet.

At high altitudes the sun's rays are more powerful and people will tan (or burn) more quickly than at sea level. If this is combined with snow cover, where light is reflected off the surface, tanning (or burning) will be quicker still. Breathing and exertion become progressively more difficult with altitude, especially over 6 or 7,000 feet. It may take time to acclimatize. Remember that La Paz, Bolivia is over 12,000 feet above sea level; Cuzco, Peru and Quito, Ecuador are each above 10,000 feet; Bogota, Colombia and Addis Ababa, Ethiopa are each above 8,000 feet; and Mexico City and Santa Fe, New Mexico are each above 7,000 feet.

Apart from the weather characteristics that affect an individual's degree of comfort, some other weather phenomena of which you should be aware are *tropical cyclones* or *hurricanes* (typhoons in Asia), and *tornadoes.*

In the Caribbean, hurricanes occur between June and November and are most frequent in August and September. During the worst of these storms, between 10 and 20 inches of rain may fall over a period of two or three days, and the very violent winds can cause severe damage. Over the Caribbean as a whole, an average of two to three hurricanes occur each year. While individual islands may go several years without experiencing a severe hurricane, and, on the larger islands, their worst effects may be confined to only one area, they are a fact of life (weather) that anybody in the travel industry should be aware of. Because they are closer to the equator, where the Coriolis force is weaker, the southern

Caribbean Islands (Aruba, Bonaire, Curaçao, Trinidad, and Tobago), are usually not affected by hurricanes.

Tropical cyclones are limited to only six regions in the world, all of them over tropical and subtropical oceans: (1) the West Indies, the Gulf of Mexico, and the Caribbean; (2) the western North Pacific, including the Philippines, the China Sea, and Japan; (3) the Arabian Sea and the Bay of Bengal; (4) the eastern Pacific coastal region off Mexico and Central America; (5) the southern Indian Ocean, off Madagascar; and (6) the western Southern Pacific in the region of Samoa, Fiji and the east coast of Australia.

Tornadoes are the smallest but most intense of all known storms. They occur most frequently in the United States (particularly in Texas, Oklahoma, Kansas, and western Missouri), and in Australia. The tornado is a small, intense cyclone in which the air is spiralling at tremendous speed (up to 250 mph). Destruction occurs both from the great wind speed and from the sudden reduction of air pressure in the vortex of the cyclonic spiral. These storms occur as parts of powerful cumulonimbus clouds traveling in advance of a cold front where atmospheric turbulance is greatest. They are most common in the spring and summer, but can occur at any time of the year.

World Population

The world that we have just described is inhabited by approximately 5 billion people, a population that is growing at a rate of about 90 million per year, or almost 250,000 per day! Demographers estimate it took some 1,700 years from the time of Christ to double the earth's population. At the current rate of growth, the earth's population is expected to reach 10 billion, or to double, by the year 2070, just 80 years from now!

Where do these more than 5 billion individuals live? They are certainly not evenly distributed throughout the continents of the world. The majority of the world's population is clustered in three principal regions (East Asia, South Asia, and Europe), and two minor concentrations (Southeast Asia and northeast North America). These five clusters, accounting for two thirds of all humanity, are located in the lowlands of the humid midlatitudes and subtropics.

Even with over 5 billion inhabitants, the world still has areas that are sparsely populated. Apart from the oceans, seas, and large lakes, the world's empty areas are the cold arctic and antarctic fringes, the hot, dry desert areas, the hot, humid tropical forests, and the higher mountain ranges and plateaus. While they support few permanent residents, these areas are not unimportant touristically—as Antarctic and Alaskan fjord cruises, Amazon jungle photo-safaris, skiing in the Andes, Alps, and Rocky Mountains, and trekking and heli-skiing in the Himalayas attest.

When population is collated by continent (Table 1), we can see that Asia, with over 3 billion people, accounts for 60 percent of the world's population, and

Table 1. POPULATION AND AREA OF CONTINENTS

	Population	% of Total	Rate of Growth (%)	Area	% of Total
Asia	3,130	60.3	1.8	17,400	30.1
Africa	642	12.4	3.0	11,700	20.2
N. America	420	8.1	0.7	9,400	16.2
S. America	288	5.5	2.2	6,900	11.9
Antarctic	0	0.0	0.0	5,400	9.3
Europe	685	13.2	0.3	3,800	6.6
Australasia and Oceania	26	0.5	1.2	3,300	5.7
World Total	5,192	100.0	1.7	57,900	100.0

Source: *The World Almanac and Book of Facts, 1990* (New York: World Almanac, 1989).

North America, with 420 million, accounts for just 8 percent. Of note, too, is that Asia, with 60 percent of the world's population, occupies only 30 percent of its land area, and North America, with only 8 percent of the world's population, has 16 percent of the land area (Table 1).

About 77 percent of the world's population, or almost 4 billion people, live in the underdeveloped or developing world—the tribal and traditional societies. Only 23 percent, or about 1.2 billion, live in the developed world, or modern societies. Moreover, the developing world is growing at an annual rate of 2.1 percent, while the developed world is only growing at an annual rate of 0.6 percent. The fastest-growing continent is Africa (currently at an annual rate of 3.0 percent). The slowest is Europe, at an annual rate of 0.3 percent (Table 1). The ten fastest-growing and ten slowest-growing countries in the world, along with their current populations, are listed in Table 2.

One manifestation of these kinds of growth rates that is obvious to the traveler is the age distribution of the population. In the developing world countries tend to have very young populations. In Kenya, for example, over 52 percent of the population is under the age of 14, and less than 5 percent is over the age of 65! In the developed world, by contrast, the population is aging rapidly. In West Germany, for instance, less than 15 percent of the population is under 14 years of age, and 21 percent is over 65.

What are some of the other salient characteristics of this population? What are these people like? Despite the fact that we are a single species with a common chromosome number (46) and the ability to interbreed, people have always distinguished different groups on the basis of some characteristic or other, the most common being race, religion, and language. It is important to realize that while these characteristics are perceived differently by different peoples and varying degrees of social significance are attached to them, they are nonetheless among the most pervasive factors affecting social and political relationships.

Table 2. POPULATION GROWTH

Slowest-Growing Countries			Fastest-Growing Countries		
	Growth Rate (% p.a.)	Pop. (Millions)		Growth Rate (% p.a.)	Pop. (Millions)
St. Kitts	−1.97	0.036	Brunei	8.62	0.316
Hungary	−0.20	10.588	UA Emirates	6.58	1.980
Grenada	−0.19	0.084	Namibia	5.30	1.301
Ireland	−0.11	3.531	Kenya	4.21	23.341
E. Germany	−0.06	16.596	Saudi Arabia	4.16	15.452
Guyana	−0.04	0.765	Ivory Coast	3.81	11.184
Montserrat	−0.01	0.012	Syria	3.74	11.569
W. Germany	0.00	60.980	Zimbabwe	3.74	9.728
Bulgaria	0.06	8.966	Maldives	3.72	0.203
Denmark	0.08	5.125	Quatar	3.70	0.328

Source: *The World Factbook, 1989* (Washington, DC: US Government Printing Office).

Race

In terms of race, Caucasoids make up 55 percent of the world's population, Mongoloids 37 percent, Negroids 7 percent, and Australoids less than 1 percent.

The Caucasoids (fair skin and eyes, light and wavy hair, prominent and narrow noses, thin lips, and abundance of body hair) are concentrated in Europe, North Africa and the Middle East, South Asia, North America, southern South America, the coastal areas of Australia, and New Zealand. Mongoloids (light yellow to brown skin, brown eyes, straight and coarse black hair, flat face and nose, broad head, epicanthic eye fold, and high cheekbones) are concentrated in eastern and southeastern Asia, northern North America, and interior South America. Negroids (black skin, black wooly hair, dark eyes, broad and flat nose, thick and everted lips, long head, and prognathous jaw), are concentrated in Africa south of the Sahara. The Australoids (dark skin and eyes, dark wavy hair, broad nose, full lips, long head) are found in interior Australia.

There are large areas of the world where there is considerable overlap or mixing of the broad racial groups. For instance, in large areas of the Soviet Union, in interior Asia, Middle and South America, a mixture of Mongoloid and Caucasoid races exist, and in northeast Africa, southeast North America, and northeast coastal South America, a mixture of Negroid and Caucasoid racial groups exist.

Religion

In terms of religious affiliation the world is much more complex, as regards both geographical distribution and religion's importance as a cultural trait. In tribal societies, and even some traditional societies, religion is an all-pervading force. Although religion plays a more modest role in most modern societies, it is still an important characteristic, and even in communist countries, where atheism is the official ideology, religion persists. The affinity between persons of the same religion clearly motivates group behavior. Unfortunately, differences in religious belief, as we shall see, also have been responsible for much historical and even recent tension and conflict in the world. Religion has had a profound effect on human societies. Religion strongly influences social institutions, social behavior, marital and other family behavior, law, and even business dealings. Ceremonial seasons (holidays, fasting periods), diet restrictions, and agricultural practices are all heavily influenced by the religious affiliation of the population concerned. Religious differences are often expressed in the landscape through distinctive styles of architecture (mosques, cathedrals, churches, and temples), and holy shrines attract huge numbers of both religious pilgrims and the more secular, less ardently religious tourists. Jerusalem, Mecca, Medina, Benares, Gaya, Rome, Canterbury, and Lourdes are just the better known of destinations that owe their attractiveness principally to religious factors.

The major religion with the most adherents is Christianity (Roman Catholicism, Protestantism, Orthodoxism, Anglicanism), claiming about a third of the world's population as practitioners. North and South America, Europe and Australasia are all predominately Christian (Table 3). After Christianity, the religion with the most adherents is Islam, with about 17 percent of the world's population either Sunni or Shii Moslems. Although it is not the dominant religion on any continent, Islam claims 39 percent of Africa's population (all in North Africa and the Sahel, and all Sunni) and 19 percent of Asia's population (Sunni in Saudi Arabia, Pakistan, Bangladesh, Malaysia, and Indonesia, and Shii in Syria and Iran).

Hinduism, with 13 percent of the world's population as adherents, is the world's third most popular religion; it is concentrated almost exclusively in India and Nepal. Buddhism, representing 6 percent of humanity, claims 10 percent of Asia as adherents, principally in China, Japan, Burma, and Thailand. Various

Table 3. ESTIMATED RELIGIOUS POPULATION (PERCENT) BY CONTINENT/REGION

Religious Group	Asia	Africa	North America	Latin America	Europe	Australasia	World
Christians	0.9	44.0	86.1	93.5	72.5	84.0	32.9
Moslems	19.1	39.0	0.9	0.1	3.8	0.0	17.4
Hindus	21.1	0.2	0.3	0.1	0.1	1.2	13.1
Buddhists	10.0	0.0	0.0	0.0	0.1	0.0	6.1
Tribal	0.8	10.3	0.0	0.2	0.0	0.3	1.8
Atheists	28.9	0.2	8.8	3.8	21.0	13.4	22.0
Other	19.2	6.3	3.9	2.3	2.5	1.1	6.7

Source: *The Universal Almanac, 1990* (Kansas City, MO: Andrews and McMeel, 1989).

tribal religions are significant in Africa, with 10 percent of that continent's population counted as adherents (Table 3).

Of note today is the relatively high percentage of humanity, 22 percent worldwide, claiming either no religious affiliation or to be atheists, with heavy concentrations in Asia (29 percent of its population) and in Europe (21 percent of its population).

There are, of course, many other religions—including Confucianism, Shintoism, Taoism, Shamanism, Bahaism, Jainism, and Judaism—with millions of adherents, but they represent individually less than 0.5 percent of humanity, and even at the national level are nowhere the dominant religion with the one exception of Judaism in Israel (and even in Israel 13 percent of the populace is Moslem). Of note is the fact that the degree of orthodoxy and the intensity of interpretation of various doctrines varies widely in all of the world's religions.

A fact worth noting is that there is typically some diversity in the religious affiliation of any individual country's population. While some countries have a high degree of homogeneity in their religious makeup, others are not very homogeneous at all. Following are the ten least homogeneous countries in terms of religious affiliation, and the ten most homogeneous (from *The World Factbook, 1989,* U.S. Government Printing Office, Washington, DC).

Least Homogeneous Countries

Sierra Leone (30% Muslim, 30% Indigenous Beliefs, 10% Christian)
Tanzania (33% Christian, 33% Muslim, 33% Indigenous Beliefs)
Trinidad and Tobago (36% Roman Catholic, 23% Hindu, 6% Muslim)
Ghana (38% Indigenous Beliefs, 30% Muslim, 24% Christian)
Congo (50% Christian, 42% Animist, 2% Muslim)
Ethiopia (45% Muslim, 35% Ethiopian Orthodox, 20% Animist)
Nigeria (50% Muslim, 40% Christian, 10% Indigenous Beliefs)
Yugoslavia (50% Eastern Orthodox, 30% Roman Catholic, 10% Muslim)
Mauritius (51% Hindu, 30% Christian, 17% Muslim)
Madagascar (52% Indigenous Beliefs, 41% Christian, 7% Muslim)

Most Homogeneous Countries

Andorra (100% Roman Catholic)
Greenland (100% Evangelical Lutheran)
Italy (100% Roman Catholic)
Saudi Arabia (100% Muslim)
North Yemen (100% Muslim)
Algeria (99% Sunni Muslim)
Mauritania (99% Muslim)
Morocco (99% Muslim)
Spain (99% Roman Catholic)
Greece (98% Greek Orthodox)

Language

Language, which serves as the vehicle of communication and means of cultural transmission, is one of the most important cultural traits. Linguists have identified as many as 4,000 different languages (divided into about twenty language families), of which 3,000 are still in use today, with probably two or three times as many dialects. Just two language families, the Indo-European and the Sino-Tibetan, account for the majority of the world's spoken languages, with about 50 percent of humanity speaking an Indo-European tongue, and 20 percent a Sino-Tibetan tongue.

There are, however, over 240 separate languages that are spoken by at least one million people in the world today, a fact that makes mapping the distribution of languages difficult, and a fact that would make communication difficult were it not for lingua francas and the emergence of English as the language of science, commerce, and trade.

At the broad world scale, the distribution of languages corresponds to that of races. Most Caucasoids speak Indo-European languages, most Mongoloids Sino-Tibetan languages, and most Negroids Niger-Congo-Bantu languages. Over time, as people have migrated, intermixed and became acculturated, the once coincident boundaries of race and language have become blurred and indistinct. Table 4 shows the principal languages of the world, estimates the number of speakers of each, and lists the regions of their predominance (where they are the standard tongues).

Most people are monolingual but many, particularly minority cultural groups, are bilingual. Few individuals or societies are truly multilingual, Switzerland being the one exception. The most widely spoken language is Mandarin Chinese, with some 840 million speakers, followed by English, Hindi, and Spanish (with 437, 338, and 331 million speakers, respectively). Russian, Arabic, Bengali, Portugese, Malay-Indonesian, Japanese, Bengali, French, and German (in that order) round out the other languages spoken by over 100 million people (Table 4).

People speaking the same language have evolved into relatively uniform blocs with fairly sharp boundaries between one language area and another. These linguistic "communities" strongly influence human behavior, particularly the association and interaction of people. Political, social, and economic organizations tend to be closely related to linguistic blocs. However, the identification of language with cultural groups or countries is not complete: some French speak German; most Irish speak English, many Peruvian Indians do not speak Spanish.

Official Languages

Official languages are political designations and are usually found in multilingual states where the existence of many different, often unrelated languages, impedes business and official government action. To make things easier, one or two languages are designated as official although those languages may not be spoken at home by the majority of the populace.

Table 4. PRINCIPAL LANGUAGES OF THE WORLD

Linguistic Family and Language	Speakers (millions)	Regions Where Language Is Standard
Indo-European		
English	437	U.S., U.K., Canada, Australia, New Zealand, Jamaica, and other former British Commonwealth countries
Hindi	338	India and Pakistan
Spanish	331	Spain, Latin America (except Brazil)
Russian	291	Russian Soviet Socialist Republic
Bengali	181	Bangladesh, West Bengal
Portuguese	171	Brazil, Portugal
German	118	Germany, Austria, Luxembourg, Switzerland
French	119	France, Belgium, Haiti, Switzerland, Quebec
Urdu	90	Pakistan, India
Punjabi	81	Punjab, Pakistan, NW India
Italian	63	Italy, Switzerland
Marathi	63	Maharashtra, India
Ukranian	45	Ukranian Soviet Socialist Republic
Sino-Tibetan		
Chinese (Mandarin)	844	China, Taiwan
Cantonese	62	China, Hong Kong
Wu	61	Shanghai, China
Vietnamese	55	Vietnam
Thai	47	Thailand
Min	46	SE China, Tiawan, Malaysia
Dravidian		
Telegu	67	Andhra Pradesh, SE India
Tamil	64	Tamil Nadu, India, Sri Lanka
Kannada	40	S. India
Japanese-Korean		
Japanese	124	Japan
Korean	69	Korea, China, Japan
Semitic-Hamitic	192	Morocco, Algeria, Tunisia, Libya, Mauritania, Egypt, Sudan, Iraq, Saudi Arabia, Kuwait, S. Yemen, Yemen, Oman, Syria, Trucial States
Austroasiatic		
Malay-Indonesian	138	Indonesia
Javanese	57	Java, Indonesia
Ural-Altaic		
Turkish	54	Turkey
Niger-Congo-Bantu	42	Kenya, Tanzania, Zaire, Uganda

Source: *World Almanac, 1990* (New York: Pharos Books, 1990).

In some instances where two languages are spoken, both may become official. For example, Canada is officially bilingual. French and English have equal status under Canadian law. Other examples include: Belgium (Flemish, French); Burundi (French, Rundi); Chad (French, Arabic); Cyprus (Greek, Turkish); Czechoslovakia (Czech, Slovak); Finland (Finnish, Swedish); Haiti (French, Creole); Israel (Hebrew, Arabic); Malawi (English, Chichewa); Pakistan (Urdu, English); Peru (Spanish, Quechua); the Philippines (Filipino, English); Rwanda (French, Kinyarwanda); the Seychelles (English, French); Somalia (Somali, Arabic); South Africa (Afrikaans, English); Swaziland (siSwati, English); Tanzania (Swahili, English); and Western Samoa (Samoa, English). Two countries, Boliva (Spanish, Quechua, Aymara) and Yugoslavia (Serbo-Croatian, Macedonian, Slovenian) are trilingual, and two, Singapore (Chinese, Malay, Tamil, English), and Switzerland (German, French, Italian, Romansch), have four official languages each.

Lingua Francas

A lingua franca is a makeshift language that is used over a wide area as a means of communication among peoples of various different languages. It typically differs from the normal daily language of its users. The best example is the use of English in India, a land of over 500 different languages, and in other parts of the former British Commonwealth. In West Africa, Hausa is used for business purposes, and Swahili is used in East Africa. Other lingua francas are Hindi (northern India), French (former French colonies), and Arabic (Islam in the West).

Dialects

A dialect is the speech of a community (region, urban area) that shares similar pronunciation, vocabulary, and grammar. Swiss German is very different from West German German, especially for those who are not native speakers of German. Similarly, Scottish and Welsh English are very different from "Oxford" English. To a much less pronounced extent, the Southern dialect of English in the United States differs from the Northern (New England) dialect.

These dialects can be both frustrating and a source of delight to travelers and often add to the charm and challenge of traveling in foreign lands. Try asking directions from a true Cockney in London or a true Liverpudlian in Liverpool in the United Kingdom.

Cultural Regions of the World

We have looked at race, religion, and language as three of the fundamental characteristics of the human species. Indeed, they are all elements of what geographers refer to as the *cultural geography* of a place or region. That is, those characteristics of a place or region that help distinguish it from other places or regions. While recognizing that there well may be differences or variations within that place or region, those differences are less pronounced than those between different places or regions.

The concept of culture has been and is constantly argued over, both in academic circles and in the mass media. However, it can generally be agreed that a culture is the way of life of a population, encompassing their ways of doing things, the behavioral traits that they have learned and passed on to successive generations. Culture consists of language, religion, music, food preferences, architecture, and taboos—in other words, a people's beliefs and values, institutions, and technology. It is expressed in the way people communicate, in the way they perceive and exploit their resources, in their architecture and art, and in the way they organize physical space.

The variety of cultures accounts for the richness of human life and fuels much of the travel industry. Witness the fascination with the medinas of Morocco's royal cities, the Indian markets of Ecuador, the rice terraces of Indonesia, and even the success of Epcot Center in Disney World. Distant places, and sometimes not-too-distant places, have their allure precisely because they are different.

Geographers and others have divided the world into cultural regions or cultural realms, the exact number of which has also been subject to lively debate. The consensus seems to settle on the thirteen world culture realms or regions defined below. A brief look at the distinguishing features of each one is instructive and is certainly something the destination consultant should be conversant with. The careful reading of a representative country's "Culturgram," (published by Brigham Young University's David M. Kennedy Center for International Studies), cited in the Appendix, is also recommended here.

Europe

Europe is a diversified, industrial, commercial, and agricultural region with an impact on world affairs that is unmatched by any other region. With about 10 percent of the world's population, Europe is highly urbanized and very literate, a population that enjoys a long life expectancy and high per capita income (Table 5).

Australia and New Zealand

Australia and New Zealand, essentially European outposts in an Asian-Pacific world, contain just 0.4 percent of the world's population. It is the most heavily urbanized population in the world (with 85 percent of its population living in urban areas). The population is very literate, enjoys a long life expectancy, and a high per capita income, second only to that of North America (Table 5).

The Soviet Union

The Soviet Union, vast in extent and very powerful in its military might and political influence, constitutes its own cultural realm and accounts for 6 percent

Table 5. SOME CHARACTERISTICS OF THE WORLD'S CULTURE REALMS

Realm	Population (millions)	% of World's Population	%Urban	Life Expectancy Female	Life Expectancy Male	Literacy Rate (%)	% Agriculture	Per Capita Income (US $)
Europe	490	10	71	75	70	99	17	8,090
Australia	19	0.4	85	77	72	99	8	9,017
Soviet Union	275	6	64	75	70	100	23	6,352
North America	263	5	75	77	73	99	10	12,127
Japan	120	2	76	79	75	99	14	8,947
Middle America	149	3	49	66	62	78	35	1,658
South America	263	5	62	67	63	82	29	2,212
SW Asia–North Africa	347	7	48	56	54	43	46	1,269
Black Africa	352	7	25	50	46	34	74	634
Indian	992	21	15	51	51	32	72	203
China	1164	24	38	69	64	86	59	938
SE Asia	397	8	36	57	54	67	66	1,106
Pacific Is.	6	0.1	29	64	60	66	41	1,764

Source: *The World Factbook, 1989* (Washington, DC: U.S. Government Printing Office).

of the world's population. Not as highly urbanized nor as affluent as Europe or Australia and New Zealand, its population nevertheless is very literate and enjoys a long life expectancy (Table 5).

North America

North America, with only 5 percent of the world's population, enjoys the highest per capita income in the world. Highly urbanized, its population has a long life expectancy, second only to Japan, and is highly literate (Table 5).

Japan

Japan, a distinct cultural region of its own, has 2 percent of the world's population. It ranks second after Australia and New Zealand in its degree of urbanization, has the longest life expectancy of any region, is very literate, and enjoys a high per capita income, ranking just behind North America and Australia and New Zealand (Table 5).

Middle America

Middle America, made up of Latin North America and the Caribbean Islands, contains 3 percent of the world's population. Most of these people live in rural areas and small towns, with a moderate life expectancy, moderate literacy levels, and only moderate per capita income levels—well below those enjoyed in North America, Australia and New Zealand, Japan, Europe, and the Soviet Union (Table 5).

South America

South America, a region shared by Portugese-influenced Brazil and a Spanish colonial domain now divided among nine separate countries, accounts for 5 percent of the world's population. Its rapidly growing, moderately urbanized population, has a moderately high life expectancy, a moderately high level of literacy, and a medium level of per capita income (Table 5).

Southwest Asia–North Africa

The Southwest Asian–North African region, sometimes referred to as the Islamic realm, holds 7 percent of the world's population. It is a predominately rural, small-town region, characterized by low life expectancy and low levels of literacy. Per capita incomes, while moderate by world standards, are much lower than those in any of the other world regions/realms discussed so far (Table 5).

Black Africa

Black Africa (that is, Africa south of the Sahara) is defined by its mosaic of hundreds of languages belonging to specific African language families as much as by race. Most of Africa's languages (as many as 1,000 different ones), belong to the Niger-Congo-Bantu family, although there are two exceptions: Madagascar's, which belong to a non-African Malay-Polynesian family; and Afrikaans (a derivative of Dutch), which is an Indo-European language spoken by 5 million whites in South Africa. With 7 percent of the world's population, Black Africa has, together with India, the lowest per capita income of the thirteen regions. Only 25 percent of its population lives in urban areas. Life expectancy, at 50 years for females and 46 for males, is the lowest in the world and literacy rates are the second lowest, just above those of India (Table 5).

India and the Indian Perimeter

The Indian realm is the poorest. Life expectancy is very low, literacy rates are the lowest in the world, and only 15 percent of its population is urbanized (Table 5). India is well defined physically, and inhabited by one of the greatest concentrations of people on earth (just over 1 billion), representing over one fifth of all humanity.

The Chinese World

The Chinese realm represents the planet's other great concentration of people with over 24 percent of the world's population. Life expectancy is moderate; literacy rates, while not as high as in the West, are much higher than Black Africa's or India's, and annual per capita income, at $938, is low. About one quarter of the population is urbanized (Table 5).

Southeast Asia

With 8 percent of the world's population, Southeast Asia is not as well defined as the Chinese or Indian culture areas and does not have a single, dominant core area of indigenous development. Rather, it is a mosaic of ethnic and linguistic groups, religions, and different economies. Per capita income levels, while modest, are higher than in China, Black Africa and India. Life expectancy is low, as are literacy rates (Table 5).

Pacific Regions

The last cultural realm, the Pacific, is defined by its physical isolation. Lying between Australasia and the Americas, the vast Pacific Ocean contains tens of thousands of islands, large and small. It is also the least populated region, with only 0.1 percent of humanity. While life expectancy is moderately high, literacy rates are low. Per capita incomes are very modest and only 29 percent of the population is urbanized (Table 5).

Most of these cultural realms originated in a particular region and, although they may have spread away from their origin, are still associated with that birthplace, or *culture hearth.* The Old World, from which the North American, South American, Australian and New Zealand, Indian, and Chinese culture realms derive their salient characteristics, has several culture hearths: Mesopotamia, Egypt, Crete, Greece, the Indus Valley, and North China. Similarly, the New World has two culture hearths, Middle America and the Andes, although the Toltecs, Aztecs, Mayas, and Incas have not had as profound an influence on subsequent cultures.

Almost all of these culture hearths, however, are major centers of tourism today. The fascination with their monuments, huge architectural constructions, and statuary is universal and enduring. Over time, people have modified the natural landscape and, depending on their industriousness and technological sophistication, have left behind a rich palette of human landscapes—a palette that stimulates exploration and understanding.

While keeping these cultural characteristics in mind, the level of development probably has more immediate significance for the traveler; it is to this topic that we turn to next.

Developed and Underdeveloped Countries

We have made several references to the developed world and to the underdeveloped or developing world. In fact, among all of the various cultural and demographic traits that have been discussed so far, this distinction is probably the most significant for the traveler. So, let us look at this distinction more closely and, more important, see what inferences can be drawn that are relevant to the traveler and destination consultant.

The large differences in standards of living between the "developed" and "underdeveloped" countries of the world would seem to constitute the basis for a classification into industrial-commercial societies and non-industrial-commercial countries. However, the non-industrial-commercial countries include the majority of the world's population and consist of an entire spectrum of countries, ranging from those in which the population lives in bands of primitive food collectors to venerable and sophisticated cultures.

Indeed, geographers have divided the underdeveloped world into tribal and traditional societies and use the term *modern* to describe the industrial-commercial societies. This is obviously a very broad generalization, since some segments of modern societies are quite underdeveloped or even backward, while many tribal and traditional societies have industrial-commercial regions or areas within their borders.

Nevertheless, this generalization holds up fairly well and is certainly useful in suggesting the general social, economic, and political conditions that characterize the lives of the world's population. What, then, are the salient characteristics of the three types of societies and what implications can be drawn for the tourists, your clients, who may visit them.

Tribal Societies

- small in scope and self-contained
- social relationships based on kinship and village community
- little or no state organization
- no clearly defined central authority
- very little if any socioeconomic hierarchy
- population works close to the land to satisfy short-range needs
- energy is derived largely from man and beasts of burden
- very little specialization of labor, very low productivity
- almost no application or knowledge of modern science
- technological level very low, ability to cope is limited
- population predominantly rural with very few, if any, large cities

Traditional Societies

- attitudes toward knowledge and technology prescientific
- birth into a specific family clan or caste determines the status of individuals
- a state organization does exist, with a hierarchic structure
- wealth derives principally from land ownership
- a small, strong wealthy ruling class exists, claims rights to the land, and exacts tribute or rent from the peasants who work it
- middle class very small
- majority of population poor and illiterate
- energy sources include people and beasts of burden, supplemented by water and wind, and increasingly by modern forms of energy
- low productivity per worker, marginal standard of living
- crop yields high per acre but low per worker-hour
- population still largely rural with some large cities, mostly administrative centers
- birth rates and death rates are high (although death rates are declining rapidly), population growth is rapid

Modern Societies

- science and technology used intensively
- status achieved through competence and achievement, although inherited social position is still important

- generally high productivity per worker, comfortable standard of living
- most of the population participates in an intricate network of impersonal relationships and is socially and geographically mobile
- agriculture employs only a small percentage of the work force
- private entrepreneurs play a large and significant role in production (unless usurped by state bureacrats, as in the case of the socialist countries)
- highly urbanized population with many large cities
- energy sources are predominantly modern with little or no reliance on man or beasts of burden
- birth rates and death rates are low, with low, or even negative, population growth

Most of the readers of this handbook are familiar enough with modern societies, their characteristics, and what these characteristics imply for the traveler. So we now turn to some of the principal characteristics of tribal and traditional societies, and what they mean to travelers.

Tribal Societies

Areas inhabited by tribal societies are frequently remote, difficult to get to, pass through, or move around in. They are also frequently inhospitable, both from the natives' point of view (e.g., some Amazon Indian tribes), and in terms of their sometimes harsh environment, which has contributed to their lack of development. There typically is a lack of toilets, doctors, dentists, drugstores, and so on. Most toiletries (such as toilet paper, toothpaste, shaving cream, and shampoo) are available in the capital cities and large towns, but not always in the smaller towns and villages.

Travel—by bus, boat, or pack animal—is difficult and protracted. In some places (Zaire, Sudan, Rwanda, Burundi, Tanzania, and Zambia, for example), the "roads" have to be seen to be believed—deep potholes, broken bridges, etc. Desert roads in places like Sudan, Chad, Mali, Niger, and Mauritania are just a set of tire tracks left in the sand. Many roads are impassable in the wet season.

Disease is prevelant, with cholera, yellow fever, typhoid, tetanus, and polio vaccinations mandatory. Tuberculin skin tests should be obtained before traveling to areas where prolonged exposure to tuberculosis is anticipated. Clients should avoid turning up at borders with expired vaccination cards, as officials may insist that they obtain the relevant injection before entering. Frequently, the same needle is used on many travelers without any sterilization between injections, so that the chance of contracting serum hepatitis can be high. Medical and dental checkups are recommended before traveling to tribal societies, since doctors and dentists are few and far between and treatment is expensive when it can be found. Since sanitation standards are low or entirely nonexistent, untreated milk or milk products should be avoided, all fruit should be peeled, and drinking water should be boiled. Swimming or bathing in fresh water should be avoided (e.g., bilharzia, an infestation of minute worms that live in the veins of the bladder and large intestine, is common in Africa).

It is often difficult to obtain visas, particularly on the road. For example, the consulate may insist on referring travelers' applications to the capital, which can take weeks. It may be necessary to have the first few pages of passports translated into the native language before applying for a visa.

Languages are usually very exotic, making it difficult to communicate unless a good guide/interpreter is present. Tribal societies are often outside the regular currency systems, therefore reliance on barter is common. Credit cards cannot be used, by and large. Maps and guidebooks are difficult to come by.

Traditional Societies

While usually less difficult to get to, and get around in, than tribal societies, traditional societies also present their own transportation problems. For example, in many parts of South America the roads are not marked and even in some major cities, such as Caracas, the streets are not marked! Many areas also experience frequent shortages of gasoline. Often it is advisable not to drive after dark, particularly in rural areas. Most fields are not fenced in and livestock is free to wander into oncoming traffic. Bicycles and other vehicles without lights are another frequent hazard.

Communications in traditional societies, while much better than the sometimes nonexistent communications in tribal societies, have their idiosyncrasies. For example, in India, the telephone system is a hit-and-miss affair. Local calls sometimes work, sometimes not. Long-distance calls are even more a matter of chance and luck—both in getting through, and in actually hearing the other party. As for international calls, sometimes it is possible to get through in 20 minutes, at other times 24 hours is not enough.

Letters home should always be mailed through the city's central or main post office; branch offices are frequently unreliable. Never send packages via surface mail in most traditional societies, as service is totally unreliable. Infrastructure is another problem. Electricity is normally widely available, but brownouts and blackouts are not uncommon.

While traditional societies are within the orbit of regular currency systems, black markets in currency exchange are common and having money transferred can be very time-consuming. Bribery or baksheesh is widespread. "Tipping" is used not so much for rewarding good service, as it is for just getting things done. Judicious baksheesh will get a seat on a crowded train, open closed doors, find a missing letter, process an application, and perform other minor miracles. One other financial-political characteristic of traditional societies is worth noting, especially in South America—with less stable and strong national economies, inflation, in some cases hyperinflation, is a fact of life. The direct consequence for travelers is that prices and therefore costs are very difficult to predict.

Similarly, bargaining is a commonly accepted practice in Africa and Asia and is expected. The concept of a fixed price is alien. Merchants in South America, however, do not always like to bargain with tourists. The assumption here is frequently that if you are rich enough to fly to South America (and you are rich, comparatively speaking), then you can well afford to spend the extra pesos. As a result, prices are standardized in each market.

Language is not as big a problem as it is in tribal societies. Because of widespread former colonial influences, one of the European languages (English, French, Spanish, etc.) is usually the second language, if not the principal one. In India, there is no "Indian" language, which is part of the reason why English is still so widely spoken over 40 years after the British left India. The country is divided into many local languages, and in many cases the state boundaries have been drawn on linguistic lines. In all there are over 14 major languages and over 200 minor languages and dialects. Many Indians have to speak English if they want to communicate with each other.

While sanitation standards are much higher than those that exist in tribal societies, and water systems in the larger cities are likely to be fairly safe, water systems in the small towns, villages, and rural areas are not safe. The use of bottled water or beer, wine, and soft drinks is advised, or water should be boiled for at least 15 minutes. A supply of Sterotabs or Halazone tablets is useful.

Why Travel to Tribal and Traditional Societies?

It must be stated, however, that while the above generalizations may make one pessimistic about travel to tribal and traditional societies, they should by no means dissuade travelers. On the contrary, as long as the traveler is aware of these characteristics and learns to accept them, then travel to and within these societies can be a particularly rewarding experience, one that simply cannot be gained by limiting oneself to the "modern world."

By staying in modern, Western-style or even Western-run hotels, and/or with Western package tours, travelers can insulate themselves from some of the more negative characteristics, but they do so at the cost of not really getting to know, and appreciating, the real character of the countries they visit.

Travel consultants or counselors in particular, though, should be aware of these characteristics and the differences between tribal, traditional, and modern societies so that they can better match the desires of their clients with potential destinations.

War Zones and Trouble Spots

The cultural differences outlined above and the frustrations produced by the differences in levels of development are often the cause of internal and even international tensions and conflict. However, despite the widespread and some-times sensationalist media coverage of the world's trouble spots, the risk to life and limb through armed conflict is not great. Certainly there are dangerous places (nobody in his right mind would travel voluntarily to Beirut, or other notorious trouble spots), but in general the host governments are not about to let tourists anywhere near potential or real hot spots.

Tourists are unlikely to get into serious trouble unless they insist on being where they are not supposed to be and doing what is forbidden. Getting caught in crossfire is a hazard, but it is extremely rare, and if tourists watch what the locals are doing, or not doing, and follow along, they should be all right. Conflict is much more likely to have an impact on tourists' trips in the form of in-conveniences—such as increased border security, delays, military checkpoints, disrupted public transport, rerouting of routes, and changes in or cancellations of particular itineraries. How inconvenient things get depends largely on what country or countries tourists are traveling in or through. Countries with serious political problems do not have much time for, or sympathy with, tourists anyway.

Predicting exactly what areas these will be is difficult if not impossible, of course, let alone trying to predict the timing of unrest. The State Department's Citizen's Alert Number (202/647-5225), in the Office of Overseas Citizen Services, and the U.S. Embassy in countries abroad, usually have good informa-tion on conditions around the world; they should be consulted if there is any doubt before traveling into countries or areas where there has been recent unrest or where that potential exists.

Worldwide Terrorism

A more recent phenomenon is terrorism. Indeed, the threat to international order from terrorism has increased markedly in the last few years, and in many respects is more disturbing to the traveler than war or hostilities, since those can be avoided, while worldwide terrorism cannot be predicted.

In its publication *Patterns of Global Terrorism: 1988,* the State Department notes that the number of international terrorist incidents has increased from 125 in 1968 to some 855 in 1988. The type of event has changed, too. In 1968, bombings accounted for 66 percent of all terrorist incidents, with armed attack and arson less frequent. In 1988, the number of bombings, while numerically larger, fell to 48 percent of all incidents, while arson, kidnapping, and assault all increased in relative importance.

Of import to you is that while the precise location and timing of terrorist incidents cannot be foreseen, the general region of occurrence can be anticipated to a degree. In the 1970s, over 70 percent of all terrorist incidents were recorded in just two regions: Europe (44 percent) and Latin America (27 percent). The Middle East–North Africa region accounted for less than 15 percent of all incidents. In the 1980s, Latin America emerged as the most dangerous region, accounting for around 60 percent of all terrorist incidents, while Europe (15 percent) declined in relative importance as a venue and Asia, with 14 percent of the incidents, saw an increase in terrorism. The Middle East–North Africa region, contrary to much popular opinion, declined to about 7 percent of all incidents. Of note is the fact that 90 to 95 percent of all incidents occur in the capital city.

Before we look at the world's principal travel destinations, a few last facets of the world's population should be explored: the political organization of states; the comparative size of countries, both in terms of geographical area and population; and the degree of urbanization and emergence of super-cities.

The Political World

Historically, of course, the political map of the world has been in a constant state of flux. Even in this century, change has been the norm. Just after World War II there were 71 independent countries. By the late 1960s, as many former colonial territories had become independent, there were 143 independent countries. Today there are 173. Everyone knows or should know where Australia and Yugoslavia are, but how many have heard of Benin, Bhutan, Burkina Faso, Comoros, Djibouti, Kiribati or Rwanda, let alone Nauru, Tuvalu, or Vanuata? Does it help to know that some of these used to be known as Upper Volta, French Somalia, the Gilbert Islands, or the New Hebrides? Consult a good atlas and a good almanac for their locations and some background information, and a good historical atlas to see how this mosaic of nation states emerged.

In addition to the 173 independent countries there are currently 31 inhabited dependencies, protectorates, possessions, or trust territories still left in the world, principally fragments of former colonial empires and almost all islands, some of them extremely remote. However, many are also major tourist destinations, so they cannot be forgotten. They are too many to show in detail on a map in this handbook, so again, consult a good atlas or globe.

One aspect of nations or countries should be noted. That is, not all are homogeneous in terms of ethnic makeup. Indeed, many, if not most, are heterogeneous. One useful distinction within heterogeneous countries is between *polyethnic* and *plural* countries. Polyethnic countries have several ethnic groups living within their borders, each tending to occupy a distinct area or region. Although each group has general allegiance to the state, their allegiances range from enthusiastic, unqualified support (Switzerland), to reluctant and sometimes very reluctant support (Nigeria, Yugoslavia, the Soviet Union). Many of these countries are former colonial territories that were welded together by the occupying colonial power and have tended to stay together under the force of inertia.

Plural societies have various ethnic groups living within their boundaries who have intermingled throughout the national territory, although they often live in segregated neighborhoods, either voluntarily or involuntarily. These groups tend to follow their own lifestyles but are integrated economically. Examples of plural societies are the United States, Malaysia and other Southeast Asian countries, and Tanzania and other East African countries.

The immediate impact of these kinds of situations is that in Switzerland, for example, the locals speak French in Geneva and Lausanne, German in Bern and Zurich, Italian in Lugano, and Romansch in the countryside around St. Moritz.

In Belgium the locals speak French in Liege, Flemish in Ghent and Antwerp. Brussels (Bruxelles), although located in the Flemish northern part of Belgium, is an enclave of predominantly French speech. Similarly, these distinct ethnic enclaves have distinctive cultural landscapes in terms of architecture, land use patterns, food preferences, and so on and add fuel to tourist dynamics. Following are the ten least and ten most homogeneous countries in the world in terms of ethnic makeup (from *The World Factbook, 1989*, U.S. Government Printing Office, Washington, DC).

Least Homogeneous Countries

Nigeria (21% Hausa, 20% Yoruba, 17% Ibo, 9% Fulani)
Kenya (21% Kikuyu, 14% Luhya, 13% Luo, 11% Kelenjin, 11% Kamba)
Ivory Coast (23% Baoule, 18% Bete, 15% Senoufou, 11% Malinke)
Bolivia (30% Quechua, 25% Aymara, 25% Mixed, 10% European)
Cameroon (31% Cameroon Highland, 19% Equatorial Bantu, 11% Kirdi, 10% Fulani)
Central African Republic (34% Baya, 27% Banda, 21% Mandjia, 10% Sara, 4% Mboum, 4% M'Baka)
Yugoslavia (36% Serb, 19% Croat, 9% Muslim, 8% Slovene, 8% Albanian)
Senegal (36% Wolof, 17% Fulani, 17% Serer, 9% Toucouleur, 9% Diola)
Surinam (37% Hindustani, 31% Creole, 15% Javanese, 10% Bushblack)
Angola (37% Ovimbundu, 25% Kimbundu, 13% Bakongo, 2% Mestico)

Most Homogeneous Countries

North Korea (100% Korean)
Algeria (99% Arab-Berber)
Austria (99% German)
East Germany (99% German)
West Germany (99% German)
Japan (99% Japanese)
Netherlands (99% Dutch)
Portugal (99% Portugese)
South Korea (99% Korean)
Bangladesh (98% Bengali)

Size of Countries

We have seen earlier how the population is distributed over the world and how it is clustered in just four major and two minor concentrations. Indeed, just the top ten countries in population size account for 3.2 billion people, or 65 percent of all humanity, and cover 39 percent of the earth's land surface. The top ten countries in terms of geographical extent or area cover 53 percent of the land area and account for 54 percent of the world's population. Of the top ten countries in each category (population and size), five (the U.S.S.R., China, the United States, Brazil, and India) appear in both categories (Table 6).

Most of the world's independent states or countries, however, are small, both in population size and geographical area. In terms of area, only eight countries have land areas of over a million square miles (Table 6), with another ten countries having land areas between half a million and a million square miles (Algeria, Indonesia, Libya, Mexico, Mongolia, Saudi Arabia, Sudan, Zaire, Iran, and Mongolia—Greenland, a dependency of Denmark is also in this size category but is not an independent country).

Ninety percent of all countries, however, are smaller than 500,000 square miles in extent and almost half (47 percent) of all countries are smaller than 50,000 square miles—about the size of Alabama or half the size of Colorado.

Figure 1 illustrates the comparative sizes of a selection of countries around the world. It is a good idea to get a basic grasp of different countries' sizes when counseling clients and organizing itineraries. People are frequently surprised by the size of Australia, for example, and with the time (and expense) involved in traveling within Australia—let alone getting there. Similarly, surprise is often expressed at the smallness of many European countries, such as Austria or Switzerland, and the close proximity of many attractions.

The whole of Europe, including European Russia (the Soviet Union west of the Urals), is approximately the same size as the United States. Individual countries, however, are much smaller. Texas (267,000 square miles) is larger than all of the non-Soviet European countries. Only France (212,000 square miles) even comes close. Both Britain and West Germany are about the same size as Oregon (albeit with populations of around 60 million each, compared to Oregon's 2 million!). Austria (32,374 square miles) is a little smaller than Maine, and Switzerland occupies only about half of this area.

No wonder, then, that it is possible (but not highly recommended) to see the major tourist attractions in just a few days. In a distance equal to that between St. Louis and Denver, one can travel through several countries, dozens of major cities, and through major linguistic and cultural areas in Europe. Only the Soviet Union, Canada, and China are larger in territory than the United States. Australia, with 2.9 million square miles, comes close.

In terms of population size, only ten countries have populations greater than 100 million (Table 6), with another eleven countries having populations between 50 and 99 million (Egypt, France, West Germany, Iran, Italy, Mexico, the Philippines, Thailand, Turkey, the United Kingdom, and Vietnam). Eighty-eight percent of all countries have a current population of less than 50 million, and a full 45 percent have populations of less than 5 million—about the same population as Missouri or the Philadelphia metropolitan area.

In terms of population density, or the degree of crowding, Monaco, Hong Kong, and Singapore lead the world, with respective densities of 28,000,

Table 6. LARGEST COUNTRIES OF THE WORLD

Country	Size			Country	Population		
	Area*	Population**	Pop. Density***		Population**	Area*	Pop. Density***
U.S.S.R.	8.649	287	33	China	1,069	3.705	288
Canada	3.851	25	6	India	833	1,266	658
China	3.705	1,069	288	U.S.S.R.	287	8.649	33
U.S.	3.623	248	68	U.S.	248	3.623	68
Brazil	3.286	154	47	Indonesia	188	0.735	255
Australia	2.966	16	5	Brazil	154	3.286	47
India	1.266	833	658	Japan	123	0.145	844
Argentina	1.065	33	30	Nigeria	115	0.356	322
Sudan	0.966	25	25	Bangladash	113	0.055	2,028
Zaire	0.905	34	37	Pakistan	110	0.310	335
Total	30.282	2,724			3,239	22.125	

Source: *The World Factbook, 1989* (Washington, DC: U.S. Government Printing Office).
* millions of square miles
** millions
*** per square mile

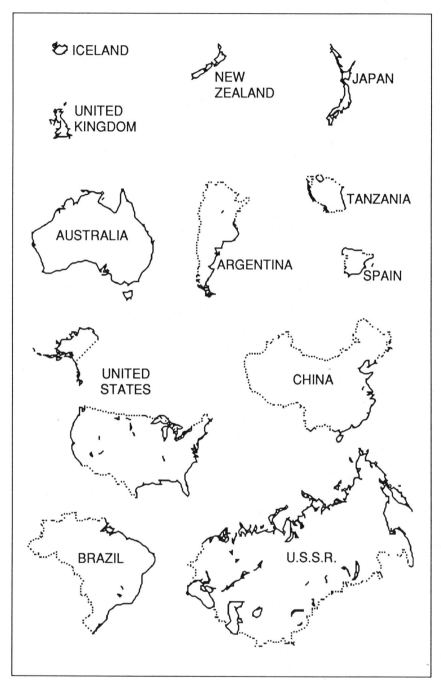

Figure 1. *Comparative Sizes of Selected Countries.*

Table 7. COUNTRIES WITH HIGHEST AND LOWEST POPULATION
DENSITIES (PER SQUARE MILE)

Ten Highest		Ten Lowest	
Monaco	28,072	Mongolia	3
Hong Kong	13,936	Mauritania	4
Singapore	11,910	Australia	5
Malta	2,934	Botswana	5
Bangladash	2,028	Canada	6
Maldavia	1,756	Iceland	6
Taiwan	1,460	Libya	6
Mauritius	1,325	Surinam	6
S. Korea	1,189	Chad	11
San Marino	958	Saudi Arabia	15

Source: *World Almanac, 1990* (New York: Pharos Books, 1990).

14,000, and 12,000 per square mile (Table 7). At the other end of the spectrum, Mongolia, Mauritania, Botswana, and Australia lead the world with population densities of just 3, 4, 5, and 5 people per square mile (Table 7). No U.S. city comes close to the population densities of Monaco or Hong Kong, and only Wyoming, with 4.9 per square mile, comes close to matching the low population densities of Mongolia or Australia.

Urbanization

One of the dominant demographic trends of the last few decades has been the growth of urban areas and the emergence of super-cities. In 1985, 45 percent of the world's population was urbanized—72 percent in the developed world, 36 percent in the developing world. By the year 2000 it is expected that 52 percent of the total population will be urbanized—75 percent in the developed world and 47 percent in the developing world. Despite these trends there still is a wide variety in the degree of urbanization in individual countries around the world. Table 8 lists the ten most and ten least urbanized countries in the world.

Of note is the increase in the number of very large cities. Today there are about one hundred urban areas in the world with populations of 2 million or more, including thirty with over 5 million, twelve with over 10 million, and four with over 15 million inhabitants (Tokyo-Yokohama, Mexico City, Sao Paulo, and New York). By the year 2000 it is expected that there will be forty-eight urban areas with populations over five million, including twenty-three with over 10 million, and six with over 15 million (Tokyo-Yokohama, Mexico City, Sao Paulo, New York, Calcutta, and Bombay). Table 9 lists the world's super-cities, those of 10 million or more inhabitants today, and those expected to reach this plateau by the year 2000—notice how many are in the developing world and how few are in the developed world.

Table 8. URBANIZATION

Most Urbanized (%)		Least Urbanized (%)	
Andorra	100	Bhutan	4
Bermuda	100	Lesotho	5
Hong Kong	100	Nepal	5
Liechtenstein	100	Rwanda	5
Monaco	100	Uganda	7
Singapore	100	Oman	8
Belgium	95	Malawi	8
W. Germany	94	Burkina Faso	9
Spain	91	Solomon Is.	9
Kuwait	90	Yemen	12

Source: *The World Almanac and Book of Facts, 1990* (New York: World Almanac, 1989).

Table 9. WORLD'S LARGEST CITIES, 1985 and 2000: WITH CURRENT POPULATIONS OR PROJECTED POPULATIONS OF OVER 10 MILLION

Urban Area	Population (millions)	
	1985	2000*
Tokyo-Yokohama, Japan	18.82	20.22
Mexico City, Mexico	17.30	25.82
Sao Paulo, Brazil	15.88	23.97
New York, U.S.	15.64	15.78
Shanghai, China	11.96	14.30
Calcutta, India	10.95	16.53
Buenos Aires, Argentina	10.88	13.18
Rio de Janeiro, Brazil	10.37	13.26
London, U.K.	10.36	10.51
Seoul, South Korea	10.28	13.77
Bombay, India	10.07	16.00
Los Angeles, U.S.	10.05	10.99
Osaka-Kobe, Japan	9.45	10.49
Beijing, China	9.25	11.17
Moscow, U.S.S.R.	8.97	10.40
Jakarta, Indonesia	7.94	13.25
Cairo-Giza, Egypt	7.69	11.13
Tehran, Iran	7.52	13.58
Delhi, India	7.40	13.24
Manila-Quezon City, Philippines	7.03	11.07
Karachi, Pakistan	6.70	12.00
Bangkok, Thailand	6.07	10.71
Dhaka, Bangladash	4.89	11.16

*Projected
Source: *The Prospects of World Urbanization, 1987* (New York: United Nations, 1987).

The rapid growth of cities in the developing world has led to slums and overcrowding, typically in shanty towns of squatter huts where the standards of hygiene and of living are appalling. The contrast between the hotel sections and shanty towns of cities like Port au Prince, Haiti; Kingston, Jamaica; and even Rio de Janeiro, Brazil—let alone Calcutta and Bombay, India—are stark. All too frequently these cities, or sections of them, are avoided by tourists, sometimes unfortunately so because they, too, have their worthy attractions.

Principal Tourist Destinations by Continent—Region and Country

The world's principal tourist destinations, ordered by continent or region, and country, are identified in this chapter. Reference maps are also included, to help you locate the destinations identified and italicized in the text. These maps should help you get a firm grasp on where these destinations actually are and help you also appreciate their locations relative to other important destinations or attractions. Such knowledge is vital in planning itineraries, in advising clients of nearby destinations that they may want to consider visiting when they have a set itinerary in mind, or, in some instances, in dissuading clients from including in their itinerary destinations that are perhaps too far apart, given certain time and cost constraints.

Since the emphasis here is on destinations at the country level, such relatively small but important destinations as Hong Kong and Singapore in Asia; Liechtenstein, Luxembourg, and Monaco in Europe; and Hawaii, Fiji, and Tahiti in Oceania have deliberately not been included. Two other tourist destinations, Bermuda and the Bahamas, which do not strictly belong in the Caribbean region (although many guidebooks include them), have similarly been left out of the discussion in this section. Rather, the details of the attractions in these destinations are included in the following chapter, which covers tourist destinations at the individual city or resort/island level.

When studying the following "country profiles" and tourist destination maps the use of a good atlas and globe is highly recommended. It is also important to note that only the principal or main tourist destinations are covered, both in terms of the countries in which they are found, and in terms of individual cities, resorts, or regions. Clearly, there are many more tourist destinations in the world than are covered here and in the next section, but these are undoubtedly the most important ones. Moreover, they are certainly the ones that every travel agent or destination consultant should be knowledgeable about, particularly regarding where they are and what makes them attractive to prospective clients.

In identifying the world's principal tourist destinations we have tried to identify not only the traditional destinations, the ones that most people are familiar with, or at least have probably heard of, but also to identify, when possible, the relatively less well known, "undiscovered gems" of the travel world. In addition, "up and coming areas" have been identified where possible. These designations should generate some thought and, we hope, some discussion. Indeed, a few of the "undiscovered gems" and "up and coming areas" designations were quite deliberately chosen to stimulate debate!

One word on the order in which the following continent/region discussion is presented. The order chosen was based on the descending order of tourism receipts as reported in the *World Almanac, 1990.* Of the world total, Europe commanded 61 percent of the world's total tourism receipts in U.S. dollars, followed by North America with 20 percent and Asia with 11 percent. Africa and the Middle East with 5 percent, South America with 4 percent, and the Caribbean with 2 percent followed. The continent/region accounting for the lowest percentage of total world tourism receipts in the late 1980s was Australia/New Zealand, with less than 2 percent.

Of interest is the identification of the top ten individual countries in terms of tourism receipts. These were, in descending order, the United States, Spain, the United Kingdom, France, West Germany, Italy, Austria, Switzerland, Canada, and Mexico. The ten countries most dependent on tourism (in terms of tourism receipts as percentages of their GNP), in descending order, were the Bahamas (59%), St. Lucia (47%), San Marino (30%), Jamaica (28%), Grenada (26%), Barbados (25%), the Seychelles (25%), Fiji (15%), St. Vincent (14%) and Jordan (12%).

Europe and the Soviet Union

Austria

Traditional Destinations

Vienna (Wien), the capital, is located in the far northeastern corner of the country on the banks of the Danube River (Figure 1). Principal attractions include the Hofberg Imperial Palace, the Museum of Fine Arts, St. Stephen's Cathedral and the Schonbrunn Palace (Austria's Versailles) just outside the city. About 160 miles to the west of Vienna near the West German border is *Salzburg,* a medieval city noted for its Baroque churches, Mirabell Palace and Gardens, and Hohensalzburg Fortress. South of Salzburg is *Zell am See,* a chic resort village.

In eastern Austria lies the *Arlberg,* with the ski resorts of *Lech, Zurs* and *St. Anton,* and the *Tyrol,* an area of breathtaking mountain scenery and the town of

Figure 1. *Austria: Principal Tourist Destinations.*

Innsbruck, known for its Altstadt (Old Town), Hofberg Palace, and two Tyrolean museums. The famous winter resort of *Kitzbuhel* is northeast of Innsbruck.

In southern Austria, in East Tyrol, is the winter and summer resort of *Lienz.* Further east is *Graz* with its Renaissance Landhaus and 15th-century cathedral.

Undiscovered Gems

The *Salzkammergut area* east of Salzberg, has the Wolfgangsee, Altersee, and Traunsee lakes and beautiful mountain scenery. *St. Gilgen* on the Wolfgangsee and *Gmunden* are the two attractive resort towns in the area. The *Worthersee area* in Corinthia, just north of the Yugoslavia border, with the resorts of *Velden* on its western end is another relatively undiscovered gem.

Up and Coming Areas

The *Tauern Range* in Styria between Salzberg and Graz with the resorts of *Grobming* and *Schladming.*

Belgium

Traditional Destinations

Brussels (Bruxelles), the capital, is in central Belgium (Figure 2), and is one of Europe's most attractive cities. It is well known for its Grand' Place, one of the continent's most beautiful squares, its Cathedral of St. Michael and its parks and museums. To the north of Brussels is *Antwerp* (Antwerpen), with its Grote Markt, fine museums and, just outside, *Mechelen,* world famous for its carillon bells.

To the northwest of Brussels is *Ghent* (Gent), with its canals, Gravensteen castle, fine town hall (Stadhuis) and museum of fine arts. Further northwest lies

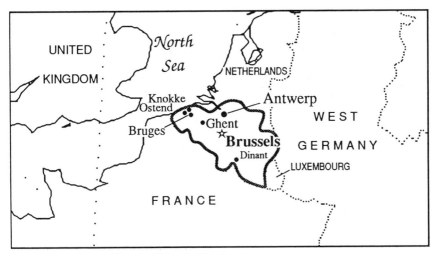

Figure 2. *Belgium: Principal Tourist Destinations.*

Bruges (Brugge), one of the continent's best-preserved medieval towns, known for its picturesque canals, canal bridges, cobbled streets, and Renaissance facades. On Belgium's North Sea coast is *Ostend* (Oostende), a beach resort, gambling center, and major ferry port. To the northeast is *Knokke,* Belgium's premier beach resort.

To the south and southeast of Brussels lie the *Ardennes,* a beautiful area of rolling hills and forests. *Dinant* is the principal resort town here.

Undiscovered Gems

Leuven, just outside Brussels to the east, is a delightful medieval town with an impressive town hall and 15th-century church.

Up and Coming Areas

Brussels itself has witnessed a remarkable rejuvination in the last few years with the influx of Eurocrats and is, today, one of Europe's most vibrant cities.

Czechoslovakia

Traditional Destinations

The capital city of *Prague* (Praha), known for its Old Town (Store Mesto), and its beautiful churches and castle (Prazky Hrad), is located in northwestern Czechoslovakia (Figure 3). To the west of Prague, near the border with the two Germanys, are the famous spa resorts of *Karlovy Vary* (Karlsbad) and *Marianski Lazue* (Marienbad).

To the southeast of Prague is *Brno,* capital of Morovia, with its Cathedral of Sts. Peter and Paul and 13th-century Spilberk Castle. The town of *Telc,* 50 miles west of Brno, is well known for its superb Renaissance architecture. *Bratislava,*

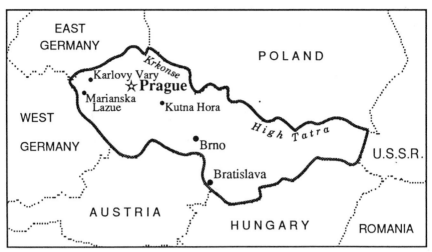

Figure 3. *Czechoslovakia: Principal Tourist Destinations.*

the capital of Slovakia, is south southeast of Prague and is known for its fine Baroque, Gothic, and Renaissance architecture.

Undiscovered Gems

Kutna Hora, southeast of Prague, has delightful Baroque houses, the ornate Vlassky drur mint, and St. Barbara's Cathedral. For stunning mountain scenery, the *High Tatras* (Vysoke Tatry) on the border with Poland in far northeastern Czechoslovakia are hard to beat.

Up and Coming Areas

The *Krkonse (Giant Mountains) area,* on the border with Poland to the northeast of Prague, offers beautiful scenery, the resorts of *Spindleruv Mlyn* and *Harrachov,* and small picturesque towns like *Litomysl, Nove Mesto,* and *Metuji.*

Denmark

Traditional Destinations

Copenhagen (Kobenhavn) is located on the eastern shore of the Danish island of Zealand (Figure 4), and is noted for its harbor area, Rosenborg Castle, Tivoli Gardens amusement park, and its intricate canal system. Some 30 miles to the north of Copenhagen is *Helsingor* (Elsinore), with its beautiful old quarter and 17th-century Kronborg Castle, less than two miles away from Sweden across the sound.

The island of *Funen* (Fyn), lies between Zealand and the Jutland peninsula to the west, and is a picturesque agricultural area. *Odense,* the birthplace of Hans Christian Andersen, has the Den Fynske Lansby open-air museum just outside town. The island of *Bornholm*, 120 miles southeast of Zealand, is a beach resort area, with picturesque fishing villages on its northern shore.

On Jutland is *Arhus* (Aarhus), noted for its Den Gamle By cultural history museum, and *Legoland*, a large amusement park built out of Lego blocks just south of Arhus.

Undiscovered Gems

Aero, an island south of Funen, has the 17th-century town of *Aeroskobing*, with its small half-timbered houses and cobblestoned streets. *Ribe*, on the western coast of southern Jutland, is another medieval town with many historical buildings.

Finland

Traditional Destinations

The Finnish capital, *Helsinki*, is located on a peninsula at the southern end of the country on the Gulf of Finland (Figure 5). It is known for its colorful open-air market, design center, rock church, and the Seurasaari open-air museum. The delightful medieval town of *Porvoo* (Borga), one of Finland's oldest towns, is just 30 miles along the coast east of Helsinki.

Turku, Finland's first capital, noted for its 14th-century cathedral, open-air crafts museum, castle, and the Sibelius museum, is located about 100 miles west of Helsinki. The *Lake District* in southeastern Finland covers about a third of the entire country, from Tampere in the west to the Soviet border, and from Lahti in the south to Lake Oulijarvi in the north. It is an area for year-round outdoor recreation with *Savonlinna* and *Kuopio* as its major resorts.

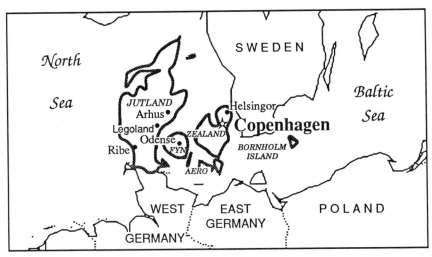

Figure 4. *Denmark: Principal Tourist Destinations.*

Figure 5. *Finland: Principal Tourist Destinations.*

In northern Finland is *Kuusamo,* noted for the white water rapids and river gorges just outside town.

Undiscovered Gems

Ramma, 60 miles north of Turku, is Finland's best-preserved medieval town.

Up and Coming Areas

Lapland (Lappi), one of the most sparsely populated areas in Europe. *Rovaniemi* is the center for exploring this region of the midnight sun.

France

Traditional Destinations

Paris, the capital and principal tourist attraction of France, is located in the north central part of the country (Figure 6). With its Eiffel Tower, Champs Elysees boulevard, Cathedral of Notre Dame, Louvre, and haute couture shopping, Paris is one of Europe's, if not the world's, major tourist destinations. To the southwest of Paris is *Chartres,* with its famous cathedral. Louis XIV's magnificent palace, *Versailles,* and *Fontainebleau* are just outside Paris.

Northwest of Paris, along France's la Manche (the English Channel) is the ritzy resort of *Deauville,* and, to its west, the very different peninsulas of *Normandy* (Normandie), with its WW II D-Day beaches (Utah, Omaha), and

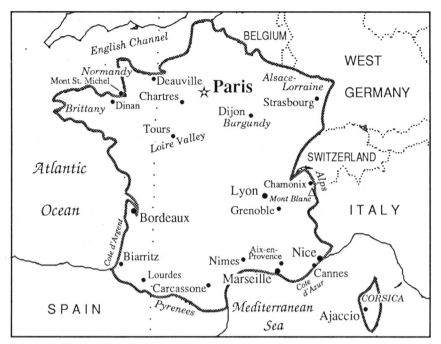

Figure 6. *Principal Tourist Destinations.*

Brittany (Bretagne), with the beautiful medieval town of *Dinan*. In between Normandy and Brittany, on the Gulf of St. Malo, is *Mont St. Michel,* an ancient abby surrounded by fortifications and built on a rock in the bay.

Southwest of Paris is the *Loire Valley* with its magnificent chateaux, such as Chambord, Chenonceau, Cheverny, and Azay-le-Rideau. Further southwest on the Gironde River is *Bordeaux,* surrounded by the world-famous wine producing regions of the Medoc (to the north), St.-Emilion, and Pomerol (to the east). France's most popular Atlantic beach resort, *Biarritz,* is 150 miles southwest of Bordeaux.

Straddling the southern border with Spain are the *Pyrenees* mountains, with Lourdes at their base. Just north of the Pyrenees and east of Toulouse is the medieval fortress city of *Carcassonne.*

On France's central Mediterranean coast is bustling *Marseille* (Marseilles), with its Old Port and side-by-side cathedrals. The surrounding region of *Provence* has the Roman aqueduct and ampitheater at *Nimes* and arena at *Arles.* Just north of Marseille is *Aix-en-Provence,* famous for its main street, Cours Mirabeau.

The *Cote d'Azur,* (Riviera) with its world-famous resorts of *St. Tropez, Cannes, Antibes, Nice,* and *Menton,* along with Monte Carlo, strung out along one of Europe's most beautiful coastlines, is east of Marseille. North of Marseille and south southeast of Paris, lies *Lyon* (Lyons), the country's second city, noted for its ornate Town Hall, Textile Museum, Old Town and superb cuisine. To the east of Lyon on the border with Italy and Switzerland, are the *French Alps*, centered on Mt. Blanc, with such world-famous winter resorts as *Chamonix*.

In the northeastern part of the country, on the border with West Germany, is *Strasbourg*, known for its 12th-century Gothic cathedral and medieval buildings.

Undiscovered Gems

The *Dabo-Wangenbourg* region of Alsace, west and northwest of Strasbourg, has picturesque mountain scenery, quiet villages with splendid half-timbered houses, well-preserved medieval fortifications, feudal castles, and excellent restaurants. The *Perigord-Quercy* area of southwestern France just east of Bordeaux and north of Toulouse has beautiful countryside, fortified towns, caves with prehistoric paintings (Grotte de Font-de-Gaume) and quaint villages.

Up and Coming Areas

The Mediterranean island of *Corsica* (Corse), southeast of Nice, has uncrowded, unspoilt beaches and the principal town of *Ajaccio*.

West Germany

Traditional Destinations

Frankfurt, noted for its medieval squares, modern skyscrapers, Palm Garden, and Old Town of Alt Sachsenhausen, is the major arrival point for most North Americans and is located in central West Germany on the Main River, a major tributary of the Rhine (Figure 7). To the northwest of Frankfurt, between Koblenz and Mainz, is the *Rhine Gorge*, the most picturesque portion of the Rhine, famous for its steep, vineyard-clad hillsides and many castles. Downstream are the cities of Koln (Cologne), and Dusseldorf. *Koln* is noted for its huge, magnificent Gothic cathedral (Dom), and *Dusseldorf*, the haute couture center of Germany, for its Konigsalle, one of the finest boulevards in Europe. Forty miles to the west of Koln, near the Netherlands border, is *Aachen*, with its 9th-century cathedral, and a spa and casino.

In northern Germany lies *Hamburg*, a major port famous for its Rathaus, Public Gardens, Hagenbeck Zoo, and its infamous St. Pauli nightlife district.

South of Frankfurt, on the Neckar just east of Mannheim is the university town of *Heidelberg* with its castle. Germany's famous *Castle Road* (Die Burgenstrasse) follows the lower Neckar valley between Heidelberg and Heilbronn to the southeast. Another famous "road," the *Romantic Road*, starts at Wurzburg, just to the northeast of Heidelberg, and continues through the medieval gem of *Rothenburg* to Fussen in the Allgau Alps on the border with Switzerland.

Figure 7. *West Germany: Principal Tourist Destinations.*

South of Heidelberg, starting at the famous spa of *Baden-Baden* east of Stuttgart, and extending all the way to the Swiss border, is the *Black Forest* (Schwartzwald). Southeast of Stuttgart is the capital of Bavaria, *Munich* (Munchen), with its former royal winter palace (Residenz), art gallery, English Gardens, and famous beer cellars and halls. South of Munich are the *German Alps,* with such winter resorts as *Garmisch-Partenkirchen,* and the royal castles of *Neuschwanstein* and *Hohenschwangau. Nymphenburg Palace* is just on the outskirts of Munich.

Surrounded by East Germany but still an integral part of West Germany, is *West Berlin,* with its Kurfurstendamn shopping street, Tiergarten park, and Dahlem Museum.

Undiscovered Gems

Lubeck, near Germany's Baltic coast northeast of Hamburg and capital of the Hanseatic cities during the Middle Ages, has a delightful, compact, and well-preserved medieval core.

Up and Coming Areas

With the crumbling of the Berlin Wall and the lowering of barriers to movement between the two Germanys, both *West* and *East Berlin* are poised to enter a new period of tourist interest.

Greece

Traditional Destinations

The capital, *Athens* (Athinai), with the Acropolis, National Archaeological Museum, Plaka nightlife section, and 11th-century Monastery of Daphni just outside town, is located at the southwestern end of the Greek mainland (Figure 8). The spectacular *Temple of Poseidon* is on Cape Sounion, 40 miles south of Athens. *The Peloponnesus,* with the ancient ruins of Corinth (Korinthos), Mycenae, Epidaurus, and Olympia, medieval villages, a beautiful coastline, and rugged interior mountains, is west of the capital.

About 100 miles northwest of Athens lies *Delphi,* an impressive archaeological site of extensive ruins 2,000 ft. above the Bay of Itea. In northern Greece are the Vicos and Aoos river canyons forming the *Vicos-Aoos National Park* near the border with Albania. Further northeast is *Thessaloniki* (Salonika), with its archaeological museum and Byzantine churches.

Off Greece's western shore lie the *Ionian islands* of Zakinthos, Kefallinia, Ithaki (Ithaca), Levkas, and *Kerkira* (Corfu), the latter known for its beautiful beaches. To the southeast of Athens in the middle of the Aegean, are the *Cyclades* (Kikladhes), the "classical" Greek islands, notably *Mykenos* (the windmill island), *Santorini* (Thira), *Paros,* and *Ios.* Further east, just off the coast of Turkey, are the *Dodecanese* (Dhodhekanisos) islands, notably *Samos, Patnos,*

Figure 8. *Principal Tourist Destinations.*

Kos, and *Rhodes,* with its ancient ruins, medieval architecture, and superb beaches.

South of the Cyclades is *Crete* (Kriti), with a fine archaeological museum in *Iraklion,* the *Knossos ruins,* and *Samaria Gorge* in the western part of the island.

Undiscovered Gems

The *Saronic islands,* just off the coast between Athens' port of Piraeus and the Parnon peninsula of the Peloponnesus are close-by, yet frequently overlooked, particularly *Poros, Hydra,* and *Spetses.*

Up and Coming Areas

The northern Aegean *Sporades islands,* particularly *Skiathos, Skopelos,* and *Skyros,* are noted for their lushly vegetated interiors, rugged coastlines, and beautiful beaches.

Hungary

Traditional Destinations

Budapest, Hungary's capital, straddles the Danube River in the north central part of the country (Figure 9), and is noted for its Castle Hill area with fine Baroque townhouses, a 13th-century cathedral, and fine museums. North of Budapest is the *Danube Bend area* where the river breaks through the Visegrad and Borzsony mountains and heads south through Hungary. The Danube Bend area is known for its river spas, resorts, Roman ruins, and picturesque villages.

To the southwest of Budapest is central Europe's largest lake, *Lake Balaton,* which is also the country's major summer resort area, with beach resorts lining

Figure 9. *Hungary: Principal Tourist Destinations.*

the lake's southern shore. *Siofok* on the southern shore and *Balatonfured* on the northern shore are the two principal resorts, notably the latter with its spas.

West of Budapest in far western Hungary on the border with Austria lies *Sopron,* a Baroque gem that is one of Europe's most picturesque towns. Esterhazy Palace, a superb Baroque structure, is in *Fertod,* just southeast of Sopron.

South of Budapest, near the border with Yugoslavia, is *Pecs,* known for its former mosques, particularly the Mosque of Pasha Ghazi Kasim, and many museums. In northern Hungary the country's other famous Baroque town, *Eger,* with its large classical cathedral, Baroque and Rococo palaces, churches, and other buildings, is located 65 miles northeast of Budapest. Beyond Eger to the north on the border with Czechoslovakia are Europe's most spectacular caves, the *Baradla Caves,* just outside Aggtelek.

Undiscovered Gems

The *Nograd valley* north of Budapest and east of the Danube Bend area, in the Nograd and Matra mountains, contains the *Paloc villages* of one of the country's many varied ethnic groups.

Up and Coming Areas

The *Matra mountains* north of Gyongyos, has both winter and summer resorts, notably *Matrafured.*

Ireland

Traditional Destinations

Ireland's capital, *Dublin,* with its beautiful Georgian architecture, Castle, museums, and galleries, and legendary pubs, is located on the central eastern coast of the country (Figure 10). South of Dublin are the *Wicklow Mountains,* an outdoor recreation area. Further south is *Waterford,* world famous for the crystal made in its Waterford Glass Factory.

Some 30 miles north of Waterford is *Kilkenny,* a market town with narrow medieval streets and buildings mixed with Georgian terraces. To the southwest of Waterford is *Cork,* with the ruins of the 15th-century Blarney Castle and its "kissing stone" just outside town to the west. *Killarney,* with its magnificent lakes and Ireland's highest mountain (3,414 ft.), is 65 miles northwest of Cork. The *Dingle* and *Iveragh Peninsulas* in County Kerry are 75 miles west of Cork and are known for their outstanding natural beauty.

North of Cork on the Shannon River is *Limerick,* noted for its King John's Castle, cathedral, art gallery and Hunt Collection. *Banratty Castle and Folk Park* is just north of Limerick. To the west, the Atlantic coastline of Clare County is especially attractive, particularly the *Cliffs of Moher* area, rising some 400–700 ft. out of the Atlantic. One of Ireland's greatest historical sights, the *Rock of Cashel,* is 36 miles southeast of Limerick.

Figure 10. *Ireland: Principal Tourist Destinations.*

North northwest of Limerick and due west of Dublin on Ireland's central Atlantic coast is *Galway,* with its many 16th- and 17th-century buildings. It is also the gateway to scenic *Connemara* to the northwest. The *Aran Islands,* home of the famous sweaters, are in Galway Bay.

Undiscovered Gems

Kinsale, a charming 18th-century port with fine bay-windowed Georgian houses lining its winding, narrow streets, and excellent restaurants, is 18 miles south of Cork at the estuary of the Bandon river.

Up and Coming Areas

The *Beara Peninsula,* one of Ireland's most beautiful and unspoiled coastal regions, is in western County Cork.

Italy

Traditional Destinations

Rome (Roma), the country's capital, is halfway down Italy's west coast on the Tyrrhenian Sea (Figure 11), and is famous for its ruins (Forum, Colosseum, baths, Pantheon), Vatican City, and sidewalk cafes. To the southeast along the coast is *Naples* (Napoli), with its National Archaeological Museum, the charming Spacca-Napoli quarter and, outside town, *Herculaneum* and *Pompeii.* Just south of Naples between Sorrento and Salermo is the spectacular *Amalfi Coast* with *Positano,* a very picturesque fishing village. Off the coast are the islands of *Capri* and *Ischia.*

The island of *Sicily* (Sicilia) lies off the boot of Italy. The city of *Palermo* and the classical ruins of *Syracuse* (Siracusa) and the *Valley of Temples* at Agrigento

Figure 11. *Italy: Principal Tourist Destinations.*

are the principal attractions. The island of *Lapari,* off Sicily's north coast, is also popular.

North of Rome is Tuscany is *Florence* (Firenze), world famous for its Renaissance buildings and art. West of Florence near the coast is *Pisa* and its leaning tower (la Torre di Pisa). The small hilltop town of *San Gimignano,* with its medieval fortress towers, is just south southwest of Florence. Northwest of Florence, with *Genoa* (Genova) in the center, is the *Italian Riviera,* stretching from the French border to La Spezia. *Portofino* and *Portovenere* on the di Levante section of the Riviera, between Genoa and La Spezia, are the two most popular areas.

North of Genoa over the Appennini Ligure range in the Po Valley is *Milan* (Milano), famous for its cathedral (Duomo), La Scala opera house, art galleries, and haute couture. North of Milan is the *Italian Lake District* with lakes *Maggiore, Como, Lugano,* and *Garda* (further east), and the snow-capped *Alps* in the distance. The *Italian Dolomites* are east and northeast of the Lake District, stretching from the Po Valley to the Austrian border, with such famous winter resorts as *Madonna di Campiglio, Val di Fassa, Val Gardena,* and *Cortina D'Ampezzo.* South of the Dolomites on the Adriatic coast lies *Venice* (Venezia), with its fantastic network of canals, St. Mark's square, and ornate palaces.

Undiscovered Gems

Ravenna, near the Adriatic coast south of Venice and east of Bologna, has superb Byzantine architecture and unique mosaics.

Up and Coming Areas

Look at the island of *Sardinia* (Sardegna), south of French Corsica, particularly its northeast coast, the *Costa Smeralda.*

The Netherlands

Traditional Destinations

Amsterdam, the capital, is located at the southwestern tip of Ijsselmeer (Zuider Zee) (Figure 12), and is noted for its canals and the beautiful 17th- and 18th-century merchants' houses that line their banks, the art collection of its National Museum, and its colorful Flower Market. *Haarlem,* just 12 miles west of Amsterdam, has one of the Netherland's most delightful medieval centers.

To the southwest of Amsterdam on the North Sea coast is *The Hague* (Den Haag), the Netherlands' seat of government, known for its medieval Binnenhof Parliament complex and art museums. The miniature Holland at *Madurodam* and the seaside resort of *Scheveningen* are also southwest of Amsterdam. *Delft,* another medieval town with tree-lined canals and magnificient Gothic and Renaissance buildings, is just southeast of The Hague. *Gouda,* famous for its cheese market, is just east of The Hague. The other famous cheese market is in *Alkmaar,* north of Amsterdam near the coast.

In the northern Netherlands, strung along the coast, are the *Wadden Islands* (Waddeneilanden), popular for their beaches.

Figure 12. *Netherlands: Principal Tourist Destinations.*

Undiscovered Gems

Try the *province of Noord-Holland,* with such historic villages as *Volendam* and *Marken,* together with picturesque medieval towns like *Monnickendam, Hoorn, Enkhuizen* and *Edam.*

Norway

Traditional Destinations

The capital, *Oslo,* with its harbor, castle, museums, and royal palace, is located at the head of Oslofjord in southern Norway (Figure 13). To the south of Oslo, along the western side of Olsofjord, are the whaling ports of *Tonsberg* and *Sandefjord.* Further southwest along the southern coast of Norway between Risor and Farsund is the country's principal beach resort area *Sonlandet.* On the southwest coast is *Stavanger,* an old fishing port and now center of Norway's oil industry.

West of Oslo on the coast across the southern Jotunheimen Mountains is the medieval city of *Bergen,* with its wooden buildings in Bryggen, Hanseatic Museum, and Stave Church. Bergen is the departure point for trips to Norway's magnificent *fjords,* particularly *Hardangefjord* to the south of Bergen, and *Sognefjord* and *Geirangerfjord* to the north. Further north along the Atlantic

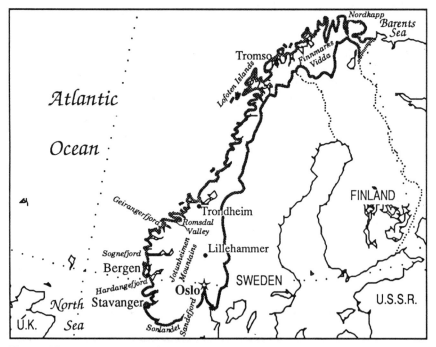

Figure 13. *Norway: Principal Tourist Destinations.*

coast is *Trondheim,* the medieval capital of Norway, with its museums, art galleries, and beautiful Nidaros Cathedral.

In northern Norway is *Tromso,* a university town, noted for its wooden cathedral and museum with Lapland exhibits. In the far northern part of the country is Europe's largest wilderness area, *Finnmarks Vidda.*

Undiscovered Gems

The *Lofoten Islands,* off the northern coast south of Tromso, are noted for their rugged beauty, jagged peaks, fjords, and picturesque fishing villages like *Nusfjord.* The *Romsdal Valley,* northeast of Geirangerfjord and southwest of Trondheim on the mainland, is a spectacular narrow valley, surrounded by some of Norway's best climbing mountains.

Up and Coming Areas

The *Jotunheimen Mountains,* between Oslo and Trondheim and centered on *Lillehammer,* famous for its Norwegian Williamsburg, the Sandvig Collection of buildings, are an area of rugged mountains, beautiful lakes and three of Norway's national parks *Ormtjernkampen, Rondane,* and *Jotunheimen.*

Poland

Traditional Destinations

The capital, *Warsaw* (Warszawa), with its fine Old Town, Royal Castle, National Museum, and Wilanow Palace and park just outside the city, is located in east central Poland (Figure 14). Some 50 miles south of Warsaw is the 17th-century palace of *Nieborow* set in a beautiful Baroque garden. About 100 miles southeast of the Capital is *Lublin,* with its 16th-century castle and old town. *Zamosc,* noted for its superb Renaissance architecture, is another 54 miles to the southeast.

One of the most attractive medieval towns in Europe, *Krakow* is 200 miles south of Warsaw. It is noted for its many well-preserved or restored medieval and Renaissance buildings, its Royal Castle, and its cathedral. Just 34 miles west of Krakow is *Auschwitz,* now a museum. South of Krakow on the Czechoslovakian border are the *Tatry (Tatra) Mountains,* known for their spectacular scenery, *Lake Morskie Oko,* and the *Koscieliska valley. Zakopane* is the main winter resort in the area.

West of Warsaw is *Poznan,* famous for its Old Market square with a fine Renassiance town hall, and old town.

On Poland's northeast Baltic coast, northwest of Warsaw and centered on Gdansk is the *Amber Coast,* with the beach resorts of *Sopot* and *Juata* on the Hel peninsula. Further west, up to the East German border, is the *Polish Riviera,* centered on the beach resort of *Kolobrzeg.* East of *Gdansk* and north of Warsaw is the *Mazurian Lake District,* famous for its nature reserves, hunting, fishing, and sailing.

Figure 14. *Poland: Principal Tourist Destinations.*

Undiscovered Gems

Wroclaw, west southwest of Warsaw and south of Poznan, is noted for its many canals ("the Venice of East Europe") bridges, and the medieval old town surrounding its Gothic cathedral.

Up and Coming Areas

The *Beskid-Slaski Mountains* just west of the Tatry Mountains in southern Poland on the border with Czechoslovakia, have the winter resorts of *Wisla* and *Szcyrk.*

Portugal

Traditional Destinations

Lisbon (Lisboa), the Portugese capital and noted for its narrow cobblestoned streets in the old Moorish quarter (The Alfama), Jeronimos Monastery, wide avenues, and many hills, lies in south central Portugal on the banks of the Tagus (Figure 15). Just to the west of Lisbon is *Queluz Palace,* Portugal's Versailles, and *Sintra* with its two Moorish palaces. On the coast west of Lisbon, just 16 and 20 miles away, respectively, are *Estoril* and *Cascais:* the former long a glamorous resort, the latter a chic beach resort.

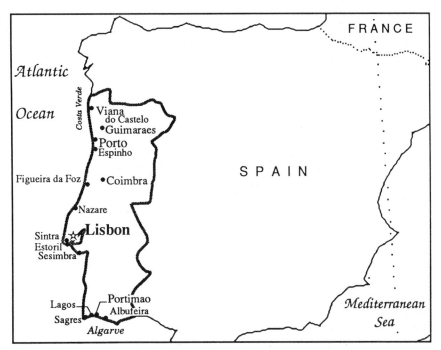

Figure 15. *Portugal: Principal Tourist Destinations.*

On Portugal's southern coast between Cape St. Vincent (Cabo de Sao Vicente) and the Spanish border is the famed *Algarve,* Portugal's premier beach resort area with the resorts of (west to east) *Sagres, Lagos, Portimao,* and *Albufeira* being especially noteworthy.

Along the Atlantic coast north of Lisbon are the beach resorts *Nazare* and *Figueira da Foz,* noted for their superb beaches. Inland from the latter is Portugal's oldest university town, *Coimbra,* with its steep, winding, tiered streets, Old University, Machado de Castro Museum, and Santa Cruz Monastery.

Further north along the Atlantic coast straddling the banks of the river Douro is *Porto* (Oporto), with its Romanesque cathedral, 19th-century stock exchange and port warehouses along the Douro. North of Porto is the *Costa Verde,* centered on the beach resort of *Viana do Castelo.* South of Porto is the gambling resort of *Espinho.*

Undiscovered Gems

The medieval village of *Guimaraes,* the country's first capital, is 32 miles northeast of Porto and is noted for its castle, palace, and beautiful Church of Our Lady of the Olive Tree.

Up and Coming Areas

The island of *Madeira,* 600 miles southwest of the mainland and 300 miles off the coast of Morocco is known for its mild climate, rocky cliffs, and mountainous interior, picturesque villages, and general "unspoiled" ambiance.

Romania

Traditional Destinations

Sometimes referred to as the "Paris of the Balkans" the capital, *Bucharest* (Bucuresti), with its Cismiqiu Park, broad avenues, and many excellent museums, is located in the southeast part of the country south of the Transylvanian Alps (Figure 16). To the east of Bucharest on the shores of the *Black Sea* are the resorts of *Constanta,* and *Mamaia.* South of Constanta are the spa resorts of *Eforie Nord* and *Mangalia,* famous for their mud baths.

North of Bucharest in the *Transylvanian Alps* is the winter sports center of *Sinaia,* also known for its monastery and royal summer palace. Just over the crest of the Transylvanian Alps is *Brasov,* a fine medieval city famous for its Black Church (Cutea Bisericii Negre). Just outside Brasov is the winter resort of *Poiana Brasov.* About 90 miles west of Brasov, at the foot of the Transylvanian Alps is *Sibiu,* another well-preserved medieval town with an excellent ethnographic museum. Northwest of Brasov and northeast of Sibiu lies yet another attractive medieval town, *Sighisoara.*

In the southwestern part of Romania at the western end of the Transylvanian Alps near the border with Yugoslavia is the Roman spa, *Baile-Herculane,* which still functions as a spa and is, indeed, one of Romania's principal spa resorts, noted for its beautiful surroundings. *Timisoara,* to the northwest, is famous for its gardens, parks, and Baroque public buildings.

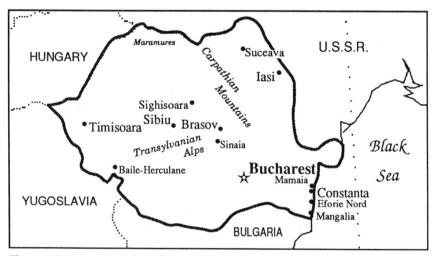

Figure 16. *Romania: Principal Tourist Destinations.*

Moldavia in the northeastern part of Romania is noted for its 15th- and 16th-century painted monasteries, famous for their frescoes covering both exterior and interior walls, many of them around *Suceava*.

Undiscovered Gems

The *Maramures region* in northern Romania, on the western side of the Carpathian Mountains near the border with the Soviet Union, is an area of unspoiled, rural villages rich in folk architecture and folklore, populated by peasants wearing traditional costumes. The town of *Iasi* in Moldavia near the Soviet border is noted for its beautiful architecture with many buildings dating from the 15th and 16th centuries.

Up and Coming Areas

Visit *Bucharest* itself now that Romanian society has opened up after the collapse of a repressive communist regime.

Soviet Union

Traditional Destinations

The Soviet Union's principal tourist destinations are all in the western part of the country, almost all in European Russia (Figure 17). *Moscow* (Moskva), the capital, is in western Russia, approximately one third of the way between

Figure 17. *Soviet Union: Principal Tourist Destinations.*

Leningrad on the Gulf of Finland and the Caspian Sea on the border with Iran. With Red Square, the Kremlin, Tretyakov Gallery and the world-famous Bolshoi Theater and Ballet, Moscow is the Soviet Union's premier tourist destination. *Leningrad,* some 400 miles to the northwest, has a State Hermitage, Winter Palace (with unquestionably one of the world's finest collections of art). The Russian "Versailles," *Petrodvorets,* is just outside Leningrad.

The Estonian capital, *Tallin,* just west of Leningrad is noted for its many medieval buildings. Further west is *Riga,* capital of Latvia, with a cathedral and medieval structures. Some 500 miles southwest of Moscow is *Kiev,* known for its Cathedral of St. Sophia.

On the southern border of the Soviet Union is the *Black Sea,* with its resorts, including *Yalta. Tbilisi,* the capital of Georgia, lies between the Black and Caspian Seas, and has such notable sights as a cathedral, a castle, and botanical gardens.

Further east in Uzbekistan, near the border with Afghanistan, are the cities of Bukhara and Samarkand. *Bukhara* is known for its Kalyan Minaret, fortress (Ark), and bazaar, *Samarkand* for its splendid madrassahs and exotic Shadi Zinda (Shakhi-Zinda) mosques and mausoleums.

Spain

Traditional Destinations

Madrid, Spain's capital, is located in the center of the country on the Castillian plateau (Figure 18). It is famous for its Prado Museum, Plaza Mayor (one of Europe's grandest), Royal Palace, and vibrant nightlife. Just south southwest of Madrid is *Toledo,* with its churches, synagogues, mosques, Alcazar, and city walls. Near Toledo is *Cuenca,* famous for its hanging houses (Casas Colgadas). North northwest of Madrid across the Sierra de Guadarrama mountains, lies *Segovia,* noted for its huge Roman aqueduct, Gothic cathedral, and magnificent Alcazar (fortress). Further northwest of the capital is the old university town of *Salamanca,* known for its varied architectural heritage and its Plaza Mayor, considered to be one of the most beautiful in Spain.

In Galicia, in the far northwestern corner of Spain, is one of the continent's most dramatic cathedrals in *Santiago de Compostela.* Another magnificent cathedral is in *Burgos,* 155 miles north of Madrid.

On the Bay of Biscay, near the French border, is Spain's largest Atlantic beach resort, *San Sebastian.* Just southeast of San Sebastian in the foothills of the Pyrenees lies *Pamplona,* world famous for its July "running of the bulls" San Fermin Fiesta. The *Pyrenees* themselves, straddling the border with France, offer dramatic Alpine scenery, particularly in the *Ordesa* and *d'Aiguestortes i Estany de Sant Maurici national parks.* The principal winter resort area in the Spanish Pyrenees is *Jaca.*

On Spain's northeast Mediterranean coast is the country's second city, *Barcelona,* noted for its elegant Rambas boulevards, cathedral, Gothic Quarter, and fine museums. Between Barcelona and the French border to the north is the

Figure 18. *Spain: Principal Tourist Destinations.*

Costa Brava. Further southwest on the Mediterranean coast is *Valencia,* with its distinctively Moorish architectural style and famous Las Fallas festival in March.

Off the Catalonian coast 100 miles southeast of Barcelona and east of Valencia are the *Balearic Islands* (Islas Baleares) of Mallorca, Menorca, Ibiza, and Formentara. *Mallorca* (Majorca) is the largest and one of the most popular resort islands of the entire Mediterranean. *Ibiza* is the rich, trendy island of the group.

In southern Spain are the three Andalusian cities: *Granada,* with its 13th- and 14th-century Alhambra complex built by the Moors; *Cordoba,* with its mosque-cathedral and Alcazar; and *Seville,* with its Gothic cathedral and Alcazar. South of Granada are Spain's highest mountains, the *Sierra Nevada,* and the ski resort of *Sol y Nieve.* Over the mountains and along the Mediterranean coast from Cabo de Gata to Tarifa is the world-famous *Costa del Sol,* with most of the beach resorts between *Malaga* and *Gibraltar. Torremolinos* is Spain's "Miami Beach," and *Marbella* the chic resort area.

Undiscovered Gems

The medieval, walled city of *Avila,* lying between the Sierra de Avila and Sierra de Gredos mountains west of Madrid, is a national monument. On the Costa Blanca south of Valencia is the beach resort of *Alicante,* with gorgeous beaches and inexpensive lodging.

Up and Coming Areas

Algeciras at the western end of the Costa del Sol, just west of Gibraltar, is a fast-developing beach resort area and jumping-off point to Morocco.

Sweden

Traditional Destinations

Sweden's capital, *Stockholm,* with its old town (Gamla Stan), Royal Palace, and Skansen open-air museum, is located in southeastern Sweden on a series of islands just inland from the Baltic Sea (Figure 19). Sweden's Versailles, *Drott-ningholms Kungliga Slott* (Royal Palace), is just outside Stockholm on Lake Malaran. Just north of Stockholm is the university town of *Uppsala,* known for its Gothic cathedral.

In northern Sweden is the winter sports resort of *Ostersund* in the province of Jantlands Lan, and, on the upper Gulf of Bothnia, the Lapp towns of *Lulea,* noted for its Lapp ethnographic museum, and *Gammelstad,* known for its old wooden buildings. In the far north, above the arctic circle, and well into the rugged mountains that Sweden shares with Norway, are the national parks of *Padjelanta* and *Stora Sjofallet.*

South of Stockholm along the Baltic coast is *Kalmar,* with its castle and 17th-century Baroque cathedral and, offshore, the island of *Oland.* At the southern tip of the country is *Ystad,* a well-preserved medieval city. The university town of *Lund,* outside Malmo, is inland to the west and known for its

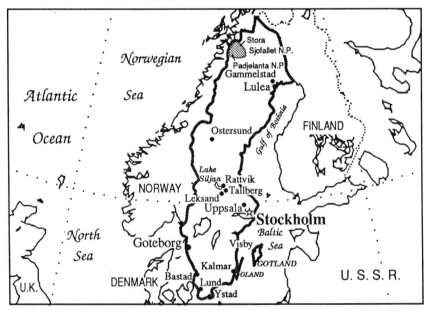

Figure 19. *Sweden: Principal Tourist Destinations.*

beautiful Romanesque cathedral and museum of old buildings. The fashionable beach resort of *Bastad* is northwest of Lund.

On Sweden's western coast is *Goteborg* (Gothenburg), with its Elfsborg Fortress, excellent Museum of Art, and Liseberg and Amusement Park. The famous *Gota Canal* runs from Goteborg to Stockholm through Ostergotland.

Undiscovered Gems

The Baltic island of *Gotland,* south of Stockholm, with the well-preserved, walled medieval town of *Visby,* is well known to Swedes but not to foreigners.

Up and Coming Areas

The *Lake Siljan area* northwest of Stockholm, with the lake resorts of *Tallberg, Rattvik,* and *Leksand,* but particularly Tallberg, is delightful.

Switzerland

Traditional Destinations

The Swiss capital, *Bern* (Berne), with its famous Clock Tower, cathedral, Bear Pits and many fine museums, is located in central, western Switzerland on the banks of the Aare (Figure 20). East northeast of Bern, at the western end of the Vierwaldstatter See, is *Lucerne* (Luzern), noted for beautiful narrow streets, colorful squares, and medieval buildings decorated with wall paintings. *Zurich,* the country's banking center, is to the northeast of Lucerne, and is known for elegant shops, Baroque guild houses and Guildhalls, and Romanesque cathedral.

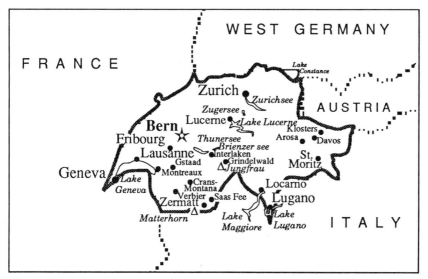

Figure 20. *Switzerland: Principal Tourist Destinations.*

Southwest of Bern is *Fribourg,* noted for its well-preserved medieval buildings. Southeast of Bern is *Interlaken,* situated between the Thunnersee and the Brienzersee. It is the gateway to the truly magnificent mountain scenery of the *Bernese Oberland* with the spectacular *Grindelwald Valley* and the equally spectacular classical U-shaped glacial *Lauterbrunnen Valley* to the southeast and south of Interlaken, respectively. *Grindelwald* is beneath the *Eiger* and *Jungfrau,* two of Switzerland's most magnificent mountains. The Lauterbrunnen Valley is known for its waterfalls and the beautiful village of *Muren* above the valley. To the southwest, at the western end of the Bernese Oberland, is the international jet-set winter resort of *Gstaad.*

Further west, in French-speaking Switzerland, is *Lake Geneva* (Lac Leman). At the lake's far western end is *Geneva* (Geneve), noted for its beautiful lakefront promenade, fine museums, old town (Vieille Ville) and active nightlife. On the lake's northern shore is *Lausanne,* with its steep streets, Gothic cathedral, and medieval old town. *Montreaux,* at the eastern end of the lake, is famous for its July jazz festival and the 13th-century Chateau de Chillon fortress outside town.

To the southeast of Lake Geneva in Valais are the winter resorts of *Verbier* and *Zermatt,* a year-round very chic resort at the foot of the famous Matterhorn on the Italian border. In Italian-speaking Ticino are the two lakeside resorts of *Locarno* on Lake Maggiore, and *Lugano* on Lake Lugano.

In eastern Switzerland in Graubunden canton are the winter resorts of *Arosa, Davos,* and *Klosters.* South of these is *St. Moritz,* perhaps the world's most famous and fashionable winter resort.

Undiscovered Gems

Saas Fe, just east of Zermatt in Valais canton is both a winter and summer resort where automobiles are banned. Here is Switzerland at its best.

Up and Coming Areas

Crans-Montana, on the north side of the Rhine in Valais, is fast becoming a first-class international winter resort.

United Kingdom

Traditional Destinations

The capital, *London,* famous for its Tower, Westminster Abbey, Buckingham Palace, fine museums, shopping, and theater, is located in southeastern England along the Thames River (Figure 21). Southeast of London in Kent is *Canterbury,* with its historic cathedral and cloister. Just outside Canterbury is *Leeds Castle,* one of the most impressive in England. South of London on the English Channel is the beach resort of *Brighton,* famous for its Royal Pavilion. Due west of London, near the Bristol Channel, is the old port of *Bristol,* known for its parish church, and the Clifton Suspension Bridge. Just 13 miles southeast of Bristol is

Figure 21. *United Kingdom: Principal Tourist Destinations.*

the ancient spa of *Bath*, with the most complete Roman remains in Britain, and elegant Georgian architecture. Britain's most famous prehistoric monument, *Stonehenge*, is 30 miles southeast of Bath on the Salisbury Plain.

Starting just north of Bristol and running in a northeastern direction are the *Cotswolds*, with their distinctive village architecture and rolling picturesque landscape. North of the Cotswolds are the two ancient cities of *Gloucester*, with its magnificent cathedral and Victorian Docks, and *Worcester*, with its famous cathedral and many half-timbered Tudor houses.

The world-renowned universities of Oxford and Cambridge are northwest and north of London, respectively. *Oxford* is particularly well-known for Magdalen College and Ashmolean Museum, and *Cambridge* for Queen's College and King's College Chapel. Across the Cotswolds to the northwest of Oxford is *Stratford-upon-Avon*, Shakespeare's birthplace, known for its Shakespearean drama.

In northern England, in Yorkshire, is the fine medieval town of *York*, with its Gothic York Minster, city walls, and excellent folk museum. North of York are the beautiful *Yorkshire Moors* and, to the northwest, the *Yorkshire Dales*. Across the Pennines to the northwest is the *Lake District*, site of one of Britain's first national parks.

In Scotland to the north and just south of the Firth of Forth lies *Edinburgh*, with its castle, "Royal Mile," elegant 18th-century townhouses and world-famous festival. Just northeast of Edinburgh across the River Forth is *St.*

Andrews, known the world over for its golf courses. In northern Scotland are the *Scottish Highlands*, beautiful, rugged mountains with some of Britain's most spectacular scenery. Off Scotland's western coast are the *Inner and Outer Hebrides*, notably the *Isle of Sky*, with its rugged coast and outdoor recreation.

Undiscovered Gems

Cornwall and *Devon*, making up the southwestern peninsula of England, are known for their spectacular coastline, desolate inland moors, picturesque villages *(Clovelly)*, and seaside resorts such as *Torquay, Truro,* and old fishing ports.

Up and Coming Areas

Wales, to the west of England, has some rugged, wild scenery both inland and along the coast, and probably more castles per square mile than any other place in Europe, together with such eccentric places as *Portmeiron*.

Yugoslavia

Traditional Destinations

The rugged, beautiful *Adriatic coast* of Yugoslavia is the country's principal tourist destination, especially the towns of Split and Dubrovnik (Figure 22). *Split*, about halfway down the coast, is noted for the Diocletian Palace that makes up a quarter of the old town, and the many other Venetian Gothic and

Figure 22. *Yugoslavia: Principal Tourist Destinations.*

Renaissance buildings. Further southeast is *Dubrovnik,* the "jewel of the Dalmation coast," a medieval fortess city. Dating from the 15th century, with intact city walls, it is remarkably well preserved and is noted for its striking architectural unity. The Adriatic coast itself, seen from the Adriatic Highway that parallels it, is one of the most beautiful in Europe.

In northern Yugoslavia along the borders with Italy and Austria is the inland resort of *Bled* in the striking *Julian Alps* (Julijske Alps). Just southeast of the Julian Alps is *Ljubljana,* capital of Slovenia and noted for its fine old town with many restored Baroque buildings. Further south, on the coast, is the elegant gambling resort of *Opatija.* Inland, over the coastal mountains, is the capital of Croatia, *Zagreb,* known for its medieval old town/upper town, Gallery of Primitive Art, other fine museums, and Yugoslavia's best nightlife. South of Zagreb is the *Plitvice Lakes National Park,* 16 lakes connected by cascading waterfalls.

Inland from Split, across the Dinaric Alps, is the winter resort of *Sarajevo,* also noted for its large Turkish bazaar, mosques, and red-tiled roofs. South of Dubrovnik is Montenegro's oldest resort, *Herceg-Novi,* known for its 11th- and 17th-century monasteries. The train ride from Bar, to the southeast, to the national capital of Belgrade is one of the more spectacular in Europe, passing through *Moraca Canyon.* Even more spectacular is *Tara Canyon,* almost 4,000 ft. deep, southeast of Sarajevo. *Belgrade* (Beograd), the country's capital, is in northeast Yugoslavia near the Romanian border and is known for its Kalemegdan fortress, Serbian Orthodox Church Museum, and National Museum. In southern Yugoslavia is the Macedonian capital, *Skopje,* with its restored 15th- and 16th-century buildings.

North America
Canada

Traditional Destinations

Toronto, Canada's largest city, known for its CN Tower, beautiful harborfront, the Royal Ontario and other fine museums, is located on the northwestern shore of Lake Ontario in southern Ontario (Figure 23). *Niagara Falls,* straddling the U.S.–Canada border is 90 miles from Toronto across Lake Ontario. To the northeast of Toronto is the capital, *Ottawa,* with impressive Gothic Parliament buildings, Rideau canal, and fine museums. Further down the Ottawa river is *Montreal,* the largest city in French-speaking Quebec Province, and noted for its old town (Vieux Montreal), and cosmopolitan atmosphere. About 127 miles further northeast is *Quebec City,* the country's oldest city with its Place Royale, Citadel, and nearby Ile d'Orleans with its well-preserved 18th-century French-Canadian heritage.

In far northeastern Canada are the Maritime Provinces of *Nova Scotia,* with historic *Halifax* and its Citadel and the spectacular *Cape Breton Highlands*

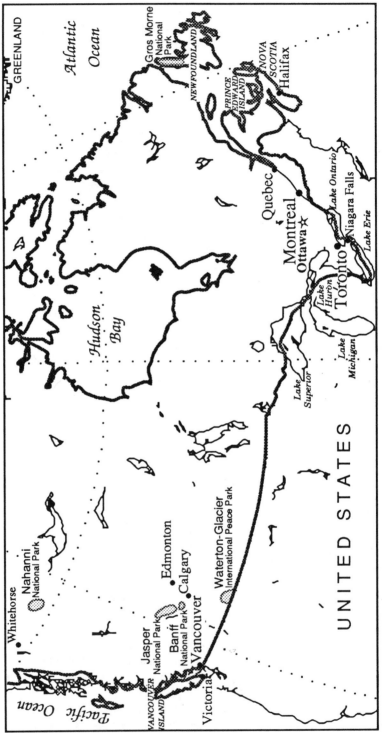

Figure 23. *Canada: Principal Tourist Destinations.*

National Park, and *Newfoundland,* with its coastal fishing villages and beautiful, rugged scenery.

In western Canada the principal tourist destinations are concentrated in the Canadian Rockies and along the coast of British Columbia. In the *Canadian Rockies* are two of North America's most spectacular national parks, Banff and Jasper. *Banff National Park,* about 80 miles west of Calgary in Alberta, is noted for its stunning mountain scenery and beautiful Lake Louise. *Jasper National Park,* north of and connected to Banff National Park, by the Icefields Parkway, has some of Canada's most majestic mountain scenery. *Waterton-Glacier International Peace Park* straddles the Alberta-Montana border south of Calgary. *Calgary* itself is a booming city, best known for the annual Calgary Stampede rodeo, and its zoo, considered to be the country's best.

Vancouver, with its world-famous Stanley Park, aquarium, and Gastown nightlife area, is on Canada's far western coast. *Victoria,* the provincial capital with its Victorian houses and manicured gardens and parks, especially Butchart Gardens, is just west of Vancouver on Vancouver Island

Undiscovered Gems

Field is just west of Lake Louise in Banff National Park. Surrounded by *Yoho National Park,* if offers little-known spectacular scenery and an uncrowded, unhurried small-town ambiance.

Up and Coming Areas

British Columbia's *Whistler-Blackcomb* ski area just northeast of Vancouver, has challenging runs, extensive terrain, excellent lifts and food, and good apres ski nightlife.

Mexico

Traditional Destinations

Mexico City (Ciudad de Mexico), the country's capital and one of the world's largest cities, known for its Zocalo, magnificent Chapultepec Park, and superb National Museum of Anthropology, is located in the central, interior part of Mexico (Figure 24). To the northwest of Mexico City are the wonderful colonial cities of *Quertaro, San Miguel de Allende, Guanajuato, Morelia,* and *Guadalajara,* with its fine Baroque buildings, museums, and crafts shopping (in San Pedro Tiaquepaque). South of Mexico City on the Pacific coast is *Acapulco,* perhaps Mexico's most famous beach resort. Up the coast to the northwest of Acapulco lie the resorts of *Ixtapa-Zihautanejo,* with its beautiful beaches, and *Manzanillo.* Still further up the coast in the state of Jalisco, is the resort of *Puerto Vallarta* on Bahia de Banderas (Bay of Flags), and in Sinaloa, *Mazatlan,* with its fine beaches, excellent fishing and El Mirador "death divers."

In northern Mexico in the state of Sonora on the Gulf of California, is the beach resort of *Guaymas,* and, inland, spectacular *Copper Canyon.* The train

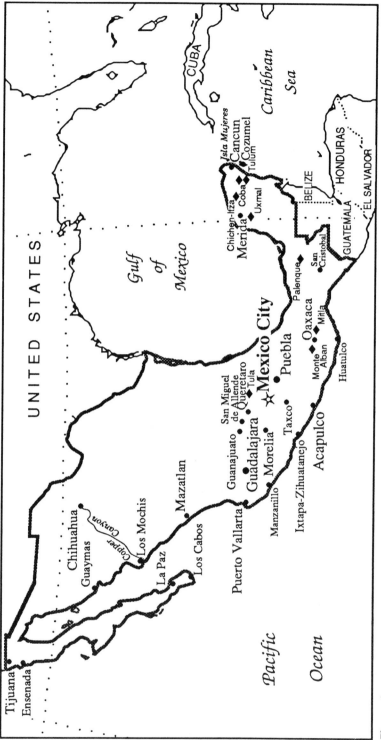

Figure 24. *Mexico: Principal Tourist Destinations.*

84

ride from Los Mochis to Chihuahua through this complex of six huge canyons is breathtaking. In the far northwestern part of Mexico is *Baja California,* a rugged, beautiful peninsula with the beach resorts of *Ensenada* at its northern end just below the California border, and, at its southern tip, *Los Cabos,* with its spectacular coastline, superb fishing, sailing, and whale watching (Jan.–Feb.).

Southeast of Mexico City in the interior highlands are the colonial cities of *Puebla, Taxco,* and *Oaxaca,* with its busy Zocalo, fine cathedral, colorful markets (the large Mercado Juarez and Saturday Indian Market), and surrounding Indian handicraft villages. Just outside Oaxaca is one of the most impressive pre-Columbian archaeological sites in Mexico, *Monte Alban. Mitla,* famous for its ornate stone mosaics, is some 30 miles southeast of Oaxaca.

The Yucatan peninsula, jutting into the Gulf of Mexico, in far eastern Mexico, has famous pre-Columbian sites, including Chichen-Itza and Uxmal. *Chichen-Itza,* some 75 miles east of Merida, is one of the largest, best-restored, and certainly most dramatic archaeological sites in the country. *Uxmal,* one of the finest and most complete complexes of pre-Columbian architecture, is just 60 miles south of Merida. On the Caribbean coast of the Yucatan are the beach resorts of *Cancun* and *Cozumel,* and offshore *Isla Mujeres,* with their superb beaches of white sand, excellent snorkeling and scuba diving, deep-sea fishing and other water sports.

Undiscovered Gems

San Cristobal, some 280 miles east of Oaxaca in the state of Chiapas near the border with Guatemala, is noted for its Baroque architecture, colorful daily market (except Sunday), and Indians in colorful traditional dress.

Up and Coming Areas

Huatulco, on the Pacific coast south of Oaxaca, is the latest beach resort to be developed by the Mexican government, and already has a Club Med and three hotels on just one of its nine beautiful bays.

United States

Traditional Destinations

America's three most visited destinations are spread out over the full length of the country—Florida, California, and Hawaii (Figure 25). *Florida,* the country's premier tourist destination, has *DisneyWorld* and a host of other theme parks around *Orlando* in the center interior of the peninsula, *Cape Canaveral* and the *Kennedy Space Center* to its east on the Atlantic coast, and a whole series of Atlantic beach resorts and cities stretching down the entire length of the coastline from Jacksonville to Miami-Miami Beach. Of particular note are: *Palm Beach-West Palm Beach* with its Mediterranean mansions; *Ft. Lauderdale* with its canals and fine museums; and *Miami-Miami Beach* with its Art Deco district, Seaquarium, and fine beaches.

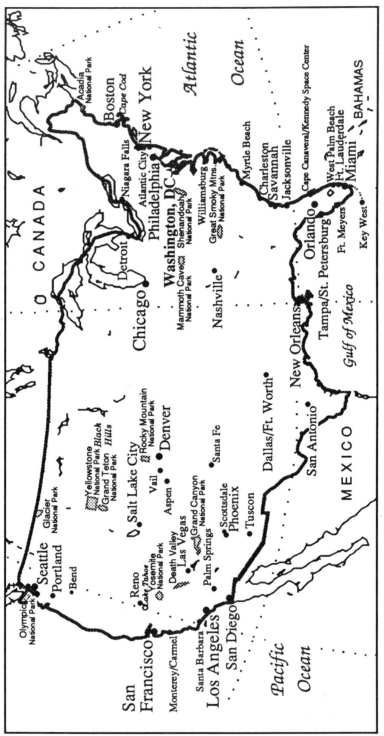

Figure 25. *United States: Principal Tourist Destinations.*

Inland from Miami is the spectacular *Everglades National Park,* the country's only subtropical wetland, famous for its birdlife. Stretching from just south of Miami into the Gulf of Mexico are the *Florida Keys* and, at their western end, *Key West,* America's "Caribbean resort." On Florida's Gulf coast, halfway up the peninsula is *Tampa-St. Petersburg* with its excellent beaches and Busch Gardens, one of the country's largest amusement parks.

Across the country, some 2,400 miles from Miami, is southern California, home of *Los Angeles,* with its film studios, Beverly Hills and Rodeo Drive, excellent museums, performing arts, and, further southeast in Orange County, Disneyland. South of Los Angeles is *San Diego,* with a magnificent harbor, world-famous zoo and Wild Animal Park. *San Francisco,* some 400 miles to the north of Los Angeles, is the other California tourist magnet with its truly magnificent natural setting, Chinatown, cable cars, Golden Gate Bridge, and cultural life. In between, along California's Highway 1, is some of the world's most spectacular coastal scenery, particularly along *Big Sur,* and delightful coastal resorts, especially *Santa Barbara, Monterey,* and *Carmel.* Inland, California offers the magnificent Sierra Nevada mountains with *Yosemite, Kings Canyon,* and *Sequoia National Parks, Lake Tahoe,* and the winter sports areas of *Squaw Valley* and *Mammoth. Death Valley,* the lowest and hottest spot in North America, is on the border with Nevada.

Some 2,400 miles into the Pacific southeast of California, are the *Hawaiian Islands,* America's other principal tourist destination. From *Waikiki,* with the world's largest concentration of hotels/motels and its famous swimming and surfing beach on Oahu, to Kauai's splendid *Waimea Canyon,* and the Big Island's *Hawaii Volcanoes* and Maui's *Haleakala National Parks,* Hawaii offers an incredible variety of attractions.

Back on the east coast of the United States, north of Florida, are the historic cities of Savannah and Charleston. *Savannah* has its beautiful squares, and Georgia's Sea Islands nearby, while *Charleston* has fine antebellum mansions, Fort Sumter, and the world-famous Magnolia Plantation and gardens 14 miles to the north. Also in South Carolina, near the border with North Carolina, is *Myrtle Beach,* one of the east coast's major beach resorts, also known for its many golf courses.

Further north along the Atlantic seaboard are *Colonial Williamsburg,* the preserved and recreated colonial town, and the capital, *Washington, DC.* Washington offers magnificent government buildings, memorials, the incredibly rich collections of the Smithsonian Institution, and nearby Alexandria with its beautifully restored 18th-century buildings. Outside the capital to the west is *Shenandoah National Park* with its Skyline Drive, and to the east, the Chesapeake Bay area with such notable communities as *Annapolis* and *St. Michaels.*

Philadelphia, with Independence Hall, the Liberty Bell, fine city townhouses, and excellent museums, is two hours to the north northeast of the capital. *Atlantic City,* the gambling mecca of the east coast, is less than 60 miles southeast of Philadelphia on the New Jersey shore. About 85 miles northeast of Philadelphia is *New York,* the nation's largest city, with its world-famous skyline, superb museums, fabulous nightlife and performing arts, and excellent shopping.

New England, in the far northeastern part of the country, offers the cultural and historial attractions of *Boston* (Faneuil Hall, Museum of Fine Arts), the beach resorts of *Cape Cod,* the winter resorts of *Stowe* and *Killington* in Vermont, and *Sugarloaf* in Maine, and such natural attractions as *Acadia National Park,* Maine.

In between the eastern seaboard and the Rocky Mountains, the United States has a number of notable tourist attractions, including *Niagara Falls* on the border with Canada, *Chicago* (magnificent skyscraper architecture, Art Institute, and other fine museums) at the south end of Lake Michigan, *Mammoth Caves* and the *Smoky Mountains National Park* further south, and the country music attractions of *Nashville* in Tennessee. On the Gulf Coast is *New Orleans,* with its French Quarter and nightlife. Texas has *San Antonio* and its River Walk, Alamo, and five missions, plus *Dallas,* with its fine museums, and Six Flags Over Texas theme park. *Mount Rushmore* in the Black Hills of South Dakota, completes the principal attractions of the area between the Rocky Mountains and the east coast.

The Rocky Mountain states in the western United States are perhaps best known for their superb natural attractions, including the magnificent *Grand Canyon* in Arizona, *Monument Valley* straddling the Arizona-Utah border, *Zion* and *Bryce National Parks* in Utah with their incredible rock formations, *Yellowstone National Park* with its thermal features and splendid wildlife, the adjacent Tetons, North America's most spectacular mountain range, in *Grand Teton National Park* in Wyoming, and *Glacier National Park* straddling the Montana-Canada border. Colorado's Rocky Mountains are also big tourist attractions, particularly the world-class winter resorts of *Vail, Aspen, Snowmass, Telluride,* and *Steamboat Springs.* Other winter resorts of note in the Rockies include *Jackson Hole* in Wyoming; *Alta, Snowbird,* and *Deer Valley* in Utah; *Sun Valley,* Idaho; and *Taos,* New Mexico.

The Rocky Mountain states also have some outstanding other attractions, such as *Santa Fe,* with its Plaza, Palace of Governors, cathedral, picturesque Canyon Road, and art galleries; *Taos* and *Pueblo de Taos* with its flat-topped adobe houses; and *Salt Lake City,* with its Temple Square, center of the Mormon Church. The nation's premier gambling mecca, *Las Vegas,* as in far southern Nevada, some 275 miles northeast of Los Angeles.

In the Pacific Northwest lies *Seattle,* with its Pioneer Square historic district, fine museums, and the stunning *Olympic National Park* across the beautiful Puget Sound. South of Seattle lies *Portland,* with its hills and parks. To the west lies the *Oregon coastline,* world famous for its rugged beauty, and to the east, the *Cascades* mountain chain of dormant and not-so-dormant volcanoes.

Undiscovered Gems

Central Oregon, centered on *Bend,* is still relatively unknown outside the West coast and has an incredible variety of attractions in addition to its almost perfect climate. On the eastern, dry and sunny side of the impressive Cascade mountains, this high desert area is Oregon's outdoor vacation mecca, with hiking, river rafting, fishing, biking, rock climbing, golfing, horseback riding, and skiing (Mt. Bachelor) all available.

Up and Coming Areas

The *Gulf coast of Florida,* particularly the *Fort Myers-Naples area* on the southwest coast of the Florida peninsula, has superb beaches, both sandy and shell-strewn (Sanibel Island), sophisticated hotels, and all the weather benefits of Florida without the crowds.

Asia
China

Traditional Destinations

Beijing, in the northeast part of China, with its Forbidden City, Temple of Heaven (Tian Tai) and Xu Beihong Museum, is the country's principal destination (Figure 26). Just outside Beijing are: the *Summer Palace* (Yitte Yuan), noted for its fine pagodas, pavilions, temples and courtyards; the *Ming Tombs* (Shi San Ling); and, the Ba Da Ling section of the *Great Wall* (Wan Li Chang Cheng).

Shanghai, China's largest city, is known for its Bund (Zhongshan Road), a boulevard along the Huangpu River, lined with European-style buildings dating from the period when foreigners were granted trading concessions in Shanghai. Also noteworthy is the *Long Hua Temple and Pagoda* (Lonh Hua Si), southwest of central Shanghai. On the southeastern coast, about 80 miles from Hong Kong, is *Guangzhou* (Canton), with its colorful Qing Ping Market, temple, and Liuhua Park.

Just southwest of Shanghai is *Hangzhou,* a resort famous for its lakes and arched bridges. *Nanjing,* further northwest from Shanghai, is known for its still-standing 14th-century walls and Ming Tomb.

Undiscovered Gems

The "Venice of China," *Suzhou,* with its canals, bridges, and many beautiful pagodas and temples is close to Shanghai, to the northwest.

Up and Coming Areas

Guilin, famous for beautiful, bizarre limestone mountains jutting out of the surrounding countryside, is one of China's most picturesque destinations. The ancient city of *Xi'an,* with its Big Goose Pagoda and, outside town, thousands of life-size terra cotta statues of horses and warriors at the entrance of the Qin Shi-huang Tom, is in Shaanxi Province, about 600 miles southwest of Beijing.

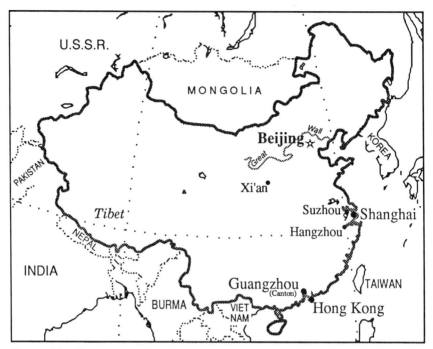

Figure 26. *China: Principal Tourist Destinations.*

India

Traditional destinations

Delhi, with its massive 17th-century Red Fort, bazaars, and mosques is in north India (Figure 27). Just 127 miles south of Delhi, in Agra, is the *Taj Mahal,* perhaps India's most famous landmark and one of the world's architectural masterpieces. Some 24 miles west of Agra is *Fatashpur Sikri,* a perfectly preserved deserted city. *Jaspur,* the walled "pink city," with its palaces, is about 160 miles south southwest of Delhi.

On India's northeast coast near the mouth of the Ganges, is *Calcutta,* known for its India Museum. About 400 miles north of Calcutta, 7,000 ft. up in the foothills of the Himalayas, is *Darjeeling,* noted for its magnificent scenery, tea plantations, and flora and fauna. On the subcontinent's southeast coast lies *Madras* with its Government Museum and Art Gallery. The fishing village of *Mahabalipuram,* just south of Madras, is famous for its shore temples.

On the country's Arabian Sea coast is *Bombay,* one of India's biggest cities, known for its Prince of Wales Museum, colorful Crawford Market, and the cave temples of Elephant Island in Bombay harbor. The former Portugese territory of Goa is 250 miles south of Bombay. It has 16th- and 17th-century churches, beautiful secluded beaches, many festivals, and a rich Portugese heritage.

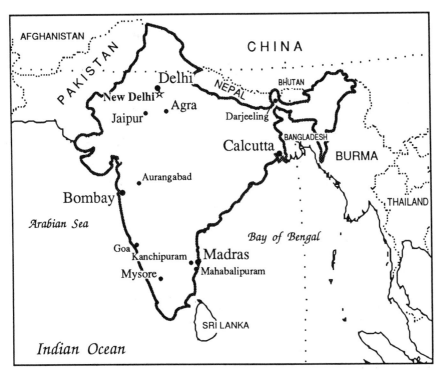

Figure 27. *India: Principal Tourist Destinations.*

Undiscovered Gems

The beautiful city of *Mysore,* about 300 miles southeast of Goa, is known for its Maharajah's Palace and crafts market.

Up and Coming Areas

Aurangabad, in Maharashta, northeast of Bombay, is at the center of a region of many important historical mounuments, temples, and shrines of India's Shivaji past, most notably the *Caves of Ajanta and Ellora. Kanchipuram,* one of India's seven sacred cities, is just southwest of Madras, and has over 150 temples dating from the 7th to 13th centuries.

Indonesia

Traditional Destinations

The island of *Bali,* just east of Java, is probably Indonesia's premier tourist destination (Figure 28). A beautiful island, Bali has extraordinary beaches and temples (particularly the Pura Taman Ayun Temple), and fascinating temple ceremonies/festivals (Odalan). *Jakarta,* the capital, is on the northwest end of Java, and is noted for its collection of porcelain in its National Museum, and old Dutch port of Sunda Kelapa. The *Bogar Botanical Gardens* are in Bogar, 40

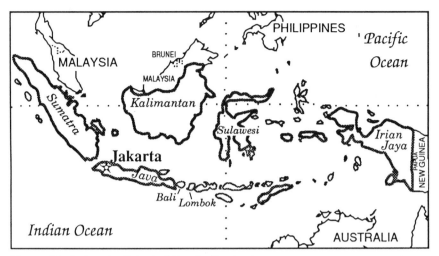

Figure 28. *Indonesia: Principal Tourist Destinations.*

miles south of Jakarta. In central Java is *Yogyakarta,* a beautiful city steeped in Javanese culture and history.

Undiscovered Gems

Lombok, Bali's neighboring island to the east, is an unspoiled island known for beautiful beaches and interior volcanic mountains.

Up and Coming Areas

The islands of *Kalimanta, Sulawesi,* and the Indonesian half of New Guinea, *Irian Juya,* are known for their exotic flora and fauna.

Japan

Traditional Destinations

Tokyo, the capital and one of the world's largest cities, is located on the south central coast of Honshu, the largest Japanese island (Figure 29). Tokyo offers the Imperial Palace, classical gardens, and the Meiji Shrine. To the north of Tokyo lies *Nikko,* noted for its fine religious architecture, particularly the Toshogu Shrine and the beautiful scenery of the surrounding Alpine region. The *Izu-Hakane-Fuji* resort area is just southwest of the capital, centered on *Mt. Fuji* (12,388 ft.). *Kamakura,* just an hour south of Tokyo, is a small fishing village known for its many temples and shrines.

Osaka, with its castle and many Kabuki and Noh theaters as well as the unique Bunraku puppet drama is west of Tokyo. Just to the north of Osaka is *Kyoto,* renowned for its temples, shrines, and beautiful gardens, and widely considered to be one of the world's most attractive cities. Just east of Osaka is *Nara,* Japan's

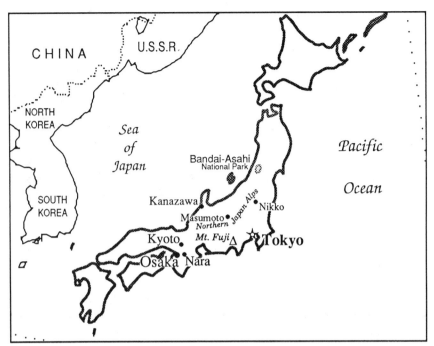

Figure 29. *Japan: Principal Tourist Destinations.*

capital in the 8th century, and often called the cradle of the country's arts, crafts, literature, and industry.

Undiscovered Gems

Kanazawa, on Honshu's northern coast, is full of ancient samurai houses and exquisitely landscaped gardens, particularly in Kenrokuen Park. The *Bandai-Asahi National Park,* in northern Honshu, has some of Japan's best mountain scenery.

Up and Coming Areas

The *Japanese Alps,* northwest of Tokyo, and their many picturesque towns and villages, such as *Takayama, Matsumoto,* with its black feudal castle, and *Ogimachi,* are gradually becoming appreciated by the visitor.

Malaysia

Traditional Destinations

Kuala Lumpur, the capital, is located on the western side of the South Malay peninsula, approximately 200 miles northwest of Singapore on the peninsula's southern tip (Figure 30). The city is noted for its mosques, National Museum,

Figure 30. *Malaysia: Principal Tourist Destinations.*

China Town, and colorful Sunday market. North of Kuala Lumpur are the *Batu Caves,* huge natural caverns containing a Hindu shrine. In the interior mountains are two hill resorts, the *Cameron Highlands* and the *Genting Highlands,* the latter with a gambling casino.

North of Kuala Lumpur, on the northwestern coast, is the island of *Penang* (Pulau Pinang), one of the Orient's most popular resorts, with splendid beaches, colonial architecture, lovely Botanical Gardens, and fine temples.

Undiscovered Gems

North of Penang, off the coast, is *Langkawi Island* (Pulau Langkawi), a tropical island paradise with superb beaches and fine scenery. *Taman Negara National Park,* in the north central part of Pahang State, is set in a tropical rain forest with exotic flora and fauna. Off the east coast of the Malay Peninsula is *Palau Tioman island,* with beautiful beaches and excellent scuba diving.

Up and Coming Areas

The states of *Sarawak* and *Saban* on the island of Borneo, particularly *Kinabalu National Park,* with 13,450 ft. Mt. Kinabalu, the highest mountain in southeast Asia, are known for beautiful nature trips that explore the region's exotic flora and fauna.

Philippines

Traditional Destinations

Manila, with its Intramuros (Walled City), the ruins of the 16th-century Spanish settlement, Fort Santiago, and world-famous sunsets over Manila Bay from Rizal park, is on the west central coast of the northern island of Luzon (Figure 31).

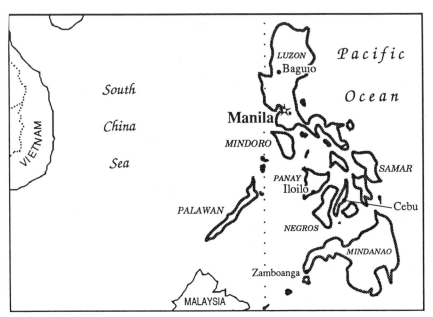

Figure 31. *Philippines: Principal Tourist Destinations.*

About 150 miles north of Manila is *Baguio,* the former summer capital and a resort town. About 5,000 ft. up in the mountains, it is considered to be one of the most beautiful areas in the Philippines, Baguio is also the jumping-off point for day trips to the incredible *rice terraces of Banaue,* carved out of the mountain sides over 2,000 years ago. The beach resort towns of *San Fernando, Bauang,* and *Agoo* are just west of Baguio on the South China Sea.

Undiscovered Gems

Some 350 miles south southeast of Manila, on Cebu Island, is *Cebu,* the Philippines' oldest Spanish settlement. On Panay, in the Visayas Islands, is *Iloilo,* a very colorful colonial city with an excellent pre-Hispanic museum.

Up and Coming Areas

Zamboanga (the city of flowers), at the western tip of Mindanao, is the center of Muslim culture in the Philippines and one of the country's most colorful, exotic cities.

South Korea

Traditional Destinations

Seoul, noted for its palaces, especially Kyongbok Palace and Changdok Palace, is South Korea's capital, and is located in the far northwest of the country, not far from the border with North Korea (Figure 32). Just south of Seoul, near Suwan,

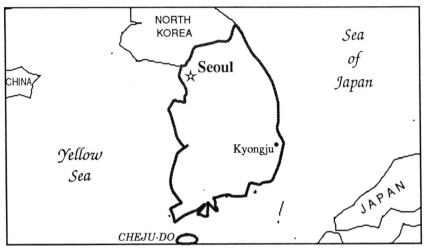

Figure 32. *South Korea: Principal Tourist Destinations.*

is the *Korean Folk Village,* a recreated Yi dynasty village complete with craft demonstrations, folk dancing, and puppet plays. *Cheju-Do island,* 50 miles off the southern coast of South Korea, with its own distinctive history and culture, is also known for *Mt. Halla,* South Korea's highest mountain.

Undiscovered Gems

Sorak-san and *Odae-san National Parks* on Korea's northeast coast, are very attractive scenically. *Hallyo Waterway National Park,* west of Pusan along the country's southern coast, is a spectacular area of rocky islands and peninsulas.

Up and Coming Areas

Kyongju, about four and a half hours southeast of Seoul on Korea's southeast coast north of Pusan, is a growing tourist destination. Capital of the Silla Dynasty, Kyongju and the surrounding countryside are full of temples, palaces, gardens, and shrines.

Taiwan

Traditional Destinations

Taipei (T'aipei), the capital, is located at the northern end of Taiwan, and is noted for its National Palace Museum with the world's most extensive and richest collection of Chinese art (Figure 33). *Taroko Gorge,* a spectacular limestone gorge, is south of Taipei. Also south of the capital and about 45 miles southeast of Taichung in the island's interior is *Sun Moon Lake,* known for its delightful mountain scenery, Buddhist temples, and a nearby aboriginal village.

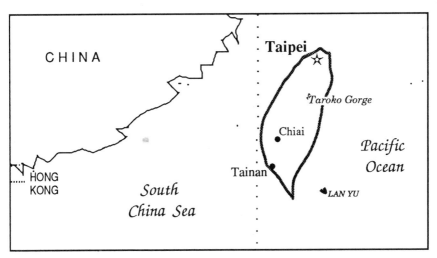

Figure 33. *Taiwan: Principal Tourist Destinations.*

On Taiwan's southwest coast is *Tainan* (T'ainan), the country's oldest city and former capital. It is noted for its many historical buildings and Confucian Temple.

Undiscovered Gems

Alishan Mountain resort is east of Chiayi. *Lan Yu* (Orchid Island), off Tiawan's southeast coast, is known for its orchids, butterflies, beaches, and Yami aboriginal inhabitants.

Up and Coming Areas

Kenting Park, near Oluanpi, at Taiwan's southern tip, is Taiwan's first National Park and international beach resort.

Thailand

Traditional Destinations

Bangkok (Krung Thep), famous for its temples, National Museum, and exotic nightlife, lies just inland at the head of the Gulf of Thailand (Figure 34). Just outside Bangkok are the *floating markets at Wat Sai* in Thonburi and the *Damnoensaduak,* about 60 miles west of the capital. *Ayutthaya,* noted for its magnificent ruins of palaces, temples, and fortifications, is just 55 miles north of Bangkok.

The beach resort of *Pattaya* is about 80 miles southeast of Bangkok on the Gulf of Thailand. *Bangsaen* is another beach resort only 60 miles from the

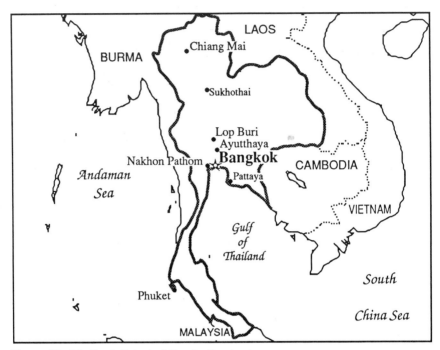

Figure 34. *Thailand: Principal Tourist Destinations.*

capital. *Nakhon Pathom,* known for its Pathom Chedi, the largest pagoda in Southeast Asia, is 50 miles west of Bangkok. Just another 20 miles away is *Kanchanaburi,* famous for the nearby bridge over the River Kwai, immortalized by the film of the same name.

In northern Thailand is *Chiang Mai,* known for its festivals, many temples, scenery, roses, and cool climate. *Doi Indhanon National Park,* Thailand's most scenic area, with the country's highest mountain, is about 60 miles from Chiang Mai.

Undiscovered Gems

Sukhothai, containing the ruins of the first Thai capital, has a beautiful natural setting and magnificent standing Buddhas. *Hua Hin,* one of the country's oldest beach resorts, is located on the western shores of the Gulf of Thailand, about 100 miles south southwest of Bangkok.

Up and Coming Areas

Phuket Island, off the west coast of the Isthmus of Kra, some 450 miles south southwest of Bangkok, is a growing beach resort area.

Africa and the Middle East
Egypt

Traditional Destinations

Cairo (Al-Qahirah), with its Egyptian Museum, impressive mosques, and Museum of Islamic Art, is located on the banks of the Nile, some 150 miles from the Mediterranean coast (Figure 35). Just outside Cairo are Egypt's premier tourist attractions, the *Pyramids of Giza* and the *Sphinx.*

Alexandria (Al-Iskandariyah), 140 miles northwest of Cairo on the Mediterranean coast, offers the Greco-Roman Museum, interesting catacombs, and King Farouk's former summer palace (Montazah Palace). Some 64 miles west of Alexandria on the Mediterranean coast lies *El Alamein* (Al-Alamayn), site of one of the decisive battles of WW II. Just a little further west is the resort of *Sidi Abdel Rahman,* with one of the best Mediterranean beaches in Egypt.

On the Nile, just over 300 miles south of Cairo, is *Luxor* (Al-Uqsur) with its Temples of Luxor and Karnak and, just outside, the Valley of the Kings, the Tombs of the Nobles, and Valley of the Queens. *Aswan,* with its Island of Elephantine, Tombs of the Nobles, and Mausoleum of the Aga Khan, is still further up the Nile, just below Lake Nasser. The reassembled *Great Temple of Abu Simbel* and the statues of Ramses II overlook Lake Nasser 170 miles southwest of Aswan.

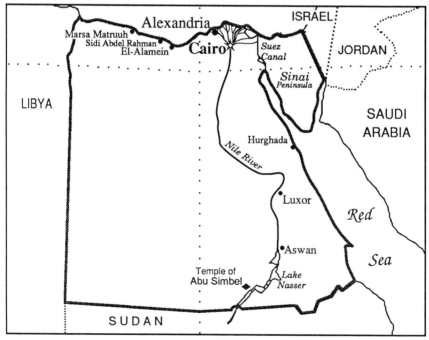

Figure 35. *Egypt: Principal Tourist Destinations.*

On Egypt's Red Sea coast is *Hurghada* (Al-Ghurdaqah), Egypt's most popular beach resort, with superb white sand beaches and excellent scuba diving.

Undiscovered Gems

Egypt's western desert oases, particularly *Kharga* and *Siwa Oasis,* near the Libyan border, where the settlements of Dakhla, Bahariyya, Farafra, and Siwa remain largely unspoiled.

Up and Coming Areas

Marsa Matruuh, with its superb beaches, is 180 miles west of Alexandria on the Mediterranean coast.

Israel

Traditional Destinations

Jerusalem, particularly the Old City, with its Western (Wailing) Wall, Dome of the Rock, and Israel Museum, is located in the center of Israel between the northern end of the Dead Sea and the Mediterranean Sea (Figure 36). *Bethlehem,* a destination of pilgrims from all over the world for centuries, is just 5 miles south of Jerusalem. *Massada,* about 70 miles south of Jerusalem, is the site of the famous Roman siege and a national symbol. Massada overlooks the *Dead Sea,* the lowest point on earth, to its east.

To the northwest of Jerusalem, on the Mediterranean coast, is *Tel Aviv-Jaffa,* Israel's principal city with its museums and active nightlife. Some 32 miles north of Tel Aviv lies the Roman capital of Judea, *Caesarea,* one of Israel's premier archaeological sites. Still further north is *Haifa,* with its Baha'i Shrine and Gardens. Across the Haifa Bay lies *Acre,* noted for the Mosque of El-Juzzar.

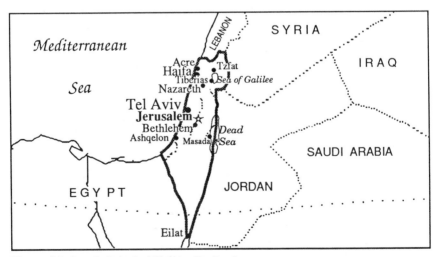

Figure 36. *Israel: Principal Tourist Destinations.*

Southeast of Haifa is *Nazareth*, and northeast of Nazareth are *Tiberias* and the *Sea of Galilee*.
In far southern Israel, at the head of the Red Sea, lies the resort of *Eilat*.

Undiscovered Gems

Tzfat, overlooking the Sea of Galilee on Mount Canaan, has a picturesque artists' quarter and an Old City famous for its small synagogues.

Up and Coming Areas

Ashqelon, on the Mediterranean just above the Gaza strip, has beautiful beaches, a Roman tomb, crusader city walls and a national park.

Kenya

Traditional Destinations

Nairobi, the modern capital city, is located in southern Kenya about halfway between the Indian Ocean and Lake Victoria (Figure 37). Kenya's principal tourist attractions are, of course, the many National Parks created to protect the country's wildlife. Just south of Nairobi lies *Nairobi National Park* and 200 miles to the southwest on the border with Tanzania is the *Masai Mara Game Reserve*, noted for its large herds of grazing animals, particularly the annual

Figure 37. *Kenya: Principal Tourist Destinations.*

migration of wildebeest. To the southeast of the capital is *Amboseli National Park,* known for its lions and cheetahs. Kenya's largest park, *Tsavo National Park,* is about halfway between Nairobi and the coastal city of Mombasa. It is known for its large herds of elephants.

On the Indian Ocean coast lies *Mombasa,* with its mosques, Arab-style houses in Old Town, colorful bazaar, and beautiful beaches.

North of Nairobi is *Aberdare National Park. Mount Kenya National Park,* with 17,058-ft. Mt. Kenya as its centerpiece, is to the northeast, and *Lake Nakuru National Park* in the Great Rift Valley, is 100 miles northwest of Nairobi. Lake Nakuru is renowned for its varied and prolific bird life.

Undiscovered Gem

The Afro-Arab town of *Lamu,* some 212 miles north of Mombasa, located offshore on Lamu Island, is almost medieval in character.

Up and Coming Areas

Lake Turkana, 475 miles north of Nairobi in northern Kenya, is one of the country's newest tourist attractions, with beautiful scenery and excellent fishing. *Malindi,* on the Indian Ocean coast north of Mombasa, is the big-game fishing center of Kenya and fast becoming a major resort area in its own right.

Morocco

Traditional Destinations

The four Imperial Cities of Morocco—Fez (Fes), Marrakesh, Meknes, and Rabat—are the country's principal tourist destinations. *Rabat,* the capital city, is on Morocco's northwest Atlantic coast (Figure 38), and is known for its Royal Palace, museums, and medina, as well as the neighboring city of *Sale. Meknes,* noted for its ramparts, gateways, mosques, and palaces, is some 60 miles east of Rabat. Another 40 miles to the northeast is *Fez,* world famous for its medina (old city). *Marrakesh,* the fourth Imperial City, lies about 250 miles to the southwest of Fez, south of Casablanca. It is known for its Djemaa el Fna square, craftsmen's souks (markets), and palaces.

Casablanca, the industrial and commercial center of Morocco, is about 90 miles southwest of Rabat on the Atlantic coast. *Tangier,* noted for its Sultan's Palace, is at the northern tip of the country, overlooking the Strait of Gibraltar.

Undiscovered Gems

Up and over the Atlas mountain passes east of Marrakesh are the remote towns or villages of *Erfoud, Ksar el Sonq, Ouarzazate, Tineghir,* and *Zagora,* each settled by a Berber tribe or clan with its unique style of clothing, and with its own Kasbah, daily market, and special crafts. One of the most spectacular natural attractions of Morocco is the Grand Canyon-like *Gorges du Dades,* just east of Zagora in the Atlas Mountains.

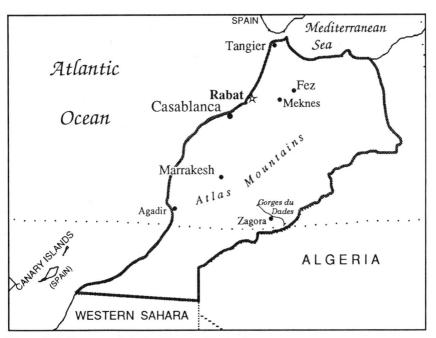

Figure 38. *Morocco: Principal Tourist Destinations.*

Up and Coming Areas

Agadir, some 325 miles south southwest of Casablanca on the Atlantic coast is the center of a growing beach resort area.

Tanzania

Traditional Destinations

The principal attractions of Tanzania, the game reserves, are all located, with one exception, in the northern part of the country between the coast and Lake Victoria (Figure 39). *Serengeti National Park,* probably Africa's most famous game reserve and best known for its lions and the spectacular annual migration of plains game, lies between Lake Victoria and the town of Arusha. To the southeast of Serengeti is *Olduvai Gorge,* site of the renowned Leakey excavations, and just east of Olduvai is *Ngorongoro Crater,* with its huge herds of plains game. To the southwest of Arusha is *Lake Manyara National Park,* noted for its birdlife, and further west is *Tarangire National Park,* famous for its black rhino. To the east of Arusha is *Arusha National Park.*

Mount Kilimanjaro (19,340 ft.), straddling the border with Kenya, is 75 miles northeast of Arusha. Along Tanzania's Indian Ocean coast, in the center, is *Dar es Salaam,* the capital, known for its National Museum, colorful market, and

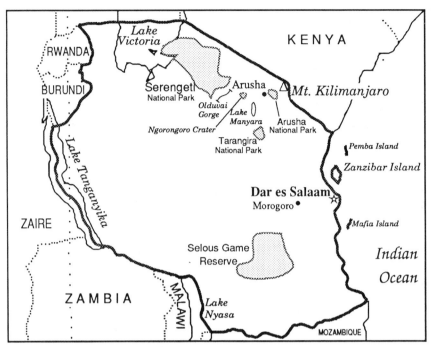

Figure 39. *Tanzania: Principal Tourist Destinations.*

beautiful waterfront. Off the coast north of Dar es Salaam are the islands of *Zanzibar* (with its Arab houses and fort), and *Pemba* (excellent beaches, superb fishing). South of Dar es Salaam is the island of *Mafia,* noted for its big-game fishing.

Undiscovered Gems

Selous Game Reserve, southwest of Morogoro, is the largest game reserve in the world, with a large elephant population, plus black rhino, hippos, and one of the last, true wilderness areas left in Africa.

Up and Coming Areas

The *Kunduchi* and *Bahari beach resorts* are 15 miles north of Dar es Salaam.

South America
Argentina

Traditional Destinations

Located in the central eastern part of Argentina near the head of the Rio de la Plata estuary (Figure 40), *Buenos Aires,* with its wide boulevards (particularly Avenida 9 de Julio), parks such as the Palermo parks, ornate buildings repre-

Figure 40. *Argentina: Principal Tourist Destinations.*

sented by the Colon Theater, fashionable districts (around San Martin Plaza), and very active nightlife centered on La Boca's Avenida Necochea, is often referred to as the Paris of South America.

Some 250 miles east of Buenos Aires on the "Atlantida" section of the Atlantic coast is *Mar del Plata,* the country's major beach resort. It has, reputedly, the largest casino in the world at *Bristol beach.* North of Buenos Aires on the border with Brazil and Paraguay, are the *Iguaza* (Iguacu) *Falls,* the widest in the world, 4 miles wide and with over 275 cataracts.

The Argentinian side of the Andes offers the ski resorts of *Las Lenas,* near Mendoza, and, further south, *Bariloche.* Bariloche is set in one of the continent's most scenic regions, the *Lake District. Patagonia,* in southern Argentina, has the *Valdes Peninsula* with its elephant seal colony, *Glacier National Park,* and *Lago Argentino National Park,* famous for its Perito Moreno glacier and icebergs. *Tierra del Fuego* at the southern end of the continent offers the adventurous traveler glaciers, waterfalls, and snow-capped mountains.

Undiscovered Gems

In the northwestern part of Argentina are the beautiful colonial cities of *Cordoba,* surrounded by the Sierras lake vacation region: *Tucuman,* (San Miquel de Tucuman) with its 18th-century colonial buildings; and *Salta,* famous for its Gaucho Parade in June. Cordoba, some 430 miles northwest of Buenos Aires, is noted for its colonial buildings, as is Tucuman. Salta, known for its beautiful churches, is also the base for breathtaking trips into the Andes.

Up and Coming Areas

Esquel, south of Bariloche, promises to be one of the premier ski resorts in Argentina, if not South America. It also offers magnificent scenery and tremendous fishing.

Bolivia

Traditional Destinations

La Paz, at 12,000 ft. the highest capital city in the world, and famous for its Indian markets, particularly the Sagaranuga and Camacho markets, and the excellent National Museum of Archaeology, is located in the far western central part of Bolivia (Figure 41). Some 42 miles from La Paz, near the southern edge of Lake Titicaca, are the pre-Inca ruins of *Tiahuanaco. Lake Titicaca* itself, at 12,600 ft. the highest navigable lake in the world, has the sacred Inca Island of the Sun and the All Souls and Saints' Days festivals in November, and the town of *Copacabana,* dating from the 16th century, on its shores. *Trinidad,* northeast of La Paz, is a safari center for trips into the Yungas or upper reaches of the Amazon Basin. South of La Paz, near Cochabamba, is *Oruro,* famous for the

Figure 41. *Bolivia: Principal Tourist Destinations.*

Diablada ceremony, performed at Carnival (late Feb. or early March), by brilliantly costumed and masked dancers.

South southeast of La Paz is Bolivia's "legal capital," *Sucre*. Known as the white city, it is full of fine art and architectural treasures with many impressive colonial buildings, particularly the Palacio Legislation and the Church of San Miguel. *Santa Cruz*, southeast of La Paz, is the starting-off point for the train ride through some of the wildest parts of Bolivia to Corumba, across the border in Brazil.

Undiscovered Gems

Just south of Sucre is *Potosi*, an old Spanish colonial town with winding streets, old mansions, and many churches with fine Romanesque or Renaissance architecture.

Up and Coming Areas

The Inca ruins at *Incallajta*, about 65 miles from Cochabamba.

Brazil

Traditional Destinations

Located on the southeastern coast of Brazil (Figure 42), *Rio de Janeiro*, with its landmark statue of Christ the Redeemer on Corcovado Peak, Sugarloaf Mountain (Pao de Acucar), Copacabana, Leme, Ipanema beaches, Carnival, and botanical gardens is one of the world's most famous cities. *Sao Paulo*, the biggest city in South America, is just over 200 miles west southwest of Rio de Janeiro, and known for its nightlife, art museum, and the Butanta Institute snake farm.

A two-hour flight from Sao Paulo on the border with Argentina and Paraguay are the world's widest waterfalls, the *Iguacu (Iguaza) Falls*, not only much wider, but also higher than Niagara Falls. Northeast of Rio is *Salvador de Bahia*, with its beautiful red tile roofs, Baroque architecture, and Carnival celebrations, considered by many to be better than those of Rio de Janeiro.

The *Amazon*, whose drainage basin occupies well over half of Brazil, is a big attraction, literally and figuratively. With thousands of species of fish, mammals, birds, and insects, it is one of the largest largely uninhabited areas left in the world, and a wildlife-lover's dream. Some 1,400 miles from the Amazon River's mouth is *Manaus*, famous for its opulent Opera House (Teatro do Amazonas) and floating market. Near the river's mouth lies *Belem*, with its Goeldi Museum and Zoo, 17th-century fort, and Festival of Candles in October.

Undiscovered Gems

Try the Gold Cities of Ouro Preto and Congonhas. North of Rio de Janeiro and 60 miles south of Belo Horizonte, *Ouro Preto*, is a truly beautiful colonial town with outstanding Baroque architecture, winding streets, and works by the Brazil-

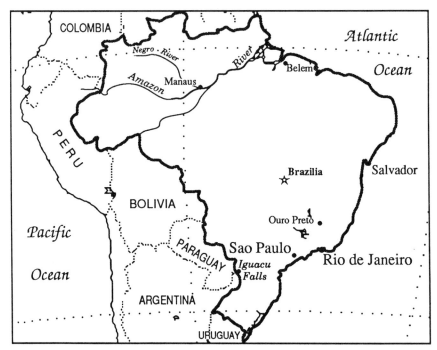

Figure 42. *Brazil: Principal Tourist Destinations.*

ian sculptor Aleijadinho. The village of *Con nhas,* just outside Ouro Preto, is famous for its Church of Bon Jesus de Matosinlos, where Aleijadinho sculpted twelve life-sized statues of the Prophets.

Up and Coming Areas

The *Pantanel region,* south of the Amazon in western Brazil, has the greatest concentration of wildlife in South America and is a growing wildlife safari center.

Chile

Traditional Destinations

Santiago with its 16th-century Plaza de Armas, superb pre-Columbian museum and excellent Museum of Colonial Art and Fine Arts Museum, is located in the center of Chile just below the Andes (Figure 43). Some 80 miles northwest of Santiago on the Pacific coast is the fashionable beach resort of *Vina del Mar.* Northeast of Santiago in the Andes is the world-famous ski resort of *Portillo,* South America's premier ski area. In northern Chile, the province of *Antofagasta* is known for its archaeological sites, with the pre-Columbian museum in *San Pedro de Atacama* especially noted.

Figure 43. *Chile: Principal Tourist Destinations.*

South of Santiago lies the spectacular *Chilean Lake District* with the Laja Falls and Lakes Villarrica (fishing, water sports), Rininahue (beautiful scenery), Puyehue (thermal baths), Llanguihue (fishing, water sports), and Todas los Santos (Esmeraldo) being especially noteworthy. Farther south still is *Punta Arenas,* starting point for the impressive *Paine Towers National Park. Easter Island,* lying 2,300 miles off the coast, is famous for its hundreds of giant statues, believed to have been placed there by peoples of Polynesian origin.

Undiscovered Gems

The *Chilean fjord area* south of the Lake District is more spectacular than the Norwegian fjords, with scenery including mountains, fjords, icebergs, and delightful fishing villages.

Colombia

Traditional Destinations

Located on the Andean plateau in the center of the country, *Bogota* is one of the oldest cities in the Americas, has a unique, superb collection of pre-Columbian Indian gold artifacts housed in the Gold Museum, the La Candelaria colonial quarter, and the excellent Archaeological Museum (Figure 44). Northeast of

Bogota is *Tunja,* site of a citadel of the ancient Chibcha Indians and a colonial city with fine churches, mansions, streets lined with overhanging balconies and a fine market (Friday). Nearby *Medellin,* the "orchid capital of the world" has a Museum of National Folklore and the Orchid Show in August.

On Colombia's Caribbean coast lies *Cartagena,* the best preserved walled city in the Americas, now a popular resort area. Nearby *Barranquilla* is known for its exciting Carnival celebration and *Santa Marta,* further along the coast, is noted for its fine beaches and the spectacular sight of a 16,000-ft. mountain rising out of the Caribbean.

Undiscovered Gems

Outside Cali, to the southwest of Bogota, is *Popayan,* a beautiful hill town with restored 16th- and 17th-century buildings and fine Holy Week processions. *Cali* itself is noted for its Feria Festival, a week-long celebration of bullfighting. To the northeast is *San Agustin Archaeological Park,* Colombia's most important archaeological site, with gigantic stone statues and pre-Columbian tombs and burial mounds.

Up and Coming Areas

One of South America's best bird-watching areas is around *Leticia* on the border with Peru and Brazil. Leticia is also the jumping-off point for trips into the Amazon jungle.

Figure 44. *Colombia: Principal Tourist Destinations.*

Ecuador

Traditional Destinations

The capital *Quito,* a World Heritage Site, with its well-preserved colonial architecture, lies in the Andes between two parallel ranges running southwest to northeast (Figure 45). It is especially famous for its many ornate churches, particularly the La Compania Church and San Francisco Church. Ecuador also has some of the continent's best Indian markets, held on different days of the week and offering excellent buys, including *Otavalo* (Sat.—woolen goods) north of Quito, and *Saquisili* (Sat.—pottery, tablecloths), *Latacunga* (Sat. and Tu.— leather goods, textiles), *Ambato* (Mon.—rugs, woolen goods, ponchos), and *Riobamba* (Sat.) south of Quito.

Guayaquil, on the Gulf of Guayaquil southeast of Quito, is a tropical city with a fine colonial section (Barrio Las Penas). The train ride (autoferro) between Quito and Guayaquil, with its many switchbacks and turns, over Urbina Pass at 11,800 ft. and past 19,200 ft. Mt. Cotopaxi, is one of the most scenic train rides in the world. *Salinas,* on the Pacific coast west of Guayaquil, is a fashionable resort with excellent beaches. About 650 miles offshore are the *Galapagos Islands.* The place where Darwin formulated his "survival of the fittest" theory of evolution, they now constitute a natural sanctuary and are world famous for their exotic wildlife.

Undiscovered Gems

Ingapirica, east of Cuenca, is Ecuador's only significant Inca archaeological site.

Up and Coming Areas

The *Equadorian Orient,* east of the Andes, is becoming an area for photographic safaris and jungle canoe trips, particularly along the *Napo River* with naturalist guides.

Panama

Traditional Destinations

The 50-mile *Panama Canal* connecting the Pacific and Atlantic oceans, one of the great engineering wonders of the world, is just east of Panama City (Figure 46). *Panama City* itself is noted for its Old Town (Panama Viejo), the National Museum of Panamanian Man, one of Latin America's finest archaeological museums, and its shopping (the Hong Kong of the Americas). Just south of Panama City, 12 miles offshore, is *Taboga Island,* with magnificent beaches and fine snorkeling. On the Caribbean coast north of Panama City are the extensive ruins of the Spanish Gold City of *Portobelo* and, further east along the coast, the *San Blas Islands* inhabited by the Cuna Indians.

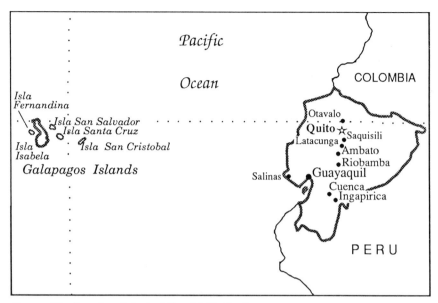

Figure 45. *Ecuador: Principal Tourist Destinations.*

West of Panama City lies the Pacific coast resort of *Playa Coronado, El Valle*, an inland mountain resort with a good Sunday handicrafts market, and *Los Santos* on the Azuero Peninsula. Los Santos is known for its adobe colonial buildings and cobblestone streets. Further west in *Chiriqui Province*, considered the most beautiful area in Panama, are the attractive mountain towns of *Boquete, Volcan*, and *Cerro Punta*.

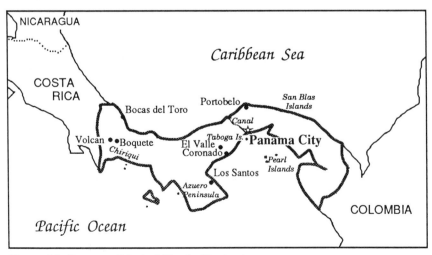

Figure 46. *Panama: Principal Tourist Destinations.*

Undiscovered Gems

The islands of the *Bocas del Toro archipelago* on the northwest coast have some of the most beautiful beaches on the Caribbean.

Up and Coming Areas

The *Pearl Islands,* including *Contadora* in the Gulf of Panama, are known for their superb fishing, swimming, snorkeling, and scuba diving.

Peru

Traditional Destinations

Machu Picchu, the spectacular Inca city high in the Andes northwest of Cuzco (Figure 47), is the principal tourist destination in Peru. At 8,200 ft., the "Lost City of the Incas," discovered in 1911, has over 200 buildings, all essentially intact except for the straw roofs. *Cuzco* itself is a delightful mix of Spanish and Inca with colonial buildings built on Inca foundations and is at the center of Peru's great archaeological region, with the major archaeological site of *Sacsahuaman, Quenco, Puca-Pucara, Tambo Machay,* and *Ollantaytambo* nearby. Cuzco's La Compania Jesuit Church is especially noteworthy and its Museum of Archaeology has a superb collection. Southeast of Cuzco is *Lake Titicaca,* the world's highest navigable lake, with the crafts center of *Puno* on its shores.

Figure 47. *Peru: Principal Tourist Destinations.*

The former center of Spanish power in the New World and the modern-day capital, *Lima,* on the Pacific coast, is a rich mix of Spanish Colonial architecture and modern skyscrapers. Its Plaza de Armas, surrounded by beautiful colonial structures, is outstanding. The train ride to the Sunday Fair in *Huancayo,* east of Lima in the Andes, is spectacular.

Along Peru's Pacific coast are two pre-Inca sites. North of Lima, near Trujillo, is *Chan Chan,* a Chima city complex spread over 9 square miles. South of Lima are the mysterious *Nazca Lines,* huge drawings on land that can only be seen from the air. Northeast of Lima in the Andes are the *Chavin Ruins.*

Undiscovered Gems

The *Callejon de Huaylas valley* north of Lima between the coastal range and the Andes, is sometimes known as the "Peruvian Switzerland" because of its snow-clad peaks and picturesque villages. *Arequipa,* south of Cuzco and west of Lake Titicaca, is a picturesque city of white volcanic stone buildings known for its colonial churches, particularly the Convent of Saint Cataline. Nearby is the *Calco Canyon,* twice as deep as Arizona's Grand Canyon.

Up and Coming Areas

Iquitos, in the far northeastern part of Peru, is the expedition center for trips into the Amazonian jungle camps with their photographic safaris.

Uruguay

Traditional Destinations

Uruguay's capital, *Montevideo,* is known for its parks, pleasant wide avenues and tree-lined streets, its Old Town, and ornate Legislative Palace, and is located on the southern coast on the estuary of the Rio de la Plata (Figure 48). The

Figure 48. *Uruguay: Principal Tourist Destinations.*

country's biggest tourist destination, however, is the *"Uruguayan Riviera,"* noted for its beautiful, white beaches, east of the capital. *Punta del Este* (La Punta) is the most famous of the Riviera resorts, which also include Atlantida, La Floresta, Solis, Piriapolis, Portezuelo, Maldonado, and Punta Ballena strung out along the Atlantic coastline east of Montevideo. *Maldonado* has a fine Museum of Art in the Americas.

Undiscovered Gems

To the west of Montevideo on the River Plate is the 17th-century Portugese settlement of *Colonia.* With its narrow cobblestone streets, rebuilt city walls, and colonial buildings in the historic section, it is a very attractive destination.

Venezuela

Traditional Destinations

Located in the mountains above and south of Venezuela's central Caribbean coastline (Figure 49), the "City of Eternal Spring," *Caracas,* is a very cosmopolitan city with some ultramodern architecture as well as a colonial center around Plaza Bolivar. Famous for its very active nightlife, Caracas also offers a fine Colonial Arts Museum. North of Caracas over the mountains is *El Litoral,* Venezuela's Riviera, with the beach resorts of *Macuto, Marbella, Niaguata, Los Caracas, Cata La Mer* and *Caraballeda Beach.*

Figure 49. *Venezuela: Principal Tourist Destinations.*

In the Venezuelan Andes, south of Lake Maracaibo, is *Merida,* another colonial city, but better known for the nearby cable car (teleferico) ride to *Pico Espejo* (15,640 ft.), the highest and longest cable car ride in the world. In the southeastern part of the country is the highest waterfall in the world, *Angel Falls,* with a total height of over 3,200 ft. *Canaima Lagoon,* downriver from Angel Falls and below the seven *Hacha Falls,* is one of Venezuela's top attractions.

Undiscovered Gems

La Guaira, Caracas's port city on the Caribbean coast, is a colonial treasure house.

Up and Coming Areas

Off Venezuela's northeastern Caribbean coast is magnificent *Margarita Island,* the "pearl island" with colonial churches, forts, fishing villages, and duty-free shops in *Porlamar.*

Caribbean

Traditional Destinations

The Caribbean's two most important island destinations, Puerto Rico and the U.S. Virgin Islands, are located in the east central part of the Caribbean (Figure 50). *Puerto Rico,* the easternmost of the Greater Antilles islands (Cuba, Jamaica, Hispaniola, and Puerto Rico), is known for historic sights in Old San Juan (Forts San Cristobal and El Morro, for example), the Condado Beach hotels section, El Yunque Rain Forest, and golf, fishing, shopping, nightlife and casinos, and fine food.

Just to the east lie the *U.S. Virgin Islands* of St. Thomas, St. John, and, a little to the southeast, St. Croix. *St. Thomas* (one of the major sailing centers of the Caribbean) is noted for its busy cruise-ship harbor in Charlotte Amalie and for its beaches, golf, fishing, scuba diving, nightlife, and food. *St. John,* just to the east of St. Thomas across Pillsbury Sound, is best known for its Virgin Islands' National Park, and Trunk Bay, widely considered to be one of the Caribbean's most beautiful. *St. Croix,* about 40 miles south of its sister islands, is known for its historic sights (Fort Frederick, Whim Greathouse), and its superb snorkeling. The *British Virgin Islands,* just northeast across The Narrows from St. John, are comparatively quiet (Virgin Gorda is virtually undeveloped), but known for their fine snorkeling and sailing.

East of the Virgin Islands are the *Leeward Islands* of the Lesser Antilles, with (in order), Anguilla, St. Martin-Sint Maarten, St. Barthelemy, Sint Eustatius, Saba, St. Kitts and Nevis, Antigua, Montserrat, and Guadeloupe in an arc curving to the southeast and south southeast of the Virgin Islands. *Anguilla* is known for its beautiful beaches and Arawak artifacts, while the half-French, half-Dutch island of *St. Martin-Sint Maarten,* one of the Caribbean's fastest-growing island destinations, is noted for its sailing, shopping in Philipsburg,

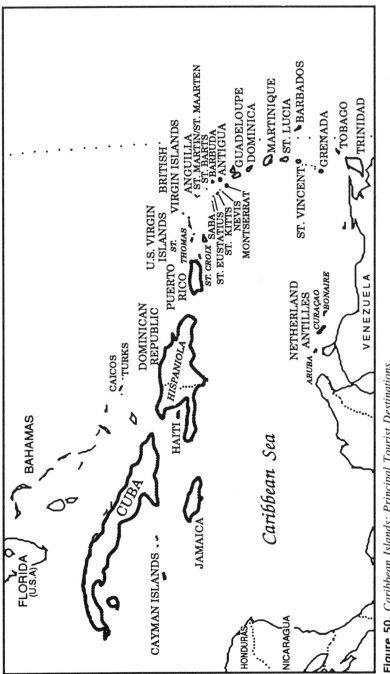

Figure 50. *Caribbean Islands: Principal Tourist Destinations.*

117

casinos and nightlife on the Dutch side, and food. *St. Barthelemy* (St. Barts) is known for its delightful French ambiance and the Baie de St. John beach, one of the Caribbean's best. Dutch-speaking *Sint Eustatius* is known for its historic sights, and neighbor *Saba* for its isolation and lack of beaches. *St. Christoper* (St. Kitts) is known for its Brimstone Hill Fortress (the Gibraltar of the Caribbean) on a 700-ft. hill overlooking the Caribbean, while *Nevis* has excellent, uncrowded beaches. The next island down in the arc, *Antigua*, is known for fine beaches, sailing, and casinos. *Montserrat* and French-speaking *Guadeloupe* are both known for their volcanic formations, plus local handicrafts on the former, and historic sights (17th-century Fort St. Charles), sailing, and fine food on the latter.

Below the Leeward Islands are the wetter *Windward Islands,* stretching south and south southwest from Dominica, just southeast of Guadeloupe, to just north of the Punta Piedras peninsula of Venezuela. In order, from north to south, they are Dominica, Martinique, St. Lucia, St. Vincent, Barbados further east, and Grenada. *Dominica,* one of the wetter Caribbean islands, is known for the Morne Trois Pitons National Park rain forest preserve and its Carib Indian reservation. French-speaking *Martinique* is noted for its tropical rain forest, beaches, sailing, and fine food. *St. Lucia* is particularly known for The Pitons, two 2,500 ft. volcanic cones jutting out of the Caribbean along the coast, a colorful waterfront market, and sailing. One of the Caribbean's best, if not the best yacht cruising area is around *St. Vincent* and the Grenadines islands to its south. St. Vincent is also known for its fine Botanic Gardens and Museum, Indian petroglyphs, and bustling Kingstown waterfront. The island of *Barbados,* while still one of the Windward Islands, lies over 100 miles east of St. Vincent further into the Atlantic. It is noted for its spectacular Bathsheba coastline, snorkeling, fine food and exciting nightlife. The last island in the chain is *Grenada,* the "Spice Island," also known for its Grand Etang tropical rain forest, historic sights, and shopping.

About 100 miles south of Grenada, just off the coast of Venezuela, are the islands of *Trinidad* and *Tobago,* both well known for calypso music, and Trinidad for golf, nightlife, its central market, and the exotic birds of the Asa Wright Nature Center. Both islands are a little hotter than the Caribbean islands to the north. Also off Venezuela's coast, some 500 miles to the west, are the Dutch islands of Aruba, Curaçao, and Bonaire. *Aruba* is known for its floating market in Schooner Harbor, casinos, and snorkeling. *Curaçao* for its 18th-century Dutch pastel houses, casinos, and shopping opportunities, among the best in the Caribbean. *Bonaire,* the easternmost of the "ABC" islands, is especially known for its scuba diving, Dutch colonial houses, and birdlife of the Washington-Slagbaii nature reserve.

To the west of Puerto Rico is the large island of *Hispaniola,* with the Dominican Republic occupying the Spanish-speaking eastern two thirds, and Haiti the French-speaking western third of the island. The *Dominican Republic* is noted for its many historic sights in colonial Santo Domingo, casinos, fishing, and especially golf courses. *Haiti,* perhaps the poorest Caribbean country/island, is noted for its primitive art and the spectacular Citadelle La Ferriere.

West of Hispaniola and south of the eastern end of Cuba, is *Jamaica,* one of the Caribbean's most popular destinations, with a scenic coastline and interior Blue Mountains, the Kingston crafts market, reggae music, beautiful beaches, and golf, fishing, nightlife, and food. Almost 200 miles to the northwest of Jamaica lie the *Cayman Islands* of Grand Cayman, Little Cayman, and Cayman Brac with their superb scuba diving, snorkeling, golf, fishing, nightlife, shopping, and on Grand Cayman one of the best beaches in the entire Caribbean, Seven Mile Beach.

In the Atlantic north of Hispaniola and outside the Caribbean proper, but included in the Caribbean islands by convention, are the *Turks and Caicos Islands,* just southeast of the Bahamas. They are especially well known for their fishing and for some of the best snorkeling and scuba diving reefs in the world.

Undiscovered Gems

The *Grenadines* are a small chain of islands south of St. Vincent in the British Windward Islands. With their beautiful snorkeling reefs and some of the best yacht cruising areas of the entire Caribbean, they constitute some of the least developed and more remote islands of the Caribbean and are also known for their superb beaches (on *Bequia*), blue lagoons (around *Canouan*), and exclusive resorts *(Palm Island). Terre de Haut,* off the southeast coast of the Basse Terre part of Guadeloupe, is another undiscovered gem, with fine scuba diving reefs and excellent French cuisine.

Up and Coming Areas

The island of *San Andres,* 120 miles off the Nicaraguan coast in the far western part of the Caribbean is administered by Colombia. A former haunt of the pirate Henry Morgan, it is a duty-free port with plenty of water sports.

Australasia
Australia

Traditional Destinations

Sydney, Australia's largest city, famous for its Opera House and magnificent harbor, lies on the southeast coast of the continent in New South Wales (Figure 51). Just west of Sydney, the *Blue Mountains National Park* offers some of eastern Australia's most spectacular scenery. A little further to the southeast is *Canberra,* the capital, with its impressive government buildings. About 500 miles north of Sydney in Queensland on the Tasman Sea coast is *Brisbane,* and the *Gold Coast,* Australia's "Miami Beach," 50 miles to the south of Brisbane.

Some 800 miles north northwest of Brisbane is *Cairns,* one of the main jumping-off points to the *Great Barrier Reef,* one of the world's great natural attractions, which parallels the coast of Queensland for 1,200 miles. Teeming with marine life, it is one of the premier snorkeling and scuba diving areas in the world.

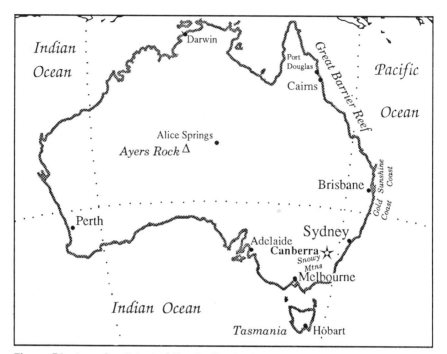

Figure 51. *Australia: Principal Tourist Destinations.*

Southwest of Sydney in Victoria on the continent's south coast is *Melbourne,* with its excellent Royal Botanic Gardens, old-world charm, and the famous Penguin Parade on nearby Phillip Island. South of Melbourne, across the Bass Straight, is the island of *Tasmania,* known for its attractive coastline, particularly its rugged west coast, and *Hobart,* with its fine museums and casino. Northwest of Melbourne in South Australia is *Adelaide,* noted for its gardens and wine cellars.

On Australia's west coast on the Indian Ocean, about 2,500 miles from Sydney, is *Perth.* Put on the international map by the recent America's Cup yacht races, Perth is known for its Kings Park, excellent museums, and ideal climate.

In Australia's interior, over 1,800 miles from Sydney, is *Ayers Rock,* a gigantic red monolith sacred to the aborigines and *Alice Springs,* the center for exploring the continent's interior.

Undiscovered Gems

Port Douglas, some 40 miles north of Cairns in the far north of Queensland, is a chic tropical resort close to the Great Barrier Reef. The *Great Ocean Road* between Torquay and Peterborough, southwest of Melbourne along the Victoria coast, is comparable to California's Highway 1 for its spectacular coastal scenery, particularly the *Twelve Apostles area.*

Up and Coming Areas

The *Sunshine Coast* north of Brisbane has superb white sandy beaches that are the equal of the much more crowded Gold Coast to the south of Brisbane. The *Snowy Mountains* in the "Australian Alps" just southwest of Canberra are the country's only alpine area, with *Thredbo* as the main ski resort.

New Zealand

Traditional Destinations

Auckland, with its extinct volcanos, two attractive harbors, and excellent Maori collection in the War Memorial Museum, is located at the northern end of New Zealand's North Island (Figure 52). *Wellington*, the capital, is on the southern tip of North Island and is noted for its cable car rides and Botanical Gardens. In the north central interior of North Island lies *Rotorua*, one of the country's principal tourist attractions, with its thermal activity, geysers, and mineral waters. The *Wanganui River* close by is famous for its jet-boat tours. Nearby are the *Glow Worm Grotto, Tongariro National Park*, and *Lake Taupo*, center of a world-renowned trout-fishing area.

   Christchurch, on the east coast of South Island, is a very "English" city with truly excellent botanic gardens. *Mount Cook National Park* is west of Christchurch in the magnificent *Southern Alps*, noted for their spectacular alpine

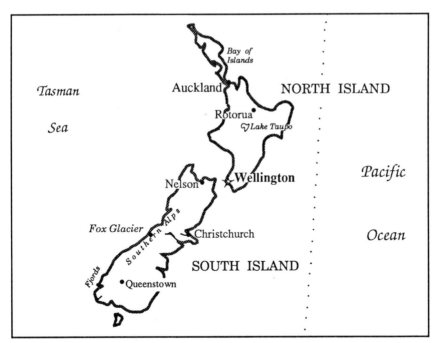

Figure 52. *New Zealand: Principal Tourist Destinations.*

scenery and Tasman Glacier. On the southwestern end of South Island are *Fjordland National Park* and *Milford Sound.*

Undiscovered Gems

The *Bay of Islands* is a water-sports paradise on North Island's northern peninsula, north of Auckland. The Fox and Franz Josef glaciers in *Westland National Park* in the west central part of South Island offer some of the world's most spectacular scenery.

Up and Coming Areas

Nelson, the South Island's most popular resort, is a budding arts and crafts center located overlooking Tasman Bay at the northern tip of South Island. *Queenstown,* on the shore of Lake Wakatipu, southwest of Christchurch in the foothills of the Southern Alps on South Island is that island's premier resort area, known for fabulous skiing, water sports, jet-boat tours (on the Shotover River), hiking, and other outdoor activities.

Individual City-Resort Destination Highlights by Continent—Region and Country

The following concise individual city or resort destination highlights, detailing the worthy sights, useful information, noteworthy side trips and local weather for cities, and the worthy sights, sports opportunities, and local weather for resorts, are provided as a resource for two reasons.

Firstly, the individual city-resort destination highlights are provided simply as a pure destination resource, so that you can become familiar with the important sightseeing attributes of the world's major travel destinations. The country profiles provided in the last section just quickly mentioned some of the distinguishing characteristics of individual destinations. This section provides the essential details. Details that you, the travel agents-destination consultant will be expected to know by an increasingly demanding traveling public.

Obviously, the more you know about a particular city or resort destination's characteristics and attractions, the more you will be able to help clients in making their destination choices, and the better you and your agency will look. The information provided is deliberately concise, and presented in an identical format to facilitate ready reference and to make comparisons between individual cities or resorts easy. There is today a wealth of information on travel destinations—in fact, probably too much information. This section attempts to get at the heart of a destination's attractions, and thus can be used as a reference tool, a "destination handbook."

Second, the individual city-resort destination highlights are provided as an information resource for you to work with. The learning process is greatly enhanced when you actually work with, touch, and manipulate the basic data.

Clearly, nothing will replace actually visiting and spending time in destinations themselves, and there is an incredible wealth of information in travel books, travel and general interest magazines, trade publications, tourist board brochures and pamphlets, and travel newsletters that you should become familiar with, but you will learn a lot by working with the information contained in this section. Pick a region of the world and, using the information presented in the following pages, construct tables comparing and contrasting the various attributes of the individual cities or resorts.

For example, how many of the Caribbean islands have golf courses? How do the Caribbean island destinations compare with those of the "mainland" Caribbean on Mexico's Yucatan peninsula? In Europe, for example, which cities offer a wealth of good museums versus monuments or historical sights? Which cities in Europe are best avoided in winter because of particularly cold weather, or which Asian destinations have a pronounced rainy "monsoon" season? Which South American destinations offer more in the way of exposure to native Indian cultures?

For clients who have extended stays in one particular destination, which resort or city destinations offer the most variety in a given region, or have readily accessible, worthwhile side trips? By combining the information in this section with the country profiles in the last section you can work out mock itineraries. Where would you recommend that a client with an interest in Baroque architecture, and two weeks to spare, travel in Europe? What about a client interested in experiencing alpine environments? And so on. Combined with a thorough understanding of world physical and cultural geography, the basics of which were presented in the first three chapters of this book, you will be armed to deal with today's traveler who is increasingly looking for a travel agent to be more than an order taker, indeed, to be a destination expert.

Europe and the Soviet Union
Innsbruck: Austria

Sights to See

Goldenes Dachl (Golden Roof), in the center of Altstadt, at the corner of Hofgasse & Herzog-Friedrichstrasse. A large balcony once used as an observation platform for watching medieval tournaments below, it is covered with a roof of heavily gilded copper shingles. The building itself houses the *Olympic Museum,* which has films and exhibits commemorating the 1964 and 1976 Winter Games held in Innsbruck.
Stadtturm (City Tower), Friedrichstrasse, opposite the Goldenes Dachl. A 14th-century Gothic tower that affords beautiful views.
Maria Theresienstrasse, S of the Goldenes Dachl at the end of Herzog-Friedrichstr. Stroll along this magnificent street, lined with Baroque palaces

and outdoor cafes, and enjoy the view of the towering Alps to the north and south.

The Hofberg (Imperial Palace), Rennweg 1, NE of the Goldenes Dachl. Originally built in the 1500s, in the 17th century it was remodeled in the Rococo style. Noted for its paintings and magnificent furniture. Open 9–4 daily.

Cathedral of St. Jacob (Dom zu St. Jakob), just W of the Hofberg and N of the Goldenes Dachl. A beautiful Baroque church known for its painted ceiling and the altarpiece painting of the Madonna by Cranach.

Hofkirche (Imperial Chapel), just S of the Hofberg. Famous for its unusual, larger-than-life bronze statues around the empty tomb of Emperor Maximilian. Open 9–5 daily.

Tyrolian Handicrafts Museum (Tiroler Volkskunstmuseum), Universitatstr. 2, next to the Hofkirche. Fine collection of handicrafts, rural furniture, implements, and costumes. Open 9–12, 2–5, M–Sa, 9–12 Su.

Tiroler Landesmuseum Ferdinandeum (Tyrolian Art Museum), Museumstr. 15, SE of the Tyrolian Handicrafts Museum. Noted for its collection of stained-glass windows and diverse painting collection. Open 9–5 M–Sa, shorter hours in winter.

Useful Information

Tourist Information (Stadtisches Verkehrsburo), Burggraben 3 (tel:53-56) and Bozner Platz 6 (tel:2077); *American Express,* Brixenstr. 3 (tel:58-2491); *Police* (tel:133 in emergencies); the nearest U.S. Consulate in Austria is in Vienna, at Boltzmanngasse 16 (tel:222/31-5511); *Taxi* (tel:27-711 or 45-500); *Post Office,* Maximillianstr. 2; *Voltage Guide,* 220 V, two round-pin outlets are used.

Special Trips/Tours

Ambras Castle (Schloss Ambras), just outside Innsbruck, to the SE, past the suburb of Pradl, makes a good side trip. Dating from the 11th century, the castle was remodeled in Renaissance style in the 16th century. It is known for its medieval weapons and art collection. Open 9–12, 2–5 daily in season.

A trip into the surrounding mountains is a real must. To the north of Innsbruck is the *Hafelekar,* 7,110 ft. above sea level, reached by cable car and funicular. You can stop off at the Seegrube stop, or go all the way up by cable car for a superb view of the mountains. South of the city, another cable-car service is operated from Igls, to the top of the *Patscherkofel mountain* (6,750 ft.), the last 800 ft. or so being by chair lift. Again, the panoramic views are just magnificent. On the way up, or down, spend some time in *Igls,* a small resort village that is a center of skiing in the winter and of hiking in the summer.

A delightful half-day trip to the **Stubai Valley,** S of Innsbruck, and its charming mountain villages like *Fulpmes* and *Telfes* will be well rewarded. At the head of the valley is the Stubaigletscher (glacier). Along the way are several cable railways that afford panoramic views of the surrounding mountain scenery.

Weather

Innsbruck's weather is changeable throughout the year. Daytime high temperatures in the summer typically get into the mid to upper 70s, dropping to the mid 50s at night. Winters can be cold and cloudy, with daytime highs in the 30s, falling to the 20s at night. Summers are normally the wettest season, with July usually being the wettest month.

INNSBRUCK: TEMPERATURES AND PRECIPITATION

Month	J	F	M	A	M	J	J	A	S	O	N	D
Average Daily Temperature												
(Fahrenheit) Max.	34	40	51	60	68	74	77	75	69	58	46	36
Min.	20	24	30	39	46	52	55	54	49	40	30	24
Average Number of Days with Precipitation												
	13	13	11	14	15	19	19	17	14	12	12	13

Salzburg: Austria

Sights to See

Hohensalzburg Fortress, overlooking Salzburg, some 500 ft. above the Salzach River, at the S end of the inner city. The largest fully preserved medieval castle in Europe. Open 9–3:30 daily; longer hours in summer. Either walk up, or catch the funicular from Festungsgasse, E of St. Peter's Abbey.

Residenzplatz, at the center of old Salzburg, N of Hohensalzburg Fortress. Complete with fountain, and the Glockenspiel tower, an 18th-century carillon with 35 bells (plays daily at 10:45 A.M. & 5:45 P.M.).

Residenz, Residenzpl. 1, on the W side of Residenzpl. A 17th-century palace of the archbishops, noted for its finely decorated Baroque staterooms and art gallery. Open 10–5 daily.

The Cathedral (Dom), Dom Platz, S of Residenzplatz. An early Baroque cathedral noted for its huge bronze doors and marble facade.

Church of the Franciscans (Franziskanerkirche), opposite the Dom on Domplatz. Noted for its high altar by Fischer von Erlach.

Collegiate Church (Collegiankirche), Universitatspl., to the NW of Dom Platz. Another masterpiece by the Viennese architect von Erlach.

Mozart's birthplace (Geburtshaus), Getreidegasse 9, N of the Collegiate Church. Full of exhibits, pictures, letters and Mozart memorabilia. You can also visit the *Mozarteum,* 9 Markartplatz (across the river), which houses the Bibliotheca Mozartiana, a library of Mozart's work and works about Mozart.

Mirabell Palace and Gardens (Mirabellschloss u garten), N across the Salzach River, on Mirabellplatz. A beautiful Baroque palace, surrounded by formal gardens, with fountains and statutes. The *Angel Staircase* is a real marvel. The N part of the gardens is now part of the Paracelsus-Kurhaus.

Hellbrunn Palace (Schloss Hellbrunn), about 5 km S of Salzburg by way of Hellbrunner Allee or Morzgerstrasse. A marvelous 17th-century summer residence of the archbishops, surrounded by a beautiful park, complete with fountains (some of which are trick fountains or spouts—watch out!), and fine sculptures. On the grounds is a well-known alpine zoo.

Useful Information

Tourist Office, Auerspergstrasse 7 (tel:80-72-3462) and Mozartplatz 5 (tel:84-7568); *American Express,* Mozartplatz 5 (tel:8425-01); *U.S. Consulate,* Giselakai 51 (tel:2-8601); *Taxi* (tel:4-4345, 7-2680 or 7-7164); *Police,* Churfurstrasse 1 (tel:4-4551 or 133 in emergencies); *Post Office,* Residenzplatz 9 (tel:84-41-2116; *Voltage Guide,* 220 V, two round-pin outlets are used.

Special Trips Tours

The *Sound of Music Tours* are an excellent way to see the area around Salzburg, one of the most beautiful in Europe. The tours leaving from the Mirabellaplatz kiosk have a good reputation. American Express, Mozartplatz 5 (tel:8425-01) also offers a tour.

Just E of Salzburg are the picturesque lakes of ***Euschlsee, Mondsee,*** and ***Wolfgangsee.*** The small towns of *St. Gilgen* and *St. Wolfgang,* both on the Wolfgangsee, are particularly worth spending some time in.

South of *Zell am See,* a chic resort village south of Salzburg, is the ***Grossglockner Hochalpenstrasse,*** one of Europe's most spectacular alpine highways (open May to November), starting at Bruck and ending at the Franz-Josefs-Hohe. If you have the time, and the weather is good, this is a truly spectacular drive. On the way back to Salzburg, between Zell am See and Bischofshofen, at Lend, a road runs south to one of Austria's most elegant spa towns, *Badgastein.*

Weather

Salzburg's weather can be changeable at all times of the year. Summer daytime high temperatures typically reach into the mid to high 70s, dropping to the mid 50s at night. Winter daytime highs are in the 30s or low 40s, falling to the 20s at night. Summer is the wettest season.

SALZBURG: TEMPERATURES AND PRECIPITATION

Month	J	F	M	A	M	J	J	A	S	O	N	D
Average Daily Temperature												
(Fahrenheit) Max.	35	41	50	60	67	73	76	76	68	57	47	36
Min.	20	25	31	39	47	51	56	55	50	41	32	25
Average Number of Days with Precipitation												
	13	13	11	14	15	18	19	17	14	13	12	12

Vienna (Wein): Austria

Sights to See

The Hofburg (Imperial Palace), Michaelerpl. The Hapsburg's town palace, a complex of several buildings ranging from early Gothic to turn of the century. It houses the *National Bibliothek* (Library), the *Imperial Apartments,* the *Schatzkammer* (royal treasury), the *Museum of Austrian Culture,* and the *Stallburg,* home of the Spanish Riding School.

Spanish Riding School (Spanische Hofreitschule), in the Hofburg complex. Haute ecole riding school. Performances by the aristocratic white Lippizaner horses prancing about the ring can be seen at 10:45 A.M. on Su and 7 P.M. on W, if you have tickets (advance reservations required). Rehearsals can be seen from 10–12 Tu–Su. from Feb.–June and Sept.–Oct., except when on tour.

Vienna Boys Choir, Mass in Schweizerhof Chapel, part of the Hofburg complex. On most Su and religious holidays; tickets required.

Albertina, Augustinerstr. 1, just SE of the Hofburg. One of the world's finest graphic arts collections, with drawings by Durer, Michelangelo, Rembrandt, and Rubens. Open 10–2 Tu, Th, & F, 10–1 & 3–6 W, 9–1 Sa & Su.

Staatsoper (Opera), 1 Opernrihg 2, across Albertina Pl. from the Albertina. An Early French Renaissance style building, rebuilt after WW II damage. Noted for its fabulous gold, crystal, and red velvet interior. Take a tour of the building if you can't get tickets.

Museum of Fine Arts (Kusthistorisches Museum), SW of the Hofburg at Maria-Theresienpl. 1. Contains one of the leading art collections in the world, thanks to the Hapsburgs. The must-see part is the entire room of Breughel (the elder) paintings. Open 10–9 Tu & F, 10–6 M, W, & Th, and 9–6 Sa & Su.

St. Stephen's Cathedral (Stephansdom), Stephanspl. 1, NE of the Hofburg. Late Romanesque and Gothic building covered with sculpture and famous for its ornate, lace-in-stone spire is one of Vienna's trademarks. Catch the elevator in the N tower for magnificent views.

The Donauturm, Donaupark, across the Danube. An 846-ft.-high viewing tower with revolving restaurants and observation deck has the city's best views.

Schonbrunn Palace (Schloss Schonbrunn), Austria's Versailles. A magnificent 18th-century Baroque building located in a park W of Vienna, it was the summer residence of the Hapsburgs. Forty-five of the palace's 1,400 rooms are open to the public. Open 9–12, 1–5 daily in summer; till 4 P.M. in winter.

Useful Information

Austrian National Information, 4 Margaretenstr. 1 (tel:587-20-00); *City Tourist Information,* 38 Kartnerstr. (tel:43-16-08-13); English-speaking City Information office in Rathaus (tel:428-00-20-85); *U.S. Embassy,* Boltzmanngasse 16 (tel:31-51-11); *Taxi* (tel:3130, 4369, 6282, or 9101); *American Express,* 1 Karntnerstrasse 21-23 (tel:515-40); *Post Office* 1 Fleischmarkt 19; *Voltage Guide,* 220 V, two round-pin outlets are used.

Special Trips/Tours

An *excursion on the Danube* with the Danube Steamship Company (DDSG), departing from Schwedenbrucke on the canal (tel:26-6535), is a delightful experience on a good day. Alternatively, *a walk in the Vienna Woods* (Wienerwald) to the S and W of the city, around the town of Mayerling, is a pleasant experience. A visit to *Hochschneeberg* (2 hours S of Vienna), near Puchberg am Schneeberg. Use the cog railway to the top of the 6,000-ft. mountain, for magnificent views in all directions.

Weather

Vienna's weather is changeable at all times of the year. Temperatures typically reach the mid 70s in the summer. Winters are moderately cold, with daytime highs in the 30s. Summer is the wet season.

VIENNA: TEMPERATURES AND PRECIPITATION

Month	J	F	M	A	M	J	J	A	S	O	N	D
Average Daily Temperature												
(Fahrenheit) Max.	34	38	47	58	67	73	76	75	68	56	45	37
Min.	25	28	30	42	50	56	60	59	53	44	37	30
Average Number of Days with Precipitation												
	15	14	13	13	13	14	13	13	10	13	14	15

Antwerp (Antwerper): Belgium

Sights to See

The Grote Markt, the main marketplace in the Old City. Surrounded by gabled Flemish guild houses, it has an impressive Renaissance Stadhuis (Town Hall) on one side, and a statue of the Roman Silvius Brabo in its center.
Cathedral of Our Lady (Onze-Lieve-Vrouw), near the Stadhuis. Dating from the 14th century, it is noted for its stained-glass windows, Gothic Tower, and Rubens's masterpieces, "Raising to the Cross," "Descent from the Cross," and "Assumption." Open 12–5 daily.
Butcher's Guild House (Vleeshuis), Vleeshouwersster. A Gothic white stone and red brick palace, it now contains the archaeological, historical, and craft industries museum. Open 10–5 Tu–Su.
Steen Castle, an impressive 9th-century fortress. It houses the National Maritime Museum. Open 10–5 daily.
Rubens House, Wapper 9. Rebuilt home and studio of the artist, where he lived for almost 30 years. It is full of treasures. Open 10–5 daily.
Royal Museum of Fine Arts, Leopold De Waelplaats 1–9. Noted for its fine collection of Flemish primitives. Open 10–5 Tu–Su.
Mayer van der Bergh Museum, noted for its Breughel's "Mag Meg" painting.

Plantin-Moretus Museum, Vrijdagmarkt 22. Devoted to the famous 16th-century printer, Plantin. It has a magnificently furnished interior and a printing plant, complete with his tools and presses, on display. A copy of one of the Gutenberg Bibles is also here. Open 10–5 daily.
Diamond Museum (Vieligheidsmuseum), Jezusstraat 28–30. Devoted to the diamond industry, of which Antwerp is a world center. Open 10–5 W–Su.
Diamond Land, Appelmansstraat 33A. Watch diamond cutters at work and see the diamond exhibition. The city's diamond industry is centered around Pelikaanstraat.
Open-Air Museum of Sculpture, Middelheim Park. Contains the works of Moore, Maillol, Rodin, and others. Open 10–dusk daily.

Useful Information

Tourist Information Pavilion, Koningin Astridplein (tel:233-0570); *Municipal Tourist Office,* Grote Markt 15 (tel:232-0103); *American Express,* Frankrijklei 21 (tel:232-5920); *Police,* Oudaan 5 (tel:231-6880 or 906 in emergencies); *U.S. Consulate,* Nationalestraat 5 (tel:225-0071 or 232-1801); *Post Office,* Groenplaats; *Voltage Guide* 110/220 V, two round-pin outlets are used.

Special Trips/Tours

An excursion *boat tour on the River Scheide* through the port of Antwerp, one of Europe's largest. Boats leave from Steen quay twice a day (May–Sept.), for this 3-hour trip.
Mechelen, residence of the Primate of Belgium, and the religious center of the country for centuries, is only 24 km from Antwerp by car. The town is world famous for its carillon bells, and many bellringers worldwide have received their training here. Visit the *Mechelen Museum* (Stradsmuseum), housed in Busleyden Manor, which illustrates local history and has a special section devoted to the Carillon. Open 10–5 W–M.
Brussels. Belgium's capital city is less than 50 km from Antwerp. With its *Grand'Place,* one of Europe's most beautiful squares, and *Gallery of Old Masters* (Musee d'Art Ancien), full of Flemish school masterpieces, it is definitely worth the trip. The fine tapestries of the time when Brussels was still the capital of the Duchy of Brabant, in the *Town Hall* (Hotel de Ville) on Grand' Place, should be seen. The view from the building's belfry is one of the best in the city. *Galeries St.-Hubert,* the oldest shopping arcade in Europe, adjoins the Grand' Place, as does the rue des Buchers, which is lined with fine restaurants.

Weather

Antwerp's weather is very variable. Summer daytime high temperatures are typically in the mid to high 60s, dropping to the mid 50s at night. Winters are cold and cloudy, with daytime highs usually in the low 40s, falling to the mid to low 30s at night. Summer and fall are normally the wettest seasons.

ANTWERP: TEMPERATURES AND PRECIPITATION

Month	J	F	M	A	M	J	J	A	S	O	N	D
Average Daily Temperature												
(Fahrenheit) Max.	41	44	48	53	59	65	67	68	66	59	50	43
Min.	33	35	37	42	49	53	56	56	53	47	40	36
Average Number of Days with Precipitation												
	15	12	11	12	11	10	12	13	10	13	15	16

Brussels (Bruxelles): Belgium

Sights to See

Grand' Place. One of Europe's most beautiful squares, dating from the 12th century. Cafes, shops, people-watching, morning flower market, and sound and light shows at 9:30 and 10:30 P.M. on summer weekends.

Town Hall (Hotel de Ville), Grand' Place. Dating from the 15th century, it is the most beautiful building in the city. See the fine tapestries of the time when Brussels was the capital of the Duchy of Brabant. The climb to the top of the belfry will be rewarded with a fine view of the city. Open 9:30–5 Tu–F, 10–4 Su. NOTE: don't miss the *Manneken-Pis,* a 17th-century statue across the rue du Lombard.

Galeries St.-Hubert, the oldest shopping arcade in Europe adjoins the Grand' Place (to the north), as does the rue des Buchers, which is lined with fine restaurants.

Place du Grand Sablon, SSE of Grand' Place. The center of Brussels' antique shop district. On weekends, the square is filled with a book and antiques market, surrounded with cafes full of people enjoying this special social scene.

Cathedral of St. Michael, blvd. de l'Imperatrice, E of Grand' Place. Dating from the 13th century, this imposing Gothic structure on top of a hill is famous for its 16th-century stained-glass windows, Baroque pulpit, and tapestries.

Brussels Park (Parc de Bruxelles), just SE of St. Michael's cathedral. A symmetrical park area, with splendid views of the surrounding buildings, including the *Parliament* (Palais de la Nation) on its N side, and the *Royal Palace* (Palais Royal) to its S.

Gallery of Old Masters (Musee d'Art Ancien), rue de la Regence 3, SW of the Palais Royal. Flemish School masterpieces, including Rubens and Breughel. Open 10–5 Tu–Su.

Palais de Justice, place Poelaert, S of Grand' Place. An immense building on a hill overlooking the older section of town.

Produce Market, place Ste. Catherine. Produce market and restaurants, especially the quai aux Briques.

Royal Art and History Museum, parc du Cinquantenaire 10. It has a large, eclectic collection, including examples of Belgian folklore.

Royal Central African Museum, in the suburb of Trevuren 13 km E of Brussels. Contains examples of art, ethnology, and natural sciences of the former Belgian Congo, now Zaire.

Useful Information

Belgium National Tourist Office, rue Marche-aux-Herbes/Grasmarkt 61, near the Grand' Place (tel:512-3030); *Tourist Information Brussels (TIB),* Town Hall, Grand' Place (tel:513-89-40); *American Embassy,* 27 blvd. du Regent (tel:513-3830); *Police* (tel:101 or 900 in emergencies); *Post Office,* pl. de la Monnaie; *American Express* pl. Louise 2 (tel:512-1740); *Taxi* (tel:511-2244); *Voltage Guide,* 220 V, two round-pin outlets are used.

Special Trips/Tours

Bruges (Brugge), one of the continent's best-preserved medieval towns, is only a 75-minute train ride NW of Brussels. It is well known for its picturesque canals, canal bridges, cobbled streets, and Renaissance facades. The *Grote Markt* (main square) is the center, with its famous octagonal tower, the *Beffroi* (Belfry), and a magnificent carillon. Go to the top of the Belfry tower for a great view of the city. Other notable sights include the 14th-century *Stadhuis* on Burg square; the *Groeninge Museum,* Dijverstraat, noted for its Flemish masters art collection; the *Gruuthuse Museum,* also on Dijverstraat; and the *Kantcentrum* (lace center), on Balstraat. On the way to or from Bruges, be sure to stop off in *Ghent* (Gent), well known in its own right for its canals, about halfway between Brussels and Bruges. Visit the *Gravensteen* (Castle of the Counts); *Sint-Michielsburg bridge;* the *Stadhuis* (town hall); and the *Museum voor Schone Kunsten* (Museum of Fine Arts) in Citadel park.

Weather

Brussels' weather is very changeable. Summer daytime high temperatures typically reach into the low 70s, falling to the 50s at night. Winter daytime highs are usually in the low 40s, dropping to the 30s at night. Despite a higher frequency of rainfall in the winter, rainfall totals are lower than during the summer.

BRUSSELS: TEMPERATURES AND PRECIPITATION

Month	J	F	M	A	M	J	J	A	S	O	N	D
Average Daily Temperature												
(Fahrenheit) Max.	40	44	51	58	65	72	73	72	69	60	48	42
Min.	30	32	36	41	46	52	54	54	51	45	38	32
Average Number of Days with Precipitation												
	21	17	17	18	16	15	17	18	13	17	20	19

Prague (Praha): Czechoslovakia

Sights to See

Old Town Square (Staromestske namesti), at the center of Prague's Old Town. Dominated by the Old Town Hall, with its famous 15th-century clock with twelve Apostles, and a bell-ringing skeleton.
Tyn Church, on the E side of Old Town Square. Noted for its twin spires, Gothic exterior, and Baroque interior.
Old-New Synagogue (Staronova Synagoga), Cervena St. in the Jewish Quarter N of Old Square. The oldest synagogue in Europe, dating from 1270.
State Jewish Museum (Statni Zidovske Muzeum), Jachymova 3, Old Town. A complex of buildings, including five synagogues, a cemetery, and a collection of Jewish artifacts. Open 9–5 M–F, Su.
Bethlehem Chapel (Betlemska kaple), Betlemske namesti, SW of Old Town Square. National hero Jan Hus preached here in the early 15th century.
Wenceslas Square (Vaclavske namesti), in Prague's New Town (Nove Mesto), SE of Old Town (Stare Mesto). The focal point of modern Prague, this square, with the statue of Vaclav 1, is surrounded by hotels, shops, and outdoor cafes.
National Museum (Narodni muzeum), Vaclavske namesti 68. Fine collection illustrating Czech history.
Charles Square (Karlovo namesti), New Town, W of Wenceslas Square. Prague's largest square, dominated by the 14th-century *New Town Hall* on its N side.
Dvorak Museum, Ke Karlovu 20, near Charles Square. An interesting museum, housing the mementoes of the Czech composer.
Charles Bridge (Karluv most), crossing the Vitava, NW of Bethlehem Chapel. Beautiful bridge connecting Old Town with Lesser Town (Mala Strana). It is lined with Baroque statues, and its defense tower affords the best view in town.
St. Nicholas Church (Kostel sv. Mikulase), Lesser Town Sq., NW of Charles Bridge. Noted for its cupola and ceiling frescoes.
Wallenstein Palace (Valdstejnsky palac), Valdstenjske namesti, N of St. Nicholas's. A beautiful 17th-century Baroque palace, housing the Ministry of Culture and a collection of 19th-century Czech paintings.
Prague Castle (Prazsky Hrad), in Hradcany above the Lesser Town. Former seat of Bohemian kings. Now the residence of Czechoslavakia's president, it also houses the *National Gallery of Art* (Narodni Galerie), known for its works by Durer and Breughel.
St. Vitus Cathedral (Katedrala St. Vita), located in the courtyard of Prague castle. Gothic structure famous for its stained-glass windows.

Useful Information

Tourist Office: Cedok, Na Prikope 18 (tel:21-27-111); *Prague Information Service,* Na Prikope 20 (tel:54-44-44); *U.S. Embassy,* Trziste 15, Lesser Town (tel:53-66-419); *Police* (tel:245-1837); *Post Office,* Jindrisska 14; *American*

Express, c/o Cedok, Na Prikope 18 (tel:212-71-11); *Voltage Guide,* 110/220 V, two round-pin outlets are used. Check the *Month in Prague,* for detailed listing of events and tourist information.

Special Trips/Tours

Prague is a good base for exploring the surrounding *Central Bohemian hills,* full of ancient castles, chateaus, fashionable health resorts, and medieval towns. *Karlstejn Castle* is less than an hour from the center of Prague. A massive fortress, it was built in the 14th century to house the Bohemian crown jewels. Its chapel is noted for its Gothic portraits and the semiprecious stones inset in the walls.

Weather

Prague experiences relatively mild winters and warm to hot summers. Summer daytime high temperatures typically reach into the high 80s, falling to the upper 40s at night. Winter daytime highs usually are in the high 40s or low 50s, dropping to the teens at night. Summer is the wet season.

PRAGUE: TEMPERATURES AND PRECIPITATION

Month	J	F	M	A	M	J	J	A	S	O	N	D
Average Daily Temperature												
(Fahrenheit) Max.	49	53	64	73	82	88	91	89	84	71	57	50
Min.	7	10	18	29	36	44	49	47	38	29	24	14
Average Number of Days with Precipitation												
	13	11	10	11	13	12	13	12	10	13	12	13

Copenhagen (Kobenhavn): Denmark

Sights to See

Amelienborg Palace, Amelienborg Square. Home of the Royal family. Closed to the public, but Amelienborg Square with its three other immense Rococo palaces is definitely worth seeing. Watch the changing of the guard every day at noon.
Den Lille Havefrue (Little Mermaid), Citadel Park, N of Amelienborg Palace. Enjoy the promenade overlooking the harbor.
Nyhavn, or the harbor area, S of Amelienborg Palace. Full of fishing boats, sailing ships, and sailors. Harbor and canal tours leave every half hour from the head of the Nyhavn canal and the Gammel Strand.
Rosenborg Castle (Rosenborg Slot), Oster Voldgade 4, W of Amelienborg Palace. A Renaissance castle with the priceless Danish crown regalia and crown jewels. Open 10–3 daily in summer, shorter hours rest of year.

Round Tower (Rundetarn), on Kobmagergade, S of Rosenborg Castle. Built in the 1600s as an observatory, it offers an excellent panorama of Copenhagen.
Christiansborg Palace, Slotsholmen Island, SW of Nyhavn and S of Rosenborg Castle. Contains the Supreme Court, Parliament, and the Royal Reception Chambers. Closed on Saturdays.
National Museum (Nationalmuseet), Fredriksholms Kanal 12, just S of Christiansborg Palace. Excellent prehistory and folk art collections, along with Viking camps and ships. Closed Mondays.
Tivoli Gardens, Vesterbrogade, W of Christiansborg Castle across H. C. Andersens Boulevard. Copenhagen's amusement park, with concert halls, theaters, restaurants, midway, etc. It is best seen in the evening, particularly on W, Sa, & Su when there are closing fireworks. Open 10–12 daily.
Christiania, ten square blocks in the Christianshavn district E of Christiansborg Palace across the Inderhavnen. "Occupied" by hippies, street people, and street entertainers.
Vor Frelsers Kirke (Our Saviour's Church), Princessegade. The view from the tower is excellent.

Useful Information

Danish Tourist Board, H. C. Andersens Blvd. 22 (tel:33-11-1325); *Copenhagen Tourist Information Office,* Banegardspladsen (tel:11-1415); *Tourist Association of Copenhagen,* in the Magasin du Nord department store, Kongens Nytorv (tel:11-4433); *U.S. Embassy,* Dag Hammerskjolds Allee 24 (tel:31-42-3144); *Taxi* (tel:31-35-3535) or 31-35-1420); *American Express,* Amagertorv 18 (tel:33-12-2301); *Police* (tel:000 in emergencies); *Post Office,* Tietgensgade 37; *Voltage Guide,* 220 V, two round-pin outlets are used; *Copenhagen This Week* will keep you up to date on local events.

Special Trips/Tours

Boat tours of the city's intricate canal system and main harbor leave from Kongens Nytorv and Gammel Strand every 30 minutes from 10 A.M. May–October (tel:01-3105). Cruises lasting 3 to 4 hours on the *Isefjord,* Denmark's oldest schooner, leave from Amaliehaven, behind the Copenhagen Admiral Hotel, Toldbodgade 24 (tel:15-1729), at 10 A.M. and 3 P.M. for trips along the sound.

Helsingor (Elsinore) is only 45 km away N of the city, and only 4 km away from Sweden across the sound. Its 17-century castle, Kronborg Castle, beautiful old quarter, good beaches, and old railway are worth a side trip.

The Open-Air Museum (Frilansmuseet), in the NW suburb of Sorgenfri, is an excellent museum housing a collection of farms, windmills, and country houses—all furnished with authentic period pieces. Closed on Mondays.

Weather

Copenhagen has a cool, temperate climate, with very changeable weather. Summer daytime high temperatures typically reach the high 60s or low 70s, falling to the mid 50s at night. Winters are relatively short and not too cold, with temperatures usually getting into the mid to high 30s. Summer and fall are the wettest seasons.

COPENHAGEN: TEMPERATURES AND PRECIPITATION

Month	J	F	M	A	M	J	J	A	S	O	N	D
Average Daily Temperature												
(Fahrenheit) Max.	36	36	41	51	61	67	71	70	64	54	45	40
Min.	28	28	31	38	46	52	57	56	51	44	38	34
Average Number of Days with Precipitation												
	17	13	12	13	11	13	14	14	15	16	16	17

Helsinki: Finland

Sights to See

Market Square, at the foot of Helsinki's Esplanade at South Harbor. A colorful open-air market that functions year round, filled with stalls selling flowers, fish, produce, baskets, and handicraft items. Don't forget to visit the coffee tent, and, especially if the weather is inclement, Kauppahalli, a busy indoor market off Market Square.

Senate Square, just N of Market Square. A large plaza dominated by the 19th-century Lutheran Cathedral, and surrounded by Neoclassical columned buildings.

Finnish Design Center, Kasarminkatu 19. Full of the superbly designed and hand-crafted products that Finland is famous for. Nothing is for sale, but it will help you decide on what to shop for later.

Art Museum of the Ateneum, Kaivokatu 2, E of Senate Square. Diverse collection, mostly by modern Finnish artists, but also some classical works.

National Museum (Kansallismuseo), Mannerheimintie 34, NW of Senate Square. Excellent collection on Finnish history, it is noted for its Gypsy and Lapp costume exhibits.

Finlandia Hall, Karamzininkatu 4, in Hesperia Park on the shore of the Toolo Bay, NE of the National Museum. A magnificent marble structure designed by Alvar Aalto.

Linnanmaki Amusement Park, N of Finlandia Hall, at the intersection of Helsingkatu & Sturenkatu. Finland's answer to Copenhagen's Tivoli. Peacock Theater in the park offers varied entertainment. Open daily, May through August.

Helsinki City Art Museum, Tamminiementie 6. Noted for its Finnish contemporary art collection.

Rock Church (Temppeliakio Church), Lutherinkatu 3, W of the National Museum. An extraordinary underground church blasted out of solid rock and capped by copper dome, this modern masterpiece was completed in 1969.

Sibelius Memorial, Sibelius Park, off Mechelininkatu, NNE of the Rock Church. Controversial monument made of tubular steel pipes.

Seurasaari Open-Air Museum, Seurasaari Island, NW of central Helsinki. A national park and open-air museum with Finnish farm and rural buildings that have been transferred from all over the country and reassembled. Folk dancers provide evening entertainment in the summer. Open daily.

Suomenlinna Fortress, S of the city center. A large old naval fortress, built in 1748 by Sweden to defend the Baltic on a series of five rocky islands. Visit any or all of the four museums. Ferries depart from Market Square at half-past the hour for the 15-minute ride. Open daily, June–Aug.

Useful Information

Helsinki Tourist Office, Pohjoisesplanadi 19 (tel:169-3.757); *Finnish Tourist Board*, Unioninkatu 26 (tel:144-511); *American Express*, c/o Travek Travel, Katajanoken Pohjoisranta 9–13 (tel:66-1631); *U.S. Embassy*, Itainen Puistotie 14b (tel:171-931); *Police* (tel:002 in emergency); *Post Office*, Mannerheimintie 11 (tel:195-51-17); *Voltage Guide*, 220 V, two round-pin outlets are used.

Special Trips/Tours

Porvoo (Borga), one of Finland's oldest towns is just 30 miles along the coast E of Helsinki. Rather than drive, catch the m/s J. L. Runeberg, which departs from Market Square for the 3-hour trip on W, F, Sa, & Su. at 10 A.M. Visit Porvoo's 15th-century Gothic Cathedral, the Municipal Museum below the cathedral, and just wander around this delightful medieval town.

Weather

While Helsinki's winters are long and cold, its summers are surprisingly warm. Daytime high temperatures typically reach into the high 60s or low 70s, dropping to around 50 at night. Winter daytime highs usually reach the mid to upper 20s, falling to the teens at night. Late winter and spring are normally the driest time of the year, with late summer and fall the wettest.

HELSINKI: TEMPERATURES AND PRECIPITATION

Month	J	F	M	A	M	J	J	A	S	O	N	D
Average Daily Temperature												
(Fahrenheit) Max.	26	25	32	44	56	66	71	68	59	47	37	31
Min.	17	15	20	30	40	49	55	53	46	37	30	23
Average Number of Days with Precipitation												
	20	18	14	13	12	13	14	15	15	18	19	20

Bordeaux: France

Sights to See

Grand Theatre, Place de la Comedie. A magnificent 18th-century building, noted for its superb colonnade and richly decorated interior.

Esplanade des Quinconces, N of the Grand Theatre. One of Europe's largest squares, beside the Garonne, noted for its impressive sculptures.

Jardin Public, NW of the Esplanade des Quinconces. Attractive gardens containing the Museum of Natural History and the Botanical Gardens.

Maison du Vin, 1 Cours du 30-Juillet, near the Grand Theatre. Offers free tastings of regional wines. Open 10:30–11:30, 2:30–4:30 M–F, 10:30–11:30 Sa.

Church of St-Seurin (Eglise St-Seurin), rue Pereire, several blocks W of the Grand Theatre. Dating from the 12th century, with a 19th-century facade, it is known for its finely decorated doorway.

Cathedrale of St-Andre, Pl. Cathedrale, SE of Eglise St-Seurin, and SW of the Grand Theatre. Dating from the 12th century, it is known for its variety of flying buttresses, and the 13th-century Porte Royale with its magnificent sculptures.

Tour Pey Berland, just E of the cathedral. A beautifully decorated belfry, which affords good views of Bordeaux.

Town Hall (Hotel de Ville), just W of the cathedral. Former 18th-century Archbishop's Palace with beautiful gardens.

Museum of Fine Arts (Musee des Beaux-Arts), Cours d'Albret, W of the cathedral. Fine collection of art. Open 10–12, 2–6, W–M, 10–12, 1–5 W–M off-season.

Aquitaine Museum (Musee d'Aquitaine), Cours d'Albret, just S of the Fine Arts Museum. Devoted to the history of this part of SW France. Open 2–6 W–M.

Pont de Pierre, spanning the Garonne, SE of the cathedral. Built in the early 19th century, it is considered one of the country's most attractive bridges.

Basilica St-Michel, Place Canteloup, S of Pont de Pierre near the Garonne. A beautiful Gothic church better known for its freestanding bell tower, the *Tour St-Michel,* at 374 ft. one of France's tallest.

Church of St-Croix (Eglise St-Croix), SE of the Tour St-Michel across rue du Hamel. Romanesque church with a beautiful facade.

Useful Information

Tourist Office (Syndicat d'Initiative), 12 Cours du 30-Juillet (tel:56-44-2841); *U.S. Consulate,* 22 Cours du Marechal Foch (tel:52-6595); *Post Office,* 52 rue Georges-Bonnac (tel:56-48-87-48); Maison du Vin, 1 Cours du 30-Juillet (lists chateaux open to visitors); *Voltage Guide* 110/220 V, two round-pin outlets are used.

Special Trips/Tours

The world-famous wine-producing regions of the *Medoc,* north of Bordeaux on the W bank of the Garonne, and *St-Emilion* and *Pomerol,* to the east on the N bank of the Dordogne, offer an opportunity to sample some of the world's best wines. Among the most notable wine chateaux (there are hundreds), are *Chateau Mouton-Rothschild* (tel:56-58-2222), *Pauillac* (noted for the Rothschilds' excellent wine museum); *Chateau Lafite* (tel:56-59-0174), Pauillac; *Chateau Latour* (tel:56-59-0051), St-Julien; *Chateau Cos d'Estournal* (tel:56-44-1137), St-Estephe; and *Chateau Margaux* (tel:56-88-7028), Margaux—all in the Medoc. While not as spectacular as the Medoc's wine chateaux, those in St-Emilion and Pomerol are still worth visiting, particularly *Chateau Villemaurine* (tel:57-43-0144), St-Emilion. The village of *St-Emilion* itself, surrounded by vineyards, is a medieval showcase and should not be missed. NOTE: prior appointments are necessary before visiting the wine chateaux.

The Perigord region, further E of Bordeaux, with its prehistoric caves, castles, country houses, and rolling hills makes an excellent side trip. The *National Museum of Prehistory* in *Les Eyzies-de-Tayac,* S of the region's capital, Perigueux, and housed in a medieval castle above the town, puts the area's prehistoric sites into perspective. Notable among these is the *Grotte de Font-de-Gaume,* famous for its prehistoric drawings, just outside Les Eyzies-de-Tayac.

The capital of the region, *Perigueux,* about 70 miles E of Bordeaux, is famous for its Roman ruins (Tour de Vesone and the Arenes amphitheater), and medieval churches (Cathedral of St-Front and the Church of St-Etienne). Further to the SE is the *Gouffre de Padirac* cave outside Rocamadour. *Rocamadour* village itself, S of Brive-la-Gaillarde, and perched on the side of a cliff, is an interesting sight, and one of the country's oldest places of pilgrimage.

The *Atlantic coast* E and SE of Bordeaux is largely unspoiled, with good beaches and some of the highest sand dunes on the continent. If you have had too much good food and wine, *Arcachon* and the small beach towns of the *Cote d'Argent* to its S, may be just the right answer. If you have the time, *Biarritz,* France's most popular Atlantic beach resort, is about 150 miles SW of Bordeaux, near the border with Spain. Nearby are *St-Jean-de-Luz,* and *Bayonne,* the center of France's Basque country, with its *Basque Museum.*

Weather

Bordeaux's summer daytime high temperatures typically reach into the high 70s, dropping to the upper 50s at night. Winter daytime highs are usually in the high 40s or low 50s, falling to the upper 30s at night. Winter is the wettest season.

BORDEAUX: TEMPERATURES AND PRECIPITATION

Month	J	F	M	A	M	J	J	A	S	O	N	D
Average Daily Temperature												
(Fahrenheit) Max.	49	51	59	63	69	75	78	78	74	65	55	49
Min.	35	36	40	43	48	54	57	56	54	47	40	37
Average Number of Days with Precipitation												
	16	13	13	13	14	11	11	12	13	14	15	17

Lyon (Lyons): France

Sights to See

Place Bellecour, in the center of Lyon, S of rue Col. Chambonnet, between the Rhone and Saone. Dating from the 18th century, it is one of Europe's biggest squares, surrounded by cafes and restaurants.

Church of St-Martin d'Ainay, SW of Place Bellecour, W of rue Victor-Hugo. Dating from the 11th century, it is Lyon's oldest church, noted for its mosaic floor.

Textile Museum (Musee Historique des Tissus), 34 rue de la Charite, E of St-Martin d'Ainay Church. Noted for its collection of fabrics, including beautiful tapestries. Open 10–12, 2–5:30 Tu–Su.

Decorative Arts Museum (Musee des Arts Decoratifs), next door to the Textile Museum. Fine collection of furniture and objets d'art. Open 10–12, 2–5:30 Tu–Su.

Town Hall (Hotel de Ville), pl. des Terreaux, N of pl. Bellecour, at the end of rue Pres. Herriot. Considered to be one of the most attractive town halls in Europe, and noted for its finely sculpted facade. Also noteworthy is the Bartholdi Fountain, pl. des Terreaux, just W of the Hotel de Ville.

Museum of Fine Arts (Musee des Beaux-Arts), on the S side of pl. des Terreaux. Excellent collection of paintings and sculpture. Open 10:45–6 W–M.

Old Lyon (Vieux Lyon), across the Saone NE of pl. Bellecour. Renovated area of Lyon that has many fine medieval and Renaissance buildings, and is full of antique shops, cafes, and art galleries.

Cathedrale St-Jean, 70 rue St.-Jean, NW of pl. Bellecour, across Pont Bonaparte in Vieux Lyon. Gothic cathedral dating from the 12th century and known for its rose window, stained glass, and 14th-century astronomical clock.

Basilica of Notre-Dame de la Fourviere, on the top of Fourviere hill, behind the cathedral. Reached by the funicular just SW of the cathedral. A 19th-century church, with magnificent views from its tower.

Gallo-Roman Museum (Musee Gallo-Romain), rue Cleberg, S of the basilica. Contains exhibits from the ruins of the two adjacent Roman theaters. Open 9–12, 2–6 M–Sa, shorter hours off-season.

Parc de la Tete d'Or, blvd. des Belges, Les Brotteaux N of cours Vitton on the E bank of the Rhone. A fine park complete with a botanical garden and zoo.

Useful Information

Tourist Office (Office de Tourisme), pl. Bellecour (tel:78-42-2575); *U.S. Consulate,* 7 quai General Sarrail (tel:246-849); *Main Post Office* is at pl. A. Poncet, just SE of pl. Bellecour; *Voltage Guide,* 110/220 V, two round-pin outlets are used.

Special Trips/Tours

The picturesque, walled medieval village of *Perouges* is some 22 miles NE of Lyon near Meximieux. Full of artisans and artists, it makes an ideal short trip if time is a constraint.

Another worthwhile short trip is to *Vienne,* known for its Roman temple and theater and medieval churches, as well as for its haute cuisine, just 18 miles S of Lyon. A Roman colony, the Roman remains include the *Temple of Augustus and Livia,* and a theater (Theatre Romain). To the S of the town's center, is the 12th-century *Cathedral of St-Maurice,* noted for its Romanesque interior sculpture. The *church of St-Pierre,* dating from the 6th century, now houses a fine sculpture collection.

If you have more time, trips to *Grenoble* or the lake resort of *Aix-les-Bains,* both SE of Lyon, are definitely worthwhile. *Grenoble* is the gateway to the French Alps, Europe's highest, and a thriving city in its own right. It is not only both a winter and summer sports center, but has a number of noteworthy sights, including the *Palais de Justice,* the 12th-century *Cathedral of Notre-Dame,* and the *Museum of Painting and Sculpture.*

Situated on the beautiful *Lac du Bourget,* some 45 mi. N of Grenoble, is one of France's largest spas, *Aix-les-Bains.* In addition to its full complement of spa facilities, there are a Roman temple and triumphal arch, the Musee du Docteur-Faure (modern art), and all kinds of water sports. Boat trips on the lake are a delight, one of which stops at Hautecombe Abbey, noted for its tombs of the kings and princes of the House of Savoy. Further N, off the A41, is Annecy, on majestic *Lac d'Annecy.* Be sure to take a boat ride on the lake and the cable car up to *Mont Veyrier* for superb panoramas of the Alps.

Weather

Lyon's summer daytime high temperatures typically reach into the high 70s or low 80s, falling to the upper 50s at night. Winter daytime highs are usually in the mid 40s, dropping to the 30s at night. Summer and early fall are the wettest seasons.

LYON: TEMPERATURES AND PRECIPITATION

Month	J	F	M	A	M	J	J	A	S	O	N	D
Average Daily Temperature												
(Fahrenheit) Max.	42	45	55	61	69	75	80	79	73	61	50	43
Min.	30	31	37	42	49	55	59	58	53	45	38	33
Average Number of Days with Precipitation												
	15	12	11	11	13	11	10	11	11	12	14	14

Marseille (Marseilles): France

Sights to See

Marseille itself, from the Notre Dame Cathedral (Basilica du Notre-Dame-de-la-Garde), pl. du Colonel Eden, on top of a 500-ft. hill overlooking the city S of Vieux Port.

The Old Port (Vieux Port). Framed by the 17th-century forts of St. Jean and St. Nicholas, and usually full of yachts and small fishing boats, this is the city's heart. Try some of Marseille's famous bouillabaisse, served at the restaurants lining the quai du Port and quai Rive Neuve in the old port.

Roman Docks Museum (Musee des Docks Romains), 28 pl. Vivaux, N of Vieux Port. Remains of old Roman docks and statuary. Open 10–12, 12–6, except Tu and W A.M.

La Major and Old La Major Cathedrals (Cathedrales de la Major), pl. de la Major, off quai de la Joliette, NW of the Roman Docks Museum. Twelfth-century Romanesque and 19th-century Romanesque/Byzantine structures side by side; famous for their domes and cupolas.

Le Panier neighborhood. Between the Vieux Port and rue du Panier, a fascinating part of Old Marseille.

Marseille Historical Museum (Musee d'Histoire de Marseille), Centre Bourse, E of the Roman Docks Museum. Houses the excavations of this ancient port city.

La Canebiere, Marseille's main street, leading out of the Vieux Port into Marseille proper. It is lined with luxury shops and inviting cafes.

Museum of Fine Arts (Musee des Beaux-Arts), Palais de Longchamp, pl. Bernex, NE of Vieux Port. Noted for its fine collection of Daumier, as well as other French artists. Open 10–12, 2–6 W–M.

Basilica of St. Victor (Basilique de St-Victor), pl. St.-Victor, just S of quai du Rive-Neuve. Known for its early Christian catacombs. Open M–Sa.

Cite Radieuse, 280 bd. Michelet, S of Vieux Port. An early 1950s housing development by Le Corbusier.

Borely Park (Parc Borely), promenade de la Plage & ave. Clotbey. Beautiful gardens, ideal for strolling.

Archaelogical Museum (Musee d'Archeologie), in the Chateau Borely is worth a visit to see its Egyptian, Greek, and Roman collections.

Chateau d'If. A 16th-century island castle, turned into a state prison, which served as the setting for Dumas's *The Count of Monte Cristo.* Boats leave for this 90-minute round trip several times every hour from the quai des Belges in the Vieux Port.

Useful Information

Tourist Office (Office du Tourisme), 4 La Canebiere (tel:91-549-111); *Taxi* (tel:91-058-080 or 91-022-020); *Public Transportation* (tel:91-776-882); *U.S. Consulate,* 12 blvd. Paul Peytral (tel:91-54-92-00 or 91-53-43-22); *Voltage Guide,* 110/220 V, two round-pin outlets are used.

Special Trips/Tours

Provence, often overlooked by visitors to the south of France, has much to offer. The Roman *Pont du Gard* (a three-tiered aqueduct), near Nimes, is spectacular, as is Nimes's *Roman temple,* the *Maison Carree,* and its Roman amphitheater. South of Nimes is *Aigues-Mortes,* a walled city set among swamps and lagoons. The *Roman arena* in Arles is similarly impressive.

Aix-en-Provence, the ancient capital of Provence, is just 31 km N of Marseille. Famous for its main street, *Cours Mirabeau,* with its fountains, cafes, shops, and 17th- and 18th-century mansions (now hotels), it also has a number of other noteworthy sights, including the *Cathedral of St. Sauveur* and an interesting museum of tapestries, the *Musee des Tapisseries.*

The *Cote d'Azur,* with its world famous resorts of St. Tropez, Cannes, Antibes, Nice, and Menton, along with Monte Carlo, strung out along one of the world's most beautiful coastlines, is only an hour or so east of Marseille. There is, of course, the sun, the beaches, and the Mediterranean itself, but these communities themselves are worth spending some time in, particularly *Nice.* The *Corniche D'Esterel,* SW of Cannes between La Napoule and St.-Raphael, has some of the most rugged coastline, best seen from the N98 road.

Weather

Marseille enjoys a Mediterranean climate, with warm to hot summers with very little rain, and mild winters. Summer daytime high temperatures typically reach into the high 70s and low 80s, dropping to the 60s at night. Winter daytime highs are usually in the mid 50s, falling to the high 30s or low 40s at night. Late fall and winter is the rainy season, with November and December normally the wettest months.

MARSEILLE: TEMPERATURES AND PRECIPITATION

Month	J	F	M	A	M	J	J	A	S	O	N	D
Average Daily Temperature												
(Fahrenheit) Max.	50	53	59	64	71	79	84	83	77	68	58	52
Min.	35	36	41	46	52	58	63	63	58	51	43	37
Average Number of Days with Precipitation												
	8	6	7	7	8	4	2	5	6	8	9	10

Nice: France

Sights to See

Promenade des Anglais, extending for miles along the Mediterranean. Just made for strolling, with a narrow pebble beach on one side, elegant hotels, restaurants, and cafes on the other, and palm trees down the center.

La Vieille Ville (The Old City), in the SE part of Nice. A veritable labyrinth of small, twisting streets and alleys and medieval buildings with overhanging balconies. Visit the Cathedral of Sainte Reparate, and one of the many markets. *The Flower Market* (Le Marche aux Fleurs), cours Saleya, near the quai des Etats-Unis. Nice's wholesale flower market. The countryside around Nice is one of France's major flower-growing areas (carnations, stock, roses, and anthemis), used to make scents and perfumes.

The Harbor (Vieux Port), off rue Cassini. Colorful yachts, boats of all kinds, and coastal steamers fill this picturesque harbor.

La Tour Bellanda, at the end of the promenade des Anglais. A beautifully situated park, with a chateau, ruins of an ancient fort-palace, later a cathedral, on top, from which there are magnificent views of Nice and the Mediterranean coast. Visit the small Naval Museum.

Matisse Museum (Musee Matisse), 164 av. des Arenes, N of the Carabacel district. An excellent collection of the artist's work, spanning his entire career. Open 10–12, 2:30–6 Tu–Sa, closed in November.

Chagall Museum (Musee National Marc Chagall), av. du Dr. Menard & blvd. de Cimiez, just NE of the railroad station. Sculptures, mosaics, sketches, lithographs, and paintings by Chagall. Open 10–7 W–M July–Sept. 10–12:30, 2–5:30 rest of year.

Russian Orthodox Cathedral, boulevard du Tzarewitch. Built for the visiting Romanovs, who frequented Nice as much as the western European aristocracy. Noted for its icons.

Useful Information

Tourist Office, Av. Thiers (tel:93-870-707); *French Riviera Tourist Board,* 55 promenade des Anglais (tel:93-445-059); *American Express,* 11 promenade des Anglais (tel:93-872-982); *Weather* (tel:93-839-111); *Taxi* (tel:93-52-3232 or 93-88-8993); *Bus Transportation* (tel:93-856-181); *Police* (tel:17); *English language tourist information* (tel:93-856-583); closest *U.S. Consulate* is in Marseille, at 12 blvd. Paul Peytral (tel:91-54-9200); *Post Office,* 23 av. Thiers; *Voltage Guide,* 110/220 V, two round-pin outlets are used.

Special Trips/Tours

Nice is an excellent base for exploring the beautiful *Cote d'Azur,* or Riviera. The world famous resorts of *St. Tropez, Cannes, Antibes,* and *Menton,* along with *Monaco* and *Monte Carlo* are strung out along the Mediterranean coast, all easily accessible by car or rail from Nice. The best beaches are between St.-Maxime and Hyeres, W of Nice. The most spectacular coastal scenery is along the *Corniche d'Esterel,* between La Napoule and St.-Raphael, SW of Cannes. Behind the Mediterranean beaches lie picturesque mountain villages like *Eze, St. Paul-de-Vence, Gourdon,* and *Grimaud,* all of which afford magnificent panoramas of the surrounding countryside.

In addition to the great natural beauty, there are the cultural jewels, such as the *Picasso Museum* in Antibes and the *Jean Cocteau Museum* in Menton. There are over 100 local festivals and events, and over 20 international festivals besides the famed Cannes Film Festival in May. Check with the Tourist Office for details. In winter, the mountains behind the coast have such ski resorts as *Auron, Isola,* and *Valberg,* all less than two hours' drive from Nice.

Monaco and nearby *Menton* with their famous casinos are just over 30 minutes from Nice by train, or less by helicopter (14 flights a day from Nice—tel:723-462)

Weather

Nice enjoys a typical Mediterranean climate with warm to hot, dry summers, and mild, relatively sunny winters. Summer daytime high temperatures usually reach the high 70s in the summer, dropping to around 70 at night. Daytime high temperatures in the winter typically are in the mid to upper 50s, falling to the 40s at night. Summers normally are dry, with little rain. Late fall and early winter are the wettest time of year.

NICE: TEMPERATURES AND PRECIPITATION

Month	J	F	M	A	M	J	J	A	S	O	N	D
Average Daily Temperature												
(Fahrenheit) Max.	54	55	57	61	66	73	78	78	74	68	61	56
Min.	47	47	50	54	59	66	71	71	67	61	54	49
Average Number of Days with Precipitation												
	5	5	7	5	5	4	1	2	4	7	7	6

Paris: France

Sights to See

Cathedral of Notre Dame, Ile de la Cite. One of the world's finest examples of Gothic architecture. A superb view of Paris can be had from the top of its towers.
Palais de Justice and Sainte-Chapelle, blvd. du Palais, Ile de la Cite. Headquarters of the early kings. Open daily 10–6, except Tu.
The Louvre, pl. du Louvre. The largest palace in the world, housing six museums. Open 9:45–5:15 W–M. While here, look around Le Marais, a very elegant area, especially place des Vosges.
Musee D'Orsay, 62 rue de Lille, along the Seine, opposite the Louvre. Devoted largely to French Impressionist paintings in the renovated Gare d'Orsay railroad station. Open 10–6 Tu–Su.
Arc de Triomphe, pl. Charles-de-Gaulle. Largest monumental arch in world. Open daily, except Tu. Magnificent views of Paris from the top. Le Fouquet's

cafe, 99 avenue des Champs-Elysees, is the place for watching the sun set over the Arc.

Champs-Elysees, Paris's world-famous boulevard, lined with shops, cafes, and trees. Take time to linger.

Eiffel Tower, Champs-de-Mars. Built in 1889, it was the world's tallest building until New York's Chrysler building was erected. Open daily. Superb views. Try the Le Jules Verne restaurant on level 2.

Le Centre Georges Pompidou, rue Rambuteau & rue St. Martin. Controversial contemporary art museum with jugglers, mimes, singers, fire-eaters, acrobats, boutiques, and magicians outside. Open daily 12–10 W–M.

Church of St. Germain-des-Pres, pl. St. Germain-des-Pres. Oldest church in Paris, surrounded by art galleries, boutiques, and cafes. (Try Aux Deux Magots, 170 blvd. Saint-Germain).

Picasso Museum (Musee Picasso), Hotel Sale, 5 rue de Thorigny. Devoted to Picasso. Open 9:45–5:15 W–M.

Useful Information

Office de Tourisme de Paris, 127 Champs-Elysees (tel:47-23-6172); *U.S. Embassy,* 2 av. Gabriel (tel:42-96-1202); *City of Paris Information Bureau,* 29 rue de Rivoli; *American Express,* 11 rue Scribe (tel:42-66-0999); *Police* (tel:42-60-3322 or 17 in emergencies); *Post Office,* 52 rue de Louvre. *Voltage Guide,* 110/220 V, two round-pin outlets are used. Check *Paris Selection* (in English and French), for events, nightlife, restaurants, shopping, etc.

Special Trips/Tours

A delightful way to see Paris is to take a cruise on one of the city's sightseeing boats, *Bateaux-Mouches,* on the Seine river. Cruises last an hour, and leave every 20 to 30 minutes from the Right Bank end of the *Pont de l'Alma* (tel:42-25-9610).

Versailles, Louis XIV's fantastic chateaux is 13 miles SW of Paris and should not be missed. The formal gardens cover 250 acres, with 600 fountains. Guided tours Tu–Su 10–3:30.

Weather

Paris enjoys a moderate climate with cool summers and mild winters. Rainfall is low but frequent, often with thunderstorms in the summer. Average daily temperatures reach the mid 70s in summer, and the mid 40s in winter.

PARIS: TEMPERATURES AND PRECIPITATION

Month	J	F	M	A	M	J	J	A	S	O	N	D
Average Daily Temperature												
(Fahrenheit) Max.	43	45	54	60	68	73	76	75	70	60	50	44
Min.	34	34	39	43	49	55	58	58	53	46	40	36
Average Number of Days with Precipitation												
	17	14	12	13	12	12	12	13	13	13	15	16

Strasbourg: France

Sights to See

Strasbourg Cathedral (Cathedral of Notre Dame), Old Town. Built on the site of an earlier Romanesque church, this 12th-century Gothic cathedral is considered to be one of France's finest medieval structures, if not Europe's. It is especially known for its richly sculpted facade, beautiful stained glass, and 16th-century astronomical clock.

Maison Kammerzell, just NW of the cathedral. A 16th-century merchant's house, noted for the fine wood carving on its half-timbered exterior.

Chateau des Rohan, place du Chateau, on the S side of the cathedral. An 18th-century palace, famous for its facades and Rococo interior. It now houses museums of archaeology, fine arts, and decorative arts, the last noted for its fine ceramics collection. Open 10–12, 2–6 daily in summer, 2–6 W–M off-season.

Musee de l'Oeuvre Notre-Dame, place du Chateau, just SW of the cathedral. Contains the originals of the cathedral's sculptures, together with a good collection of medieval and Renaissance art. Open 10–12, 2–6 daily in summer, 2–6 W–M off-season.

Suckling Pigs Market (place du Marche-aux-Cochons-de-Lait), just SW of the Musee de l'Oeuvre Notre-Dame. Picturesque square surrounded by medieval buildings.

Museum of Modern Art (Musee d'Art Moderne), housed in an old custom house, west of the Suckling Pigs Market. Good collection of paintings and sculptures. Open 10–12, 2–6 daily, 2–6 W–M off-season.

Alsace Museum (Musee Alsacien), 23 quai St.-Nicolas, S of the cathedral across the Ill river over the Pont du Corbeau. Devoted to the folk art, costumes, furniture, and implements of Alsace. Open 10–12, 2–6 daily in summer, 2–6 W–M off-season.

Church of St. Thomas, place St. Thomas, SW of the cathedral, back across the Ill. A 13th-century church known for its mausoleum of Maurice de Saxe.

La Petite France (Little France), sometimes known as the Tanner's Quarter (Quartier des Tanneurs), W of St. Thomas's church. Famous district of Strasbourg with many 16th-century, half-timbered houses lining its narrow streets and canals.

Useful Information

Tourist Office, Place Gutenberg (tel:88-32-5707), and at the Palais des Congres, ave. Schutzenberger (tel:88-35-0300); *U.S. Consulate,* 15 ave. d'Alsace (tel:35-3104); *Main Post Office* is between ave. de la Marseillaise & ave. de la Liberte, SE of the pl. de la Republique; *Voltage Guide,* 110/220 V, two round-pin outlets are used.

Special Trips/Tours

On a good day a *short cruise on the Ill River* (day or evening) is a very pleasant way to see Strasbourg and its immediate surrounding. Boats leave from near the

Chateau des Rohan. Longer river *cruises on the Rhine* are also offered, leaving from Promenade Dauphine.

Just W and NW of Strasbourg is the beautiful *Dabo-Wangenbourg* region of Alsace, known for its picturesque mountain scenery and quiet villages. If you have more time, a drive S to *Colmar,* via the famous *Route du Vin* through a string of delightful wine villages, along the foothills of the *Vosges mountain region* of Alsace, is a real must-do side trip. Note only will you get to see a relatively unspoiled part of rural France with many superb scenic vistas, but you will pass through such fascinating villages as *Rosheim, Obernai, Mittlebergheim, Dambach, Ribeauville, Riquewihr,* and *Kaysersberg.* Many of these have splendid half-timbered houses, well-preserved medieval fortifications, feudal castles, and excellent restaurants—take your time!

Two excursions off the Route du Vin, into the *Vosges* proper, are especially worthwhile. *Mont Ste.-Odile,* W of Obernai, is a ridge surrounded by a prehistoric wall, with a shrine of Ste.-Odile. The views of the Vosges are magnificent. The other attraction is *Haut-Koenigsbourg,* a restored medieval castle built on a 2,500-ft. peak W of Selestat that affords tremendous views of the surrounding countryside.

Colmar itself, some 40 miles S of Strasbourg, is famous for its *Unterlinden Museum,* housed in a former Dominican convent, with its chapel paintings and 13th-century cloisters and its medieval old town with narrow, winding streets and beautiful 16th- and 17th-century houses.

About 95 mi. W of Strasbourg is the old university town of *Nancy,* famous for its fine Baroque architecture. Noteworthy sights include *Place Stanislas,* a magnificent 18th-century square surrounded by beautiful palaces on all sides, with wrought-iron gates; the late Gothic *Ducal Palace* (Palais Ducal), housing the *Historical Museum of Lorraine* (Musee Historique Lorraine); and the *Franciscan Church* (Eglise des Cordeliers), noted for its tombs of the Dukes of Lorraine.

Weather

Strasbourg's summer daytime high temperatures typically reach into the mid 70s, dropping to the upper 50s at night. Winter daytime highs are usually in the low 40s, falling to the 30s at night. Summer is the wettest season.

STRASBOURG: TEMPERATURES AND PRECIPITATION

Month	J	F	M	A	M	J	J	A	S	O	N	D
Average Daily Temperature												
(Fahrenheit) Max.	43	45	54	60	68	73	76	75	70	60	50	44
Min.	34	34	39	43	49	55	58	58	53	46	40	36
Average Number of Days with Precipitation												
	17	14	12	13	12	12	12	13	13	13	15	16

Cologne (Koln): West Germany

Sights to See

Cologne Cathedral (Dom), opposite the main train station. One of the world's best examples of High Gothic architecture, and the largest Gothic building in the world. Built between the 13th and 19th centuries, this huge, truly magnificent structure is famous for its stained-glass windows, towering spires (515 ft.), and ecclesiastical art. The climb to the top of the south spire (328 ft.) will be rewarded with superb views of the city.

Roman-Germanic Museum (Romisch-Germanisches Museum), Roncalliplatz 4, just S of the cathedral. Fine collection of artifacts from the original Roman colony, including the famous Dionysus mosaic. Open 10–5 Tu, F–Su, 10–8 W–Th.

Wallraf-Richartz Museum, Rheingarten, between the cathedral and the Rhine. Superb collection of European painting, both classical and modern. Open 10–8 Tu–Th, 10–6 F–Su.

Old Town Hall (Rathaus), U. Taschenm., S of the cathedral. Dating from the 15th century and rebuilt in the 20th, it is noted for its Hanseatic Chamber.

Church of St. Maria im Kapitol, off Cacilienstr. S of the cathedral. One of the city's many Romanesque churches, built on the foundations of a Roman Temple in the 11th century. It is noted for its huge crypt and beautifully carved medieval doors.

Hohestrasse, running N-S, just E of the cathedral. Cologne's principal shopping street, a pedestrian mall, lined with boutiques and department stores, and full of activity in the evenings.

St. Gereon's Church, off Gereonstr., W of the cathedral. Dating from the 11th century, this unusual Romanesque church is noted for its long choir.

Schnutgen Museum, St. Cacilien's Church (Cecilia), at the W end of Cacilienstr., SW of the cathedral. Fine collection of religious art and sculpture. Open 10–5 Tu–Su.

St. Severinus Church, at the S end of Severinstrasse, S of the cathedral. Dating from the 11th century, it is known for its carved stalls and wall hangings.

Severinstorburg, just S of St. Severinus Church. One of the few remaining old fortified town gates.

Useful Information

Tourist Information Office (Verkehrsamt), am Dom opposite the cathedral's western portal (tel:221-3345); the closest *U.S. Embassy/Consulate* is in Bonn, at Deichmanns Ave. (tel:228/3391); *American Express,* Burgmauerstr. 14; *K.D. German Rhine Line,* Frankenwerft 15 (tel:2-0880); *Voltage Guide,* 110/220 V, two round-pin outlets are used.

Special Trips/Tours

A *Rhine cruise* is a real must if you have the time. The K.D. German Rhine Line (tel:2-0880) offers a wide itinerary of cruises, from the 5-day Rotterdam–Basel trip, to the short Cologne to Koblenz trip. The *Rhine gorge* section between Koblenz and Mainz is the most picturesque portion, famous for its steep, vineyard-clad hillsides, small villages, and many castles.

About 55 miles SE of Cologne, located at the junction of the Moselle with the Rhine, is *Koblenz.* One of the principal embarkation points for Rhine cruises, it also has a number of noteworthy sights, including the 12th-century *Liebfrauen-kirckhe* (Church of Our Lady); *St. Castor's Church;* and the 19th-century *Ehrenbreitstein Fortress* across the Rhine.

In the SW suburb of Bruhl is *Schloss Augustusburg,* the 18th-century residence of the Archbishop of Cologne. Lavishly decorated and furnished, it is famous for its staircase and surrounding gardens. Nearby is the *Phantasialand Amusement Park,* the largest such recreation park in Germany, with boat, gondola, car, and train rides, a bobsled run, and entertainment.

The Imperial City of *Aachen* (Aix-la-Chapelle) with its 9th-century *cathedral,* the *Elisenbrunnen spa,* and a *casino,* is 40 miles W of Cologne. The *Cathedral* is noted for its Konigsstuhl (Charlemagne's throne), and Schatzkammer (Treasury), containing one of Europe's most valuable ecclesiastical treasures. The *International Casino Bad Aachen* is NE of the cathedral.

Dusseldorf, just N of Cologne on the Rhine, makes an interesting side trip from Cologne. It is especially known for its very fashionable shopping street and promenade, the *Konigsallee.*

Weather

Cologne's weather is changeable at all times of the year. Summer daytime high temperatures typically reach the high 70s, dropping to the upper 50s at night. Winter daytime highs are usually in the upper 30s, falling to the low 30s at night. Summer is the wet season, although precipitation is frequent year-round.

COLOGNE: TEMPERATURES AND PRECIPITATION

Month	J	F	M	A	M	J	J	A	S	O	N	D
Average Daily Temperature												
(Fahrenheit) Max.	38	41	51	60	69	74	77	76	69	58	47	39
Min.	29	30	35	42	49	55	58	57	52	44	38	32
Average Number of Days with Precipitation												
	17	15	12	14	14	14	14	14	13	14	16	16

Dusseldorf: West Germany

Sights to See

Dusseldorf itself from the Rhine Tower, a 600-ft.-plus telecommunications tower on the bank of the Rhine. The view is splendid and on a clear day you can see the Koln cathedral and the Netherlands. The tower is just S of Rheinknie-brucke.

Old Town (Altstadt), Dusselfdorf's lively playground, with pubs, discos, old brewery houses, restored medieval townhouses, boutiques, galleries, and restaurants. See the *Jan Wellem Memorial,* a fine Baroque equestrian statue by Grupello, in front of the Rathaus.

Karlstadt, immediately to the S of Altstadt. A culturally diverse district with antique shops, artists' studios, a food market, cafes, and the splendid Baroque *Maxkirche* (St. Maximilian's Church).

Konigsalle (the "Ko"), just E of Altstadt and Karlstadt, and the piece de resistance of the city. One of the finest boulevards in Europe. Laid out by Napoleon, this short, but broad avenue, lined with trees and divided down the middle by a canal, is probably Germany's most fashionable.

North Rhine–Westphalia Art Collection (Kunstsammlung Nordrhein-Westfalen), Grabbenplatz 5, N of the "Ko." Noted for its collection of Meissen porcelain and 20th-century art, particularly paintings by Chagall, Picasso, Klee, and others. Open 10–5 Tu–Su.

Hofgarten, a very attractive park dating from 1770 on the N edge of downtown.

Goethe Museum, Jagerhofstr. & Kaiserstr. in the Hofgarten. Known for its large collection of Goethe's manuscripts, first editions, drawings, and other memorabilia. Open 10–5 Tu–Su.

Municipal Art Gallery (Kunstmuseum), Ehrenhof 5. Fine collection of paintings and sculpture from the Middle Ages to the 20th century. Open 10–5 Tu–Su.

Hetjens Museum, Palais Nesselrode, Schulstr. 4. Renowned for its ceramic art collection.

Art Hall (Stadtische Kunsthalle), 4 Grabbeplatz. Devoted to contemporary artists, including many from the city's large art community.

Useful Information

Dusseldorf Tourist Association, Immermannhof (tel:35-05-05) for general information, sightseeing tours, tickets for theaters, etc.; closest *U.S. Embassy/ Consulate* is in Bonn, at Deichmanns Ave. (tel:228/3391); *Public Transportation* (tel:57-50-58); *German Rhine-Steamship Co.* (tel:32-60-72); *Taxi* (tel:33-333); *American Express,* Heinrich-Heine Alle 14 (tel:80-222); *Police* (tel:110 in emergency); *Post Office,* Charlottenstr. 16 (tel:16-30); *Voltage Guide* 220 V, two round-pin outlets are used.

Special Trips/Tours

Schloss Benrath, just S of Dusseldorf, makes a good short side trip. Surrounded by beautiful parkland, this late-18th-century Rococo castle houses a natural history museum. Open 10–5 Tu–Su, shorter hours off-season.

A Rhine cruise is a real must if you have the time. Short boat trips leave from the Rathausufer along the banks of the Rhine. Cologne (Koln), just S of Dusseldorf, is a major embarkation point for Rhine cruises. The picturesque

Rhine Gorge section, between Koblentz and Mainz, is the most beautiful portion, famous for its steep hillsides, small villages, and many castles.

Cologne (Koln), with its magnificent cathedral, one of the world's largest and most beautiful Gothic churches, is only 48 km S of Dusseldorf, a 35-minute drive on the autobahn. The cathedral itself, the *Kolner Dom,* begun in the 13th century, is definitely a must. The long climb to the top of one of its two towers will afford great views. Also worth seeing, opposite the cathedral, is the *Roman-Germanic Museum,* as is the *Wallraf-Richartz Museum,* which has one of Europe's greatest art collections.

Weather

Dusseldorf's weather is very changeable. Summer daytime high temperatures are typically in the low to mid 70s, falling to the mid 50s at night. Winter daytime highs are usually in the upper 30s, dropping to the high 20s at night. Precipitation is fairly evenly distributed through the year, with summers, particularly July and August, being somewhat wetter.

DUSSELDORF: TEMPERATURES AND PRECIPITATION

Month	J	F	M	A	M	J	J	A	S	O	N	D
Average Daily Temperature												
(Fahrenheit) Max.	38	39	47	55	65	71	72	72	69	60	48	40
Min.	29	29	33	40	46	50	54	53	50	45	37	31
Average Number of Days with Precipitation												
	17	17	14	15	13	14	15	16	14	14	16	17

Frankfurt: West Germany

Sights to See

Hauptwache, An Der Hauptwach square, at the W end of Zeil. A beautifully reconstructed Baroque building in a square right in the center of the city. Sit in one of the cafes and watch the world go by.

Goethe House (the Goethehaus), Grosser Hirschgraben 23, SW of the Hauptwache. Birthplace of Goethe. Fine collection of original furnishings, along with the adjoining *Goethe museum* with its Goethe period pieces. Open 9–6 M–Sa, 10–1 Su.

Romerberg, a large medieval square at the historic center of Frankfurt, SE of the Hauptwache and E of the Goethe House, with the fountain of justice in its center. On its W side is the 15th-century *City Hall* (Romer). Visit the emperors' coronation hall. Also preserved after WW I are the Gothic church of St. Nicholas (with its modern clock-orchestra), and the *Cathedral of St. Bartholomew* (the Dom), dating from the 15th century, known for its carved pews and murals, and site of all German coronations.

Alt-Sachsenhausen. Frankfurt's Greenwich Village, S of the Romerberg, across the Main river. An old, cobblestoned section of Frankfurt filled with taverns, shops, restaurants, and nightclubs. Try the Henninger Tower revolving restaurant, on Hainer Weg, and enjoy the view from the top.

Stadel Institute of Art and Museum Gallery (Stadelsches Kunstinstitut und Stadtische Galerie), Schaumainkai 63, SW of the Romerberg in Sachsenhausen. One of Europe's best art collections. Open 10–5 Tu–Su.

Palm Garden (Palmengarten), NW of the Hauptwache via Bockenheimer Landstrasse. One of Europe's best-known botanical gardens. Take a walk through the extensive gardens and greenhouses and admire the 12,000 varieties of plants and thousands of orchids and cacti. Sunday concerts are given in the park. Open 9–8 daily, May–Aug., to dusk rest of the year.

Senckenberg Museum of Natural History, Senckenberganlange 25, SSW of the Palmengarten. Huge dinosaurs and a large prehistoric collection. Open 9–5 daily.

Telecommunications Tower (Fernmeldeturm), Rosa Luxemburgstrasse, N of the Palmengarten in the Ginnheim section of NW Frankfurt. At 1,086 ft., it is the tallest structure in West Germany. The view of the city and surrounding countryside from either the revolving restaurant or observation deck is superb.

Useful Information

The *German National Tourist Office's main office* is at Beethovenstrasse 69 (tel:7-5721); the *Frankfurt Tourist Association* has information offices in the main railway station (tel:22-1288 and 28-7486; *U.S. Consulate*, Siesmayerstrasse 21 (tel:7-5305-0); *American Express*, Steinweg 5 (tel:21-051); *Voltage Guide*, 220 V, two round-pin outlets are used.

Special Trips/Tours

The Germans take their spas very seriously indeed, and the area around Frankfurt has a number, stretching from Wiesbaden to Bad Wildungen. *Bad Homberg*, N of Frankfurt (once a favorite with European royalty) is worth visiting. It has a casino, and just outside of town, at Saalburg, the best-preserved Roman fort in Europe.

Further N of Frankfurt, is the university town of *Marburg*. The houses of the old city are clustered beneath the towering 13th-century *castle*. Locals frequently wear the old costumes and during the summer months the castle hosts folk plays, concerts, and festivals. Dating from the 13th century, and noted for its golden shrine and stained glass, Marburg's finest building is *St. Elizabeth's Church*.

Weather

The weather can be very variable at all times of the year, and from year to year. Summer daytime high temperatures typically reach the mid to high 70s, falling to the high 50s at night. Winter daytime highs usually reach the high 30s and low 40s, dropping to around 30 at night. Summer is the wet season.

FRANKFURT: TEMPERATURES AND PRECIPITATION

Month	J	F	M	A	M	J	J	A	S	O	N	D
Average Daily Temperature												
(Fahrenheit) Max.	38	41	51	60	69	74	77	76	69	58	47	39
Min.	29	30	35	42	49	55	58	57	52	44	38	32
Average Number of Days with Precipitation												
	17	15	12	14	14	14	14	14	13	14	16	16

Hamburg: West Germany

Sights to See

Rathaus, a Renaissance-style structure with a tall clock tower. Noted for its vaulted ceilings, doorways, festival hall, and decorated interior generally.
Hamburg Art Gallery (Kunsthalle), Glockengiesserwall 1, NE of the Rathaus. Fine collection of 16th- to 20th-century art, particularly noted for its Expressionist pieces.
Decorative Arts and Crafts Museum (Museum fur Kunst und Gewerbe), Steintorpl. 1, E of the Rathaus. Excellent collection of handicrafts and furnishings, some from medieval times.
St. Michael's Church (St. Michaeliskirche), Ost-West Strasse, SW of the Rathaus. The cupola is accessible by elevator, for a good view of the city. A walk through the Fleete neighborhood around St. Michael's will make you think that you are still in the Middle Ages.
The Krameramtswohnungen, Krayenkamp 10, E of St. Michaeliskirche, really old, but well-preserved, apartments built for the widows of guild members in medieval times.
Hamburg harbor (Hamburg Hafen). Boats leave the St. Pauli wharf, SE of St. Michaeliskirche, every 30 minutes in summer (twice daily rest of year), for tours of this fascinating, bustling harbor, one of the world's busiest. Take the one-hour Grand Tour of the port by Hadag steamer.
Hamburg Fish Market (Fischmarkt), between Hexenberg and Grosse Elbestrasse, on the waterfront near St. Pauli. A colorful market every Sunday morning from 5 to 9:30, with fresh fish, flowers, produce, plants, and animals (pets) for sale.
Public Gardens (Planten und Blomen), near the Dammtor Station, NW of the Rathaus. Beautiful gardens. While here, stop by the *TV Tower* (Fernsehturm), across Karolinestrasse from the gardens, and enjoy the view of Hamburg from its revolving *Skyline Restaurant* or observation platform. Open 9–11 daily.
Hagenbeck Zoo, in the NW suburb of Stellingen. Considered to be one of the world's best zoos, it is noted for its open enclosures. Open 8–dusk daily.

Useful Information

Tourist Office, Bieberhaus, opposite the main railroad station, Glockengiesserwall (tel:30-05-1245), and at Gerhart-Hauptmann-Platz (tel:324-758); *American*

Express, Rathausmarkte 5 (tel:33-1141); *U.S. Consulate,* Alsterufer 27 (tel:441-061); *Police* (tel:110 in emergency); *Taxi* (tel:441-0111 or 682-001); *Post Office,* Kirchenallee, next to the main railroad station; *Voltage Guide,* 220 V, two round-pin outlets are used.

Special Trips/Tours

One of the nicest ways to see sections of Hamburg is to take an *Alster Cruise around the Aussenalster,* a lake-like branch of the Elbe. During the summer, ferries leave from the Jungfernstieg quayside for the 60-minute round trip daily from 10:15 to 5:15.

Welcome Point (Wilkomm-Hoft), at the Schulauer Fahrhaus on the Elbe at Wedel, just NW of Hamburg, is an interesting spot. Incoming and outgoing vessels are greeted or bid farewell as they sail past, flags are dipped, the ship's national anthem is played, and greetings are extended in the ship's national tongue. Visit the *Bottleship Museum* (Buddelschiff-Museum). Open 8–sunset (10–6 for the museum).

Lubeck, capital of the Hanseatic cities during the Middle Ages, is just a short railroad trip, or drive from Hamburg. This former "Queen of the Hanseatic League," with its compact, medieval core, wealth of preserved historic buildings, and famous *Holstentor* (huge twin-towered gates at the entrance to the city), is well worth a visit.

Weather

Hamburg's summer daytime high temperatures typically reach into the low 70s, falling to the mid 50s at night. Winter daytime highs are usually in the mid to high 30s, dropping to the upper 20s at night. Rainfall is pretty evenly distributed, although July and August tend to get slightly more rain.

HAMBURG: TEMPERATURES AND PRECIPITATION

Month	J	F	M	A	M	J	J	A	S	O	N	D
Average Daily Temperature												
(Fahrenheit) Max.	36	37	44	55	64	69	73	72	66	55	45	39
Min.	28	28	31	38	45	51	55	54	49	43	37	31
Average Number of Days with Precipitation												
	18	16	13	14	14	14	17	16	15	17	18	18

Heidelberg: West Germany

Sights to See

Heidelberg Castle (Schloss), Neue Schloss-Strasse, above Heidelberg. Dating from the 16th century, it is considered to be one of the finest examples of German Renaissance architecture. The castle ruins are noted for the courtyard, and Otto Heinrich (Ottheinrichsbau) and Friedrichs (Friedrichsbau) buildings. The terrace offers superb views of the town and Neckar Valley. Open 9–1, 2–5 daily.

German Pharmacy Museum (Apothekenmuseum), Heidelberg Castle. Noted for its 17th-century laboratory. Open 10–5 daily.

Konigsstuhl (Kings Seat), behind and above the castle. Reached by the funicular (Bergbahn) from Kornmarkt. At 1,864 ft., it affords magnificent panoramas of the surrounding countryside from the TV tower.

Grand-Ducal Palace, Karlsplatz, below the castle. Formerly the court of the grand dukes of Baden, it now houses the Academy of Sciences. Noted for its reception rooms with their period furnishings.

Church of the Holy Ghost (Heiliggeistkirche), Hauptstr., W of Karlsplatz. Late Gothic structure that served as the burial place for the electors.

Haus zum Ritter, Hauptstr., opposite the Holy Ghost Church. Fine building (now a hotel), famous for its Renaissance front.

University Library, Grabenstrasse, S of Hauptstrasse, SW of the Hotel Ritter. Known for its Manesse Codex, illustrated medieval lyric poetry. Open 11–noon daily.

Student Jail (Karzer), 2 Augustinergasse, N of the University Library in the old student quarter. Known for its graffiti and drawings. Open 9–5 M–Sa.

Palatinate Museum (Kurpfalzisches Museum), Hauptstr. 97, NW of the University Library. Fine painting and sculpture collection, plus an archaeological collection, including the jawbone of "Heidelberg man." Open 10–5 Tu–Su.

Philosopher's Way (Philosophenweg), on the N band of the Neckar across the Old Bridge (Alte Brucke). This path, leading through the woods to Saint's Mountain lookout, an amphitheatre, and the ruins of the 9th-century St. Michael's Basilica, offers the best views of Old Town Heidelberg.

Useful Information

Tourist Information, outside the Hauptbahnhof (Railroad Station) (tel:277-35); *American Express,* Friedrich-Ebert-Anlage 16 (tel:2-9001); the closest *U.S. Consulate* is in Frankfurt, at Siesmayerstr. 21 (tel:75/30-5500); *Emergency* (tel:110); *Post Office,* across from the main station; *Voltage Guide,* 110/220 V, two round-pin outlets are used.

Special Trips/Tours

Germany's famous *Castle Road* (Die Burgenstrasse) follows the lower *Neckar Valley,* between Heidelberg and Heilbronn to the SE. With its dozen or so castles and fertile vineyards, it has some of the most attractive scenery in southern Germany. Particularly notable are *Neckarsteinach* with its four castles; *Hirschhorn;* the spa town of Eberbach; *Zwingenberg Castle; Burg Hornberg* at Neckarzimmern; *Schloss Guttenberg;* and medieval *Bad Wimpfen.*

 Heilbronn itself has many interesting sights, including the *Town Hall* with its 16th-century astronomical clock and *St. Kilian's Church,* noted for its high altar.

NOTE: boat tours along the Neckar to Neckarsteinach and back are operated by the *Rhein-Neckar-Fahrgastschiffahrt GMBH* (tel:2-0181), and are worthwhile. The old Imperial city of *Speyer* is about an hour's drive or train ride SW of Heidelberg on the W bank of the Rhine. Its 11th-century *Romanesque Cathedral* (Dom) is particularly noted for its Imperial burial vault and crypt. The *Palatinate Historical Museum,* just S of the cathedral, is worth visiting.

North of Speyer, and NW of Heidelberg, is another cathedral city, *Worms.* Like Speyer's cathedral, *Worms Cathedral* (Dom St. Peter), was constructed in the High Romanesque style in the 11th and 12th centuries and is a very impressive structure.

On the way to or from Worms or Speyers, stop by 18th-century *Schloss Schwetzingen,* summer residence of the Electors of the Palatinate, just 7 miles W of Heidelberg. Its world-famous landscaped gardens, noted for their great Rococo detail, are definitely worth seeing. Open 8–8 daily, April–Sept.

Weather

Heidelberg's weather is changeable year-round. Summer daytime high temperatures typically reach the upper 70s, falling to the high 50s at night. Winter daytime highs are usually in the high 30s, dropping to the low 30s at night. Precipitation is fairly evenly distributed throughout the year, although summer is the wettest season.

HEIDELBERG: TEMPERATURES AND PRECIPITATION

Month	J	F	M	A	M	J	J	A	S	O	N	D
Average Daily Temperature												
(Fahrenheit) Max.	38	41	51	60	69	74	77	76	69	58	47	39
Min.	29	30	35	42	49	55	58	57	52	44	38	32
Average Number of Days with Precipitation												
	17	15	12	14	14	14	14	14	13	14	16	16

Munich (Munchen): West Germany

Sights to See

The Palace (The Residenz), Residenzstr. The restored former royal winter palace of the Wittelsbachs. The complex includes, the Rococo *Altes Residenztheater,* and the *Schatzkammer* (treasury), known for its jewelry collection. Developed from the 18th to 19th centuries, it is an impressive document of European cultural development, with Renaissance, Baroque, Rococo, and Classic styles. Open 10–4:30 Tu–Sa, 10–1 Su.

Residenz Museum, in the SW section of the palace. Excellent collection of art and furnishings. Open 10–4:30 Tu–Sa, 10–1 Su.

Old Pinakothek (Alte Pinakothek), Barerstrasse 27, NW of the Residenz. West Germany's most important art gallery, with 14th- to 18th-century paintings, particularly N European and Italian. Open 9–4:30 Tu–Su, and 7–9 Tu and Th.
New Pinakothek (Neue Pinakothek), across the street, concentrates on European art and sculpture of the 19th century. Open same hours as Alte Pinakothek, except on Th evenings, when it is closed.
Bavarian National Museum, Prinzregentenstr. 3, NE of the Residenz. Fine Gothic, Renaissance, and folk art collections. Known for its wood and stone sculptures, tapestries, and armor collections. Closed M.
English Gardens (Englischer Garten), just NW of the Bavarian National Museum, across Lerchenfeldstr. With lakes, pavilions, outdoor cafes, and a Japanese teahouse, this 18th-century park is the city's summer playground. The *Haus der Kunst,* just S of the Japanese teahouse, has a fine art collection.
Cathedral of Our Lady (Frauenkirche), Frauenplatz, SW of the Residenz. With its twin domed towers this late Gothic brick church is a landmark and symbol of the city, with important works of art. An elevator goes to the top of the N tower, affording magnificent views of the city; and, on a clear day, the Alps.
Hofbrauhaus, Am Platz 9, SE of the Residenz. A landmark beer hall that epitomizes the "good life" of Munich. It is surrounded by other beer halls, taverns, and wine rooms.
German Museum (Deutsches Museum), on an island in the Isar River, SSE of the Residenz. The world's largest technical-scientific museum, with over 300 rooms of working displays. See the electrical show and the planetarium. Open 9–5 daily.
Olympiaturm TV tower, the Olympic Village, NW Munich. On a clear day the view from the terrace of this 943-ft. tower is magnificent.

Useful Information

The City Tourist Office (tel:239-11), has information counters at the airport and in the main railway station (Hauptbahnhof) near the Bayerstr. exit, and at Sendlingerstr. 1; *U.S. Consulate,* Koenigenstr. 5 (tel:2-3011); *Police* (tel:110); *American Express,* Int. Promenadeplatz 6 (tel:219-90); *Post Office,* opposite the main railroad station (tel:53-88-0732); *Taxi* (tel:2-1611); *Voltage Guide,* 220 V, two round-pin outlets are used.

Special Trips/Tours

Nymphenburg Palace (Schloss Nymphenburg), just on the outskirts of the city. This Rococo royal summer residence is set in magnificent gardens. Open 9–12:30, 1:30–4 Tu–Su from April–Sept. (opens an hour later in winter).
Augsburg, a 40-minute train ride from Munich, was founded by the Romans in 15 B.C., and really flourished in the 15th and 16th centuries. Its cathedral, over

1,000 years old, is particularly famous for its stained-glass windows. Augsburg's medieval Rathaus is also well known.

Organized day trips from Munich by bus to *Garmisch-Partenkirchen, Oberammergau,* and the royal castles of *Neuschwanstein* ("mad Ludwig's") and *Hohenschwangau* (more authentic but not as spectacular), in the Bavarian Alps, should not be missed if time permits.

Weather

Weather can be very changeable at all times of the year. Summer daytime high temperatures are typically in the low 70s, falling to the 50s at night. Winter daytime highs are usually in the mid 30s, dropping to the 20s at night. Summer is the wet season.

MUNICH: TEMPERATURES AND PRECIPITATION

Month	J	F	M	A	M	J	J	A	S	O	N	D
Average Daily Temperature												
(Fahrenheit) Max.	35	38	48	56	64	70	74	73	67	56	44	36
Min.	23	23	30	38	45	51	55	54	48	40	33	26
Average Number of Days with Precipitation												
	16	16	13	15	15	17	16	16	13	13	15	15

Stuttgart: West Germany

Sights to See

The view of Stuttgart and surrounding countryside from the observation platform or restaurant (492 ft.) of the *Television Tower* (Fernsehturm) S of Stuttgart on the Hoher Bopser, off Hohenheimerstr.

Wurttemberg Provincial Museum (Wurttembergisches Landesmuseum), Old Castle (Altes Schloss), on the Planie in central Stuttgart. Excellent collection of medieval art, the Wurttemberg Crown Jewels, costumes and musical instruments, and Swabian artifacts. Open 10–5 Tu–Su.

Schiller Platz, just to the W of the Altes Schloss. Monument to Schiller, together with a colorful market on Tu, Th, and Sa. *Stiftskirche,* SW corner of Schiller Platz. Dating from the 12th century, rebuilt in the 15th, and reconstructed in the 20th century, this Gothic church is noted for its Renaissance statues of the Counts of Wurttemberg.

New Castle (Neues Schloss), NE of the Altes Schloss, across the Planie. The former residence of the Kings of Wurttemberg, this huge Baroque palace now houses governmental offices of Baden-Wurttemberg.

State Gallery (Staatsgalerie), Konrad-Adenauer-Str. 30-32, NE of Neues Schloss. Excellent art collection, including works of the Dutch Masters, and the modern German Expressionists. Open 10–5 Tu–Su.

Castle Garden (Schlossgarten), N of the State Gallery and E of the main railroad station. In a city known for its parks, this one is noted for its fountains, mineral springs, and modern Planetarium.

Wilhelma Zoological Botanic Gardens, on the W bank of the Neckar, N of central Stuttgart in Bad Cannstatt. Known for its hothouses and aquarium in the park of the former summer residence of Wilhelm I.

Daimler-Benz Museum, Mercedes-Benz Works, Unterturkheim, E of Stuttgart. Superb collection of cars and car engines.

Useful Information

Tourist Office (Touristik Zentrum i Punkt), Klett Passage, Main Railroad Station, and at Lautenschlagerstr. 3 (tel:22-28240); *U.S. Consulate,* Urbanstr. 7 (tel:21-0221); *American Express,* Lautenschlagerstr. 3 (tel:208-90); *Post Office,* Bolzstr. 3; *Voltage Guide,* 110/220 V, two round-pin outlets are used.

Special Trips/Tours

The beautiful old university town of *Tubingen,* situated on the W bank of the Neckar, is a short drive (26 miles) SW of Stuttgart. Its gabled medieval houses, *Marktplatz* and half-timbered *Town Hall,* ancient university, and famous *Platanenallee,* an avenue of trees on a manmade island in the Neckar, make it a worthwhile side trip.

Further afield and due W of Stuttgart, is Germany's most elegant spa, *Baden-Baden,* at the northern edge of the Black Forest (Schwarzwald). Full of stately hotels, it is an international health resort, with one of the world's most formal and elegant casinos. Noteworthy sights to see include the *Kurhaus* and *Casino,* the *Lictentaler Allee* park promenade, and the *Neues Schloss* (New Castle). If you have the time, the road running S to *Freudenstadt* passes through some of the Black Forest's most magnificent scenery. From Freudenstadt it is a very pleasant drive back to Stuttgart via Tubingen.

On the Danube about 55 miles SE of Stuttgart is *Ulm,* site of the *Minster,* the largest Gothic church in the country after Cologne's Cathedral. Dating from the 14th century, its 528-ft. tower is reputedly the highest church tower in the world. The Minster is also noted for its superbly carved choir stalls. Other noteworthy sights in Ulm include the *Municipal Museum* and the restored *Gothic Town Hall.*

One of the most beautiful market squares in Germany, the *Marktplatz,* is in *Schwabisch Hall,* about 30 miles NE of Stuttgart. Known for its uniform architectural style, the *Marktplatz* is surrounded by the Baroque Town Hall (Rathaus) on one side, and the steps leading up to the 15th-century St. Michael's Church on the other. Outside Schwabisch Hall is the Benedictine abbey-fortress of *Comburg* (Gross-Comburg).

Weather

Stuttgart's weather is very changeable throughout year. Summer daytime high temperatures are typically in the low 70s, falling to the 50s at night. Winter daytime highs are usually in the upper 30s, dropping to the 20s at night. Although summer is the wettest season, precipitation is frequent year-round.

STUTTGART: TEMPERATURES AND PRECIPITATION

Month	J	F	M	A	M	J	J	A	S	O	N	D
Average Daily Temperature												
(Fahrenheit) Max.	36	38	48	55	64	70	73	72	67	56	45	37
Min.	25	26	31	38	45	51	55	54	49	41	34	28
Average Number of Days with Precipitation												
	16	15	13	15	14	16	16	15	13	14	15	16

West Berlin: West Germany

Sights to See

Kaiser Wilhelm Memorial Church (Gedachtniskirche), Breitscheidpl. A war-damaged Romanesque church that has been preserved in its ruined state as a reminder of WW II. The view of Berlin from the top floor of the adjacent *Europa Center* is excellent and particularly interesting at night. Open daily.

Kurfurstendamm (Ku'damm), running W from the Kaiser Wilhelm Memorial Church. West Berlin's "Main Street," lined with luxury hotels, cafes, shops, and theaters.

Tiergarten, NE of the Kaiser Wilhelm Memorial Church. A magnificent public park, originally a royal hunting preserve, now containing Berlin's zoo with, reputedly, more species than any other zoo in the world. Open 9–6 daily.

Brandenburg Gate, at the end of Strasse des 17 Juni, at the E end of the Tiergarten. Once the "Arch of Triumph" of Germany's capital. Located just across the Wall in East Berlin, it can be seen from the top of the Tiergarten's *Victory Column* (Siegessaule), or from the observation platform on The Wall itself.

The Wall, a sight to see and ponder in its own right, especially before it's all torn down. An impressive exhibition about the Berlin Wall, its history and the daring attempts by people in the eastern sector to escape to the West, can be seen in the *House at Checkpoint Charlie,* Friedrichstr. Open 9–8, M–Sa.

Reichstag (Deutscher Reichstag), Pl. der Republik. At the E end of the Tiergarten, N of the Brandenburg Gate. Germany's former parliament building, rebuilt since fire damaged it before the war, it is now used for political conclaves, when the West German parliament makes a point of meeting once a year in Berlin to stress the fact that the city is an integral part of Germany.

Museum of Arts and Crafts (Kunstgewerbemuseum), opposite the Philharmonie, off Kemperplatz, SW of the Brandenburg Gate. An impressive collection of handicrafts. Closed M.

Dahlem Museum, Arnimallee 23–27, in SW West Berlin. An enormous complex of seven museums, it contains one of the finest collections of paintings in

Germany, particularly the Old Masters in the Gemaldegalerie with 26 Rembrandts. Open 9–5 Tu–Su.
Charlottenburg Palace (Schloss Charlottenburg), NW of Kaiser Wilhelm Memorial Church, on Luisenpl. Berlin's Versailles. A complex of half a dozen major museums, including the Egyptian Museum, devoted to the art and artifacts of Egypt. Open 9–5 Sa–Th.

Useful Information

The Tourist Center, Europa-Center on Budapesterstr. 2 (tel:262-6031); *U.S. Consulate,* Clayallee 170 (tel:819-55-23 or 819-50-19); *Taxi* (tel:6902 or 26-1026); *American Express,* Ku'damm 11 (tel:882-7575); Police (tel:110 in emergency); *Post Office* (tel:313-9799), Bahnhof Zoo; *Voltage Guide:* 220 V, two round-pin outlets are used.

Special Trips/Tours

No trip to West Berlin would be complete without at least a quick visit to *East Berlin.* Four-hour bus tours leave at 2 P.M. every day opposite the Kaiser Wilhelm Memorial Church. Highlights of the trip include the *Pergamon Museum* and the *Russian war memorial* at Treptow.

Weather

Berlin's weather can be changeable at all times of the year. Summer daytime temperatures normally reach the low to mid 70s. Winters are rather cold, with daily high temperatures in the mid 30s, dropping into the 20s at night. Summer is the wettest season.

BERLIN: TEMPERATURES AND PRECIPITATION

Month	J	F	M	A	M	J	J	A	S	O	N	D
Average Daily Temperature												
(Fahrenheit) Max.	35	37	46	56	66	72	75	74	68	56	45	38
Min.	26	26	31	39	47	53	57	56	50	42	36	29
Average Number of Days with Precipitation												
	17	15	12	13	12	13	14	14	12	14	16	15

Athens (Athinai): Greece

Sights to See

The Acropolis. Despite the damage of time and the work of reconstruction, it is undoubtedly the monument of Western Civilization. Located on a 500-ft. rock, 300 ft. above most of the rest of the city, it dominates Athens. Includes the

Parthenon, Temple of Athena Nike, Erechtheon. Open 7:30–7:15, M–Sa, 8–4:45 Su.

Acropolis Museum. Remains of earlier constructions on the Acropolis and many works of art discovered in the Acropolis. Open same hours, except closed on Tu A.M.

National Archaeological Museum, 28 October St. One of the world's great museums with a superb sculpture collection. Open 8–7 Tu–Sa, 9–5 Su.

Agora (Stoa of Attalos), entrance on Adrianou. The excavated main marketplace of ancient Athens. The Stoa is now a museum of excavated artifacts. Open 7:30–7:15 M–Sa, 8–5 Su.

Plaka. 19th-century section of town nestled against the Acropolis. The winding streets are full of shoppers and tavernas. It is one of the city's centers of nightlife.

Byzantine Museum, 22 Vassilias Sophias St. Unique collection of Byzantine icons, frescoes, and mosaics. Open 9–3 Tu–Sa, 9–2 Su.

Syntagma Square, at the center of modern Athens, full of cafes, people. The *Changing of the Guard ceremony,* by soldiers in traditional dress (evzones), at the Unknown Soldier Memorial at the E side of the square, is best seen on Sundays at 11 A.M., when an entire regiment is present. Otherwise it can be seen daily at 20 minutes before the hour.

St. George's Chapel, Lycabettus Hill. The view from this small chapel is the best in town.

Useful Information

The National Tourist Organization of Greece (NTOG), 2 Karageorgis Servias on Syntagma Square (tel:322-2545 or 322-3111); *Tourist Police,* 7 Syngrou (tel:923-9224); *U.S. Embassy,* 91 Vasilissis Sophias (tel:721-2951); *American Express,* 2 Ermou St., Syntagma Sq. (tel:324-4975); *Post Office,* 100 Eolou St., Syntagma Sq.; *Voltage Guide* 110/220V, two round-pin outlets are used.

Special Trips/Tours

The 11th-century *Monastery of Daphni,* just outside Athens, is famous for its superb Byzantine mosaics. Open 9–3 M–Sa, 9–2:30 Su.

The *Temple of Poseidon,* on Cape Sounion, 40 miles S of Athens is spectacular, as is the ride along the coastal road to reach it. If time permits, stop off in the town of *Vouliagmeni* on the way.

Delphi, an archaeological site of extensive ruins 2,000 ft. above the Bay of Itea and less than 100 miles NW of Athens, is one of the most impressive sights in the country. Stop at the museum, and on the way there, or back, be sure to visit the village of Archova for a glimpse of relatively unspoiled Greece.

Weather

An outstanding feature of the Greek climate is the large amount of sunshine. Summers are warm or even hot with almost no cloud or rain for three months. Temperatures typically reach the high 80s and low 90s, and Athens can experience some of the worst smog in Europe on calm days. In winter, the weather is generally mild, with daytime highs in the mid to upper 50s, falling to the 40s at night. Winter is the wettest season.

ATHENS: TEMPERATURES AND PRECIPITATION

Month	J	F	M	A	M	J	J	A	S	O	N	D
Average Daily Temperature												
(Fahrenheit) Max.	55	57	60	68	77	86	92	92	84	75	66	58
Min.	44	44	46	52	61	68	73	73	67	60	53	47
Average Number of Days with Precipitation												
	16	11	11	9	8	4	2	3	4	8	12	15

Budapest: Hungary

Sights to See

The view of Budapest itself from the top of *Gellert Hill,* on the Buda side of the Danube, is superb. Visit the *Citadel,* a 19th-century fort built by the Habsburgs. *Castle Hill* (Var hegy), N of the Citadel. The center of medieval Buda, with narrow, cobbled streets, and delightful squares. Walk through the picturesque Fortuna utca area with its fine Baroque townhouses, particularly along Becsi Kapu ter, near Fortuna ter, which has a number of superb examples.
Matthias Church, Castle Hill. Coronation site of Hungarian Kings. Dating from the 13th century, the cathedral has been rebuilt and undergone many transformations, but is still magnificent.
Fisherman's Bastion, built to protect the cathedral, it affords another excellent vantage point for viewing Budapest.
National Gallery, Szent Gyorgyter 2, on Castle Hill, just S of Matthias Church. Housed in the former Royal Palace, itself being restored, the gallery has an impressive collection of Hungarian art.
Historical Museum of Budapest, in the Royal Palace. Noted for its exhibits from earlier palace excavations, and archaeological remains of Buda. The terrace affords a wonderful panoramic view of the city.
Margaret Island (Margitsziget), right in the middle of the Danube, N of Castle Hill. This park is very active in the summer with concerts, plays, sporting events, and film festivals.
Museum of Fine Arts (Szepmuveszeti muzeum), Dozsa Gyorgy ut 41, next to Varosliget Park, in Pest. Noted for its fine drawing collection, along with many paintings by the Italian and Flemish masters.
National Museum. Muszeum Korut 14–16, in Pest opposite Gellert Hill, SW of the Fine Arts Museum. The history of Hungary is highlighted. The crown jewels collection is worth seeing by itself.
St. Stephen's Basilica, Bajcsy-Zsilinszky utca, in Pest, NW of the National Museum. Noted for its beautiful dome, tall spires, and interior murals.

Parliament of Hungary, Szechenyi rakpart, on the Pest side, NW of St. Stephen's and S of Margitsziget. A huge neo-Gothic building on the banks of the Danube.
Turkish Baths of Rudas Furdo, Dobrentei ter 9, & Kiraly Furdo, Fo u 85. Huge-domed baths, with reclining benches in arched rooms. Built by the Ottomans, they will provide you with a unique experience.

Useful Information

IBUSZ (Hungarian tourist bureau), V, Tanucs Krt. 3c (tel:42-31-40); *Tourinform,* V, Suto ut 2 (tel:17-9800); *U.S. Embassy,* V, Szabadsag ter 12 (tel:12-6450 or 32-89-33); *Foreign Language Information* (tel:172-200); *IBUSZ Hotel and Tour Information* (tel:184-848); *American Express,* IBUSZ, Petofi ter 3 (tel:18-4848); *Post Office,* next to Keleti and Nyugati railroad stations; *Voltage Guide,* 220 V, two round-pin outlets are used.

Special Trips/Tours

A *horse-drawn carriage* ride through the cobblestone streets of Budapest's Castle Hill District on a good day is wonderful. The carriages usually line up in *Trinity Square* just in front of Matthias Church for the 15-minute rides.
A *Danube cruise* is a worthy, memorable experience. If time is short, an evening cruise aboard the *Setahajo,* complete with music, dancing, and cocktails, is recommended. Boats leave for the 3-hour cruise from below the Duna Inter-Continental, Apaczai Csere Janos ut 4, at 5:30 and 9:00 P.M. If time is not a constraint, IBUSZ offers several tours of the *Danube Bend* area. Contact them at the address given above.

Weather

Budapest's weather is very changeable. Summers are usually warm to hot, with daytime highs in the low 80s, dropping to the 60s at night. Winters can be cold, with a lot of snow cover. Winter daytime high temperatures typically reach the mid 30s, falling to the 20s at night. Spring and early summer are normally the wettest times of the year, due to the frequent thunderstorms.

BUDAPEST: TEMPERATURES AND PRECIPITATION

Month	J	F	M	A	M	J	J	A	S	O	N	D
Average Daily Temperature												
(Fahrenheit) Max.	34	39	50	62	71	78	82	81	74	61	47	39
Min.	25	28	35	44	52	58	62	60	53	44	38	30
Average Number of Days with Precipitation												
	13	12	11	11	13	13	10	9	7	10	14	13

Cork: Ireland

Sights to See

Old Cork, the area around Grand Parade, South Mall, and St. Patrick's St., between the N and S channels of the River Lee. The commercial and financial center of the city, full of 18th-century buildings.
Crawford Municipal Art Gallery, Emmet Pl. Paintings and sculpture of Irish artists, together with fine pieces of Cork silver and glass. Open 10–3:30 M–Sa.
St. Anne's Church (Shandon steeple), Eason's Hill, on the N side of the River Lee. An early-18th-century Protestant church, noted for the fine views of Cork from its tower balcony as much as anything. Open 9:30–6 daily during the summer, shorter hours the rest of the year.
St. Mary's Cathedral, off Leitrim St., on the N bank. Just N of St. Anne's Church. Noted for its large tower and ornate interior. Red Abbey Tower, off Mary Street, on the S bank. The only remnant of medieval Cork monasteries.
St. Finbarre's Cathedral, Bishop Street, on the S bank W of the Red Abbey Tower. A late-19th-century structure that is a fine example of the French Gothic style.

Useful Information

Tourist Information Office, Monumet Bldg., 42 Grand Parade (tel:27-3251); nearest *U.S. Embassy* is in Dublin, at 42 Elgin Rd., Ballsbridge (tel:01-688777); *American Express,* Casey Travel Ltd., 60 South Mall; *Taxi* (tel:22317 or 961311); *Emergency* (tel:999 for police, fire, or ambulance); *Post Office,* Oliver Plunkett St.; *Voltage Guide:* 220 V, two round-pin outlets or three square-pin outlets are used.

Special Trips/Tours

The ruins of the 15th-century **Blarney Castle** are five miles W of Cork. The *Blarney (Kissing) Stone,* which most visitors kiss to obtain the gift of eloquence, is set in the tower's battlements. Even if you do not kiss the stone, the views from the 120-ft. tower will make the trip worthwhile. Open daily.
Fota Island, 8 miles E of Cork on the road to Cobh is also worth visiting. A 750-acre park with a wildlife park and arboretum surrounds Fota House, a fine Irish-Regency mansion. It is noted for its excellent collection of 18th- and 19th-century Irish landscape paintings. Open 11–6 M–Sa, 2–6 Su, April–Sept.
Some 18 miles S of Cork City at the Bandon river estuary is **Kinsale,** a charming 18th-century port with bay-windowed Georgian houses lining its winding, narrow streets. *St. Multose Church,* dating from the 12th century, is noted for its fine west tower, north transept, and ornamental portal. Kinsale also has a reputation as a gourmet center, with its "Good Food Circle," a group of restaurants known for their excellent seafood and other dishes. Try *Le Toucan,* Milk Market (tel:021-772233).
Killarney, with its magnificent lakes and nearby Macgillycuddy's Reeks with 3,414-ft. Carrantuohill, Ireland's highest mountain, is only 65 miles N of Cork

on the N20. Take one of the CIE coach tours of the area. Be sure to visit *Muckross House,* with its landscaped gardens, folk museum, and craft shops. Also try and catch a performance of the Siamsa National Folk Theatre troupe (tel:066-23055) at the Great Southern Hotel annex or in nearby Tralee.

If you have more time on your hands, a trip to the western part of County Cork via the N71 through the villages of Clonakilty, Skibbereen and Bantry to the *Beara Peninsula,* one of Ireland's most beautiful and unspoiled coastal regions, is a must. The peninsula, stretching westward between Bantry Bay and the Kenmare River estuary, is straddled by the rugged Caha Mountains (do drive over Tim Healy Pass), which afford magnificent views of the coastal cliffs, islands offshore, and beautiful beaches. The western tip of the peninsula, around *Allihies,* is the most attractive.

Weather

Cork has a cool, temperate climate characterized by mild, rainy weather. Summer daytime high temperatures typically reach into the high 60s, dropping to the mid 50s at night. Winter daytime highs are usually in the upper 40s, falling to the upper 30s at night. Rainfall is well distributed throughout the year, although fall and winter are the wet seasons.

CORK: TEMPERATURES AND PRECIPITATION

Month	J	F	M	A	M	J	J	A	S	O	N	D
Average Daily Temperature												
(Fahrenheit) Max.	47	48	52	56	61	66	68	68	64	58	52	49
Min.	36	37	39	42	45	51	54	53	50	45	40	38
Average Number of Days with Precipitation												
	15	11	12	11	11	10	11	11	12	12	14	16

Dublin: Ireland

Sights to See

The Georgian architecture of the *Customs House,* the *Four Courts,* and the *Bank of Ireland* headquarters, is some of the world's best. The buildings on *Merrion and Fitzwilliam Sqs., St. Stephen's Green* and adjoining streets reflect Georgian elegance at its best.

National Museum, Kildare St. just N of St. Stephen's Green. Full of Irish antiquities and Celtic Art, including the famous Tara brooch, and a noteworthy silver collection. Open 10–5 Tu–Sa, 2–5 Su.

National Gallery, Merrion St. W., behind the National Museum. Fine collection of Old Masters and Irish painters. Open 10–6 M–F, 2–5 Su.

Trinity College Library, College Green, just NW of the National Gallery. Famous for its *Book of Kells,* an 8th-century illuminated manuscript considered to be one of the best examples of early Christian art. Open 10–4:45 M–F, 10–12:45 Sa.

Dublin Castle, Cork Hill, off Lord Edward Street, W of Trinity College along Dame Street. A 13th-century Norman stronghold and once the seat of British power. It includes a Heraldic Museum, state apartments, and a Genealogical Office. Open 8–6:30 M–F, 2–5 Sa–Su.

Christ Church Cathedral, Christ Church Place, just W of the Castle. Founded in the 12th century by the Norman knight, Strongbow, it is an excellent example of early Gothic architecture.

St. Patrick's Cathedral, St. Patrick's St., S of Christ Church. Built in the 13th and restored in the 19th century, it is the longest cathedral in Ireland. It contains the tomb of Jonathan Swift.

Chester Beatty Gallery of Oriental Art, 20 Shrewsbury Rd., in the suburb of Ballsbridge. One of the world's premier collections, particularly the miniatures and manuscripts. Open Tu–F.

The Marino Casino, Malahide Road. A classical garden temple in the plan of a Greek cross. A superb example of 18th-century European architecture in miniature.

Useful Information

Irish Tourist Board (Bord Failte), on Baggot Street Bridge (tel:765-871); *Dublin Tourism,* 14 Upper O'Connell St. and 51 Dawson St. (tel:747-733); *U.S. Embassy,* 42 Elgin Road, Ballsbridge (tel:688-777); *American Express,* 116 Grafton St. (tel:772-874); *Taxi* (tel:766-666 or 761-111); *Emergency* (tel:999 for fire, police, or ambulance); *Post Office,* O'Connell St. (tel:728-888); *Voltage Guide,* 220 V, two round-pin outlets or three square-pin outlets are used.

Special Trips/Tours

To get the flavor of Ireland, drive down the coast on the N11 to Bray, through the beautiful ***Glen of the Downs*** on to Wicklow. Turn W to the small village of Rathdrum in the beautiful ***Avonmore Valley,*** through Laragh to ***Glendalough*** in Co. Wicklow. One of Europe's most famous centers of learning in the 10th and 11th centuries, Glendalough has some of the most extensive complexes of monastic ruins in Ireland. On the way back N to Dublin, visit the 19th-century estate village of ***Enniskerry,*** and ***Powerscourt Gardens,*** known for its fine waterfall, the highest in Ireland.

Weather

Dublin enjoys a mild, changeable climate with very rare extremes of heat or cold. Summer temperatures typically reach the mid 60s, falling to the low 50s at night. Winters are mild, with highs usually in the upper 40s, dropping to the low 30s at night. Summer and fall are normally the wettest seasons.

DUBLIN: TEMPERATURES AND PRECIPITATION

Month	J	F	M	A	M	J	J	A	S	O	N	D
Average Daily Temperature												
(Fahrenheit) Max.	46	47	51	55	60	65	67	67	63	57	51	47
Min.	34	35	37	39	43	48	52	51	48	43	39	37
Average Number of Days with Precipitation												
	13	10	10	11	10	11	13	12	12	11	12	14

Galway: Ireland

Sights to See

Eyre Square, the city's focal point. It contains the J. F. Kennedy Memorial Gardens, the O'Connaire Monument, and the 17th-century Browne's Gateway.
Lynch's Castle, Shop & Francis Eglin Sts., SW of Eyre Square down William St. An early-17th-century tower house, once the residence of a prosperous merchant, now a bank. It is noted for its gargoyles.
St. Nicholas's Church, Market & Lombard Streets, just W of Lynch's Castle. Dating from the 14th century, it is the largest medieval church in Ireland. It is also known as the church where Columbus is said to have prayed before sailing to America.
Catholic Cathedral (Cathedral of St. Nicholas and Our Lady Assumed into Heaven), Earl's Island in the middle of the River Corrib, NW of St. Nicholas's Church. A modern Renaissance-style structure, noted for the fine mosaics in the side chapel.
Salmon Weir Bridge, across the R. Corrib, E of the Cathedral. Salmon can be seen leaping upstream to the breeding grounds in Lough Corrib.
Downtown Galway. The city has a good concentration of 16th- and 17th-century houses, particularly in the area around Market, Shop, Middle, and Abbeygater Sts.
Galway City Museum, at the SW end of Merchants Road. Exhibits illustrating the history of the city. Open 10–1, 2:30–5:30 M–Sa, 3–6 Su. NOTE: climb the spiral staircase to the gallery for fine panoramas of the city and harbor.
Spanish Arch, Long Walk, next to the museum. A section of the old town wall and gateway built in the late 16th century to protect the unloading Spanish ships.

Useful Information

Irish Tourist Office, Aras Failte, Victoria Place (tel:63081); *American Express,* c/o Ryan's Travel, 27 William St. (tel:64631); the nearest *U.S. Embassy* is in Dublin, at 42 Elgin Rd., Ballsbridge (tel:01-688777); *Taxi* (tel:55919 or 63333); *Emergency* (tel:999 for fire, ambulance, or police); *Voltage Guide,* 220 V, two round-pin or three square-pin outlets are used.

Special Trips/Tours

The rich and beautiful scenic diversity of *Connemara,* just to the NW of Galway, is easily accessible. Ranging from the stark beauty of the "Twelve Bens" mountain range and the rocky headlands and bays of the rugged coastline, to the simple, charming coastal and interior villages, Connemara should not be missed.

The quick way to *Clifden,* some 50 miles NW of Galway, and the region's principal town, is via the N59. But the coastal route through such picturesque villages as Spiddal, Costelloe, Screeb, Carna, and Roundstone is more rewarding. Clifden is an early-19th-century market town and fishing harbor, with the Twelve Bens mountains hemming it in. Along the coast to the NE of Clifden, is *Killary Harbor,* a fjord-like estuary, with the tiny village of *Leenaun* at its head. The road N through Delphi to the delightful fishing village of *Louisburgh,* is especially scenic. On the way back to Galway, drive through Leenaun to *Maam,* a small village situated in a beautiful valley, and on to *Cong.* Visit the 12th-century Augustinian abbey ruins, and nearby late-19th-century *Ashford Castle,* now a hotel.

One of the most interesting trips to be made in this part of Ireland is to the *Aran Islands* in Galway Bay. Home of the famous Aran sweaters, these wind-swept, treeless islands are almost the last outpost of traditional Irish ways. Significant sights, apart from the stark beauty of the islands themselves, include *Dun Aengus,* one of the finest prehistoric stone forts in Europe, on Inishmore Island. The islands can be reached by ferry from Galway City or from Rossaveal Harbor in Connemara, or by plane from Carnmore Airport N of Galway. Contact the Tourist Office for details.

Weather

Galway has a cool, temperate climate characterized by frequent rainy weather. Summer daytime high temperatures typically reach into the mid 60s, dropping to the mid 50s at night. Winter daytime highs are usually in the high 40s, falling to the low 40s at night. Rainfall is plentiful, and well distributed throughout the year, although late fall and early winter are the wettest times of the year.

GALWAY: TEMPERATURES AND PRECIPITATION

Month	J	F	M	A	M	J	J	A	S	O	N	D
Average Daily Temperature												
(Fahrenheit) Max.	49	49	52	55	59	62	64	65	62	58	53	50
Min.	40	40	42	43	47	51	54	55	52	48	44	42
Average Number of Days with Precipitation												
	20	15	14	13	13	13	15	15	16	17	18	21

Limerick: Ireland

Sights to See

King John's Castle, E side of Thomond Bridge on the banks of the River Shannon. An impressive early-13th-century castle, with massive round towers, and 10-ft.-thick walls. Open during the summer months.

Treaty Stone, across the Shannon at the W end of the bridge. The Treaty of Limerick was reportedly signed on this stone in October, 1691, after the Irish had heroically defended the castle during a long siege by William of Orange.

St. Mary's Cathedral, Nicholas & Bridge Sts., just S of King John's Castle. Dating from the 12th century, and subsequently rebuilt and augmented, it is noted for its 15th-century black oak misericords. Open 9–1, 2:30–5:30 daily in summer, 9–1 in winter.

Custom House, Patrick St. & Charlottes Quay, across the Abbey River, S of St. Mary's. Noted for its elegant pilastered front.

City Wall and Devil's Battery, between New Rd. & Old Clare St., E of the Custom House. Fragments of the former city walls, and a section famous as a scene of fierce resistance against the Williamites.

St. John's Cathedral, Cathedral Place, S of the Devil's Battery. A 19th-century Gothic Revival structure, its spire, at 280 ft., is the tallest in Ireland.

Limerick Museum, St. John's Square, opposite the Cathedral. Fine collection of archaeological finds.

Limerick Art Gallery, People's Park on Perry Square, half a mile SW of St. John's Square. Fine collection of modern Irish painting.

Hunt Collection, National Institute for Higher Education, 3 miles NE of Limerick on the Dublin Road. Superb collection of Celtic antiquities, including Bronze Age ornaments and weapons; medieval bronzes and enamels; and 18th-century Irish porcelain and silverware. Open 9:30–5:30 M–Sa, April–Oct.

Useful Information

Tourist Office, The Granaray, Michael St (tel:31-7522); the closest *U.S. Embassy* is in Dublin, at 42 Elgin Rd., Ballsbridge (tel:01-688777); *Taxi* (tel:48844 or 46230); *Emergency* (tel:999 for ambulance, fire, and police); *Voltage Guide,* 220 V, two round-pin or three square-pin outlets are used.

Special Trips/Tours

Bunratty Castle and Folk Park, some 8 miles NW of Limerick on the N18 to Ennis. Built in the 15th century, it has a huge rectangular keep, or tower, offering fine panoramas of the surrounding countryside. It is well known for its superb furniture, tapestry, and stained-glass windows. The castle is also famous for its nightly medieval banquets. The *Bunratty Folk Park* adjacent to the castle has an interesting collection of country cottages, housing various working, traditional craft exhibits.

The Atlantic coastline of Clare County is especially attractive, especially the *Cliffs of Moher* area, just NW of the village of Liscannor. Rising some 400 to 700 ft. out of the Atlantic, the cliffs offer dramatic views of the coastline, and on a clear day the Aran Islands. *O'Brien's Tower,* on the highest point of the cliffs, has a visitors' center. On the way, stop in *Ennis* and see the ruins of the 13th-century *Franciscan friary,* noted for its sculptures.

Some 36 miles SE of Limerick, via the N24 to Tipperary, and the N74 E to Cashel, is one of the country's greatest historical sights, the splendid *Rock of Cashel.* A 200-ft. limestone rock rising out of the surrounding countryside, it is crowned with a group of ruins, including a huge 13th-century cathedral and earlier tower. Cormac's Chapel, by the cathedral's south transept, is particularly noteworthy. Take one of the conducted tours from 10–7 daily, June–Sept.; shorter hours the rest of the year.

Weather

Limerick has a cool, temperate climate characterized by mild, frequently rainy weather. Daytime high temperatures in the summer typically reach into the high 60s, dropping to the mid 50s at night. Winter daytime highs are usually in the upper 40s, falling to the upper 30s at night. Rainfall is well distributed throughout the year, although fall and winter are the wettest times.

LIMERICK: TEMPERATURES AND PRECIPITATION

Month	J	F	M	A	M	J	J	A	S	O	N	D
Average Daily Temperature												
(Fahrenheit) Max.	47	48	52	56	61	66	68	68	64	58	52	49
Min.	36	37	39	42	45	51	54	53	50	45	40	38
Average Number of Days with Precipitation												
	15	11	12	11	11	10	11	11	12	12	14	16

Waterford: Ireland

Sights to See

Waterford Glass Factory, Cork Road, 2 miles SW of the city center. World-famous factory, considered by many to produce some of the world's finest crystal. Guided tours demonstrate glass blowing, cutting, and polishing skills. Tours should be booked well in advance (tel:051-7331), or make arrangements through most of the Tourist Offices in Ireland. Tours start at 10:15, with the last one at 2:30. NOTE: closed on weekends and usually the last week in July and first two weeks in August.
Reginald's Tower, Corner of Parade Quay & The Mall. A large, 80-ft.-high, circular stone fortress built in the early 11th century as a Norse stronghold. It now houses a historical and maritime museum. Open 10–12:30, 2–5 M–Sa, 10:30–12:30 Su, April–Sept.

City Hall, The Mall, close to Reginald's Tower. Built in 1788, it is noted for its collection of Thomas F. Meagher (a native son who became a Governor of Montana) memorabilia and its fine Waterford glass chandelier.
French Church, Bailey's New St., just N of the City Hall. A 13th-century Franciscan Friary, used by the Huguenots in the 17th century.
Christchurch Cathedral, Cathedral Sq., off Lady Lane, just W of City Hall. A late-18th-century Baroque building.
St. Olaf's Church, just NW of Christchurch Cathedral. Originally a Danish church, rebuilt by the Normans, it is noted for the fine carving in its pulpit.
Holy Trinity Cathedral, Barronstrand St., down High St., NW of St. Olaf's. A late-18th-century Neoclassical structure, known for its fine interior.
Chamber of Commerce, Gt. Georges St., across Barronstrand St. and to the west of Holy Trinity Cathedral. A handsome, late-18th-century Adam-style building, noted for its oval staircase.
Dominican Friary, O'Connell & Bridge Sts., 4 blocks NW of the Chamber of Commerce. The tower of St. Saviour's is the only remaining part of an early-13th-century friary. The frescoes over the church's altar are worth seeing.

Useful Information

Tourist Office, 41 The Quay (tel:75788) closest *U.S. Embassy* is in Dublin, at 42 Elgin Road, Ballsbridge (tel:01-688777); *Taxi* (tel:75222); *Emergency* (tel:999 for police, fire, and ambulance); *Voltage Guide,* 220 V, two round-pin or three square-pin outlets are used.

Special Trips/Tours

The historical town of *Wexford,* home to the internationally famous Wexford Opera Festival in late October of every year, is 39 miles E of Waterford via the N25. Notable sights include *Westgate Tower,* the sole surviving section of the town's former Norman walls; *Bull Ring square;* and the *Gothic Revival Twin Churches* on Rowe & Bride Sts.

Kilkenny, a market town with narrow medieval streets and buildings, mixed with handsome Georgian terraces, and an important ecclesiastical and government center since the 6th century, is 30 miles N of Waterford. It is particularly well known for its castle and fine cathedral. *Ormonde Castle,* dating from the 12th century and rebuilt in the 13th century and 19th centuries, has massive drum towers. It is also noted for its main hall and tower dining room, decorated with period furnishings. Open daily, June–Sept. *St. Canice's Cathedral,* St. Canice's Place, is the second largest medieval cathedral in Ireland. Its tomb sculptures and the unusual domed roof of its round tower are notable. Open daily.

On the way to or from Kilkenny, visit the ruins of *Jerpoint Abbey.* A magnificent 12th-century Cistercian monastery, it is just outside Thomastown, off the N9 to Carlow. The abbey's restored cloister with its fine figure sculptures, and the knights' tombs are worth seeing.

Weather

Waterford has a cool, temperate climate characterized by mild, rainy weather. Summer daytime high temperatures are typically in the high 60s, dropping to the mid 50s at night. Winter daytime highs are usually in the upper 40s, falling to the high 30s at night. Rainfall is well distributed throughout the year, although late fall and early winter is the wettest time.

WATERFORD: TEMPERATURES AND PRECIPITATION

Month	J	F	M	A	M	J	J	A	S	O	N	D
Average Daily Temperature												
(Fahrenheit) Max.	47	48	52	56	61	66	68	68	64	58	52	49
Min.	36	37	39	42	45	51	54	53	50	45	40	38
Average Number of Days with Precipitation												
	15	11	12	11	11	10	11	11	12	12	14	16

Florence (Firenze): Italy

Sights to See

Piazza del Duomo–Santa Maria del Fiore Cathedral complex. The Cathedral itself, the Gothic campanile, and the baptistry with its bronze doors by Ghiberti. The climb to the dome is rewarded with spectacular views. Open 7–12:30 and 2:30–6 daily.
Church of St. Lawrence (Chiesa di San Lorenzo), NW of the Duomo on Piazza San Lorenzo. Early Renaissance building by Brunelleschi.
Medici Chapels (Cappelle Medicee), behind the church on the Piazza degli Aldobrandini. Contains the famous tombs of the Medici, designed by Michelangelo.
The Academy (Galleria dell'Accademia), Via Ricasoli 6, NNE of the Duomo. Noted for its Florentine paintings and Michelangelo's *David* outside. Open 9–2 Tu–Sa, 9–1 Su.
National Museum (Museo Nazionale or Museu del Bargello), Via del Proconsolo 4, SSE of the Duomo. Housed in the Bargello, it contains the best of Florentine sculpture. Open 9–2 Tu–Sa, 9–1 Su.
Palazzo Vecchio, Piazza della Signoria, S of the Duomo. The 13th-century residence of the Medicis. See the Salon of the Five Hundred (Sala dei Cinquecento).
Uffizi Gallery (Galleria degli Uffizi), Piazza del Signoria, just SW of Palazzo Vecchio. The most important art collection in Italy, particularly the works from the 13th to 18th centuries. Open 9–7 Tu–Sa, 9–1 Su.
Ponte Vecchio, just SW of the Uffizi. The only bridge over the Arno to survive WW II damage, it is lined with jewelry shops and is a masterpiece.
Pitti Palace (Palazzo Pitti), S of the Arno, just S of the Ponte Vecchio. A 15th-century palace that became the seat of the Medici grand dukes in the 16th century. Visit the Palatine Gallery and the Gallery of Modern Art.

Boboli Gardens (Giardino di Boboli), just SE of the Pitti Palace. One of best examples of Italian gardening. Full of fountains and statuary. Open 9–6:30 daily in the summer.

Useful Information

Tourist Information Office (Azienda Autonoma di Turismo), Via Tornabuoni 15 (tel:21-6544); *Ente Provinciale per il Turismo,* Via A. Manzoni 16 (tel:247-8141); *U.S. Consulate,* Lungarno Amerigo Vespucci 38 (tel:29-8276); *Taxi* (tel:4798 or 4390); *American Express,* c/o Universalturismo, via Guicciardini 49r (tel:27-8751); *Police* (tel:113 for emergencies); *Post Office,* Via Pellicceria, off p. della Repubblica; *Voltage Guide,* 220 V, two round-pin outlets are used.

Special Trips/Tours

For one of the most *famous views of Florence and the Arno* valley, drive to the terrace of the *Piazzale Michelangelo,* at the end of the *Viale dei Colli,* S of Florence (running from the Porta Romano).

In summer the *Estate Fiesolana* fills the old Roman theater in **Fiesole** with concerts, opera, theater, ballet, and movies. This villa town, with its 11th-century cathedral, Roman ruins, and superb views of the surrounding Tuscan countryside, is less than 30 minutes NE of Florence.

Pisa and its leaning tower (la Torre di Pisa) is only 51 miles W of Florence. The top of the inclining tower, which serves as a campanile, or belfry, for the Pisa Cathedral, affords a dramatic view of the town. Be sure to see the *Piazza dei Cavalieri.*

Siena, about 43 miles S of Florence, and originally an Etruscan city, is also worth a day side trip. Its *Piazza del Campo* is one of Europe's most beautiful medieval squares, with the 13th-century *Palazzo Pubblico* (Town Hall) on its S side. The *Gothic Siena Cathedral* (Duomo di Sienna) is also a "must see." If you will be in the area around July 2 or August 16, try and see Siena's *Corsa del Palio* medieval festival held in the Piazzo del Campo.

Weather

Florence has a typical Mediterranean climate with mild winters and hot, dry summers. Summer daytime high temperatures are typically in the low to mid 80s, dropping to the 60s at night. Winter daytime highs reach the low to mid 50s, falling to the 40s at night. Winter is the wettest season.

FLORENCE: TEMPERATURES AND PRECIPITATION

Month	J	F	M	A	M	J	J	A	S	O	N	D
Average Daily Temperature												
(Fahrenheit) Max.	52	55	59	66	74	82	87	86	79	71	61	55
Min.	40	42	45	50	56	63	67	67	62	55	49	44
Average Number of Days with Precipitation												
	8	9	8	6	5	4	1	2	5	8	11	10

Milan (Milano): Italy

Sights to See

Milan Cathedral (Duomo), Piazza del Duomo. World's biggest Gothic cathedral and second largest church (after Rome's St. Peter's). Noted for its beautiful stained-glass windows and the marvelous panorama of Milan from its roof, among the statues and gargoyles. Open 7–7 daily, roof open Tu–Su.
Royal Palace (Palazzo Reale), Piazza del Duomo 12. See the art exhibits in the Royal Apartment, and visit the Museo del Duomo, which illustrates the 400-plus years of construction of the cathedral.
Galleria Vittorio Emanuele, next to the Duomo. Some of Italy's most exclusive shops are found here.
La Scala (Teatro alla Scala), Piazza del Scala, N of Duomo. The world's most famous opera house, built in 1776–1778. Try to get tickets to any performance.
Scala Museum (Museo della Scala), next to La Scala. Fine collection of La Scala memorabilia. Open daily.
Poldi-Pezzoli Museum (Museo Poldi Pezzoli), Via Manzoni 12, NE of La Scala. Notable private art collection, bequeathed to Milan in the late 19th century. Noted for its silverware, embroidery, and china collection, as well as its paintings. Open 9:30–12:30, 2:30–6, Tu–W; Th–Su until 5:30.
Brera Palace and Art Gallery (Palazzo e Pinacoteca di Brera), Via Brera 28, N of La Scala. One of Italy's great museums, with the works of Tintoretto, Titian, Raphael, Rubens, and Rembrandt well represented. Open 9–2 Tu–Sa, 9–1 Su.
Sforza Castle and Art Gallery (Castello Sforzesco e Museo d'Arte), Piazza Castello, NW of the Duomo. A huge 15th-century castle built by the Sforza family. Noted for its excellent sculpture collection, including Michelangelo's unfinished *Rondonini Pieta*. Open 9:30–12:15, 2:30–5:30 Tu–Su.
Da Vinci's Last Supper in the refectory adjacent to the Church of St. Mary of Grace (Santa Maria delle Grazie), Piazza Santa Maria delle Grazie, W of Sforza Castle. Still undergoing painstaking restoration. The church itself also has some fine 15th-century frescoes. Open 9–1:30, 2–6:30 Tu–Sa.
St. Ambrose's Basilica and Museum (Basilica e Museo di Sant'Ambrogio), Piazza Sant'Ambrogio, S of Sforza Castle. Noted for its atrium and 9th-century high altar. Open Tu–Su.
Leonardo da Vinci National Museum of Science and Technology, Via San Vittore 21, W of the S. Ambrogio Basilica. Fine collection illustrating the history of science and technology. Open 9–5 Tu–Su.

Useful Information

Tourist Office (APT), Piazza del Duomo (tel:809-662) & Stazione Centrale (tel:669-0532); *American Express,* Via Brera 3 (tel:855-71); *U.S. Consulate,* via Principe Amedeo 2/10 (tel:65-2841); *Police* (tel:113 in emergencies); *Post Office,* Via Cordusio 4; *Voltage Guide,* 220 V, two round-pin outlets are used.

are magnificent. NOTE: Mt. Vesuvius is still an active volcano. It has erupted an average of once every 35 years over the past 300 (the last one was in 1944).

Capri can be reached by hydrofoil from Naples or Sorrento, or by ferry in 40 minutes from Naples. The best-known excursion on the island is to the Blue Grotto (Grotta Azzurra), best seen around the lunch hour.

Ischia, the largest island in the Bay of Naples. Can be reached by motorboat or ferry from Naples in 60 and 90 minutes, respectively. Very popular with Italians, the island is well known for the health resorts centered on its many hot springs. For information on steamers and hydrofoils, contact Caremar, Molo Beverello, Piazza Municipio (tel:31-3882).

The Amalfi Coast (Costa Amalfitana). A drive along the scenic Amalfi Drive on the S coast of the Sorrento peninsula is a delight. Stop and see the *Amalfi Cathedral* (Amalfi Duomo), and *Positano,* a very picturesque fishing village.

Weather

Naples has a typical Mediterranean climate, with mild winters and hot, generally dry summers. Daytime high temperatures in the summer typically reach into the high 70s or low 80s, dropping to the 60s at night. Winter daytime highs reach the mid 50s, falling to the low 40s at night. Winter is the wettest season.

NAPLES: TEMPERATURES AND PRECIPITATION

Month	J	F	M	A	M	J	J	A	S	O	N	D
Average Daily Temperature												
(Fahrenheit) Max.	53	55	59	65	72	79	84	84	79	71	63	56
Min.	40	41	44	48	54	61	65	65	61	54	48	44
Average Number of Days with Precipitation												
	11	10	9	8	7	4	2	3	5	9	11	12

Rome (Roma): Italy

Sights to See

Roman Forum (Foro Romano), via dei Fori Imperiali. An archaeological site, containing the Arch of Titus, Romulus's Tomb, and Augustus's Palace, that was once the commercial, civil, and religious center of ancient Rome. Open 9–6 M, W–Sa, 12–6 Su.

The Colosseum, Piazza del Colosseo, just E of the Forum. The enduring symbol of ancient Rome, it was an arena for entertainment, gladiator and wild animal fights. Open 9–7 M–Sa.

Baths of Caracalla (Terme di Caracalla), via delle Terme Caracalla, S of the Colosseum. Ancient Rome's largest public baths. Closed M.

S. Giovanni in Laterano, Piazza San Giovanni, SE of the Colosseum. Cathedral of Rome. Church of the popes until 1307, it is known for its cloister.

S. Maria Maggiore, Piazza S. Maggiore, NE of the Colosseum. Neoclassical basilica dedicated to the worship of St. Mary, known for its coffered ceiling. *Piazza del Campidoglio,* Just NW of the Forum. Beautifully designed square by Michelangelo. *Museo Capitolino,* Piazza del Campidoglio. Noted for its Greek and Roman antiquities. Open 9–2 Tu–Sa, 9–1 Su. *Pantheon,* Piazza della Rotonda, NW of the Forum. The best-preserved ancient Roman building. *Piazza Navona,* just W of the Pantheon. A 17th-century Baroque square, and one of Rome's most historical. Have a cup of cappuccino in one of the sidewalk cafes and enjoy. *Spanish Steps,* Piazza di Spagna, NNE of the Pantheon. Also famous for its Bernini fountain. Excellent view from the top of these French-built steps. *The Vatican,* across the Tiber, W of Piazza Navona across the Ponte Vittorio Emanuele. The headquarters of the Roman Catholic world, and a country in its own right. General audiences are held by the Pope every Wednesday at 11 A.M. during the winter and 6 P.M. on St. Peter's Square during the summer. *St. Peter's Basilica* (Basilica di San Pietro), with Michelangelo's Pieta, is open daily to 7 P.M. in summer, to 6 P.M. in winter. *Vatican Museum,* Viale Vaticano. One of the world's great collections. Closed on Sundays. *Castel Sant'Angelo,* Lungotevere Castello, on the banks of the Tiber, E of the Vatican. Originally Hadrian's mausoleum, it now houses the *National Military Museum.* View Rome from its terrace. Closed Mondays.

Useful Information

Italian Tourist Office (ENIT), Via Maghera 2 (tel:497-1282); *Provincial Tourist Office* (EPT), Stazione Termini (tel:48-25-4078); *U.S. Embassy,* 119A Via Vittorio Veneto (tel:46-741); *American Express,* Piazza di Spagna 38 (tel:72-2801); *Thomas Cook,* Via Veneto 9–11; *Vatican Information Office,* P. San Pietro (tel:698-4866 or 698-4466); *Radio Taxi* (tel:3570, 3875, 4994, or 8433); *Emergency* (tel:113 for police, fire, ambulance); *Post Office,* P. San Silvestro 28 (tel:67-71); *Voltage Guide,* 220 V, two round-pin outlets are used. NOTE: consult *This Week in Rome* or *A Guest in Rome* (available at newsstands) for an English language guide and information on theaters, galleries, etc.

Special Trips/Tours

On weekends, *boat excursions on the Tiber River* leave from Lungotevere Dante 271 (tel:637-0268); reservations are necessary. The archaeological site of *Ostia Antica,* just 15 miles SW of Rome provides a glimpse of a classical Roman city. Closed Mondays. A short bus or train ride away (19 miles E of Rome) is *Tivoli,* a charming hilltop town, famous for its gardens, fountains, waterfalls, and villas, especially *Villa d'Este* and Hadrian's villa, *Villa Adriana*. Open 9–11:30 Tu–Su.

Weather

Rome enjoys a typical Mediterranean climate with mild, wet winters and hot dry summers. Summer high temperatures typically reach the mid 80s, dropping to the 60s at night. Winter daytime highs usually reach the mid 50s, falling to the 40s at night.

ROME: TEMPERATURES AND PRECIPITATION

Month	J	F	M	A	M	J	J	A	S	O	N	D
Average Daily Temperature												
(Fahrenheit) Max.	52	55	59	66	74	82	87	86	79	71	61	55
Min.	40	42	45	50	56	63	67	67	62	55	49	44
Average Number of Days with Precipitation												
	8	9	8	6	5	4	1	2	5	8	11	10

Venice (Venezia): Italy

Sights to See

Grand Canal (Canal Grande). Venice's main waterway, lined with over 200 marble palaces built between the 12th and 18th centuries. Best seen by boat, you can board a "vaporetto" (motor-boat bus) at either end (San Marcos or the station). Make sure it is the slow one (accelerato); relax and enjoy.
St. Mark's Square (Piazza San Marco). A huge marble square, widely considered one of the world's finest, lined on three sides with arcades housing shops and cafes, complete with flocks of pigeons and people.
St. Mark's Basilica (Basilica di San Marco), Piazza San Marco. Dating from the 11th century, it has magnificent mosaics, and the famous Pala d'Oro altarpiece, a gold Byzantine bas-relief. Open 9:30–4:30 daily.
Campanile of St. Mark (Campanile di San Marco), on the SE corner of Piazza San Marco. Rebuilt bell tower of St. Mark's Basilica. The views from the top are magnificent.
Doge's Palace (Palazzo Ducale), adjoining the basilica, the reception rooms have paintings by many of Italy's finest artists, especially Tintoretto's *Paradise* in the Great Council Chamber. Guided tours end with a visit to *Piombi Prison* reached by the *Bridge of Sighs* (Ponte dei Sospiri), behind the Palace. Open 8:30–6:30 daily.
Torre Del'Orologio, Piazza San Marco, north of St. Mark's. The view from its campanile is marvelous. Open 10–7:30 daily.
San Giorgio Maggiore, on the Isola di S. Giorgio, SE of St. Mark's Square, across the Canale di S. Marco. Palladio's superb church with Tintoretto's famous

Last Supper and *Gathering of Manna.* The view from the top of the church's campanile is breathtaking.

Academy of Fine Arts (Galleria dell'Accademia), Campo della Carita, across the Grand Canal, W of St. Mark's Square. Houses Venice's best works of art. Open 9–2 Tu–Sa, 9–1 Su.

Great School of S. Rocco (Scuola Grande di S. Rocco), Campo San Rocco, NNW of the Academy of Fine Arts. Contains over 50 of Tintoretto's works, including the *Crucifixion.*

Useful Information

Azienda Autonoma di Soggiorno e Turismo, 4089 Rialto, Palazzo Martinengo (tel:52-303-13 or 52-303-99); APT (Tourist Office), San Marco 71F (tel:52-263-56); *American Express,* San Marco 1471 (tel:520-0844); *Police* (tel:113 in emergencies; otherwise 520-0754); nearest *U.S. Consulate* is in Milan, at Via Principe Amedeo 2/10 (tel:2/652-841); *Post Office,* salizzada Fontego dei Tedeschi; *Voltage Guide,* 220 V, two round-pin outlets are used.

Un Ospite di Venezia (A Guest in Venice) is a bilingual booklet published weekly listing special events, up-to-date museum schedules, and entertainment.

Special Trips/Tours

No visit to Venice can be complete without a boat ride down the **Grand Canal.** Boats leave from either end (San Marco or the station). The No. 1 and No. 2 lines both ply the Grand Canal and go to the Lido, while the No. 5 line, the Circolare, circumnavigates the city. If time permits, a *ride in a gondola* (as much as $30 per hour), especially in the evening, is worthwhile. The *canal ferries* (traghetti) crisscrossing the Grand Canal at various points between the bridges are real bargains.

The lagoon trips to the islands of *Murano, Burano,* and *Torcello,* leaving from the Fondamenta Nuova are worthwhile. **Murano** is an ancient center of glass blowing and molding. Its *Glassworks Museum* (Museo Vetrario) has an excellent collection of Venetian glass. *Burano* is a center of the Venetian lace industry and a picturesque fishing village. *Torcello,* the first colony of the Venetian lagoon, has an 11th-century cathedral worth seeing. The island-town of *Chioggia,* at the S end of the Venetian lagoon, makes for an interesting side trip. Not only for its own attractions (canals, narrow streets, 17th-century cathedral and its campanile), but also because of the opportunity to cruise the lagoon. Boats leave for the two-hour cruise from the Riva degli Schiavoni, off the Piazza San Marco.

Weather

Venice has a distinctive climate. Summers are hot and sunny, with daytime high temperatures in the low 80s, falling to the 60s at night. Winter daytime highs usually reach the mid to upper 40s, dropping to the mid 30s at night. Rainfall is well distributed throughout the year.

VENICE: TEMPERATURES AND PRECIPITATION

Month	J	F	M	A	M	J	J	A	S	O	N	D
Average Daily Temperature												
(Fahrenheit) Max.	42	46	53	62	70	76	81	80	75	65	53	46
Min.	33	35	41	49	56	63	66	65	61	53	44	37
Average Number of Days with Precipitation												
	6	6	7	9	8	8	7	7	5	7	9	8

Liechtenstein

Sights to See

Vaduz, the principality's capital, and home to about 5,000 of the nation's 25,000 inhabitants. Beautifully situated in the Rhine valley, surrounded by vineyards and the towering Alps.

Art Gallery (Gemaldegalerie), Stadtle 37, in the same building as the National Tourist Office, Vaduz. Noted for its excellent Rubens collection in the Prince's Gallery (from the Prince's private art collection). The gallery also has a number of paintings by the other Old Masters. Open varied hours.

Post Office Museum (Briefmarkenmuseum), Stadtle 37, Vaduz. A philatelist's dream, full of Liechtenstein's famous and valuable decorative stamps, known among stamp collectors the world over for their fine engraving. Open 10–12, 2–6 daily.

National Museum (Landesmuseum), Stadtle 43, just S of the Post Office Museum. Well known for its medieval weapons collection. It also has interesting exhibits on the country's folklore and history. Open varied hours.

The Castle (Schloss Vaduz), above Vaduz to the east. The palace itself, home to Prince Franz Josef II, is not open to the public, but the grounds are, and they afford nice vistas of Vaduz below and the surrounding Alps.

Triesenberg, a small village above Vaduz past Vaduz Castle. A small skiing center in winter and a center of hiking in the summer. Visit the *Walser Museum.*

Masescha and Malbun, higher in the Alps N of Triesenberg. Small villages in beautiful Alpine settings, commanding excellent panoramas of the surrounding mountains. *Malbun,* at 5,200 ft. is a growing international skiing center, although still small. A chair lift to the top of *Bettlerjoch Peak,* where at almost 7,000 ft. there is a restaurant, will be rewarded with spectacular views.

Gutenberg Castle, above the village of Balzers, in the south of Liechtenstein. An impressive medieval castle that formerly belonged to the Hapsburgs.

Useful Information

Liechtenstein National Tourist Office, Stadtle 37, Vaduz (tel:6-6288); *Vaduz Tourist Office,* Vaduz (tel:2-1443); closest *U.S. Consulate* is in Zurich,

Switzerland at Zillokerstr. 141 (tel:41/01/55-2566 Swiss); *Voltage Guide*, 220 V, two round-pin outlets are used.

Special Trips/Tours

Chur, Switzerland, with its beautiful Romanesque cathedral, is less than an hour's drive S of Vaduz along the Rhine. One of Switzerland's oldest towns, with many 15th- to 17th-century buildings in its old town, it also has other noteworthy sights in addition to the cathedral, including the *Bishop's Court* surrounding the Hofplatz, the *Cathedral Museum,* and St. Lucius Church.

Near Chur, to the E and SE, are the famous resorts of *Arosa, Davos,* and *Klosters,* which offer some of the best skiing in the winter, and great hiking in the summer. You can catch a train from Chur to Arosa and explore the village, or take the *cable-car ride* up a neighboring peak for marvelous panoramic views. Davos has the *Davos-Parsenn-Bahn* funicular, which makes the surrounding mountains accessible, either from the Hohenweg station (7,281 ft.), or the Weissfluhjoch station (8,737 ft.).

Bregenz, on the Bodensee (Lake Constance) in Austria is just an hour or so N of Vaduz. Bregenz has a well-preserved medieval section. If you have the time, take a steamer ride on the Bodensee. Closer to Vaduz is the medieval town of *Feldkirch,* Austria, with its *Schattenburg Castle.* Further up the valley is the village ski resort of *Schruns,* with another impressive cable-car ride, the *Hochjockbahn.*

Weather

Liechtenstein's weather is typical of other Alpine communities. Summer daytime high temperatures typically reach into the high 70s, dropping into the mid 50s at night. Winter daytime highs usually are in the mid to upper 30s or low 40s, falling to the 20s at night. Summer is the wet season, with July normally being the wettest month, although the frequency of precipitation is fairly high year-round.

LIECHTENSTEIN: TEMPERATURES AND PRECIPITATION

Month	J	F	M	A	M	J	J	A	S	O	N	D
Average Daily Temperature												
(Fahrenheit) Max.	34	40	51	60	68	74	77	75	69	58	46	36
Min.	20	24	29	39	46	52	55	54	49	40	31	24
Average Number of Days with Precipitation												
	13	13	11	14	15	19	19	17	14	12	12	13

Luxembourg

Sights to See

Luxembourg City, formerly one of the strongest fortresses on the continent, was founded in 963 A.D. The remains of the city's 50-odd defensive forts, linked by miles and miles of tunnels, the famous casements carved out of solid rock, can be toured in summer.

Cathedral of Our Lady of Luxembourg, a late Gothic structure, noted for its beautiful stained-glass windows.

Fish Market (Marche aux Poissons), the oldest part of the city.

Museum of Natural History, Marche aux Poissons. Fine mineralogy, paleontology, and zoology exhibits.

Museum of History and Art, Marche aux Poissons. Has interesting archaeological, historic, folkloric, and art collections.

Place d'Armes, Luxembourg City's social center, surrounded by pleasant cafes.

Grand-Ducal Palace, dating from the late 16th century, and renovated in the 19th century, it is known for its fine Renaissance facade. Not open to the public.

United States Military Cemetery, Hamm, about 3 miles east of Luxembourg City. Burial place for 5,000 American soldiers, including General George S. Patton, Jr.

Echternach, a beautiful medieval town, on the frontier with Germany, with patrician houses, narrow streets, and ancient ramparts. Don't miss the town's 7th-century *Benedictine Abbey,* noted for its vaults painted with frescoes dating from the early 12th century.

Vianden, a beautiful town dating from the 9th century, and N of Echternach on the Sure river, is definitely worth visiting. Old ramparts with watchtowers encircle this town, and *Vianden Castle,* one of the largest feudal castles in this part of Europe, is an architectural jewel. Also visit the Folklore Museum.

Clervaux, in the northernmost part of Luxembourg, is the site of the *Benedictine Abbey* of *St. Maurice and St. Maur,* and the fine 12th-century feudal *Clervaux Castle.* The castle houses the "Family of Man" photographs of E. Steichen, a native son. Open 10–5 daily.

Useful Information

Grand Duchy National Tourist Office, place de la Gare (tel:48-1199) & place d'Armes (tel:2-2809); *American Express,* 6-8 rue Drigier (tel:49-6041); *U.S. Embassy,* 22 blvd. E. Servais (tel:46-0123); *Moselle River Tours* (Navigation Touristique de la Moselle), 32 rte. de Thionville, Grevenmacher (tel:75-8275); *Police* (tel:49-4949); *Post Office,* 25 rue Aldringern; *Voltage Guide,* 110/220 V, two round-pin outlets are used.

Special Trips/Tours

A visit to *Luxembourg's wine area* (The "Circuit Viticole") is a delight when the weather is good. The tours consist of a visit to the cellars of Wellenstein, a walk through the vineyards, followed by a boat trip and a wine tasting in the castle of *Stadbredimus*. Contact Vins-moselle, Chateau de Stadbredimus (tel:69-8314), or the Tourist Office.

A *Moselle River trip* aboard the "Princesse Marie-Astrid," between Schengen and Wasserbillig with stops along the way, is a good way to see rural Luxembourg. Contact Navigation Touristique de la Moselle at the address or phone number above.

Weather

Luxembourg enjoys a temperate climate without extremes. Summer daytime high temperatures typically reach into the low 70s, dropping to the mid to low 50s at night. Winter daytime highs are usually in the upper 30s or low 40s, falling to the low 30s at night. Rainfall is pretty evenly spread throughout the year, although summer is the wettest time of year, with August normally getting the most rain.

LUXEMBOURG: TEMPERATURES AND PRECIPITATION

Month	J	F	M	A	M	J	J	A	S	O	N	D
Average Daily Temperature												
(Fahrenheit) Max.	37	40	49	57	65	70	73	71	66	56	44	39
Min.	29	31	35	40	46	52	55	54	50	43	37	33
Average Number of Days with Precipitation												
	20	16	14	13	15	14	14	15	16	15	19	20

Monaco

Sights to See

Oceanographic Museum (Musee Oceanographique), Ave. St-Martin, at the end of Jardins de St-Martin. This world-famous museum and research institute, directed by Jacques-Yves Cousteau, has one of Europe's finest aquariums on its lowest level. The marine mammal skeletons and zoological exhibits on the ground floor are fascinating.

Cathedral of Monaco, off rue du Tribunal, W of the Oceanographic Museum. Modern cathedral in Romanesque style containing the tombs of the Princes of Monaco.

Prince's Palace (Palais du Prince), pl. du Palais, NW of the cathedral. Some portions of the palace date from the 13th century (the Grimaldi family has been ruling the principality since about then), this picture-postcard palace is known for its 16th- and 17th-century frescoes, and its superb throne room (the Salle du Trone). Also worth seeing is the palace's *Art Gallery* with its Napoleonic collection, and the Prince's stamp collection. Open 9–12:30, 2–7 daily, July–Sept. Changing of the Guard, Place du Palais. This colorful ceremony takes place at 11:55 A.M. daily.

Exotic Garden (Jardin Exotique), W of the Palais du Prince across blvd. Rainier III. Noted for its large cacti collection (over 9,000 varieties of cacti and succulents) and prehistoric caves.

Museum of Prehistoric Anthropology, Jardin Exotique. Archaeological finds from the caves, along with some Roman artifacts, are displayed.

Monte Carlo Casino (Casino de Monte Carlo), N of the Monaco-Ville peninsula, behind the modern Monte Carlo Congress Centre. Surrounded by beautiful gardens, this ornate structure, complete with crystal chandeliers and its Salle Granier theater and various gaming rooms, is world famous. Even if you don't wish to gamble, you should see the inside of this magnificent casino, a far cry from its gaudy cousins elsewhere along the Cote d'Azur. Opens at 10 A.M. daily.

Useful Information

Tourist Information, 2A blvd. des Moulins (tel:30-8701); *American Express,* 35 blvd. Princess Charlotte; nearest *U.S. Consulate* is in Marseille, France, at 12 blvd. Paul Peytral (tel:33/91/549-200); *Police* (tel:17); *English language information* (tel:50-0751); *Voltage Guide,* 110/220 V, two round-pin outlets are used.

Special Trips/Tours

Monaco is an excellent base for exploring the beautiful *Cote D'Azur,* or Riviera. The world-famous resorts of *St. Tropez, Cannes, Nice, Antibes,* and *Menton* are strung out along the coast, and all are easily accessible by car or train from Monaco. The best beaches are between St.-Maxime and Hyeres to the W of Nice. The most spectacular coastal scenery is found along the *Corniche d'Esterel,* between La Napoule and St.-Raphael, SW of Cannes. Behind the Mediterranean beaches lie picturesque mountain villages like *Eze, St. Paul-de-Vence, Gourdon,* and *Grimaud,* all of which afford magnificent panoramas. In winter, the mountains behind the coast have such ski resorts as *Auron, Isola,* and *Valberg,* all only an hour or two's drive from Monaco.

In addition to the great natural beauty, there are the cultural jewels, such as the *Picasso Museum* in Antibes, the *Chagall* and *Matisse Museums* in Nice, and the *Jean Cocteau Museum* in Menton. There are over 100 local festivals and events, and over 20 international festivals besides the famed *Cannes Film Festival* in May. Check with the Tourist Information Office for details.

Weather

Monaco enjoys a Mediterranean climate, with warm to hot, dry summers and mild, relatively sunny winters. Daytime high temperatures typically reach into the high 70s in the summer, falling to around 70 at night. Winter daytime highs usually are in the mid to upper 50s, dropping into the 40s at night. Summers normally are dry, with little rain. Late fall and early winter are the wettest time of the year.

MONACO: TEMPERATURES AND PRECIPITATION

Month	J	F	M	A	M	J	J	A	S	O	N	D
Average Daily Temperature												
(Fahrenheit) Max.	54	55	57	61	66	73	78	78	74	68	61	56
Min.	47	47	50	54	59	66	71	71	67	61	54	49
Average Number of Days with Precipitation												
	5	5	7	5	5	4	1	2	4	7	7	6

Amsterdam: Netherlands

Sights to See

Amsterdam's canals, particularly the four concentric tree-lined canals (the *Keizergracht, Prinsengracht, Herengracht* and *Singel).* Their banks are lined with beautiful 17th- and 18th-century merchants' houses. A tour boat ride around the canals is a perfect introduction to the city. Operators along the Rokin, Camrak, and Nassaukade run tours. In the evenings between April and October, the canals are illuminated by thousands of lights, and cheese and wine are served by candlelight on some boats.

Royal Palace (Koninklijk Paleis), Dam Square. Baroque structure noted for its opulent interior. Open 12:30–4 P.M. M–F. Summer only.

New Church (Nieuwe Kerk), next to the Royal Palace. A late-Gothic structure dating from the 16th century. Open 11–4 M–F, 12–5 Su.

Old Church (Oude Kerk), on Ouderkerksplein. Offers outstanding views of the city. Noteworthy itself. Open 10–5, M–Sa.

Anne Frank House, 263 Prinsengracht, W of the Dam. See the attic where Anne Frank and her family hid from the Nazis. Exhibits on the city and its Jews during WW II. Open 9–5 M–Sa, 10–5 Su.

National Museum (Rijkmuseum), 42 Stadhouderskade. Has one of the finest art collections in the world, particularly the works of the Dutch masters (Rubens, Van Dyck, Rembrandt, Vermeer, Bosch, and Hobbema). Open 10–5 Tu–Sa, 1–5 Su.

Vincent Van Gogh Museum, 7–11 Paulus Potterstr. Over 200 of the artist's paintings, but also works of Toulouse-Lautrec. Open 10–5 Tu–Sa, 1–5 Su.

Stedelijk Museum, 13 Paulus Potterstr. Fine collection of modern art. Open 1–5 daily.

National Shipping Museum, 1–7 Kattenburgplein. Devoted to the seafaring side of Dutch history. Ship models, atlases, sea charts, and navigation tools. Open 10–5 Tu–Sa, 1–5 Su.

Useful Information

Amsterdam Tourist Office (VVV), Stationsplein 10, in front of the *Central Railway Station* (tel:26-6444); *American Express,* Damrak 66 (tel:26-2042); *Thomas Cook,* Dam 19 (tel:6-5511); *U.S. Consulate,* Museumplein 19 (tel:79-

0321 or 64-5661); *Taxi* (tel:77-7777); *Police Emergency* (tel:22-2222); *Post Office*, Nieuwezijds Voorburgwal 182 (tel:555-89-11): *Voltage Guide*, 220 V, two round-pin outlets are used.

Special Trips/Tours

Haarlem, just 12 miles W of Amsterdam, has one of the Netherlands's most delightful medieval centers. Centered around the *Grote Markt* (marketplace), with its 13th-century *Stadhuis* (town hall), former Renaissance *Vleeshal* (meat market) and 18th-century *Vishal* (fish market), and 15th-century *St. Bavorkerk*, Haarlem's old town is definitely worth visiting. The *Frans Hals Museum*, Groot Heiligland 62, is also of interest.

The province of **Noord-Holland** is very attractive, and just over 30 minutes from Amsterdam are historic villages such as *Volendam* and *Marken*, together with picturesque medieval towns like *Monnickendam, Hoorn, Enkhuizen,* and *Edam.*

Weather

Weather can be very changeable from day to day at all times of the year. Summer daytime high temperatures typically hover in the low 70s, dropping to the 50s at night. Winter daytime highs are usually in the 40s, falling to the low 30s at night. Rainfall is well distributed throughout the year, although somewhat heavier and less frequent in the summer.

AMSTERDAM: TEMPERATURES AND PRECIPITATION

Month	J	F	M	A	M	J	J	A	S	O	N	D
Average Daily Temperature												
(Fahrenheit) Max.	40	42	49	56	64	70	72	71	67	57	48	42
Min.	31	31	34	40	46	51	55	55	50	44	38	33
Average Number of Days with Precipitation												
	22	19	16	16	14	14	17	18	19	20	21	21

The Hague (Den Haag): Netherlands

Sights to See

Binnenhof Parliament. Site of Holland's parliament, this complex of buildings, courtyards, archways, and halls dating from the 13th century is very impressive, particularly the medieval Hall of Knights (Ridderzaal). Take one of the guided tours. Open 10–4 M–Sa.

Mauritshuis Museum, Jacob de Witt Huis, Kneuterdijk 6, next to the Binnenhof. Superb collection of Dutch and Flemish Old Masters, it houses the Royal art collection. Open 10–5 M–Sa, 11–5 Su.

Gemeente Museum, Stadhoudersplaan 41. Excellent modern art collection, with Van Gogh, Picasso, Monet, and particularly Mondrian well represented. It

also has an interesting collection of 15th-century musical instruments. Open 10–5 Tu–Sa, 1–5 Su.
Bredius Museum, Prinsegracht 6. Dutch Old Masters are highlighted. Open 2–5 Tu & Th.
Lange and Korte Vorhout, two magnificent streets in the center of the city with beautiful houses and an interesting antiques market on Lange Voorhout.
Peace Palace, Carnegieplein 2. Home to the International Court of Justice and Academy of International Law. Open 10–12, 2–4 M–F.
Madurodam, Haringkade 175. A scaled-down (1:25) model town with model structures characteristic of Dutch towns and villages, including replicas of every famous building and monument in the Netherlands. Open 9:30–10:30 daily, shorter hours in winter.
Scheveningen, a suburb of The Hague, is a famous seaside resort that has recently undergone a radical facelift. Stroll along its promenade (Strandweg) and pier, and visit the casino in the Kurhaus Hotel.

Useful Information

VVV (Tourist Office), Kon. Julianaplien 30 (tel:546-200); *U.S. Embassy,* Lange Voorhout 102 (tel:624-911); *American Express,* Venestr. 20 (tel:540-1919); *Police* (tel:222-222 in emergency); *Post Office,* Nobelstr. & Prinsenstr. (tel:71-94-49); *Voltage Guide,* 220 V, two round-pin outlets are used.

Special Trips/Tours

Delft, just 7 miles SE of The Hague, is a delightful medieval town, with stately tree-lined canals, and magnificent Gothic and Renaissance structures. In the Delftware factories *De Porceleyne Flex,* Rotterdamseweg 196, and *De Delftse Pauw,* Delftweg 133, you can see how the famous Delft Blue pottery is still being made by hand. The *Prinsenhof Museum* on Agathaplein has a fine collection of tapestries and paintings. Open 10–5 Tu–Sa, 1–5 Su, June–Aug.

The oldest university town in Holland, *Leiden,* is a short trip NE of The Hague, off the A4 to Amsterdam. It is famous for its many fine museums, observatory, and botanical gardens. Particularly notable are the *National Museum of Ethnology* (Rijksmuseum voor Volkenkunde), Steenstraat 1; and the *National Antiquities Museum* (Rijksmuseum van Oudheden), Rapenburg 28, with its Egyptian Temple of Taffah.

The *Bulbfield Region.* If you are in the Netherlands in April or May, the famous daffodils, tulips, and hyacinths will be in bloom. The area around *Oegstgeest, Noordwijkerhout, De Zilk,* and *Hillegom,* between The Hague and Amsterdam, is well signposted with bulb-viewing routes. From the end of March through May, *Lisse,* between Leiden and Haarlem, hosts the world-famous *Keukenhof National Flower Exhibition.*

Holland's second city, *Rotterdam,* makes for an interesting side trip if you have more time. Almost completely destroyed during WW II, the rebuilt city is strikingly modern, and has a number of worthwhile sights, including the

Lijnbaan pedestrian shopping precinct; the views from the 600-ft. *Euromast,* Parkhaven 20; the world-famous modern art collection at the *Boymans Van Benningen Museum,* Mathenesserlaan 18-20; the city's restored and renovated western quarter of *Delfshaven,* including the *Pilgrimskerk,* on Voorstraat, where the Pilgrim Fathers prayed before departing for the New World; and a *Spido boat trip* around the world's largest port.

Weather

The Hague has a mild climate, with very changeable weather, both from day to day and from year to year. Summer daytime high temperatures typically reach the low 70s, dropping to the mid 50s at night. Winter daytime highs usually reach into the 40s, falling to the 30s at night. Rainfall is well distributed throughout the year. It tends to rain less frequently in the summer, but total precipitation is higher.

THE HAGUE: TEMPERATURES AND PRECIPITATION

Month	J	F	M	A	M	J	J	A	S	O	N	D
Average Daily Temperature												
(Fahrenheit) Max.	40	42	49	56	64	70	72	71	67	57	48	42
Min.	31	31	34	40	46	51	55	55	40	44	38	33
Average Number of Days with Precipitation												
	22	19	15	16	14	14	17	18	19	20	21	21

Bergen: Norway

Sights to See

Bergen itself from Mount Floien, a 1,000-ft. mountain rising out of the city to its east, reached by funicular railway (from Vetridsalmenningen). The view of Bergen and its harbor is magnificent. Open daily April–Oct.

Torget fishmarket, at the SE end of the main harbor (Vagen). Choose fish from open tanks, and watch the fishermen clean your choice.

Bryggen (The Wharf), on the E side of the main harbor (Vagen). Medieval wooden buildings with a museum and center for arts and crafts.

Hanseatic Museum, Bryggen quay, just NE of Torget. The Museum, depicting the life of medieval merchants, is housed in a well-preserved 16th-century wooden building. Open daily in the summer.

St. Mary's Church (Mariakirke), just NE of Bryggen Museum, N of the Hanseatic Museum. Romanesque and Gothic church dating from the 12th century.

Bergenhus Fortress, NW of St. Mary's church. Noted for its 16th-century Rosenkrantz Tower and restored 13th-century King Haakons Hall (Hakonshallen).

Old Bergen Open-Air Museum, Elsesro, Sandviken, NE of St. Mary's Church. A recreated town with some thirty-five 18th- and 19th-century wooden houses representative of the period's architecture.

Rasmus Meyer's Collection, adjacent to Lille Lundgardsvatnet, on Rasmus Meyer's Alle, S of the Torget. A small museum with excellent works by Norwegian naturalists, impressionists, and expressionists. Open 11–4 M–F, 12–3 Su.

Bergen Aquarium, in front of Nordnesparken at the end of the peninsular W of the main harbor (Vagen). One of the largest in Scandinavia. Open 10–6, longer hours in the summer.

Maritime Museum, Sydneshaugen, W of the Meyer Collection. A fascinating collection illustrating the development of shipping from the Old Norse period to the present. Open 11–2 Su–F.

Stave Church, Fantoft. Built in the early 12th century in Sognefjord, this pagoda-style wooden church was moved to its present site. A 15-minute bus ride (#14, 15, or 16) from downtown Bergen.

Troldhaugen, on Nordas Lake, about 20 minutes outside Bergen at Hop. The home of Edvard Grieg, Norway's most famous composer.

Useful Information

Tourist Office, Torgalmenning Pavilion (tel:32-1480); *Bergen Guide Service,* Slottsgaten 1 (tel:05-32-7700); *American Express,* Winge Travel Bureau, Karl Johansgate 33 1–3 (tel:42-91-50); closest *U.S. Embassy* is in Oslo, at Drammensveien 18 (tel:2/44-85-50); *Taxi* (tel:32-2222); *Police* (tel:002); *Voltage Guide,* 220 V, two round-pin outlets are used.

Special Trips/Tours

Bergen is the departure point for *fjord trips,* with coastal express steamers to the North Cape as well as boat trips to Hardanger, Sogne, and Nord fjords. For a day trip to *Hardangefjord,* with stops at Lofthus and Odda, two picturesque resorts on the fjord, contact the Hardanger Sunnhordlandske Steamship Co., 191 Strandgaten (tel:32-0077). For 2-day steamer cruises of the *Nordfjord* and the *Sognefjord area,* contact Fylkesbaatane I Sogn Og Fjordane, 197 Strandgaten (tel:32-4015). Your travel agent or the Tourist Information Office at Torgalmenning in Bergen will also help you arrange these trips.

There are morning and afternoon hydrofoils to the oil boomtown of *Stavanger,* with its 11th-century Anglo-Norman *cathedral, Ledaal Museum,* and beautiful Lyse fjord.

Weather

Bergen's climate and weather are heavily influenced by the Atlantic Ocean. Cloud cover is common, and rainfall is frequent and heavy. Summers are mild to warm, with daytime highs usually in the mid 60s, falling to the 50s at night. Winters are cold, with daytime highs in the upper 30s, falling to the low 30s at night. Precipitation is fairly heavy all year, but late fall and early winter is typically the wettest time of year.

BERGEN: TEMPERATURES AND PRECIPITATION

Month	J	F	M	A	M	J	J	A	S	O	N	D
Average Daily Temperature												
(Fahrenheit) Max.	38	38	43	49	58	61	66	65	59	52	46	41
Min.	31	30	33	37	44	49	54	54	49	43	38	34
Average Number of Days with Precipitation												
	20	17	16	19	15	17	20	20	22	23	21	22

Oslo: Norway

Sights to See

Oslo Harbor. Modern harbor with cruise ships, cargo vessels, ferries, and fishing boats.

City Hall (Radhus), Radhusplassen, overlooking the harbor. Decorated with murals, paintings, and sculptures of contemporary Norwegian artists. Open 10–2 M–Sa, 6–8 M, W.

National Gallery (Nasjonalgalleriet), Universitetsgate 13, N of the Radhus. Norway's major art museum, with an excellent 19th- and 20th-century collection of Norwegian and European artists. Open 10–4 M–F, 10–3 Sa, 12–3 Su, 6–8 W, Th.

Historical Museum, Frederiksgate 2, just NW of the National Gallery. Fine historical and ethnographic collections, particularly from the Viking era. Open daily.

Royal Palace (Det Kongelige Slott), at NW end of Karl Johansgate, NW of the Radhus. Watch the *changing of the guard* at 1:30 daily.

Oslo Cathedral (Oslo Domkirke), Stortorvet, E of the Radhus. A 17th- and 19th-century building known for its stained-glass windows and ceiling decorations.

Akershus Castle and Fortress, Radhusgate, SE of the Radhus. A 14th-century fortress jutting into Oslo's harbor. Rebuilt in the 17th century when a Renaissance castle was added. Offers a good view of Oslo from the bluffs. The Resistance Museum in the fortress is worth visiting. Open 10–4, M–F.

Norwegian Folk Museum (Norske Folkmuseet), Bygdoy Peninsula SW of the Radhus (take the ferry from the pier in front of the Radhus). A park containing 18th- and 19th-century buildings from all over Norway, including the famous 13th-century stave, or log church. Every Sunday at 7:30 P.M. you can either watch, or take part in, folk dancing. Open 10–6 daily.

Viking Ship House (Vikingskiphuset), Bygdoy Peninsula. A museum with collections of utensils, jewelry, and artifacts from the Viking period (A.D. 800–900), together with three Viking longships.

Frogner Park (a.k.a. Vigeland Park), NW of the Radhus. A large park in the W part of Oslo, noted for its Gustav Vigeland stone sculptures.
Munch Museum, Toyengate 53, E of the Radhus in E. Oslo. Devoted exclusively to the paintings, lithographs, and woodcuts of Edvard Munch. Open 10–8 Tu–Sa, 12–8 Su.
Tryvannstornet Tower (radio tower), a 390-ft. observation tower on a hill in the suburbs of Oslo, reached by a 25-minute walk from the Frognerseteren Station on the Holmenkollen rail line, has by far the best view of the city and its environs. The *Ski Museum* (Ski Museet) on your way up the hill is worth seeing.

Useful Information

Oslo Tourist Information, Radhuset (City Hall) (tel:42-7170); *U.S. Embassy*, Drammensveien 18 (tel:44-8550); *Taxi* (tel:348); *American Express* c/o Winge Travel, Karl Johans Gate 33 (tel:42-9150); *Police* (tel:002); *Post Office*, Dronningensgate 15 (tel:40-7823; *Voltage Guide*, 220 V, two round-pin outlets are used.

Special Trips/Tours

Harbor Sightseeing Tours, boats leave the piers in front of City Hall. The *Vestfjord Cruise*, lasting two hours, daily from May to mid-Sept., is popular. Boats also leave from the pier opposite City Hall.

About two hours S of Oslo are the two old whaling ports of *Sandefjord* and *Tonsberg*. See the Verstfold Folk Museum in Tonsberg, along with the fortress. In Sandefjord, visit the *Whaling Museum*.

Weather

Oslo's weather is changeable throughout the year. Summer daytime high temperatures are typically in the high 60s or low 70s, falling to the 50s at night. Winter daytime high temperatures usually reach into the high 20s or low 30s, dropping to the high teens at night. Summer is the rainy season.

OSLO: TEMPERATURES AND PRECIPITATION

Month	J	F	M	A	M	J	J	A	S	O	N	D
Average Daily Temperature												
(Fahrenheit) Max.	28	30	39	50	61	68	72	70	60	48	38	32
Min.	19	19	25	34	43	50	55	53	46	38	31	25
Average Number of Days with Precipitation												
	15	12	9	11	10	13	15	14	14	14	16	17

Warsaw (Warszawa): Poland

Sights to See

Old Town (Stare Miasto), restored after the destruction of WW II, particularly the central *Rynek Starego Miasta*, or market square, one of the finest in eastern Europe with its re-created Baroque houses.

Historical Museum of the City of Warsaw (Muzeum Historyczne Miasta Warszawy), Rynek Starego Miasta 48. Known for its scale models of Warsaw from prehistoric to modern times.
Cathedral of St. John, just S of Rynek Starego Miasta off ul. Swietojanska. A rebuilt 14th-century Gothic church noted for its tombs of famous Poles.
Madame Curie-Sklodowaka Museum, ul. Freta 16 just NW of the Rynek. Madame Curie's birthplace, filled with memorabilia.
Royal Castle, pl. Zamkowy, SE of the Rynek, Old Town. Originally built between the 14th and 18th centuries and destroyed during WW II, this recently restored palace is one of Europe's most attractive. The symbol of Warsaw, *King Sigismund's Column,* sits in front.
Monument to the Heroes of the Ghetto, ul. Zamenhofa & ul. Anielewicza, just W of Old Town. Commemorates those who died in the Jewish ghetto that was destroyed by the Nazis in WW II.
National Museum (Muzeum Narodowe), ul. Jeorzolimskie 3, SW of Old Town. Noted for its superb collection of 8th- to 12th-century Coptic art and Polish art of the last 200 years. Open Tu–Sa.
Palace of Culture (Palac Kultury), pl. Defilad, off Marszalkowska, W of the National Museum. Housing theaters, restaurants, meeting halls, and scientific institutions, this skyscraper's interest lies more in the spectacular views it offers from its observation terrace, rather than any intrinsic qualities.
The Royal Route, between the Royal Castle and Lazienkowski Palace, further to the S along ul. Krakowskie-Przedmiescie, ul. Nowy Swaiat, Al. Ujazdowskie. Lined with historic residences, Baroque churches, palaces, ancient monuments, and fine restored or reconstructed buildings.
Frederick Chopin Museum, (Muzeum Towarzystwa im. Fryderyka Chopina), Academy of Fine Arts, ul. Krakowskie-Przedmiescie 5. Reconstructed interior of Chopin's home.
Lazienkowski Palace and Park, al. Ujazdowskie at the end of the Royal Route. Home to the last of Poland's kings, and known for its collection of 17th- and 18th-century art. Do spend some time in the gracious surrounding park.

Useful Information

Tourist Offices: ORBIS, ul. Bracka 16 (tel:26-0271); *Tourist Office* (ALMA-TUR), ul. Kopernika 23 (tel:26-3512); *U.S. Embassy,* Aleje Ujazdowskie 29/31 (tel:28-3041); *American Express,* c/o ORBIS, Marszalkwska 142; *Post Office,* Swietokrzyska & Jasna; *Police* (tel:997); *Voltage Guide,* 220 V, two round-pin outlets are used.

Special Trips/Tours

Wilanow Palace and Park. This Baroque palace on the S side of Warsaw, former residence of King Jan Sobieski, has a particularly fine collection of antiques and paintings. Further S, on the same road, is the medieval castle of *Czersk.*

If you have more time, **Kracow,** the former capital of Poland, and one of Europe's most beautiful medieval towns (undamaged by WW II), is about 200 miles S. The city's *Wawel,* a 16th-century castle, is worth the trip alone. Its paintings, furniture, tapestries, and architectural splendor are a sight to behold.

WARSAW: TEMPERATURES AND PRECIPITATION

Month	J	F	M	A	M	J	J	A	S	O	N	D
Average Daily Temperature												
(Fahrenheit) Max.	32	32	42	53	67	73	75	73	66	55	42	35
Min.	22	21	28	37	48	54	58	56	49	41	33	28
Average Number of Days with Precipitation												
	15	14	11	13	11	13	16	13	12	12	12	16

Lisbon (Lisboa): Portugal

Sights to See

The Alfama, the old Moorish quarter, situated between the Tagus River and St. George's castle. It is relatively easy to get momentarily lost in this old district of Lisbon, but the balconies, archways, courtyards, terraces, and people that you will encounter are delightful. *Miradouro de Santo Luzia* square offers magnificent views of the Alfama and harbor.
St. George's Castle (Castelo Sao Jorge), Rua Costa do Castelo. Its ramparts afford excellent views. Enjoy the gardens within the castle. Open 8–sunset daily.
Lisbon Cathedral, Largo da Se, S of St. George's Castle. Dating from the 12th century. Noted for its ambulatory and tombs.
Praca do Comercio (Black Horse Square), SW of the cathedral on the banks of the Tagus River. Well-proportioned square lined with classical buildings.
National Museum of Ancient Art (Museu Nacional de Arte Antiga), Rua das Janelas Verdes 95, W of Praca do Comercio. Full of treasures. Open 10–5 Tu–Su.
Praca Rossio, NW of St. George's Castle. The city's main square, complete with bronze fountains, flower vendors, and a statue of Dom Pedro IV.
Avenida da Liberdade, NW of Praca Rossio. Lisbon's Champs-Elysees, with a mixture of art nouveau and modern buildings.
Gulbenkian Foundation Museum (Museu Calouste Gulbenkian), Av. de Berna, N of Praco Marques de Pombal. Excellent collection of French Impressionists and contemporary Portuguese artists. Open 10–5 Tu–Su.
Belem section of Lisbon, W of central Lisbon. Escaped much of the 1755 earthquake damage to the rest of Lisbon, it consequently has some of the best-preserved architecture.
Jeronimos Monastery (Mosteiro dos Jeronimos), Praco do Imperio, Belem. Probably the finest example of the Manueline style (Portugal's unique contribu-

tion to architecture), it is noted for its intricately sculptured cloisters and south portal.

Belem Tower (Torre de Belem), Av. Marginal, Belem, SW of the monastery. A five-story Renaissance tower (Gothic inside) marking the spot from which the great Portuguese discoverers of the 15th centuries sailed, with great views of the city.

National Coach Museum, Praco Afonso de Albuquerque, Belem, SE of the monastery. Luxury and state coaches from the 17th to 19th centuries. Open 10–5 Tu–Su.

A Bullfight at Cascais Praca da Touros, from April to October, usually on Sundays. (NOTE: bulls are not killed in Portuguese fights.)

Useful Information

Palacio Foz (Tourist Information), Praca dos Restauradores (tel:346-3643); *Directorate General for Tourism* (Direccao-Geraldo Turismo), Av. Antonio Augusto de Aguiar 86 (tel:57-5091); *U.S. Embassy,* Av. das Forca Armadas (tel:726-6600); *American Express,* Star Travel Service, Praca dos Restauradores 14 (tel:53-9871); *Police* (tel:115 or 36-6141); *Post Office,* Praca do Comercio (tel:346-3231); *Voltage Guide,* 220 V, two round-pin outlets are used.

Special Trips/Tours

Queluz Palace, Portugal's Versailles, is just 10 miles outside Lisbon. Dating from the 18th century, it is noted for its beautiful gardens. In summer, chamber music concerts are held in the palace. Open 10–5 W–M. *Estoril and Cascais,* 16 and 20 miles W of Lisbon, respectively, are also worth visiting. The former has a gambling casino, nightclubs, and glamour, while the latter rivals St. Tropez as a chic beach resort. *Sintra,* with its two palaces, the *National Palace,* built on the ruins of a Moorish fortress, and *Pena Palace,* is only some 20 miles NW of Lisbon.

Weather

Lisbon enjoys a Mediterranean climate. Summer daytime high temperatures are typically in the high 70s or low 80s, falling to the 60s at night. Winter daytime highs reach the mid to high 50s, dropping to the 40s at night. Winter is the wet season.

LISBON: TEMPERATURES AND PRECIPITATION

Month	J	F	M	A	M	J	J	A	S	O	N	D
Average Daily Temperature												
(Fahrenheit) Max.	57	59	63	67	71	77	81	82	79	72	63	58
Min.	46	47	50	53	55	60	63	63	62	58	52	47
Average Number of Days with Precipitation												
	15	12	14	10	10	5	2	2	6	9	13	15

Bucharest (Bucuresti): Romania

Sights to See

Cismigiu Park, in central Bucharest. A fine example of why Bucharest is sometimes referred to as "the Paris of the Balkans." The park has lakes, gardens, springs, fountains, grottoes, and beautiful meandering walkways.
National Art Museum (Muzeul de Arta S.R.R.), Str. Stirbei Voda, E of Cismigiu Gardens. Extensive collection of Romanian and Western classical art, housed in the former Royal Palace.
Romanian Athenaeum, off Calea Victoriei, NE of the National Art Museum. A Neoclassical structure housing Bucharest's beautiful concert hall. It is especially noted for its elaborate interior.
National History Museum (Muzeul de Istoriei de Romania), Calea Victoriei 12, S of the National Art Museum. Noted for its collection of ancient Romanian gold objects.
Folk Art Museums (Muzeul de Arta Populara), Calea Victoriei. Good collection of folk art objects.
George Enescu Museum, Calea Victoriei 141. Interesting exhibits devoted to the Romanian composer.
Theodor Aman Museum, Calea A. Rosetti 8. The life and work of this Romanian painter are displayed.
Village Museum, on the edge of Herastrau Park (Parcul Herastrau) in Soseaua Kiseloff, N of Piata Victoriei. An open-air museum, it has examples of village architecture from all over Romania. The peasant homes are fully furnished.
Minovici Museum of Feudal Art, Dr. Minovici Str. 3, near Herastrau Park. Interesting feudal collection.

Useful Information

ONT (National Tourist Office), Blvd. Magheru 7 (tel:14-5160), and Gare du Nord train station (tel:052); *Police* (tel:055 or 061 in emergency); *U.S. Embassy,* Strada Tudor Arghezi 7–9 (tel:10-4040), near the Intercontinental Hotel; *Romanian Automobile Club,* Blvd. Poligrafiei 3; *American Express,* at the ONT Office, Blvd. Magheru 7; *Voltage Guide,* 110/220 V, two round-pin outlets are used.

Special Trips/Tours

Mogosoaia Palace, some 9 miles W of central Bucharest in the countryside, makes a pleasant trip. Formerly the palace of Prince Brancoveanu, this ornate, early-18th-century structure now houses a museum of feudal art.
About three hours N of Bucharest by car or train, across the Transylvania Alps, is the medieval city of *Brasov.* Noteworthy sights include the *Black Church,* Cutea Bisericii Negre, noted for its Gothic architecture and 19th-century calliope. Brasov is also a good base for visiting the *Castle of Bran,* often,

erroneously, thought to be the home of Count Dracula. He did, apparently, spend some time there. The nearby resort town of *Poiana Brasov* is worth lingering in.

Weather

Bucharest experiences a continental-type climate with cold, snowy winters and warm to hot summers. Summer daytime high temperatures usually reach the mid 80s, falling into the low 60s or high 50s at night. Winter daytime highs are typically in the upper 30s, dropping to the low 20s or high teens at night. Late spring and summer are the wettest seasons, with July normally being the wettest month. Winter precipitation comes in the form of snow.

BUCHAREST: TEMPERATURES AND PRECIPITATION

Month	J	F	M	A	M	J	J	A	S	O	N	D
Average Daily Temperature												
(Fahrenheit) Max.	34	38	50	64	74	81	86	85	78	65	49	39
Min.	19	23	30	41	51	57	60	59	52	43	35	26
Average Number of Days with Precipitation												
	11	9	9	11	13	12	10	7	5	7	12	10

Leningrad: Soviet Union

Sights to See

State Hermitage: Winter Palace (Godudarstvenni Ermitazh: Zimnniy Dvoryets), entered from the Dvorcovaja embankment. Unquestionably one of the finest collections of art and antiquities in the world in a magnificent building noted for its huge rooms and long halls. *Malachite Hall,* where the czar entertained, is quite spectacular. Open 10:30–6 Tu–Su.

Summer Gardens, Kutuzov Embankment (Naberezhnaya Kutuzova). A large park, with a summer palace for Peter the Great, laid out in 1704. Noted for its classical sculptures. Open daily. The palace is open daily, except Tu, May–Nov.

Palace Square (Dvortsovaya Pl.), between the Winter Palace and the Admiralty Building. Site of Bloody Sunday in 1905 and the storming of the Winter Palace in October 1917.

St. Isaac's Cathedral (Isaakievsky Sobor), Isaakyevskaya Square. Noted for its huge, gold-covered dome, which also affords a superb view of Leningrad. Open 11–6 W–Tu.

Peter the Great Monument, Decemberists Square (Dekabristov Pl.). Falconet's statue, which inspired Pushkin's famous poem, "The Bronze Horseman."

Peter and Paul Fortress (Petropavlovskaya Krepost), on an island in the Neva River. Originally built in 1703 to protect St. Petersburg from the Swedes, it became a political prison under the czar, where many a revolutionary was jailed. Inside the fortress is the *Peter and Paul Cathedral* (Petropavlovsky Sobor), noted for its tall, thin golden spire. Open 10–6 Th–Tu in summer; shorter hours off-season.

Russian Museum (Gosudarstvenni Russky Musei), Inzhenernaya Ul 4/2. Excellent collection of traditional Russian art from the 10th century to the present. Open 10–6 W–M. Also see the *Ethnographical Museum of the Peoples of the USSR*, in a wing of the Russian Museum. Open Tu–Su.

Piskarevskoye Memorial Cemetery, Piskarevsky Prospekt in the NE part of Leningrad. Burial site for the 500,000 victims of the WW II blockade.

Useful Information

Intourist Service Bureau, Leningrad Hotel, Vyborgskaya Naberzhnaya 7 (tel:542-0616); *U.S. Consulate,* Ul. Petra Lavraova 15 (tel:274-8235); *Post Office,* Ul. Soyuza Sviazi 9; *American Express,* Ul. Gertsena 36 (tel:311-5215); *Theater Information* (tel:542-0777); *Voltage Guide,* 220 V, two flat, parallel-blade or two round-pin outlets are used.

Special Trips/Tours

Petrodvorets, the Russian Versailles, begun by Peter the Great, is 30 minutes away from central Leningrad by hydrofoil. Perhaps more interesting than the Grand Palace itself are the 300-acre park that surrounds it and the incredible systems of fountains that are scattered around the park and gardens. Watch out for the "joke fountains!" Open 11–6 Tu–Su, closed the last Tu of each month. Hydrofoils leave from the dock in front of the Winter Palace.

The *Pavlovsk Palace,* a gift from Catherine II to her son Paul in 1777, is just outside Pushkin (the Czar's village), some 15 miles S of Leningrad. Open Sa–W. In Pushkin itself is the *Catherine (Yekaterininsky) Palace,* a Baroque masterpiece noted for its exquisite interior, and fanciful stucco moldings and lacy balcony grilles on its exterior.

Weather

Leningrad enjoys one of the mildest climates in the Soviet Union. Summer daytime high temperatures typically reach into the high 60s, dropping to the mid 50s at night. Winters tend to be rather drab, with very little sunshine, and cold. Daytime highs usually reach into the 20s, falling to the low teens and below at night. Summer is the wettest season, with July and August normally receiving the most rain.

LENINGRAD: TEMPERATURES AND PRECIPITATION

Month	J	F	M	A	M	J	J	A	S	O	N	D
Average Daily Temperature												
(Fahrenheit) Max.	19	22	32	46	59	68	70	69	60	48	35	26
Min.	8	11	18	33	42	51	55	55	47	39	28	18
Average Number of Days with Precipitation												
	21	17	14	12	13	12	13	14	17	18	18	22

Moscow (Moskva): Soviet Union

Sights to See

Red Square (Krasnaya Ploshchad), the centerpiece of Moscow and site of the May Day and Revolution Memorial Day parades. It is surrounded by the Kremlin, the Lenin Mausoleum, St. Basil's Cathedral, and GUM, Moscow's huge department store.

Lenin's Mausoleum (Mausolei V. I. Lenin), Red Square. A red granite structure housing Lenin's body. Catch the changing of the guard ceremony, held every hour.

The Kremlin, seat of the Soviet government overlooking Red Square. This huge complex, surrounded by a wall 20 ft. high, contains the *Grand Kremlin Palace,* meeting place of the Supreme Soviet of the U.S.S.R. (not open to the public); *Cathedral Square,* site of three multidomed Russian Orthodox cathedrals (Annunciation, Archangel, and Assumption) which now are museums; and the Armory Museum, full of czarist treasures. Try and get the separate tickets for the Museum's Diamond Fund section.

St. Basil's Cathedral (Pokrovsky Sobor), Red Square. Perhaps Russia's most famous building with its brilliant onion-shaped domes. Commissioned by Ivan the Terrible in the 16th century. The interior is noted for its frescoed chapels. Open 9:30–5:30 W–M.

GUM, Red Square. Russia's largest department store.

Tretyakov Gallery (Gosudarstvennaya Tretakovskaya Galereya), near the Novokuznetskaya Metro Station, across the Moskva from the Kremlin. Probably the best collection of icons, Russian paintings, and sculpture. Open 10–8 Tu–Su.

Novodyevichy Convent, Novodyevichy Proyed & Bolshaya Pirogovskaya, near the Sportivnaya Metro Station. The convent's Smolensk Cathedral houses a fine applied arts museum and is a particularly beautiful structure itself. Open 10:30–5:30 daily.

Pushkin Museum of Fine Arts (Gosudarstvenni Musei Izobrazitelnikh Iskusstv im A. S. Pushkina), near the Kropotkinskaya Metro Station. Fine collection of Oriental and European Renaissance art and modern French paintings. Open 12:30–7:30 W–F, 10–5 Sa–Su.

Exhibition of Economic Achievements (Vistavka Dostizheny Narodnono Khozyaistva SSSR-VDNC), Prospect Mira, near the VDNKH Metro Station. Varied hours.

Moscow's Metro. The stations are immaculately clean and decorated with original art. If you can only see one, make it the Mayakovskaya station.

Useful Information

Central Intourist Office, Prospekt Marksa 16 (tel:229-4206); *Central Excursion Bureau,* Ul. Gor'kova 3–5, next to the Intourist Hotel at Ul. Gor'kova 3–5 (tel:203-6962); *Taxi* (tel:225-0000, or 227-0040); *American Express,* Ul. Sadovaya-Kuringskaya 21A (tel:254-4305); *U.S. Embassy,* Ul. Chaikovskovo 19–23 (tel:252-2451); *Post Office,* Ul. Gor'kova 7; *Voltage Guide,* 220 V, two flat, parallel-blade or two round-pin outlets are used.

Special Trips/Tours

A boat trip on the Moskva River is a good way to get a feel for Moscow's impressive architecture. Hour-long trips leave the pier near the Kiev Metro Station. The *Arkhangelskoye Estate,* an architectural monument of the 18th and 19th centuries set in a very picturesque park with pavilions, sculptures, and decorative stairways, is 10 miles from central Moscow. The museum inside the palace has a good collection of European paintings and sculptures. Open 10–5 W–Su, May–Sept. Closed on the last Friday of each month.

Weather

Moscow's summer daytime high temperatures typically reach into the low 70s, dropping to the mid 50s at night. Winter daytime highs usually are in the high teens or 20s, falling to the low teens or lower at night. The summer months normally get the most precipitation, although it is fairly frequent all year.

MOSCOW: TEMPERATURES AND PRECIPITATION

Month	J	F	M	A	M	J	J	A	S	O	N	D
Average Daily Temperature												
(Fahrenheit) Max.	15	22	32	50	66	70	73	72	61	48	35	24
Min.	3	8	18	34	46	51	55	53	45	37	26	15
Average Number of Days with Precipitation												
	18	15	15	13	13	12	15	14	13	15	13	23

Barcelona: Spain

Sights to See

Barcelona Cathedral (La Seu), Barrio Gotico. Catalan Gothic building known for its fretted spires, lacy windows, and cloisters covered with semitropical vegetation. Views from the SW tower are excellent.
Federico Mares Museum, next to the cathedral. Housed in what was formerly the Royal Palace of the Counts of Barcelona, it has a superb sculpture collection.
Gothic Quarter (Barrio Gotico), the old medieval area of tiny streets surrounding the cathedral. Full of antique shops, people, and street musicians.
Ramblas Boulevards, or promenades, actually composed of five separate boulevards that replaced the city walls that once circled the old town. An elegant street, with outdoor cafes, bird and flower markets, and crowds of people, stretching from the Plaza de Cataluna to the port.
Picasso Museum (Museo Picasso), E of the cathedral in the Gothic Palau Aguilar on Calle Montcada. Traces the chronology of the artist's work. Open 9:30–2 & 4:30–8 Tu–Sa, 9:30–2 Su.

Temple of the Holy Family (Templo Expiatori de la Sagrada Familia), Plaza de la Sagrada Familia, N of the cathedral. Antonio Gaudi's partially completed neo-Gothic church famous for its Nativity facade. Take the elevator to the towers. Open 9–9 daily.
Museum of Catalonian Art (Museo de Arte de Cataluna), National Palace, Montjuich Park, on the S side of the city. Contains Romanesque and Gothic artifacts from small churches all over Catalonia. Probably the best collection of Romanesque paintings in the world. Open 9–2 Tu–Su.
Spanish Village (Pueblo Espanol), Montjuich Park. See artisans and craftsmen at work in this reconstructed village. During the summer at night, the fountains in the park are illuminated with changing color lights. Ride the cable car from Miramar on Montjuich Hill, to La Barceloneta for a great view of the city.
Archeological Museum (Museo Arqueologico), Montjuich Park. Known for its Roman and Greek exhibits. Open 9:30–1, 4–7 Tu–Sa, 9:30–2 Su.

Useful Information

Tourist Information Office, Gran Via de las Cortes Catalanas 658 (tel:301-7443) and Plaza de San Jaime (tel:318-2525); *U.S. Consulate,* Via Layetana 33 (tel:319-9550); *American Express,* Passeig de Gracia 101 (tel:217-0070); *Police* (tel:091 in emergencies); *Taxi* (tel:300-3811, 330-0804); *Post Office,* Pl. d'Antoni Lopez; *Voltage Guide,* 220 V, two flat parallel-blade, or two round-pin outlets are used.

Special Trips/Tours

Montserrat (Montsagrat), the sacred mountain, about 37 miles NW of Barcelona, is one of Spain's principal tourist attractions. The Benedictine *Montserrat Monastery,* reached by cableway from the road above the village of Collbato, was founded in the 9th century. The new monastery, begun in 1765, is noted for its *Basilica* with a wooden image of the Virgin (Santa Imagen, or *Black Madonna*), which has attracted pilgrims for centuries. The monastery's library and museums are also noteworthy. The views from the *Turo de San Jeronimo* peak (4,000 ft.), above the monastery, are magnificent.
   If you have more time on your hands, the *Costa Brava,* Spain's own Riviera, is between Barcelona and the French border to the north. With a spectacular coastline, it is one of the most popular vacation areas in Europe, with excellent hotels, exciting nightlife, and, of course, the beach. If you go, visit *Alicante,* the area's main town, known for its Moorish castle.

Weather

Barcelona enjoys a Mediterranean climate with mild winters and hot, dry summers. Summer daytime highs typically reach the high 70s and low 80s. Rainfall is low, although heavy downpours of thundery rain are characteristic of this coastal area. Fall tends to be the wettest season. Winter temperatures reach the mid to high 50s, falling to the mid 40s at night.

BARCELONA: TEMPERATURES AND PRECIPITATION

Month	J	F	M	A	M	J	J	A	S	O	N	D
Average Daily Temperature												
(Fahrenheit) Max.	55	57	60	65	71	78	82	82	77	69	62	56
Min.	43	45	48	52	57	65	69	69	66	58	51	46
Average Number of Days with Precipitation												
	5	5	8	9	8	6	4	6	7	9	6	6

Cordoba: Spain

Sights to See

Mosque-Cathedral (Mezquita-Catedral), between Cardenal Gonzales and Cardenal Herrero. Once the principal mosque of the western Islamic world, it still is one of the world's largest mosques. Begun in 785 and later enlarged, it was converted to a cathedral in the 13th century, resulting in a mix of architectural styles. It is noted for its impressive interior with over 850 columns, its Patio de los Naranjos (Courtyard of Orange Trees), its colorful carved roof structure, and its Mihrab (chapel-shrine). The top of the 16th-century tower affords excellent views of Cordoba. Open 10:30–1:30, 4–7 daily.

Alcazar (Alcazar de los Reyes Cristianos), just SW of the Mezquita-Catedral. This 14th-century fortress with massive walls and towers is known for its beautiful gardens, which are illuminated at night, and for its Moorish baths. Open 9:30–1:30, 5–8 daily.

Roman Bridge (Puente Romano), over the Guadalquivir river, S of the Mezquita-Catedral. Actually a Moorish bridge built over the Roman foundations.

Tower of the Calahorra (Torre de la Calahorra), at the S end of the Roman bridge. A huge Arab defensive tower now housing the Municipal Museum. Open 9:30–1:30, 5–8 daily.

Synagogue, Calle Judio, Jewish Quarter (Barrio Judio), just NW of the Mezquita-Catedral. Dating from the 14th century, it is noted for its plaster work, characteristic of the Mudejar art of the period. Open 9:30–1:30, 3:30–6:30 daily.

Municipal Museum of Bullfighting (Museo Taurino), Plaza Bulas, opposite the Synagogue. Interesting collection of bullfighting memorabilia. Open 9:30–1:30, 4–7 Tu–Sa, 9:30–1:30 Su.

Almodovar Gate (Puerta de Almodovar), just N of the Synagogue. A well-preserved Moorish gate that governed access to the Jewish ghetto.

Julio Romero de Torres Museum, Plaza del Potro, NE of the Mezquita-Catedral. Devoted to the works of the city's most famous artist, known for his paintings of nude women. Open 10–2 daily.

Provincial Archaeological Museum (Museo Arqueologico Provincial), Plaza Jeronimo Paez, a few blocks NW of Plaza Bulas. Fine collection of Iberian, Visigothic, and Moorish artifacts. Open 10–2, 5–8 Tu–Sa, 10–2 Su.

Marquis of Viana Palace (Palacio de los Marqueses de Viana), Plaza de Don

Gome, N of the archaeological museum and E of Plaza de Colon. Noted for its beautiful patios and leatherwork collection. Open 9–2 daily in summer.

Useful Information

Provincial Tourist Office, C. Torrijos 10 (tel:47-1235); *Municipal Tourist Office,* 3 Plaza de Juda Levi (tel:29-0740); closest *U.S. Embassy/Consulate* is in Madrid, at Serrano 75 (tel:1/276-3400); *Police* (tel:29-3537); *Post Office,* Calle Cruz Conde 15 (tel:47-8267); *Voltage Guide:* 110/220 V, two flat, parallel-blade or two round-pin outlets are used.

Special Trips/Tours

Just 4 miles W of Cordoba are the ruins of **Medina Azahara,** the Versailles of Cordoba, built in the 10th century. In this palace-town built by a 10th-century caliph, are interesting exhibits of ceramic, ornamental, and wrought-iron pieces taken from the excavations in the Medina Azahara Museum at the site. The **Cordovan Mountains** just behind Cordoba also have a number of other worthwhile points of interest as well as affording the opportunity to see the countryside. These include the Gothic cloister at the 15th-century *Monastery of San Jeronimo de Valparaiso;* the castle of *Almodovar del Rio;* and *Las Ermitas,* a group of hermitages.

Following all, or part, of the **Wine Highway** (Ruta del Vino), which passes through a series of delightful villages and towns, makes another good side trip. The route passes by *Montemayor,* off the Seville road, with its castle; *Moriles* and *Montilla,* further S, two towns famous for their wines; and, further S still, *Aquilar de la Frontera,* with several fine churches, notably the Santa Maria de Soterrano and Nuestra Senora del Carmen and fine Plaza San Jose. *Lucena,* a center of the Andalusian wine trade, is further along the route, and has a noteworthy church, San Matero. All along the way, you can visit the wine cellars, bodegas, and wine-tasting rooms.

Weather

Cordoba has one of the hottest climates in Europe. Summer daytime high temperatures are typically in the high 90s, falling to the upper 60s at night. Winter daytime highs are usually in the low 60s, dropping to the low 40s at night. October through March is the "wet" season, although rainfall is low all year.

CORDOBA: TEMPERATURES AND PRECIPITATION

Month	J	F	M	A	M	J	J	A	S	O	N	D
Average Daily Temperature												
(Fahrenheit) Max.	59	63	69	74	80	90	98	97	90	78	68	60
Min.	42	44	48	52	56	63	67	68	64	57	50	44
Average Number of Days with Precipitation												
	8	6	9	7	6	1	0	0	2	6	7	8

Granada: Spain

Sights to See

Alhambra, a huge complex of palaces, military fortifications, and gardens built by the Moors in the 13th and 14th centuries, comprised of over 50 courts, pavilions, gates, towers, halls, and palaces. The most notable sights within the Alhambra are listed here.

Charles V's Palace (Palacio de Carlos V), Alhambra, just inside the main entrance, the Gate of Justice, on the E side of the Plaza de los Alijibes. It is considered to be the best example of Renaissance architecture in Spain.

Museum of Fine Arts (Museo Provincial de Bellas Artes), Palacio de Carlos V. Fine collection of paintings and sculpture. Open 10–2 M–Sa.

Alhambra Museum (Museo de la Alhambra), Palacio de Carlos V. Devoted to Hispanic-Muslim art. Open 10–2 M–Sa.

Palace of the Alhambra (Palacio Arabe), N of Palacio de Carlos V, Alhambra. Dating from the 14th century, it is noted for its superb Islamic palace architecture, exemplified in its Court of Myrtles (Patio de los Arrayanes), Hall of the Ambassadors (Sala de los Ambassadores), Hall of the Two Sisters (Sala de las Dos Hermanas), Court of Lions (Patio de los Leones), and the beautiful Patio de Daraxa.

Alcazaba, at the W tip of the Alhambra. The oldest part of the complex, a 9th-century Moorish fortress, it lies in ruins with only its outer walls and massive towers still standing.

Ladies' Tower (Torre de las Damas), just E of the Hall of the Two Sisters outside the Alhambra Palace. Probably the best of the Alhambra's many towers.

Generalife (Palacio del Generalife), located on Cerro del Sol, overlooking the Alhambra, just to its east. The summer palace of the Moorish kings, it was completed in 1319, and is especially noted for its *Patio de la Acequia* and beautiful gardens. NOTE: both the Alhambra and Generalife are open daily, although some rooms are not open on Sunday. From May to September the buildings are usually illuminated every Saturday evening between 10 and 12.

Cathedral (Santa Maria de la Encarnacion), W of the Alhambra, across Calle de los Reyes Catolicos. Dating from the 16th century, it is considered to be Spain's finest Renaissance-style church and is best known for its paintings, stained glass, and richly decorated interior. The *Royal Chapel* (Capilla Real), on the S side of the cathedral, was built in late Gothic style as the mausoleum of the Catholic Monarchs Ferdinand and Isabella. Both open 11–1, 4–7 daily.

La Cartuja, Calle Real de la Cartuja, in the suburbs of Granada. A splendid Carthusian monastery known for its Baroque sacristy. Open 10–1, 3–7 daily.

Useful Information

Tourist Office, C. de Libreros 2 (tel:22-1022); closest *U.S. Embassy or Consulate* is in Madrid, at Serrano 75 (tel:1/276-3400); *American Express*, Viajes Bonal, Av. Calvo Sotelo 19 (tel:27-6312); *Police* (tel:27-8300); *Post Office*, Puerta Real, off Reyes Catolicos (tel:22-4835); *Voltage Guide:* 110/220 V, two flat parallel-blade or two round-pin outlets are used.

Special Trips/Tours

A drive into the beautiful *Sierra Nevada* range just S of Granada is rewarding. Spain's highest mountains, they reach to over 11,000 ft., the higher peaks being snow-covered much of the year. One of the tallest peaks, *Pico de Veleta* (11,388 ft.), is almost accessible by car via one of the highest mountain roads in Europe, which passes through the ski resort area of *Sol y Nieve,* and stops at 11,132 ft., just below the summit of Veleta. The revolving restaurant, or the summit itself, affords magnificent panoramas, especially to the south.

Spain's world-famous *Costa del Sol* (Coast of the Sun) stretching between Cabo de Gata and Tarifa along the Mediterranean coast of Andalusia, is just over 60 miles away over the Sierra Nevada range via the N323 to Motril. To the west is the Cave of Nerja (Cueva de Nerja) outside Nerja, famous for its paleolithic paintings, and, further still, *Malaga,* with its 16th-century *cathedral,* and 10th-century *Alcazaba* (fortress) with an archaeological museum and beautiful gardens. *Torremolinos,* Spain's Miami Beach, is just W of Malaga, with an excellent beach and active nightlife.

Weather

Granada enjoys a Mediterranean climate with hot, dry summers and mild, wetter winters. Summer daytime high temperatures typically reach into the low 80s, dropping to the low 70s or high 60s at night. Winter daytime highs are usually in the low 60s, falling to the 40s at night. Although precipitation is very low year-round, winter is the "wet" season.

GRANADA: TEMPERATURES AND PRECIPITATION

Month	J	F	M	A	M	J	J	A	S	O	N	D
Average Daily Temperature												
(Fahrenheit) Max.	60	61	64	68	72	78	83	84	81	73	67	62
Min.	46	47	51	55	59	65	70	71	68	60	54	49
Average Number of Days with Precipitation												
	6	4	5	5	3	1	0	1	3	5	4	5

Madrid: Spain

Sights to See

Prado Museum, Paseo de Prado. With over 5,000 paintings from all over Europe, the Prado has one of the world's finest collections of art. It is particularly rich in Spanish, Flemish, and Italian paintings. Open 10–5:45 Tu–Sa, 10–1:45 Su.

Plaza Mayor, located in the most picturesque part of old Madrid, this 17th-century square, built for celebrations and competitions by Philip III, is one of Europe's grandest public squares.

Plaza Puerto del Sol (Times Square of Madrid).

The streets of Old Madrid between Puerta del Sol and the Royal Palace, provide a fascinating look at a medieval city. Full of pedestrians at night.
Museum of the Royal Academy of Fine Arts of San Fernando (Museo de la Academia Real de Bellas Artes de San Fernando), C. Alcala 13, between Puerta del Sol & Plaza de la Cibeles. Superb collection of Spanish, Flemish, and Italian paintings and sculptures, including many by El Greco, Murillo, and Goya. Open 9–7 Tu–Su.
Royal Palace (Palacio Real), Calle de Bailen. A huge, 18th-century Neoclassical structure with an elegant facade. There are guided tours in English, and during the summer, a sound and light show in the Sabatini Gardens. Open 10–12:45 and 4–5:45 M–Sa, 10–12:45 Su.
Royal Armory (Armeria), in the southwest wing of the Royal Palace. Probably the world's greatest collection of armor, including grisly torture gadgetry. Open the same hours as the Palace.
National Archaeological Museum (Museo Arqueologico Nacional), Calle Serrano 13. Excellent Iberian, Greek, Phoenician, Carthaginian, Roman, Muslim, and medieval items. See the life-size reproductions of prehistoric cave paintings from Altamira. Open 9:30–1:30, 4–8 Tu–Su.
Museo Lazaro Galdiano, C. Serrano 122, housed in a turn-of-the-century palace has another excellent collection, especially of paintings and antiques. Open 10–2 Tu–Su. Closed in August.

Useful Information

Municipal Office of Tourist Information, Plaza Mayor 3 (tel:266-5477); *National Tourist Office,* C. Princesa 1, Pl. de Espana (tel:241-2325); *U.S. Embassy,* C. Serrano 75 (tel:276-3400); *American Express,* 2 Plaza de las Cortes (tel:429-2875); *Police* (tel:091); *Post Office,* Pl. de la Cibeles (tel:521-8195); *Voltage Guide:* 220 V, two flat parallel-blade, or two round-pin outlets are used.

Special Trips/Tours

The *bullfighting season* in Madrid runs from April to October. Fights are on most Sundays and frequently on Thursdays, with starting times varying throughout the late afternoon. The large main ring is the *Plaza de Toros* at Ventas. Tickets can be bought at the ring or from the "taquillas" on Calle de la Victoria.

The monastery-palace-mausoleum *San Lorenzo de El Escorial* in the foothills of the Sierra De Guadarrama, 30 miles NW of Madrid, built in the 16th century, is definitely worth a trip.

Weather

Summers are generally hot and dry. Daytime highs reach the mid to high 80s in the summer. Winters have frequent cold spells, but daytime highs usually get into the upper 40s. Spring and early summer are the wettest times of the year.

MADRID: TEMPERATURES AND PRECIPITATION

Month	J	F	M	A	M	J	J	A	S	O	N	D
Average Daily Temperature												
(Fahrenheit) Max.	47	52	59	65	70	80	87	85	77	65	55	48
Min.	35	36	41	45	50	58	63	63	57	49	42	36
Average Number of Days with Precipitation												
	8	7	10	9	10	5	2	3	6	8	9	10

Seville: Spain

Sights to See

Cathedral, just S of the Plaza de San Francisco. Dating from the early 15th century, it is one of the world's largest and richest Gothic cathedrals, and is noted for its impressive interior, its Capilla Real (with its woodcarving), Patio de los Naranjos (Court of Orange Trees), paintings (Montanes's crucifix), and altarpieces. Open 10:30–1:30 and 4:30–6:30 daily.

La Giralda Tower, at the NE corner of the Cathedral. Seville's principal landmark, it is a 305-ft. tower, built in the 12th century as the minaret of the Great Mosque, which was later razed. Views from the top are magnificent. Open the same hours as the cathedral.

The Alcazar, S of the cathedral on Plaza del Triumfo. A Moorish fortress that was modified in the 14th century by the Christians, it is noted for its superbly decorated interior rooms—especially the Hall of the Ambassadors (Salon de Embajadores), and the Court of the Dolls (Patio de las Munecas)—and its fine gardens. Open 9–8 daily.

Hospital de la Caridad, Plaza de Jurado, just W of the Alcazar. Founded in the late 17th century by Miguel de Manara (reputedly Don Juan), it is famous for its paintings by Valdes Leal and Murillo. Open 10–1:30, 4–7 daily.

Tower of Gold (Torre del Oro), Paseo de Colon, overlooking the Guadalquivir river. A 13th-century Moorish tower that affords fine views of Seville and contains a small Maritime Museum. Open 10–2 Tu–Sa, 10–1 Su.

Town Hall (Ayuntamiento), Plaza de San Francisco, N of the Cathedral. A fine Renaissance building noted for its Plateresque east front.

Casa de Pilatos, Plaza de Pilatos, NE of the Ayuntameinto. One of the finest of Seville's many palaces, it was built in 1540 and is known for its Mudejar architectural style and beautiful patio.

Museum of Fine Arts (Museo de Bellas Artes), Pl. del Museo, W of Casa de Pilatos. One of Spain's most important art museums, especially noted for its collection of works by Murillo, Leal, and Zurbaran. Open 10–2, 4–7 Tu–F, 10–2 Sa–Su.

Santa Cruz Quarter (Barrio de Santa Cruz), between Plaza Triunfo and Jardines de Murillo, E and NE of the Alcazar. A labyrinth of narrow, picturesque streets with beautiful courtyards full of flowers.

Maria Luisa Park (Parque de Maria Luisa), S of Plaza de Juan de Austria. Full of tiled fountains, flowers and shrubs, and pavilions left over from the Spanish-American Exhibition of 1929. The Plaza de Espana and Palacio Centrale on its NE side is especially attractive.

Archaeological Museum (Museo Arqueologio Provincial), Plaza de America, Maria Luisa Park, in the S part of central Seville. Good collection of prehistoric and Roman antiquities. Open 10–2 Tu–Su.

Useful Information

Tourist Office, 21b Avenida de la Constitucion (tel:22-1404); *American Express,* Viajes Alhambra, 3 Coronel Sequi (tel:21-2923); the closest *U.S. Embassy/ Consulate* is in Madrid, at C. Serrano 75 (tel:1/276-3400); *Post Office,* 32 Avenida de la Constitucion; *Police,* Plaza de la Gavidia (tel:22-8840 or 091 in emergency); *Voltage Guide:* 110/220 V, two flat parallel-blade or two round-pin outlets are used.

Special Trips/Tours

Just 6 miles NW of Seville near the village of Santiponce are the *Roman ruins of Italica.* Founded in 206 B.C., the remains of a huge amphitheater and traces of houses, streets, a fountain, and cisterns can be seen.

Some 20 miles NE of Seville is the ancient city of *Carmona.* Dominated by its Alcazar (fortress) and surrounded by fortified walls, it is known for its San Pedro church and the Roman cemetery (Necropolis Romana) with over 900 tombs, outside town.

The countryside around *Jerez de la Frontera,* about 70 miles SW of Seville, is famous for its vineyards, which produce some of the world's best sherries. Guided tours of the many bodegas (wine cellars) are offered, along with the obligatory sampling afterward. About 20 miles E of Jerez de la Frontera is the spectacular town of *Arcos de la Frontera,* one of the many that mark the famous *Ruta de los Pueblos Blancos* (route of the white towns), stretching from the Costa de la Luz to the Costa del Sol. Situated on a hilly outcrop with the Guadalete river flowing around it, the town is filled with whitewashed houses and narrow, winding streets. Medieval castle ruins and the 15th-century *Church of Santa Maria* make it still more appealing, but best of all are the truly superb views of the surrounding countryside.

Weather

Seville has one of the hottest climates in Europe. Summer daytime high temperatures are typically in the high 90s, falling to the upper 60s at night. Winter daytime highs are usually in the low 60s, dropping to the low 40s at night. October through March is the "wet" season, although rainfall is low year-round.

SEVILLE: TEMPERATURES AND PRECIPITATION

Month	J	F	M	A	M	J	J	A	S	O	N	D
Average Daily Temperature												
(Fahrenheit) Max.	59	63	69	74	80	90	98	97	90	78	68	60
Min.	42	44	48	52	56	63	67	68	64	57	50	44
Average Number of Days with Precipitation												
	8	6	9	7	6	1	0	0	2	6	7	8

Gothenburg (Goteborg): Sweden

Sights to See

Elfsborg Fortress, a 17th-century castle built on an island guarding the harbor. Boats leave from Stenpiren, just W of Packhus Platsen where the Stora Hamnkanal meets the Gota Alv, several times daily.

Gustav Adolfs Torg, on the N bank of the Stora Hamnkanal E of the Stenpiren. Large square with the 19th-century Exchange on its N side, and the 18th-century Town Hall, noted for its inner courtyard, on its W side.

Crown House (Kronhuset), Kronhusgaten, NW of Gustav Adolfs Torg. Dating from 1643, it is the oldest secular building in the city, and is now a historical museum.

Kronhusbodarna, next to the Crown House. Turn-of-the-century shops and handicrafts center, with craftsmen demonstrating the old techniques.

Kungsportsavenyn (Avenyn), starting at the S end of Ostra Hamngaten, S of Gustav Adolfs Torg, running SE past the Grand Theater (Stora Teatern), to Gotaplatsen. Gothenburg's main street.

Museum of Applied Art (Rohsska Konstlojdmuseet), on Vasagatan, just W of the Avenyn. Noted for its textile, furniture, glass, porcelain, gold, and silver collections.

Gotaplatsen, a large plaza at the head of Kungsportsavenyn, the city's principal boulevard, with the famous Poseidon Fountain by Carl Milles at its center.

Museum of Art (Konstmuseet), Gotaplatsen. Excellent collections of both the Old Masters and 20th-century artists. One of the best museums in Europe.

Liseberg Amusement Park, to the SE of Gotaplatsen. One of Europe's largest and finest, complete with gardens, ponds, cafes and restaurants, and amusement park rides. Open May–September.

Industrial Museums, Avagen 24, just N of Liseberg. Historical exhibits illustrate three centuries of industrial development.

Maritime Museum and Aquarium, Stigbergstorget, W of the central part of the city. Ship models from Viking to modern times. Both tropical fish and fish from Sweden's waters are on display in the aquarium.

Fish Market (Feskekorkan), Rosenlundsgaten, W of the Ship Museum. A colorful fish and seafood market. Catch the morning auction at 7 A.M. every morning.

Useful Information

The Gotesborgskortet (Key to Gothenburg), available from the Tourist Office, is a good value. It includes free use of public transport, free parking, a sightseeing trip with Paddan, a boat trip to Elfborg Fortress, a bus sightseeing trip, admission to Liseberg and all museums, and much more. *Tourist Office,* Basargaten 10 (tel:10-0740); closest *U.S. Consulate Embassy* is in Stockholm at Strandvagen 10 (tel:08/783-5300); *American Express* (tel:21-7510); *Emergency* (tel:90-000) *Voltage Guide,* 110/220 V, two round-pin outlets are used.

Special Trips/Tours

An excellent way to see Gothenburg, particularly its harbor, Sweden's largest, is to take one of the **Paddan sightseeing boats,** which cruise the city's canals and harbor. Tours leave from the dock at Kungsportsplatsen, opposite the main Tourist Office. **Elfsborg,** the 17th-century island fortress, makes another interesting excursion.

If you have the time (three days), the **Gota Canal Cruise** to Stockholm is definitely well worth it. Steamers leave from Gothenburg several times a week from May through August, winding their way through rivers, canals, and lakes. If time is a constraint, it is possible to combine part of the cruise with a train trip. For more information and tickets, contact: *Rederiaktiebolaget Gota Kanal,* Hotellplatsen 2 (tel:31-1776).

Weather

Gothenburg's weather, like that of the rest of Scandinavia, is very changeable from day to day and from season to season. Summer high temperatures typically reach into the high 60s or low 70s, dropping to the mid 50s at night. Winters are long and cold, with daytime highs usually in the mid 30s, falling to the mid 20s at night. The wet season is in late summer/early fall with July and August normally the wettest months.

GOTHENBURG: TEMPERATURES AND PRECIPITATION

Month	J	F	M	A	M	J	J	A	S	O	N	D
Average Daily Temperature												
(Fahrenheit) Max.	34	34	39	49	60	66	70	68	61	51	43	38
Min.	26	25	29	37	45	53	57	56	50	43	37	32
Average Number of Days with Precipitation												
	15	12	10	12	10	12	14	14	16	15	16	17

Stockholm: Sweden

Sights to See

Royal Palace (Kungl. Slottet), Gamla Stan. See the changing of the Guard at noon and the royal apartments and Royal Armory inside. Open 10–3 Tu–F.

Old Town (Gamla Stan), once a slum, it has been transformed into a very fashionable district with many of Sweden's snazziest antique shops, galleries, boutiques, restaurants, and people crowded into narrow, twisting, cobbled pedestrian streets.

Storkyrkan Cathedral, Gamla Stan, just SW of the Royal Palace. A 13th-century church known for its 15th-century statue of St. George and the Dragon.

Stortorget, Gamla Stan, S of the cathedral. Cobbled central square surrounded by 14th-century merchants' houses and sidewalk cafes.

Riddarholm Church, on the S side of Birger Jarlstorg, on Riddarholmen island just W of Gamla Stan. Dating from the 13th century, it is the burial place of Swedish monarchs.

National Museum, NE of the Royal Palace, at the S tip of the peninsula of Blasieholmen. Sweden's Louvre. Once a week in July and August the museum is transformed into a concert hall. Open 10–4 W–Su, 10–9 Tu.

Museum of Modern Art (Moderna Museet), Skeppsholmen, SE of the National Museum. One of Europe's best contemporary art museums, it has an excellent collection of American and European pop art. Open 11–9 Tu–F, 11–5 Sa–Su.

Skansen Open-Air Museum, Djurgarden, E of Skeppsholmen. Sweden's Williamsburg, a restoration of antique and rural Sweden. Open 11–5 daily. Visit the folk art *Nordic Museum* (Nordiska Museet).

Wasa Museum (Vasavarvet), at the W end of Djurgarden. Houses the *Wasa,* royal flagship, which sank on her maiden voyage out of Stockholm's harbor in 1628.

City Hall (Stadshuset), Hantverkargatan 1, Kungsholmen, W of Gamla Stan. Site of the Nobel Prize dinner. Excellent view of the city and some of its 14 islands from the top.

Kaknastornet, on the E edge of the city. This 508-ft. TV tower offers fantastic views of the city.

Useful Information

Swedish Tourist Association, Hamngatan 27 (tel:22-32-80), is the best place for maps, posters, guidebooks, and cultural calendars; *Emergency* (tel:900-00); *Police* (tel:769-5100); *Taxi* (tel:15-0000); *U.S. Embassy,* Strandvagen 10 (tel:783-5300); *American Express,* Birger Jarlsgaten 1 (tel:14-3981); *Sweden-House* (Stockholm Information Service and Swedish Tourist Board), Kungstradgarden (tel:789-2000); call *Miss Tourist* (tel:22-1840) for a summary of the day's events in English; most hotels have copies of *This Week in Stockholm* for a review of current events; *Tourist-Taxis* (tel:15-0400) has bilingual drivers; *Post Office,* Vasagaten 28-34; *Voltage Guide,* 220 V, two round-pin outlets are used.

For summer visitors the city is issuing *Key to Stockholm* cards (Stockhomskortets) entitling holders to unlimited free travel on buses, subways, and suburban railways. A free boat excursion to Drottningholm Palace is included.

Special Trips/Tours

Boat tours of the city that allow you to get on and off as you wish leave on the half-hour from the front of the Grand Hotel. A steamer trip to *The Skerries*, an archipelago of thousands of islands stretching from the outskirts of Stockholm 30 miles into the Baltic Sea, can be made aboard the steamer *Nooskar*, which makes the less-than-4-hour trip to Sandhamn (Sweden's Newport) daily. Do try the lunch at the *Royal Swedish Yacht Club* (open to the public).

Drottningholms Kungliga Slott (Royal Palace), on an island in Lake Malaren, sometimes referred to as Sweden's Versailles, has splendid gardens, a theater museum, and a theater. Open from April to September, 10–5:30 daily, and accessible by boat (about an hour's trip), which leaves from Klara Malarstrand, near City Hall, or from Stadhusbron.

Weather

Summer weather is very changeable in Stockholm. The high latitude produces long hours of daylight during the summer and short days in the winter. Summer temperatures reach into the high 60s or low 70s. Winter temperatures reach the mid 30s. August is the wettest month.

STOCKHOLM: TEMPERATURES AND PRECIPITATION

Month	J	F	M	A	M	J	J	A	S	O	N	D
Average Daily Temperature												
(Fahrenheit) Max.	30	30	37	47	58	67	71	68	60	49	40	35
Min.	23	22	26	34	43	51	57	56	49	41	34	29
Average Number of Days with Precipitation												
	16	14	10	11	11	13	13	14	14	15	16	17

Bern (Berne): Switzerland

Sights to See

Clock Tower (Zeitglockenturm), at the W end of Kramgasse. Dating from the 12th century, this medieval clock tower with its beautiful mechanical dancing figures is the city's focal point. Be sure to catch the mechanical show, which starts at 4 minutes before the hour.

Albert Einstein House, Kramgasse 49. Einstein lived here from 1902 to 1907. Open 10–5 Tu–Su.

Berne Cathedral (Munster), in the heart of the Old City, SE of the Clock Tower across Munstergasse. A beautiful 15th-century Gothic structure known for its long steeple. The long climb to the top of the tower will be rewarded with the best view in town. Open 10–12, 2–5 M–Sa, 11–12, 2–5 Su.

Bear Pits (Barengraben), across the Nydeggbrucke E of the cathedral. Home of Berne's heraldic animals. Open 7–6 daily in summer, 8:30–4 in winter.

Barenplatz, the city's main square, W of the Clock Tower. Enjoy a light snack or drink in one of the outdoor cafes.

Art Museum (Kunstmuseum), Holderstrasse 12, NW of Barenplatz and the Clock Tower. An excellent collection of Swiss artists and an outstanding collection of the works of Paul Klee, together with some Impressionist works. Open 10–5 W–Su, 10–9 Tu.

PTT Museum, Helvetiaplatz 4, S of the Clock Tower across the Kirchenfeldbrucke. Noted for its extensive collection of rare stamps.

Swiss Alpine Museum, Helvetiaplatz 4, adjacent to the PTT Museum. Good exhibits on the history of mountaineering and on the scenery and cultural life of the Swiss Alps.

Berne Historical Museum (Bernisches Historisches Museum), Helvetiaplatz 5, across from the Swiss Alpine and PTT museums. The city's history is interestingly portrayed. Noted also for the medieval tapestries. Open 9–5 Tu–Sa, 10–5 Su, shorter hours in winter.

Natural History Museum, Bernestrasse 15, just SSE of the Berne Historical Museum. Excellent. One of the continent's best. Noted for its many dioramas and large collection of minerals, crystals, and precious stones from the Swiss Alps.

Useful Information

Tourist Office, Railway Station (tel:22-7676); *Police* (tel:117); *American Express,* Bubenberg 11 (Tel:22-9401); *U.S. Embassy,* Jubilaumstrasse 93 (tel:43-7011); *Post Office,* Schanzenpost 1; *Voltage Guide,* 110/220 V, two round-pin outlets are used.

Special Trips/Tours

Interlaken, some 35 miles SE of Berne, is the gateway to the magnificent *Bernese Oberland* with its spectacular alpine scenery and the delightful villages and small towns along the shores of lakes Thun and Brienz. *Thun,* with its castle and street arcades, picturesque *Spiez,* and the woodcarver's town of *Brienz,* are all worth lingering in. For a really spectacular trip, though, head into the mountains to the Yosemite-like *Lauterbrunnen valley* and Murren, or to *Grindalwald,* a resort village just below Eiger.

If the weather is good—and only if it is—the railway trip to *Jungfraujoch* (11,333 ft.) is breathtaking. The Jungfrau railway climbs up, through, and inside the Eiger and Monch mountains to Jungfraujoch station, stopping at two stations on the way, each of which has huge panoramic windows. From the summit station an elevator takes you to the *Sphinz terrace* (11,720 ft.), the views from which are truly impressive. Trains leave from Interlaken E station, or Kleine Scheidegg.

Lucerne, with its medieval covered wooden bridges, houses, and beautiful town squares, famous *Glacier Gardens,* water tower, and *Lion Monument,* is a delightful city, and not far from Berne (56 mi. to the E). Of the city's many beautiful churches, the *Jesuit's Church,* a Rococo fantasy in pastels, is the most stunning.

Weather

Berne's weather is changeable at all times of the year. Summers are generally warm but wet. Daytime highs typically reach the low to mid 70s, falling to the 50s at night. Winters can be cold, with daytime high temperatures in the high 30s or low 40s, dropping to the 20s at night. Summer and early fall are the wettest seasons, with July usually getting the most rain.

BERNE: TEMPERATURES AND PRECIPITATION

Month	J	F	M	A	M	J	J	A	S	O	N	D
Average Daily Temperature												
(Fahrenheit) Max.	36	41	51	59	67	73	76	75	69	57	45	37
Min.	26	28	34	40	47	53	56	56	51	43	35	29
Average Number of Days with Precipitation												
	14	13	12	13	14	15	14	14	12	12	12	13

Geneva (Geneve): Switzerland

Sights to See

St. Pierre's Cathedral (Cathedrale St. Pierre), Vieille Ville. Constructed between the 12th and 13th centuries and, for a time, Calvin's church. The view from the North Tower is excellent. Open 9–7 daily, June–Sept. The Tower is open from 11:30–5:30.

Old Town (Vieille Ville), the old section of town, with narrow, winding streets and beautiful homes with ubiquitous flower boxes, surrounds St. Pierre's.

Place du Bourg-de-Four, SE of St. Pierre's, with the 18th-century Palais de Justice.

Art and History Museum (Musee d'Art et d'Histoire), 2 rue Charles Galland, SE of St. Pierre's. A fine collection of applied art and archaeology, and an especially good modern art gallery on the top floor. Open 10–5 Tu–Su.

Museum of Old Musical Instruments (Musee d'Instruments Anciens de Musique), 23 rue Lefort, just E of the Art and History Museum. Noted for its beautiful stringed instruments, some of which are played by visiting musicians. Open 3–6 Tu, 10–12 & 3–6 Th, 8–10 F.

Baur Collection, 8 rue Monier-Romilly, SE of the Art and History Museum. Excellent Oriental ceramics collection. Open P.M. only, Tu–Su.

Watch Museum (Musee d'Horlogerie), 15 rte. de Malagnou, SE of the Museum of Old Musical Instruments. Superb collection of watches, clocks, and music boxes from the 16th century to the present. Closed Mondays.

Petit-Palais, 2 Terrasse St. Victor, S of the Art and History Museum. Excellent collection of modern art in a delightful 19th-century palace. Open 2–6 M, 10–12 & 2–6 Tu–Su.

Jean-Jacques Rousseau Museum, Promenade des Bastions, SW of St. Pierre's. Historical museum of the Reformation. See the Reformation Monument under the Prom. de la Treille nearby.

Promenade on the Quais, N of St. Pierre's on the shores of Lake Geneva. Stroll along the quai du Mont-Blanc to the *Botanical Gardens,* then to the quai des Bergues, over the Pont des Bergues or Pont du Mont-Blanc to the Promenade du Lac and the *Jardin Anglais* (English Garden) with its famous "Horloge Fleurie," a large clock decorated with flowers.

Jet d'Eau, on Geneva's lakefront, off quai G. Ador. The world's highest fountain, shooting water 500 ft. into the air.

Palais des Nations, ave. de la Paix, N of the Pont du Mont-Blanc. Former League of Nations palace, now the home of the European section of the U.N.

Useful Information

Tourist Office, Gare Cornavin (Train station) (tel:45-5200); *U.S. Consulate,* 11 Route de Pregny, in the Geneva suburb of Chambesy (tel:733-5537 or 44-2330); *American Express,* 7 rue du Mont-Blanc (tel:731-7600); *Taxi* (tel:141 or 21-3333); *Police* (tel:117 in emergencies); *Post Office,* 16 rue des Gares; *Voltage Guide,* 220 V, two round-pin outlets are used.

Special Trips/Tours

Steamer trips along Lake Geneva (Lac Leman), calling at both French and Swiss ports, leave the landing stage at the Jardin Anglais (English Garden). Alternatively, the "Mouettes genovoises," a fleet of small boats, provide a shuttle service (March–Oct.) from one quay to another and as far as the narrowest part of the lake for magnificent views of the city, chateaux, and city parks.

If you have more time on your hands and would like to see Alpine Switzerland from a different vantage point, then the *Glacier Express* package tour may be the answer. The Glacier Express is a 150-mile narrow-gauge railway adventure operating all year. The $7\frac{1}{2}$-hour trip crosses 291 bridges and passes through 91 tunnels connecting the highest peaks and glaciers of the Eastern Alps with those of the Western Alps. Contact the Tourist Office in Geneva.

Weather

Geneva's summer daytime high temperatures typically reach into the mid to upper 70s, falling to the high 50s at night. Winter daytime highs are usually in the low to mid 40s, dropping to around 30 at night. Summer is the wet season.

GENEVA: TEMPERATURES AND PRECIPITATION

Month	J	F	M	A	M	J	J	A	S	O	N	D
Average Daily Temperature												
(Fahrenheit) Max.	38	42	51	59	66	73	77	76	69	58	47	40
Min.	29	30	36	42	49	55	58	58	53	44	37	31
Average Number of Days with Precipitation												
	11	9	9	9	11	11	9	11	10	10	11	10

Zurich: Switzerland

Sights to See

Fraumunster Church, Munsterhof square, Old Town. A 12th-century Gothic church, known for its chapel with new stained-glass windows by Marc Chagall. Open 9–6 daily May–Sept.

Zunfthaus zur Meisen, Munsterhof square, opposite the Fraumunster. Fine late-Baroque guild-house, which now houses the Swiss National Museum's ceramic collection. Open daily.

St. Peter's Church, N of the Fraumunster. Its Gothic tower has the largest clockface in Europe.

Guildhalls along the Limmatquai, Limmatquai, E of the Fraumunster on the opposite side of the Limmat river. Dating from the 17th and 18th centuries. Try the *Zunfhaus zur Schmiden* restaurant, Marktgasse 20, to get a feel for their marvelous interiors complete with ornate friezes and ceilings.

Nagelihof, off Limmatquai 42. A reconstructed square with cafes, shops, movies, and generally superb atmosphere.

Grossmunster Cathedral, Grossmunster Pl., just E of the Fraumunster across the Munsterbrucke. Switzerland's largest Romanesque cathedral, reputedly founded by Charlemagne. Noted for its frescoes and stained-glass windows (some by Giacometti). It was the center of the Reformation under Zurich's own Calvin, Ulrich Zwingli. Open 9–6 M–F, 9–5 Sa, during services Su.

Kunsthaus (Fine Arts Museum), Heimplatz, E of the Grossmunster. A huge collection of Western paintings and sculpture, particularly of the 20th century, including works of Picasso, Chagall, and Klee. Open 2–5 M, 10–9 Tu–F, 10–5 Sa–Su.

The Quaibrucke (Quay Bridge), S of the Fraumunster, located where the Limmat River and Lake Zurich meet. Offers the city's best views.

Swiss National Museum (Schweizerisches Landesmuseum), Museumstrasse 2, just N of the main railroad station N of the Fraumunster. Contains the largest and most complete collection of Swiss artifacts and art, which tell the story/history of Switzerland.

Bahnhofstrasse, extends from the railroad station S to the lake. The main street and the country's most prestigious shopping area.

Buhrle Collection, Zollikerstrasse 172, S of the Fraumunster along Lake Zurich near the Zurichhorn Park. One of the world's finest private collections of European Art. Open 2–5, Tu & F only.

Reitberg Museum, Gablerstrasse 15, SW of the Fraumunster, off Seestrasse. Contains some of the finest Eastern antiquities in the world. Open 10–5 Tu–Su.

Useful Information

Zurich Tourist Office, Bahnhofplatz 5 (tel:211-4000); *U.S. Consulate,* Zollikerstr. 141 (tel:55-2566); *American Express,* Bahnhofstrasse 20 (tel:211-8370); *Taxi* (tel:44-4441); *Police* (tel:117); *Post Office,* Hauptbahnhof; *Voltage*

Guide, 220 V, two round-pin outlets are used. The Tourist Office distributes *Spotlights on Zurich,* a bilingual bimonthly publication covering local events. The *Zurich Weekly Official,* issued every Friday, has detailed events of the coming week.

Special Trips/Tours

Boat trip on Lake Zurich. Boats depart on 90-minute to 4-hour cruises from Burkliplatz, at the lake end of Bahnhofstrasse. In summer there are special lunch cruises that, on a beautiful day, are just delightful. Contact *Zurichsee Schiffahrtsgesellschaft* (tel:482-1033) or the *Zurich Tourist Office* (tel:211-4000).

Many of the villages around Zurich have retained their original character, especially those with timbered houses, as in **Regensberg,** a walled medieval village about 20 minutes from Zurich. *Eglisau, Stammheim,* and *Marthalen,* with their renowned vineyards, are worth seeing to get a feel for rural Switzerland.

Weather

Summer daytime high temperatures are usually in the low to mid 70s, falling to the 50s at night. Winter daytime high temperatures usually reach the high 30s, dropping to the high 20s at night. Summer is the wet season.

ZURICH: TEMPERATURES AND PRECIPITATION

Month	J	F	M	A	M	J	J	A	S	O	N	D
Average Daily Temperature												
(Fahrenheit) Max.	36	41	51	59	67	73	76	75	69	57	45	37
Min.	26	28	34	40	47	53	56	56	51	43	35	29
Average Number of Days with Precipitation												
	14	13	12	13	14	15	14	14	12	12	12	13

Bath: England

Sights to See

Roman Baths, Abbey Church Yard in the center of Bath. Uncovered in the 18th century, these almost perfectly preserved hot-spring baths are one of the best examples of Roman remains in the country. Open 9–6 daily April–Oct., 9–5 M–Sa, 11–5 Su rest of the year.
Roman Baths Museum, adjoining the Roman Baths. Excellent collection of Roman antiquities. Open same hours as the Baths.
The Pump Room, upstairs from the Baths. A large Classical-style 18th-century building, noted for its hot-spring fountain. Open same hours as the Baths.
Bath Abbey, across the yard from the Baths. Started in 1499, this Perpendicular-style church is known for its large windows and fan vaulting. Open 9–5:30 M–Sa.

Assembly Rooms, Bennett St., N of the Baths. Renovated 18th-century ball-room and social meeting place, noted for its magnificent crystal chandeliers. **Museum of Costume,** in the Assembly Rooms, Bennett St. Superb collection, covering the 17th century to the present. Open 9:30–6 M–Sa, 10–6 Su, April–Oct., 10–5 rest of the year.
The Circus, at the N end of Gay St., just W of the Assembly Rooms. Superb example of Georgian architecture, with some notable former residents having occupied some of these townhouses.
Royal Crescent, at the end of Brock St., also in the NW part of Bath. Another fine example of residential Georgian architecture.
Number One Royal Crescent, Royal Crescent. A finely restored 18th-century townhouse complete with authentic period furniture and decorations. Open 11–5 Tu–Sa, March–Oct.
Pulteney Bridge, spanning the Avon River, just NE of the baths. A shop-lined structure with three arches.
Holburne of Menstrie Museum, Great Pulteney St., across Pulteney Bridge. Noted for its fine collection of miniatures, silver, glass, and furniture, in addition to its Old Masters. Open 11–5 Tu–Sa, 2:30–6 Su.

Useful Information

Tourist Information Centre, Abbey Churchyard (tel:46-2831)—the Centre also publishes the monthly *What's On;* closest *U.S. Embassy* is in London, 24–31 Grosvenor Sq., W1 (tel:01-499-9000); *American Express,* Bridge & Great Pulteney Sts.; *Public Transportation* (tel:6-4446); *Emergency* (tel:999 for police, fire, or ambulance); *Post Office,* New Bond St.; *Voltage Guide:* 220 V, two round-pin or three square-pin outlets are used.

Special Trips/Tours

Just outside Bath, 6 miles NW of Aylesbury is **Waddesdon Manor,** a French Renaissance-style chateau built for Baron Ferdinand de Rothschild in the 1870s. It is noted for its fine collection of French royal decorative art and English 18th-century portraits. Open 2–6 W–Su, April–Oct.

Further afield is the delightful small town of **Wells,** in Somerset, some 20 miles southwest of Bath. *Wells Cathedral,* dating from the 12th century, is one of the most beautiful in the country. It is particularly noted for the several hundred statues on its west front, and the astronomical clock in the north transept. Vist *Vicar's Close,* a particularly well-preserved street of 14th-century houses in Wells.

Stonehenge, Britain's most famous prehistoric monument, is about 30 miles SE of Bath on the Salisbury Plain, 10 miles N of Salisbury. Dating from between 1850 and 1400 B.C., this magalithic structure, consisting of two concentric rings of huge standing stones surrounding an inner horseshoe formation of smaller stones, is the largest of its kind in Europe. Nearby is **Wilton House,** 9 miles NW of Salisbury, noted for its great hall and beautiful gardens. A magnificent

16th-to-19th-century house, it also has a superb collection of paintings, furniture, and sculpture. Open 11–6 Tu–Sa, 1–6 Su, April–Oct.

Nearby *Salisbury,* with its 13th-century *cathedral* known for its decorated tower and spire (the tallest in England) and general medieval charm, is also worth visiting if you have the time.

Weather

Bath has a cool temperate climate with frequent and rapid changes of weather common. Summer daytime high temperatures are typically in the high 60s, dropping to the mid 50s at night. Winter daytime highs are usually in the mid 40s, falling to the upper or mid 30s at night. There is a high percentage of cloud cover, and precipitation is well distributed throughout the year, with fairly frequent rainfall.

BATH: TEMPERATURES AND PRECIPITATION

Month	J	F	M	A	M	J	J	A	S	O	N	D
Average Daily Temperature												
(Fahrenheit) Max.	45	45	50	56	61	68	69	69	64	58	51	46
Min.	35	35	38	41	46	51	54	55	51	46	41	37
Average Number of Days with Precipitation												
	16	13	12	12	12	12	13	14	14	15	16	17

Birmingham: England

Sights to See

City Museum and Art Gallery, Chamberlain Square, in central Birmingham. Fine archaeological, historical, and natural history exhibits, and the most comprehensive collection of art outside London. The *Art Gallery* is particularly noted for its superb collection of Pre-Raphaelite paintings and drawings. Open 10–5 M–Sa, 2–5 Su.

Council House, immediately S of the City Museum and Art Gallery. Built in the 1870s as a Venetian palace in the classical Renaissance style, it contains fine sculpture, mosaics, marble statues, and ornate furnishings.

Town Hall, Colmore Row & New Street, opposite the City Museum and Art Gallery. Modeled after a Roman temple with Corinthian columns, it is a fine example of Victorian architecture.

Central Library, opposite the Town Hall, across Paradise Circus. Noted for its *Shakespeare collection,* the largest outside the United States.

St. Philip's Cathedral, Temple Row, east of the Town Hall. An 18th-century Renaissance-style church noted for its stained-glass windows.

Museum of Science and Industry, Newhall & Charlotte Sts., N of the Town Hall. Fine collection, including steam engines, machine tools, motor vehicles, electronic equipment, and musical instruments.

St. Chad's Cathedral, St. Chad's Circus, E of the Museum of Science and Industry. First Roman Catholic cathedral built in England after the Reformation. It is known for its superb 15th-century Flemish and German artwork.

Barber Institute of Fine Art, Bristol Road, W of central Birmingham. Houses the University of Birmingham's rich collection of Old Masters.

Aston Hall, Aston Park, N of the Civic Centre. A red brick 17th-century Jacobean mansion, noted for its period furniture, oak staircase, and intricate plasterwork.

Useful Information

Tourist Information Centre, 2 City Arcade (tel:643-2514); *Public Transportation* (tel:236-8313); nearest *U.S. Embassy* is in London, at 24–31 Grosvenor Sq., W1 (tel:01-499-9000); *Emergency* (tel:999 for police, fire, or ambulance); *Voltage Guide:* 220 V, two round-pin or three square-pin outlets are used.

Special Trips/Tours

The ancient city of *Worcester* is less than an hour's drive SSW of Birmingham via the M5. Situated on the banks of the River Severn, it is famous for its cathedral and the many half-timbered Tudor houses that line many of its streets. *Worcester Cathedral* is noted for its interior vaulting, elegantly carved bosses and capitals, and Norman Crypt. New Street, Fish Street, and Friar Street are especially attractive. Other sights worth seeing include the *Guildhall,* the *Commandery* on Sidbury St., the *Royal Worcester Porcelain Factory,* and the *Dyston Perrins Porcelain Museum* next door on Severn St.

Stratford-upon-Avon is just 25 miles S of Birmingham on the A34. You can visit Shakespeare's birthplace on Henley St., Ann Hathaway's Cottage just outside town in Shottery village, and several other historic buildings. A performance of the world-famous *Royal Shakespeare Company* (tel:0789-29562 for booking seats and 0789-69191 for information on seat availability) should be seen if at all possible.

On the way back to or from Birmingham, travel via *Warwick* (only 9 miles NE of Stratford on the A46), the site of what many consider to be the finest medieval fortress in England—*Warwick Castle.* Dating from the 14th century, it is noted for its magnificent battlements and fine collection of furniture, paintings, sculpture, porcelain, and weapons. Open 10–5:30 daily.

Weather

Birmingham has a cool, temperate climate with frequent and rapid changes in weather fairly common. Summer daytime high temperatures typically get into the high 60s, dropping to the mid 50s at night. In winter, daytime highs are usually in the mid 40s, falling to the mid 30s at night. Precipitation is fairly well distributed throughout the year, although the late summer, fall, and early winter tend to be the wettest seasons.

BIRMINGHAM: TEMPERATURES AND PRECIPITATION

Month	J	F	M	A	M	J	J	A	S	O	N	D
Average Daily Temperature												
(Fahrenheit) Max.	42	43	48	54	60	66	68	68	63	55	48	44
Min.	35	35	37	40	45	51	54	54	51	45	40	37
Average Number of Days with Precipitation												
	17	15	13	13	14	13	15	14	14	15	17	18

Brighton: England

Sights to See

Royal Pavilion, Pavilion Parade, near Old Steine in central Brighton. An elaborate, eccentric palace in the Oriental style, built for Price Regent in the early 19th century by architect John Nash. The state and private apartments are full of objets d'art of the Regency period. Open 10–6:30 daily, June–Sept.
Brighton Art Gallery and Museum, Church St., just W of the Royal Pavilion. Fine collection of paintings, costumes, and pottery. Open 10–5:45 Tu–Sa.
The Lanes, centered around North St., East St., and King's Road SW of the Royal Pavilion. Part of the original fishing village, the area is now full of art shops, antique dealers, bookshops, cafes, pubs, and boutiques.
Brighton Aquarium and Dolphinarium, Marine Parade, just E of Palace Pier. The largest aquarium in the country, with hundreds of marine, tropical, and freshwater species. Dolphins perform in the indoor Dolphinarium. Open 9–5 daily.
Volk's Electric Railway, along the waterfront between Palace Pier and the Brighton Marina. A 19th-century electric train that runs for about a mile. Open 10–5:30 daily, May–Oct.
Brighton Marina, Marine Parade, E of Palace Pier. The largest yachting marina in Europe. Vist *H.M.S. Cavalier,* a WW II destroyer. Open 9–dusk daily.
British Engineerium, Nevill Rodl, Hove, about 3 miles W of Brighton. Large exhibition of British engineering know-how, featuring motors and steam engines. Open 10–5 daily.
Preston Manor, Preston Park, off A23, just N of Brighton. Dating from the early 18th century, this Edwardian country house has a fine collection of furniture, portraits, silver, and family memorabilia. Open 10–5 Tu–Su.

Useful Information

Tourist Information Centre, Marlborough House, 54 Old Steine (tel:23755); *American Express,* 66 Churchill Sq. (tel:21242); *Public Transportation* (tel:606600); *Taxi* (tel:24245 or 27282); *Emergency* (tel:999 for police, fire, or ambulance); nearest *U.S. Embassy* is in London at 24–31 Grosvenor Square, W1 (tel:01-499-9000); *Voltage Guide:* 220 V, two round-pin or three square-pin outlets are used.

Special Trips/Tours

Brighton is an excellent base for exploring the *South Downs,* a long ridge of chalk hills running parallel to the coast. Designated an area of outstanding natural beauty, the Downs can be seen from the A27. Places worth stopping in are *Lewes,* with its castle and many medieval houses, and *Arundal,* which also has a castle and half-timbered houses. *Arundal Castle,* a Norman stronghold restored in the 18th and 19th century, is set in beautiful grounds, and is noted for its fine portraits and 16th-century furniture collection. Open 1–5 Su–F, April–Oct.

Petworth, on the N edge of the Downs, N of Arundal, is another picturesque village. *Petworth House,* a large 17th-to-19th-century mansion situated in a great park, is just outside the village. It is especially noted for its picture gallery, and ancient sculpture collection. Open 2–6 Tu–Su, April–Oct.

Some 30 miles along the coast E of Brighton is Pevensey, built around the imposing *remains of a Roman fort,* within which the Normans built a castle. *Pevensey Castle* is open 9:30–6:30 M–Sa, 2–6:30 Su, March–Oct., shorter hours rest of the year. Vist the *Old Minthouse,* on High St., which is noted for its eclectic collection of Victoriana. Open 9–5 M–F, 10–4 Su. On the way to or from Pevensey, stop off at *Beachy Head,* a promontory 3 miles W of Eastbourne, for a fine vantage point of this part of the S. Coast.

Weather

Brighton has a cool temperate climate, with frequent and rapid changes in weather throughout the year. Summer daytime high temperatures typically reach into the mid 60s, dropping to the mid 50s at night. Winter daytime high temperatures are usually in the high 40s to low 50s, falling to the upper 30s at night. Rainfall is fairly uniform throughout the year, although the fall and winter months normally receive the most precipitation.

BRIGHTON: TEMPERATURES AND PRECIPITATION

Month	J	F	M	A	M	J	J	A	S	O	N	D
Average Daily Temperature												
(Fahrenheit) Max.	43	44	50	56	62	69	71	71	65	58	50	45
Min.	36	36	38	42	47	53	56	56	52	46	42	38
Average Number of Days with Precipitation												
	15	13	11	12	12	11	12	11	13	13	15	15

Bristol: England

Sights to See

Bristol Cathedral, between Deanery & Anchor Rds., S of College Green. Dating from the 12th century, it has been augmented and modified right up to Victorian times. It is noted for its choir, the rectangular chapterhouse, and its nave.

St. Marks Chapel (Lord Mayor's), College Green, opposite the cathedral. Dating from the 13th century, and once the chapel of a hospital, it is known for its Flemish and French stained glass.

Georgian House, 7 Great George Street, to the NW of the cathedral. A late-18th-century mansion that is a museum with fine period furniture, portraits, and miscellaneous pieces. Open 10–1, 2–5 M–Sa.

Cabot Tower, behind the Georgian House on Brandon Hill. Erected as a monument to Cabot's discovery of North America, it affords fine views of the city.

City Museum and Art Gallery, Queen's Road. Fine archaeological, historical, geological, and natural history exhibits in the museum, and paintings in the art gallery. Open 10–5 M–Sa.

Red Lodge, Park Row, near the Museum. A fine 16th-century museum-house that is noted for its superbly furnished and decorated rooms.

St. Stephen's Church, Corn St. Noted for its Gothic windows. Walk around this lovely old area, up Corn St. to the Cross, the heart of old Bristol, which, unfortunately, was badly damaged in WW II.

Theatre Royal, King Street in the harbor area, E of the cathedral. The oldest English theater, it currently is the home of the Bristol Old Vic Company.

Ye Llandoger Trow Inn, King Street. A half-timbered 17th-century inn in which Defoe met Alexander Selkirk, who allegedly told the story Defoe made famous in *Robinson Crusoe.*

St. Mary Redcliffe, Redcliffe Way, across Redcliffe Bridge, SE of King St. Dating from the 14th and 15th centuries, it is considered by many to be England's most attractive parish church. It is known for its pure Perpendicular Gothic style, the hexagonal north porch, and its choir.

Clifton Suspension Bridge, spanning the Avon Gorge in Clifton, the residential district W of central Bristol. Designed in the 1820s and finished in 1864, this 702-ft.-long, 245-ft.-high bridge by Brunel is an architectural wonder.

Useful Information

Tourist Information Centre, Colston House, Colston St. (tel:29-3891); *American Express,* 15 Colston St. (tel:27-7491); *Public Transportation* (tel:553231); nearest *U.S. Embassy* is in London, at 24–31 Grosvenor Sq., W1 (tel:01-499-9000); *Emergency* (tel:999 for ambulance, fire, or police); *Voltage Guide:* 220 V, two round-pin or three square-pin outlets are used.

Special Trips/Tours

The ancient spa of *Bath,* one of the country's most attractive towns, is only 13 miles SE of Bristol. It is famous for its elegant Georgian architecture, best seen in the NW part of town in Gay St., *Queen Square,* the *Circus,* and *Royal Crescent.* The most complete Roman remains in Britain, the *Roman Baths* and *Pump Room* are also in Bath, off Abbey Church Yard. The adjacent late-15th-century *Bath Abbey* is noted for its impressive fan vaulting.

The old city of *Gloucester,* NE of Bristol along the M5, with its magnificent *cathedral,* dating from the 11th century, and *Victorian docks,* is worth a day trip. The cathedral, College St., is noted for its beautiful choir, cloister, and its 14-century stained-glass east window. In the SW part of the city, the unique Victorian docks of Gloucester have remained virtually unchanged, and are remarkably well preserved. On the way to or from Gloucester, visit 12th-century **Berkeley Castle,** off the A38, 134 miles SW of Gloucester. A splendidly preserved Norman castle overlooking the Severn river, it is known for its great hall, dungeon, and state apartments with fine tapestries, furniture, silver, and paintings. Open 11–5 M–F May–Aug., shorter hours the rest of the year.

Weather

Bristol has a cool, temperate climate with frequent and rapid changes of weather fairly common. Summer daytime high temperatures are typically in the high 60s, dropping to the mid 50s at night. Winter daytime highs are usually in the mid 40s, falling to the 30s at night. Precipitation is reasonably well distributed throughout the year.

BRISTOL: TEMPERATURES AND PRECIPITATION

Month	J	F	M	A	M	J	J	A	S	O	N	D
Average Daily Temperature												
(Fahrenheit) Max.	45	45	50	56	61	68	69	69	64	58	51	46
Min.	35	35	38	41	46	51	54	55	51	46	41	37
Average Number of Days with Precipitation												
	16	13	12	12	12	12	13	14	14	15	16	17

Cambridge: England

Sights to See

Queen's College, Queen's Lane off Silver St. Dating from 1448, it is noted for its red brick First Court, centerpiece of the most complete complex of medieval buildings in Cambridge.

King's College Chapel, King's College, off King's Parade. Built between 1446 and 1515 of white limestone, it is a masterpiece of late Gothic architecture. Famous for its fan-vaulted ceiling, choir stalls, Rubens's "The Adoration of the Magi" behind the altar, and its stained-glass windows. Evensong services are held at 5:30 Tu–F, and 3:30 Su during university terms only.

Trinity College, N of King's College on Trinity St. Founded in 1546, it is the largest college in Cambridge, with its oldest buildings surrounding the two-acre Great Court.

Wren Library, dating from 1676, is known for its old oak bookcases, and fine limewood carvings. Library is open noon–2 M–F.

St. John's College, St. John's St., N of Trinity College. Known for its impressive gateway with its turrets and gilded coat of arms.

The Bridge of Sighs, with its tracery windows, leads over the River Cam to the College Grounds.

Round Church, Bridge & St. John's Sts. Dating from c.1130, it is one of the few Norman round churches in England.

Magdalene College (pronounced "maudlin"), N of St. John's College, off Bridge St., on the W side of the Cam. Famous for its *Pepys Library* in the Second Court, containing the library which Samuel Pepys bequeathed to his old college. Library is open 11:30–12:30 and 2:30–3:30 M–Sa.

Folk Museum, Castle & Northampton Sts., opposite Magdalene College. Fine exhibits depicting life in Cambridge and the surrounding countryside. Open Tu–Su.

Jesus College, Jesus Lane, E of the Round Church. Known for its 15th-century gate tower and stained-glass chapel.

Emmanuel College, St. Andrew's & Downing Sts., S of Jesus College. The college of many of the Pilgrim Fathers. A window in the Chapel, designed by Wren, commemorates John Harvard, the principal founder of Harvard University.

Fitzwilliam Museum. Trumpington Street, SW of Emmanuel College via Downing St. Excellent collection of Egyptian, Greek, Roman, and Chinese objets d'art, Old Masters, and European ceramics. Open 10–2 Tu–Sa, 2–5 Su (the upstairs gallery is open from 2–5, Su–F).

Useful Information

Tourist Information Office, Wheeler Street (tel:32-2640); *American Express,* 25 Sidney Street (tel:35-1636); *Emergency* (tel:999 for police, fire, or ambulance); *Taxi* (tel:31-3131, 35-2222); nearest *U.S. Embassy* is in London, at 24–31 Grosvenor Square, W1 (tel:01-499-9000); *Voltage Guide:* 220 V, two round-pin, or three-prong rectangular blade outlets are used. NOTE: Cambridge is a functioning university town, so many areas such as private living quarters are off-limits. Indeed, during examination periods, whole colleges may be off-limits—check with the college porters, or look for notices.

Special Trips/Tours

If the weather is good, the best way to see and enjoy Cambridge's marvelous architecture is to **rent a punt and explore the "Backs,"** a stretch of the Cam behind the colleges. These famous long, flat-bottomed boats either are self-propelled and steered by a long pole or can be rented complete with a "chauffeur"—very advisable if you're a novice! Rental locations are at Mill Lane, off Silver St., and Quayside, off Bridge St.

The small, ancient market town of *Ely,* with its magnificent *cathedral,* is only 16 miles NE of Cambridge. Dating from the 7th century, it is noted for its 14th-century octagonal lantern tower and very ornate Lady Chapel. The cathedral is open 7:30–7 M–Sa, 7:30–6 Su.

Weather

Cambridge has a cool, temperate climate with rapid changes in weather quite common. Summer daytime high temperatures typically reach into the high 60s or low 70s, dropping to the mid 50s at night. Winter daytime highs are usually in the mid 40s, falling to the mid 30s at night. Precipitation is fairly well distributed throughout the year, although winter is normally the wet season.

CAMBRIDGE: TEMPERATURES AND PRECIPITATION

Month	J	F	M	A	M	J	J	A	S	O	N	D
Average Daily Temperature												
(Fahrenheit) Max.	43	44	50	56	62	69	71	71	65	58	50	45
Min.	36	36	38	42	47	53	56	56	52	46	42	38
Average Number of Days with Precipitation												
	15	13	11	12	12	11	12	11	13	13	15	15

Canterbury: England

Sights to See

Canterbury Cathedral, Christchurch Gateway. Built over five centuries, it is a beautiful example of the Transitional style between Norman and Early English architecture. Seat of the Archbishop of Canterbury, Primate of All England, and leader of the worldwide Anglican Communion, the cathedral is historically the most important in England. It is expecially noted for its nave, the screen between the nave and choir, the fan vaulting of the interior central tower, and the huge choir and its glasswork. Climb the stairs of the northeast tower for a splendid view of the city.

The Martyrdom, northwest transept of the Cathedral. A stone tablet marking the spot where Thomas Becket was murdered in 1170.

The Cloister, built in the late 14th and early 15th centuries, it is particularly spacious and known for the over 800 painted roof-bosses.

St. Augustine's Abbey Ruins, Longport, just E of the Cathedral. Founded in the 7th century by St. Augustine. The Tudor Fyndon Gate complex is an annex of King's School, the oldest "public school" in the country. Open 9:30–6:30 M–Sa, 2–6:30 Su.

St. Martin's Church, close to the Abbey. Considered to be the oldest surviving church in England. Dating from the 7th century, its walls contain Roman bricks.

Royal Museum and Art Gallery, 18 High Street. Works of local artists are displayed, along with local archaeological and historical exhibits. Buff's Regimental Museum is part of the museum. Open 10–5 M–F.

Eastbridge Hospital, High St., between Westgate and the cathedral. Former hostel to pilgrims in the Middle Ages. Open 10–1, 2–5 M–Sa.

Westgate Museum, St. Peter's Street, W of the cathedral. The only surviving medieval city gate, its tower now houses a small museum, with a collection of armor and relics of the prison it once was. Open 10–1, 2–5 M–F, April–Sept., shorter hours Oct.–March.

Canterbury Castle, Castle St. & Rheims Way, SW of the cathedral. Only a late Norman tower is left in the ruins of the large 11th-century castle.

Dane John Mounds and Gardens, near the castle. This prehistoric mound affords fine views of the central part of Canterbury. The remains of the old town walls can be seen in the gardens.

Useful Information

Tourist Office, 34 St. Margaret's St. (tel:76-6567 for a recorded message on current and upcoming events); *Taxi* (tel:6-0333, 45-6363, or 45-4105); nearest *U.S. Embassy* is in London, at 24–31 Grosvenor Sq., W1 (tel:01-499-9000); *Emergency* (tel:999 for police, fire, or ambulance); *Voltage Guide:* 220 V, two round-pin or three square-pin outlets are used.

Special Trips/Tours

Leeds Castle, one of the most impressive castles in the country, is just outside Maidstone, Kent, some 16 miles W of Canterbury via the A252 and A20. The 9th-century castle was built on two islands in the middle of a lake, set in over 500 acres of landscaped parkland. Originally a Norman stronghold, it was converted into a royal palace by Henry VII. Its interior is noted for the fine paintings, antiques, and medieval Flemish tapestries. Open 11–5 daily, April–Oct., 12–4 Sa & Su only Nov.–March.

The hilly area of the *North Downs* forms the backbone of Kent to the SW and W of Canterbury. The open, rolling farmland, mixed with woodlands, offers fine panoramas of the surrounding countryside. In W Kent are two of England's stately country homes, *Knole,* and *Penshurst Place,* which can be seen on a drive back to London, via Ashford, through the picturesque villages of Bidden-den, Sissinghurst, Goudhurst, Lamberhurst, and via Tonbridge and Sevenoaks. Penshurst Place, on the B2176 SW of Tonbridge, a magnificent gray stone Tudor mansion noted for its beamed Great Hall, is open 1–5:30 daily April–Sept. Knole, just outside Sevenoaks, is one of the largest and finest country houses in England. Dating from the 15th century, with many later additions, it is famous for its state rooms with their superb furniture, paintings, tapestries, and silver. Open 11–5 W–Sa, 2–5 Su, April–Oct.

Weather

Canterbury has a cool, temperate climate with frequent and rapid changes in weather common year-round. Summer daytime high temperatures typically reach into the low 70s, dropping to the mid 50s at night. Daytime highs in the winter are usually in the mid 40s, falling to the 30s at night. Precipitation is well spread out during the year, although late summer and fall tend to be the wettest seasons.

CANTERBURY: TEMPERATURES AND PRECIPITATION

Month	J	F	M	A	M	J	J	A	S	O	N	D
Average Daily Temperature												
(Fahrenheit) Max.	43	44	50	56	62	69	71	71	65	58	50	45
Min.	36	36	38	42	47	53	56	56	52	46	42	38
Average Number of Days with Precipitation												
	15	13	11	12	12	11	12	11	13	13	15	15

Edinburgh: Scotland

Sights to See

Edinburgh Castle, Princes Street Gardens. Among other things it contains "the Crown Jewels" of Scotland. The oldest building in Edinburgh, the 11th-century *Queen Margaret's Chapel,* is located within the castle's walls. The view of the city from the castle is splendid. Open 9:30–6 M–Sa, 11–6 Su.

The "Royal Mile," the oldest part of Edinburgh, between Edinburgh Castle and Holyrood Palace to the east. It is lined with 16th- and 17th-century houses and other historic buildings.

St. Giles Cathedral, High St., between George IV Bridge & South Bridge, E of the Castle. The 15th-century "High Kirk" of Scotland. Famous for its openwork spire supported by flying buttresses. Open 9–5 daily.

Parliament House, Parliament Square, just behind the cathedral. A 17th-century building that once housed the Scottish Parliament and today functions as Scotland's supreme court. Open Tu–F.

National Gallery, on the Mound, NW of the cathedral. Fine collection of Scottish and English paintings, together with a collection of Old Masters, including the Bridgewater "Madonna" of Raphael. Open 10–5 M–F, 2–5 Su.

Museum of National Antiquities, Queen & Duke Sts., N of the National Gallery. A real find for those interested in Celtic history. Open 10–5 M–Sa, 2–5 Su.

The Palace of Holyroodhouse (the Buckingham Palace of Edinburgh), at the E end of the "Royal Mile." The official residence of the Queen when in town. Conducted tours start every 45 minutes. The music room and the northwest tower are particularly worth seeing. Open 9:30–5:15 M–Sa, 11–4:15 Su.

Arthur's Seat, Holyrood Park, to the S of the palace. On a good day, the view from the top of this 823-ft. extinct volcano is excellent.

Scottish National Gallery of Modern Art, Inverleith House in the botanic gardens. Henry Moore sculptures and drawings by Picasso and Rouault abound. Open 10–6 M–Sa, 2–6 Su.

Useful Information

Scottish Travel Centre, St. Andrews Sq.; *Scottish Tourist Board,* 5 Waverly Bridge (tel:332-2433); *City of Edinburgh Tourist Centre,* 3 Princes St. (tel:557-

1700); *U.S. Consulate,* 3 Regent Terrace, (tel:556-8315); *Tele-Tourist Information Service,* for coming attractions and daily events (tel:246-8031 May–Sept.); *American Express,* 139 Princes St. (tel:225-7881); *Taxi* (tel:228-1211); *Post Office,* 2 Waterloo Pl. (tel:550-8314); *Voltage Guide:* 220 V, two round-pin or three square-pin outlets are used.

Special Trips/Tours

St. Andrews, across the River Forth about 75 miles NE of Edinburgh, is a picturesque university town and famous the world over for its golf courses. St. Andrews has the oldest clubhouse in the world (the Royal and Ancient), and is the worldwide arbiter of the game. St. Andrews is also one of the leading historic centers in Scotland, with a cathedral and castle ruins. The *ruins of St. Andrews Castle* stand on a promontory, affording fine views of the coast.

A trip into the **Scottish Highlands** should not be missed. Breathtakingly beautiful, these rugged mountains afford not only spectacular scenery, but a wealth of folk festivals during the summer. If you can't get to the far NW, at least try to see *Ben Nevis,* Britain's highest mountain (4,406 ft.), the summit of which offers magnificent panoramas of Highland Scotland. The road from Fort William to Inverness, passing *Loch Lochy* and its two castles, *Loch Oich,* and *Loch Ness* (home to Nessie!), passes through some of Britain's most beautiful scenery. The road (E120) back S over the *Grampians* is also scenic, going through *Pitlochry* and *Perth,* with *Glamis Castle* just NE of Perth.

Weather

Edinburgh's weather is notoriously changeable. Summer daytime high temperatures typically reach into the mid 60s, dropping to the low 50s at night. Winters are cold and damp, with daytime highs usually in the 40s. Summer is the wet season.

EDINBURGH: TEMPERATURES AND PRECIPITATION

Month	J	F	M	A	M	J	J	A	S	O	N	D
Average Daily Temperature												
(Fahrenheit) Max.	42	43	46	51	56	62	65	64	60	54	48	44
Min.	34	34	36	39	43	49	52	52	49	44	39	36
Average Number of Days with Precipitation												
	17	15	15	14	14	15	17	16	16	17	17	18

London: England

Sights to See

Tower of London, Tower Hill, EC3. Crown Jewels, Beefeaters, armor, uniforms, and historic relics. Open 9:30–5 M–Sa, 2–5 Su.

Tower Bridge Walkway, Tower Bridge, close to the Tower of London. Reached by elevator at North Tower entrance. Magnificent views. Open 10–6:30 daily.

St. Paul's Cathedral, Ludgate Hill, EC4. Wren's masterpiece. Tours start at 11 A.M. and 2 P.M. Excellent vistas of London from the dome. Open 8–5 daily.
British Museum, Great Russell Street, WC1. One of the world's truly great museums, full of treasures. Open 10–5 M–Sa, 2:30–6 Su.
National Gallery, Trafalgar Square, WC2. Masterpieces galore. Open 10–6 M–Sa, 2–6 Su.
Houses of Parliament, Palace of Westminster, Westminster, SW1. Seat of power. Apply at the U.S. Embassy for a Strangers Gallery pass to hear debates.
Westminster Abbey, Parliament Square, SW1. Burial place of the great. Open 9–5 daily. Closes for Sunday services. Check the Enquiry Desk for excellent guided tours by Vergers.
Cabinet War Rooms, King Charles St., SW1. Churchill's auxiliary WW II command post frozen in a 1945 timewarp. Open 10–6 Tu–Su.
Buckingham Palace, The Mall, SW1. The royal family's residence. Majestic, but not open to the public.
Changing of the Guard at Buckingham Palace. In summer, it takes place daily at 11:30 A.M. Advisable to get there early.
St. James, Green, and Hyde Parks. Speaker's corner, boating, riding, picnicking, and military bands.
Victoria & Albert Museum, South Kensington, SW7. Excellent collections of fine and applied arts. Open 10–5:50 M–Sa, 2:30–6 Su.
The Wallace Collection, Manchester Square, W1. Fine collection of Baroque paintings, armor, and 18th-century French furniture. Open 10–5 M–Sa, 2–5 Su.

Useful Information

British Tourist Authority's Tourist Information Centre, 64 St. James St., SW1; *Britain Travel Centre,* 12 Regent Street, Piccadilly Circus (tel:730-3400); the *London Tourist Board* (tel:730-0791) has branches in Selfridges, Harrods, Victoria Station, and Heathrow Underground. The *City of London Information Centre* (tel:606-3030) is at St. Paul's Churchyard, EC4, and also at the Tower of London. For *recorded information on the day's events,* call 246-8041 (246-8007 for children's events). *London Taxi Guide,* 3 Elystan St., SW3, (tel:584-3118) for personal, individualized tours; *Taxi* (tel:286-6010, 286-4848, or 272-3030); *London Transport's 24-hr. info. line* (222-1234); *Emergency* (tel:999 for ambulance, fire, police); *U.S. Embassy,* 24–31 Grosvenor Square, W1 (tel:499-9000); *American Express,* 6 Haymarket, SW1 (tel:930-4411); *Voltage Guide:* 220 V, two round-pin or three-prong rectangular blade outlets are used.

Special Trips/Tours

On a good day London can be seen from a cruise boat on the River Thames. Upstream, the *Royal Botanical Gardens* at Kew are worth a visit. Downstream, *Greenwich,* the *Cutty Sark,* Sir Francis Chichester's *Gipsy Moth IV,* and the *National Maritime Museum.* *"Water buses" or cruise boats* can be boarded at Tower Pier, Charing Cross Pier, or Westminster Pier. London Transport has excellent unconducted *double-decker bus tours* every hour from Marble Arch, Baker St., Piccadilly Circus, and Grosvenor Gardens.

Weather

Rapid changes of weather are common. Summer daytime high temperatures are typically in the high 60s or low 70s, dropping to the 50s at night. Winter daytime highs only reach the mid 40s. It does tend to rain quite a bit, so take a "brolly" along. Summer and fall are the wet seasons.

LONDON: TEMPERATURES AND PRECIPITATION

Month	J	F	M	A	M	J	J	A	S	O	N	D
Average Daily Temperature												
(Fahrenheit) Max.	43	44	50	56	62	69	71	71	65	58	50	45
Min.	36	36	38	42	47	53	56	56	52	46	42	38
Average Number of Days with Precipitation												
	15	13	11	12	12	11	12	11	13	13	15	15

Oxford: England

Sights to See

Christ Church, St. Aldates, S of Carfax. Founded in 1525, it is known for its quadrangle, Tom Quad, the largest in Oxford, and its Hall, full of interesting portraits. See the Picture Gallery on Oriel Sq.
Christ Church Cathedral, on the E side of Tom Quad, off St. Aldates. One of the country's smallest cathedrals, it is also the college chapel of Christ Church. Noted for the double arcading of its nave.
Merton College, Merton Street, just to the E of Christ Church. Founded in 1266, it has some of the most interesting buildings. Merton Street itself is very attractive.
High Street, at the end of Merton St. With the 15th-century Magdalen Tower at its E end, this half-mile-long street has been called "the finest street in England."
Magdalen College (pronounced "maudlin"), at the E end of High St. Founded in 1458, it is considered to be the most attractive of the Oxford colleges. Visit the Botanic Gardens opposite the entrance.
Radcliffe Camera, Radcliffe Square, behind St. Mary's the Virgin, on High St., W of Magdalen. An early 18th-century rotunda of the Anglo-Italian style. It is a reading room of the Bodleian Library.
Bodleian Library, Radcliffe Square. One of the great libraries of the world, and one of the oldest.
New College Chapel, New College Lane, immediately to the NE of Radcliffe Square. Noted for its stained-glass windows.
Sheldonian Theatre, Broad Street, N of the Bodleian. Built by Sir Christopher Wren in the 1660s.

Blackwells Bookshop, 50 Broad Street, opposite the Sheldonian Theatre. World famous, it is one of the finest and largest bookshops in the world.
Ashmolean Museum, Beaumont & St. Giles Sts. The oldest museum in England, this Neoclassical building houses a superb collection of art and antiquities, including Far Eastern art, classical sculptures, Greek and Roman pottery, jewelry, and an outstanding collection of drawings and prints. Open 10–4 Tu–Sa, 2–4 Su.

Useful Information

Oxford Information Centre, St. Aldates St. (tel:72-6871); *What's On in Oxford* (recorded message—tel:24-4888); closest *U.S. Embassy* is in London, 24–31 Grosvenor Square, W1 (tel:01-499-9000); *American Express* c/o Bailey Travel Agency, 99 St. Aldates St. (tel:79-0099); *Taxi* (tel:24-9743); *Emergency* (tel:999 for police, ambulance, and fire); *Post Office,* 102 St. Aldates St.; *Voltage Guide:* 220 V, two round-pin or three square-pin outlets are used. NOTE: Oxford is a functioning university town, so many areas, such as private living quarters, are off-limits. Indeed, during examination periods, whole colleges may be off-limits—check with the college porters, or look for notices.

Special Trip/Tours

On a good day, a leisurely ***boat ride on the Thames*** (called the Isis here) or Cherwell rivers is a delightful experience. Rowboats or punts can be rented at either the *Folly Bridge* at the S end of St. Aldates St., or *Magdalen Bridge* at the E end of High St.
 Blenheim Palace, home of the 11th Duke of Marlborough and birthplace of Sir Winston Churchill, is 8 miles N of Oxford in Woodstock. A huge Baroque mansion built in the early 18th century, it is noted for its excellent collection of furniture, paintings, and porcelain. Open 11–6 daily, mid-March–Oct.

Weather

Oxford has a cool, temperate climate. Frequent and rapid changes of weather are common throughout the year. Daytime high temperatures typically are in the high 60s or low 70s, dropping to the mid 50s at night. Winter daytime highs are usually in the mid to upper 40s, falling to the 30s at night. Precipitation is spread out through the year, although winter is the wettest season.

OXFORD TEMPERATURES AND PRECIPITATION

Month		J	F	M	A	M	J	J	A	S	O	N	D
Average Daily Temperature													
(Fahrenheit)	Max.	43	44	50	56	62	69	71	71	65	58	50	45
	Min.	36	36	38	42	47	53	56	56	52	46	42	38
Average Number of Days with Precipitation													
		15	13	11	12	12	11	12	11	13	13	15	15

Stratford: England

Sights to See

Shakespeare's Birthplace, Henley St. A modest, half-timbered Tudor house, furnished with period pieces, where Shakespeare was born in 1564. The adjoining museum houses a library and exhibits of period costumes. Open 9–6 M–Sa, 10–6 Su, April–Oct., shorter hours rest of the year.
Harvard House, High St., S of the birthplace. A half-timbered house built in 1696, owned by the mother of John Harvard, founder of Harvard University. Nicely furnished with period pieces. Open 9–1, 2–6 M–Sa, 2–4 Su, April–Sept.; shorter hours the rest of the year.
Nash's House, High St., just S of, and on the opposite side of the street from, Harvard House. Houses the New Place Museum with archaeological exhibits.
New Place, next door on Chapel St., marks the site of Shakespeare's house, now only foundations. See the "Great Garden," and the "Knot Garden" behind the remaining foundations. Open 9–6 M–Sa, 2–6 Su, April–Oct.; shorter hours the rest of the year.
Hall's Croft, Old Town Rd., S of New Place. Considered to be one of the finest Tudor houses in town. Home of the Bard's eldest daughter, it is well furnished with period pieces. Linger in the garden. Open 9–6 M–Sa, 2–6 Su, April–Oct.; shorter hours the rest of the year.
Holy Trinity Church, off Old Town Rd. & College La. on the banks of the Avon. Shakespeare's grave is on the north side of the chancel.
Royal Shakespeare Theatre, Southern & Chapel Lanes, on the Avon. See the *Picture Gallery and Museum,* on the upper floor, noted for its paintings and sculpture of Shakespeare and well-known actors and actresses who have appeared in the Bard's plays. There are also stage-settings and costume exhibits. Open 9–6 M–Sa, 2–6 Su, April–Oct. and 9–4 M–Sa, Nov–March.
Anne Hathaway's Cottage, in Shottery, 1 mile W of Stratford. The birthplace of Shakespeare's wife, it has been remarkably well preserved. Open 9–6 M–Sa, April–Oct., shorter hours Nov.–March.
Mary Arden's House, in Wilmcote, 4 miles NW of Stratford. Farmhouse home of Shakespeare's mother. Open 9–6 M–Sa, 2–6 Su, April–Oct.; 9–4 M–Sa, Nov.–March.

Useful Information

Tourist Information Centre, 1 High St. (tel:29-3127); *Stratford-upon-Avon Tourist Information Phone* (tel:6-7522); *Royal Shakespeare Theatre Box Office recorded message* (tel:6-9191); *American Express,* High Street (tel:29-3582); closest *U.S. Embassy* is in London, 24–31 Grosvenor Square, W1 (tel:01-499-9000); *Emergency* (tel:999 for police, fire, and ambulance); *Taxi* (tel:6-9999); *Voltage Guide:* 220 V, two round-pin or three square-pin outlets are used.

Special Trips/Tours

Warwick Castle, a magnificent medieval fortress with splendid battlements overlooking the Avon is about 10 miles NE of Stratford on the A46 to Coventry.

Complete with towers, dungeons, and armory, it is especially noted for the fine collection of furniture, paintings, porcelain, and sculptures in the state rooms. Open 10–6 daily. The town of *Warwick* itself should not be missed. It is full of half-timbered Elizabethan houses and at the center of town is the church of *St. Mary,* noted for its beautiful *Beauchamp Chapel* on the south side of the choir.

Some 10 miles from Stratford is **Ragley Hall,** 2 miles SW of Alcester, which is 8 miles NW of Stratford. The 17th-century home of the Seymour family, it is known for its superb great hall and fine gardens. Open 1:30–5:30 Tu–Su, April–Sept. The town of **Worcester,** some 26 miles W of Stratford, has an imposing Early English *cathedral,* known for its spacious interior and finely carved bosses and capitals. New, Fish, and Friar Streets have some fine half-timbered Tudor houses.

Weather

Stratford has a cool, temperate climate with frequent and rapid changes in the weather. Summer daytime high temperatures typically reach into the high 60s, dropping to the mid 50s at night. Winter daytime highs are usually in the low 40s, falling to the mid 30s at night. Precipitation is spread uniformly throughout the year, although its frequency increases during the winter months.

STRATFORD: TEMPERATURES AND PRECIPITATION

Month		J	F	M	A	M	J	J	A	S	O	N	D
Average Daily Temperature													
(Fahrenheit)	Max.	42	43	48	54	60	66	68	68	63	55	48	44
	Min.	35	35	37	40	45	51	54	54	51	45	40	37
Average Number of Days with Precipitation													
		17	15	13	13	14	13	15	14	14	15	17	18

York: England

Sights to See

York Minster, St. Duncombe & Bootham Sts. One of the largest medieval churches in northern Europe. Particularly famous for its 14th- and 15th-century stained-glass windows. Its nave and transepts are also noteworthy. Climb to the top of the lantern tower for excellent panoramas. Don't miss the octagonal chapterhouse off the N transept. Open daily, although restricted during services. **Undercroft Museum,** underneath York Minster. Roman and Norman foundations, revealed during excavations to strengthen the central tower's foundations, can be seen, along with other historical exhibits.
Treasurer's House, immediately behind the Minster, standing on the site of the Roman Imperial barracks. The 17th-century house contains a fine collection of furniture and art. Open 10:30–6 daily, April–Oct.

City Walls, with a total remaining length of almost 3 miles, these medieval fortifications, following the old Roman walls, offer splendid views of York. The sections just N of York Minster, between Bootham and Monk Bars (gates), are the best.

Yorkshire Museum, Museum Street, W of the minster. Noted for its fine archaeological and geological collections, particularly Roman antiques. Open 10–5 M–Sa, 1–5 Su. The ruins of St. Mary's Abbey, and the *Hospitium* (abbey guest house), known for its Roman collection, are in the Museum Gardens.

York Art Gallery, Exhibition Square, off Bootham St., N of the museum. Noted for its Italian works and Old Masters collection. Open 10–5 M–Sa, 2:30–5 Su.

Old York, between York Minster and the Castle Museum. The city center is full of narrow streets, with the upper stories of the heavily beamed and gabled houses leaning toward each other. The Shambles is the best known, but *Stonegate* is probably the finest.

Castle Folk Museum, Tower Street. Housed in a former 18th-century prison, the museum's Kirk collection is the nucleus for one of England's best folk museums. Noted for its reconstructions of streets and shops, and craftsmen's workshops. Open 9:30–6:30 M–Sa, 10–6:30 Su, April–Sept., shorter hours Oct–March.

Clifford's Tower, on the Castle grounds. A mid-13th-century structure noted for its unusual quatrefoil shape. Open 9:30–6:30 M–F & Su, April–Sept., shorter hours Oct.–March.

Jorvik Viking Centre, Coppergate, N of Clifford's Tower. A detailed underground reconstruction of a row of streets in the York of the Viking era, with workshops, houses, and wharves. Open daily.

National Railway Museum, Leeman Rd., adjacent to the railway station. Superb collection of locomotives, rolling stock, and other railway memorabilia. Open 10–6 M–Sa, 2:30–6 Su.

Useful Information

Tourist Information Centre, De Grey Rooms, off Exhibition Square (tel:62-1756) and at the railway station; *Taxi* (tel:5-4579 or 2-2333); *Emergency* (tel:999 for fire, ambulance, and police); nearest *U.S. Embassy* is in London, 24–31 Grosvenor Square W1 (tel:01-499-9000); *Voltage Guide:* 220 V, two round-pin or three square-pin outlets are used.

Special Trips/Tours

Castle Howard, a huge, magnificent 18th-century Palladian mansion is just outside Malton, 18 miles NE of York on the A64. It has a famous collection of porcelain, paintings, and furniture, and is surrounded by extensive grounds, with lakes and fountains. The costume galleries in the stable court are excellent. Open 11:30–5 daily, Mar 25–Oct.

Some 23 miles N of York is the village of *Thirsk,* home of the veterinary office of James Herriot, the author of *All Creatures Great and Small.* For information on the *James Herriot walking tours* (James Herriot's Yorkshire), ask your travel agent or phone R & I Country Tours, Grassington (tel:0756/75-2757). The *Yorkshire Dales National Park,* an area of great natural beauty, is just a few hours drive NW of York. On its E edge is the attractive cathedral town of Ripon. The ruined Cistercian *Fountains Abbey* and adjacent *Studbury Royal* formal garden are noteworthy.

Harewood House, one of the great country houses of England, is 25 miles W of York outside Harewood. An 18th-century neoclassical mansion, it contains a superb collection of Chippendale furniture, English and Italian paintings, and Chinese porcelain. The grounds are magnificently landscaped, and contain a bird garden and tropical paradise garden. Open daily April–Oct., Su only in Feb., March, and Nov.

Weather

York has a cool, temperate climate, with frequent and rapid changes of weather fairly common. Summer daytime high temperatures typically reach into the high 60s, dropping to the 50s at night. Winter daytime highs are usually in the mid 40s, falling to the mid 30s at night. Rainfall is well distributed throughout the year.

YORK: TEMPERATURES AND PRECIPITATION

Month	J	F	M	A	M	J	J	A	S	O	N	D
Average Daily Temperature												
(Fahrenheit) Max.	43	44	49	55	61	67	70	69	64	57	49	45
Min.	33	34	36	40	44	50	54	53	50	44	39	36
Average Number of Days with Precipitation												
	17	15	13	13	13	14	15	14	14	15	17	17

Zagreb: Yugoslavia

Sights to See

Old Town/Upper Town (Gornji Grad), located on the top of a hill, it is Zagreb's oldest section, with its medieval character still intact.
St. Mark's Church, Gornji Grad. Noted for its sculptures by Yugoslavian artist Ivan Mestrovic and its colorful mosaic tile roof.
Mestrovic Gallery, Mletacka 8, close to St. Mark's. Contains some of the works of the country's best-known sculptor, Ivan Mestrovic. Open 10–1, 5–7 Tu–Sa, 10–1 Su.
St. Stephen's Cathedral, N of Trg Republike below Gornji Grad. Noted for its austere 300-ft. Gothic towers and thick fortifications.
Republic Square (Trg Republike), Lower Town (Donji Grad). A large, spacious, and tree-lined square.
Dolac Market, just above Republic Square. A colorful morning market with vendors from the surrounding countryside plying their wares.

Gallery of Primitive Art, Cirilmetodska 3. An excellent collection of Yugoslav Naive art by Croatian peasant painters. This "school" of painting has become world famous. Open 11–1, 5–8 daily.
Archaeological Museum, 19 Zrinjski Square, Donji Grad. Its collection spans the prehistoric to medieval times and is noted for its coin collection and its Egyptian mummy with some interesting well-preserved Etruscan text.
Ethnographic Museum, Mazuranicev Trg 14. Known for its collection of traditional Yugoslavian costumes, general folk collections, and interiors of peasant homes. Open 9–1 Tu–Su, 5–7 W–Th.
Museum of the City of Zagreb, Opatricka 20. Exhibits devoted to the life and history of this capital of Croatia. An excellent museum of its kind. Open 9–1 M–Sa, 2–7 Tu–Th, 10–1 Su.

Useful Information

Tourist Office, Zrinjevac 14 (tel:41-1883); *American Express,* Zrinjevac 17 (tel:42-7623); *U.S. Consulate,* Brace Kavurica 2 (tel:44-4800); *Police* (tel:92); *Post Office,* Branimirova 4, next to the main train station; *Voltage Guide:* 220 V, two round-pin outlets are used.

Special Trips/Tours

Ljubljana, the capital of Slovenia, about 74 miles NW of Zagreb, makes a nice trip. Surrounded by the *Julian Alps* (Julijske Alps), the city's old quarter, dating from the 16th century, has been restored to its original Baroque style. About 30 miles from Ljubljana is the mountain resort of *Bled* on beautiful *Lake Bled.* Be sure to visit the museum in the lakeside castle.

Plitvice Lakes, a national park some 80 miles S of Zagreb past Karlovac, is known for its 16 lakes connected by cascading waterfalls. Just magnificent.

Zagreb is the ideal stepping-off point to the marvelous *Adriatic coast* of Yugoslavia. The *Adriatic Highway* (Jadranska Magistrala) parallels the coast, one of the most beautiful in Europe. On the way you will pass through unspoiled medieval towns, Greek and Roman ruins, picturesque fishing villages, and fashionable beach resorts with coastal mountains on one side, and the shimmering Adriatic and its hundreds of islands on the other. Two towns are especially worth seeing: *Split* and *Dubrovnik.*

Split is clearly the most accessible from Zagreb, and is full of Venetian Gothic and Renaissance buildings, medieval churches and towers. Split is built into and around the 4th century *Emperor Diocletian's palace* (Dioklecijanova Palata), famous for its *Cathedral of Sveti Duje,* with its fine sculpture and carvings. The *Archaeological Museum* (Arheoloski Muzej), is known for its Roman artifacts.

Dubrovnik, the "Pearl of the Adriatic," is some 124 miles S of Split. A 15th-century walled city, it is remarkably well preserved, and its architectural unity is strikingly beautiful. Particularly noteworthy sights include the *Maritime Museum* in St. John's Fortress, the *Franciscan Monastery,* and the *Dominican Cloister* and *Museum.* The short *boat cruises along the Riviera* should not be missed.

Weather

Zagreb enjoys warm to hot summers, with cold winters. Summer daytime high temperatures typically get into the high 70s or low 80s, dropping to the high 50s at night. Winter daytime highs are usually in the high 30s or low 40s, falling to the low 30s or 20s at night. Late spring and early summer tend to be the wettest times of the year.

ZAGREB: TEMPERATURES AND PRECIPITATION

Month	J	F	M	A	M	J	J	A	S	O	N	D
Average Daily Temperature												
(Fahrenheit) Max.	36	41	51	63	72	79	81	82	75	64	50	42
Min.	25	27	33	44	54	59	61	62	54	48	35	30
Average Number of Days with Precipitation												
	14	13	12	13	14	13	9	9	8	11	14	14

North America
Calgary: Canada

Sights to See

Calgary itself, best seen from the *observation terrace* of the 628-ft.-tall *Calgary Tower,* 9th Ave. & Centre St. Or have a leisurely meal in the revolving restaurant, and enjoy the view. Open 7:30–midnight M–Sa, 7:30–11 Su.
Glenbow-Alberta Institute, 9th Ave. & 1st St. SE., just across 9th Ave. from Calgary Tower. A combination art gallery, museum, and library, it is best known for its Indian and Eskimo artifact collection. Open 10–6 Tu–Su.
Fort Calgary Interpretive Centre, 750 9th Ave. SE., E of the Institute. Site of the original Northwest Mounted Police Fort. Exhibits illustrate local history. Open 10–6 W–Su.
Calgary Zoo and Prehistoric Park, Memorial Dr. & 12th St. E., on St. George's Island, E of Fort Calgary. Canada's largest and best zoo, together with particularly lifelike, full-size dinosaur reproductions in a fern-filled swamp. Open 9–5:30 M–W, 9–8:30 Th–Su.
Devonian Gardens, Toronto-Dominion Square, 8th Ave. & 3rd St. SW., just NW of Calgary Tower. A 2.5-acre climate-controlled garden paradise with some 140 varieties of plants, waterfalls, fountains, reflecting pools, and little bridges. Open 9–9 daily.
Calgary Centennial Planetarium, 701 11th St. SW., W of the Devonian gardens. Noted for its Star Chamber's special effects, ranging from exploring the universe to the laser light/sound shows. Open 1:30–9 daily.
Alberta College of Art Gallery, 1407 14th Ave. NW. An excellent contemporary arts gallery.

Heritage Park, W of 14th St. & Heritage Dr. SW., on a peninsula in the Glenmore Reservoir. A fine re-created pioneer village, complete with blacksmith, general store, Indian village, mining camp, streetcars, steam trains, ranch, and a paddle-wheeler. Open 10–6 daily, May–Sept., weekends Sept.–Oct.

Fish Creek Park, Canyon Meadows Dr. & Macleod Trail SE., at the S end of the city. A huge wildlife reserve, with walks and park interpreters. Visit the Bow Valley Ranch and the Visitors' Centre.

Useful Information

Calgary Tourist and Convention Bureau, 1300 Sixth Ave SW., (263-8510) for information on cultural groups, individual performances, facilities, and events in the Calgary area; *Emergency* (999 for police, fire, ambulance); *Calgary Stampede Information* (261-0101); *Taxi* (273-5759 or 255-6555).

Special Trips/Tours

Banff National Park. Canada's oldest, is just over 80 miles W of Calgary via Hwy. 1. Open all year, the park is both a summer hiking, climbing, camping, riding, fishing, and boating center and a winter skiing center. Although the park tends to be crowded in the summer, the scenery is spectacular. The resort town of Banff has two museums worth seeing: the *Natural History Museum,* 112 Banff Ave, and the *Parks Canada Natural History Museum,* 93 Banff Ave. For magnificent panoramas of Banff and the surrounding mountains, take the gondola up *Mount Norquay* (8,275 ft.), just outside Banff off Trans-Canada Hwy. 1 on Mount Norquay Road. *Lake Louise,* 35 miles NW of Banff, is a truly beautiful lake surrounded by mountains. If you have the time, take the day's drive from Lake Louise W to *Golden,* through the adjoining *Yoho National Park,* S to *Radium Hot Springs,* and NE to Hwy 1 N of Banff.

Jasper National Park, which contains some of Canada's most majestic mountain scenery, is N of Banff National Park via the *Icefields Pkwy.,* a drive that has to rank among the most beautiful in the world. Not as crowded as Banff NP, it is also open all year. Just inside the S edge of the park is the *Columbia Icefield,* the largest sheet of glacial ice (150 sq. miles) in N. America S of the Arctic circle. Although this ice sheet is not visible from the Parkway, three of the glaciers, Athabasca, Dome, and Stutfield, are. Visit the *Icefield Centre.* The *Jasper Tramway,* just S of Jasper, via Hwy. 93 and Whistler Mountain Rd., affords magnificent panoramas of the park. Take a boat cruise on *Maligne Lake.*

Weather

Summer daytime high temperatures typically reach into the low to mid 70s, dropping to around 50 at night. Winter daytime highs are usually in the teens to 20s, falling to the single digits and below at night. June through August is the wettest period.

CALGARY: TEMPERATURES AND PRECIPITATION

Month	J	F	M	A	M	J	J	A	S	O	N	D
Average Daily Temperature												
(Fahrenheit) Max.	12	20	33	50	64	72	77	73	65	58	33	19
Min.	−5	1	11	30	38	47	52	48	41	36	15	2
Average Number of Days with Precipitation												
	12	9	10	8	12	15	14	12	9	9	10	11

Edmonton: Canada

Sights to See

Edmonton itself from the 33rd floor of Vista 33, the Alberta Telephone Tower, 11120 100th St. Magnificent panoramas of the city and surrounding countryside, plus a telecommunications museum. Open 10–8 daily.

Edmonton Art Gallery, 2 Sir Winston Churchill Sq., just N of Vista 33. Fine and applied arts exhibits. Open 10:30–5 M–W, 10:30–8 Th–F.

Muttart Conservatory, 98th Ave. & 96A St., SE of Vista 33, across the MacDonald Bridge. Four pyramid-shaped greenhouses with tropical, arid, and temperate houses, and a house for changing seasonal displays. Open daily 11–9, June–Aug, 11–6 rest of the year.

Alberta's Legislative Building, 109th St. & 97th Ave., SW of Vista 33, just N of the N. Saskatchewan River. Noted for the electronic carillon in its dome, elegant interior, and provincial greenhouses on its terrace. Open daily 9–8:30.

Provincial Museum of Alberta, 12845 102nd Ave., W of Vista 33. Excellent exhibits on Alberta's natural and human history. Open daily 9–8 Victoria Day–Labour Day, 9–5 Tu–Su rest of year.

Edmonton Space Sciences Centre, 142nd St. & 11th Ave., Coronation Park, NW of downtown Edmonton. Excellent displays, including a planetarium, an IMAX theater, science exhibits, games, and models. Open daily 10–10.

Fort Edmonton Park, Whitemund Dr., 5 miles SW of downtown Edmonton on the S bank of the North Saskatchewan River. Fine reconstruction of the 1840s Hudson Bay Company fort and pioneer village that started it all. Costumed workers demonstrate various pioneer skills. Live performances on Su and holidays. Open daily 10–6, Victoria Day–Labour Day.

West Edmonton Mall, 87th Ave. & 107th St., NW of Fort Edmonton Park, across the N. Saskatchewan River. The world's largest mall is a shopping mall and amusement park rolled into one, with some 800 shops, a hotel, a Fantasyland (including submarine rides), a 5-acre World Waterpark, an ice rink, and an 18-hole miniature golf course. Has to be seen to be believed! Open 10–10 M–Sa, 10–8 Su.

Useful Information

Travel Alberta (427-4321), 10025 Jasper Ave; *Edmonton Tourism Visitor Information Center* (422-5505), 9797 Jasper Ave; *Emergency* (911); *Taxi* (462-3456); *Public Transportation* (421-4636); *Weather* (468-4940).

Special Trips/Tours

Jasper National Park, containing some of Canada's most majestic mountain scenery, is about 222 miles W of Edmonton on Hwy. 16. Just inside the S boundary of the park is the *Columbia Icefield,* the largest sheet of glacial ice (150 sq. miles) in North America S of the Arctic circle. Visit the Icefield Centre. The *Jasper Tramway,* just S of Jasper, via Hwy. 93 and Whistler Mountain Road, affords magnificent panoramas of the park. Take a boat cruise on *Maligne Lake.*

South of Jasper National Park on the *Icefields Pkwy.* (itself one of the most beautiful drives in the world), is *Banff National Park,* with equally spectacular scenery. The resort town of Banff has two museums worth seeing: the *Natural History Museum* and the *Parks Canada Natural History Museum. Lake Louise,* 35 miles W of Banff, is a truly beautiful lake, surrounded by magnificent mountains.

Some 24 miles N of Edmonton, via Hwy. 28 to Bon Accord, and Lilly Lake Rd., N of Bon Accord, is the *Alberta Wildlife Park,* a 1,000-acre refuge with over 100 species of animals from all over the world. Open daily 10–7 Apr.– Sept., 10–5 rest of year.

Rocky Mountain House National Historic Park is SW of Edmonton, just E of Jasper and Banff National Parks and the rugged wilderness areas of Rocky Mountain Forest Reserve. The park contains the remnants of several fur trading posts. During July and August, park interpreters in period costumes demonstrate late-18th- and 19th-century crafts and skills, and the visitor center offers fascinating glimpses of life on the frontier. Open daily 10–8 May–Labour Day, 8:30–5 M–F, 9–4:30 Su rest of year. Take Hwy. 2 to Red Deer 97 miles S of Edmonton, and then Hwy. 11 and 11A W of Red Deer for about 50 miles.

Weather

Edmonton has a continental climate with long, severe winters and short, warm summers. Summer daytime high temperatures typically reach into the low to mid 70s, falling to the upper 40s at night. Winter daytime highs are usually in the teens or low 20s, dropping to the single digits or below at night. May through August is the wet period.

EDMONTON: TEMPERATURES AND PRECIPITATION

Month	J	F	M	A	M	J	J	A	S	O	N	D
Average Daily Temperature												
(Fahrenheit) Max.	15	22	34	52	64	70	74	72	62	52	34	21
Min.	–4	1	12	28	38	45	49	47	38	30	16	5
Average Number of Days with Precipitation												
	12	9	10	8	12	15	14	12	9	9	11	12

Halifax: Canada

Sights to See

Halifax Citadel National Historic Park, Citadel Hill, overlooking downtown Halifax. Dating from 1828, this large star-shaped masonry fort is one of the best surviving examples of 19th-century fortification in North America. Has two museums and a good audiovisual presentation, "The Tides of History." During the summer, soldiers in period uniforms demonstrate garrison duties. Open daily 9–6 June–Labour Day, 9–5 the rest of the year.
Nova Scotia Museum, 1747 Summer St., just SW of the Citadel. Devoted to the province's history. Open 9:30–5 M–Sa, 1–5:30 Su, May–Oct., 9:30–5 Tu–Sa the rest of the year.
Halifax Public Gardens, Spring Garden Rd., opposite the Nova Scotia Museum. Considered among the finest gardens in Canada. Open daily.
Art Gallery of Nova Scotia, 6152 Coburg Rd., just SW of the Public Gardens. Noted for its collection of regional folk art. Open 10–5:30 M–Sa, noon–5:30 Su.
Province House, Prince & Hollis Sts., below the citadel. Dating from 1811, it is considered to be one of the finest examples of Georgian architecture in North America. Open 9–4:30 M–F.
Historic Properties, between Duke and Buckingham Sts., on the waterfront. Restored early-19th-century buildings. In the summer a replica of *Bluenose,* a famous schooner, is docked here, offering harbor cruises (422-2678).
St. Paul's Church, Barrington & Duke Sts., near Province House. Halifax's oldest existing building. Open 10–4 M–F, June–Aug.
Maritime Museum of the Atlantic, 1675 Lower Water St., just SE of Province House. An excellent marine history collection, including the historic hydrographic vessel, *C.S.S. Acadia,* docked in the museum's wharf. Open 9:30–5:30 M–Sa, 1–5:30 Su, May 15–Oct 15, 9:30–5 Tu–Su the rest of the year.
York Redoubt, Herring Cover Rd., just outside Halifax to the S, off Hwy. 253. A national historic site, the 200-year-old fort overlooks the harbor, offering fine views of the coastline. Open daily 10–6, June 15–Labor Day.

Useful Information

Nova Scotia Tourist Bureau, Historic Properties (424-4247); *U.S. Consulate,* Cogswell Tower, Suite 910, Scotia Square (429-2480); *Taxi* (422-1551 or 422-4433).

Special Trips/Tours

A harbor cruise aboard the Bluenose II schooner, a replica of the famous 19th-century fishing schooner, is an excellent way to get to see Halifax. The schooner leaves from her wharf at Historic Properties (422-2678 or 424-4247).
    Peggy's Cove, a famous artists' community, is one of the many fishing villages strung out along Nova Scotia's rugged S coast. Some 30 miles SW of Halifax, off Rte. 333, it is one of the best-preserved fishing villages in Canada,

with an old lighthouse, weatherbeaten wharves, and plenty of fishing and sailing boats. Further down the coast is the fishing port of *Lunenburg*, dating from the 1750s, and home port of the original *Bluenose*. On the dockside, housed in waterfront buildings and on two historic ships (a fishing schooner and a trawler), is the *Fisheries Museum of the Atlantic*. The museum has excellent displays and exhibits, including an aquarium, a gallery, and a movie theater. Open daily 9:30–5:30 May 15–Oct. 31.

If you have several days to spare, a trip through Scottish Nova Scotia (New Scotland) along the truly spectacular *Cabot Trail* around Cape Breton Island should not be missed. Although a long drive from Halifax, it will reward you with beautiful scenery as the trail circles the E and W shores of the island along the edge of the very rugged *Cape Breton Highlands National Park* (drive in a clockwise direction). In Baddeck, at the S end of the Cabot Trail, is the *Alexander Graham Bell National Historic Park*, containing a museum displaying working models, papers, and exhibits commemorating the 37 years that Alexander Bell lived in Baddeck.

Weather

Halifax has a cool maritime climate with very changeable weather year-round. Daytime high temperatures in the summer are typically in the mid 70s, falling to the mid 50s at night. Winter daytime highs are usually in the low 30s, dropping into the teens at night. Nova Scotia is one of the least sunny regions of Canada. Precipitation is fairly evenly spread throughout the year.

HALIFAX: TEMPERATURES AND PRECIPITATION

Month	J	F	M	A	M	J	J	A	S	O	N	D
Average Daily Temperature												
(Fahrenheit) Max.	32	31	38	47	59	68	74	74	67	57	46	35
Min.	15	15	23	31	40	48	55	56	50	41	32	21
Average Number of Days with Precipitation												
	17	14	15	14	14	14	13	12	12	13	14	15

Montreal: Canada

Sights to See

Notre-Dame Basilica, place d'Armes. Noted for its larger altar and organ, wood carvings, and paintings. Open daily.

Vieux Montreal, between rues McGill, Notre-Dame, and Bern, along the riverbank. Site of the first settlement, with many 17th- and 18th-century buildings still standing—indeed, well preserved.

Place Jacques Cartier, between St. Paul & Notre-Dame. Restored 19th-century houses, restaurants, a flower market, and outdoor cafes.

Chateau de Ramezay, 280 rue Notre-Dame E. Excellent historical museum in the former home of the early French governors, offices of the West Indian Company, residence of English governors, and U.S. generals during the American occupation of 1775 and 1776. Open 10–4:30 Tu–Su.

Vieux Port, waterfront at the foot of place Jacques Cartier. A summertime entertainment complex, with daily movies, dancing, theater, puppet shows, and clowns. At night, the Montreal Symphony Orchestra or other ensembles play.

Underground Montreal, place Ville Marie, entered through the Queen Elizabeth Hotel, 900 Dorchester Blvd. A network of subterranean commercial and residential complexes, known as "places," designed by I. M. Pei and linked by the Metro system. The place *Ville Marie* was the first, but the plushest is *Westmount Plaza,* noted for its high fashion salons. Metro to Atwater. Shops open 9–6 M–W, 9–9 Th, F, 9–5 Sa.

Botanical Garden. 4101 Sherbrooke St. Over 25,000 species and varieties of flora. Open daily.

Mount Royal Park, Mount Royal. Planned by New York's Central Park architect, Frederick Law Olmsted, it offers an excellent panorama of the city from its Mount Royal Chalet lookout, or the Westmount Lookout.

St. Joseph's Oratory, 3800 Queen Mary Rd. A famous shrine, with basilica, oratory museum, and religious arts gallery. Open 8–10 daily.

Museum of Fine Arts, 1379 Sherbrooke W. Canada's oldest art museum, noted for its excellent collection of Canadian, European, and Eastern art. Open 11–5 Tu–Su.

Dow Planetarium, 1000 St. Jacques W. Programs are narrated in English and French on alternate hours. Open Tu–Su. Closed most of September.

Ile Ste. Helene and Ile Notre Dame, St. Lawrence River, across the Ponts de la Concorde and Jacques Cartier. The former has a military museum, aquarium, theater, a park, and La Ronde (an amusement park with pubs and restaurants). The latter has the "Man and His World" exhibits preserved from EXPO 67. Open 8–midnight daily from mid-June to Labour Day.

Useful Information

Tourist Office, 2 Place Ville Marie, University St. (873-2015), and Dominion Square, 1241 Peel St. (871-1595); *Tourist Bureau Kiosks,* Dominion Square & place Jacques Cartier (871-1595) are both open June through September; *American Express,* 1141 blvd. de Maison-neuve (284-3300); *U.S. Consulate,* Place Desjardins (281-1886); *Police* (934-2121); *Ambulance* (842-4242).

Special Trips/Tours

St. Lambert Lock, St. Lawrence Seaway, Rte. 15 across Victoria Bridge. The beginning of the famous system of locks and canals that allow oceangoing ships to navigate all the way through to the Great Lakes. The locking procedure can be witnessed from the observation tower, which also affords great views of Montreal. Open May–October.

Ottawa, Canada's capital city, is only 127 miles W from Montreal via Hwys. 40 and 417. Be sure to visit the Parliament Buildings, on a promontory above Ottawa River, and the outdoor Sparks Street Mall, lined with boutiques, specialty shops, flower vendors, rock gardens, historic buildings, and full of people.

Weather

Montreal's summers are quite warm, with lots of sunshine. Daytime highs reach into the high 70s, dropping into the mid to high 50s at night. Winters are very cold, however. Daytime high temperatures typically get into the low 20s, falling to the single digits at night. Precipitation is fairly even year-round, falling as snow in winter, usually covering the ground from mid-December to mid-March.

MONTREAL: TEMPERATURES AND PRECIPITATION

Month	J	F	M	A	M	J	J	A	S	O	N	D
Average Daily Temperature												
(Fahrenheit) Max.	20	21	32	50	63	73	79	75	66	53	38	23
Min.	3	3	15	30	42	53	58	55	47	37	25	9
Average Number of Days with Precipitation												
	13	13	13	11	12	12	12	11	12	12	13	15

Ottawa: Canada

Sights to See

Parliament Buildings, Parliament Hill, overlooking the Ottawa River. Perhaps Canada's best-known landmark, these impressive Gothic buildings with their distinctive green copper roofs, dating from the 1850s, were rebuilt after a 1916 fire. Noted for the Peace Tower that tops the Centre Block, with its carillon and national memorials. Tours 9–9:30 daily, July–Labour Day, 9–4:30 rest of year.
Changing the Guard Ceremony, Parliament Buildings. Performed by the Foot Guards and Grenadier Guards in front of the Centre Block daily at 10 A.M., June 24–Aug. 28.
The view from Nepean Pont, to the N of and below the Parliament Buildings, by the Alexandria Bridge over the Ottawa River, is beautiful.
Rideau Canal, running from just NE of the Parliament Buildings, where it joins with the Ottawa River, to Kingston, Ontario and to Lake Ontario. One of the city's main recreation areas, during the summer it is full of boats and canoes, and during the winter it is a skating rink. Boat tours leave from the Ottawa Locks daily, May–Oct.
National Gallery of Canada, 380 Sussex Dr., E of the Parliament Buildings. Fine collection of Canadian art, plus representative works of the Masters. Open 10–5 Tu daily May–Sept., 10–5 Tu–F rest of year.
Sussex Drive, running from near the National War Memorial, off Wellington St., NW and N along the Ottawa River to *Rockcliffe Park Village,* Ottawa's most

exclusive residential area, and home to many of the diplomatic corps. The official residence of the Canadian prime minister is at *24 Sussex Dr.,* opposite the *Government House,* the residence of the governor-general.

Currency Museum, 245 Sparks St., just S of the Parliament Buildings. Principally devoted to exhibits illustrating the history of Canadian currency, it also has interesting exhibits on the development of Chinese, Greek, Roman, and other currencies. Open 10:30–5 daily, May–Labour Day, 10:30–5 Tu–Sa, 1–5 Su the rest of the year.

Sparks Street Mall, between Elgin and Lyon Sts. A pleasant pedestrian mall with department stores, boutiques, sculptures, rock gardens, entertainment, fountains, and artwork on display.

National Museum of Science and Technology, 1867 St. Laurent Blvd., S of the downtown area. Hands-on museum with antique carriages, steam engines, automobiles, and aircraft on display. Open 10–8 daily, May–Labour Day, 9–5 Tu–Su the rest of the year.

Royal Canadian Mounted Police Stables, St. Laurent Blvd. & Sandridge Rd. Where the Mounties and their horses train for the famous *Musical Ride.* Call in advance for the schedule (993-2723).

Useful Information

Visitor and Convention Bureau, National Arts Centre, 65 Elgin St (237-5158); *National Capital Commission,* 161 Laurier Ave (996-1811); *U.S. Embassy,* 100 Wellington St (238-5335); *American Express,* 220 Laurier St. W. (563-0231); *Taxi* (238-1111); *Public Transportation* (741-4390); *Post Office,* 313 Rideau St. (992-4760).

Special Trips/Tours

The Department of Agriculture's *Central Experiment Farm and Agricultural Museum* are located off Prince of Wales Dr. in the southern part of Ottawa, and make an interesting diversion. Well known for its ornamental flower gardens and large arboretum, the Central Experimental Farm also has livestock barns and fields of various crops, which can be seen from a horse-drawn wagon tour during the summer months. The museum illustrates the development of farming techniques. The farm is open 8:15–dusk daily, the museum 9:30–5 daily.

Gatineau National Capital Community Park, a 90,000-acre wilderness and recreation area, is just 15 minutes NW of Ottawa, across the river in Quebec. Noted for its scenery, fishing, boating, swimming, and hiking opportunities, it provides a welcome respite from the urban world. Open daily. About an hour's drive SE of Ottawa, via Hwys. 417 and 138, is *Cornwall* on the St. Lawrence River. Headquarters of the St. Lawrence Seaway Authority, it is also the site of the *Moses-Saunders Power Dam,* a huge hydroelectric facility jointly owned by New York and Ontario. The dam's information center is worth seeing. Open 10–5 daily July–Aug. Nearby, on Cornwall Island, is a re-created *Indian Village and museum,* depicting 18th-century Indian life. Open 8:30–3 M–F, May–Sept.

Weather

Ottawa experiences very variable weather. Summer daytime high temperatures are typically in the mid to high 70s, dropping to the 50s at night. Winter daytime highs are usually in the 20s, falling to the single digits at night. Precipitation is fairly evenly spread throughout the year, with snow on the ground from December to March.

OTTAWA: TEMPERATURES AND PRECIPITATION

Month	J	F	M	A	M	J	J	A	S	O	N	D
Average Daily Temperature												
(Fahrenheit) Max.	21	22	33	51	66	76	81	77	68	54	39	24
Min.	3	3	16	31	44	54	58	55	48	37	26	9
Average Number of Days with Precipitation												
	13	12	12	11	11	10	11	10	11	12	12	14

Quebec City: Canada

Sights to See

Place Royale, at the center of Lower Town. Small cobblestoned square that marks the beginning of French colonization of North America. Largest concentration of 17th- and 18th-century buildings on continent.

Notre-Dame-des-Victoires, Place Royale. Dating from the late 17th century, it is known for its fine interior woodwork and commemorative paintings. Open 8–5 daily May–Oct., shorter hours the rest of the year.

La Promenade des Gouverneurs, Upper Town. A walkway that extends half a mile from Dufferin Terrace to ave. Cap Diamant beside the Citadel. Affords magnificent views of the Saint Lawrence River. Reached by the funicular at rues Petit-Champlain & Sous-le-Fort.

Citadel, on the summit of Cap Diamant, some 350 ft. above the Saint Lawrence River. Dating from the 1820s, this huge star-shaped fortress is noted for the *Changing of the Guard ceremony* at 10 A.M. daily, and the ceremonial retreat at 7 P.M., Tu, Th, Sa & Su, mid–June to Aug. Closed from December to February, except to groups.

Musee du Fort, 10 rue Ste. Anne, N of the Citadel. See the sound and light show reenacting battles and sieges of Quebec. Open 9–6 M–F, 1–5 Sa–Su during spring and summer, shorter hours the rest of the year.

Quebec Seminary (Seminaire de Quebec), cote de la Fabrique, off rue St. Famille, E of place d'Armes. A cluster of 17th-century buildings, known for its courtyard, chapel, and Mon. de Laval's commemorative hall. Open 9:30–5:30 M–Sa, 12–5:30 Su.

Musee du Seminaire, 9 rue de l'Universite, NE of place d'Armes. Fine collection of religious and secular paintings, 19th-century scientific instruments, silver jewelry, and stamps. Open 10–4 W–Su, May–Oct., shorter hours the rest of the year.

Artillery Park (Parc de l'Artillerie), just N of Porte Saint-Jean, NW of place d'Armes. Drop by the visitors center. Open 1–6 M, 10–6 Tu–Su, July–Aug., shorter hours the rest of the year.
Battlefield Park (Parc des Champs-de-Bataille), SE of the citadel. Surrounds the Plains of Abraham, site of the battle between Wolfe and Montcalm in 1759. Plaques explain the battle.
Musee du Quebec, 1 Av. Wolfe-Montcalm, in Battlefield Park. Good collection of Quebec fine arts. Open 9:15–4:45 M–Su. 9:15–10:45 P.M. W.

Useful Information

Tourist Office (Maison du Tourisme de Quebec), 12 rue Sainte-Anne (643-2280); *Information Center of the Tourism & Convention Bureau,* 60 rue d'Auteuil (692-2471); *U.S. Consulate,* 2 Place Terrasse (692-2095); *Police* (694-6123); *American Express,* 2270 Leon Harmel, Ste-Foy (681-0008); *Taxi* (525-5191 or 522-2001).

Special Trips/Tours

A Quebec City Cruise. The M/V Louis Jolliet leaves the quai Chouinard, 10 rue Dalhousie, daily at 10 A.M. for 1-hour cruises of the harbor, and at 2 P.M. for the 90-minute cruise to Ile d'Orleans, mid-June–Labour Day.
  The Basilica of Ste.-Anne de Beaupre, a world-famous shrine, is on the N shore of the St. Lawrence, 22 miles NE of Quebec City. A striking Romanesque-style building, rebuilt in the 1920s after suffering fire damage, it contains the Miraculous Statue and the forearm bone of Ste.-Anne. It is also noted for its beautiful interior craftsmanship, especially the fine ceiling mosaics in the nave. Open 6:30–9 daily, June–Sept., shorter hours the rest of the year. On the way to Ste.-Anne de Beaupre, see *Montmorency Falls,* at the intersection of Autoroute 40 & Hwy. 360. Surrounded by a provincial park, the waterfall drops 274 ft.
Ile d'Orleans, an island in the St. Lawrence, is just downstream from Quebec City, and well worth the trip. It is reached either by road, via the bridge opposite Montmorency Falls, or by boat (see Quebec City Cruises above). Relatively isolated for many years, the island has preserved its 18th-century French-Canadian heritage remarkably well. Take Hwy. 368, which circles the island. *Manoir Mauvide-Genest,* located at the entrance to Saint-Jean village, is considered to be one of the most beautiful rural buildings in Quebec. It has a restaurant, small museum, and a summer theater. The *Laurentides Reserve* in the Laurentian Mountains makes a nice side trip. NW of Quebec City via Hwy. 175, it is a vast reserve of wooded uplands with moose, beaver, bear, and other kinds of wildlife.

Weather

Quebec City's summer daytime high temperatures typically reach into the mid 70s, dropping to the mid 50s at night. Winter daytime highs are usually in the high teens or 20s, dropping to the single digits at night. Precipitation is fairly even through the year, falling as snow during the winter.

QUEBEC CITY: TEMPERATURES AND PRECIPITATION

Month	J	F	M	A	M	J	J	A	S	O	N	D
Average Daily Temperature												
(Fahrenheit) Max.	18	20	31	45	61	72	76	73	64	51	36	22
Min.	2	4	15	29	41	52	57	54	47	37	24	9
Average Number of Days with Precipitation												
	14	14	14	12	13	14	13	12	13	13	14	17

Toronto: Canada

Sights to See

Toronto itself, from the observation deck or revolving restaurant 1,122 ft. up the *CN Tower,* 301 Front St. (the world's tallest free-standing structure). There is another deck at 1,500 ft. Open 10–10 daily.

Ontario Place, Lakeshore Blvd. Large theme park with a Children's Village, a pavilion with Ontario exhibits and restaurants, an amphitheater, and a cultural center. Open 10–1 A.M. M–Sa, 10–11 Su, May–Sept.

Harbourfront, 235 Queen's Quay W. A recreation and cultural complex, with cafes, a railway museum, and a year-round antiques and flea market. Open 9–9 daily.

Ontario Parliament Buildings, Queen's Park Crescent at University Ave. Visit the Visitors' Gallery to listen to a question period. Guided tours daily in the summer; weekends during the winter. Open 8:30–3:30. Concerts are held in Queen's Park during summer evenings.

The Royal Ontario Museum, 100 Queen's Park Crescent, next to the parliament buildings. Canada's largest museum, noted for its excellent science, art, and archaeology exhibits, as well as its Chinese collection. Open 10–9 M–Sa, 12–8 Su.

Chinatown, centered around University Ave. & Dundas St. W. The usual assortment of shops, markets, and restaurants.

Nathan Phillips Square and City Hall, Bay & Queen Sts. Named after the mayor whose vision built this modern building, complete with reflecting pool with fountains and a bronze Henry Moore sculpture.

Art Gallery of Ontario, Dundas St. W. between McCaul & Beverley Sts. Noted for its Henry Moore Sculpture Center. Open 11–5:30 Tu–Su, 11–9 W, Th.

Casa Loma, 1 Austin Terrace, near Davenport & Spadina Rds. A splendid 98-room castle built by wealthy industrialist Sir Henry Pellat in the early 1900s. Open 10–4 daily, 10–5 in summer.

Eaton Centre, 220 Yonge St. A large three-level gallery with over 300 shops, boutiques, and restaurants and the famous Eaton's department store.

Ontario Science Centre, 770 Don Mills Rd. at Eglinton Ave. E., Don Mills. Famous for its excellent scientific and technological exhibits. Demonstrations, films, and multimedia shows along with participatory exhibits. Open 10–6 daily. *Black Creek Pioneer Village,* Jane St. & Steeles Ave. A restored 19th-century town, with guides in period costumes demonstrating various tasks. Open daily during the summer.

Useful Information

Metropolitan Toronto Convention and Visitors Association, Eaton Center, 207 Queen's Way W. (368-9990) and 220 Yonge St. (979-3143); *Visitor Information Centre,* City Hall main lobby, Queen & Bay Sts. (392-7341); *U.S. Consulate General,* 360 University Ave. (595-1700); *American Express,* 167 A Yonge St. (868-1044); *Weather* (676-3066); *Road Reports*—Ontario 248-3561), (U.S.- 964-3094); *Taxi* (363-5611 or 366-6868); *Toronto Transit Commission,* Public Transportation (484-4544); *Emergency* (911 for fire, police, ambulance).

Special Trips/Tours

A 15-minute ferry ride to the Toronto Islands, Lake Ontario, just offshore, makes an interesting trip. No cars, only pedestrians and bicycles allowed. *Centre Island* has picnic grounds, restaurants, and boating facilities.

From June 14 through September 2, the 95-ft. schooner *Challange* makes 2-hour *harbor tours* daily, starting at 10 A.M. It is moored at the Queen's Quay Terminal Bldg. at the foot of York St. (366-0612).

Niagara Falls, due S of Toronto across Lake Ontario, is some 90 miles away via the QEW Hwy. Water from Lake Erie (571 ft. above sea level) flowing to Lake Ontario (243 ft. above sea level) created the falls, divided by an island. The *Horseshoe (Canadian) Falls* are 176 ft. high and 2,100 ft. wide, and the *American Falls* are 182 ft. high and 1,076 ft. wide. Ride the *Maid of the Mist* sightseeing boat that takes you to the bottom of the Horseshoe Falls.

Weather

Summer daytime highs are typically in the mid to high 70s, dropping to the high 50s at night. Winters are cold, with daytime highs usually in the 30s, falling to the teens and low 20s at night. Precipitation is pretty evenly divided throughout the year, coming in the form of snow during winter.

TORONTO: TEMPERATURES AND PRECIPITATION

Month	J	F	M	A	M	J	J	A	S	O	N	D
Average Daily Temperature												
(Fahrenheit) Max.	30	30	37	50	63	73	79	77	69	56	43	33
Min.	16	15	23	34	44	54	59	58	51	40	31	21
Average Number of Days with Precipitation												
	16	12	13	12	13	11	10	9	12	11	13	13

Vancouver: Canada

Sights to See

Stanley Park, at the foot of W. Georgia St. One of the finest natural parks in the world, surrounded by the sea on three sides, and full of lakes, lagoons, gardens, and trails, together with tennis courts, cafes, restaurants, a zoo, and an aquarium. Walk along the promenade.

Vancouver Aquarium, Stanley Park. The country's largest and best, with over 9,000 specimens, and killer whale and dolphin shows. Open 10–5 M–F, 10–6 Sa & Su in summer, 10–5 daily rest of year.

Vanier Park, 1100 Chestnut. Contains an excellent planetarium, the *Vancouver Museum* (illustrating the area's history and native cultures; open 10–5 daily), a maritime museum (open 10–5 daily), and the Royal Canadian Mounted Police schooner.

Harbour Centre Observation Deck, 555 W. Hastings St. The view from this 500-ft. observation deck or the lounge is spectacular. See the movie, "Vancouver Discovery Show" shown in the Centre. Open 10–10 Su–Th, 10–midnight F & Sa.

Gastown, bordered by Water, Alexander, Columbia, and Cordova Sts. Renovated warehouses, with boutiques, antique shops, galleries, and restaurants. Enjoy the gaslight fixtures and see the only steam clock in the world, at Cambie & Water Sts.

Chinatown, centered on East Pender St., is the second largest such community in North America, after San Francisco's. Full of sidewalk markets and gilded and elaborately decorated shops.

Vancouver Art Gallery, 750 Hornby St. Housed in an old courthouse, it is known for its collection of works by Emily Carr, a native artist. Open Tu–Su.

Museum of Anthropology, NW. Marine Dr. University of British Columbia campus. Noted for its excellent collection of Indian art and artifacts, and totem poles. Open 12–9 Tu, 12–7 W–Su in summer; 12–9 Tu, 12–5 W–Su the rest of the year.

Van Dusen Botanical Gardens, 5251 Oak St. An outstanding collection of native and exotic plants arranged in different sections to show geographical origin and botanical relationships.

MacMillan Bloedel Place, at Oak Street & 37th Ave., offers a participatory presentation explaining the nature of British Columbia's forests. Open 10–9 daily in summer, 10–6 the rest of the year.

Capilano Canyon and Suspension Bridge, Capilano Rd., North Vancouver. A long footbridge spans a spectacular, heavily wooded gorge in a beautiful park with colorful gardens, complete with totem poles and life-size carvings of Indians. Open 8–10 daily in summer; 8–5 the rest of the year.

Capilano Fish Hatchery, 4500 Capilano Park Rd., noted for its architecturally acclaimed showcase facility. Open 8–dusk daily.

Useful Information

Vancouver Tourism, 562 Burrard Street (682-2222); *Tourism B.C. Information Center,* 800 Robson St. (668-2300); *British Columbia Ferries* (669-1211); *U.S. Consulate,* 1075 W. Georgia St. (685-4311); *Emergency* (911); *Weather* (273-8331); *Travelers Aid* (683-2531); *Highway Information* (277-0112); *Taxi* (681-3311, 681-2181, or 731-9211); *Ski Information* (669-SNOW).

Special Trips/Tours

Ride the *Grouse Mountain Skyride aerial tramway* from the parking lot to the top of Grouse Mountain (3,974 ft.), and enjoy the magnificent view of the city and environs. At the end of Capilano Rd. in North Vancouver. Open 10–10 daily.

The *Royal Hudson steam train ride* from North Vancouver to Squamish, up the Howe Sound, is definitely worth it, whether you are a steam buff or not. The scenery is magnificent, and you can come back on the cruise boat, *M/V Britannia.* Trains leave at 10:30 W–Su July–Aug., and W & Su in May and June (987-5211). Call 687-9558 for information on the motorboat's schedule and also train/ship or ship/train combination tours.

Victoria, the provincial capital, is a short ferryride and less than an hour's drive away, on Vancouver Island, across the Strait of Georgia. Replete with Victorian houses, manicured gardens, parks, fish & chips restaurants, and lawn-bowling greens. Walking along Government Street, with its small restaurants, sweetshops, and Tudor-style buildings, will make you appreciate its Victorian charm. Visit *Bastion Square, Thunderbird Park,* the *Provincial Museum,* and the famous *Butchart Gardens.*

Weather

Vancouver's climate is influenced by its proximity to the ocean, with mild winters and warm summers. The weather is very changeable. Daytime highs in the summer typically reach the mid 70s, falling to the 50s at night. Winters are very cloudy and wet, with frequent coastal fog. Temperatures usually get into the 40s and drop to the low 30s at night. July and August typically have much less rain than the other months.

VANCOUVER: TEMPERATURES AND PRECIPITATION

Month	J	F	M	A	M	J	J	A	S	O	N	D
Average Daily Temperature												
(Fahrenheit) Max.	41	44	50	58	64	69	74	73	65	57	48	43
Min.	32	34	37	40	46	52	54	54	49	44	39	35
Average Number of Days with Precipitation												
	20	17	17	14	12	11	7	8	9	16	19	22

Victoria: Canada

Sights to See

Inner Harbor, downtown Victoria. Busy harbor with yachts, ferries, and sea planes overlooked by the splendid *Empress Hotel,* famous for its afternoon teas.

Parliament Buildings, Belleville St., overlooking the harbor. Seat of British Columbia's provincial government. Ornate Victorian buildings surrounded by lush gardens, they are known for their elaborate interiors. Tours daily, May–Labour Day.

Royal British Columbia Museum, 675 Belleville St., to the E of the Parliament Buildings. Excellent collection of the human and natural history of British Columbia. Noted for its Indian art. Open daily 9:30–7, May–Labour Day, 10–5:30 rest of year.

Thunderbird Park, Douglas & Belleville Sts., next to the Royal British Columbia Museum. Known for its collection of Indian totem poles. Open daily.

Helmcken House, 638 Elliot Street, next to Thunderbird Park. Pioneer house with period furnishings and medical instruments. Open daily 10–5.

Crystal Garden, 713 Douglas Street, NE of Thunderbird Park across Belleville St. A tropical conservatory, with walkways, an aviary, and a waterfall. Open daily.

Pacific Undersea Gardens, 440 Belleville Street, N of the Parliament Buildings in the Inner Harbor. Billed as the world's only undersea theater, it features scuba diving shows with an octopus. Open daily 9–9 May–Oct., 10–5 rest of year.

Maritime Museum of British Columbia, 28 Bastion Square, N of the Pacific Undersea Gardens, off Wharf St. Interesting collection of maritime artifacts, ships, models, figureheads, etc. Open daily 10–6 July–Labour Day, 10–4 rest of year.

Bastion Square, overlooking the Inner Harbor. An area of renovated 19th-century buildings surrounding a courtyard.

Butchart Gardens, in Brentwood, 14 miles N of Victoria, off Hwy. 17. World famous manicured gardens full of beautiful native and exotic flowers, complete with English, Japanese, and Italian gardens. Concerts are held during summer evenings. Open daily 9–9 May–Sept., 9–4 rest of year.

Fable Cottage and Estate, 5187 Cordova Bay Road, via Hwy. 17. Thatched cottages and animated gnomes surrounded by flower gardens on an oceanfront estate. Open daily 9:30–dusk April–Oct.

Useful Information

Greater Victoria Visitor Information Center, 812 Wharf Street (382-2127); *Tourism B.C.,* 1117 Wharf Street (387-1642); *B.C. Ferry* (386-3431); *Weather* (656-3978); *Taxi* (382-4235, 383-7111); *Public Transportation* (382-6161).

Special Trips/Tours

A guided tour of Victoria on one of the many red London double-decker buses will get you in the mood to see this quintessentially British city. Buses leave from the Inner Harbor along Belleville Street.

A day-long *train ride on the Esquimalt & Nanaimo Railroad,* operated by VIA Rail (383-4324), to Courtenay and back provides a scenic journey along the E coast of Vancouver Island past dense forests, lakes, and an Indian reservation and over Malahat summit (1,000 ft.). Trains leave Victoria's Russell St. Station at 8:15 A.M., stopping briefly in Nanaimo and Courtenay, and arriving back in Victoria before 6:00 P.M.

Vancouver Island's natural, rugged beauty can best be seen by driving NNW on Hwy. 1 to Nanaimo (73 miles), on to Parksville (another 23 miles), and then heading W over the island on Hwy. 4 to the *fishing villages of Ucluelet and Tofino* and the *Pacific Rim National Park.* The park is known for its long, sandy beaches, rugged headlands, dense rainforests, rocky islands, snowcapped mountains, and abundant wildlife. On the way there, or on the way back, stop off in Nanaimo and visit the *Nanaimo Centennial Museum,* 100 Cameron Street, with its fine exhibits illustrating Vancouver Island's history.

Vancouver, British Columbia, is less than an hour's drive and a short ferry-ride away across the Strait of Georgia. With its magnificent natural setting and world-famous *Stanley Park,* its excellent *Vancouver Aquarium,* fine museums, and its *Gastown nightlife area,* the city of Vancouver should not be missed.

Weather

Victoria has a cool maritime climate, with mild winters and warm summers and very changeable weather year-round. Daytime highs in the summer typically reach into the mid 70s, falling to the 50s at night. Winters are very cloudy and wet with frequent coastal fog. Temperatures usually get into the 40s, dropping to the low 30s at night. July and August have much less rain than the other months.

VICTORIA: TEMPERATURES AND PRECIPITATION

Month	J	F	M	A	M	J	J	A	S	O	N	D
Average Daily Temperature												
(Fahrenheit) Max.	41	44	50	58	64	69	74	73	65	57	48	43
Min.	32	34	37	40	46	52	54	54	49	44	39	35
Average Number of Days with Precipitation												
	20	17	17	14	12	11	7	8	9	16	19	22

Winnipeg: Canada

Sights to See

The panorama of Winnipeg from the 31st-floor observation deck of the *Richardson Building,* Portage Ave. & Main St., is the city's best.

Winnipeg Commodity Exchange, Portage Ave. & Main St. One of the largest grain exchanges in the world. Watch the trading from a special gallery. Open 9:30–1:15 M–F.

Manitoba Museum of Man and Nature, Main St. & Rupert Ave., just N of the Richardson Building. Exhibits and audiovisual presentations illustrating the relationship of man and nature in Manitoba. Also noted for its planetarium. Open 10–9 M–Sa, 12–9 Su, May–Sept., 10–5 Tu–Su the rest of the year.

Ukrainian Cultural and Educational Centre, 184 Alexander Ave. E, N of the Manitoba Museum of Man and Nature. Ukrainian folk art and history is featured. Open 10–4 Tu–Sa, 2–5 Su.

Winnipeg Art Gallery, 300 Memorial Blvd., SW of the Commodity Exchange. Fine collection of Canadian and European art, but noted for its collection of Eskimo sculpture. Open 11–5 Tu–Sa, 12–5 Su.

Legislative Building, SSE of the Commodity Exchange, on the Assiniboine River, between Kennedy and Osborne Sts. Imposing Neoclassical building noted for its Italian marble grand staircase, and the bronze statue, Golden Boy, on top of its dome. Tours 8:30–4:30 daily.

Osborne Street Village, Osborne St., between River and Stradbrook Aves., just SE of the Legislative Building. One of Winnipeg's principal shopping areas.

Dainavert, 61 Carlton St., just E of the Legislative Building. The former home of prominent politician Sir Hugh John McDonald, it is full of period Victorian antiques. Open 10–6 Tu–Th, Sa–Su, June–Aug., 12–4:30 Tu–Th, Sa–Su the rest of the year.

Assiniboine Park, 2799 Roblin Blvd., just W of the downtown area, off Corydon Ave. A conservatory, an English garden, a miniature railway, and a zoo. Park open 7–10 daily, zoo 10–8 daily.

Living Prairie Museum and Nature Preservation Park, 2795 Ness Ave., W of downtown on the N side of the Assiniboine River from Assiniboine Park. A remnant of the original prairie grasslands that once covered so much of Canada and the U.S., with exhibits, nature walks, and lectures on this surprisingly diverse ecological community. Open 10–6 M–F, 1–5 Sa–Su, July–Labour Day, 8–4:30 daily the rest of the year.

Royal Canadian Mint, 520 Lagimodiere Ave., in St. Boniface suburb SE of downtown Winnipeg. Watch the minting process from a viewing gallery in one of the world's most modern mints. Open 9–3 M–F.

Useful Information

Travel Manitoba Visitor Reception Center, Legislative Building, Broadway & Osborne Sts. (945-3777); *Winnipeg Convention and Visitors Bureau,* 375 York (943-1970); *Attractions Recorded Information* (942-2535); *Public Transportation* (284-7190); *Weather* (983-2050).

Special Trips/Tours

Several boat lines offer *sightseeing cruises* on the Red and/or Assiniboine rivers, in addition to evening cruises offering live entertainment and dinner. Contact

Rouge Line Boat Tours (669-2824); or *Gray Line Paddlewheel Riverboat Tours* (339-1696).

About 21 miles NE of Winnipeg, outside Selkirk, is **Lower Fort Garry National Historic Park,** an original 19th-century fur-trading post with restored buildings and period furniture, along with costumed interpreters. Open 9:30–6 daily May–Labour Day (204/482-6843).

The **Mennonite Village Museum,** near Steinbach, is just over 30 minutes SE of Winnipeg via the Trans-Canada Hwy. (Hwy. 1) and Hwy. 12. A replica of one of the original Mennonite villages, it has 20 furnished buildings, a gristmill, and period farm equipment. Open 9–8 M–Sa, 12–8 Su July–Aug., shorter hours in June and Sept.

About an hour's drive E of Winnipeg on the Trans-Canada Highway (Hwy. 1), is **Whiteshell Provincial Park.** If you enjoy hunting, canoeing, fishing, or just getting away from it all, this is the area. *Falcon Lake* offers sailing, boating, and other recreational opportunities. The park's 365-ft.-deep *West Hawk Lake* is thought to have been formed by a meteor.

Weather

Winnipeg has a continental climate with short, warm summers and long, very cold winters. Summer daytime high temperatures typically reach into the upper 70s, dropping to the 50s at night. Winter daytime highs are usually in the teens, or low 20s, falling to the minus single digits or teens in the winter. Precipitation is heaviest in June and July.

WINNIPEG: TEMPERATURES AND PRECIPITATION

Month	J	F	M	A	M	J	J	A	S	O	N	D
Average Daily Temperature												
(Fahrenheit) Max.	7	12	27	48	65	74	79	76	65	51	30	15
Min.	−13	−9	5	27	39	50	55	51	43	31	13	−3
Average Number of Days with Precipitation												
	12	11	9	9	10	12	10	10	9	6	9	11

Acapulco: Mexico

Sights to See

Avenida Costera Miguel Aleman, running parallel to the beach along Acapulco Bay. Most of the resort's large hotels, restaurants, shops, and night spots are located along this wide avenue.

Fort San Diego (Fuerte de San Diego), Morelos, off Av. Costera Miguel Aleman near the yacht harbor. Dating from the late 18th century, the fort now houses a museum.

Plaza Juan Alvarez (The Zocalo), the city's main square, SW of the Fort. Picturesque.

Acapulco Cathedral, Plaza Juan Alvarez. A Moorish-Byzantine structure built in the 1930s.

Quebrada divers, La Quebrada, next to the El Miradore hotel, SW of the cathedral. Spectacular dives from 130-ft.-high cliffs into the ocean below are made by these Acapulco divers. Dives are made at 1:30, 7:30, 8:30, 9:30 and 10:30 P.M.

Laguna de Coyuca, some 6 miles W of Acapulco. A freshwater lagoon, surrounded by dense tropical vegetation, full of exotic birds.

Playa Condesa, in the center of Acapulco Bay, between the Hyatt Continental and El Presidente hotels. Perhaps the most fashionable beach in Acapulco today.

Cultural and Convention Center (Centro Cultural y de Convenciones), at the E end of Acapulco Bay, off Av. Costera Miguel Aleman & Cristobal Colon. Contains a theater, a small archaeological museum, and folk art exhibits along with its conference halls.

Papagayo Park (Parque Papagayo), straddling the Av. Costera Miguel Aleman, at the underpass at the end of the strip. A beautiful park in a beautiful location.

Puerto Marques, a picturesque fishing village 8 miles E of Acapulco, situated on a beautiful bay.

Sports

Boating: all kinds of boats, including sailboats, are available for rent on the bay beaches. *Puerto Marques* and *Playa Caleta* are especially good spots. Glass-bottom-boat rides are also offered. Check with your hotel for information on bay cruises. Contact *Fiesta* or *Bonanza* (tel:2-2055) for yacht cruises.

Fishing: fishing boats leave from the *Malecon,* downtown waterfront. *Divers de Mexico* (tel:2-1398), Av. Costera Miguel Aleman 100, rents boats.

Golf: both the *Acapulco Princess Hotel* (tel:4-3100); and the *Pierre Marques Club de Golf* (tel:4-2000) at Revolcadero Beach have 18-hole courses. There is a 9-hole course in front of the Elcano hotel on Av. Costera Miguel Aleman.

Horseback Riding: horses can be rented at the *Revolcadero Beach,* and at *Pie de la Cuesta.*

Parasailing: most of the parachute rides operate on *Condesa Beach,* NOTE: it can be dangerous.

Snorkeling and Scuba Diving: snorkeling equipment is available at most of the principal hotels. For scuba equipment rental, instruction, and guided dives, contact *Divers de Mexico* (tel:2-1398), Av. Costera Miguel Aleman 100; or *Hermanos Arnold* (tel:2-1877), at the Hornos Beach. *Roquetta Island* is the diving spot.

Swimming: under Mexican law, all beaches are public. The best beaches for swimming, not just sunbathing, are *Caleta, Caletilla, Condesa, Homos, Hornitas,* and *Puerto Marques* E of Acapulco. The open Pacific Ocean beaches typically have heavy surf and undertow.

Tennis: many of the hotels have good tennis courts, some of which allow non-guests to play. The courts at the *Club de Tenis Alfredo* (tel:4-0024), Pradc

29; and at the *Villa Vera Racquet Club* (tel:4-0333), Villa Vera Hotel, Lomas del Mar are open to the public.

Water Skiing: all the major hotels have tow boats available. Popular spots are the *Caleta Beach* and *Puerto Marques*. Contact the *Escuela de Skiis* (tel:2-1551) for instruction.

Weather

Acapulco has a sunny, tropical climate with fairly uniform temperatures year-round. Summer daytime high temperatures typically reach into the low 90s, falling to the high 70s at night. Winter daytime highs are normally in the high 80s, dropping to the low 70s at night. The wet season is from June through October.

ACAPULCO: TEMPERATURES AND PRECIPITATION

Month	J	F	M	A	M	J	J	A	S	O	N	D
Average Daily Temperature												
(Fahrenheit) Max.	88	88	88	90	90	91	90	91	90	90	90	88
Min.	72	72	72	73	77	77	77	77	75	75	73	72
Average Number of Days with Precipitation												
	1	0	0	0	3	13	14	13	16	9	2	1

Cancun–Isla Mujeres: Mexico

Sights to See

Beaches on the island of Cancun. Superb beaches of white sand, palm groves, and banks of coral.

Archaeological Museum of Cancun, Convention Center at the E tip of the island. A small museum featuring local Mayan artifact exhibits.

CEDAM Marine Museum, Club Akumal, near the Playa Blanca hotel on Cancun island. Relics of 15th- and 18th-century shipwrecked galleons are featured.

Avenida Yaxchilan, mainland Cancun City (Ciudad de Cancun). Has some of the best shops and restaurants.

Ruins of El Rey, between Punta Cancun and Punta Nizuc. Mayan remains in the Puuc style, including truncated pyramids topped by temples.

Isla Mujeres (Island of Women), 5 miles long and up to a mile wide, it lies off the Yucatan peninsula, some 6 miles N of Cancun. Reached by air or ferry. Ferries leave from Punta Sam and Puerto Juarez.

Playa Cocos, on the N side of Isla Mujeres. The best beach on the island.

El Garrafon, at the S end of Isla Mujeres. A bay with a federally protected coral reef teeming with exotic tropical fish.

Maya Temple, on a hill at the southern tip of the island near El Garrafon beach.

Dating from the 10th century, it was constructed to honor the fertility goddess Ix-Chel.

Isla Contoy, N of Isla Mujeres, it is a bird sanctuary, with flamingoes, pelicans, frigate birds, and other species. Reached by boat from Isla Mujeres.

Sports

Boating: Cancun: all kinds of boats, motor and sail, are available in Cancun. Arrangements for rentals can be made through your hotel. Windsurfing is big here, contact *Windsurfing Cancun* (tel:4-2023). ISLA MUJERES: rentals at *El Presidente Caribe* (tel:2-0146).

Fishing: CANCUN: the waters off Cancun are abundant in sport fish. Boats can be rented, or charters arranged at *Club Lagoon Marina* (tel:3-1111); *Mauna Loa Marina* (tel:3-0072); *El Presidente Marina* (tel:3-0200); or through *Aventurismo* (tel:3-0315); and *Pez Vela* (tel:3-0992). Alternatively, your hotel can make all the arrangements. ISLA MUJERES: check with your motel. Fishing trips out to *Isla Contoy* are popular.

Golf: CANCUN: there is an 18-hole course designed by Robert Trent Jones at *Pok-Ta-Pok* (tel:3-0871). ISLA MUJERES: no golf course.

Parasailing: CANCUN: parachute tows are available on the resort island's beaches. NOTE: parasailing can be dangerous. ISLA MUJERES: no facilities at the moment.

Snorkeling and Scuba Diving: CANCUN: excellent snorkeling and scuba diving spots can be found around Cancun. The area off *Playa Tortugas' dock* is a popular snorkeling spot, and there are several excellent reefs between Cancun and Isla Mujeres. Contact: *Scuba Cancun* (tel:3-0315). ISLA MUJERES: the *El Garrafon coral reef* at the southern end of the island is the best spot.

Swimming: CANCUN: the hotel zone on Cancun has excellent beaches—all public under Mexican law. The *North Shore* has the safest beaches, with little surf. The Caribbean, or eastern, side of Cancun has fine beaches, but experiences strong currents and undertow. ISLA MUJERES: the best swimming beach is *Playa Los Cocos,* on the N side of the island.

Tennis: CANCUN: most of the island resort hotels have their own tennis courts; some even allow non-guests to play. Check with your hotel. ISLA MUJERES: as of the moment there are no tennis courts on the island.

Water Skiing: CANCUN: the *lagoon* behind Cancun's beachfront is the best place for water skiing. Arrangements can be made through your hotel. ISLA MUJERES: check with Hotel *El Presidente Caribe* (tel:2-0146).

Weather

Cancun's summer daytime high temperatures typically reach into the low 90s, falling to the mid 70s at night. Daytime highs in the winter are normally in the low 80s, falling to the mid 60s at night. June and September are the "wet months."

CANCUN: TEMPERATURES AND PRECIPITATION

Month	J	F	M	A	M	J	J	A	S	O	N	D
Average Daily Temperature												
(Fahrenheit) Max.	83	85	89	92	94	92	92	91	90	87	85	82
Min.	62	63	66	69	72	73	73	73	72	71	68	64
Average Number of Days with Precipitation												
	0	1	2	5	10	9	8	8	12	4	3	0

Cozumel: Mexico

Sights to See

Cozumel's beaches, particularly Playa San Juan beach in the NW and Playa San Francisco beach in the SW part of the island. Magnificent white sand beaches, many fringed by palms, overlooking crystal-clear water.

Palancar Reef, at the SW tip of the island. Considered by many to be one of the world's finest, it is especially noted for its black coral.

The Malecon (waterfront boulevard) in San Miguel de Cozumel. The focal point of the small town, Avenida Rafael E. Melgar has many of the town's shops, restaurants, and nighttime activities.

Chancanab Lagoon, a small freshwater lake about 4 miles S of San Miguel. The crystal-clear water, connected to the ocean by underground channels, is an ideal swimming and snorkeling spot.

Cozumel Island itself. The single road that loops around the island takes you through jungle, and then along the beautiful E coast. NOTE: most of the beaches here are unsafe, due to the strong undertow.

El Cedral Mayan temple ruins, just E of Playa San Francisco, in the SW part of the island. One of the many relatively undistinguished Maya sites on Cozumel, but one of the more accessible.

Tulum, about 60 miles S of Puerto Morelos on the mainland of the Yucatan. The only known Maya coastal fortress city, the *Castillo,* its most prominent structure, is perched on 40-ft.-high cliffs above the Caribbean. The *Temple of the Frescoes* is noted for its 13th-century wall paintings.

Xel-ha, some 7 miles N of Tulum on the coast, is a fascinating nature reserve, with a cove (caletas), freshwater lake, and Maya remains in and around the lagoon.

Sports

Boating: all kinds of boats, both motor and sail, are available for rent in Cozumel. Arrangements are typically made through your hotel. Windsurfing is popular, and windsurfers can be rented on the beach in front of hotels *El Sol Caribe, El Presidente,* and *Mayan Plaza.*

Fishing: the waters off Cozumel are abundant with sport fish. Contact *Club*

Nautico (tel:2-1113); the *Cabanas del Caribe Hotel* (tel:2-0072); or the *Mayan Plaza Hotel* (tel:2-0411).
Golf: there are no regular golf courses on Cozumel.
Parasailing: tows can be had along the beaches north of San Miguel.
Snorkeling and Scuba Diving: hotels along the beaches S of San Miguel tend to cater to divers and many have dive shops. These include *El Sol Caribe* (tel:2-1700); *La Ceiba* (tel:2-0816); *El Presidente* (tel:2-0322); *Galapago Inn* (tel:2-0627). Otherwise, contact *Discover Cozumel* (tel:2-0280); *Aqua Safari* (tel:2-0101); or *Fantasia Divers* (tel:2-0816). The best reefs for snorkeling or scuba diving are the *Palancar, Gonzalez, Maracaibo,* and *Punta Norte reefs.* The *Chancanab lagoon* is another popular spot for snorkelers.
Swimming: under Mexican law all beaches are public. The beaches N and S of San Miguel are generally safe, but those on the island's E side, facing the Caribbean, are not. Strong undertows make them hazardous. The *Playa San Juan* in the northwest and the *Playa San Francisco* beach in the southwest are two of the best.
Tennis: many of the major hotels have good courts, including the *El Presidente, Cozumel Caribe, Mayan Plaza, Sol Caribe,* and the *La Ceiba.*
Waterskiing: the beaches north of San Miguel offer waterskiing. Make arrangements through your hotel.

Weather

Cozumel enjoys a superb climate, with warm to hot temperatures all year through, and very little rainfall. Summer daytime high temperatures typically get into the low 90s, dropping to the mid 70s at night. Daytime highs in the winter months normally reach the low 80s, falling at night to the mid 60s. June and September are the "wet" months.

COZUMEL: TEMPERATURES AND PRECIPITATION

Month	J	F	M	A	M	J	J	A	S	O	N	D
Average Daily Temperature												
(Fahrenheit) Max.	83	85	89	92	94	92	92	91	90	87	85	82
Min.	62	63	66	69	72	73	73	73	72	71	68	64
Average Number of Days with Precipitation												
	0	1	2	5	10	9	8	8	12	4	3	0

Guadalajara: Mexico

Sights to See

Plaza de Armas, in the center of the city. Known for its fine pavillion or kiosk.
Government Palace (Palacio de Gobierno), on the E side of Plaza de Armas. A fine 17th-century Baroque building, noted for its beautiful ornamentation and murals by the well-known artist Jose Orozco.

Cathedral, on the N side of Plaza de Armas, with its facade facing the Plaza de la Liberacion. Dating from the late 16th century, it is comprised of many architectural styles. Noted for its many altars and fine ornamentation. The towers afford fine views.

State Museum (Museo del Estado de Jalisco), Plaza de la Rotunda, one block N of the cathedral. Fine collection of Mexican and European paintings, along with pre-Columbian artifacts, and colonial arts and crafts. Open 10–4 Tu–Sa, 10–1 Su.

Church of Santa Monica, Calle de Santa Monica & San Felipe, just NW of the cathedral. Especially noted for its Baroque facade.

Degollado Theater (Teatro Degollado), Plaza de la Liberacion, opposite the cathedral. A large Neoclassical building, known for its interior frescoes.

Hospicio Cabanas, Calle Hospicio, 6 blocks E of the cathedral. An early-19th-century Neoclassical structure with 23 patios, noted for the frescoes by Orozco in a former chapel, including *The Four Horsemen of the Apocalypse.* Open 10–4 Tu–Sa, 10–1 Su.

Market Hall (Mercado Libertad), between Rodriguez & Javier Mina across the Plaza de Toros from Hospicio Cabanas. Huge building housing vendors of every kind.

Parque Agua Azul, Calzada Independencia Sur & Constituyentes, near the main train station. A beautiful park containing a bird sanctuary. *Casa de las Artesanias,* near Constituyentes, has folk art and crafts exhibits.

Archaeological Museum (Museo de Arqueologico de Occidente), Plaza Juarez, on Independencia, opposite Parque Agua Azul. Fine collection of pre-Hispanic art. Open 10–2, 4–6 M–Sa.

Orozco Museum (El Museo Orozco), Aurelio Aceves 27. Paintings and drawings by this famous muralist.

Useful Information

Tourist Office, Morelos 102 (tel:14-8686) & Av. Chapultepec Norte 15 (tel:15-7506); *Federal Tourist Office,* Plaza Tapatia (tel:13-1605); *U.S. Consulate,* Progreso 175 (tel:25-2700); *American Express,* Lopez Mateos 447 (tel:30-0200); *Police* (tel:17-6060).

Special Trips/Tours

The SE suburb of *San Pedro Tlaquepaque* is a crafts shopping mecca. Centered around the restored *El Parian,* and along Av. Independencia, are a great many shops selling ceramics, glass, antiques, jewelry, clothing, and leather goods. Tlaquepaque's zocalo, El Parian, is the place to go for mariachi music, particularly on Sunday evenings. Be sure to visit the *Museo Regional de la Ceramica y las Artes Populares de Jalisco,* on Av. Independencia.

Some four miles beyond Tlaquepaque is the suburb of *Tonala,* also noted for its fine pottery, particularly its soft-blue glazed ceramics. It doesn't have the range of shops that exist in Tlaquepaque, but is less crowded and in some respects a more pleasant place to visit. Best time is on Sunday, a market day.

Mexico's largest lake, *Lake Chapala,* is only 26 miles S of Guadalajara on Mex. 44. A longtime favorite of visitors, it offers beautiful scenery and a number of picturesque villages around its shores. *Ajijic* and *Jocotepec* are especially worth visiting. Ajijic is a writers' and artists' retreat and a center for handicrafts. Jocotepec is an attractive fishing village.

Weather

Although in the tropics, Guadalajara enjoys a moderate climate due to its altitude. Summer daytime high temperatures are typically in the high 70s, dropping to the high 50s at night. Winter daytime highs are usually in the low 70s, falling to the high 40s at night. June to September is the wet season.

GUADALAJARA: TEMPERATURES AND PRECIPITATION

Month	J	F	M	A	M	J	J	A	S	O	N	D
Average Daily Temperature												
(Fahrenheit) Max.	69	73	79	84	82	78	77	77	76	73	71	70
Min.	46	47	50	55	60	61	58	57	56	53	50	48
Average Number of Days with Precipitation												
	4	5	9	14	17	21	27	27	23	13	6	4

Guanajuato: Mexico

Sights to See

Guanajuato itself from the Carratera Panoramica, a scenic loop road that circles the city, off the Irapuatio Road at the N edge of Guanajuato.
Union Garden (Jardin de la Union), in the center of Guanajuato. One of the city's most popular parks, with concerts on Tu, Th, & Su evenings.
Juarez Theater (Teatro Juarez), opposite the Union Garden. Dating from the late 19th century, it is noted for its Moorish interior and Doric columns. Open M–F.
San Diego Church, just N of the Juarez Theater. Dating from the 1660s and rebuilt in the 18th century, it is an outstanding example of Churrigueresque art.
La Parroquia, Plaza de la Plaz, N of Union Garden. Built in the late 17th century, this church houses the famous wooden image of the Virgin Mary, *La Virgin de Santa Fe de Guanajuato,* considered the oldest piece of Christian art in Mexico.
Church of La Compania, Pocitos & Navarro, N of Union Garden. Dating from the late 18th century and restored in the 19th, it is also a fine example of Churrigueresque art.
Diego Rivera Museum, Calle Pocitos 47, NW of the Church of La Compania. Birthplace of Diego Rivera, with period furniture on the first floor and many of the artist's works on the upper floors.
State Historical Museum, Mendizabel & Cinco de Mayo, W of the Diego

Rivera Museum. Housed in a huge early-19th-century grain warehouse, the *Alhondiga de Granaditas,* that figured prominently during the War of Independence. Noted for its pre-Columbian artifacts, handicrafts, and murals by Chavez Morado. Open Tu–Su.

Hidalgo Market (Mercado Hidalgo), Av. Juarez, just S of the Alhondiga de Granaditas. The city's principal market, housed in a large, vaulted, iron and glass building. Open daily.

The Pantheon (Cemetery), SW of Union Garden. Catacombs lined with some 100 well-preserved mummies in glass caskets. Open daily 9–6.

Useful Information

Tourist Office, Av. Juarez & Cinco de Mayo (tel:2-1574 or 2-0086); *Post Office,* Ayuntamiento 25; *Police* (tel:2-02666); closest *U.S. Consulate* is in Mexico City, at Reforma 305 (tel:5-211-0042).

Special Trips/Tours

About 12 miles outside town is the **Monumento a Cristo Rey,** a 53-ft.-tall bronze monument of Jesus Christ dedicated in 1956, on top of a mountain, Cerro del Cubilete, 8,550 ft. above sea level. The trip there and back offers fine panoramas of the surrounding mountains.

The Guanajuato area is famous historically for its productive silver mines; one in particular, the **Valenciana Mine,** is variously estimated to have produced 20 to 30 percent of the entire world's silver in the 17th and 18th centuries. It is still producing today and visitors can look around and even look down the 1,700-ft.-deep main shaft. It is 3 miles NW of Guanajuato, on the Dorlores Hidalgo Hwy.

Also in Valenciana is a really beautiful mid-18th-century church, the **Iglesia de San Cayetano.** Known for its ornate interior, fine paintings, and altars trimmed with gold leaf, it is an excellent example of a colonial church in the Churrigueresque style.

Some 2 miles outside Valenciana, on the road to Marfil, is the **Hacienda San Gabrielde Barrera,** a stunning, recently restored 18th-century hacienda. It is furnished in the Spanish Colonial style and is surrounded by a variety of formal gardens. Open daily 9–6:30.

Leon, the Guanajuato state's largest city, is about an hour W of Guanajuato. Mexico's principal shoe-manufacturing city, it offers a chance to see some of Mexico off the tourist path. Many of the downtown buildings are colonial, and it has a fine central plaza, or zocalo, and a colorful market.

Weather

Guanajuato has a warm temperate climate. Summer daytime highs typically reach into the mid 70s, dropping to the mid 50s at night. In winter, the highs are usually in the upper 60s, falling to the mid to low 40s at night. June through September is the wettest period.

GUANAJUATO: TEMPERATURES AND PRECIPITATION

Month	J	F	M	A	M	J	J	A	S	O	N	D
Average Daily Temperature												
(Fahrenheit) Max.	66	69	75	77	78	76	73	73	74	70	68	66
Min.	42	43	47	51	54	55	53	54	53	50	46	43
Average Number of Days with Precipitation												
	4	5	9	14	17	21	27	27	23	13	6	4

Ixtapa-Zihuatanejo: Mexico

Sights to See

Palmar Bay, Ixtapa, at the foot of the Sierra Madre mountains, is lined with the ultramodern hotels that make up the town of Ixtapa, founded in 1975 by FONATUR.

Ixtapa beaches, particularly *Playa Hermosa,* known for its tall rock formations.

Zihuatanejo Bay (Bahia de Zihuatenejo), about 6 miles SE of Ixtapa. Noted for its beautiful beaches, surrounded by wooded hills and rocky headlands. The beaches are *Playa Principal* (the most crowded); *Playa Madera* (where most of the hotels are); *Playa de la Ropa* (good swimming and the most beautiful); and *Playa de las Gatas* (good snorkeling and diving, and accessible by foot or boat only).

Paseo del Pescador, Zihuatanejo's waterfront, with beautiful views of the bay and its headlands, and its waterfront restaurants.

Zihuatanejo's Pier, Paseo del Pescador. The village's water-sport activity center.

Zihuatanejo's Market, Paseo del Cocotal, between Antonio Nava & Catalina Gonzalez. Has good buys in handicrafts, pottery, and jewelry.

Zihuatanejo itself, particularly the cobblestoned side streets off the waterfront. You can catch a glimpse of the quiet fishing village that Zihuatanejo was just over 14 years ago.

Isla Ixtapa (Isla Grande), 10 miles offshore. A wildlife sanctuary noted for its exotic birds and small, secluded beaches. Reached by boats from Zihuatanejo's pier and Ixtapa beach.

Morrodelos Pericos, another island N of Isla Ixtapa, known for its bird life and beaches.

Costa Grande (Big Coast), between Ixtapa/Zihuatanejo and Acapulco, 150 miles to the SE. Highway 200 parallels this stunning coastline with its tropical vegetation and beautiful, unspoiled beaches.

Sports

Boating: *Playa Quieta,* Ixtapa, has sailboats and windsurfing boards for rent. Rental boats are also available at the *downtown pier* in Zihuatanejo.

Fishing: fishing boats can be rented from *Playa Quieta* in Ixtapa or from the *downtown pier* in Zihuatanejo. Otherwise, contact the *Sociedad Cooperativa* (tel:4-2056), which arranges fishing trips.

Golf: the 18-hole Robert Trent Jones–designed course at the *Palma Real Golf and Tennis Club* (tel:4-2280), is across from the Sheraton in Ixtapa.

Horseback Riding: horses can be rented at *Playa Linda,* N of Playa Quieta.

Parasailing: the *Riviera del Sol* (tel:4-2406); *Holiday Inn* (tel:4-2396); and the *Dorado Pacifico* (tel:4-3060) hotels in Ixtapa all offer tows. NOTE: parasailing can be dangerous.

Snorkeling and Scuba Diving: Isla Ixtapa and *Playa Las Gatos* are the two best snorkeling and scuba diving spots and both have equipment rentals and instructors. *La Casa del Mar* (tel:4-2119) in Zihuatanejo rents equipment.

Swimming: La Quieta in Ixtapa, and *La Ropa* and *Las Gatas beaches* in Zihuatanejo are all popular.

Tennis: many of the hotels have courts for their guests. The *Palma Real Golf and Tennis Club* (tel:4-2280), has lighted courts that are open to the public.

Weather

Ixtapa-Zihuatanejo has a sunny, tropical climate with fairly uniform temperatures year-round. Summer daytime high temperatures typically reach in the low 90s, falling to the high 70s at night. Winter daytime highs are normally in the high 80s, dropping to the low 70s at night. The wet season is from June through October.

IXTAPA-ZIHUATANEJO: TEMPERATURES AND PRECIPITATION

Month	J	F	M	A	M	J	J	A	S	O	N	D
Average Daily Temperature												
(Fahrenheit) Max.	88	88	88	90	90	91	90	91	90	90	90	88
Min.	72	72	72	73	77	77	77	77	75	75	73	72
Average Number of Days with Precipitation												
	1	0	0	0	3	13	14	13	16	9	2	1

Los Cabos: Mexico

Sights to See

Los Arcos (El Arco), a natural rock arch at Land's End where the Gulf of California meets the Pacific. Accessible by boat.

Playa Medano (Rafa's Beach), Cabo San Lucas. A popular swimming beach.

Playa Santa Maria, 7 miles from San Lucas, it is one of the most secluded beaches in the area.

Chileno Bay, 8 miles from San Lucas. Known for its crystal-clear water, good diving and snorkeling, and swimming.

Parish Church, San Jose del Cabo. Built on the site of an early-18th-century church, it was the first mission in the area.

Paseo Mijares, San Jose del Cabo. Especially noted for its colorful flowers.
Coastline between Cabo San Lucas and San Jose del Cabo. Spectacular
coastline with beautiful beaches, interrupted by rocky headlands.
Sierra de la Laguna National Park, outside El Pescadero N of Cabo San
Lucas. Only place in Baja California with pine forest and running water.
Whale watching in season (peaks in Jan.–Feb.). The whales can easily be seen
from the shore, or from whale-watching boats. Check with your hotel for details.
La Paz, capital of Baja California Sur, with its *Museum of Anthropology, Shell
Market,* and *old colonial buildings,* is worth visiting if you have the time. Some
140 miles N of Cabo San Lucas, you can take Hwy. 9 through El Pescador one
way, and Hwy. 1 through Miraflores and El Triunfo the other way.

Sports

Boating: boats can be rented from the water sports center on *Playa Medano.*
Cabo Acuadeportes (tel:3-0022), at the Hacienda Beach hotel, Cabo San Lucas,
rents sailboats and windsurfers.
Fishing: the *Sea of Cortez* is world famous for its fishing, particularly the
Gordo Bank, off the coast of San Jose del Cabo. All the hotels can arrange for
fishing charters, many of them having their own fishing fleets. Otherwise,
contact *La Laguna Fishing* (tel:2-0211) at the El Presidente; or *Amigos del Mar*
(tel:3-0022) at the Solmar.
Golf: there is a 9-hole course in San Jose del Cabo in the Hotel Zone.
Horseback Riding: contact *Ramon's Horse Rentals* in front of the Cabo San
Lucas and Hacienda Beach (tel:3-0022) hotels in Cabo San Lucas.
Parasailing: tows are available on *Playa Medano.* NOTE: parasailing can be
dangerous.
Snorkeling and Scuba Diving: contact *Cabo Acuadeportes* at the Hacienda
Beach (tel:3-0022) or Cabo San Lucas hotels for rentals equipment.
Swimming: many of the area's beaches, especially those on the Pacific, are
unsafe for swimming because of the strong undertow. *Playa Chilena,* just S of
the Cabo San Lucas hotel, and *Playa Medano* (Rafa's Beach), are popular
swimming beaches.
Tennis: the *San Jose del Cabo Golf Course* also has tennis courts. In San Jose
del Cabo the *Palmilla* (tel:2-0583), the *Posado Real* (tel:2-0155), and the
Stoutter *El Presidente* (tel:2-0211) all have courts. In Cabo San Lucas, the
Hacienda Beach (tel:3-0022), *Twin Dolphin,* and *Cabo San Lucas* hotels all have
good courts.

Weather

Cabo San Lucas and San Jose del Cabo are famous for their dry, hot climate with
350 days of sunshine per year. Summer daytime highs are typically in the low to
mid 90s, falling to around 80 at night. Winter daytime highs are usually in the
mid 70s, dropping to the upper 50s at night. Late summer and fall are the wettest
seasons.

CABO SAN LUCAS: TEMPERATURES AND PRECIPITATION

Month	J	F	M	A	M	J	J	A	S	O	N	D
Average Daily Temperature												
(Fahrenheit) Max.	73	75	79	84	88	93	94	95	95	85	82	74
Min.	55	57	60	64	69	76	80	80	78	72	64	56
Average Number of Days with Precipitation												
	2	1	2	1	1	1	7	8	6	2	3	5

Mazatlan: Mexico

Sights to See

Cathedral, on the Zocalo, Av. Angel Flores & Juarez. A neo-Gothic structure, noted for its fine interior.

Aquarium (Acuario Mazatlan), Av. de los Deportes, off Av. del Mar. Over 250 species of fish in several large tanks. Open 10–6 Tu–Su.

Sea Shell City Museum, Loaiza 407, off Av. del Mar. A notable collection of shells and objects made from shell.

Fisherman's Monument, a local landmark on the ocean side of the Malecon, at the foot of Najera.

El Mirador "death divers," above Olas Atlas beach at Paseo Claussen. Young divers plunge into the ocean at high tide on most afternoons or evenings.

El Faro lighthouse, at the tip of the peninsula S of El Mirador. At 525 ft., it is one of the highest in the world, not so much due to the structure itself, but because of its elevation above the sea. The views are spectacular.

Fiesta Yacht Cruise. An approximately 3-hour cruise around the harbor and bay, with nature guides and entertainment. Cruises leave at 10 A.M. and 2:30 P.M. from El Faro.

Isla de la Piedra, E of Mazatlan's dock area. The boats leave from Av. del Puerto. The island has some beaches and a village, and is popular with the local population.

Sports

Boating: sailboats and speedboats can be rented along *Playa Norte* directly N of town, or along the Las Gaviotas beach beyond Punta Cameron. The fashionable *Sabalo beach* still further north also has facilities. Contact *Agua Sports Center,* Sabalo Beach Rd. (tel:3-3333).

Fishing: this is the sport in Mazatlan, with excellent sport fishing year-round. Contact: *Flota Faro* (tel:1-2824); *Flota Perla* (tel:1-7271); *Flota Estrella* (tel:2-3878); *Aviles Brothers* (tel:1-3728) or *Mike's Sportfishing* (tel:1-2824).

Golf: the *El Cid Resort* (tel:3-3333) some 5 miles N of town on Sabalo Beach Rd. has an 18-hole course. *Club Campestre de Mazatlan,* International Rd., has a 9-hole course.

Horseback Riding: Sabalo Beach N of town along Av. Cameron-Sabalo has rental stables.

Hunting: duck hunting is a big sport in Mazatlan, particularly in the *Caimanero Lagoon* area. Contact the *Aviles Brothers* (tel:1-3728), or make arrangements through your hotel.

Parasailing: parachute tows are available along the northern beaches—*Playa Norte, Las Gaviotas,* and *Sabalo.* The *Holiday Inn Mazatlan,* Sabalo Beach Rd. (tel:3-2222), offers parasail rides.

Snorkeling and Scuba Diving: although not very popular here, some of the hotels do have rental equipment, notably *Hotel Playa Mazatlan* (tel:3-4444), Las Gaviotas Beach. Or contact the *Agua Sports Center* (tel:3-3333) next to the El Cid Resort on Sabalo Beach Rd.

Swimming: under Mexican law all beaches are public. *Playas Norte, Las Gaviotas,* and *Sabalo,* north of town are the popular beaches. *Sabalo Beach* is probably the best. NOTE: there are strong currents offshore, so caution is advisable.

Tennis: the *El Cid Resort* (tel:3-3333), Sabalo Beach Rd., has the best courts, which can be rented by non-guests.

Waterskiing: tows are available along the northern beaches.

Weather

Mazatlan has a warm to hot tropical climate. Summer daytime high temperatures typically reach into the 90s, dropping to the high 70s at night. Winter daytime highs are usually in the high 80s, falling to the low 70s at night. The wet season extends from June through October.

MAZATLAN: TEMPERATURES AND PRECIPITATION

Month	J	F	M	A	M	J	J	A	S	O	N	D
Average Daily Temperature												
(Fahrenheit) Max.	88	88	88	90	90	91	90	91	90	90	90	88
Min.	72	72	72	73	77	77	77	77	75	75	73	72
Average Number of Days with Precipitation												
	1	0	0	0	3	13	14	13	16	9	2	1

Merida: Mexico

Sights to See

Plaza Mayor (Plaza de la Independencia). The commercial and cultural center of Merida.

Palacio Montejo, on the S side of the Plaza Mayor. Now a bank, this former Montejo family palace, dating from the 16th century, is noted for its Plateresque facade and beautifully furnished interior. Open daily.

Merida Cathedral, on the E side of Plaza Mayor. A twin-towered, large 16th-century structure that dominates the plaza.

Government Palace (Palacio de Gobierno), on the NE corner of the Plaza Mayor. A late-19th-century building noted for its murals.

Franciscan Church of the Third Order, Calle 60, one block N of Plaza Mayor. Considered to be one of the town's most attractive churches.
La Ermita de Santa Isabel, Calles 66 & 77, SW of Plaza Mayor. Known for its garden with Maya and Toltec statues.
Museum of Anthropology and History, Palacio Canton, Paseo Montejo & Calle 43, N of Plaza Mayor. Fine collection of pre-Columbian and Maya artifacts. Open Tu–Su.
Paseo Montejo, a splendid, tree-lined, 8-block-long boulevard, dotted with 19th-century mansions and monuments.
Municipal Market (Mercado Municipal), Calles 67 & 56. Colorful market full of sisal products, and clothing vendors.

Useful Information

Merida Tourist Office, Palacio Municipal, Plaza Mayor, and the *State Tourist Office,* Estado de Yucatan (tel:24-9290), Calle 60 between 57 and 59; *U.S. Consulate,* Paseo Montejo & Av. Colon (tel:5-5409); *Police* (tel:1-3782); *Post Office,* Calles 56 & 65. *Merida's horse-drawn carriages* (calesas) leave from Parque Cepeda Peraza, Calle 60, one block N of Plaza Mayor.

Special Trips/Tours

One of the largest and best restored, and certainly most dramatic, archaeological sites in Mexico is ***Chichen-Itza,*** some 75 miles E of Merida on Hwy. 180. A sacred center of the Mayas for over 700 years, and the 11th- and 12th-century political and religious center of the region under the Toltecs, it extends over a 3-square-mile area. Especially noteworthy among the site's many superb buildings, are *El Castillo* or Pyramid of Kukulkan, affording magnificent views of the site from its top platform; the *Great Ball Court* (Juego de Pelota), the largest of its kind in Mesoamerica; the *Temple of the Warriors* (Templo de los Guerreros) and the mysterious *Group of the Thousand Columns (Grupo de las Mil Columnas); the Sacred Cenote* (Cenote Sagrado), a sacrificial well; and *El Caracol* (the Sanil), an observatory. Don't miss the sound and light show in English at 9 P.M.

The world-famous Maya site of ***Uxmal,*** considered to be one of the finest and most complete complexes of pre-Columbian architecture in Mexico, is just 60 miles S of Merida. Particularly outstanding among the site's magnificent Mayan structures, are the 125-ft. *Pyramid of the Magician* (Piramide del Adivino), which affords superb views of Uxmal from its top; the *Nunnery Quadrangle* (Cuadrangulo de las Monnjas), noted for its carved rain-god masks; the *Governor's Palace* (Palacio del Gobernador), known for its ornate frieze carvings; and the *Dovecot* (Polomar), known for its unusual lattice-design roof comb. Don't miss the sound and light show in English at 9 P.M.

Some 14 miles S of Uxmal on Hwy. 261 is ***Kabah.*** A rather neglected and largely unrestored Maya site, Kabah is famous for its *Palace of the Masks* (Codz-Poop), noted for its stylized carved mask facade. Also noteworthy is the *Arch of Kabah* (Arco de Kabah). A short distance along Hwy. 261, a road turns left to the archaeological sites of *Sayil* and *Labna*. The former is dominated by the terraced *Palace* (Palacio), with a facade decorated with fine carvings. Labna also has its *Palace* (Palacio), but is best known for the superb, richly decorated *Arch of Labna* (Arco de Labna).

Weather

Merida has a tropical climate with hot, humid weather in the summer, and warm, dry winters. Summer daytime high temperatures typically reach into the low 90s, dropping to the low 70s at night. Winter daytime highs are usually in the low 80s, falling to the low 60s at night. The wet season lasts June to October.

MERIDA: TEMPERATURES AND PRECIPITATION

Month	J	F	M	A	M	J	J	A	S	O	N	D
Average Daily Temperature												
(Fahrenheit) Max.	83	85	89	92	94	92	92	91	90	87	85	82
Min.	62	63	66	69	72	73	73	73	73	71	67	64
Average Number of Days with Precipitation												
	8	6	6	5	10	19	20	19	20	17	12	9

Mexico City: Mexico

Sights to See

The Zocalo (Plaza de la Constitucion). At the center of Mexico City, this is one of the largest squares in the world, occupying a former Aztec marketplace and the site of the famous Halls of Montezuma.

Metropolitan Cathedral (Catedral Metropolitana), N side of the zocalo. Started in 1573, this cathedral, full of art treasures, is also noted for the facade of its chapel.

National Palace (Palacio Nacional). Official residence of Spanish viceroys and now the presidents of Mexico. Known for its Diego Rivera murals in the center patio, it also houses the *National Archives* and the *Bonito Juarez Museum*. Open 10–6 M–F.

Palace of Fine Arts (Palacio de Bellas Artes). Corner of Juarez & San Juan. An opulent opera house, built of Italian marble and famous for its murals by Rivera and others. Open 10:30–6:30 Tu–Su.

Chapultepec Park (Bosque de Chapultepec). One of the world's oldest and most magnificent parks. In addition to playgrounds, picnic areas, and an amusement park, it contains museums, two zoos, restaurants, miniature trains, a lake, and fountains. The terraces and rooftop garden of Chapultepec Castle afford excellent views of this sprawling metropolis.

National Museum of Anthropology (Museo Nacional de Antropologia), on Reforma in Chapultepec Park. One of the finest museums in the world, full of Aztec, Maya, and modern-day Indian treasures. Open 9–7 Tu–Sa, 10–6 Su.

National University (Ciudad Universitaria), Insurgentes Sur, on the S side of the city. Famous for its modern architecture, exterior murals, and mosaics. *Siquieros Cultural Polyforum,* Insurgentes Sur 700, on the S side of city. Known for its mural paintings by Siquieros. Open daily. *Shrine of the Virgin of Guadalupe* (Basilica de la Virgen de Guadalupe), N of the city via Insurgentes Norte. Noted for a cloak on the main altar, which has an image of the Virgin Mary imprinted on it, from a 16th century Indian who had an apparition of the Virgin Mary and was directed to build a church in her honor.

Useful Information

Tourist Ministry Information Desk, Av. Juarez 92 (tel:250-0123), and at Amberes & Londres (tel:525-9380) in the Pink Zone; *U.S. Embassy,* Reforma 305 (tel:211-0042); *Benito Juarez International Airport* (tel:571-3600); *Taxi* (563-8618); *American Express,* Hamburgo 75 (tel:525-8428); *Direccion General de Proteccion al Turista* (tel:250-0151 or 250-0493); *Police* (tel:588-5100); *Cultural and Arts Information* (tel:512-3633); *Ticket Agency* for cultural and sporting events, Palacio de Bellas Artes lobby (tel:534-4924).

Special Trips/Tours

Pyramids of Teotihuacan (Piramides de Teotihuacan), about an hour's drive N of the city, via Av. Insurgentes Norte and the toll road. Built between A.D. 400 and 800, this is the site of the Pyramids of the Sun and Moon and the Temple of Quetzalcoatl. See the sound and light show presented at 7 P.M. Tu–Su. *Taxco,* located about 115 miles SW of Mexico City, halfway to Acapulco, is a very picturesque community, with narrow, cobbled streets, pink and white stucco houses with red tile roofs, colonial balconies filled with potted plants, and silversmiths everywhere. See the *Cathedral of Santa Prisca,* and ride the aerial tramway to the Hotel Montetaxco and enjoy the view.

Weather

Mexico City enjoys a warm temperate climate. Summer daytime highs typically reach the mid 70s, dropping to the mid 50s at night. In winter, the highs are usually in the upper 60s, falling to the mid to low 40s. Summer is the rainy season, particularly the months of July and August. Summers can be smoggy.

MEXICO CITY: TEMPERATURES AND PRECIPITATION

Month	J	F	M	A	M	J	J	A	S	O	N	D
Average Daily Temperature												
(Fahrenheit) Max.	66	69	75	77	78	76	73	73	74	70	68	66
Min.	42	43	47	51	54	55	53	54	53	50	46	43
Average Number of Days with Precipitation												
		4	5	9	14	17	21	27	27	23	13	6	4

Oaxaca: Mexico

Sights to See

Zocalo (Plaza de Armas), the focal point of Oaxaca. With its tree-shaded benches, bandstand, and cafes in the arcades surrounding the square, it is one of the most active in the country.

Government Palace (Palacio de Gobierno), on the S side of Plaza de Armas. Noted for its interior mural depicting Oaxaqueno history.

Cathedral of Oaxaca, on the NW corner of the Plaza de Armas. Dating from the 16th century, it is known for its wooden clock, ornate Baroque facade, and engraved glass windows. Open 8–1, 4:30–8 M–Sa, mass on Su.

Oaxaca Market (Mercado Juarez) two blocks S of the Zocalo at Las Casas & Flores Magon. A large and colorful indoor and outdoor market, best seen on Saturday when Indians from the surrounding countryside sell their wares.

Church of Santo Domingo, Gurrion & M. Alcala, five blocks N of Plaza de Armas. A truly magnificent example of Baroque art, it is famous for its superb interior decorations, especially the ornate Chapel of the Rosary. Open 8–1, 4:30–8 M–Sa, Su before masses.

Regional Museum of Oaxaca (Museo Regional de Oaxaca), in the convent adjoining the Church of Santo Domingo. Excellent Indian archaeological and ethnological collection, including the Mixtec Treasure. Open 10–6 Tu–F, 10–5 Sa–Su.

Rufino Tomayo Museum (Museo de Arte Prehispanico Rufino Tamayo), Calle Morelos 503, three blocks N of Plaza de Armas. The artist's personal collection of pre-Hispanic objects from the main Indian cultures of Mexico. Open 10–2, 4–7 W–M.

Church of La Soledad (Basilica de la Soledad), Independencia & Galeana, five blocks W of the Zocalo. One of the most important shrines in southern Mexico, with its statue of the Virgin of Solitude.

Saturday Market, off Las Casas, across the railroad tracks, on the outskirts of town. One of the liveliest and most genuine Indian markets in Mexico. Open every day and busy in the mornings, it is best seen on Saturday mornings.

Useful Information

Tourist Office, Palacio Municipal, Independencia 607 (tel:6-3810); *State Tourist Office,* Morelos & Cinco de Mayo (tel:6-4828); *U.S. Consulate,* Grupo Consular, 817 Av. Hidalgo (tel:6-0654); *Post Office,* Independencia & Alameda Park; *Police,* Calle Aldama (tel:6-5988).

Special Trips/Tours

Monte Alban, considered to be one of the most impressive pre-Columbian archaeological sites in Mexico, is only 6 miles SW of Oaxaca. Monte Alban served a succession of different peoples as a cult and ceremonial site for over 2,500 years, and once covered an area of over 15 sq. miles. Especially notable structures on the Gran Plaza, include the *North Platform* (Plataforma Norte); *Ball Court* (Juego de Pelota); *Palace* (Palacio); *Building H* (Edificio H); *Mound J* (Monticulo J); *Palace of the Dancers* (Palacio de los Danzantes); and *South Platform* (Plataforma del Sur). A platform on top of the South Platform has the best overall view of this magnificent site. Be sure to see *Stela 1* (Estela 1), one of the best preserved and finest, just NW of the South Platform; and *Tomb 104* (Tumba 104), NW of the North Platform.

The archaeological site of *Mitla* is some 30 miles SE of Oaxaca. Although not as imposing as Monte Alban, it is famous for its ornate stone mosaics. The *Group of the Columns* (Grupo de las Columnas) in the E part of the site is the most interesting complex.

Weather

Oaxaca has a tropical climate that is ameliorated by its 5,000-ft. altitude. Summer daytime high temperatures typically reach into the high 70s or low 80s, dropping to around 60 at night. Winter daytime high temperatures usually hover around 70, falling to the low 50s at night. The rainy season is from May to October.

OAXACA: TEMPERATURES AND PRECIPITATION

Month	J	F	M	A	M	J	J	A	S	O	N	D
Average Daily Temperature												
(Fahrenheit) Max.	69	72	78	80	81	79	76	76	77	73	71	69
Min.	49	50	54	58	61	62	60	62	60	57	53	50
Average Number of Days with Precipitation												
		4	5	9	14	17	21	27	27	23	13	6	4

Puerto Vallarta: Mexico

Sights to See

Malecon (seafront promenade), facing the Bahia de Banderas N of the Rio Cuale. The focal point of Puerto Vallarta, with the main hotels, restaurants, nightspots, and shops.

Bahia de Banderas (Bay of Flags). A huge bay, some 30 miles long, on which the town is located. The beaches S of Rio Cuale, including Playa del Sol, Las Amapas, and Playa las Estacas, are popular.

Church of Guadalupe, just E of the zocalo. The town's only real landmark, albeit an undistinguished one.

Gringo Gulch, a few blocks uphill from the church, N of Rio Cuale. Locale of some wealthy North American homes, including that of Elizabeth Taylor.

Cuale Island (Isla Del Rio Cuale), between the two branches of the Rio Cuale. Snack bars, restaurants, craft market, mariachi bands, shopping stalls, and a small museum.

Los Arcos (The Arches), rock formations jutting out of the ocean some 6 miles S of Puerto Vallarta.
Mismaloya, about 7 miles S of town. Location of the filming of the "Night of the Iguana," which put Puerto Vallarta on the map.
Yelapa (the meeting place). A picturesque freshwater lagoon, with waterfall, at the S end of Bahia de Banderas. The small fishing village is reached by boat, which leaves Vallarta from the marina pier.

Sports

Boating: just about any kind of boat can be rented along the beaches, particularly *Playa del Sol,* or in any of the major hotels.
Fishing: the waters off Puerto Vallarta are abundant with sport fish. Fishing boats leave from the *Marina* and *the pier* at the N end of Malecon. Make arrangements through your hotel.
Golf: there is an 18-hole course N of the airport, at *Club de Golf Los Flamingos* (tel:2-2703).
Horseback Riding: most of the principal beaches have horses for rent. *Yelapa beach* is very popular. Among the hotels, the following offer rides: *Krystal Vallarta* (tel:2-2165), and *Holiday Inn* (tel:2-1700), both on Airport Rd., and *Playa de Oro* (tel:2-0348), Av. De la Gaza, off Airport Rd.
Parasailing: the *Krystal Vallarta* (tel:2-1459), N of Airport Rd., and the *Holiday Inn* (tel:2-1600), on Airport Rd., offer parasailing.
Snorkeling and Scuba Diving: contact *Chico's Dive Shop* (tel:2-1895), on the Malecon; or *Silent World Diving* (tel:2-1700), Holiday Inn, Airport Rd.
Swimming: under Mexican law, all beaches are public. The best-known beaches include the *Playa de las Glorias, Las Palmas,* and *Vallarta de Oro* N of the Rio Cuale. South of the Rio Cuale, they include *Playa del Sol, Las Amapas, Conchas Chinas,* and *Las Estacas.*
Tennis: most of the principal hotels have courts for guests, sometimes allowing non-guests to play for a fee. The *John Newcombe Tennis Center* (tel:2-3156), at the Plaza Vallarta, Paseo de las Glorias, is open to all.

Weather

Puerto Vallarta has a sunny, tropical climate. Summer daytime highs are typically in the low 90s, failing to the high 70s at night. Winter daytime highs are usually in the high 80s, dropping to the low 70s at night. The wet season is from June through October.

PUERTO VALLARTA: TEMPERATURES AND PRECIPITATION

Month	J	F	M	A	M	J	J	A	S	O	N	D
Average Daily Temperature												
(Fahrenheit) Max.	88	88	88	90	90	91	90	91	90	90	90	88
Min.	72	72	72	73	77	77	77	77	75	75	73	72
Average Number of Days with Precipitation												
	1	0	0	0	3	13	14	13	16	9	2	1

San Miguel de Allende: Mexico

Sights to See

Parochial Church (La Parroquia), Plaza Allende in central San Miguel de Allende. Noted for its pseudo-Gothic facade and tower, designed and constructed by Indian architect Zerefino Gutierrez, who reportedly was inspired by postcard pictures of French cathedrals.

House of the Counts of Canal (Palacio de los Condes de Canal), on Plaza Allende. An excellent example of Spanish Colonial architecture, this 18th-century mansion now houses a bank. Open 9–1:30 M–F.

Ignacio Allende's House (Casa de Don Ignacio Allende), Calles Canal & Cuna de Allende, just off Plaza Allende. Birthplace of Allende, co-leader, with Miguel Hidalgo, of the Mexican independence revolution. Open Tu–Su.

Church of the Conception (Las Monjas), Calle Canal & Hernandez Macias, just W of Plaza Allende. A large, domed, late-19th-century structure known for its sculptures and collection of paintings. Open daily.

Allende Institute (Instituto Allende), Calzada Ancha de San Antonio 4, in the SW part of San Miguel. World-famous art school, attracting students from throughout the Americas. Housed in an old hacienda, the institute has a number of galleries open to the public and hosts frequent concerts and plays.

Useful Information

Tourism Office, Plaza Allende (tel:2-1747); *Post Office,* Correos 16 (tel:2-0089); *Police* (tel:2-0022); *Taxi* (tel:2-0192, 2-0290); closest *U.S. Embassy* is in Mexico City, at Reforma 305 (tel:5-211-0042).

Special Trips/Tours

Joining one of the *house and garden tours* of the city's mansions is an excellent way to see the interiors of these colonial gems. Tours leave from the Public Library (Biblioteca Publica), Calle Insurgentes 25, every Sunday at 11:30 (tel:2-0293).

Queretaro, site of some of the main battles of the Mexican War of Independence and one-time capital of Mexico (in 1840), is just SE of San Miguel de Allende. Dating from the 15th century, Queretaro is famous for its many fine examples of Spanish Colonial architecture, and some of Mexico's best ecclesiastical architecture. Especially noteworthy are the *Palacio Municipal,* the original Casa de la Corregidora (former home of the heroine of the 1810 War of Independence), on Plaza de la Independencia; the *Museo Regional,* Calle Juarez, housed in the former monastery next to the Church of San Francisco; and the Mexican Baroque *Federal Palace* (Convento de San Agustin), Calle Allende S. 14.

Excellent examples of ecclesiastical architecture are the *Church of Santa Rose de Viterbo,* Gral. Arteaga & Calle E. Montes; the *Church of Santa Clara,* Plaza de Santa Clara, with its ornate interior and rich nunnery; the *Church of San Francisco,* Plaza Obregon. Also notable is the city's *Neptune Fountain,* Calles Allende & Madero, fed by water brought into the city by a Spanish aqueduct (acueducto) built in the early 18th century, with 74 arches. Queretaro's *Plaza de Toros Santa Maria,* is one of Mexico's best *bullrings,* attracting matadors from Spain and all over Mexico (Nov.–Feb. is the main season).

If you have more time, the Toltec capital of *Tula,* one of Mexico's most interesting archaeological sites, is off the Queretaro–Mexico City road (Hwy. 57D) on State Hwy. 126.

Weather

San Miguel has a warm temperate climate. Summer daytime high temperatures typically reach into the mid 70s, dropping to the mid 50s at night. Winter daytime highs are usually in the mid 60s, falling to the low 40s at night. The wettest period is from June through September.

SAN MIGUEL: TEMPERATURES AND PRECIPITATION

Month	J	F	M	A	M	J	J	A	S	O	N	D
Average Daily Temperature												
(Fahrenheit) Max.	66	69	75	77	78	76	73	73	74	70	68	66
Min.	42	43	47	51	54	55	53	54	53	50	46	43
Average Number of Days with Precipitation												
			4	5	9	14	17	21	27	27	23	13	6	4

Anchorage

Sights to See

Anchorage Historical and Fine Arts Museum, 121 W. 7th Ave. Native Alaskan prehistoric artifacts, together with contemporary native arts and crafts. Open 9–6 M–Sa during the summer, shorter hours the rest of the year.
Alaska Native Arts and Crafts Association, 425 D St. Showroom full of traditional and contemporary Alaskan native crafts.
Heritage Library, the National Bank of Alaska Building, Northern Lights Blvd. & C St. Gold-rush exhibits and Alaskan native artifacts. Open 1–4 M–F.
"Parade of Alaska History" **Mural,** Alaska Mutual Bank, 5th & F Sts. A fine, 160-ft.-long, bas-relief depicting the state's illustrious history.
Elderberry Park, at the W end of 5th Ave., overlooking the Knik Arm of Cook Inlet. Watch for the Bore Tide, and whales, if you're lucky.
Anderson House, Elderberry Park. One of Anchorage's first homes, now fully restored as a museum. Open 1–4 Tu–Su.
Captain Cook's Statue, Resolution Park, just N of Elderberry park at the end of 3rd Avenue. Commemorates the nearby landing of the famous captain.
Earthquake Park, at the W end of Northern Lights Blvd. Time-mellowed result

of the 1964 earthquake (8.6 on the Richter scale). Affords magnificent views of Mt. McKinley, weather permitting.

Elmendorf Wildlife Museum, Elmendorf Air Force Base, Bldg. 4803, Boniface & Glenn Hwy. Fine collection of mounted Alaskan wildlife arranged in displays by region of the state. Open 8–5 M–F, 10–3 Sa.

Fort Richardson Wildlife Center, Fort Richardson, 10 miles N of Anchorage on Glenn Hwy. Collection of mounted Alaskan wildlife trophies. Open 9–5 M–F, 10–4 Sa, 12–4 Su in summer; 9–5 M–F the rest of the year.

Alaska Zoo, O'Malley Rd., off Seward Hwy., 10 miles S of downtown Anchorage. Over 40 species of the state's animal and bird wildlife. Open 10–6 daily during the summer, shorter hours the rest of the year.

Useful Information

Anchorage Convention and Visitors Bureau, 201 E. 3rd Ave. (276-4118); *Log Cabin Visitor Information Center* (274-3531), W. 4th Ave. & F St. (Open May–Sept.); *Recorded Message of the Day's Events* (276-3200); *Cultural Events Recorded Message* (276-2787); *National Park Service Office,* 540 W. 5th Ave. (271-4243).

Special Trips/Tours

Time permitting, no visitor to Anchorage should pass up the opportunity to visit the truly spectacular *Denali National Park and Preserve,* encompassing over six million acres of wilderness and North America's highest mountain, *Mount McKinley (Denali),* 20,320 ft. Reached by car or bus via Hwy. 3 (George Parks Hwy.), by air, or by train (Alaska Railroad, 265-2494), the park's entrance is 240 miles from Anchorage. Stop at the Riley Creek Information Center for park orientation and enjoy. NOTE: Mount McKinley is hidden by cloud or fog much of the time.

The *Portage Glacier Recreation Area* is about 45 miles S of Anchorage, off the Seward-Anchorage Hwy. The glacier spawns icebergs, which calve off the face of the glacier and float in Portage Lake. Drop by the Visitors Center (open Memorial Day–Labor Day). Be sure to take the chairlift up *Mt. Alyseka* for great views.

Continuing along the Seward-Anchorage Hwy. will bring you to *Seward,* an ice-free port at the mouth of Resurrection Bay at the base of the Chugach Mountains. Destroyed by the 1964 earthquake, the town has been rebuilt and is the center of a popular fishing and recreational area and an important port. Surrounded by high mountains and icefields, it is an attractive community in a magnificent setting. The *Seward Community Library,* 5th Ave. & Adams Street, shows free movies of the 1964 earthquake's damage.

Seward is an excellent base for exploring the splendid *Kenai Fjords National Park* on the SE side of the Kenai Peninsula. Covering a coastal mountain range and the Harding Icefield, it has a rugged and spectacular coastline. The park's headquarters are in Seward. Inland, the *Kenai National Wildlife Refuge* in Soldotna, off the Sterling Hwy., is home to moose, Dall sheep, black bears, bald eagles, wolves, and other wildlife. Visit the *Refuge Visitor Center in Soldotna* and see the films and dioramas (Open 8–4:30 daily).

Weather

Anchorage's summer daytime high temperatures are typically in the mid 60s, dropping to the high 40s at night. Winters are comparatively mild, with daytime highs usually in the 20s or 30s, falling to the single digits at night. The wet season is from August to October. Cloud and fog are common.

ANCHORAGE: TEMPERATURES AND PRECIPITATION

Month	J	F	M	A	M	J	J	A	S	O	N	D
Average Daily Temperature												
(Fahrenheit) Max.	19	27	33	44	54	62	65	64	57	43	30	20
Min.	5	9	13	27	36	44	49	47	39	29	15	6
Average Number of Days with Precipitation												
	7	6	5	4	5	6	10	15	14	12	7	6

Atlanta

Sights to See

Peachtree Center, 230–233 Peachtree St. NE. Full of interesting shops and restaurants, and of architectural interest. The view from the revolving restaurant, the Sun Dial, on the 70th floor of Peachtree Plaza Hotel is superb. Open daily.
Woodruff Park, between Peachtree, Pryor, & Edgewood Sts., S of the Peachtree Center. Especially popular at lunchtime, with its street entertainers.
High Museum of Art, 1280 Peachtree at 15th St. Particularly known for its decorative arts. The museum building itself is noteworthy. Open 10–5 Tu–Sa, 12–5 Su. The museum's downtown annex is at 133 Peachtree St. NE. (open 11–6 M–F).
Martin Luther King, Jr. Historic District, between Jackson & Boulevard Sts., in the Sweet Auburn area of NE Atlanta. The district includes the civil rights leader's birthplace, 501 Auburn Ave.; the Ebeneezer Baptist Church, 407 Auburn Ave., where he and his father pastored; and the Freedom Hall Complex. Open 9–5 daily.
Georgia State Capitol, Washington St., between Martin Luther King Jr. Dr. & Mitchell St. Noted for its gold leaf dome, it contains the Georgia State Museum of Science and Industry. Open 9–4:30 M–F, 10–2 Sa, 1–3 Su.
The Wren's Nest, 1050 Gordon St. The home of Joel Chandler Harris, author of the Uncle Remus stories. Open 9:30–5 M–Sa, 2–5 Su.
Paces Ferry Road area, N of downtown. One of the most beautiful residential areas in the South. See the Governor's Mansion, 591 West Paces Ferry Rd.

(Open 10–11:45 Tu–Th); the Swan House and the Tullie Smith House, 3099 Andrews Dr. (Open 10–4 M–Sa, 2–4 Su.). *Grant Park*, between Atlanta Ave. & Memorial Dr., downtown. Contains the city zoo, noted for its reptile collection, and the Cyclorama, reputedly the largest painting-in-the-round, depicting the 1864 Civil War Battle of Atlanta. Open 9–5 daily. *Fernbank Science Center*, 156 Heaton Park Dr. NE. One of the largest planetariums in the country, together with natural science exhibits, the original Apollo 6 Space Capsule, a botanical garden, and a 65-acre "forest" with walking trails. Open 8:30–5 M, 8:30–10 Tu–F, 10–5 Sa, 1–5 Su. *Atlanta Botanical Garden*, Piedmont Park, Piedmont Ave. at South Prado. A conservatory, a Japanese Garden, and Herb and Rose Gardens. Open 9–4:30 M–Sa, 12:30–4:30 Su. *Carter Presidential Center*, N. Highland & Cleburne Aves., E. of downtown. Memorabilia of President Carter's White House years. Open 9–5 daily.

Useful Information

Atlanta Convention and Visitors Bureau, 235 Peachtree NE, Suite 1414 (521-6600); *Taxi* (681-2280 or 522-0200); *Travelers Aid* (523-0585); *Multi-Lingual Visitor Assistance*, 800/356-8392); *MARTA* (Public Transportation) *Schedule Information* (848-4711); *Atlanta Airport Shuttle* (766-5312). The *Atlanta Preservation Center 4041* 522-4345, conducts walking tours of historic districts in Atlanta.

Special Trips/Tours

Georgia's Stone Mountain Park, 16 miles E of Atlanta, off Hwy. 78 in Stone Mountain (404/498-5600). Famous for its large relief sculpture on the N face of one the world's largest exposed granite rocks. Also has a paddle-wheel steamer, cable-car ride, golf course, ice skating rink, steam locomotive ride, antebellum plantation, and much more. Open 10–9 in summer, 10–5:30 rest of the year.

    Marietta, Georgia, about 30 minutes NW of Atlanta, via I-75N and Hwy. 112W. *Historical Marietta Square*, originally built in 1834, is now surrounded by restored buildings and warehouses filled with art galleries, boutiques, antique shops, and restaurants. The Marietta Welcome Center (429-1115) offers historic tours.

    Six Flags Over Georgia (948-9290), considered one of the country's better amusement theme parks, is some 14 miles W of the city off I-20 via the Six Flags exit. Particularly known for its roller coaster, the "Great American Scream Machine." Open 10–10 daily, June–Aug., 10–10 weekends, March–May, and Sept.–Nov.

Weather

Atlanta summers tend to be hot and humid, with daytime highs in the mid to high 80s. Winters are mild, with daytime highs usually in the low 50s and low temperatures typically above freezing. Rainfall is fairly heavy throughout the year, although winter tends to be a little wetter than the other seasons.

ATLANTA: TEMPERATURES AND PRECIPITATION

Month	J	F	M	A	M	J	J	A	S	O	N	D
Average Daily Temperature												
(Fahrenheit) Max.	51	54	62	71	79	86	87	86	82	72	61	52
Min.	35	37	43	51	60	67	70	69	64	54	43	37
Average Number of Days with Precipitation												
	12	11	11	10	10	11	13	12	8	7	8	11

Baltimore

Sights to See

Harborplace, Pratt & Light Sts. This is Baltimore's answer to Boston's Faneuil Hall. The two glass-enclosed pavilions are full of shops, boutiques, restaurants, stalls, kiosks, and people. On weekends and holidays musicians, mimes, magicians, and jugglers can be seen performing outside. The *best view of the city* and harbor is from the observation deck of the *World Trade Center,* between Piers 1 & 3 in the inner harbor, which also has interesting exhibits. Open 10–4:30 M–F, Su, 10–10 Sa.
The National Aquarium, Pier 3, Inner Harbor. One of the most interesting aquariums in the world, with over 5,000 specimens, audiovisual displays, and a tropical rain forest on the top floor. Open 10–5 M–Th, 10–8 F–Su.
Maryland Science Center, Inner Harbor. Innovative displays and an excellent planetarium. Open 10–10 M–Sa, 12–8 Su.
U.S.S. Constellation, Pier 1, Inner Harbor. The U.S. Navy's oldest warship, this frigate has daily tours. Open 10–8 daily.
Fort McHenry National Monument at the foot of Fort Ave., S of the Inner Harbor. Site of the United States's successful repulsion of British forces in 1814, which inspired Francis Scott Key's "The Star-Spangled Banner." Open 9–8 daily in summer, 9–5 in winter.
Charles Center, between Liberty & Charles Sts. opposite Hopkins Plaza. An area of fountains, plazas, and office and apartment buildings, Hopkins Plaza has frequent free concerts, and chamber music and jazz performances.
Edgar Allen Poe Home, 203 N. Amity St. Poe lived here in the 1830s. Open 12–3:45 W–Sa. His grave can be seen nearby in the cemetery at Fayette & Greene Sts.
Lexington Market, 400 W. Lexington at Eutaw. Indoor market and an Arcade with over 100 kiosks and shops. Open 8:30–6 M–Sa.
Walters Art Gallery, Charles & Centre Sts. Excellent collection with particular emphasis on medieval art and manuscripts. Open 11–5 Tu–Su.

Baltimore Museum of Art, Art Museum Dr., near N. Charles & 31st Sts. Famous for its French Postimpressionist, primitive art, and modern sculpture collections. Open 10–4 Tu–F, 11–6 Sa–Su.

B & O Railroad Museum, 901 W. Pratt St. Fine collection of locomotives, including the nation's first passenger and freight station, and a well-preserved 1884 roundhouse. Open 10–4 W–Su.

Useful Information

Baltimore Office of Promotion and Tourism, 34 Market Place, Suite 310 (752-8632); *Visitor Center,* Pratt & Pier 4 (837-4636); *Recorded Message of Events and Shows* (837-4636); *Taxi* (685-1212, 947-3333 or 235-0300); *Travelers Aid Society* (685-3569).

Special Trips/Tours

Baltimore is a major port city. Although small, the *Inner Harbor* is just that, an inner harbor. Outside the immediate inner harbor, lies a fascinating *port complex,* with a chrome smelter, the world's largest processor of teas and herbs (McCormick & Co.), a working shipyard, automobile import docks, and, at Sparrow's Point, one of the world's largest integrated iron and steel mills. For a narrated 90-minute tour of all of this, by boat, catch either the *Patriot II or III* (685-4288), which leave from the inner harbor daily April–Oct. An alternative is to tour the harbor on either a historic skipjack, the *Minnie-V* (522-4214), or on a clipper, the *Clipper City* (539-6063).

Annapolis, Maryland's charming state capital and the yachting capital of the East Coast, is only 24 miles S of Baltimore on the Chesapeake Bay via Hwy 2. With its own thriving arts community (ballet, chorale, opera, and symphony), it offers something for every kind of visitor. Stop by the Tourism Council, 171 Conduit St. (301/268-8687) or take the *Historic Annapolis Tour* (267-8149). The action is centered around the harbor and along Main Street.

If you have more time, and the traffic is not too heavy, *St. Michaels,* across the Bay Bridge from Annapolis on the other side of the Chesapeake Bay, makes a delightful side trip. Just W of Easton, off Hwy. 50, this relatively unspoiled old port community offers a glimpse of Maryland's E shore as it might have been. Visit the *Chesapeake Bay Maritime Museum,* Mill St., and try the crab at the *Crab Claw,* overlooking the harbor.

Weather

Baltimore's summers are hot and can be muggy. Daytime highs are typically in the low to mid 80s, falling to the 60s at night. Winters are moderately cold, with highs in the 40s and daytime lows usually in the high 20s and low 30s. Precipitation is fairly evenly distributed throughout the year.

BALTIMORE: TEMPERATURES AND PRECIPITATION

Month	J	F	M	A	M	J	J	A	S	O	N	D
Average Daily Temperature												
(Fahrenheit) Max.	42	43	51	63	74	82	86	84	78	67	54	44
Min.	28	28	35	45	56	65	69	67	61	50	40	31
Average Number of Days with Precipitation												
	11	10	12	11	11	11	11	11	8	8	9	10

Boston

Sights to See

Boston Common, between Beacon & Tremont Streets. The country's oldest park, and just right for a respite on a good day. Call 267-6446 for information on activities.

State House, Beacon St., opposite the Common. A gold-domed 18th-century building known for its basement Archives Museum. Open 9–5 M–F.

Faneuil Hall, Congress & North Sts. Built in 1742, this hall has been a meeting- and marketplace ever since. Open 9–4:30 daily.

Faneuil Hall Marketplace (Quincy Market), between N. & S. Market Sts., adjacent to Faneuil Hall. The prototype urban renewal project with over 150 shops, restaurants, boutiques, and stalls. Open daily.

New England Aquarium, Central Wharf, at the foot of State St. on the Waterfront. Over 2,000 species of fish, including the world's largest collection of sharks in the largest glass-enclosed saltwater tank. Open 9–6 M, Tu, & Th, 9–9 W & F, 9–7 Sa & Su.

Beacon Hill, between Boston Common and Longfellow Bridge. Centered on Mt. Vernon and Pinckney Sts., this area is full of stately old townhouses.

Newbury Street, Back Bay. Boston's fashionable shopping district. Art galleries, boutiques, and cafes.

Museum of Fine Arts, 465 Huntington Ave., along the Fenway. One of world's great art museums, with superb Egyptian and Asian collections. Open 10–5 Tu–Su, W till 10.

Paul Revere's House, 19 North St. Home of the Revolutionary hero, and Boston's oldest wooden house. Open 9:30–5:30 daily.

Museum of Science and Charles Hayden Planetarium, Science Park, Charles River Dam. Excellent museum. Open 9–4 Tu–Th, 9–10 F, 10–5 Sa–Su.

U.S.S. Constitution (Old Ironsides), Boston Naval Shipyard, Charlestown. The oldest commissioned ship in the U.S. Navy. Adjoining shoreside museum. Open 9:30–3:50 daily. Visit the adjacent Bunker Hill Pavilion.

Boston Tea Party Ship and Museum, Congress St. Bridge at Fort Point Channel. Replica of one of the original ships in the Boston Tea Party, along with an adjacent museum. Open 9–dusk daily.

Harvard Yard, Harvard University, Cambridge. The center of the nation's oldest university (1636). For information on campus tours check at the Holyoke Center.
The Fogg Art Museum-Arthur Sackle Museum, 32 Quincy St. (495-2387), is worth visiting if you are on the Harvard campus, as is the Botanical Museum on Oxford St. (495-1910), famous for its exhibit of glass flowers. Open 9–4 M–Sa, 1–4:30 Su.

Useful Information

Visitor Information Center, City Hall, Congress St., Hancock Tower, 200 Clarendon St., and Boston Common (536-4100); *Taxi* (426-8700, 536-5000, or 536-7000); *Travelers Aid,* 911 Atlantic Avenue (542-7286); *MBTA* (Public Transportation) (722-5215); *Boston Harbor Cruises* (227-4320); *Whale Watch Cruises* (742-8830); *Sightseeing by Helicopter,* Boston Skyview, Inc. (542-5244); *Boston Sightseeing Tours* (899-1454).

Special Trips/Tours

Many of the principal sights identified above, are located along the *"Freedom Trail."* A bold red stripe on the sidewalks leads visitors on this 2-mile-long tour of Boston's historic sites. An information kiosk in the center of the pedestrian mall on Tremont St., adjacent to Boston Common, will get you oriented. If you don't want to walk, *Brush Hill Tours* offers a "Freedom Trail Shuffle" on trolley cars with commentary (436-4100). The view of the city from the 50th-floor observatory of the *John Hancock Tower,* Copley Sq., is spectacular.

Just 35 miles SE of Boston on Hwy. 3 is *Plymouth,* site of *Plymouth Rock,* on Water St., the place where the Pilgrims landed. Nearby, moored at State Pier, is *Mayflower II,* a reproduction of the early Pilgrim ships. Costumed guides re-create life and conditions experienced on board. Open daily 9–5, April–Nov. See *Pilgrim Hall,* Chilton & Court Sts., one of the oldest public museums in the country. Open 9:30–4:30 daily.

Weather

Boston's summers are hot, with daytime highs usually in the high 70s or low 80s, dropping to the 60s at night. Winters can be cold, with daytime highs in the high 30s and low 40s, falling to the 20s at night. Precipitation is uniform throughout the year.

BOSTON: TEMPERATURES AND PRECIPITATION

Month	J	F	M	A	M	J	J	A	S	O	N	D
Average Daily Temperature												
(Fahrenheit) Max.	36	37	43	54	66	75	80	78	71	62	49	40
Min.	20	21	28	38	49	58	63	62	55	46	35	25
Average Number of Days with Precipitation												
	12	10	12	11	11	10	10	10	9	9	10	11

Charleston

Sights to See

Fort Sumter, entrance to Charleston Harbor. The first shots of the Civil War were fired here. Boats (the only means of access) leave the Municipal Marina, Calhoun St. & Lockwood Dr., daily at 9:30 & 2:30.

The Battery & White Point Gardens, East Bay & Murray Blvd. Site of former gallows for hanging pirates, the gardens provide an excellent vantage point of the harbor and Fort Sumter.

Charleston's antebellum mansions include *Hayward-Washington House,* 87 Church St., built in 1772, and famous for its period furniture; *Nathaniel Russell House,* 51 Meeting St., known for its interior decorations, detailing, and furniture; *Edmonston-Allston House,* 21 E. Battery St.; and the *Marigault House* 350 Meeting St., noted for its 18th-century kitchen and period furnishings. Open 10–5 daily.

St Michael's Church, Broad & Meeting St. Noted for its Palladian Doric portico, tall steeple, and fine interior. Open 9–4 M–F, 9–12 Sa.

Old Slave Mart Museum, 6 Chalmers St., devoted exclusively to Black history and crafts. Open M–Sa.

The Old Exchange and Provost Dungeon, Broad at East Bay, a British prison during the Revolution. See the movie "Dear Charleston." Open daily.

Huguenot Church, Church & Queen Sts. A fine example of Gothic architecture, it is one of the few remaining Huguenot churches in the country. Open 10–12:30, 2–4 M–F.

Gibbes Art Gallery, 135 Meeting St. Fine collection of American paintings, especially portraits relating to Southern history, and an excellent collection of miniatures. Open 10–5 Tu–Sa, 1–5 Su & M.

Charleston Museum, 360 Meeting St. Oldest municipal museum in the country, known for its collection of early state art pieces and its reproduction of a Confederate submarine. Open 9–5 daily.

The Citadel, Military College of South Carolina, Hampton Park & Moultrie St. Established in 1842, it is one of the last three military state colleges in the United States. Known for its museum of military artifacts, and its precision drill team, which can be seen at 3:45 P.M. on Fridays during the school year.

Useful Information

Visitor Center, 85 Calhoun St. (722-8338); *Taxi* (577-6565, 722-8383, or 722-4066); *DASH,* Downtown Area Shuttle (724-7368); *SCE & G,* City Bus Service (722-2226); *Your Charleston Connection,* 64 Calhoun St. (723-8145), provides a free shuttle to the Historic District, and has tickets for carriages and other major attractions.

Special Trips/Tours

Horse-drawn carriage rides through the historic district are offered by the Charleston Carriage Co., 96 N. Market St. (577-0042) 9–dusk daily. The carriages leave from the above address, with a free shuttle to 96 Market St. from the Visitor Center and downtown hotels. Night rides on a cool evening are particularly romantic. *Old South Carriage Tours* (723-9712), and *Palmetto Carriage Works,* Inc., 8 Guignard St. (723-8145) also offer horse-drawn carriage tours.

An unusual park, *Charles Towne Landing,* located on SR 171 between US 17 and I-26 at 1500 Old Towne Rd., about 3 miles NW of downtown Charleston, makes an interesting side trip. On the site of the first permanent English settlement in South Carolina, it offers tram tours, restored buildings, a trading ship replica, and an interpretive center. Open 9–6 daily June 1–Labor Day; 9–5 the rest of the year.

Patriots Point Naval and Maritime Museum, across the Cooper River off US 17 in Mt. Pleasant, just E of downtown Charleston, offers the chance to see firsthand an aircraft carrier (the *U.S.S. Yorktown*), a nuclear-powered merchant ship (the *Savannah*), a destroyer, a Coast Guard cutter, and a submarine. Open 9–6 April–Oct; 9–5 the rest of the year.

The world-famous *Magnolia Plantation and Gardens,* is about 14 miles N on SC Rte. 61. Considered to be one of the most beautiful gardens in the world, this 300-year-old plantation is known for its colonial estate garden with its camellias, and one of the largest collections of azaleas in the world. Includes a petting zoo, a mini horse ranch, a wildlife refuge, a herb garden, horticultural maze, boat tours, and canoeing. Open 8–6 daily.

Less than 4 miles from Magnolia Plantation on SR 61 are the oldest landscaped gardens in America, *Middleton Place,* noted for its landscaped terraces, intricate walks, and camelias, azaleas, roses, magnolias, crepe myrtles, and other ornamentals. The house contains a museum, and a restored stableyard features working exhibits on 18th-century crafts and artifacts. Open 9–5 daily.

Weather

Charleston summers are hot, with daily highs in the mid to high 80s. Daily lows average in the 70s from June through September. Winters are mild, with daytime highs in the high 50s, falling to the mid 40s at night. July and August are the wettest months.

CHARLESTON: TEMPERATURES AND PRECIPITATION

Month	J	F	M	A	M	J	J	A	S	O	N	D
Average Daily Temperature												
(Fahrenheit) Max.	58	59	66	73	80	86	88	87	83	75	66	59
Min.	43	44	50	57	66	73	75	75	71	61	51	44
Average Number of Days with Precipitation												
	10	9	9	8	8	11	13	13	10	6	7	9

Chicago

Sights to See

Chicago's magnificent skyscrapers. Views of the city can be seen from either the Skydeck on the 103rd floor of the *Sears Tower,* Wacker & Adams, or from the *John Hancock Building* observation dock, 875 N. Michigan Ave. Both are open 9–midnight daily.

Chicago ArchiCenter, 330 S. Dearborn Avenue. The best place to learn about the city's architecture. Open 9–4:30 M–Sa.

Water Tower Place, N. Michigan Avenue at Pearson St. A vertical shopping mall with an eight-story atrium. Afterwards, stroll along N. Michigan Ave., "The Magnificent Mile," with its internationally known shops.

The Water Tower, N. Michigan & Chicago Aves. The sole survivor of the Great Fire of 1871. Now a visitors information center. Open 9–5 daily.

Chicago Historical Society, Clark St. at North Ave. Known for its outstanding collection of President Lincoln's belongings, as well as its pioneer crafts demonstrations. Open 9:30–4:30 M–S, 12–5 Su.

State of Illinois Building, 100 W. Randolph. A new, very controversial three-sided building, with a 20-story ethereal atrium. Open 9–5 M–F.

Art Institute of Chicago, Michigan Ave. at Adams St. Excellent collection, noted particularly for its Impressionist paintings. Open 10–7 daily in summer, odd hours the rest of the year: call 443-3600.

Chicago Board of Trade, Jackson at La Salle St. Go to the visitor's gallery and watch the activity in this, the world's largest grain exchange. Open 9–2 M–F.

Field Museum of Natural History, S. Lake Shore Dr. at Roosevelt Rd. Outstanding museum. Open 9–5 daily.

Shedd Aquarium, 1200 S. Lake Shore Dr. at Museum Point. The world's largest with over 5,000 specimens. Famous for its coral reef exhibit. Open 9–5 daily.

Adler Planetarium, 1300 S. Lake Shore Dr. at Museum Point. Noted for its antique instrument collection and out-of-the-ordinary skyshow. Open 9:30–9 daily June 16–Aug. 31; 9:30–4:40 daily rest of year.

Museum of Science and Industry, S. Lake Shore Dr. at 57th St. Chicago's number-one attraction, noted for its working exhibits. Open 9:30–4 M–F, 9:30–5:30 Sa, Su.

Oriental Institute of the University of Chicago, 1155 E. 58th St. Small but superb collection. Open 10–4 Tu–Sa, 12–4 Su. Walk around the delightful campus (but only during the day), of one of the nation's top research universities.

Public sculpture and art in the plazas of downtown buildings. For example: the Picasso sculpture, *Chicago's Picasso,* Richard J. Daley Plaza, Washington & Clark; Miro's *Chicago,* across the street from Daley Plaza; Chagall's *Four Seasons,* First National Plaza, Monroe & Dearborn; Calder's *Universe,* Sears Tower Lobby, and his *Flamingo,* Federal Center Plaza, Adams & Dearborn.

Useful Information

Chicago Tourism Council Visitors Information Center, 163 E. Pearson, Water Tower, N. Michigan (280-5741); *Chicago Visitor Eventline* (225-2323 for taped information on theater, sports, and special events); *Jazz Hotline* (666-1881); *Mayor's Office of Special Events* (744-3315); *Sports Information* (976-1313); *CTA* (public transportation information, 836-7000); *Travelers Aid* 327 S. LaSalle St. (435-5000); *Taxi* (829-4222, 561-1444, or 248-7600).

Special Trips/Tours

Boat trips on the Chicago River and into Lake Michigan, are offered by Wendella Sightseeing, 400 N. Michigan Ave. (337-1446).

Architectural tour of Oak Park. The Oak Park Tour Center, in the Frank Lloyd Wright home and studio, 158 N. Forest (848-1978), operates walking tours through this delightful community with its 25-odd Frank Lloyd Wright buildings, and numerous Queen Anne and Victorian gingerbread houses.

Weather

Chicago has a continental climate with hot summers and cold winters. Summer daytime highs are usually in the high 70s or low 80s, falling to the mid 60s at night. Winters are cold, with daytime highs usually in the low 30s, dropping to the 20s at night. The wettest time of the year is summer.

CHICAGO: TEMPERATURES AND PRECIPITATION

Month	J	F	M	A	M	J	J	A	S	O	N	D
Average Daily Temperature												
(Fahrenheit) Max.	32	34	43	55	65	75	81	79	73	61	47	36
Min.	18	20	29	40	50	60	66	65	58	47	34	23
Average Number of Days with Precipitation												
	11	10	12	11	12	11	9	9	9	9	10	11

Cincinnati

Sights to See

Fountain Square South, W. 5th & Vine Sts. A shopping complex, a skywalk (Pogue's Arcade), and a fountain, with frequent free events and concerts. The view of the city from the top of Carew Tower is superb.

Contemporary Arts Center, 115 E. 5th St., just E of Fountain Square. Famous for its multimedia exhibits, but also a fine collection of modern art. Open 10–5 M–Sa.

Taft House Museum, 316 Pike, NE of the Contemporary Arts Center. Former home of President Taft, known for its portraits and Chinese porcelains. Open daily.

Cincinnati Art Museum, Eden Park, NE of the immediate downtown area, off Gilbert Ave. Excellent collection. Open 10–5 Tu–Sa, 12–4 Su.
Irwin M. Krohn Conservatory, Eden Park. One of the largest public greenhouses in the world. Open 10–5 M–Sa, 10–6 Su.
Natural History Museum, 1720 Gilbert Ave., at the W edge of Eden Park. Famous for its cavern and waterfall exhibit and its life-size dioramas of Indian life. Open Tu–Su.
Cincinnati Zoo, 3400 Vine St. & Forest Ave. One of the best in the country. Noted for its rare white Bengal tigers and gorillas. Open 9–8 M–Su in summer, 9–6 in winter.
Union Terminal, 1031 Western Ave. This Art Deco building has the world's highest unsupported dome. Open 10–5:30 M–W, 10–5:30 Sa, and 12–5 Su.
Cincinnati Fire Museum, 315 W. Court St., NE of Fountain Square. Fine collection of restored antique firefighting equipment. Open 10–4 Tu–Sa.
College Football Hall of Fame, Kings Mill, off I-71, just NE of Cincinnati. Memorabilia of college football stars, coaches and teams, with multimedia displays, films, and entertainment. Open 9–7 daily in summer, 10–5 the rest of the year.
Kings Island, on Kings Island Dr., just SW of Kings Mill, off I-71. One of America's better theme parks, known for the world's longest wooden roller coaster. Open 9–10 Su–F, 9–11 Sa, Memorial Day–Labor Day.

Useful Information

Convention and Visitors Bureau, 300 W. 6th St. (621-2142); *Taxi* (241-2100, 761-5007); *Public Transportation* (621-4455); *Weather* (241-1015); *Recorded Announcement of Cultural Events & Shows* (421-4636); check the free *Downtowner* for details on current and upcoming events, and entertainment information.

Special Trips/Tours

Day cruises on the Ohio River are offered by the *Riverboat Princess,* leaving from Coney Island (232-4052), off I-275 at exit 72. Cruises leave at 2 and 3 Tu–Su, and at 7 Tu–Th. *B & B Riverboats* (606/261-8500) offer a 60-minute narrated sightseeing cruise of the Ohio river from Covington, across the river (May–Oct.).
Further afield, just NE of Dayton, is the *U.S. Air Force Museum* at Wright-Patterson Air Force Base. Known for its Apollo spacecraft exhibits and over 150 aircraft, it is the world's largest military aviation museum. Open 9–5 M–F, 10–6 Sa–Su.
Kentucky's world-famous *Bluegrass region* is not far from Cincinnati. Centered around Lexington, 78 miles S of Cincinnati via I-71 and I-75, the Bluegrass region is noted for its thoroughbred horse farms and estates and beautiful rolling hills. The *Kentucky Horse Park* (606/233-4303), just NW of Lexington off I-75

(exit 120), is devoted to the region's unique heritage. The park contains the *International Museum of the Horse* and the *American Saddle Horse Museum*. Take a carriage ride through the park, a working farm, to see many of the 32 breeds of horse stabled at the park. Polo matches are held every Sunday afternoon. Trail rides are available. Open 9–7 daily Memorial Day–Labor Day, 9–5 the rest of the year.

Weather

Cincinnati's summers are warm, with frequent heat waves. Daytime highs typically reach the mid to high 80s, dropping to the 60s at night. Winters are cold, with daytime highs usually in the 40s, falling to the 20s at night. Precipitation is fairly well distributed throughout the year. September and October tend to be the driest months, relatively speaking.

CINCINNATI: TEMPERATURES AND PRECIPITATION

Month	J	F	M	A	M	J	J	A	S	O	N	D
Average Daily Temperature												
(Fahrenheit) Max.	43	45	55	66	76	84	88	86	80	69	55	45
Min.	27	29	37	47	56	65	69	67	61	49	38	29
Average Number of Days with Precipitation												
	12	10	12	12	11	11	10	9	8	8	10	11

Cleveland

Sights to See

The panorama of Cleveland itself from the observation deck of the 52-story *Terminal Tower,* Public Square. Tremendous views of this large, industrial city spread out along the shores of Lake Erie.

Cuyahoga River or Harbor cruise aboard the *Goodtime II* passenger boat (481-5001). An excellent way to see "the Flats" industrial area, and the lakefront area. Cruises leave from the E. 9th St. pier, Memorial Day–Labor Day.

The Mall, between Lakeside & St. Clair Aves., and E. 6th & E. 4th Sts. The heart of Cleveland, surrounded by government buildings.

The Arcade, 401 Euclid Ave., just S of the Mall. A renovated 19th-century marketplace full of interesting boutiques, galleries, and restaurants, with free lunchtime entertainment.

Cleveland Museum of Art, 11150 East Blvd., University Circle, E of the downtown area. One of the country's better museums, with an excellent, diverse collection. Open Tu–Su.

Cleveland Museum of Natural History, Wade Oval, University Circle, just N of the Museum of Art across Wade Park. Known for its exhibits on prehistoric and North American Indian life. Open 10–5 M–Sa, 1–5:30 Su.

Western Reserve Historical Society, 10825 East Blvd., University Circle, NE of the natural history museum. A library, historical museum and an auto/aviation museum with over 200 antique vehicles and airplanes. Open 10–5 Tu–Sa, 12–5 Su.

Rockefellᵒr Park Greenhouse, 750 E. 88th St., NNE of the University Circle area toward Lake Erie via Martin Luther King Blvd. The greenhouse contains tropical plants and a Japanese garden, and is surrounded by landscaped grounds. Open 9:30–4:30 daily.

NASA Lewis Research Center, 21000 Brookpark Rd., next to Cleveland Hopkins International Airport, W of downtown Cleveland. The visitor center has exhibits, films, and lectures on space exploration, satellites, energy, and jet propulsion. Open 9–4 M–F, 10–3 Sa, 1–5 Su.

Useful Information

Cleveland Convention & Visitors Bureau (621-4110), 3100 Tower City Center; *Events Phone* (621-8860); *Weather* (931-1212); *Taxi* (881-1111, 623-1500); *Public Transportation* (621-9500).

Special Trips/Tours

Sea World of Ohio is just SE of Cleveland, off SR 43 near Aurora. An 80-acre marine life park with shows by killer whales, dolphins, seals and other marine life, it also has water ski shows. Open 9–7 daily Memorial Day–Labor Day.

Akron, the rubber capital of the world, is 40 miles S of Cleveland on I-77. The home of such companies as Goodyear, Goodrich, General Tire, and Firestone, it offers two outstanding attractions: *Quaker Square,* and *Stan Hywet Hall and Gardens. Quaker Square,* at 120 E. Mill St., includes the renovated Quaker Oats Co. factory buildings, which house boutiques, galleries, restaurants, and hotels. Open 11–11 M–Sa, 12–9 Su. The *Stan Hywet Hall and Gardens* (216/664-3103), 714 N. Portage Path in Akron's NW section, is listed in the National Register of Historic Places. A fine 70-acre natural garden, together with a Japanese garden, surrounds a Tudor Revival mansion. The 65-room mansion is furnished in 14th-century period pieces, and is particularly noted for its interior details, as well as its stained-glass and leaded windows. Open 10–4 Tu–Sa, 1–4 Su.

If you have the time, the *Pro Football Hall of Fame* is in Canton, another 20 miles S on I-77. Located at 2121 Harrison Ave., NW. (216/456-8207), the hall features memorabilia and films of football greats, plus a research library.

On the way back to Cleveland, between Akron and Cleveland, stop by *Hale Farm and Village,* some 5 miles SE of Bath off the I-77 (exit 143). A 19th-century farm and restored village is re-created, complete with craftspeople demonstrating various period skills. Open 10–5 Tu–Sa, 12–5 Su, May–Oct.

Weather

Cleveland has a continental climate with warm, humid summers and cold winters. Summer daytime highs are typically in the mid 80s, falling to the 60s at night. Winter daytime highs are usually in the upper 30s, dropping to the 20s at night. Precipitation is fairly evenly spread throughout the year.

CLEVELAND: TEMPERATURES AND PRECIPITATION

Month	J	F	M	A	M	J	J	A	S	O	N	D
Average Daily Temperature												
(Fahrenheit) Max.	37	39	49	61	72	81	85	83	77	65	50	39
Min.	22	23	32	42	52	61	65	63	57	46	35	26
Average Number of Days with Precipitation												
	14	12	14	12	12	12	11	10	9	9	11	13

Dallas

Sights to See

Downtown Dallas. Go to the revolving lounge, restaurant, or observation deck on top of the *Hyatt Regency Tower,* 400 S. Houston St., for a magnificent view of this sprawling, fast-growing Texas city.

Reunion Tower of Dallas, 300 Reunion Boulevard. A 50-story tower topped by a huge geodesic sphere. The view from the observation deck is spectacular. Open 9:30–midnight daily.

Dallas City Hall, between Akard and Ervay Streets on Marilla St. Designed by I. M. Pei and surrounded by a plaza with fountains.

Old City Park, Gano & St. Paul Sts. Pioneer log cabins, restored shops and Victorian homes, a railroad depot, a bank, a church, and rural craft demonstrations. Open 10–4 Tu–F, 1:30–4:30 Sa–Su.

Nieman-Marcus, Main & Ervay (downtown), North Park, and Prestonwood Mall. Dallas's top department store.

Texas School Book Depository, 506 Elm. The place where Lee Harvey Oswald hid and shot President John F. Kennedy.

John F. Kennedy Memorial, Market & Main Sts. An open, white monument marks the spot where Kennedy was hit.

Museum of Natural History, Ranger Circle, Fair Park. Noted for its collection from the Southwest. Open 9–5 M–Sa, 1–5 Su.

Dallas Museum of Art, 1717 N. Harwood. Excellent pre-Columbian art and African sculpture collections and a fine sculpture garden with works of Henry Moore and Ellsworth Kelly. Open 10–5 Tu–Sa, 12–5 Su.

Health and Science Museum, Fair Park. Anatomy, astronomy (plus a planetarium), and geology exhibits. Open 9–5 Tu–Sa, 1–5 Su.

The Midway. On weekends May–Sept., and during the State Fair (Oct.), this fairground is full of exciting, thrilling rides, food stands, and people. Visit the Hall of State, noted for its giant murals. Open daily.

Dallas Zoo, Marsalis Park, 621 E. Clarendon Dr., off I-35E. Fifty-four acres of mammals, reptiles, amphibians, and birds in a park-like setting. Open 9–6 in summer, 9–5 the rest of the year.

Biblical Arts Center, 7500 Park La., at Boedeker. Noted for its 30-minute light and sound presentation of the "Miracle at Pentecost" painting and its collection of art. Open 10–5 Tu–Sa, 1–5 Su.
The Age of Steam Museum, The Midway. A railroad buff's delight. Open Su and during State Fair in Aug.
Southfork, off Murphy Rd., via Hwy. 75 and Farm Road 544. A private home that is not open to the public, but nevertheless the much-photographed fictional home of J. R. and the Ewing "family."

Useful Information

Dallas Convention and Visitors Bureau, 1507 Pacific (954-1482); *Union Station Visitor Center,* 400 South Houston (954-1111); *Dallas Transit System* (826-2222); *Taxi* (426-6262); *Weather* (654-0161); *Time* (844-1111); *Events Information* (954-1111).

Special Trips/Tours

Fort Worth is only 30 miles W of Dallas and offers a number of worthwhile attractions, including the *Fort Worth Stockyards* with its Cowtown Coliseum (indoor rodeo); *Kimbell Art Museum,* 3333 Camp Bowie Blvd., famous for its excellent collection of portraits and Renaissance art (open 10–5 Tu–Sa, 1–5 Su); the *Amon G. Carter Museum of Western Art,* 3501 Camp Bowie Blvd., noted for its Western and American art collection (open 10–5 M–Sa, 1–5 Su); *Sundance Square,* downtown, which is surrounded by boutiques, craft shops, art galleries, and restaurants. Also visit the *Sid Richardson Collection of Western Art,* 309 Main St., noted for its Remington and Russell paintings. The *Fort Worth Museum of Science and History,* 1501 Montgomery St., on Amon Carter Square, is also well worth visiting. Open 9–5 M–Sa, 1–5 Su.
Six Flags Over Texas, between Dallas and Fort Worth, off I-30, at Hwy. 360. If you have children along, or if you are young at heart, stop off on the way back from Fort Worth and spend some time in this theme park, complete with rides, entertainment, and a narrow-gauge railroad. Open daily May–Sept.; closed Nov.–March; weekends only in April and Oct. (640-8900).
International Wildlife Park, 601 Wildlife Pkwy., Grand Prairie, between Dallas and Fort Worth. Drive through or catch the park-operated train and see some of the 2,500 exotic animals in 360 acres of natural environment. Open 9:30–6:30 daily, March–Nov. (263-2203).

Weather

Dallas summers are very hot, but relatively dry. Daytime highs reach into the 90s, dropping to the 70s at night. Winters are warm, with daytime highs typically in the upper 50s and low 60s. Temperatures usually stay above freezing. April and May are the wettest months.

DALLAS: TEMPERATURES AND PRECIPITATION

Month	J	F	M	A	M	J	J	A	S	O	N	D
Average Daily Temperature												
(Fahrenheit) Max.	55	60	67	75	82	90	94	94	88	78	66	57
Min.	36	40	46	55	63	71	75	74	68	57	47	38
Average Number of Days with Precipitation												
	9	7	7	9	9	7	5	6	6	7	6	7

Denver

Sights to See

Denver Art Museum, 100 W. 14th Avenue. A spectacular building in its own right (over a million specially faceted glass tiles were used in the curved structure), it is particularly noted for its excellent Indian collection. Open 9–5 Tu–Su, 12–5 M.

Colorado History Museum, 1400 Broadway. Fine collection, especially in the Heritage Center. Open daily.

Denver Public Library, 1357 Broadway. Noted for its excellent collection on Western history. Open M–Sa.

Molly Brown House, 1340 Pennsylvania St. Famous home of the "unsinkable Molly Brown." Open 10–4 M–Sa, 12–4 Su. Stroll around the neighborhood, Capitol Hill, the site of luxurious homes once owned by mining tycoons.

Larimer Street, between 14th & 19th Sts. Lined with art galleries, boutiques, silversmiths, cafes, and craft shops in restored Victorian buildings. Also *Larimer Square* (14th & 15th), with its cluster of shops and restaurants.

United States Mint, 320 W. Colfax. Watch money being stamped and printed and see some of the gold bullion. Open 8:30–5 M–F.

State Capitol, between 14th Ave. & Colfax, at Sherman Ave. See the rotunda, and climb the steps for a spectacular view from the top on a clear day. Open 9–3:30 M–F.

Denver Museum of Natural History, City Park, between 17th and 23rd Aves., and York St. & Colorado Blvd. Noted for its dioramas of wildlife in natural settings. In the Coors Mineral Hall is one of the largest gold nuggets ever found in Colorado. Open 9–5 M–Su. Visit the nearby *Gates Planetarium,* with its star shows and "Laserdrive" show, and catch a film in the five-story by eight-story *IMAX theater.* Open 11–8 M–Su.

Denver Botanic Gardens, 1005 York St., in Cheeseman Park. Tropical to tundra flora, together with Japanese teahouses and an herbarium. Open 9–4:45 M–Su. Elitch Gardens, 38th Ave. & Tennyson St. An amusement park with brilliant floral gardens, rides, a summer theater, and picnic grounds. Open 10–11 daily in summer; 5–11 F, 10–11 Sa & Su the rest of the year.

Coors Brewery, 13th & Ford Sts., in Golden just W of Denver. Tour this huge brewery, and get a free taste of this famous "Rocky Mountain" beer in the tasting room. Open 9–4 M–Sa, closed holidays.

Buffalo Bill Memorial Museum and Grave, Lookout Mountain Park, 5 miles W of Golden off US 6. The museum has artifacts of the Old West and depicts the life of William F. Cody. The view, of the Denver metropolitan area and the Rocky Mountains to the west, from the observation deck on top of the museum is spectacular. Open 9–5 daily, May–Oct., 9–4 Tu–Su the rest of the year.

Useful Information

Denver Convention & Visitors Bureau, 225 W. Colfax Ave. (892-1112); *Tourist Information* (892-1505); *Taxi* (777-7777 or 861-2323); *Historic Denver Tours,* 1340 Pennsylvania Street (863-1398); *Time and Weather,* (639-1311); *Road conditions* (west, mountains 639-1111); *Travelers Aid,* 17th Ave. & Grant St. (832-8194); *Guestguide Magazine* and the monthly *Denver Magazine* are two good sources of information.

Special Trips/Tours

Rocky Mountain National Park, just over an hour from Denver via Hwy. 36, NW through Boulder and Lyons, is one of the highest regions of the country. With 67 named peaks over 12,000 ft., it has some truly spectacular scenery. The park is also a notable wildlife sanctuary. Open all year, although many facilities are available only from June to Sept., it is well worth the trip. For a terrific panorama of the Rocky Mountains, take the *aerial tramway* to the top of Prospect Mountain from Estes Park, where the park headquarters are located (586-2371). For park information, call 586-2385. Call 586-9561 and 586-4000, for weather information and road conditions.

Colorado Springs, home of the *U.S. Air Force Academy,* a thriving summer resort, high-tech center, and gateway to *Pikes Peak,* is 70 miles S of Denver on I-25. The major attraction is Pikes Peak (14,110 ft.), which can be climbed, driven up (via Rte. 24), or ascended via the *Pikes Peak Cog Railway* (685-5401). The railway leaves from Manitou Springs (515 Ruxton Ave.), 3 miles W of town on Rte. 24, May–Oct.

Weather

Denver summers are dry and warm. Winters are relatively mild, given the altitude of 5,000 ft. Summer daytime highs are typically in the high 70s, falling to the low 50s at night. Winter daytime highs are normally in the upper 30s or 40s, dropping to the high teens at night. Summer is the wet season.

DENVER: TEMPERATURES AND PRECIPITATION

Month	J	F	M	A	M	J	J	A	S	O	N	D
Average Daily Temperature												
(Fahrenheit) Max.	38	40	46	55	64	75	80	79	72	59	48	39
Min.	16	20	24	31	40	49	55	54	45	36	25	19
Average Number of Days with Precipitation												
		6	6	8	9	11	9	11	10	7	6	5	5

Detroit

Sights to See

Renaissance Center (RenCen), Civic Center between E. Jefferson St. and the riverfront. The centerpiece of Detroit's hoped-for downtown revival, this city-within-a-city contains shops, restaurants, theaters, a hotel, and offices. View the city from the revolving bar on the top floor of the Westin Hotel.

Philip A. Hart Plaza, Civic Center. Noted for its computerized fountain, the plaza also hosts ethnic festivals and concerts in the summer and ice skating in the winter.

Belle Isle, to the NE of the RenCen in the middle of the Detroit River, is connected with the city by a bridge at E. Jefferson Ave. & E. Grand Blvd. Visit the Dossin Great Lakes Museum, and the fine displays in the Whitcomb Conservatory. Open 9–6 daily.

Detroit Institute of Arts, Woodward & Kirby Aves., in the Cultural Center N of the RenCen. An excellent and comprehensive collection of Old Masters and more modern art. Known for Diego Rivera's mural "Detroit Industry." Open 9:30–5:30 Tu–Su.

Detroit Historical Museum, Cultural Center, adjacent to the Institute of Arts. Noted for its reconstruction of the Old City, and exhibits on Detroit's development. Open 9:30–5 W–Su.

Detroit Science Center, Cultural Center, John R. St. & Warren Ave. Hands-on exhibits, workshops, and demonstrations on science and technology. Open 9–4 Tu–F, 10–7 Sa, noon–7 Su.

Historic Fort Wayne Military Museum, 6325 W. Jefferson at Livernois, on the banks of the Detroit River S of the RenCen. Dating from the mid-19th century, it was a Civil War training center. Contains exhibits on the city's military history, together with an Indian Museum. Open 9:30–5 W–Su May–Sept.

Greenfield Village, Village Rd. & Oakwood Blvd., in Dearborn, a suburb just SW of Detroit. A unique collection of homes and shops, spanning 300 years, moved from all over America, complete with crafts and trade demonstrations. Among some of the historic structures are the homes of Noah Webster, the Wright brothers, and Henry Ford, and the Menlo Park laboratory of Thomas Edison. Visitors can ride on antique cars, a steam train, and a paddlewheel steamboat during the summer. Open 9–5 daily.

Henry Ford Museum, Village Rd. & Oakwood Blvd., in Dearborn, adjacent to Greenfield Village. Twelve acres of artifacts of early American technology, including a decorative arts collection, thousands of machines, and splendid antique automobiles. Open 9–5 daily.

Useful Information

Detroit Convention & Visitors Bureau, 100 Renaissance Center, Suite 1950 (259-4333); *Visitors Bureau Tourist Information "What's Line"* (298-6262);

Taxi (963-7000, 834-3300); *Public Transportation Information* (833-7692); *Weather* (976-1111); *Boblo Island Information* (259-7500).

Special Trips/Tours

On a good day, a trip to **Boblo Island** amusement park in the Detroit River is enjoyable, not only for the 90-minute ferry ride each way, but also for the recently renovated rides, shows, and attractions. The ferries leave from Detroit Dock behind the Joe Louis Sports Arena, off Jefferson St., after 9:30 A.M. Open 11–varying times, May 25–Labor Day. NOTE: moonlight cruises featuring local bands are also available (259-7500).

The Canadian city of **Windsor,** Ontario is just a short drive across the Ambassador Bridge, off I-75 between Porter & Howard Sts., or through the Detroit-Windsor Tunnel, next to the RenCen. Although not too different from Detroit itself, Windsor does have some noteworthy sights, including the *Art Gallery of Windsor,* 445 Riverside Drive W. (open 10–5 Tu, Th–Sa); the *Peace Fountain* in Coventry Gardens at Riverside Dr. E. & Pillette Rd.; and the fine *Jackson Park–Queen Elizabeth II Sunken Gardens,* Tecumseh Rd. & Quellette St. The *Dieppe Gardens,* Riverside Dr. & Quellette St. afford good views of Detroit across the river. NOTE: U.S. residents should carry identification papers.

Weather

Detroit has a continental climate with warm to hot and humid summers and cold winters. Summer daytime high temperatures typically reach into the high 70s or low 80s, dropping to the 60s at night. Winter daytime highs are usually in the low to mid 30s, falling to the 20s or high teens at night. Precipitation is well distributed throughout the year, with May and June normally being the wettest months.

DETROIT: TEMPERATURES AND PRECIPITATION

Month	J	F	M	A	M	J	J	A	S	O	N	D
Average Daily Temperature												
(Fahrenheit) Max.	31	32	42	55	67	77	82	80	73	60	46	35
Min.	19	18	27	37	48	58	63	62	55	44	33	24
Average Number of Days with Precipitation												
	13	12	13	11	13	9	9	10	10	12	14	

Fort Lauderdale

Sights to See

Intracoastal Waterway cruise aboard the Paddlewheel Queen. An excellent way to see the Gold Coast's canals. Sightseeing cruises depart at 2 P.M., dinner cruises at 7:30, from 2950 NE. 32nd St. (564-7659).

Discovery Center, 231 SW. 2nd Ave. A hands-on creative learning center/ museum dedicated to various art, history, and science subjects. Open 10–5 Tu–Sa, 12–5 Su.

King-Cromartie House, next to the Discovery Center at 229 SW. 2nd Ave. Restored turn-of-the-century house noted for its fine period antiques and furniture. Open 10–5 Tu–Sa, 12–5 Su.

Fort Lauderdale Museum of Art, 1 E. Las Olas, just E of the Discovery Center. Fine, diverse collection of art, ancient and modern. Open 10–5 W–Sa, 12–5 Su.

Fort Lauderdale Historical Museum, 219 SW. 2nd Ave., just N of the Discovery Center. Devoted to local artifacts and regional history. Open 10–4 M–Sa, 1–4 Su.

Ocean World, 1701 SE. 17th St., SE of the Discovery Center. Performances by porpoises, sea lions, and dolphins, along with a shark moat, and a three-story aquarium. Open 10–6 daily.

International Swimming Hall of Fame, 1 Hall of Fame Dr., off Seabreeze Blvd., NE of Ocean World. Museum housing swimming memorabilia adjoining the Olympic pool that hosts many of the world's top swimming meets. Open 10–4 M–Sa, 1–4 Su.

Las Olas Boulevard, from the downtown area W toward the ocean. This is Fort Lauderdale's chic shopping street, with expensive boutiques and restaurants.

Malibu Castle, 1999 SW. 33rd Pl. Amusement park and arcade with waterslides, miniature golf, carousels, haunted houses, bumper boats, etc. Open noon–11 M–F, 10–midnight Sa.

Six Flags Atlantis, 2700 Stirling Rd., Hollywood, S of Fort Lauderdale. Billed as the world's largest water theme park. Open 10–5 daily, March–Dec.

Seminole Indian Reservation, 3551 N. State Rd., Hollywood, just SSW of Fort Lauderdale. The Indian Village has a museum, gift shop, and demonstrations of alligator wrestling as well as snake and turtle shows, along with big-time bingo. Open daily.

Boca Raton, N of Fort Lauderdale on the Atlantic, one of Florida's most attractive cities, and one of the nation's wealthiest, is noted for its Spanish Revival architecture.

Morikami Japanese Park and Museum of Culture, 4000 Morikami Park Rd., Delray Beach, between Fort Lauderdale and Palm Beach. Noted for its fine Japanese Garden, and changing exhibits of Japanese folk arts. Open 10–5 Tu–Su.

Sports

Boating: Bill's Sunrise Rentals, 301 Seabreeze Ave. (467-1316); *Bahia Mar Small Boat Rentals,* Bahia Mar Yacht Basin (467-6000); and *Susi's Watersports,* 2000 E. Sunrise Blvd. (463-7874) all rent small boats.

Fishing: the *Bahia Mar Yacht Basin* (525-7174), 800 Seabreeze Ave., is the home port for several deep-sea fishing charter boat operators. *Pier 66* and *Marina del Americana* also have fishing boat rentals.

Golf: there are over 50 golf courses in the area. Those open to the public include *American Golfer's Club* (564-8760), 3850 N. Federal Hwy.; *Bonaventure GC* (389-8000), 200 Bonaventure Blvd.; and *Rolling Hills GC* (475-3010), 3501 W. Rolling Hills Circle, Davie.
Horseback Riding: contact the *Bar-B Ranch* (434-6175), 4601 SW. 128th Ave., or *Saddle Up Stables* (434-1808), 5125 SW. 76th Ave., both in Davie.
Snorkeling and Scuba Diving: *Lauderdale Diver* (467-2822), 1134 SE. 17th St., and *Divers Haven* (524-2112), 1530 Cordova Rd., both offer lessons and guides. *Boca Raton Beach* and *Deerfield Beach,* N of Pompano Beach, are two popular snorkeling and scuba diving spots.
Swimming: Fort Lauderdale's 27 miles of beaches are all open to the public. The *"strip"* between Sunrise & Las Olas Blvds., is the most crowded. The *John U. Lloyd Beach State Recreation Area* at the S end is less crowded, and *Hugh Taylor Birch State Park* has a fine beach. *Dania Beach,* between Fort Lauderdale and Hollywood to the S, is one of the least developed beach areas.
Tennis: most of the principal hotels have courts, but most are not open to the public. Public courts include *George English Park,* 1101 Bayview Dr., and *Holiday Park,* Sunrise Blvd.
Water Skiing: *Lake Osborne* is a popular spot. Contact *Mike Seipel's Barefoot International* (964-3346), 2600 W. Lantana Rd., Lantana.

Weather

Fort Lauderdale's summer daytime high temperatures typically reach into the high 80s, dropping to the mid 70s at night. Winter daytime highs are usually in the mid 70s, falling to the low 60s at night. Summer and early fall are the wettest seasons.

FORT LAUDERDALE: TEMPERATURES AND PRECIPITATION

Month	J	F	M	A	M	J	J	A	S	O	N	D
Average Daily Temperature												
(Fahrenheit) Max.	74	75	78	80	84	86	88	88	87	83	78	76
Min.	61	61	64	67	71	74	76	76	75	72	66	62
Average Number of Days with Precipitation												
	9	6	7	7	12	13	15	15	18	16	10	7

Fort Myers-Naples

Sights to See

Thomas Edison's Winter Home, 2350 McGregor Blvd., off SR 867, just SW of Fort Myers. The inventor's winter home, where he perfected the light bulb. Guided tours include the house with Edison's original furnishings, his laboratory and workshops, a museum displaying his inventions, and his botanical garden. Open 9–4 M–Sa, 12:30–4 Su.

Fort Myers Historical Museum, 2300 Peck St., Fort Myers. Exhibits illustrating local history. Open 9–4 Tu–F, 1–5 Sa–Su.

Caloosahatchee River cruise. Boats leave from the Fort Myers City Yacht Basin (Oct.–April) for cruises as far inland as Lake Okeechobee, affording a unique perspective on this part of the Everglades.

Waltzing Waters, 18101 US 41 SE, Fort Myers. Water, light and laser shows. Open 9–9 daily.

Sanibel and Captiva Islands, SW of Fort Meyers via Hwy. 867. Famous for their excellent fishing and incredible seashells, the latter attracting collectors from around the world. Beware of the "Sanibel Stoop"!

Ding Darling National Wildlife Refuge, on the N side of Sanibel Island. Canoe trails, bird-watching tower, wildlife drive, and interpretive trails. Open daily, dawn to dusk.

Collier County Museum, 3301 Tamiami Trail E., just SE of Naples. Exhibits depicting the region's history. Open 9–5 M–F.

African Safari Park, US 41 & Fleischmann Blvd. Guided safari train rides through 70 acres of "jungle." Also trained animal shows. Open 9:30–5:30 daily.

Corkscrew Swamp Sanctuary, NE of Naples on Sanctuary Rd., off I-75 via Hwy. 846. A National Audubon Society wilderness and wildlife sanctuary, famous for its colony of American wood storks and bald cypress trees. Open 9–5 daily.

Big Cypress National Preserve, E of Naples, traversed by Alligator Alley (SR 84) and Tamiami Trail (US 41). Huge area noted for its bald and dwarf cypress trees, mangrove forests and abundant wildlife. Drop by the Visitor Information Center at the Oasis Ranger Station, 20 miles E of Ochopee on US 41. Airboat rides are available.

Everglades National Park, to the S and E of the Big Cypress National Preserve. The largest subtropical wilderness in the United States, it is famous for its mangrove forests, tropical flora, and rare birds. Really worthwhile is *The Shark Valley Tram Tour,* which departs from Shark Valley, off US 41 W of Monroe and Paolita. The two-hour tour includes a 30-minute stop at an observation tower overlooking this magnificent sawgrass wilderness. Tours operate 9–4 daily, weather permitting (305/221-8455). *Everglades National Park Boat Tours* leave the park's ranger station outside Everglades City, off US 41 via SR 29, at the NW corner of the National Park, 9–4:30 daily (813/695-2591).

Sports

Boating: FORT MYERS: *Happy Sailboat Rentals* (463-3351), 1010 Estero Blvd., rents all kinds of boats in addition to sailboats. NAPLES: *Naples Beach Hotel and Golf Club* (261-2222), 851 Gulf Shore Blvd., North Naples, rents sailboats.

Fishing: FORT MYERS: deep-sea charters are available at *City Marina* (334-2348) and *Golf Star Marina* (463-2224), Fort Myers Beach. NAPLES: contact the *Queen* (774-3149), Naples Boat Haven Marina.

Golf: FORT MYERS: *Bay Beach Golf Club* (463-2064), 7401 Estero Blvd., and *Cape Coral Golf and Racquet Club* (542-3191), 4003 Palm Tree Blvd., Cape Coral, are courses open to the public. NAPLES: *Riviera Golf Club* (744-1081), Hwy. 864; *Golden Gate Inn & Country Club* (813/455-1010), 4100 Golden Gate Pkwy.; and *Naples Beach Hotel and Golf Club* (261-2222), 851 Gulf Shore Blvd., N., have courses open to the public.

Snorkeling and Scuba Diving: NAPLES: *Sealandia Scuba Center* (261-3357), 625 8th St. S., rents gear.

Swimming: pretty near all of the area's beaches are fine, particularly the stretch between Fort Myers Beach and Naples. *Sanibel Island* and *Captiva Island,* of course, are famous for their white beaches and shell collectors.

Tennis: FORT MYERS: *Cape Coral Golf and Racquet Club* (542-3191), 4003 Palm Tree Blvd., Cape Coral, and *Lehigh Country Club* (369-2121), 225 E. Joel Blvd., Lehigh Acres, have tennis courts open to the public. NAPLES: *Naples Beach Hotel and Golf Club* (261-2222), 851 Gulf Shore Blvd., N., has tennis courts open to the public.

Weather

Fort Myers-Naples summer daytime high temperatures are typically around 90, falling to the mid 70s at night. Winter daytime highs are usually in the mid 70s, dropping to the 50s at night. Summer is the wet season.

FORT MYERS-NAPLES: TEMPERATURES AND PRECIPITATION

Month	J	F	M	A	M	J	J	A	S	O	N	D
Average Daily Temperature												
(Fahrenheit) Max.	75	76	80	85	89	90	91	91	90	85	80	75
Min.	52	53	57	62	66	72	74	74	73	67	59	54
Average Number of Days with Precipitation												
	6	7	7	6	8	14	18	16	14	9	5	6

Hartford

Sights to See

Wadsworth Atheneum, 600 Main St. With one of the largest collections of American art in the country, it is also noted for its collection of Great Masters in the adjacent *Avery Art Memorial* and Colt firearms in the affiliated *Morgan Memorial.* Open 11–5 Tu–Su, May–Oct.

The view from the top of the Travelers Tower, 1 Tower Square, just N of the Atheneum, is the best in the city. Open 10:30–2:30 daily (reservations required, 277-0111).

St. Joseph's Cathedral, 140 Farmington Ave., W of the Atheneum. A modern structure, known for its huge stained-glass windows. Open daily.

Old State House, Main & State Sts., just NW of the Atheneum. A fine Colonial red brick building dating from 1796, now a museum with colonial furniture. Open 10–5 Tu–Sa, 12–5 Su.

State Capitol, Capitol Hill in Bushnell Park. A gold-domed capitol made of Connecticut marble, and known for its bas-reliefs and historical exhibits. Open daily.

Harriet Beecher Stowe House, Nook Farm, 73 Forest St., W of the State Capitol. The restored house of the famous author of *Uncle Tom's Cabin.* Open 9:30–4:30 daily June–Aug., 9:30–4 Tu–Sa, 1–4 Su rest of year.

Mark Twain Memorial, Nook Farm, 351 Farmington Ave., next to the Stowe house. A Victorian Gothic house occupied by Twain in this 19th-century writer's community. Noted for its interior decorations. Open the same hours as Stowe House.

Elizabeth Park Rose Gardens, 915 Prospect Ave., NW of the Twain House. Considered to be one of the country's most beautiful municipal rose gardens, with over 500 varieties (peak season is late June, early July). Open dawn–dusk daily.

Trinity College Chapel, Trinity College, Summit & Vernon Sts., S of downtown Hartford. A beautiful neo-Gothic structure.

Useful Information

Greater Hartford Convention and Visitors Bureau (728-6789), 1 Civic Center Plaza; *Visitors Center,* Old State House, 800 Main St. (522-6766), *Connecticut Division of Tourism* (566-2496), 210 Washington St.; *Public Transportation* (525-9181); *Taxi* (666-6666); the *Hartford Courant* provides detailed entertainment information.

Special Trips/Tours

Just W of Hartford, in Farmington off I-84, is the *Hill-Stead Museum* (203/677-9064), off Mountain Rd. It is noted for its excellent collection of French Impressionists and Chinese porcelains. Open 2–5 W–Su. Also in Farmington, at 37 High St., is the *Stanley-Whitman House* (203/677-9222), dating from the early 18th century and full of period furnishings. Open 1–4 Tu–Su, May–Oct.

Just over 50 miles SE of Hartford on Long Island Sound is *Mystic,* Connecticut with its famous *Mystic Seaport Museum* (203/572-0711) on SR 27. A truly outstanding re-created mid-19th-century seaport, complete with shops, homes, craft demonstrations, four historic ships, and a working historic preservation shipyard. Festivals and parades are held year-round. A turn-of-the-century steamboat, *Sabino,* makes excursions on the Mystic River, May–Oct. Open 9–5 daily, April–Oct., 9–4 the rest of the year.

Mystic also has another noteworthy attraction, the mystic *Marinelife Aquarium* (203/536-3323), off I-95 at exit 90. With over 6,000 species of

marine life, it also has dolphin, sea-lion, and whale demonstrations in its Marine Theater. Open 9–6 daily, July–Labor Day, 9–4:45 the rest of the year.
Just E of Mystic, in Groton, is the *U.S.S. Croaker Submarine Memorial* (203/448-1616), a WW II submarine you can board and see in a guided tour.
Open 9–5 April–Oct., 9–3 the rest of the year. Local operators also offer cruises along the Thames River past the submarine berths of the U.S. Submarine Base (203/445-8111). *Project Oceanology* (203/448-1616), offers educational cruises with marine scientists. Cruises leave from the *U.S.S. Croaker* Submarine Memorial, 359 Thames St., Sa–M, W early June–Labor Day. Call for reservations.

About 34 miles SSW of Hartford is *New Haven,* home of *Yale University,* which offers a number of noteworthy attractions, including the *Peabody Museum of Natural History* (203/436-0850), 170 Whitney Ave.; the *Yale Center for British Art* (203/436-3909), 1080 Chapel St.; the *Beinecke Rare Book and Manuscript Library* (203/436-8438), High & Wall Sts; and the *Yale University Art Gallery* (203/436-0574), 1111 Chapel St.

Weather

Harford's summer daytime high temperatures typically reach into the high 70s and low 80s, falling to around 60 at night. Winter daytime high temperatures are usually in the upper 30s, dropping to the low 20s at night. Precipitation is fairly evenly distributed throughout the year.

HARTFORD: TEMPERATURES AND PRECIPITATION

Month	J	F	M	A	M	J	J	A	S	O	N	D
Average Daily Temperature												
(Fahrenheit) Max.	37	37	46	56	68	76	82	80	73	63	51	40
Min.	22	21	29	38	48	57	63	62	55	45	35	25
Average Number of Days with Precipitation												
	12	10	12	11	11	11	10	9	9	9	10	10

Houston

Sights to See

Sam Houston Park, Allen Pkwy. & Bagby St. Some of the city's oldest buildings are restored, depicting the lifestyle of 19th-century Houstonians. Conducted tours leave from 515 Allen Pkwy. Open daily.
Museum of Natural Science, 5800 Caroline St. (Hermann Park). Noted for its oil and space exhibits. Open 12–5 Su, M, 9–5 Tu–Sa.
Houston Zoological Gardens, S. Main & Bissonnet (Hermann Park). One of the country's best, known for its Tropical Bird House and children's zoo. Open 10–6 M–F, 10–dusk Sa & Su.

Tranquillity Park, downtown Houston in the Civic Center. Commemorates the historic Apollo 11 moon landing. Features a cascading fountain with five stainless-steel stacks resembling rockets, and an exact replica of the famous footprint that Neil Armstrong left on the moon.

Museum of Fine Arts, 1001 Bissonnet. Excellent collection, especially Indian art and Remington paintings. Also noted for its Impressionist and Postimpressionist works. The building itself was designed by Mies van der Rohe. Open 10–5 Tu–Sa, 1–6 Su.

Museum of Printing History, Graphic Art Conference Center, 1324 W. Clay. Antique printing equipment, ancient documents, etchings, and engravings. Open 10–4 M–F.

Rothko Chapel, 3900 Yupon St. A nondenominational chapel, noted for its large, abstract canvases by Russian-born painter Mark Rothko. Open 10–5 daily.

Bayou Bend Collection, 1 Westcott St., off Memorial Dr. Noted for its excellent collection of 17th- and 18th-century American furniture and decorative arts. Open 10–2:30 Tu–F, 10–1 Sa.

Astrodomain, Kirby Dr. & I-610. A fantastic entertainment complex that includes the Astrodome (home of the Oilers and Astros), the Astrohall, the Astroarena, and Astroworld (a theme amusement park). Open daily, June–Aug., weekends in spring and fall.

Galleria Center, 5015 Westheimer. Oppulent shopping mall with a ground-floor skating rink. Open daily.

Port of Houston. Take a free boat tour of the harbor by calling the Port of Houston, Gate 8, Clinton Dr. (225-4044) and making reservations well in advance, or go to the observation platform on Wharf 9.

Useful Information

Houston Convention and Visitors' Council, 3300 Main St. (523-5050); *Taxi* (523-6080, 654-4040, or 236-1111); *Travelers Aid* (654-8072); *Airport Shuttle* (668-0011); *Weather* (529-4444); *Time* (844-7171).

Special Trips/Tours

The *Lyndon B. Johnson Space Center,* some 25 miles SE of Houston via I-45 and NASA Rd. 1, is a worthwhile trip. The Visitor Orientation Center (Bldg. 2) has spacecraft exhibits, including craft that have flown in space, photographs, paintings, a lunar roving vehicle, and a lunar module. The auditorium shows NASA films. Guided tours of the *Mission Control Center* and the *Skylab Training Room* are available with reservations (483-4321). Open 9–4 daily.

San Jacinto Battleground, Farm Rd. 134, off Hwy. 225, is about 21 miles E of downtown Houston. Site of Texas's independence victory over Mexico. Ride the elevator to the observation deck 489 ft. up the monument, and see the Museum of Texas History, and visit the WW I and WW II battleship *Texas.* Open 10–6 daily.

Weather

Houston's summers are long, hot, and humid, its winters warm and short. Summer daytime highs typically reach the high 80s or low 90s, with temperatures dropping to the 70s at night. Winter daytime highs are usually in the 60s and low 70s, falling to the mid 40s at night. Rainfall is pretty uniformly spread throughout the year.

HOUSTON: TEMPERATURES AND PRECIPITATION

Month	J	F	M	A	M	J	J	A	S	O	N	D
Average Daily Temperature												
(Fahrenheit) Max.	62	65	72	78	94	90	92	93	88	81	71	63
Min.	44	46	54	60	66	72	74	74	70	61	52	45
Average Number of Days with Precipitation												
	9	8	8	7	7	8	10	10	8	5	8	10

Jacksonville

Sights to See

Cummer Gallery of Art, 829 Riverside Ave. Fine collection of fine and decorative arts, especially noted for its early Meissen porcelain. Open 10–4 Tu–F, 12–5 Sa.
Jacksonville Art Museum, 4160 Boulevard Center Drive. Known for its pre-Columbian artifacts and impressive collection of Chinese porcelains. Open 10–4 Tu–F, 1–5 Sa–Su.
Jacksonville Museum of Arts and Sciences, 1025 Gulf Life Dr. Exhibits on Florida Indians, pioneer life, and wildlife, along with a planetarium. Open 9–5 Tu–F, 11–5 Sa, 1–5 Su, longer hours in July and Aug.
Friendship Fountain, next to the Arts and Sciences Museum. A 120-ft.-high fountain, lighted at night.
Fort Caroline National Memorial, about 10 miles E of Jacksonville, near Monument & Fort Caroline Rds. A reconstructed 16th-century fort commemorating the original French colonial settlement. Open 9–5 daily.
Kingsley Plantation State Historic Site, Fort George Island, E of Jacksonville, N of the St. Johns River. Early-19th-century home of Zephanish Kingsley, one of the wealthiest plantation owners of the period. Open 8–5 daily.
Fernandina Beach, Amelia Island, N of Jacksonville, just S of the state border. Noted for the concentration of fine Victorian houses and stores in its National Historic District.
Fort Clinch State Park, Amelia Island. Known for its huge brick and masonry 19th-century fort. Fort open 9–5 daily.

Useful Information

Jacksonville's Convention and Visitor Bureau, 33 S. Hogan St. (904/353-9736); *St. Augustine's Visitor Information Center,* 10 Castillo Dr. (824-3334); *24-Hour Artline Hotline* (353-1405).

Special Trips/Tours

Established in 1565, the nation's oldest permanent settlement, *St. Augustine,* is some 39 miles SSE of Jacksonville, off I-95. Still preserving traces of its Spanish origins, the old city has narrow streets lined with walled patios and stucco houses, some of which hold various craftspeople demonstrating their particular skills. The *San Augustin Antiguo* (The Restoration Area), straddling St. George St., N of Hypolita St. is particularly attractive.

The multimedia presentation at the *Visitor Information Center,* 10 Castillo Dr. (824-3334), provides a good introduction to the city. Starting from the Visitor Center, just N of San Augustin Antiguo, and heading generally S, are the following sights: *City Gate,* San Marco Ave., the only remaining part of the city's defensive perimeter; *Castillo de San Marcos,* 1 Castillo Dr., E of the City Gates, the oldest masonry fort in the United States, built in 1672–1695; *Old School House,* 14 St. George St.; *Sanchez House,* 105 St. George St., with furnishings dating from the 18th century; *Old Drug Store,* Orange & Cordova Sts.; *San Augustin Antiguo Museum Houses,* St. George & Cuna Sts.; *Cathedral of St. Augustine,* 35 Treasury St., dedicated in 1797; *Government House,* W block of the plaza; *Flagler College,* 70 King St., the former Ponce de Leon Hotel; *Zorayada Castle,* 83 King St., a 1:10 scale replica of a Spanish castle; *Lightner Museum,* King & Cordova Sts., excellent Victoriana collection; *Old Store Museum,* 4 Artillery Lane, former turn-of-the-century C. F. Hamblen Store with thousands of curios; *Ximenez-Fatio House,* 20 Aviles St., noted for its period furnishings; and the *Oldest House,* 14 St. Francis St., used as a residence since the early 1600s.

From mid-June to mid-August, at the St. Augustine Amphitheatre, 2 miles S on SR A1A, a dramatic musical pageant, the *Cross and Sword,* reenacts the founding of St. Augustine. Shows at 8:30 M–Sa (471-1965). Nearby, also off SR A1A on Anastasia Island, is the *St. Augustine Alligator Farm,* with alligators and crocodiles and Florida wildlife shows every hour from 10–5 (824-3337).

Marineland of Florida, farther S on SR A1A, features dolphins and penguins. Dating from the 1930s, it is Florida's oldest marine attraction. Open 9–5 daily.

Weather

Jacksonville's summer daytime high temperatures typically reach into the high 80s and low 90s, falling to the 70s at night. Winter daytime high temperatures

JACKSONVILLE: TEMPERATURES AND PRECIPITATION

Month	J	F	M	A	M	J	J	A	S	O	N	D
Average Daily Temperature												
(Fahrenheit) Max.	65	67	72	79	85	88	90	90	86	79	71	66
Min.	44	46	50	57	64	70	72	72	70	62	51	45
Average Number of Days with Precipitation												
	9	6	7	7	12	13	15	15	18	16	10	7

are usually in the upper 60s or low 70s, dropping to the 40s at night. Summer and early fall are the wettest seasons.

Key West

Sights to See

Key West from the Conch Tour Train that covers most of the principal sights in old and new Key West. The "trains" leave from Mallory Sq. and Roosevelt Ave. (294-5161).

Ernest Hemingway House and Museum, 907 Whitehead St., An elegant, mid-19th-century Spanish Colonial mansion, where Hemingway lived and wrote *For Whom the Bell Tolls* and *A Farewell to Arms* in the 1930s. Open 9–5 daily (294-1575).

Audubon House and Gardens, Whitehead & Green Sts. See the audiovisual presentation and film that shows some of Audubon's 1830s paintings of local birds. Open 9–12, 1–5 daily (294-2116).

East Martello Gallery and Museums, 3500 S. Roosevelt Blvd. Changing art shows featuring the works of prominent local artists, together with displays illustrating the Key's history. Open 9:30–5 daily (296-3913).

Mel Fisher's Treasure Exhibit, Green & Front Sts. Exhibits of the treasures found on the 17th-century Spanish galleons *Atocha* and *Santa Margarita* and on underwater archaeology. Open 10–6 daily (296-9936).

Lighthouse Military Museum, 938 Whitehead St. Collection of Key West naval history items, together with a Florida lighthouse display. Open 9:30–5 daily (294-0012).

Municipal Aquarium, Whitehead St. & Mallory Sq. Collection of local marine life in one of the country's first open-air aquariums. Open 10–6 daily (296-9936).

Offshore coral reefs, from the glass-bottom sightseeing boats *Fireball* or *Coral Princess.* Boats leave from the foot of Duval St. several times daily (296-3287 or 296-6293).

Sunset at Mallory Square Dock. A crazy "tradition" in Key West. Sometimes spectacular sunsets are watched by hordes of people who are simultaneously "entertained" by street performers, magicians, and other assorted characters.

John Pennekamp Coral Reef State Park, Key Largo, off US 1. Especially noted for the glass-bottom-boat tours (2–3 hours) out to the only coral reef off the continental United States. Open 8–sunset daily (451-1621).

Bahia Honda Recreation Area, Bahia Honda Key, midway between Key West and Key Largo. Excellent state park, with the whole island devoid of the commercialization that has marred much of the keys. Fine beaches. (872-2353).

Fort Jefferson National Monument, Tortugas Keys, some 68 nautical miles W of Key West. Built between 1846 and 1876, the fort has had a checkered history, and is a fine example of 19th-century coastal fortification. Reached by seaplane (Key West Seaplane Service, 5603 W. Jr. College Rd., Key West (294-6978). Open daily 8–sunset.

Sports

Boating: contact *Key West Charter Co., Inc.*, 165 Key Haven Rd. (294-3737); *Amiral's Passports to Paradise* (294-0011). *Fireball* (296-6293) and *Coral Princess* (296-3287) both offer sunset cruises in addition to glass-bottom-boat trips viewing the coral reefs.

Fishing: contact *Charterboat Amorous*, Amberjack Pier (296-5375); *Charterboat Seabreeze*, Oceanside Marina (294-6027); *Charterboat Billfisher*, 2828 Seidenberg Ave. (296-9969); *Charterboat Tenacious Too*, Garrison Blight Marina (296-4417). For fishing trips to the Tortugas, contact *Yankee Capts.* and *Yankee Freedom*, Land's End Marina (294-7009), and *Tortugas Unlimited, Inc.*, Safe Harbor Marina, Stock Island (296-0111).

Golf: the *Key West Resort*, Key West (294-5232) has a championship-quality Rees Jones 18-hole course.

Parasailing: contact *Amiral's Passports to Paradise* (294-0011); or *Parasail*, Smother's Beach (296-2554).

Snorkeling and Scuba Diving: contact *Key West Pro Dive Shop*, 1605 N Roosevelt Blvd. (296-3823); *Amiral's Passports to Paradise* (294-0011); *Island Angler*, Boog Powell's Marina (294-6356); *Capt's Vicki Wilderness Guide* (294-9731); *Reef Raiders Dive Shop*, MM 4.5, US 1, Stock Island (294-0660); or *Angler's Marine*, Boog Powell's Marina (296-4384).

Spearfishing: *Carol J's Key West Dive Center*, 2319 Roosevelt Blvd. (296-3661) offers spearfishing.

Tennis: some of the resort hotels have tennis courts. There are public courts at *Bayview Park*, near Truman & Eisenhower Dr.

Underwater Photography: contact *Admiral Bushy & Sons Snorkeling*, Land's End Marina (294-0011).

Waterskiing: contact *Sky & Ski*, MM 4.5, US 1, Stock Island (296-5165); or *Marriott's Casa Marina Resort*, 1500 Reynold's St. (294-2192).

Windsurfing: contact *Windsurfing Key West*, 700 Waddell Street (296-8897).

Weather

The Florida Keys enjoy a subtropical climate with a long, hot summer and very sunny winter. Summer daytime high temperatures typically reach into the high 80s, dropping to the mid 70s at night. Winter daytime highs are usually in the mid 70s, falling to the low 60s at night. The rainy season extends from May through October.

KEY WEST: TEMPERATURES AND PRECIPITATION

Month	J	F	M	A	M	J	J	A	S	O	N	D
Average Daily Temperature												
(Fahrenheit) Max.	74	75	78	80	84	86	88	88	87	83	78	76
Min.	61	61	64	67	71	74	76	76	75	72	66	62
Average Number of Days with Precipitation												
	9	6	7	7	12	13	15	15	18	16	10	7

Las Vegas

Sights to See

The Strip, Las Vegas Blvd., S of the city along US 91. Home of the Circus Circus, Riviera, Stardust Hotel, Silver Slipper, Desert Inn, Frontier Hotel, The Castaways, Sands Hotel, Caesar's Palace, Flamingo, Barbary Coast, Dunes, MGM Grand, Dunes, Aladdin, Marina, Tropicana, and others. All attempting to outdo the others with glitter, neon lights, entertainment, and gaming lures. *Las Vegas itself* can be seen from the Top of the Landmark, 364 Convention Center Drive.

Circus Circus, 2880 Las Vegas Blvd. Clowns, acrobats, dancers, fire-eaters, and trapeze and high-wire artists entertain the gamblers two stories over the casino floor. One of the few family-oriented casinos in the city.

Caesar's Palace, 3570 Las Vegas Blvd. The city's most elegant casino. Not just a casino, it also contains an exclusive shopping arcade (the Appian Way), the Garden of the Gods, and The World of Caesar, a Disney-style ride through a miniature city of Rome, complete with laser-powered sound, 3-D video projections, and other special effects.

Downtown Casinos area, centered around Fremont & 1st Sts. The older, more seedy section of town, although the Golden Nugget is relatively new. Known for *Glitter Gulch,* a 40-ft.-high wall of lights that extends for several blocks.

Liberace Museum, 1775 E. Tropicana Ave. See his collection of pianos, cars, and fantastic costumes. Of special note is the Czar Nicholas uniform, a piano played by Chopin, and a concert grand owned by George Gershwin. Open 10–5 M–Sa, 1–5 Su.

Imperial Palace Auto Collection, Imperial Palace Hotel, 3535 Las Vegas Blvd. S. Over 200 classic and historic automobiles, antique fire engines, buses, motorcycles, and horse-drawn carriages. Open 9:30–11:30 daily.

Museum of Natural History, University of Nevada campus. Noted for its collection of Indian artifacts and desert exhibits. Open 9–5, M–F, 10–5 Sa.

Old Nevada, W of Las Vegas on Charleston Blvd. A thematic reproduction of a Nevada boomtown, with recreated buildings, melodrama, gun fights and hangings, museums and shops. Open daily.

Red Rock Canyon, 15 miles W of Las Vegas off Hwy. 160. A striking recreational area, offering hiking, exploring, and some camping and picknicking. Drop by the Visitors' Interpretation Center.

Mount Charleston (almost 12,000 ft.), 40 minutes from Las Vegas via Hwys. 95 and 39, offers a respite from the heat and tremendous views of the surrounding Amargosa Desert.

Useful Information

Las Vegas Chamber of Commerce, 2301 E. Sahara Avenue (457-4664, or 457-5544 for a 24-hour recorded message); *Las Vegas Convention and Visitors Authority,* 3150 Paradise Rd. (733-2323) for up-to-date information on floor shows and buffet specials; *Taxi* (382-7100, 382-4444, or 384-6111); *Weather* (736-6141); *Gamblers Anonymous* (385-7732, call 24 hours a day).

Special Trips/Tours

Hoover Dam and Lake Mead, 30 miles S of Las Vegas on Boulder Hwy. (US 93). Hoover Dam, over 700 ft. high, created Lake Mead, one of the largest man-made lakes in the world, and supplies electricity to Las Vegas and California. Take the tour of the dam, which includes a visit to the powerhouse (702/293-8367). You can also take a boat trip to the Dam from Boulder City, on the *Echo,* which departs at 10:30 and 3 daily. *Scenic air tours* of the Grand Canyon or Lake Mead are available from Las Vegas or Boulder City. Contact *Scenic Airlines* (739-1900); *Lake Mead Air* (293-1848); or *Paradise Travel Service* (739-6481).

Death Valley National Monument, is only 140 miles W of Las Vegas via Rts. 95 and 190. One of the hottest places in the world (134 degrees), it contains the lowest point in the country (282 ft. below sea level). It is also breathtakingly beautiful. Stop by the Visitors Center (714/786-2331), and be sure to see *Scotty's Castle,* and *Furnace Creek Inn and Ranch.*

Weather

Las Vegas enjoys one of the sunniest climates in the country. Summers are hot, but dry. Daytime highs reach into the high 90s and low 100s, dropping to the 60s at night. Winters are warm, with daytime highs in the 60s and lows in the 30s. Rainfall is very low all year.

LAS VEGAS: TEMPERATURES AND PRECIPITATION

Month	J	F	M	A	M	J	J	A	S	O	N	D
Average Daily Temperature												
(Fahrenheit) Max.	60	67	72	81	89	99	103	102	95	84	71	61
Min.	29	34	39	45	52	61	68	66	57	47	36	30
Average Number of Days with Precipitation												
	2	2	2	1	1	1	2	2	1	1	1	2

Los Angeles

Sights to See

Universal Studios, 3900 Lankershim Blvd. Famous for its movie studio show, stunt show, "Jaws" shark attack, and simulated earthquake, on the tour tram. Open 8–6 daily July & Aug., 10–3:30 the rest of the year (877-2121).

Olivera Street, site of the old Spanish-Mexican pueblo, now full of Mexican shops, food vendors, and restaurants. Open 10–8 daily.

Downtown Los Angeles (yes, there is one!). The top of *City Hall,* Main & Los Angeles Sts., affords an excellent view of the city; the *Bradbury Building's* interior is an architectural gem; *Grand Central Public Market* is an old-fashioned bustling food market; the *Bonventura Hotel* is a futuristic structure with an interesting atrium.

Mann's (Grauman's) Chinese Theater, 6925 Hollywood Blvd. Its world-famous forecourt has celebrity footprints and handprints immortalized in cement. It is worth seeing almost any movie that is playing just to see the ornate interior.
Hollywood Wax Museum, 6767 Hollywood Blvd. Full of the likenesses of film stars, together with a good documentary on the Academy Awards and winners. Open daily.
Los Angeles County Museum of Art, 5905 Wilshire Blvd. Houses a superb collection. Open 10–5 Tu–F, 10–6 Sa & Su. See the *La Brea tar pits* and the *Page Museum of La Brea Discoveries* next door. Open 10–5 Tu–Su.
Farmers Market, W. Third St. & Fairfax Ave. Over 150 food shops, markets, and services, together with clothing and gift shops. Open 9–6 M–Sa, 10–5 Su, longer hours in summer.
Beverly Hills, one of the most affluent and prestigious addresses in southern California. Shop or just browse along *Rodeo Drive* (between Wilshire & Santa Monica Blvds.), one of the world's most chic shopping streets.
Ports o' Call Village, Berth 77 at the foot of Harbor Fwy., San Pedro. Almost 90 shops, boutiques, restaurants, and snack bars, in a re-created shipping village right on the harbor. Boats leave here for harbor tours and whale-watching trips in season. Open daily.
Queen Mary and Spruce Goose, Queen Mary exit on Long Beach Fwy, Long Beach. Tours of both one of the largest ships and the largest airplane in the world. Open 10–6 daily.
Knott's Berry Farm, 8039 Beach Blvd., Buena Park, SE of downtown Los Angeles. Six theme parks rolled into one, with entertainment. Open 9–12, Su–F, 9–1 A.M. Sa Memorial Day–Labor Day, 10–6 M–F, 10–10 Sa, 10–7 Su the rest of the year.
Movieland Wax Museum, 7711 Beach Blvd., Buena Park. Over 200 figures of movie and TV stars. Open 9–10 daily April–Labor Day, 10–9 the rest of the year.
Disneyland, 1313 Harbor Blvd., Anaheim, about 40 minutes from downtown Los Angeles, in Orange County. No trip to southern California would be complete without a visit to Walt Disney's fantasyland amusement park. Great for kids and parents alike. Open 9–midnight daily in summer, similar hours the rest of the year. (714/999-4000).

Useful Information

Greater Los Angeles Visitors and Convention Bureau, 515 S. Figueroa St. (624-7300); *Southern California Rapid Transit District* (626-4455); *Police* (625-3311); *Travelers Aid* (625-2501); *Taxi* (988-8515, 481-1234, 627-7000, 653-5050); *Weather* (554-1212).

Special Trips/Tours

A drive along Mulholland Drive at night, especially between the San Diego and Hollywood Fwys. The view from this road that follows the crest of the Santa

Monica Mountains is just superb, giving you some idea of the size of this sprawling metropolis.

A day cruise to Catalina Island, one of the Channel Islands, some 26 miles offshore. The approximately 2-hour one-way boat trip is offered by *Catalina Cruises,* with boats leaving from either downtown Long Beach or San Pedro (795-2334).

A drive along Hwy. 1, through *Malibu,* up to the coastal town of *Santa Barbara.* On a good day the drive is magnificent. Stop off at the *J. Paul Getty Museum,* 17985 Pacific Coast Hwy. (Hwy. 1) (open 10–5 M–F in summer, Tu–Su the rest of the year). While in Santa Barbara, visit the picturesque *Mission,* the Santa Barbara Co. *Courthouse,* 1100 Anacapa St., *El Paseo,* off De La Guerra St., and, *Stearns Wharf,* for beautiful views of the harbor and mountains behind. Try the *Famous Enterprise* fish restaurant on lower State St.

Weather

Los Angeles enjoys a Mediterranean climate. Summer daytime high temperatures typically reach into the high 70s and low 80s, dropping to the low 60s or high 50s at night. Winter daytime highs are normally in the mid 60s, falling to the 40s at night. Winter is the wet season.

LOS ANGELES: TEMPERATURES AND PRECIPITATION

Month	J	F	M	A	M	J	J	A	S	O	N	D
Average Daily Temperature												
(Fahrenheit) Max.	65	66	67	70	72	76	81	82	81	76	73	67
Min.	46	47	48	50	53	56	60	60	58	54	50	47
Average Number of Days with Precipitation												
	6	6	6	4	2	1	0	0	1	2	3	6

Miami-Miami Beach

Sights to See

Miamarina, 5th St. & Biscayne Bay. Take a 2-hour cruise of Biscayne Bay aboard the *Island Queen* (379-5119).

Metro-Dade Cultural Center, 101 W. Flagler St. Houses the *Historical Museum of South Florida* (Spanish, Indian, and maritime exhibits); the *Center for the Fine Arts* (featuring traveling exhibitions and the public library). Open 10–6 M–F, noon–6 Sa & Su.

Planet Ocean, 3979 Rickenbacker Causeway, Virginia Key. Films and exhibits on the world's oceans. Experience an indoor hurricane. Open 10–6 daily.

Miami Seaquarium, Rickenbacker Causeway, opposite Planet Ocean. World's largest tropical marine aquarium, with some 10,000 fish and mammals, including performing seals and dolphins. Open 9–6:30 daily.

Museum of Science and Space Planetarium, 3280 South Miami Ave. Known for its coral-reef and Everglades exhibits. Open 9–10 M–Sa, noon–10 Su.
VillaVizcaya, 3251 S. Miami Ave. See how the other half lived. Former home of James Deering of International Harvester, full of European antiques and art. Now the Dade County Art Museum. Open 9:30–4:30 daily.
Parrot Jungle, 11000 SW. 57th Ave. Thousands of tropical birds flying free. Watch one of the 40-minute trained bird shows. Open 9:30–5 daily.
Fairchild Tropical Gardens, 10901 Old Cutler Road, Coral Gables. Take the tram ride through this lush, exotic garden of tropical and subtropical plants. Open daily.
Little Havana, Calle Ocho (Eighth Street). Center of the large Cuban community in Miami. Full of restaurants serving authentic Latin food.
Miami Beach. Renovation and redevelopment have stayed the recent decline of this formerly world-class resort area. Famous for such hotels as the *Fontainebleau Hilton* and others along Collins Avenue. Stroll along the boardwalk between 21st & 46th Sts.
Art Deco District, Southern Miami Beach, between 6th and 23rd Sts., has over 800 buildings designed in the Art Deco style and pastel colors of the 1930s.
Miami Beach Garden and Conservatory, 2000 Convention Center Dr. Known for its impressive display of native flora.
Miccosukee Indian Village, 25 miles W of Miami on US 41 (Tamiami Trail). Tribal members, clad in traditional garb, create and exhibit patchwork, basketry, and other crafts. Open 9–5:30 daily.

Useful Information

Greater Miami Convention & Visitors Bureau, 4770 Biscayne Blvd. (539-3000) or 555 17th St. (673-7070); *Metrobus* (638-6700); *Taxi* (532-5555, or 888-8888); Information on *activities in the city's parks* (579-2568); *Travelers Aid* (643-5700); *Weather* (661-5065).

Special Trips/Tours

Take a *Cruise along the coast* with *Nikko's Gold Coast cruises,* which leave Haulover Marina, 10800 Collins Avenue (945-5461). Or take a *helicopter flight* over Miami Beach. Flights leave year-round from Watson Island on MacArthur Blvd. (377-0934).

Everglades National Park, part of this country's only subtropical wetland, is only about an hour's drive from Miami. The park entrance is on Rt. 27, 12 miles SW of Homestead, off Hwy. 1. Stop at the *Visitors Center* (305/247-6211) and get your bearings on this unique ecological system.

Weather

Miami's summers are hot and humid, with daytime highs typically in the mid to high 80s, dropping to the mid 70s at night. Winters are very warm and sunny, with daytime highs in the mid 70s, falling to the 60s at night. The wettest time of the year is summer and fall.

MIAMI: TEMPERATURES AND PRECIPITATION

Month	J	F	M	A	M	J	J	A	S	O	N	D
Average Daily Temperature												
(Fahrenheit) Max.	74	75	78	80	84	86	88	88	87	83	78	76
Min.	61	61	64	67	71	74	76	76	75	72	66	62
Average Number of Days with Precipitation												
	9	6	7	7	12	13	15	15	18	16	10	7

Milwaukee

Sights to See

Milwaukee Art Museum, 750 N. Lincoln Memorial Dr., on the lakefront. Fine, diverse collection, particularly of 19th- and 20th-century European and American art. Open 10–5 Tu–W, F–Sa, 12–9 Th, 1–6 Su.

Charles Allis Art Library, 1630 E. Royal St., N of the Art Museum off Prospect Ave. Fine collection of artifacts from all over the world, together with American and European period furniture housed in an English Tudor mansion. Open 1–5 W–Su.

Milwaukee Public Museum, Civic Center, 800 W. Wells St., W of the Art Museum in the center of downtown. An excellent, large natural history collection. It is noted for its realistic exhibits of the streets of Old Milwaukee, Indian settlements, a Mexican street, and a European village, among others. Open 9–5 daily.

Joan of Arc Chapel, Marquette University, 601 N. 14th St., just SW of the Public Museum across Hwy 43. Transported, stone by stone, from the village of Chasse in France, where Joan reputedly kissed one of the stones before her death. It is a fine example of medieval Gothic architecture. Open 10–4 daily.

The Pabst Mansion, 2000 W. Wisconsin Ave. The Flemish Renaissance former home of Frederick Pabst, the beer baron. Noted for its fine interior. Open 10–3:30 M–Sa.

Miller Brewery, 4251 W. State St. Take a tour of this, one of the city's two large breweries, and sample some free beer. Open 9–3:30 M–Sa in summer, 9–3:30 M–F the rest of the year. The other one, of course, is the *Pabst Brewery,* 915 Juneau Ave.

Mitchell Park Conservatory, 524 S. Layton Blvd. Rain forest, desert, and seasonal floral displays in three glass domes, each seven stories high. Open 9–5 M–F, 9–8 Sa–Su.

Villa Terrace, 2220 N. Terrace Ave. A good decorative arts museum in an Italian-style villa. Open 1–5 W–Su.

Milwaukee County Zoo, 10001 W. Bluemound Rd., about 6 miles W of downtown, off US 18. One of the country's best zoos, noted for its natural habitat settings in continental groups. Open 9–5 M–Sa, 9–6 Su, Memorial Day-Labor Day, 9–4:30 daily the rest of the year.

Useful Information

Visitor Information Center, 756 N. Milwaukee (273-3950) and 161 W. Wisconsin (276-6080); *Taxi* (271-1800, 933-2266); *Public Transportation* (344-6711); *Weather* (936-1212); *Fun Line* (799-1177) for local entertainment information.

Special Trips/Tours

Old World Wisconsin (594-2116), is just outside Eagle, off SR 67, some 20 miles SW of Milwaukee. A large, interesting outdoor museum with over fifty 19th-century buildings, depicting a village, a farm, and farmsteads of the period. Interpreters, in full costume, are on hand to explain the life of 19th-century immigrants. Open 10–5 daily May–Oct.

The capital of Wisconsin, *Madison,* is 77 miles due W of Milwaukee on I-94. A beautiful city, *Madison* has a number of noteworthy sights, including the *State Capitol,* a fine Roman Renaissance structure; *Frank Lloyd Wright's Unitarian Church,* 900 University Bay Dr., S of downtown; the *Madison Art Center,* 211 State St., known for its collection of 19th-century Japanese prints; and the *U.S. Forest Products Laboratory* (608/264-5600), Gifford Pinchot Dr. (take one of the fascinating tours at 2 P.M. M–Th).

About an hour's drive N of Madison on I-90 is the town of Wisconsin Dells, center for the state's premier natural attraction, the *Dells of the Wisconsin River.* A natural gorge, famous for its unusual geological formations, it can be seen on one of the guided sightseeing trips offered by *Dell Boat Tours* (608/254-8336) through the Upper and Lower Dells. Boats leave from the Upper Dells Landing, and the Lower Dells Landing at Wisconsin Dells, every 30 minutes, 8–6 daily May–Oct. *Storybook Gardens,* just S of Wisconsin Dells, are worth visiting.

If you've come this far, you should not miss the *Circus World Museum* (608/356-8341) in Baraboo, a few miles S of Wisconsin Dells off Hwy. 12, on SR 13. The original winter quarters of the Ringling Bros. Circus, it has a fantastic collection of circus wagons and an antique carousel, and offers circus performances, parades, and sideshows. Open 9–6 daily May–Sept., 9–9 July–Aug.

Weather

In the summer, Milwaukee's daytime high temperatures typically reach into the high 70s, falling to the 60s at night. Winter daytime highs are usually in the 30s, dropping to the 20s at night. Precipitation is fairly evenly distributed throughout the year.

MILWAUKEE: TEMPERATURES AND PRECIPITATION

Month	J	F	M	A	M	J	J	A	S	O	N	D
Average Daily Temperature												
(Fahrenheit) Max.	32	34	43	55	65	75	81	79	73	61	47	36
Min.	18	20	29	40	50	60	66	65	58	47	34	23
Average Number of Days with Precipitation												
	11	10	12	11	12	11	9	9	9	9	10	11

Minneapolis-St. Paul

Sights to See

The view of the Twin Cities from one of the restaurants at the top of the IDS building, off Nicollet Mall, or from the observation deck of the *Foshay Tower* (open Sa–Su), 9th St. & 2nd Ave., in Minneapolis, is magnificent.

Walker Art Center, 725 Vineland Pl., SW of downtown Minneapolis. Excellent collection of 20th-century American and European art. Open 10–8 Tu–Sa, 11–5 Su. The center also houses the *Guthrie Theater,* home of one of America's premier repertory companies.

Minneapolis Institute of Arts, 2400 3rd Ave. S., SE of the Walker Art Center. Superb collection of sculpture, paintings, prints, and drawings from a wide variety of cultures. Open 1–5 Tu–W, F–Sa, 10–9 Th, 12–5 Su.

American Swedish Institute, 2600 Park Ave., near the Arts Institute across I-35W. Swedish-American art and ethnic exhibits housed in a fine stone mansion. Open noon–4 Tu–Sa, 1–5 Su.

Minnesota Zoological Gardens, 12101 Johnny Cake Ridge Rd., Apple Valley, S of Minneapolis on Hwy 35. One of the country's best zoos, it is noted for its trail system of exhibit areas, Aquarium, and Sky Trail monorail. Open 10–6 daily, May–Oct., 10–4 the rest of the year.

State Capitol, University Ave. between Cedar & Wabasha Sts., St. Paul. Noted for the large variety of marble, limestone, sandstone and granite used in its construction. It also has one of the largest unsupported domes in the nation. Tours offered 9–4 M–F, 10–3 Sa, 1–3 Su.

St. Paul's Cathedral, 239 Selby Ave., SW of the Capitol. A scaled-down replica of St. Peter's in Rome, it is noted for its dome and Shrine of Nations. Open daily.

Science Museum of Minnesota 30 E. 10th St., St. Paul, just SE of the Capitol. With fine displays on natural history, anthropology, biology, and technology, it is particularly known for its programs on space and science. The *Omnitheatre,* in the Science Center, on Wabasha, is especially noteworthy. Open 9:30–9 M–Sa, 11–9 Su.

City Hall and Courthouse, between St. Peter & Wabasha, and 4th St. & Kellogg, St. Paul, S of the Science Museum, near the Mississippi River. Fine contemporary structure, known for the marble concourse and council-chamber painting. Open 8:30–4:30 M–F.

Useful Information

Minneapolis Convention & Tourist Commission Booth, 1219 Marquette Ave. (348-4313); *St. Paul Chamber of Commerce and Convention Bureau,* 445 Minnesota St. (297-6985); *Taxi* (Minneapolis: 333-3331, 824-4444; St. Paul: 292-1616, 222-4433); *Weather* (452-2323); *Art Events Hotline* (870-3131); the monthly *Minneapolis-St. Paul Magazine* is a good source for entertainment information details.

Special Trips/Tours

Valleyfair (445-7600), a turn-of-the-century amusement park, is just outside Shakoppee, SW of Minneapolis, and W of Bloomington, off I-35W, via SR 101. Attractions include roller coasters, an IMAX theater, a river raft ride, water log flume, ferris wheel, and music and dance shows. Open 10–8 daily, Memorial Day–Labor Day.

The *St. Croix river gorge,* about 25 miles NE of Minneapolis, offers a number of attractions, including the *Dalles of the St. Croix,* noted for their unusual rock formations, and *Interstate State Park,* also noted for its unusual geological formations. The *museum* in the Interstate State Park is worth visiting. Open 9:30–5:30 daily May–Sept. *Sightseeing cruises* through the Dalles of the St. Croix are offered by Taylors Falls Scenic Boat Tours (465-6313) daily, May–Sept. If you are more adventurous, the *St. Croix National Scenic River* further N, offers excellent canoeing.

The *Mayo Medical Museum,* in Rochester, Minnesota, just over 100 miles SSE of Minneapolis, is definitely worth a side trip if you have the time. Located at 1st St. & 3rd Ave., it is especially noted for its life-size anatomical models of the human body, and its fascinating exhibits. Open 9–9 M–F, 9–5 Sa, 1–5 Su (507/284-3280).

Weather

Minneapolis-St. Paul experiences a continental climate with warm summers and cold winters. Summer daytime high temperatures are typically in the high 70s or low 80s, falling to around the 60s at night. Winter daytime highs are usually in the 20s, dropping to the teens or below at night. The wet season is from April to September.

MINNEAPOLIS: TEMPERATURES AND PRECIPITATION

Month	J	F	M	A	M	J	J	A	S	O	N	D
Average Daily Temperature												
(Fahrenheit) Max.	22	25	38	56	68	77	83	80	72	59	40	27
Min.	6	8	22	36	48	58	63	61	52	41	26	12
Average Number of Days with Precipitation												
	8	7	8	10	12	12	9	9	9	9	7	8

Nashville

Sights to See

The Grand Ole Opry, 2802 Opryland Drive. A country music lover's heaven, with over 20 acts performing every Friday and Saturday night year-round. Reserved-seat tickets sell out months in advance. The box office opens at 9 A.M. on Tuesday for general admission tickets to shows for that week. Arrive early (889-3060).

Opryland USA, Opryland USA and Music Valley Dr. interchanges on Briley Pkwy. A theme park centered on music (country, bluegrass, and everything else) with rides, restaurants, and a showboat. Open 10–10 daily in summer, weekends in spring and fall.

The Country Music Hall of Fame and Museum, 4 Music Square E. Country music star memorabilia. Included is RCA's *Studio B* (806 17th Ave. S), one of the most famous recording studios of the 50s and 60s, where greats like Elvis, Dolly Parton, and others recorded their early hits. Open 8–8 daily, June–Aug., 9–5 the rest of the year.

Barbara Mandrell Country, 1510 Division Street (242-7800). The family life and career of this star are highlighted. Open 9–5 daily from November 17 to March 28; 9–6 Su–Th, March 29–May 2.

The Ryman Auditorium, 116 5th Ave. N. Home of the Grand Ole Opry between 1943 and 1974. Full of mementos of the stars.

Fort Nashborough, 170 1st Ave. N. Partly reconstructed late-18th-century fort. Costumed guides re-create the everyday life of the times. Open 9–4 Tu–Sa.

Belle Meade Mansion, Harding Rd. & Leak Ave. US 70S. Known for its ornate cornices. Open 9–5 M–Sa, 1–5 Su. The Parthenon, Centennial Park, 25th Ave. N. & West End Ave. A full-size replica of the ancient Athenian Parthenon built in granite. Noted for its huge bronze doors. Contains casts of the Elgin Marbles from the original Parthenon. Open 9–5 Tu–Sa, 1–5 Su.

Tennessee Botanical Gardens and Fine Arts Center, 7 miles W of Nashville on Forrest Park Dr. via West End Ave. and Belle Meade Blvd. A museum with formal gardens, horticultural exhibits, and both a boxwood and Japanese sand garden. Open 9–5 Tu–Sa, 1–5 Su.

Music Village USA, Music Village Blvd., Hendersonville, about 8 mi. NE of Nashville on US 31E. Special exhibits, museums, and live performances. Open 9–9 in summer, 9–5 rest of year.

House of Cash, 700 Johnny Cash Pkwy., Hendersonville, near Music Village USA. Museum containing memorabilia of the Cash and Carter families. Also known for its Frederic Remington bronze collection. Open daily.

Useful Information

Tourist Information Center, Exit 85 on I-65N just E of downtown Nashville (242-5606); *Nashville Chamber of Commerce,* 161 4th Ave. N. (259-3900);

MTA (Public Transit 242-4433); *Travelers Aid* (256-3168); *Weather* (361-6417); *Taxi* (256-0101 or 254-5031).

Special Trips/Tours

Tours of the Homes of the Stars are offered by *Grand Ole Opry Tours,* 2808 Opryland Dr. (889-9490); *Country and Western Tours,* 2416 Music Valley Drive (883-5555); *Stardust Tours,* 1504 Demonbreun St. (244-2335); and *Gray Line,* 501 Broadway (244-7330).

Attend a Nashville taping of a show for the Nashville Network, or a syndicated network show like "Hee Haw" or Tom T. Hall's "Pop Goes the Country Club." Call the Opryland information center (615/889-6611). For "This Week in Country Music," call 615/791-1077, and for tickets to the "Music City Nows Country Awards Show," phone 615/244/5187.

Some 12 miles E of Nashville, via I-40E or I-65N to the Old Hickory Blvd. exit, is *The Hermitage* mansion, the plantation home of President Andrew Jackson. Dating from the early 19th century, it has the original furniture and furnishings, and many of the personal effects of Jackson. Guided tours by hostesses dressed in period costumes add to the charm. Open 9–5 daily (889-2941).

Weather

Nashville summers can be hot, with daytime highs typically in the mid to upper 80s, falling to around 70 at night. Winters are mild, with daytime high temperatures usually in the high 40s or low 50s, falling to the 30s at night. Winter and spring tend to be the wettest seasons.

NASHVILLE: TEMPERATURES AND PRECIPITATION

Month	J	F	M	A	M	J	J	A	S	O	N	D
Average Daily Temperature												
(Fahrenheit) Max.	47	50	59	69	78	86	89	88	82	72	58	49
Min.	31	33	40	49	58	67	70	68	62	50	40	33
Average Number of Days with Precipitation												
	12	11	12	11	11	11	11	9	8	7	9	11

New Orleans

Sights to See

Jackson Square, 700 Chartres St., Vieux Carre. Formerly the town square of the French colonial settlement. Full of people, artists and their wares, and surrounded on two sides by the fine Pontalba apartment buildings with their distinctive cast ironwork balconies.

St. Louis Cathedral, 700 Chartres St., across from Jackson Square. An 18th-century Spanish building, known for its painted ceilings and imported Belgian altar.

The Cabildo, Chartres & St. Peters Sts. next to the cathedral. Formerly the headquarters of Spanish rule, now part of the Louisiana State Museum, with interesting displays of New Orleans's French and Spanish heritage. Open 10–9 Tu–Su, 10–6 Su.

Jackson Brewery, 620 Decatur St., directly across from Jackson Sq. Former old "Jax" beer brewery, now an ongoing jazz and food festival, with Louisiana foodstuffs, Mardi Gras memorabilia, antiques, gourmet chocolates, jewelry, designer clothing stores, and live or piped music. Open daily.

Bourbon Street, full of honky-tonks offering live jazz, bars, strip joints, and peep shows. Despite the latter, there are enough jazz clubs playing into the earlier hours of the morning to distinguish it from most other big-city red-light districts.

Preservation Hall, 726 St. Peter St. Home of traditional Dixieland jazz. Open 8:30–12:30 nightly.

Garden District, between Jackson & Louisiana Avenues. Take the St. Charles Streetcar from Canal Street to Carrolton and get off and explore this former center of 19th-century opulence, with its fine Victorian and Greek Revival mansions.

Audubon Park, next to Tulane University. Reboard the St. Charles Streetcar to the park with its statues, lagoons, stables, and zoo. Either take the streetcar back to the French Quarter or catch the steamboat to Canal Street. The *Cotton Blossom* leaves the zoo at 11:30, 2:15, and 5 (586-8777).

Louisiana Maritime Museum, 2 Canal St. at the Mississippi River, in the International Trade Mart building. Good collection on the river's commercial shipping history, along with a collection of model ships, boats, and naval paraphernalia. Open daily. While here, go to the *Viewpoint observation deck* on top of the Trade Mart building for an impressive panorama of the city and port. Open 9–5 daily.

Musee Conti Wax Museum, 917 Conti. One of the world's best wax museums, depicting the romantic and sometimes bizarre history of New Orleans. Famous for its voodoo display and haunted dungeon. Open 10–5 daily.

New Orleans Museum of Art, City Park, near N. Carrolton & Esplanade Aves. Noted for its ancient glass and pottery collection, along with an outstanding collection of Renaissance art. Open 10–5 Tu–Su.

Useful Information

New Orleans Tourist Information Center, 529 St. Ann St. (566-5031); *Taxi* (525-3311 or 522-9771); *Travelers Aid Society* (525-8726); *Time* (529-6111); *Weather* (525-8831); *American Express,* 134 Carondelet St. (586-8201); *Regional Transit Authority* (Public Transportation 569-2721); *Ticketmaster* (888-8181, outlets all over New Orleans).

Special Trips/Tours

A steamboat ride along the Mississippi on the *Bayou Jean Lafitte,* which leaves the Toulouse Street Wharf on a trip through the bayou country. The *Cotton Blossom* steamboat also makes daily trips into the bayou country (586-8777). The *President* steamboat tours up and down the river daily from the dock at the foot of Canal St. (522-3030), as does the steamboat *Natchez,* which leaves from the Toulouse St. Wharf at Jackson Square (586-8777).

Walking Tours of the French Quarter are offered by the "Friends of the Cabildo" at 9:30 and 1:30 M–Sa.

Weather

New Orleans summers are hot and humid, with daytime highs typically in the high 80s or low 90s, falling to the mid 70s at night. Winters are very warm, with daytime highs in the mid to upper 60s, dropping to the low 50s or upper 40s at night. June, July, and August are the wettest months.

NEW ORLEANS: TEMPERATURES AND PRECIPITATION

Month	J	F	M	A	M	J	J	A	S	O	N	D
Average Daily Temperature												
(Fahrenheit) Max.	62	65	71	77	83	88	90	90	86	79	70	64
Min.	47	50	55	61	68	74	76	76	73	64	55	48
Average Number of Days with Precipitation												
	10	12	9	7	8	13	15	14	10	7	7	10

New York

Sights to See

Empire State Building, 34th St. and 5th Ave. (736-3100). The view from this world-famous Art Deco building, either from the open 86th-floor observation deck, or the glass-enclosed 102nd floor, is spectacular. Open daily, 9:30–11:30.

Midtown Manhattan, from 34th Street to 59th Street and from river to river. This is quintessential New York, containing the greatest concentration of tall buildings, best restaurants, big businesses, art galleries, best bargain basements, and exclusive shopping areas. It also is the center of the theater, concert, and opera districts and has the brightest lights.

Central Park. Over 800 acres of landscaped and wooded grounds. A horse-drawn hansom cab ride through the park is a delight. Cabs are for hire at the Plaza entrance on Central Park South.

World Trade Center, Liberty and West Sts., with an enclosed observation deck on the 107th floor and an open-air promenade on the 110th floor. The views on a clear day are truly spectacular. Open daily, 9:30–9:30. Tickets are sold on the mezzanine level of Tower Two.

South St. Seaport and Fulton Fish Market, Fulton St. between South and Water Sts. Home to the fish market, and also to the South St. Seaport maritime museum, it is full of restaurants, cafes, food market stalls, and retail outlets along Schermerhorn Row (renovated 19th-century warehouses). Open 10–10.
Chinatown, centered around Mott, Bayard, and Pell Sts. This little more than 10-square-block area is a genuine Chinese neighborhood, full of pseudo pagodas, emporiums, bright street banners, stalls and shop windows filled with exotic displays, delightful aromas, and the place where the Chinese themselves shop. See the *Chinese Museum* at 7 Mott Street (open weekdays).
Little Italy, centered around Mulberry St., just N of Chinatown. Reputedly one of the safest areas in the city, it is full of bakeries, restaurants, produce markets, cafes, and people, particularly during the festivals of San Gennaro (Sept.) and St. Anthony (June).
Greenwich Village, centered around Washington Square. Visit Grove Court or the Morton Street Pier on the Hudson River. Full of restaurants, cafes, art galleries, musicians, mimes, and street people.
Statue of Liberty, Liberty Island, Upper New York Bay. Ferries depart regularly from Battery Park, 8:30–4 daily.
Museum of Modern Art 1 W. 53rd Street (708-9400). The collection is superb and is arranged in chronological order. Closed Wed.
Metropolitan Museum of Art, 5th Ave. at 82nd St. One of the world's finest museums. Closed Mon.
The Guggenheim Museum, 5th Ave. between E. 88th and E. 89th Sts. Modern art housed in a building designed by Frank Lloyd Wright. Closed Mon.
American Museum of Natural History, Central Park West and W. 79th St. (873-4225). An excellent collection of anthropological and natural history exhibits. Open daily.
Brooklyn Heights, Brooklyn. An area of classic brownstones and picturesque streets. Visit Montague Street and view Manhattan from Brooklyn Promenade.

Useful Information

New York Convention and Visitors Bureau, 2 Columbus Circle (397-8222); *Information Desk,* 30 Rockefeller Plaza (489-2950); *Times Square Information Center,* 43rd St. off 8th Ave.; *International Center,* 151 W. 51 St., hotel reservations and tour information for foreign visitors (921-8205), open 9–8 M–F; *Weather* (976-1212); *Travelers Aid* (944-0013); *TKTS* has booths at 47th and Broadway and on the mezzanine level of Tower Two of the World Trade Center (354-5800), offering day-of-performance half-price tickets for theater. *Bryant Park Music & Dance Booth,* 42nd St. off 6th Ave., has half-price tickets for music and dance events (382-2323).

Special Trips/Tours

Guided *boat trips around Manhattan* (approx. 3 hours), are provided by *Circle Line Cruises,* and are an excellent way to appreciate the grandeur of New York.

Boats leave from Pier 83, at W. 42nd St. and the Hudson River, from mid-April until mid-November (563-3200). Even more spectacular, is a *helicopter ride around Manhattan* provided by *Island Helicopter,* E. 34th St. & the East River (683-4575). More conventional bus tours are offered by *Gray Line,* 900 8th Ave. (397-2600), and *Short Line Tours,* 166 W. 46th St. (354-5122).

Weather

New York experiences changeable weather all year. Summers can be hot and humid, with daytime highs in the high 70s and low 80s. Winter temperatures usually reach daytime highs in the high 30s and low 40s. July and August are the wettest months.

NEW YORK: TEMPERATURES AND PRECIPITATION

Month	J	F	M	A	M	J	J	A	S	O	N	D
Average Daily Temperature												
(Fahrenheit) Max.	37	38	45	47	68	77	82	80	79	69	51	41
Min.	24	24	30	42	53	60	66	66	60	49	37	29
Average Number of Days with Precipitation												
	12	10	12	11	11	10	12	10	9	9	9	10

Orlando

Sights to See

Walt Disney World, 25 minutes SW of Orlando off I-4 at the EPCOT Center Drive. The world-famous total destination resort, including the renowned Magic Kingdom's six theme lands and the futuristic *EPCOT Center* with its Future World, World Showcase, and Living Seas attractions. Also contained in the complex are golf courses, a nature preserve, a campground, a major hotel/eating/shopping complex, two minor theme parks—Discovery Island and River Country—and now Disney/MGM Studio and Pleasure Island entertainment complex.
Sea World, off I-4 at Rte. 528 SW of Orlando. A huge (135-acre) marine-life park featuring performing killer whales, dolphins, sea lions, and otters. Be sure to see the World of the Sea aquarium, "Shark Encounter," and "Fountain Fantasy." Open 9–7 daily, longer hours during the summer.
Six Flags Stars Hall of Fame, 6825 Starway Dr., adjacent to Sea World off I-4 at Rte. 528. Over 200 life-size wax figures from the stage, screen, and TV. Open 10–10 daily.
Universal Studios Florida, Kirkman Rd., off I-4 SE of Orlando. Features rides, shows, and attractions based on Hollywood motion pictures, including *E.T., Back to the Future, King Kong,* and *Ghostbusters.* Open 9–9 daily.
Gatorland Zoo, off US 441 near Bennett Road, S of Orlando. The world's largest alligator farm, with alligators in their natural habitat. Open daily.

Wet 'N Wild 6200 International Dr., off I-4 at exit SR 435S. Considered to be one of the best water theme parks, complete with water slides and flumes, wave pool, raging rapids, and a water roller coaster. Open 9–8 daily in summer, 10–5 the rest of the year.

Loch Haven Park, between Mills & Orange Aves., downtown Orlando. The city's cultural and educational center, the park contains three museums and a theater.

Morse Gallery of Art, 133 E. Wellbourne Ave., Winter Park, a suburb just NE of Orlando. Noted for its excellent Tiffany collection. Open 9:30–4 Tu–Sa, 1–4 Su.

Beale-Maltbie Shell Museum, Rollins College campus, Park & Holt Aves., Winter Park. Fine collection of seashells, with over 100,000 species represented among the 2 million shells. Open 10–4 M–F.

Useful Information

Orlando Chamber of Commerce, 75 E. Ivanhoe Blvd. (425-1234), frequently offers discount coupons to the area's major attractions; *Orlando Tourist Information Center,* 8445 International Dr., Suite 152 (351-0412 and 363-5871); *Walt Disney World* (824-4321); *Cultural Events Information* (843-2787); *Public Transportation* (841-8240); *Taxi* (422-4455, 422-4561, or 859-7514); *Emergency* (911).

Special Trips/Tours

About an hour's drive SW of Orlando via I-4, US 27, and SR 540 are the *Florida Cypress Gardens,* a 200-acre botanical garden with over 9,000 varieties of plants and flowers. There are 13 themed Gardens of the World, winding walkways, and boat rides. Be sure to see the water skiing show. Open 8:30–6 daily.

At the junction of I-4 and US 27, on the way to or from Cypress Gardens on the former site of Circus World, is *Boardwalk and Baseball.* Featuring thrill rides, a midway, and live entertainment shows, the complex has baseball games, baseball cages, and pitching machines. For hours, call 800/826-1939 or 305/422-0643.

Bok Tower Gardens, some 40 minutes S of Disney World in Lake Wales near the junction of US 27 and SR 60, is worth the trip. Beautifully landscaped gardens and a nature preserve surround the tower, noted for its carillon recitals, given daily at 3 P.M. Open 8–5:30 daily.

Kennedy Space Center and the Cape Canaveral Air Force Station, the site of NASA's blast-offs is about 50 miles E of Orlando via the Bee Line Expressway or SR 50. Two-hour bus tours of the Space Center and Air Force Station originate at Spaceport USA and stop at several of the facilities depending on activity at the spaceport. The Air Force Station is also open for drive-through tours on Sunday. Be sure to stop by the Visitors Center on Rte. 405 and see the IMAX movies and exhibits. Open 9:15–sunset daily, subject to operational conditions. Call 800/432-2153 for launch information.

Weather

Orlando enjoys a particularly sunny climate, especially in the winter months. Summer daytime high temperatures typically reach into the high 80s, falling to the low 70s at night. Winter daytime highs are usually in the 70s, dropping to the 50s at night. Summer is the wet season with frequent thunderstorms.

ORLANDO: TEMPERATURES AND PRECIPITATION

Month	J	F	M	A	M	J	J	A	S	O	N	D
Average Daily Temperature												
(Fahrenheit) Max.	70	72	76	81	87	89	90	90	88	82	76	71
Min.	50	51	56	61	66	71	73	73	72	66	57	51
Average Number of Days with Precipitation												
	6	7	7	6	8	14	18	16	14	9	5	6

Palm Beach-West Palm Beach

Sights to See

Palm Beach's Mediterranean Mansions, particularly along Ocean Blvd. With over 200 mansions, most built in the 1920s and 1930s, and many in the Spanish Revival style, Palm Beach is full of historic houses. *Villa Mizner,* 3 Via Mizner, the former home of Addison Mizner, and *Mar al Lago,* 1100 S. Ocean Blvd., former home of Marjorie Merriweather Post, are notable.

Whitehall, Whitehall Way, off Coconut Row. Completed in 1902 by Henry Flagler, Florida's premier land developer, this mansion is noted for its elegantly furnished interior. Open 10–5 T–Sa, noon–5 Su.

Breakers, S. County Rd. Palm Beach's legendary, landmark hotel, built in 1925 on the site of an earlier hotel built by Flagler. Its Italian Renaissance exterior remains largely unchanged, and its magnificent interior should be seen, even if you're not fortunate enough to be a guest.

Bethesda-by-the-Sea Church, S. County Rd., just S of the Breakers. Fine example of modified Gothic design.

Hibel Museum of Art, 150 Royal Poinciana Plaza. Devoted to the works of Edna Hibel, including paintings, lithographs, and porcelains. Open 10–5 Tu–Sa, 1–5 Su.

Society of the Four Arts, Four Arts Plaza, off Royal Palm Way. A library, art museum, auditorium, and sculpture and botanical gardens. Open 10–5 M–Sa, 2–5 Su, Dec.–April, weekends only the rest of the year.

Worth Avenue ("The Avenue"), Palm Beach's three-block-long, world-famous shopping street. Cartier, Godiva, Gucci, Saks, Sotheby Parke Bernet, and so on.

Norton Gallery of Art, 1451 S. Olive Ave., West Palm Beach. Excellent collections of American and European modern art, and a fine Chinese art display. Open 10–5 Tu–Sa, 1–5 Su.

Lion Country Safari, on US 98/441 and SR 80 (Southern Blvd.), W of I-95. Fenced game preserve and theme park. Open 9:30–5:30 daily.

Loxahatchee National Wildlife Refuge, SW of West Palm Beach, and due W of Boynton Beach on Hwy 804. Over 250 species of birds, alligators, Florida panthers, bald eagles, Florida sandhill cranes, and other rare animals in the eastern Everglades. Open daily.

Sports

Boating: Frey's Sailing Center (845-7952), Blue Heron Blvd., rents sailboats.
Fishing: contact the *Shamrock* (842-4850), 336 E. Blue Heron Blvd., Riviera Beach; the *B-Love Fleet* (588-7612), 314 E. Ocean Avenue., Lantana; or the *Sailfish Marina* (844-1724), 98 Lake Dr., Palm Beach Shores, for charter fishing boats. *Lake Okeechobee* offers many opportunities for freshwater fishing.
Golf: several of the area's hotels/resorts have their own golf courses for guests. Golf courses open to the public include the *West Palm Beach Country Club* (582-2019), 7001 Parker Ave.; the *North Palm Beach Country Club* (626-4343), 901 US 1, North Palm Beach; and the *PGA's National Golf Club* (627-1804), 1000 Avenue of the Champions, Palm Beach Gardens.
Polo: the area's principal polo grounds are *Royal Palm Polo Club* (994-1876), 6300 Clint Moore Rd.; *Palm Beach Polo and Country Club* (793-1113), 13198 Forest Hill Blvd.; and *Gulfstream Polo Field* (965-2057), Lake Worth Rd.
Snorkeling and Scuba Diving: Coastal Sport & Dive Shop (965-0524), 2407 10th Ave. N., Lake Worth, rents diving gear. *Singer Island,* just N of Palm Beach, is a popular snorkeling spot.
Swimming: most of Palm Beach's beaches are restricted to residents and hotel/ resort guests. There is a public beach just south of Worth Avenue, between Australian & Hammon Aves.
Tennis: most of the area's hotels/resorts have courts for guests only, but there are courts open to the public at *Lake Worth Racquet & Swim Club* (967-3900), 4090 Coconut Rd., Lake Worth; *Seaview Avenue Tennis Courts* (655-5341), 340 Seaview Ave., Palm Beach, and *John Price Park,* Lake Worth Rd.
Waterskiing: Mike Seipel's Barefoot International (964-3346), 2600 W. Lantana Rd., Lantana, offers tows on *Lake Osborne.*

Weather

Palm Beach's summer daytime high temperatures typically reach into the high 80s or low 90s, dropping to the mid 70s at night. Winter daytime highs are usually in the mid 70s, falling to the upper 50s at night. Summer and fall are the wettest seasons.

PALM BEACH: TEMPERATURES AND PRECIPITATION

Month	J	F	M	A	M	J	J	A	S	O	N	D
Average Daily Temperature												
(Fahrenheit) Max.	75	76	79	83	86	88	90	90	88	84	79	76
Min.	56	56	60	65	69	72	74	74	75	70	62	57
Average Number of Days with Precipitation												
		9	6	7	7	12	13	15	15	18	16	10	7

Philadelphia

Sights to See

Independence Hall, 5th & Chestnut. Site of the signing of the Declaration of Independence and writing of the Constitution. Open 9–5 daily, 9–8 in summer.
Congress Hall, 6th & Chestnut. Seat of Congress between 1790 and 1800, and home of the Bill of Rights. Open 9–5 daily.
Old City Hall, 5th & Chestnut. Home of the first U.S. Supreme Court. See the audiovisual show of post-Revolutionary life in Philadelphia. Open 9–5 daily.
Liberty Bell Pavillion, Independence Mall, Market & 5th St. Houses the Liberty Bell. Open 9–5 daily, 9–8 July–Aug.
Elfreth's Alley, between Front & 2nd Sts. Dating back to the late 17th century, it is lined with 200-year-old houses.
Philadelphia Museum of Art, 26th & Parkway. Excellent museum, the steps of which were featured in "Rocky." Open 10–5 Tu–Su.
Franklin Institute Science Museum, 20th & Parkway. Well known for its Fels Planetarium, it has excellent displays. Open 10–5 M–Sa, 12–5 Su.
City Hall, Broad & Market Sts. An elaborate landmark building in the center of the city. Offers good views from its tower on a clear day. Open 9–4:30 M–F.
United States Mint, 5th & Arch Sts. Take the self-guided tour of the minting process, and see the historic coin collection in the Relic Room. Open 9–4:30 M–Sa.
Rittenhouse Square, one of the most elegant downtown residential areas in the city, with restored brownstones and newer high-rise apartment buildings, guarded by uniformed doormen. Concerts and art and flower shows are held in the square during the spring and summer. The adjoining Walnut and Locust Sts. are worth strolling down.
Italian (Rocky's) Market, 9th St. & Washington Ave. in South Philly, is a genuine ethnic produce and meat market bustling with activity and full of character.
Society Hill, around Walnut & Pine Sts. between Front & 7th. The city's ritzy neighborhood, with 17th- and 18th-century townhouses on cobblestoned streets with old-fashioned lampposts. Visit the restaurants, boutiques, and craft shops in Head House Square, 2nd & Pine, and the art galleries on South Street between 3rd & 4th. Try the Hogies at *Jim's Steaks,* 4th & South Sts.
Penn's Landing, at the foot of Chestnut & Walnut Sts. & the Delaware River. Moored alongside are a square-rigger; a steel sailing ship; the *U.S.S. Olympia* from the Spanish-American War; and a WW II submarine, all of which can be boarded and toured. Open 10–6 daily.
Boathouse Row, East River Dr. Victorian boathouses along the E bank of the Schuylkill River, N of the Museum of Art. Best seen at night from across the river, when they are all illuminated with hundreds of small lights.

Useful Information

Visitors Information Center, 16th St. at J. F. Kennedy Blvd, next to City Hall (636-1666); the *Philly Fun Phone* (568-7255) is a recorded message of current things to see and do; *Taxi* (922-8400, 728-8000); *Police* (231-3131); *Greater Philadelphia Cultural Alliance* (735-0570) for cultural events update; *SEPTA* (Public Transportation, 574-7800); *Travelers Aid Society* (922-0950); *Central City Ticket Office,* 1422 Chestnut St. (564-3686) for cultural & sporting event tickets.

Special Trips/Tours

A horse-drawn carriage ride, on a good day, through colonial Philadelphia is a real delight. Carriages depart from Chestnut between 5th & 6th Sts. daily. Or take the 90-minute candlelight walking tour, offered by Centipede Tours (564-2246), that leaves City Tavern, Second & Walnut Sts., at 6:30 W–Sa, May–Oct.

Longwood Gardens, 30 miles SW of the city on US 1 in Brandywine Valley, on the former private estate of Pierre S. Du Pont, are spectacular, complete with Conservatory, Italian fountains, terraces, waterfalls, greenhouses, and a famous bonsai collection. Open 9–6 daily, April–Oct., 9–5 the rest of the year. Catch the 9:15 P.M. fountain displays on Tu, Th, and Sa (215/388-6741).

Weather

Philadelphia experiences changeable weather throughout the year. Summers tend to be hot, with daytime highs in the mid to high 80s, frequently with humidities to match. Winters can be cold, with daytime highs typically in the high 20s or low 30s. July and August are the wettest months.

PHILADELPHIA: TEMPERATURES AND PRECIPITATION

Month	J	F	M	A	M	J	J	A	S	O	N	D
Average Daily Temperature												
(Fahrenheit) Max.	40	41	49	61	72	80	85	83	76	66	53	43
Min.	26	27	33	43	54	62	68	67	60	50	39	30
Average Number of Days with Precipitation												
	12	11	12	11	11	10	11	11	8	8	9	10

Phoenix

Sights to See

Arizona State Capitol Museum, W. Washington & 17th Ave. Known for its interior murals depicting the state's history. In its restored wings are exhibits of relics and documents of early Arizona. Guided tours are given at 10 and 2. Open 8–5 M–F.

Heard Museum, 22 E. Monte Vista. Excellent Western and Indian collections, especially the artifacts from ancient Indian civilizations in Arizona. Open 10–5 M–Sa, 1–5 Su.

Heritage Square, 6th St. & Monroe St. An 1880s city block preserved as a park, with a Victorian mansion, museums, shops, restaurants, and an open-air bath house. Open daily.

Pueblo Grande Museum and Indian Ruins, 4619 E. Washington. Former 200 B.C.–A.D. 1400 Hohokam Indian settlement. A self-guiding trail leads to a mound overlooking the remains of Indian dwellings and canals. Open 9–4:45 M–Sa, 1–4:45 Su.

Desert Botanical Gardens, Papago Park, 1201 N. Galvin Pkwy. The garden is devoted exclusively to arid land plants of the world, and is famous for its cactus collection. Open 8–sunset.

Phoenix Art Museum, 1625 N. Central. Excellent collection of Southwest contemporary art. Open Tu–Su.

Scottsdale. A re-created Western community complete with hitching posts and Western fronts, it is known for its art galleries, craft shops, and golf courses. Stroll along Fifth Avenue and browse in the Indian arts and crafts galleries.

Cosanti Foundation, 6433 E. Double Tree Ranch Road, Scottsdale. Architect Paolo Soleri's workshop, complete with a model of *Arcosanti,* his megalopolis of the future, along with some of his sculpture. Open 9–5 daily, reservations required (948-6145).

Taliesin West, E. Shea Blvd. & 108th St., Scottsdale. Frank Lloyd Wright's architectural school and winter home. Open 10–4, Oct–May; by appointment during the rest of the year (948-6670).

Rawhide, 23023 N. Scottsdale Rd., Scottsdale. Escape into the nostalgia of the Old West. Shootouts, stagecoach rides through the desert, and shops. Open 5–midnight M–F, noon–midnight Sa & Su.

Useful Information

Phoenix and Valley of the Sun Convention and Visitors Bureau, 505 N. 2nd St. (254-6500); *Scottsdale Chamber of Commerce,* 7333 Scottsdale Mall, Scottsdale (945-8481); *Arizona Office of Tourism,* 1100 W. Washington St. (542-3618); *Visitor Information Hotline,* recorded message (252-5588); *Time* and *Weather* (258-7600); *Phoenix Transit System Information* (257-8426); *Taxi* (252-5071, 257-1818, or 253-8294).

Special Trips/Tours

Tonto National Monument, off Rte. 88 in the Mazatzal Mountains E of Phoenix, makes an interesting side trip. Contains the well-preserved cliff dwellings of the Salado Indians. The drive through the mountains and canyons, and past the Apache, Canyon, and Roosevelt lakes is spectacular. Open 8–5 daily. Stop and visit *Tortilla Flat,* a resurrected ghost town, E of Canyon Lake.

    Sedona and the Red Rock Canyon. At the S end of Oak Creek Canyon, about 2 hours N of Phoenix, via I-17 and Hwy. 179 off I-17 at Rimrock. A center for the traditional and contemporary arts, Sedona is full of art galleries. Visit the *Tlaquapaque* complex of specialty shops. *Jeep rides* through the rugged Red Rocks area are available daily (602/282-5000).

On the way back to Phoenix, travel on Alt. 89 through Cottonwood and visit *Tuzigoot National Monument.* Some 2 miles E of Clarkdale, it is noted for its 12th-century pueblo ruins. In Prescott, the *Smoki Museum* on Arizona Ave. has a fine collection of ceramics and artifacts from surrounding pueblo ruins. Open 10–4:30 Tu–Sa, noon–4:30 Su.

For those with more time, there is, of course, the *Grand Canyon,* incomparably beautiful at any time of the year. Best seen from the South Rim, which has extensive facilities and a visitor's center (602/638-7888). For *Canyon mule trips,* call 602/638-2401. *Helicopter tours* are also available (638-2419 or 638-2688) as are *airplane flights* over the Canyon (638-2618 or 638-2407).

Weather

Phoenix enjoys one of the sunniest climates in the nation. Summers are very hot, although bearable because of the low humidity. Summer daytime highs are typically in the high 90s or low 100s, dropping to the high 60s or low 70s at night. Winters are warm, with daytime highs usually in the 60s, falling to the low 40s or high 30s at night. Although July and August are the two "wettest" months, precipitation is very low throughout the year.

PHOENIX: TEMPERATURES AND PRECIPITATION

Month	J	F	M	A	M	J	J	A	S	O	N	D
Average Daily Temperature												
(Fahrenheit) Max.	65	69	75	82	91	101	104	101	97	86	75	66
Min.	39	43	47	53	60	69	77	76	69	56	45	40
Average Number of Days with Precipitation												
	4	4	4	2	1	1	5	6	3	2	3	4

Pittsburgh

Sights to See

Downtown Pittsburgh can best be seen from the summit of Mt. Washington on the W side of the Monongahela River, reached via the *Duquesne Incline cable railway* on W. Carson St. or the *Monongahela Incline* on E. Carson St.

Station Square, at the foot of the Monongahela Incline. An old railroad terminal converted to a shopping and dining mall.

Point State Park, at the confluence of the Allegheny, Monongahela, and Ohio rivers in downtown Pittsburgh. Noted for its fountain, and, within the park, *Fort Pitt Museum* which has exhibits on the early history of western Pennsylvania. Museum open 9–5 W–Sa, 12–5 Su.

Cathedral of Learning, University of Pittsburgh, Bigelow Blvd. & 5th Ave., E of the Golden Triangle. A Gothic skyscraper noted for its 18 Nationality Classrooms, decorated to represent the city's ethnic heritages, on the first floor. Open 9:30–3:30 M–Sa, 11–3:30 Su.

Carnegie Institute Museum of Natural History, 4400 Forbes Ave., close to the cathedral. Known for its dinosaur, mammal, and Indian artifacts exhibits. Open 10–5 Tu–Sa, 1–5 Su.
Carnegie Museum of Art, 4400 Forbes Ave. Fine Impressionist and Postimpressionist collection. Open 10–5 Tu–Sa, 1–5 Su.
Phipps Conservatory, Schenley Park, just S of the Carnegie Institute. Rare tropical and domestic flowers and plants in 13 showhouses, including a Japanese garden. Open 9–5 daily.
Frick Art Museum, 7227 Reynolds St. in Point Breeze. Noted for its Old Masters Renaissance collection, as well as Renaissance and French decorative arts and Chinese porcelains. Open 10–5:30 W–Sa, 12–6 Su.
Buhl Science Center, Allegheny Sq., on the N side across the Allegheny River. Participatory science and technology exhibits, a planetarium, and laserium concerts Th–Su eve. Open 1–5 Tu–F & Su, 10–5 Sa.
Hartwood Acres, 215 Saxonburg Boulevard, North Mills. An over-600-acre re-creation of an English country estate, with an English Tudor mansion as its centerpiece. During the summer months Hartwood is the scene of free jazz and classical music concerts. Open 10–3 Tu–Sa, noon–3 Sun, April–Dec.
Pittsburgh Zoo, Highland Park. Over 2,000 animals on display. Noted for its Aqua Zoo and Reptile House. Open 9–5 M–Sa, 10–5 Su.

Useful Information

Pittsburgh Convention and Visitors Bureau, 4 Gateway Center, Suite 514 (281-7711); *Daily Events,* recorded information (391-6840); *Taxi* (665-8123, 681-3131, or 833-3300); *Weather* (936-1212); *Public Transportation Information* (231-5707).

Special Trips/Tours

On a good day, a cruise on one of Pittsburgh's three rivers can be delightful. *Sightseeing cruises* aboard boats of the *Gateway Clipper Fleet* depart daily between June and Labor Day from the dock at Station Sq. on the Monongahela. Dinner and moonlight cruises are offered as well (355-7980 or 355-7979).

About 20 miles NW of Pittsburgh along the Ohio River is *Old Economy Village* in Ambridge. A two-block area contains some 18 original structures of the 19th-century German-immigrant Harmony Society.

Further afield is *Frank Lloyd Wright's Fallingwater,* at the Kaufmann Conservation on Bear Run: a landmark structure, especially noted for its large balconies cantilevered from huge boulders. Drive SE of Pittsburgh on US 51 through Uniontown, continue on US 40 to Farmington, turn left on Hwy. 381 to Fallingwater, just outside Mill Run. Open 10–4 Tu–Su, April–Nov.

Fort Necessity National Battlefield is just W of Farmington off US 40. A replica of the Fort originally built by George Washington commemorates the Battle of Great Meadows, which began the French and Indian War in the 1750s. Open 10–5 daily.

Weather

Pittsburgh has a moderate continental climate and experiences changeable weather throughout the year. Summer daytime high temperatures usually reach into the low 80s, falling to the mid 60s at night. Winter daytime highs are typically in the high 30s, dropping to the 20s at night. Precipitation is well distributed throughout the year, although July and August are normally the wettest months.

PITTSBURGH: TEMPERATURES AND PRECIPITATION

Month	J	F	M	A	M	J	J	A	S	O	N	D
Average Daily Temperature												
(Fahrenheit) Max.	38	39	49	61	72	80	84	82	76	64	51	41
Min.	24	23	31	41	52	60	64	63	57	46	36	27
Average Number of Days with Precipitation												
	16	14	15	13	13	12	12	10	9	10	12	14

Portland (OR)

Sights to See

Oregon Art Institute, 1219 S.W. Park Ave. Fine collection of art from the Renaissance to the present. It is particularly noted for its Pacific Northwest Native American art. Open 11–7 Tu–Th, 11–9:30 F, 12–5 Sa–Su.

Oregon Historical Society, 1230 S.W. Park Ave., opposite the Art Museum. Fine archaeological, anthropological, and historical exhibits, together with dioramas on Indian life. Open 10–4:45 M–Sa.

Pioneer Courthouse Square, 701 S.W. 6th Ave., just NE of the Historical Society. The heart of Portland, and busy day and night.

Portland Building, 1120 S.W. 5th Ave. Controversial post-modern building, whose controversiality is heightened by a huge copper sculpture, *Portlandia,* over the main portico.

Old Town, straddling Burnside, between 1st & 5th Aves. A restored, renovated area of boutiques, restaurants, and antique shops.

Washington Park, W of downtown Portland, off Burnside Rd. Located in the hills overlooking Portland, it offers superb views of the city and is known for its *Rose Test Gardens,* and *Japanese Garden.* Open daily.

Washington Park Zoo, 4001 S.W. Canyon Rd., in the SW part of the park, off US 26. Especially noted for its large Asian elephant herd. Open 9–7 daily, May–Sept., shorter hours the rest of the year.

Oregon Museum of Science and Industry, 4015 S.W. Canyon Rd., Washington Park, next to the zoo. A hands-on museum, known for the Kendall Planetarium and laser show. Open 9–9 Tu–Sa, 9–6 Su–M.

Western Forestry Center, 4033 S.W. Canyon Rd., Washington Park, next to the Science and Industry Museum. Interesting exhibits on Northwest forestry and logging. Open 9–6 daily in summer, 10–5 daily the rest of the year.

Useful Information

Visitors Information Center (275-9750), 26 S.W. Salmon; *Weather* (255-6660); *Taxi* (227-1212, 227-1234); *Public Transportation* (233-3511); *Local Events Hotline* (233-3333).

Special Trips/Tours

A drive along the Columbia River Highway through the spectacular *Columbia River Gorge,* E of Portland, makes an interesting side trip from Portland. The gorge is famous for its many impressive waterfalls cascading down sheer cliffs, especially the 600-ft. *Multnomah Falls.* Be sure to stop and see the *Bonneville Dam,* and its Bradford Island Visitor Center (503/374-8820) with its displays, observation deck, theater, and underwater viewing room where migrating fish can be seen negotiating the fish ladder. Open 9–6 daily Memorial–Labor Day, 9–5 the rest of the year.

The *Mt. Hood Wilderness Area,* SE of Portland, also offers spectacular scenery. It can be reached either by continuing along the Columbia River Highway to Hwy. 35 at Hood River, and then turning S on the *Mt. Hood Loop Hwy.* (SR 35), which goes through the Mt. Hood National Forest, or more directly from Portland via Hwy. 26 through Sandy and Brightwood. *Mt. Hood,* at 11,239 ft., is Oregon's highest mountain, with several glaciers. *Timberline Lodge,* on the S side of Mt. Hood, is definitely worth seeing.

Mount St. Helens National Volcanic Monument, encompassing Mount St. Helens and the surrounding area that was devasted by its 1980 eruption, is about 50 miles N of Portland in Washington State. SRs 503 and 504 off I-5 afford access to the area, with Forest Service information portals at Yale Park, W of Cougar on SR 503. The U.S. Forest Service's Mount St. Helens National Volcanic *Monument Visitor Center* (206/864-6699), is in *Lewis and Clark State Park,* off I-5 at exit 68, about 30 miles N of Longview.

Heading in the opposite direction from Portland is the equally spectacular scenery of the *Oregon coastline,* world famous for its rugged beauty. The drive from Astoria down the Pacific coast as far as you have time for will be richly rewarded as the coastline, paralleled by US 101, offers truly magnificent scenery, historic fishing villages, and unspoiled beaches. The *Maritime Museum* in Astoria is worth visiting.

Closer to Portland is *Champoeg State Park* (503/678-1251), outside Newberg, just SW of the city, off SR 99W. Site of the first provincial government on the Pacific coast, in 1843, the park has a number of museums depicting pioneer life. Open 8–4:30 M–F, 9–5 Sa–Su.

Weather

Portland has a wet, mild climate. Summer daytime high temperatures are typically in the upper 70s, falling to the mid 50s at night. Winter daytime highs are usually in the 40s, dropping to the 30s at night. Winter is the wet season.

PORTLAND: TEMPERATURES AND PRECIPITATION

Month	J	F	M	A	M	J	J	A	S	O	N	D
Average Daily Temperature												
(Fahrenheit) Max.	44	48	54	61	66	72	77	77	71	62	53	46
Min.	34	36	39	43	47	53	56	56	52	47	41	37
Average Number of Days with Precipitation												
	19	17	17	14	13	10	3	4	8	12	17	19

St. Louis

Sights to See

Gateway Arch, at the Levee on the riverfront. The view from the top of this 630-ft. arch is impressive. Rides up the monument 8:30–9:30 daily in summer, 9–5:30 the rest of the year. Visit the *Museum of Westward Expansion* between the two base columns. Open 10–10 daily in summer, 9–6 the rest of the year.

Laclede's Landing, between Veterans and Eads bridges N of the Arch. The old downtown section of the city, now renovated, and full of restaurants, galleries, and bars.

St. Louis Sports Hall of Fame, Busch Memorial Stadium, between Gates 5 & 6, at Walnut St. A sports-fan's delight. Open daily.

St. Louis Union Station, 18th & Market Street. A restaurant, shopping and entertainment center with its own hotel. Open 10–9 M–Th, 10–10 F & Sa, 12–7 Su.

St. Louis Cathedral, Lindell Blvd. & Newstead Ave. A huge structure famous for its interior mosaics. Open 7–6 daily.

Anheuser-Busch Brewery 610 Pestalozzi St. Take the one-hour tour, sample the beer and see the famous Clydesdales' stables. Open 9–4 M–Sa in summer, 9:30–3:30 M–F rest of the year.

Missouri Botanical Garden (Shaw's Garden), 2101 Tower Grove. Famous for its Japanese Garden, Scented Garden for the blind, and a geodesic-domed tropical greenhouse. Open 9–7:30 daily May–Oct., 9–5 daily the rest of the year.

Soulard Market, 7th St. & Lafayette. A colorful indoor and outdoor market humming with activity, particularly on Saturday mornings.

Maryland Plaza, between Kingshighway & Euclid Avenue. Full of shops, restaurants, boutiques, and galleries.

Gallery of Art, in Steinberg Hall, Forsyth & Skinker Blvds. The first art museum west of the Mississippi. Noted for its collection of 19th- and 20th-century American paintings. Open 10–5 M–F, 1–5 Sa.

St. Louis Science Center, 5100 Clayton Ave. in Forest Park. A planetarium, museum of science and natural history, and a medical museum have been combined into one educational and entertainment complex. Open daily.

St. Louis Zoo, Forest Park. One of the nation's better zoos, famous for its huge walk-through aviary and landscaped areas in its "Big Cat Country." Open 9–5 daily.

Useful Information

Convention and Visitors Bureau, 10 S. Broadway, Suite 30 (421-1023); *Travelers Aid,* 809 North Broadway (241-5820); *St. Louis Fun Phone* (421-2100); *Dial & Dine,* for information on restaurants, entertainment, and hot spots, including location, hours, dress code, and price range (441-DINE); *Taxi* (652-3456, 361-2345, or 531-4545); *Public Transportation information* (231-2345); *Time & Temperature* (321-2522); *Weather Forecast* (321-2222).

Special Trips/Tours

On a good day, take a *daytime or moonlight cruise on the Mississippi* aboard *The President,* America's biggest cruising riverboat. Daytime cruises last about $2\frac{1}{2}$ hours and leave at noon from the foot of the Arch daily. Moonlight cruises leave at 8 P.M., returning at 11, W–Su. (621-4040). Shorter cruises (one hour) of the historic port of St. Louis can be taken on the *Huck Finn* or *Tom Sawyer Riverboats* (621-4040), also leaving from the boat docks below Gateway Arch.

Hannibal, home of Mark Twain, is 80 miles NW of St. Louis along the Mississippi River. Visit the *Mark Twain Boyhood Home and Museum,* 208 Hill Street (open 8–5 daily), and, if you haven't had enough of riverboats, take a one-hour cruise on the *Mark Twain Riverboat,* leaving from the Center St. landing (221-3222).

Six Flags Over Mid-America, 25 miles SW of St. Louis off I-44 at the Allentown Road exit, is one of the better amusement theme parks in the country. With over 100 rides, from roller coasters to whitewater rapids, it has something for everybody, including musical and variety shows. Open daily May–Sept., weekends only mid-April–May, and late Sept.–mid-Oct. (938-4800).

Weather

St. Louis has a continental climate with hot summers and cold winters. Summer daytime high temperatures typically reach the mid to high 80s, falling to the high 60s at night. Winters are relatively cold with daytime highs usually in the mid 40s and lows in the 20s. The late spring and early summer are normally the wettest seasons.

ST. LOUIS: TEMPERATURES AND PRECIPITATION

Month	J	F	M	A	M	J	J	A	S	O	N	D
Average Daily Temperature												
(Fahrenheit) Max.	40	43	54	65	75	84	88	87	80	68	54	43
Min.	24	26	36	47	57	66	71	69	62	50	38	28
Average Number of Days with Precipitation												
	9	9	11	11	11	11	9	8	8	8	8	9

Salt Lake City

Sights to See

Temple Square, between N. & S. Temple Streets and W. Temple & Main Streets. Center of the Mormon Church. Within the enclosed square are the *Temple,* holding the ordinances sacred to the Mormon faith (closed to non-Mormons); the *Tabernacle,* home of the world-famous Mormon Tabernacle Choir; and an information center. Guided tours leave from the information center. Choir rehearsals are open to the public on Thursday at 8 P.M. You can also listen to the Tabernacle's magnificent *organ* (one of the world's finest), every day at noon. Open 8–9 daily in summer; 9–7:30 the rest of the year.
Church Office Building, Temple Square. Houses the world's largest *genealogical collection,* accessible to Mormons and non-Mormons alike. The observation deck at the top of the building affords a great view of Salt Lake City and environs. Open 9–4:30 M–F, 9:30–4 Sa.
Beehive House, 67 E. Temple & State Sts. Former home of Brigham Young and the first Governor's Mansion, now a museum. Open 9:30–4:30 M–Sa, 10–2:30 Su.
Promised Valley Playhouse, State Street, between 1st & 2nd South Sts. Religiously inspired dramatization of the Mormon history and faith is presented. Free tickets can be obtained at the Temple Square visitors center.
Pioneer Memorial Museum, 300 N. Main St. Excellent collection of pioneer relics. The adjacent Carriage House houses antique farm machinery and vehicles. Open 9–5 M–Sa, 1–5 Su, May–Oct.
State Capitol, Capitol Hill. A splendid granite and marble building, topped with a huge copper-covered dome, with many exhibits on Utah's art and products. Guided tours are offered 8–5 M–F.
Trolley Square, South & 7th East Streets. Shops, boutiques, restaurants, theaters and street musicians in old restored trolley barns. Open 10–9 daily.
Hansen Planetarium, 15 S. State St. Shows at 2, 4:30, & 7 M–Sa, 2 & 4:30 Su. See the rock-laserium show.
Pioneer Troll State Park, 2601 Sunnyside Ave., Emigration Canyon. *"This is the Place"* monument commemorating Brigham Young's decision to settle in the Great Salt Lake valley. The visitors' center has audiovisual exhibits chronicling the Mormons' journey from Illinois. Open 9–9 in summer, 9–4:30 in winter.

Useful Information

Salt Lake Convention and Visitors Bureau, 180 South West Temple (521-2822); *Visitor Information Center,* Trolley Square, and 600 E. 530 south; *Travelers Aid* (328-8996); *Utah Travel Council,* Council Hall, Capitol Hill (538-1030); *Taxi* (521-2100, 363-5014, or 359-7788); *Events Information* (533-TIPS); *Weather* (524-5133).

Special Trips/Tours

Great Salt Lake State Park, Saltair beach, 16 miles W on I-80. Take a walk into this remnant of Lake Bonneville, and float in the warm, very salty (15–25%) water, but do not get your head wet—the salty water will sting! Watch the flies and mosquitoes too. The lake's waters have been rising dramatically recently, so contact the state parks (533-6011) for access information before you go.

The *Wasatch Mountains ski resorts* of Alta, Deer Valley, Park City, and Snowbird, famous for their deep powder snow, are all close to Salt Lake City, and worth visiting no matter what time of year. Park City, a one-time mining town, is full of shops, boutiques, and restaurants. Snowbird has an aerial tram, which in addition to ski duty, also runs from June to October up to the 11,000-ft. Hidden Peak, offering riders spectacular views of the Wasatch Mountains. Open 11–8 daily.

Just N of Salt Lake City, outside Farmington, off I-15 is the *Lagoon Amusement Park* (801/451-0101), featuring a Pioneer Village. Attractions in this re-created frontier settlement include a rodeo stadium, train and stagecoach rides, and musical entertainment. Open daily, Memorial Day–Labor Day.

Weather

Salt Lake City's summers are hot, but dry, with daytime highs typically reaching the high 80s or low 90s. Winters can be cold, with daytime highs in the 40s, and temperatures falling to the 20s or high teens at night. Temperatures in the minus teens have been recorded in January and February. Winters get the most precipitation, mostly in the form of snow.

SALT LAKE CITY: TEMPERATURES AND PRECIPITATION

Month	J	F	M	A	M	J	J	A	S	O	N	D
Average Daily Temperature												
(Fahrenheit) Max.	35	41	51	62	73	82	92	90	79	66	49	40
Min.	17	24	31	38	45	52	61	60	49	40	28	22
Average Number of Days with Precipitation												
	10	9	10	9	8	5	4	6	5	7	7	10

San Antonio

Sights to See

Paseo del Rio (River Walk). An arm of the San Antonio River curves through the downtown area of the city, and San Antonio has taken magnificent advantage of it. Some 20 ft. below street level, the River Walk is an oasis, with cafes, boutiques, restaurants, and lush foliage lining its length. Ride a paddleboat from under Market St. bridge, or take a barge trip, some of which offer candlelight dining (430 E. Commerce St. 222-1701).

The Alamo, Alamo Plaza, just NE of the River Walk. Legendary site of the defeat of Davy Crockett, Jim Bowie, and others by Santa Ana's Mexican force of 5,000 in Texas's 1836 independence struggle. Open 9–5:30 M–Sa, 10–5:30 Su. *Long Barracks Museum and library,* 315 Alamo Plaza. An excellent museum. Be sure to see the 30-minute film, "Remember the Alamo." Open 9–5:30 daily. *La Villita.* San Antonio's first residential neighborhood, bounded by the river and Nueva, S. Alamo, & Villita Sts., just S of the River Walk entrance. Restored stone patios and adobe buildings, with artisans and outdoor cafes. Open daily. *HemisFair Plaza,* Alamo & Market Sts., E of La Villita across Alamo St. The 1968 World's Fair was held here, leaving exhibition buildings, the most notable of which are the *Institute of Texan Culture* (open 9–5 Tu–Su), and the *Tower of the Americas,* a 622-ft. tower that offers the best view of the city from its observation deck. Open 7–midnight daily. *Hertzberg Circus Collection,* 210 W. Market St., just N of La Villita. Excellent collection of circus memorabilia and artifacts. Open 9–6 M–Sa. *El Mercado,* 515 W. Commerce St. The city's original marketplace with renovated Spanish buildings & Mexican merchants. Open daily. *Spanish Governor's Palace,* 105 Military Plaza. Known for its original Spanish furnishings. Open 9–5 M–S, 10–5 Su. *San Antonio Museum of Art* 200 W. Jones Ave., N of the immediate downtown area. Diverse collection, but noted for its excellent pre-Columbian sculpture and pottery and fine Mexican folk art. Open 10–5 M–Sa, 12–5 Su. *Witte Museum,* 3801 Broadway, N of the Museum of Art. Fine exhibits on science and the natural history of Texas. Open 10–5 M, W–Sa, 12–5 Su. *McNay Art Institute,* 6000 N. New Braunfels. Excellent small collection of Postimpressionist European art. Open 9–5 Tu–Sa, 2–5 Su.

Useful Information

Convention and Visitors Bureau, 210 S. Alamo St. (299-8123); *Visitor Information Center,* 321 Alamo Plaza (299-8155); *Taxi* (222-2151, 226-4242); *VIA Metropolitan Transit Information* (227-2020); *Weather* (681-0100).

Special Trips/Tours

Follow the *Mission Trail* and visit San Antonio's five missions, including *Mission San Antonio De Valero* (The Alamo). If time is short, just see *Mission San Jose,* 6539 San Jose Dr., 6 miles S of San Antonio on US 281 (229-4770), and *Mission Concepcion,* 807 Mission Rd. (229-5732). The former, particularly known for its "Rosa's Window," and referred to as the "Queen of the Missions" is the largest and is enclosed by a large compound with historical artifacts on display. The latter, is the oldest unrestored church in the United States and famous for its original frescoes. Both are open daily.

    Austin, Texas's bustling state capital is 78 miles NE on I-35. Considered by many to be one of the most livable cities in the country, it is home to the large University of Texas and home of progressive country-western music. See the huge *State Capitol,* on Congress Ave. (open 9–4:30 daily), and the *Laguna Gloria Art Museum,* 3890 W. 35th St. (open 10–5 Tu–Sa, 1–5 Su). The area around East Sixth St. has a lot of nightclubs and bars with live music.

Sea World of Texas (512/225-4903), 10500 Sea World Dr., is 18 miles NW of downtown San Antonio, at the junction of Ellison Dr. and Westover Hills Blvd., off Hwy. 151. The 1,250-acre park, billed as the world's largest marine-life park, offers over 20 shows and exhibits, with shows by killer whales, dolphins, sea lions, walruses, and other performing marine life. In addition, it has a *Penguin Exhibit,* a *Reef Presentation,* a *Shark Exhibit,* and is combined with *Cypress Gardens West.* Open 9–7 daily, longer hours in summer.

Weather

San Antonio has a sunny climate. Due to the relatively low humidity, summers, although hot, are not usually unpleasant. Summer daytime highs are typically in the 90s. Winters are also sunny, and mild with daytime highs in the 50s and low 60s. Temperatures usually don't drop much below the low 40s.

SAN ANTONIO: TEMPERATURES AND PRECIPITATION

Month	J	F	M	A	M	J	J	A	S	O	N	D
Average Daily Temperature												
(Fahrenheit) Max.	56	60	68	75	83	91	94	94	89	77	67	58
Min.	37	40	47	55	64	72	75	76	69	56	48	39
Average Number of Days with Precipitation												
	9	7	7	9	9	8	6	6	7	6	7	8

San Diego

Sights to See

San Diego Zoo, Balboa Park. One of the finest, if not the finest, in the world. Take the Skyfari Aerial Tramway or one of the guided bus tours. Open 9–6:30 daily in summer, 9–5 the rest of the year.

Museum of Man, El Prado, Balboa Park. Excellent anthropological and archaeological exhibits. Open 10–4:30 daily.

Aerospace Museum, Ford Bldg., Balboa Park. Known for its fine collection of antique planes. Open 10–4:30 daily.

Reuben H. Fleet Space Theater, Park Boulevard, Balboa Park. Simulated space travel theater, plus astronomy exhibits and laser demonstrations on weekends. Open 9:45–9:30 Su–Th, 9:45–10:30 F & Sa.

San Diego Museum of Art, N. side of El Prado, Balboa Park. Contemporary sculptures, Asian arts, early American decorative arts and works of the European masters. Open 10–5 Tu–Su.

Mission San Diego De Alcala, 10818 San Diego Mission Rd., in Mission Valley, off I-8. The first of California's missions, dating, at its present site, from 1774. Open 9–5 daily.

Old Town Plaza, San Diego & Mason Streets, off Rte. 8. The original downtown San Diego, with adobe buildings and Spanish courtyards. Visit *Junipero Serra Museum* (open 9–4:45 Tu–Sa, 12–4:45 Su), in Presidio Park, and *Casa de Estudillo,* the home of San Diego's former Mexican commandente. Open 10–5 daily. Free guided short tours of Old Town leave from the Plaza.

San Diego Historical and Union Newspaper Museums, 2606 San Diego Ave. Excellent collections. Open 10–5 Tu–Su.

Mission Bay Park, Mission Bay Drive, off I-5. A huge waterfront recreation area, with lots of facilities for golfing, waterskiing, sailing, swimming, and restaurants.

Sea World, Mission Bay Park. A large oceanarium with performing dolphins, seals, otters, and a killer whale. Open 9–dusk daily.

Maritime Museum, 1306 N. Harbor Dr. on the Embarcadero. A square-rigged merchantman, a ferryboat, and a steam yacht are berthed here. Open 9–8 daily. On weekends, U.S. Navy ships are open to visitors off Broadway Pier.

Seaport village, Harbor Dr. & Kettner Blvd. Waterfront complex of restaurants, boutiques, a transplanted Flying Horse Carousel, and a lighthouse. Open 10–9 daily.

Gaslamp Quarter, just S of downtown, centered on Fifth Ave. A renovated 16-block area with gas lamps, brick sidewalks, and Victorian architecture.

Cabrillo National Monument, S end of Cabrillo Memorial Dr. at Point Loma, overlooking the city and harbor. A statue commemorates Carbrillo's 1542 landing. There is also an historic lighthouse and a whale overlook to observe the annual gray whale migrations (Dec.–Feb.). Open 9–5:15 daily.

Mingel International Museum of World Folk Art, 4405 La Jolla Village Dr. Excellent collection of American quilts, African bark textiles, and Japanese ceremonial items. Open 11–5 Tu–Sa, 2–5 Su.

Useful Information

Convention and Visitors Bureau, 1200 3rd Ave., Suite 824 (232-3101); *Visitor Information Center,* 11 Horton Plaza (236-1212) and 2688 E. Mission Bay Dr. off I-5, Mission Bay (276-8200); *Telephone Recording of Events & Shows* (239-9696); *Taxi* (234-6161, 232-6566, or 234-4477); *Travelers Aid* (232-7991); *San Diego Transit* (233-3004); *Weather* (289-1212); *Arts/Entertainment Hotline* (234-2787).

Special Trips/Tours

If you're not already "zooed out" the *San Diego Wild Animal Park* in Escondido, some 30 miles N of San Diego (234-6541) is definitely worth a trip. You can see the animals, in very large enclosures designed to simulate their natural habitats as much as possible, from the Wgasa Bush Line Monorail. Open 9–8 daily, 9–5 in winter.

Tijuana, Mexico is less than 20 miles S of San Diego, accessible by car or by trolleys that leaves from the Amtrak Terminal, C. Street & Kettner Blvd. and terminate at San Ysidro at the border. Prices are a bargain, although you can only bring back $400 worth duty free.

Weather

San Diego enjoys a Mediterranean climate, with warm, dry summers and mild, slightly wetter winters. Summer daytime temperatures typically reach the low to mid 70s, dropping to the mid 60s at night. Winter daytime highs are in the mid 60s, falling to the low 50s or upper 40s. Winter is the wet season.

SAN DIEGO: TEMPERATURES AND PRECIPITATION

Month	J	F	M	A	M	J	J	A	S	O	N	D
Average Daily Temperature												
(Fahrenheit) Max.	63	63	64	66	67	69	73	74	73	71	69	65
Min.	47	48	50	53	56	59	63	64	62	57	52	48
Average Number of Days with Precipitation												
	6	7	7	4	3	1	1	1	1	3	4	6

San Francisco

Sights to See

Chinatown. This 24-block area centered on Grant Ave. represents the largest Chinese community outside Asia, complete with fine restaurants, shops, temples, and museums. The Chinese Cultural Foundation, 750 Kearny St. (986-1822, open 10–4 Tu–Sa), offers walking tours.

Fisherman's Wharf, along the Embarcadero and Jefferson St. at the foot of Mason, Jones, and Leavenworth Sts. A famous waterfront section, replete with fishing boats (which usually return in the afternoon to the pier at the foot of Jones and Leavenworth Sts.), cargo ships, seafood restaurants, and markets. Visit *The Cannery,* a complex of shops, galleries, and restaurants, and the *National Maritime Museum* in Aquatic Park (open 10–6 daily).

Ghirardelli Square, across from the Maritime Museum, at the foot of Polk and Larkin Sts. A collection of boutiques, galleries, restaurants, and plazas in an old chocolate factory. Open daily.

Pier 39, on the Embarcadero, near Fisherman's Wharf. An entertainment complex with shops, restaurants, seafood booths, playgrounds, and a marina. Try Swensen's.

Union Square, Powell & Geary Sts. Flanked by the very elegant St. Francis Hotel and some of the city's finest shops, this square offers a respite with concerts, fashion shows, and flower displays.

Cable Car Barn Museum, Washington & Mason Sts. Not only a museum, but also the powerhouse for the current cable-car system. Open 10–5 daily.

Coit Tower, Telegraph Hill Blvd. The view from the top of this 210-ft. column is just spectacular on a good clear day. Open 10–4:30 daily.

The Golden Gate Bridge. The tallest and one of the longest single-span suspension bridges in the world. You can either drive or walk across. The view of San Francisco from the small park at the first exit N of the bridge is spectacular.

Golden Gate Promenade. Between Aquatic Park & Golden Gate Bridge, this shoreline area offers a beautiful walk past a marina, two military museums—Fort Point and The Presidio Army Museum (open 10–4 Tu–Su)—and the Palace of Fine Arts, which houses the Exploratorium, a fascinating collection of pieces on perception. Open W–Su.

Golden Gate Park, over 1,000 acres with bike paths, bridle paths, three lakes, sports fields, a Rose garden, an outdoor music concourse, and the really beautiful Japanese Tea Garden, a fine example of Oriental landscaping.

M. H. de Young Memorial Museum, Golden Gate Park Music Concourse. A good collection of traditional arts of Africa, the Pacific, and the Americas. Open 10–5 W–Su.

Asian Art Museum, next to the de Young museum. Excellent Oriental collection. Open 10–5 daily.

California Academy of Sciences, Golden Gate Park Music Concourse. Noted for both its aquarium and planetarium. Open 10–5 daily.

Useful Information

San Francisco Visitor and Convention Bureau, 1390 Market St. (391-2000); *Visitor Information Center,* Powell & Market Sts. (974-6900); *Travelers Aid* (868-1503); *Weather* (936-1212); *Daily Events* (391-2001); *Taxi* (626-2345, 552-1300).

Special Trips/Tours

A cable car ride, especially on the Hyde Park line, which goes from the intersection of Powell & Market Sts. over Nob and Russian Hills to Victorian Square. *Alcatraz Island.* Run by the National Park Service, this notorious federal penitentiary offers a grim reminder of the rigors of prison life. Boats for the 2-hour tours leave from Pier 41 (546-2805). Advance tickets can be purchased through Ticketron. Open 8:45–5 June–Oct.; 8:45–2:45 the rest of the year. *Bay cruises: The Red and White Fleet,* Pier $43\frac{1}{2}$, near Fisherman's Wharf, and Pier 41 (546-2810), and *The Blue and Gold Fleet,* Pier 39 (781-7877), offer year-round cruises past Alcatraz Island, the Golden Gate Bridge, and the Marin County shoreline. Taking a *dinner cruise in the bay at night* is particularly delightful. Contact *Hornblower Yachts,* Pier 33, The Embarcadero (434-0300).

Weather

San Francisco's summer daytime high temperatures typically reach the mid to high 60s, dropping to the low 60s at night. Winters are mild and moderately wet, with daytime highs in the upper 50s, falling to the high 40s at night.

SAN FRANCISCO: TEMPERATURES AND PRECIPITATION

Month	J	F	M	A	M	J	J	A	S	O	N	D
Average Daily Temperature												
(Fahrenheit) Max.	55	59	61	62	63	66	65	65	69	68	63	57
Min.	47	48	50	53	56	59	63	64	62	57	52	48
Average Number of Days with Precipitation												
	11	10	10	6	4	2	0	0	2	4	7	10

Santa Fe

Sights to See

Plaza de Santa Fe, at the heart of downtown Santa Fe. Laid out by decree of the King of Spain in 1610, the Plaza has been the center of cultural and social gatherings since then. It is surrounded by shops, restaurants, galleries, and the Palace of the Governors.

Palace of the Governors, N side of the Plaza on Palace Ave. Dating from 1610, it is the oldest continually occupied government building in the country. It now houses historical exhibits for the Museum of New Mexico. Open 9–4:45 daily, Tu–Su in winter.

Museum of Fine Arts, across Union Avenue from the Palace of the Governors. Fine collection of 20th-century and traditional Southwestern art and contemporary Indian paintings. Open 9–4:45 daily, Tu–Su in winter.

Sena Plaza, East Palace Ave., to the E of the Palace of the Governors right off the Plaza. The courtyard of a former 38-room adobe hacienda, now divided into shops and offices.

St. Francis Cathedral, Cathedral Place, one block E of the Plaza. A beautiful 19th-century French Romanesque structure, noted for its adobe chapel and the carved wooden statue of the Madonna. Open 5–6 daily.

San Miguel Mission, Old Santa Fe Trail & De Vargas St., S of the Plaza across the Santa Fe River. The oldest mission church in the country, noted for its wooden reredos (alter screens). Open 9–11:30, 1–4:30 daily.

Canyon Road, running SE of downtown Santa Fe along the Santa Fe River. One of the oldest and most picturesque streets in the country. Formerly the center of the local art colony, it still is lined with galleries, studios, cafes, and restaurants.

Cristo Rey Church, Upper Canyon Rd. & Camino Cabra. One of the largest adobe structures in the world, it was built in 1940 to house an 18th-century hand-carved stone reredo (altar screen), moved from St. Francis' Cathedral. Open 6:30–7 daily.

Museum of International Folk Art, 706 Camino Lejo off the Santa Fe Trail, SE of downtown. Excellent folk art collection. Open 9–4:45 Tu–Su.

Wheelwright Museum of the American Indian, next to the folk art museum. Indian arts and artifacts. Especially noteworthy is the Navajo ceremonial art exhibit. Open 10–5 M–Sa, 1–5 Su in summer; Tu–Su in winter.

Laboratory of Anthropology, also on Camino Lejo next to the folk art museum. Excellent native American pottery, textile, jewelry, and basket collection on display. Open 9–5 M–F.

Useful Information

Santa Fe Convention and Visitors Bureau, 200 W. Marcy St. (984-6760); *New Mexico State Travel Division,* 1100 St. Francis Dr. (827-0291); *Santa Fe Chamber of Commerce,* 333 Montezuma at Guadalupe (983-7317); *Taxi* (982-9990, 988-1211).

Special Trips/Tours

Some 80 miles N of Santa Fe at the foot of the beautiful Sangre de Cristo mountains, is *Taos.* Actually comprised of three villages (the original Spanish town of Taos itself, now essentially an art colony; the Taos Indian *Pueblo de Taos;* and the Indian farming village of *Rancho de Taos*), Taos constitutes a fascinating blend of Spanish, Indian, and Anglo cultures. In Taos itself, the central plaza and its many surrounding art galleries are worth exploring in depth. Two blocks E of Taos Plaza is the restored home of *Ernest L. Blumenschein* on Ledoux St., now a showcase for Blumenschein's paintings and those of other Taos painters. Open 9–5 daily; 10–4 during winter. Less than 3 miles N of the Plaza is *Pueblo de Taos,* made up of flat-topped adobe houses and a five-story, terraced pueblo, a communal dwelling housing almost 2,000 members of the conservative Indian tribe. Contact the tribal office (758-8626) for information on tribal ceremonies and/or feast days that may be taking place during your visit, and which you may be allowed to watch. Open 8–sunset daily. In *Ranchos de Taos,* 4 miles S, is the magnificent 18th-century adobe brick church, the *Mission of St. Francis of Assisi,* noted for its massive abutments and buttresses. If you have the time, the indirect route to Taos via Hwys. 4, 76, and 3 (the High Road), through the communities of *Chimayo, Cordova, Truchas,* and *Trampas,* is very rewarding.

Weather

At 7,000 ft., Santa Fe has warm to hot summers with very low humidity, and cold, dry winters. Summer daytime high temperatures typically reach into the high 70s, dropping to the 50s at night. Winter daytime highs are usually in the 40s, falling to the 20s or high teens at night. July and August receive the most precipitation.

SANTA FE: TEMPERATURES AND PRECIPITATION

Month	J	F	M	A	M	J	J	A	S	O	N	D
Average Daily Temperature												
(Fahrenheit) Max.	40	43	51	59	68	78	80	79	73	62	50	40
Min.	19	23	29	35	43	52	57	56	49	38	28	20
Average Number of Days with Precipitation												
	6	6	7	6	7	6	13	12	8	5	4	6

Savannah

Sights to See

Riverfront Plaza and River Street along the Savannah River at the foot of Bull Street. Former 19th-century cotton warehouses have been converted to gift shops, restaurants, pubs, and small boutiques. The bordering concourse of parks is ideal for strolling and ship-watching.

Factor's Walk, on the river bluff above River Street. Noted for its narrow iron bridgeways over cobblestone ramps connecting the cotton factor's buildings to the bluff.

Bull Street, from City Hall on Bay St. to Forsyth Park. Famous for its five beautiful squares, each with a distinctive monument or fountain.

Telfair Academy of Arts and Sciences, 121 Barnard St. on Telfair Sq., two blocks W of Wright Sq. on Bull St. Housed in the Telfair Mansion, noted for its unique Octagon Room. Museum wing has fine collection of American and European paintings, prints, drawings, porcelain, and costumes. Open 10–5 Tu–Sa, 2–5 Su.

Owens-Thomas House and Museum, 124 Abercorn St., off Oglethorpe Sq. E of Wright Sq. Considered to be one of the best examples of English Regency architecture in America. Fine period furniture and notable 18th- and 19th-century European and Chinese porcelain. Open 10–5 Tu–Sa, 2–5 Su. Closed in September.

Davenport House, 119 Habersham St., on Columbia Sq. just E of the Owens-Thomas House. American Federal-style house. Noted for its elliptical staircase and period furniture. Open 10–4:30 M–Sa, 1:30–4:40 Su.

Museum of Antique Dolls, 505 E. President St. between Columbia & Greene Sqs. Fine collection of dolls, doll furniture, and toys. Open 10–5 Tu–Sa. Closed Sept.

Juliette Gordon Low Birthplace, Oglethorpe & Bull Sts., S of Wright Sq. A Regency-style house, birthplace of the founder of the Girl Scouts, with a collection of Girl Scout memorabilia. Open 10–4 M–Sa, 11–4:30 Su. Closed W.

Fort Jackson, 3 miles E of downtown Savannah on President St. on the S bank of the Savannah River. The oldest (dating from 1809) remaining brickwork fort in the city, it has displays and artifacts depicting the history of Savannah and coastal Georgia. Open 9–5 daily Memorial Day–Labor Day, 9–5 Tu–Su the rest of the year.

Useful Information

Savannah Visitors Center, 301 W. Broad St. (944-0456); *Taxi* (964-1500, 927-7466); *Public Transport* (233-5767); *Fort Pulaski National Monument* (786-5787); *Carriage Tours of Savannah* (236-6756); *Police* (232-4141). Check the *Savannah Evening Press* for entertainment details.

Special Trips/Tours

Historic Savannah, with its beautiful squares, trees hung with Spanish moss, and elegant antebellum houses, is made for walking—by far the best way to appreciate this city. Indeed the Savannah Visitors Center has mapped out several *self-guided walking tours* with carefully marked routes outlined by signs. Most of the sights listed above can be seen on the walking tours. Self-guided driving tours are similarly marked.

Just 15 miles E of Savannah on US 80, on the E end of Cockspur Island, is one of the best-preserved coastal forts on the eastern seaboard, *Fort Pulaski.* Part of the Third System of forts designed to protect the coasts of the United States, and now a national monument, the fort was built between 1829 and 1847. This massive irregular pentagon, surrounded by a moat crossed by a drawbridge, is especially noted for its fine brick arch masonry in the casemated galleries. The fort's Visitors Center contains exhibits on the fort's history, and the fort itself illustrates Civil War–era garrison life. Open 8:30–6:45 daily, Memorial to Labor Day; 8:30–5:15 daily the rest of the year (768-5787).

About 69 miles S of Savannah, and 10 miles N of Brunswick, GA on US 17 is the *Hofwyl-Broadfield Plantation.* Dating from the early 19th century, this former rice plantation is now a 1,200-acre wildlife preserve with a museum illustrating the history of the area's rice industry. Hofwyl, the plantation's house, is noted for its original furnishings. Open 9–5 Tu–Sa, 2–5:30 Su (264-9263).

Georgia's *Golden Isles,* or *Sea Islands,* lie just off the coast S of Savannah. Famed as a refuge used by Blackbeard in the 18th century and used as sugar and indigo plantations in the 19th, these islands now are one of Georgia's major resort areas. *St. Simons, Sea Island, and Jekyll Island* are the only islands accessible by car. Apart from the fine beaches, *St. Simons* offers Fort Frederica, the Museum of Coastal History, and Christ Church as notable sights; while *Jekyll Island* offers the famous Millionaires' Village, composed of the former summer "cottages" of the Morgan, Gould, Goodyear, Pulitzer, and Rockefeller families.

Weather

Savannah has an almost subtropical climate with hot humid summers and mild winters. Summer daytime high temperatures typically hover around 90, falling to around 70 at night. Winter daytime highs are usually in the low to mid 60s, dropping to the 40s at night. June through September is the wettest time of the year with frequent afternoon thunderstorms.

SAVANNAH: TEMPERATURES AND PRECIPITATION

Month	J	F	M	A	M	J	J	A	S	O	N	D
Average Daily Temperature												
(Fahrenheit) Max.	63	64	70	77	85	90	91	91	86	78	69	63
Min.	41	42	47	54	62	69	71	71	67	56	46	40
Average Number of Days with Precipitation												
	10	9	9	8	8	11	13	13	10	6	7	9

Seattle

Sights to See

Seattle Center, Broad & Thomas Sts. Former site of the 1962 World's Fair. Ride to the top of the *Space Needle* (607 ft.) and enjoy the view of Seattle, the Puget Sound, and the Cascade mountains from the observation deck or revolving restaurant. Visit the *Food Circus,* 305 Harrison Street, and enjoy cuisine from around the world, or go for a ride in the *Fun Forest Amusement Park,* 370 Thomas St. Open 10–6 daily.
Pacific Science Center, 200 2nd Ave. N., next to the Space Needle. Excellent astrospace exhibits, a laserium, and an oceanographic model of the Puget Sound. Open 9–6 M–F, 9–9 Sa & Su.
Seattle Aquarium, Pier 59, at the foot of University St., adjacent to Waterfront Park. Famous for its "viewing room," or Underwater Dome, which takes you beneath Puget Sound waters for an intimate view of sea life. Open 10–7 daily in summer, 10–5 the rest of the year.
Pike Place Market, 1st Ave. between Pike & Virginia Sts. Full of colorful vendors, musicians, arts and crafts booths, and restaurants. Open M–Sa.
Seattle Art Museum, Volunteer Park, Broadway & Prospect St. Noted for its excellent Oriental collection, and one of the two Tiepolo ceilings in America. Open 10–5 Tu & W, 10–9 Th, 10–5 F & Sa, 12–5 Su.
Museum of History and Industry, 2161 East Hamlin St. An interesting collection tracing Seattle's history, with mementos of the Gold Rush and a Boeing exhibit. Open daily.
Pioneer Square Historic District between Yeslor Way & the Kingdome on the city's S side. An historic preservation area, full of restored Victorian buildings, boutiques, and restaurants. Take the *Underground Tour* (682-4646), and visit the *Klondike Gold Rush Historic Park,* 117 S. Main, and trace its history.
International District, between King & Dearborn Sts. and 5th & 8th Aves. A joint Chinese and Japanese community, with the characteristic Oriental shops, temples, and restaurants. (Try *Nikko's,* 1306 King Street 322-4641, the largest sushi bar in town). Visit the *Wing Luke Memorial Museum,* 414 8th Ave., which commemorates the Chinese immigration to the Northwest. Open Tu–F.
University of Washington Arboretum, Lake Washington Blvd. between E. Madison & Montlake. Famous for its Japanese Tea Garden. Open 11–5 daily.
Lake Washington Ship Canal and Hiram M. Chittenden Locks, within Seattle where Salmon Bay, Lake Union, and Lake Washington connect to Puget Sound, Gilman Ave., NW of Seattle Center. The locks are some of the largest in the world. Watch the trout and salmon run up the fish ladder from a viewing window.

Useful Information

Seattle Visitors Bureau, 666 Stewart St. (461-5890); *Travelers Aid,* 909 4th Ave. (447-3888); *Metro Transit* (447-4800); *Taxi* (622-1717, 622-6500, 292-0569);

Weather (382-7246); *Mountain Pass road conditions* (464-6010); *TICKETMAS-TER,* The BON, 3rd & Pine Street (628-0888); *Washington State Ferries* (464-6400).

Special Trips/Tours

Seattle Harbor Tour. One-hour narrated trips along the waterfront and past the shipyards are offered on boats that leave Pier 56 at the foot of Seneca Street (623-1445).

Puget Sound Ferry Ride. Take an inexpensive boat trip along the E shore of the Puget Sound, either just to Bremerton or to Winslow on Brainbridge Island (35 minutes). Ferries leave from Pier 52 (464-6400), S of Waterfront Park.

Victoria, BC is only 4 hours away, via the British Columbia Steamship Co.'s *Princess Marguerite,* which sails daily at 8 A.M. from Pier 69 (682-8200), N of Waterfront Park. Return trips are in the late afternoon. Or you can cut that time in half by catching the *Island Jet Foil to Victoria,* which leaves at 7 A.M. and 12 noon (623-3645).

Weather

Seattle's climate is very much influenced by the Pacific Ocean. Winters are mild and summers are warm. Seattle is cloudy much of the time and has a large number of rainy days. Summer daytime highs reach the high 60s to low 70s, and temperatures fall into the low 50s at night. In winter, daytime highs are typically in the 40s, with lows in the mid to upper 30s. Temperatures rarely fall into the teens. Winter is the wettest season.

SEATTLE: TEMPERATURES AND PRECIPITATION

Month	J	F	M	A	M	J	J	A	S	O	N	D
Average Daily Temperature												
(Fahrenheit) Max.	45	48	52	58	64	69	72	73	67	59	51	47
Min.	36	37	39	43	47	52	54	55	52	47	41	38
Average Number of Days with Precipitation												
	18	16	16	13	12	9	4	5	8	13	17	19

Tampa-St. Petersburg

Sights to See

Ybor City State Museum, 1818 9th Avenue, Ybor City, in the heart of Tampa's Latin Quarter. Devoted to exhibits on the local cigar industry. Open 9–12, 1–5 Tu–Sa (247-6323).

The Wines of St. Augustine, 1205 8th Avenue, across from Ybor Square. Florida's first winery. Tasting sessions from 11–5 M–Sa. (273-0070).

Henry S. Plant Museum, Plant Hall, University of Tampa, 401 W. Kennedy Blvd. Housed in the Moorish Tampa Bay Hotel, the museum has a collection of

furniture and paintings from this former fashionable resort hotel. Open 10–4 Tu–Sa (253-3333).
Seminole Culture Center, 5221 N. Orient Rd., N of I-4, NE of Ybor City. A Seminole village with craft demonstrations, alligator wrestling, snake shows, and a museum. Open 9–5 M–Sa, 12–6 Su (623-3549).
Museum of Science and Industry, 4801 E. Fowler Ave., N of the Seminole Culture Center, off N. 56th St. The largest museum in Florida, noted for its "hands-on" exhibit and simulated hurricane. Open 10–4:30 daily. (985-6531).
Busch Gardens (The Dark Continent), 3000 Busch Blvd., SR 580, off I-275 (exit 33), 8 miles NE of downtown Tampa. Rides, live entertainment, shops, shows, and bird and animal exhibits. Ride the monorail through the Serengeti Plain. Open 9:30–6 daily, 9–8 during the summer (971-8282).
Salvador Dali Museum, 1000 3rd St. S., St. Petersburg, along Bayboro Harbor. Excellent collection of works by the surrealist. Open 10–5 Tu–Sa (823-3767).
St. Petersburg Museum of Fine Arts, Beach Dr. & 2nd Ave. NE, just N of the Salvador Dali Museum. Interesting collection of decorative arts, and oriental and pre-Columbian art and paintings. Open 10–5 Tu–S, 1–5 Su (896-2667).
MGM's Bounty Exhibit 345 2nd Ave. NE, next to the Municipal Pier. A full-size replica of *H.M.S. Bounty,* used in the filming of *Mutiny on the Bounty.* Open 9–7 daily (896-3117).
Sunken Gardens, 1825 N. 4th St., N of the Fine Arts Museum. Over 7,000 varieties of tropical plants and flowers, and a large walk-through aviary. Open 9–5:30 daily. (896-3186).
London Wax Museum, 5505 Gulf Blvd, St. Petersburg Beach. Over 100 life-size figures created by London's Madame Tussaud's. Open 9–10 M–Sa, noon–10 Su (360-6985).
Pass-a-Grille Beach, across the Pinellas Bayway on St. Petersburg's Gulf coast, S of St. Petersburg Beach. Considered to be the best of the city's many fine beaches.

Sports

Boating: TAMPA: contact *Bay Harbor Inn* (sailboats), 7700 Courtney Campbell Cswy. (885-2541). ST. PETERSBURG: contact *Annapolis Sailing School,* Sheraton St. Petersburg Marina and Tennis Resort (867-1151); *Gulfcoast Sailboats* 9600 W. Gulf Blvd., Treasure Island (367-4444); *Suncoast Rent-a-Boat* 945 Gulf Blvd., Madeira Beach (360-6623). For powerboat rentals, contact *Suncoast Boat Rentals* (360-1822).
Fishing: TAMPA: contact *Suncoast Charters* (864-3106). ST. PETERSBURG: contact *Suncoast Sailing Center,* Clearwater Beach Marina (581-4662); *Daytona Cat,* Madeira Beach (391-6111); *Florida Fisherman,* Madeira Beach (393-1947). Alternatively, check with your hotel for charter fishing boat information.
Golf: there are some 19 golf courses and golf resorts in the area, including the *Rocky Point GC* (884-5141) and the *Babe Zaharias GC* (932-4401) in Tampa;

the *Dunedin CC,* Dunedin (733-2484); and the *Pasadena GC* (348-9329) in St. Petersburg.
Tennis: the area has a number of good tennis resorts, including *Bardmoor CC,* Largo (392-1234); *Belleview Biltmore Hotel,* Clearwater (442-6171); *Gulf Island Resort,* Hudson (862-5491), and *Innisbrook Resort and GC,* Tarpon Springs (937-3124). For the public court closest to you, call Tampa's recreation department (238-6451), or St. Petersburg's (442-0229).
Windsurfing: contact *Windsurfing Florida Suncoast,* Beachcomber Resort, St. Petersburg Beach (360-3783); or *West Coast Water Sports,* Gulfview Blvd., Clearwater Beach (443-1902).

Weather

Tampa-St. Petersburg enjoys a sunny, subtropical climate, with hot summers and mild winters. Summer daytime high temperatures are typically in the low 90s, falling to the low 70s at night. Winter daytime highs are normally in the 70s, dropping to the low 50s at night. The rainy season extends from June to September with many short, heavy thunderstorms.

TAMPA: TEMPERATURES AND PRECIPITATION

Month	J	F	M	A	M	J	J	A	S	O	N	D
Average Daily Temperature												
(Fahrenheit) Max.	71	72	77	81	88	91	92	92	89	83	76	71
Min.	50	52	55	61	67	71	73	73	71	65	56	51
Average Number of Days with Precipitation												
	6	7	7	6	8	14	18	16	14	9	5	6

Washington, DC

Sights to See

Washington Monument The Mall, 15th St. between Independence and Constitution Aves. The view from the top of this 555-ft. obelisk is excellent. Open 8–midnight in summer, 9–5 the rest of the year.
Lincoln Memorial, Memorial Circle between Constitution & Independence Aves., The Mall. Columned white marble building with the Gettysburg and Second Inaugural addresses inscribed on the interior walls. Open 24 hours.
Jefferson Memorial, South Basin Drive, SW., The Mall. A domed temple with a bronze statue of Jefferson and inscriptions of Jefferson's quotations. Open 24 hours.
Vietnam Veterans Memorial, W end of the mall. A deceptively simple and moving monument dug into the earth; it is especially haunting at night. Open 24 hours.
The National Gallery of Art, 6th St. & Constitution Ave. One of the world's finest collections of Western art. Open 10–5, M–Sa, 10–9 Su, and in summer.

Smithsonian Institution, 1000 Jefferson Dr. SW. The Mall. A vast collection of museums, galleries, and research organizations, including the *National Museum of Natural History,* Constitution Ave. at 10th St.; *National Museum of American History,* Constitution Ave. between 12th & 14th Sts.; *National Air and Space Museum,* Independence Avenue, between 4th & 7th Sts.; *Hirshhorn Museum* and *Sculpture Garden,* Independence Ave. at 8th St.; *Freer Gallery of Art,* 12 St. & Jefferson Dr. SW.; and the *National Museum of African Art,* next to the Freer Gallery. All are open 10–5:30 daily, longer hours in the summer, and free.

The Capitol, 1st St. between Constitution & Independence Aves. Catch the 40-minute guided tours that leave from the Rotunda every quarter hour. Open 9–4:30 daily.

The Library of Congress, 1st St. between E. Capitol & B Sts. The world's largest and richest library. Open 8:30–9 M–F, 8:30–6 Sa & Su.

The White House, 1600 Pennsylvania Ave. Tours start at the East Gate on E. Executive Ave. Open 10–noon Tu–Sa, 10–2 in summer.

The Supreme Court, 1st St. between Maryland Ave. & E. Capitol Street NE. Sessions (normally from October through June) are open to the public on a first-come, first-served basis. Open 9–4:30 M–F

Washington Cathedral, Massachusetts & Wisconsin Aves. Noted for its stained-glass windows and stone carving (still in progress).

Georgetown, centered around the intersection of M St. & Wisconsin Ave. Home to many of Washington's elite and also the city's prime nightlife center. Visit the *Georgetown Park Mall* on M Street.

Arlington National Cemetery, in Arlington, directly across the Potomac from Washington. It contains the graves of many famous Americans. The changing of the guard ceremony at the Tomb of the Unknown Soldier is worth seeing. Open 8–5 daily, 8–7 during the summer.

Useful Information

Washington Convention and Visitors Association, 1212 New York Ave. NW. (789-7000); *Visitors Center,* Great Hall, Department of Commerce, 14th & Pennsylvania Ave. (789-7000); *Information Center,* Union Station, Massachusetts & Delaware Ave., NE. (289-1908); *Travelers Aid* (347-0101); *Weather* (936-1212); *Smithsonian Dial-A-Museum,* recorded information on daily events (357-2020); *Smithsonian Visitor Information* (357-2700); *Metrorail/Metrobus Information* (637-2437); *Taxi* (544-1212, 387-6200).

Special Trips/Tours

The easiest way for the first-time visitor to see the principal sights is to take the *Tourmobile,* a tram that shuttles among 14 stops with commentary (554-7950). Washington Boat Lines, Inc., runs daily *cruises along the Potomac* from April through mid-October, leaving from the foot of Wisconsin Avenue in Georgetown and Lincoln Memorial (554-8000). *Old Town Alexandria, Virginia,* just S of

National Airport, across the Potomac from Washington DC, is a delightful community with a very large concentration of beautifully restored 18th-century buildings. Try *Gadsby's Tavern,* 138 N. Royal St. (548-1288).

Weather

Washington's summers tend to be hot and muggy, with daytime highs in the mid to high 80s. Winters are moderately cold, with daytime highs in the low to mid 40s. Fall and spring are both delightful seasons. Precipitation is spread fairly uniformly throughout the year, although July and August are the wettest months.

WASHINGTON: TEMPERATURES AND PRECIPITATION

Month	J	F	M	A	M	J	J	A	S	O	N	D
Average Daily Temperature												
(Fahrenheit) Max.	42	44	53	64	75	83	87	84	78	67	55	45
Min.	27	28	35	44	54	63	68	66	59	48	38	29
Average Number of Days with Precipitation												
	11	10	12	11	12	11	11	11	8	8	9	10

Asia
Beijing: China

Sights to See

Forbidden City (Imperial Palaces), in the center of Beijing. The largest and best-preserved complex of ancient buildings in China. Covering some 250 acres, with some 800 buildings and 9,000 rooms slowly being renovated, it has been turned into a splendid museum, with a priceless collection of Chinese bronzes, jade, paintings, and porcelain among other outstanding objects. The whole complex, dominated by the palaces' huge golden roofs, can be seen to best advantage from the top of *Coal Hill* (Meishan), just N of the Shenwu Gate in Jingshan Park.
Tiananmen Square, the largest public square in the world, just outside the Forbidden City. Takes its name from the huge gate (Gate of Heavenly Peace) on its N side that was built in 1412.
Great Hall of the People, on the W side of Tiananmen Square. Site of the National People's Congress conventions, and receptions of foreign statesmen.
Monument to the People's Heroes, on the S side of Tiananmen Square. A tall granite obelisk, with an inscription in Chairman Mao's calligraphy.
Museum of Chinese History and Museum of the Chinese Revolution, in the same building on the E side of the square. Huge museums, the first covering prehistory to the 1839–1842 Opium War, the second covering modern history from the Opium War to the present.

Mausoleum of Mao Zedong, behind the Monument to the People's Heroes. The sarcophagus rests on a bier surrounded by flowers shipped in from all over China. Twice-weekly CITS tours are conducted.

Beihai Park, just NW of the Forbidden City. Beautifully landscaped with artificial hills, pavilions, temples, halls, bridges, and covered walkways. Be sure to visit the "Hall Which Receives the Light" and the Jade Pavilion in the Round City, standing to the west (left) of the main entrance. Also catch the barge across the lake to see the Nine Dragon Screen.

Xu Beihong Museum, 53 Xinjiekou Beidajie, Xicheng District. Best gallery for traditional Chinese paintings, oils, gouaches, and sketches. Open 9–5 Tu–Su.

Temple of Heaven (Tian Tan), a cluster of ceremonial buildings in SE Beijing. One of the most popular attractions, these 15th-century structures have been restored several times. The most important one, the "Hall of Prayer for Good Harvests" (Qi Nian Dian), is notable in that it is constructed entirely of wood without any nails.

Useful Information

China International Travel Service (CITS), 6 Chang An Dong Daji (tel:75-7181); *U.S. Embassy,* Xiu Shui Bei Jie 3 (tel:53-3831); *Taxi* (tel:55-7461); *Voltage Guide:* 220 V, two round-pin or two flat, angled blade outlets are used.

Special Trips/Tours

The Great Wall (Wan Li Chang Cheng). The Ba Da Ling section of this 3,000-mile wonder, a tourist attraction for thousands of years, is only 43 miles NW of Beijing, just a two-hour bus ride away. It is also accessible by train.

The Ming Tombs (Shi San Ling), are about 30 miles north of Beijing near Changping. The 13 tombs lie in a natural amphitheater, approached by a road lined with statues of man and animals. The Chang Ling tomb of the 15th-century Emperor Yong La is the most impressive. The exhibition rooms of the Ding Ling tomb of the 16th-century Emperor Wan Li show the possessions of the emperor and the mausoleum itself can be explored.

The Summer Palace (Yi He Yuan), is about 9 miles NW of Beijing's center, and is noted for its fine pagodas, pavilions, temples, and courtyards. The main building is the Hall of Benevolence and Longevity. On the lake, at the W end of the covered walk, is the famous marble boat, completed by the Empress Dowager Ci Xi. Be sure to ride the ferry on Lake Kun Ming.

Weather

Beijing experiences hot, humid semitropical summers with daytime high temperatures typically in the mid to high 80s, falling to the low 70s or high 60s at night. Winters are cold with frequent frost and light snow. Daytime highs usually reach into the mid to upper 30s, dropping to the teens at night. Summer is the wet season, with July and August normally receiving the most rain.

BEIJING: TEMPERATURES AND PRECIPITATION

Month	J	F	M	A	M	J	J	A	S	O	N	D
Average Daily Temperature												
(Fahrenheit) Max.	34	39	52	70	81	88	88	86	79	68	48	37
Min.	14	18	30	45	55	64	70	68	57	43	28	18
Average Number of Days with Precipitation												
	3	3	3	4	6	8	13	11	7	3	3	2

Guangzhou (Canton): China

Sights to See

Temple of the Six Banyan Trees (Liu Rong Temple), on Liu Rong St., between Haizhu & Chaoyang Rds. in central Guangzhou. Equally noted for its adjacent 9-story pagoda.

Huaisheng Mosque, Guang Ta Lu Street, just S of the temple. Originally founded in the 7th century to serve the large Moslem colony that had become established in the city. The present structure is much more recent, and the minaret's balcony affords excellent views of the city.

Liuhua Park, between Dongfeng Rd. & Xicun Highway, W of Renmin Road. It is known for its lakes, covered walks, and arched stone bridges.

Guangzhou Orchid Garden, at the corner of Jiefang & Huanshi Rds., NE of Liuhua Park. Hundreds of varieties of orchid, together with groves of rare tress, a teahouse, and gazebo.

Zen Hoi Tower, Yue Xiu Park, just E of the orchid garden. The last vestige of the city wall that once defended the city. Visit the city museum in the tower and enjoy the fine views.

Roman Catholic Cathedral, just off the foot of Haizhu Rd. near the Zhu Jiang (Pearl) River. A mid-19th-century Gothic structure, with twin spires.

Sha Mian Island, E of the foot of Liwan Rd. in the Zhu Jiang (Pearl) River. Specifically created as a foreign enclave in the 1860s from a sandbank in the river. The setting is one of the most delightful in the city, with all manner of boats plying the Zhu Jiang (Pearl) River on one side, and old Colonial British and French buildings on the other side.

Qing Ping Market, Qingping Lu, opposite the bridge to Sha Mian Island. A very colorful market with every kind of animal and fowl being sold.

National Peasant Movement Institute, Zhonshan & Yuexiu. Located in a well preserved temple, the institute contains the office of Mao Zedong, who headed the institute in the 1920s.

Exhibition Hall of the Revolution, next to the Institute. Noted for its collection of photographs and writings of Mao Zedong and Zhou Enlai.

Useful Information

Chinese International Travel Service (CITS), Rm. 2366 Dong Fang Hotel, 120 Liu Hau Rd. (tel:66-2427), and 179 Huanshi Lu (tel:66-1369), next to the

Railway Station; *U.S. Consulate*, Dong Fang Hotel, 120 Liu Hau Rd. (tel:66-9900); *Public Security Bureau* (Foreigners' Section, tel:33-1060); *Voltage Guide:* 220 V, two round-pin or two flat, angled blade outlets are used.

Special Trips/Tours

Bai Yun Shan (White Cloud Mountain), is a hot-springs resort area in the NE suburbs of Guangzhou. From *Moxing Ling* (Star Touching Peak), you get a fine panorama of Guangzhou spread out below, as well as the Pearl River delta, one of China's important rice-growing regions. The *Cheng precipice* is considered to be a major tourist attraction among the Chinese. Express buses leave from Guangwei Lu, or you can take a taxi.

Some 15 miles SW of Guangzhou is *Foshan,* well known for its Shiwan pottery, and paper-cutting tradition. Formerly a famous religious center, its *Temple of the Ancestors* dates from the 10th century.

Weather

Guangzhou has a subtropical climate, with hot, humid summers with much heavy rain, and mild winters. Summer daytime high temperatures typically reach into the high 80s, dropping to the upper or mid 70s at night. Winter daytime highs are usually in the mid 60s, falling to the upper to mid 50s at night. The rainy season is from May through September.

GUANGZHOU: TEMPERATURES AND PRECIPITATION

Month	J	F	M	A	M	J	J	A	S	O	N	D
Average Daily Temperature												
(Fahrenheit) Max.	65	66	71	77	84	89	91	90	88	85	75	69
Min.	49	49	56	65	72	76	77	77	77	67	59	53
Average Number of Days with Precipitation												
	7	7	10	15	16	18	16	15	12	6	5	5

Shanghai: China

Sights to See

The Bund (Zhongshan Road), along the Huangpu River. Lined with the impressive buildings of banks, clubs, hotels, and a customs building built in the 19th century by foreigners granted concessions in Shanghai.
The Mandarin's Garden (Yu Yuan Yu), off Zhongshan Rd., at Fu Yu & An Ren Sts. in the old Chinese Town S of the Bund. Built by the Pan family in the 16th century, it is noted for its many halls and pavilions, bridges, and towers. The Yu Yuan Bazaar in the garden is worth seeing.
Temple of the Town Gods (Cheng Huang Miao), adjacent to the Mandarin's Garden. One of the few surviving such temples in China.

Garden of the Purple Clouds of Autumn (Qiu Xia Pu), behind the Temple of the Town Gods. Known for its ornamental lake and pavilions.

Five-Star Pavilion Teahouse (Wu Xing Ting), opposite the Mandarin's Garden. Set in the middle of an ornamental lake, this pentagon is surrounded by zigzag bridges and dozens of small shops.

Shanghai Museum, at the E end of Nanjing Rd. on Henan Nanlu. A fine collection of bronzes, paintings, ceramics, and Han dynasty clay tomb figurines. Open 9–11:45 and 1–4:45 M–Sa.

Temple of the Jade Buddha (Yu Fo Si), near the intersection of Changshou & Jiang Ning Rds., NW of central Shanghai. Famous for its white-jade Buddha, brought from Burma in the 1880s. Open 8–5 daily.

Children's Palace, near the intersection of Nanjing and Yunan Roads. The best known of Shanghai's many dancing, singing, music, painting, and handicraft schools for children.

Shanghai Industrial Exhibition, off Zhonglu, just W of Shaanxi Nanlu. A permanent exhibition of Chinese industrial products, many of them made in Shanghai.

Useful Information

China International Travel Service (CITS), 66 Nanjing Donglu (tel:21-7200), and 33 Zhongshan Rd. E. (tel:32-4960); *U.S. Consulate,* 1469 Huai Hui Lu (tel:336-880); *Business Center,* 59 Maoming Nan Lu (tel:37-0115); *Huangpo River Tourism Service* (tel:21-1098); *Voltage Guide:* 220 V, two round-pin or two flat, angled blade outlets are used.

Special Trips/Tours

A *Huangpu River Trip* is one of the best ways to see Shanghai, and one of the most relaxing, since Shanghai traffic is just shocking and the main sights are some distance apart. Tour boats leave from the dock on the Bund near the Peace Hotel at 1:30 daily, and in the evening in the summer months, and last over 3 hours. The boats reach the Yangtse River and you will see an incredible variety of craft plying the river.

Long Hua Temple and Pagoda (Long Hua Si), SW of central Shanghai, near the Huangpu River, is famous for its 7-story pagoda, the only one in Shanghai. A noted example of southern Chinese architecture, the pagoda was made of brick in the 10th century, with exterior balconies made of wood.

Weather

Summers in Shanghai are hot and humid, with daytime high temperatures typically reaching into the high 80s or low 90s, dropping to the mid to low 70s at night. Winter weather is very changeable, but daytime highs are normally in the upper 40s, falling to the mid 30s at night. The wet season extends from June through September, with June normally the wettest month.

SHANGHAI: TEMPERATURES AND PRECIPITATION

Month	J	F	M	A	M	J	J	A	S	O	N	D
Average Daily Temperature												
(Fahrenheit) Max.	46	47	55	66	77	82	90	90	82	74	63	53
Min.	33	34	40	50	59	67	74	74	66	57	45	36
Average Number of Days with Precipitation												
	6	9	9	9	9	11	9	9	11	4	6	6

Hong Hong

Sights to See

Hong Kong, is best seen from the *summit of the Peak.* The view of the city, its harbor, and outlying islands from this vantage point is just superb, day or night. Take the Peak Tram, a funicular railway, from Garden Rd., to the top of Victoria Peak (1,809 ft.).

Causeway Bay, E of central Hong Kong. A shopping district with market stalls and department stores.

Wangchai, between Causeway Bay and central Hong Kong to the E of the Central District. The girlie bar center of Suzie Wong fame.

Tiger Balm Gardens, a public park built by the Haw Par brothers, promoters of the patent medicine, "Tigar Balm." Full of bizarre Chinese sculptures. See the jade collection in the park's Haw Par Mansion.

Man Mo Miu, at the top of Ladder St. on Hollywood Rd. The oldest Miu (temple) in Hong Kong.

Poor Man's Night Club Macao Ferry Terminal's parking lot. After the cars leave in the evening, the vendors and their stalls take over.

Aberdeen, a floating town on the SW side of Hong Kong island, with junks, sampans, trawlers, and floating restaurants. Take a sampan tour (30 minutes). Try the Jumbo Restaurant.

Ocean Park, Sham Shui Kok Peninsula. One of the wood's largest oceanariums, with performances by a variety of marine mammals.

Tsim Sha Tsui District of Kowloon, centered along Nathan Rd. Just as busy as central Hong Kong, crowded with hotels, shops, nightclubs, neon signs, traffic, and tourists.

Ocean Terminal, behind the Hong Kong Hotel, near the intersection of Canton & Salisbury Roads, Kowloon. A large shopping complex, together with the newer, adjacent Ocean Centre Complex.

Planetarium and Space Museum, Salisbury Rd, near the Star Ferry Terminal on the waterfront, Kowloon.

Sung Dynasty Village, Laichikok in North Kowloon. A modern re-creation of a Chinese Village dating from the 10th to 13th centuries.

Po Lin Monastery, outside Tung Chung on Lantau Island. An impressive, ornate structure, famous for the statue of Buddha, SE Asia's tallest, just outside.

Useful Information

Hong Kong Tourist Association (HKTA), 35th Floor of the Connaught Centre, HK Island, and the Star Ferry Concourse, Kowloon; *Tourist Office* (tel:5-24-4191); *U.S. Consulate,* 26 Garden Rd. (tel:23-9011); *Voltage Guide:* 220 V, three-prong rectangular blade outlets are used.

Special Trips/Tours

Apart from making sure that you use the cross-harbor *Star Ferry* at least once (rather than the MTR underground railway), the ferries to *Lantau, Cheung Chau, and Peng Chau islands* are an excellent, and cheap, way to see Hong Kong. They leave from the Outlying Island Services Pier on Connaught Rd., central Hong Kong.

Weather

Hong Kong has a tropical monsoon climate, with hot, wet summers, and mild, relatively dry winters. Summer daytime high temperatures typically reach the high 80s, falling to the upper 70s at night. Winter daytime highs are usually in the mid 60s, dropping to the mid 50s at night. May through September is the monsoon season, with heavy rainfall.

HONG KONG: TEMPERATURES AND PRECIPITATION

Month	J	F	M	A	M	J	J	A	S	O	N	D
Average Daily Temperature												
(Fahrenheit) Max.	64	63	67	75	82	85	87	87	85	81	74	68
Min.	56	55	60	67	74	78	78	78	77	73	65	59
Average Number of Days with Precipitation												
	4	5	7	8	13	18	17	15	12	6	2	3

Bombay: India

Sights to See

Prince of Wales Museum, off Wellington Circle, Fort Bombay (downtown). One of India's best museums, it is noted for its Indian miniature paintings and collections of jade, crystal, and china artifacts. Open 10–5:30 Tu–Su, longer hours during summer.
Johangir Art Gallery, adjoining the Prince of Wales Museum. Contemporary exhibits. Open 10–5 Tu–Su.
Gateway of India, Apollo Bunder, S of the Prince of Wales Museum. A yellow basalt stone arch, Bombay's principal landmark.
Flora Fountain (Hutatma Chowk), a major landmark at the center of downtown Bombay.
Rajabai Tower, Bombay University, just W of Hutatma Chowk. The clock tower, above the university library, affords fine views of downtown Bombay.

Crawford Market (Mahatma Phule Market), Dadabhoy Naoroji & Lokmanya Tilak Rds., NW of Victoria Terminus Station. Very colorful, bustling flower, fruit, vegetable, meat, and fish market.

Marine Drive (Netaji Subhash Rd.), along the shoreline of Back Bay, W of Rajabai Tower. Famous promenade.

Taraporowella Aquarium, Netaji Subhash Rd. Good collection of tropical fish. Open 11–8 Tu–Su.

Chowpatty Beach, at the N end of Marine Drive. Busy, famous beach known for its annual Ganesh Chaturthi festival, and its kulfi and ice cream vendors.

Hanging Gardens (Pherozeshah Mehta Gardens), on the top of Malabar Hill, NW of Chowpatty Beach. Formal gardens, known for their topiary (shrubs trimmed into ornamental shapes). Fine views of Bombay, too.

Victoria and Albert Museum, Veermata Jijabai Bhonsle Udyan (formerly Victoria Gardens), N of the downtown area near the Byculla Station. Exhibits on Bombay and W. India. Open 10:30–5 Tu–Su.

Useful Information

Government of India Tourist Office, 123 Maharashi Karve Road, Churchgate (tel:29-3144); and at the Taj Mahal Intercontinental, Apollo Bunder; *Maharashtra Tourism Development Corporation,* Express Tower, Nariman Point (tel:202-1713); *U.S. Consulate,* Lincoln House, 78 Bhulabhai Desai Rd. (tel:822-3611); *Voltage Guide:* 220 V, two round-pin outlets are used.

Special Trips/Tours

A magnificent series of 7th- and 8th-century, rock-cut cave temples, noted for their large sculptured interiors, are located on *Elephanta Island,* the area's principal tourist attraction, 6 miles NE of Apollo Bunder in Bombay harbor. The island can be reached by the launches that leave regularly from the Gateway to India, Apollo Bunder, except during rough weather. Try to avoid going on weekends, the crowds are huge.

Krishnagri Upavan National Park, about 26 miles N of Bombay, is noted for the 2nd-century Buddhist Kanheri Caves. Particularly worthwhile is the Great Chaitya Cave. The park also contains lakes, picnic spots, and a Lion Safari Park. Open 9–5 Tu–Su.

The marvelous Shivaji past can be witnessed in many locations in Maharashtra, but perhaps most notably in the *caves of Ajanta and Ellora,* near Aurangabad, some 230 miles NE of Bombay. With its many Mughul monuments and tombs, especially the *mausoleum of Aurangzeb's Begum (Bibi ka Maqbara),* which is a replica of the Taj Mahal, Aurangabad is a good base for exploring the area. At *Ajanta,* some 60 miles NE of Aurangabad, the famous Buddhist caves are noted for their well-preserved frescoes as well as their sculptures. The marvelous Buddhist, Jain, and Hindu Brahmanic rock-cut temples at *Ellora,* are about 15 miles NW of Aurangabad. They are considered to be among the most important historical monuments in India. The *Kailash Temple,* for example, has a 100-ft.-high shrine and numerous galleries depicting scenes from Shiva myths. On the way, about halfway to Aurangabad, visit the massive hilltop fortress at *Daulatabad.*

The *scenic train trip to Pune,* just over 100 miles SE of Bombay is worthwhile. Noteworthy sights include the *Raja Kelkar Museum,* with its traditional Indian arts collection; the *Aga Khan Palace;* and the *Empress Gardens,* with the moated Ganesh temple.

Weather

Bombay has a tropical, monsoon climate. Summers are hot and humid, with daytime high temperatures typically in the high 80s, dropping to the high 70s at night. Winter daytime highs are usually in the low 80s, falling to the upper 60s at night. The rainy (monsoon) season lasts from June to September with very heavy and frequent rainfall.

BOMBAY: TEMPERATURES AND PRECIPITATION

Month	J	F	M	A	M	J	J	A	S	O	N	D
Average Daily Temperature												
(Fahrenheit) Max.	83	83	86	89	91	89	85	85	85	89	89	87
Min.	67	67	72	76	80	79	77	76	76	76	73	69
Average Number of Days with Precipitation												
		1	1	0	0	1	14	21	19	13	3	1	0

Calcutta: India

Sights to See

Fort William, the Maiden, off the Strand on the banks of the Hooghly River. Built by the British in the 1770s. Not open to the public, but impressive.

The Maiden, surrounding Ft. William. The Central Park of Calcutta. A huge recreational park with gardens, reservoirs, cricket and soccer fields, and monuments. The view from the top of the Shahid Minar (Ochterlony Monument), at the N end, is worth the climb.

Victoria Memorial at the S end of the Maiden. A massive, white marble, domed building that is a museum with an excellent collection of British Raj memorabilia, with fine Indian and Persian miniatures. Open 10–5 Tu–Su.

St. Paul's Cathedral, opposite the Victoria Memorial. White Gothic building noted for its stained glass.

Academy of Fine Arts, Cathedral Rd., next to the cathedral. Noted for its fine collection of old textiles and miniatures. Open 3–8 Tu–Su.

Indian Museum, 27 J. Nehru Rd., E of Fort William. India's best museum, and one of Asia's best too. Excellent, comprehensive collection. Especially noted for its archaeological section and art collection. Open 10–5 Tu–Su.

B.B.D. Bagh (Dalhousie Square), N of Fort William, at the commercial center of Calcutta.
Writers Building, N side of B.B.D. Bagh. A huge, late-19th-century building that housed the clerks of the East India Co., and now houses those of the W. Bengal State Govt.
Marble Palace, Muktarambabu St., E of B.B.D. Bagh. Claims to have the world's largest collection of Victorian sculptures and paintings. Open 10–4 Tu–W, F–Su.
Nakoda Mosque, N of B.B.D. Bagh, between Chittaranjan Avenue & Rabindra Sarani. Huge red sandstone mosque right in the middle of a bustling commercial area.
Sitambara Jain Temple, Raja Dinendra St., NE of the Nakoda Mosque. Noted for its inlaid precious stones.
Howrah Station, S of the Howrah Bridge on the W side of the Hooghly River. Calcutta's main railroad station, unbelievably crowded, a sight to behold! So is the traffic across the Howrah Bridge.

Useful Information

The Government of India Tourist Office, 41 Shakespeare Sarani (tel:44-3521); *West Bengal Tourist Information Center,* 3/2 B.B.D. Bagh (tel:23-8271); *American Express,* 21 Old Court House St. (tel:23-6281); *U.S. Consulate,* 5/1 Ho Chi Minh Sarani (tel:44-3616); *Voltage Guide:* 220 V, two round-pin outlets are used.

Special Trips/Tours

If you have the time, a trip especially by train, to *Darjeeling* is an absolute must. Located about 400 miles N of Calcutta, 7,000 ft. up in the Himalayan foothills between Nepal and Bhutan, the town is world famous for its truly magnificent scenery, tea plantations, and surrounding flora and fauna. Seeing the sun rise over *Kanchenjunga* (28,209 ft.) and other Himalayan peaks, from Tiger Hill, some 7 miles S of Darjeeling outside Ghoom, is a must. If you're lucky, you may even catch a glimpse of *Mt. Everest* (29,028 ft.).

Nor is the incredible scenery the only attraction in *Darjeeling* and its surrounding area. The town itself has several noteworthy sights, including the *Dhirdham Temple, Lloyd Botanical Gardens, Zoological Park,* and the *Himalayan Mountaineering Institute,* just outside Darjeeling, with a fine collection of mountaineering equipment and an interesting relief model of the Himalayas. Just outside Ghoom is the *Ghoom Buddhist Monastery,* with its image of the Maitreya Buddha.

Darjeeling is reached by train, or plane (to the airport at Bagdogra—and then by road or train). The ride on the *"Toy Train"* between New Jalpaiguri (near Bagdogra), and Darjeeling is the real highlight of the trip. NOTE: you do need a permit to travel to Darjeeling; check with your travel agent or hotel.

Weather

Calcutta has a hot, humid, subtropical climate. Summer daytime high temperatures typically reach into the low to mid 90s, dropping to the high 70s at night. Winter daytime highs are normally in the low 80s, falling to the high 50s at night. The monsoon season lasts from June until September.

CALCUTTA: TEMPERATURES AND PRECIPITATION

Month	J	F	M	A	M	J	J	A	S	O	N	D
Average Daily Temperature												
(Fahrenheit) Max.	80	84	93	97	96	92	89	89	90	89	84	79
Min.	55	59	69	75	77	79	79	78	78	74	64	55
Average Number of Days with Precipitation												
	1	2	2	3	7	13	18	18	13	6	1	1

Delhi: India

Sights to See

Red Fort, Old Delhi, just S of the Yamuna Bridge. Dating from the mid-17th century, this massive red sandstone fort was built at the peak of Moghul power. Inside are the Halls of Public and Private Audience (Diwan-i-Am and Diwan-i-Khas); the Pleasure Palace (Rang Mahal); the Pearl Mosque (Moti Masjid); and the Royal Baths (hammams). Catch the *sound and light show* each evening. Tickets available from ITDC, L Block, Connaught Place (tel:42-336).
Chandni Chowk Bazaar, along Old Delhi's main street, Chandni Chowk, just W of the Red Fort. A crowded, colorful shopping area where bargaining is the norm.
Jama Masjid Mosque, just SW of the Red Fort across Netaji Subhash Marg. India's largest mosque, it also dates from the 1640s. Constructed of red sandstone and white marble, it is noted for its tall minarets. Open 7–12, 2–5 daily.
Connaught Place, SW of the Jama Masjid Mosque, at the N end of New Delhi. The business and tourist center of Delhi.
National Gallery of Modern Art, Jaipur House, just SE of the India Gate on Zakir Hussain Marg. noted for its collection of works by Amrita Shergil. Open 10–4 Tu–Su.
Purana Qila, E of India Gate toward the Yamuna River, across Mathura Rd. A mid-16th-century fort, on the site of Indraprastha, the original city of Delhi. Noted for its Sher Shah's mosque.
National Museum, Janpath, just S of Rajpath, W of the India Gate. Excellent art, anthropological, and archaeological collections. Noted for its Indian stone, bronze, wood, and terracotta sculptures dating from the 2nd and 3rd centuries B.C. Open 10–5 Tu–Su.

Rashtrapati Bhavan (Presidential Palace), on Raisini Hill, at the W end of Rajpath, W of the National Museum. Closed to the public. Noted for its Moghul-style gardens.

Humayun's Tomb, Mathura Road, SE of the India Gate along Zakir Hussain Marg. An impressive, mid-16th-century Moghul mausoleum. Open sunrise–sunset.

Qutab Minar Tower, some 9 miles S of Delhi. Dating from 1199, this 230-ft. tall, ornately decorated tower, is considered to be an outstanding example of early Afghan architecture. The *Quwwat-ul-Islam Mosque,* at the foot of the Qutab Minar, is famous for its 5th-century Iron Pillar. Open sunrise–sunset.

Useful Information

Tourist Information Office, 88 Janpath (tel:32-0005); *Delhi Tourism Corporation,* N Block, Connaught Place (tel:46-356); *U.S. Embassy,* Shanti Path, Chanakyapuri (tel:60-0651); *American Express,* A Block, Connaught Place; *General Post Office,* Baba Kharak Singh Marg & Ashoka Rd.; *Voltage Guide:* 220 V, two round-pin outlets are used.

Special Trips/Tours

The *Taj Mahal,* perhaps India's most famous landmark, is in Agra, only some 127 miles S of Delhi. Built of marble between 1631 and 1653, this mausoleum of Empress Mumtaz Mahal is widely considered to be one of the world's architectural masterpieces. Especially noted for its graceful lines, it is also famous for the intricate, detailed patterns of semiprecious stones inlaid into the marble. Open sunrise–10 P.M.

Although the Taj Mahal is undoubtedly Agra's main attraction, the town also has two other noteworthy sights: massive Agra Fort, and the Itmad-ud-Daulah tomb. *Agra Fort,* built in the mid-16th century, with its huge, 70-ft.-high walls of red sandstone and its moat, is in the center of Agra on the banks of the Yamuna River, W of the Taj Mahal. Inside the fort are the beautiful, white marble, *Moti Masjid* (Pearl Mosque); *Diwan-i-Am* (Hall of Public Audience); *Diwan-i-Khas* (Hall of Private Audience); *Jahangiri Mahal* (Red Palace); and the octagonal *Musamman Burj tower.* On the other side of the Yamuna River, N of Agra Fort, is the tomb of *Itmad-ud-Daulah,* noted for its inlaid precious stones. Open sunrise–sunset.

Some 24 miles W of Agra, is the perfectly preserved, deserted city of *Fatehpur Sikri,* capital of the Moghul Empire in the late 16th century. The *Jama Masjid mosque* is especially noteworthy.

Weather

Summers are very hot, with daytime high temperatures typically in the high 90s or low 100s, falling to the low 80s or high 70s at night. Winter daytime highs are in the 70s, dropping to the 40s at night. The rainy season extends from June through September.

DELHI: TEMPERATURES AND PRECIPITATION

Month	J	F	M	A	M	J	J	A	S	O	N	D
Average Daily Temperature												
(Fahrenheit) Max.	70	75	87	97	105	102	96	93	93	93	84	73
Min.	44	49	58	68	79	83	81	79	75	65	52	46
Average Number of Days with Precipitation												
	2	2	1	1	2	4	8	6	4	1	1	1

Goa: India

Sights to See

Bom Jesus Basilica, Old Goa. Dating from the 16th century, it is famous for the tomb and remains of St. Francis Xavier. It is also noted for its richly decorated yet simple interior.

Cathedral of St. Catherine (Se Cathedral), across the square from the Basilica of Bom Jesus, Old Goa. Also dating from the 16th century, this large Portugese Gothic cathedral (the largest Christian church in Asia), is known for its magnificent altars.

St. Francis of Assisi Church and Convent, Old Goa. A simple 17th-century structure, known for its gilded, carved woodwork, and rich stucco ceilings.

St. Cajetan Church, Old Goa. Mid-17th-century church, modeled on the Basilica of St. Peter in Rome.

Mangesh Temple, between Old Goa and Ponda, SE of Old Goa. This Goan Hindu shrine is noted for its ornate, baroque interior, and 7-story lamp tower.

Margao Covered Market, in Margao, some 20 miles SE of Panaji, and SW of Ponda. The best market in Goa.

Colva Beach, W of Margao. Beautiful white sand, palm trees, warm, clear turquoise water. Considered the best of the fabled Goan beaches.

Secretariat Building, on the banks of the R. Mandovi, in Panaji, the state capital, W of Old Goa. Formerly a Muslim palace.

Church of the Immaculate Conception, Church Square (Largo da Igreja), Panaji. A 16th-century structure, noted for its baroque facade and tall, twin towers.

Fontainahas residential area, behind the Church of the Immaculate Conception, Panaji. Narrow, winding streets, old houses with overhanging balconies, red tiled roofs—you might be forgiven if you thought you were in Portugal!

Baga Beach, just N of the infamous Calangute beach, W of Mapusa, and NW of Panaji. One of Goa's best.

Anjuna Beach, W of Mapusa. As famous (infamous) for its "free spirits," as for its natural attractions.

Chapora Beach, N of Anjuna beach. Beautiful, secluded beach. Chapora Fort, on the headland S of the Chapora River, is the best-preserved of the many Portugese forts in Goa.

Useful Information

Tourist Office, Tourist Home, Pato Bridge, Panaji (tel:2757); the closest *U.S. Consulate* is in Bombay, at Lincoln House, 78 Bhulabhai Desai Rd. (tel:022/ 822-3611); *Voltage Guide:* 220 V, two round-pin outlets are used.

Special Trips/Tours

Further afield in N. Karnataka (formerly Mysore), E of Goa, at Hampi, are the medieval *Vijayangar Ruins.* The former capital of one of the largest Hindu empires, the superb ruins are spread over 10 square miles in a magnificent natural setting. Noteworthy sites within the ruins include the *Vittala Temple,* known for its sculptures; the *Veerupaksha Temple;* and the *Lotus Mahal and Watchtower.*

About 300 miles SE of Goa, is the beautiful city of *Mysore,* a craft and incense-manufacturing center. The major attraction, of course, is its *Maharajah's Palace,* one of the largest palaces in India. Built in 1912, the palace is richly decorated in a jumble of styles and, on Sundays and holidays, spectacularly illuminated with thousands of lights. Open 10:30–5:30 daily. The *Deveraja Market* and the *Kaveri Arts* and *Crafts Emporium,* are good bets for local crafts. Just S of Mysore is *Chamundi Hill,* with its famous 17th-century statue of Nandi (Shiva's Bull), and, on top, the Sri Chamundeswari Temple and Tower.

Some 25 miles E of Mysore, in *Somnathpur,* is the exquisite 13th-century *Sri Channakeshara Temple,* famous for its wonderful stone sculptures. Many consider it to be one of the most beautiful buildings in the world. About 10 miles N of Mysore are the ruins of *Tipu Sultan's capital on Srirangapatnam,* with its *Daria Daulat Bagh* summer palace; *Sri Ranganatha Hindu temple; Tipu's mausoleum,* the Gumbaz; and *Tipu's old fort and dungeons.* Just over 60 miles N of Mysore is the giant statue of *Gomateswara,* above the town of Sravanbelagola. Almost 60 ft. tall and carved out of a single piece of rock, it is one of the most important Jain pilgrimage centers in India. Several Jain temples and monasteries in the area are also worth visiting.

Weather

Goa has a tropical, monsoon climate. Summers are hot and humid, with daytime high temperatures typically in the high 80s, falling to the upper 70s at night. Winter daytime highs are usually in the low 80s, dropping to the high 60s at night. The rainy season lasts from June through September.

GOA: TEMPERATURES AND PRECIPITATION

Month	J	F	M	A	M	J	J	A	S	O	N	D
Average Daily Temperature												
(Fahrenheit) Max.	83	83	86	89	91	89	85	85	85	89	89	87
Min.	67	67	72	76	80	79	77	76	76	76	73	69
Average Number of Days with Precipitation												
	1	1	0	0	1	14	21	19	13	3	1	0

Madras: India

Sights to See

Fort St. George, South Beach Rd., just N of the Cooum River, on the Bay of Bengal. Built in the 1650s by the British East India Co., it now houses government offices. The *Fort Museum* has a fine collection of East India Co. and British Raj memorabilia. Open 9–5 Sa–Th.

St. Mary's Church, Fort St. George. Dating from the 1670s, it was the first English church in India.

Government Museum and Art Gallery, Pantheon Road, SW of Fort St. George. Fine anthropological, archaeological, and natural history collection, but especially noted for its excellent collection of South Indian bronzes. Open 8–5 Sa–Th.

Parthasarathy Temple Triplicane High Rd., SE of the Government Museum. Dating from the 8th century, and rebuilt in the 16th, it is dedicated to Lord Krishna.

St. George's Cathedral, off Chetti Rd., S of the Government Museum. Early-19th-century structure.

San Thome Cathedral South Beach Rd., E of St. George's Cathedral along the Bay of Bengal. Dating from the early 16th century, it is believed to contain the remains of St. Thomas the Apostle.

The Marina, the long stretch of sandy beach along the Bay of Bengal, N of San Thome Cathedral. In the evenings, fishing boats still come ashore.

Kapaleswarer Temple, off Kutchery Rd., W of San Thome Cathedral. Shiva temple that is noted for its finely carved tower (gopuram).

Guindy Deer Park and Madras Snake Park, at the S edge of Madras. Beautiful park, famous for its black buck Indian antelope. Located inside Guindy Deer Park, the Snake Park contains most types of Indian snake, along with many other reptiles. Open 9–6 daily.

Useful Information

The Indian Government Tourist Office, 154 Anna Salai (tel:88-685); *Tamil Nadu Tourism Development Corporation,* 143 Anna Salai, (tel:84-0752); *U.S. Consulate,* Mount Rd. (tel:473-040); *Voltage Guide:* 220 V, two round-pin outlets are used.

Special Trips/Tours

Kanchipuram, one of India's seven sacred cities, is just 40 miles SW of Madras. One of India's most spectacular temple cities, with some 150 temples dating from the 7th to 13th centuries A.D., it should not be missed. Especially noteworthy are the *Kailasanatha, Ekambareshwara, Varadarajaswamy,* and *Vaikuntaperumal temples.* The *Ekambareshwara Temple,* one of the largest Kanchipuram temples, is famous for its tall gopuram (190-ft. tower), huge outer stone wall, and interior hall. The *Kailasanatha Temple,* one of the oldest, is noted for its remnants of 8th-century murals. The *Varadarajaswamy Temple* is especially known for its many pillared hall, each of which is covered with sculptured figures. The *Vaikuntaperumal Temple* is also noted for its elegant sculptures.

About the same distance S of Madras on the coast, is the fishing village of *Mahabalipuram,* famous for its shore temples. With about 70 rock-cut monoliths and monuments, it, too, should not be missed. Its magnificent beach also makes it appealing. Particularly noteworthy are the *Krishna Mandapam,* with its pastoral scene carvings; the nearby *Arjuna's Penance,* a huge relief sculptured on a rock face; a group of Rathas (temple chariots), the *Five Rathas,* monolithic monuments carved out of solid rock; and the 8th-century *Shore Temples,* surrounded by dozens of stone bulls.

Further afield in Tamil Nadu is *Thanjavor* (Tanjore), another town with a number of beautiful temples built during the Chola dynasty of the 9th to 13th centuries. Just over 200 miles SW of Madras, the town has India's tallest ancient monument, the *Brihadesvara Temple,* with its 13-tiered tower. Surrounded by fortified walls and a moat, this superb temple is also known for its painted murals, huge Nandi guarding the gateway to the inner courtyard, and carved stonework. Near the temple is a huge 16th-century palace containing the *Thanjavor Art Gallery,* which has a fine collection of Chola bronze sculptures.

Weather

Madras has a hot and humid tropical monsoon climate. Summer daytime high temperatures are typically in the high 90s or low 100s, dropping to the low 80s or high 70s at night. Winter daytime highs are usually in the mid 80s, falling to the high 60s at night. The rainy season extends from July through December.

MADRAS: TEMPERATURES AND PRECIPITATION

Month	J	F	M	A	M	J	J	A	S	O	N	D
Average Daily Temperature												
(Fahrenheit) Max.	85	88	91	95	101	100	96	95	94	90	85	84
Min.	67	68	72	78	82	81	79	78	77	75	72	69
Average Number of Days with Precipitation												
	2	1	1	1	1	4	7	8	7	11	11	5

Bali: Indonesia

Sights to See

Museum Bali, between Jalan Surrapati & Jalan Sugianjar, just E of Letda Sudu Wisnu, central Denpasar. Excellent collection of prehistoric and modern Balinese art. Open 8–12 Tu–Th, Su, and 8–11 A.M. F–Sa.

Pura Jagatnatha Temple, next to the Museum Bali. The state temple, dedicated to the supreme god, Sanghyang Widi. The throne is made of white coral.

Bali Arts Centre, at Abiankapas at the E end of Denpasar, along Jalan Hayam Wuruk. Exhibits of modern Balinese paintings and wood carving, plus dances and recitations of classical literature. Open 8–5 Tu–Su.

Kuta Beach, S of Denpasar on the W side of the isthmus to the Bukit peninsula. Fine palm-fringed beach, noted for its sunsets.

Sanur, SE of Denpasar. Bali's premier resort area. There is a beach market with food stalls and the offshore reef is accessible at low tide.

Pura Luhur Ulu Watu Temple, at the W tip of the Bukit peninsula S of Denpasar. Situated at the edge of a 300-ft. cliff, this 10th-century temple is noted for its unusual arched gateway.

Museum Puri Lukisan (Museum of Fine Arts), Ubud, N of Denpasar. Excellent collection of modern Balinese art housed in buildings surrounded by beautiful gardens with statues and fountains. Open 8–4.

Monkey Forest, Monkey Forest Rd., just S of Ubud. A small remnant of jungle, inhabited by a troop of monkeys. Visitors stroll through, passing out peanuts.

Goa Gajah (Elephant Cave), between Ubud and Pejeng. An 11th-century Buddhist or Hindu monastery/shrine, known for its elaborately carved entrance.

Kertha Gosa (Hall of Justice), Klungkung, E Bali. A superb example of the Klungkung architectural style.

Pura Besakih Temple, some 3,000 ft. up on the slopes of Gunung Agung mountain in E Bali. This complex of 30 separate temples/shrines, over 1,000 years old, is Bali's largest and holiest temple.

Tanah Lot Temple, on a huge offshore rock, on Bali's SW coast, SW of Kediri on the main Denpasar-Tabanan-Negara road. One of Bali's most spectacular temples.

Pura Taman Ayun Temple, Mengwi, just NE of Kediri. Surrounded by a wide moat, this large state temple is considered to be one of Bali's most beautiful.

Mt. Batur Crater and Lake Batur, N Bali. Reached by the road to Penelokan via Tampaksiring N of Denpasar. Panoramic views and the Pura Ulun Danu temple. Visit the Kintamani market on the W rim.

Useful Information

Bali Government Tourist Office, Renon Civic Centre, Denpasar; closest *U.S. Embassy* is in Jakarta, at Jalan Medan Merdeka Selatan 5, (tel:21/360-360); *Main Post Office,* Jalan Puputan Raya between Sanur and Denpasar; *Emergency*—contact your hotel; *Voltage Guide:* 110/220 V, two round-pin outlets are used.

Special Trips/Tours

Just a short flight or a somewhat longer ferry ride away is *Lombok,* Bali's neighboring island to the E. An unspoiled island about the same size as Bali, it is known for its beautiful beaches and interior volcanic mountains, topped by the 12,228-ft. *Rinjani.* Notable sights include *Cakra,* a crafts center, the *Pura Meru temple* outside Cakra, the *Lingsat temple complex* N of Narmada, the *Sembulan Valley* below *Mount Rinjani,* and *Senggigi Beach* N of Ampenan.

Weather

Bali's daytime high temperatures are remarkably uniform throughout the year, reaching into the high 80s, falling to the mid to low 70s at night. Although typically short in duration, rainfall is heavy with frequent thunderstorms. The wet season is from December through March.

BALI: TEMPERATURES AND PRECIPITATION

Month	J	F	M	A	M	J	J	A	S	O	N	D
Average Daily Temperature												
(Fahrenheit) Max.	84	84	85	86	87	86	86	87	87	87	69	84
Min.	74	75	74	74	74	72	70	70	70	72	74	74
Average Number of Days with Precipitation												
	18	17	15	11	9	7	5	4	5	8	12	14

Jakarta: Indonesia

Sights to See

Medan Merdeka (Freedom Square), in the center of the city. Dominated by the city's landmark National Monument (Monas), a 400-ft. structure topped by a gold-plated flame. Beneath the Monas is a gallery of dioramas depicting Indonesia's struggle for independence. Good panoramic views from the top of the Monas.

National Museum (Gedang Gajah), on Jalan Merdeka Barat, immediately W of the square, across Jalan Husni Thamrin. Noted for its superb ceramics, along with its fine exhibits of archaeological, ethnological, and historical artifacts. Open 8–2 Tu–Th, 8–11 A.M. F–Sa, 8–3 Su.

Textile Museum, on Jalan Satsuit Tuban W of the National Museum. Known for its fine batik and weaving collection. Open the same hours as the National Museum.

Merdeka Palace, on the NW corner of the square. The official residence of the president. Not open to the public.

Istiqial Mosque, just NE of the square. An impressive, massive modern structure.

Pasar Baru Market, N of the mosque across Jalan Dr. Sutomo. Try some of the dishes from the food stalls in this colorful market.

Jakarta City museum, Taman Fatahillah Square, in Kota (Old Jakarta), N of Medan Merdeka near Kota Station. Noted for its collection of colonial Dutch artifacts, and exhibits tracing the city's development. Open Tu–Su.

Wayang Museum, Fatahillah Square. Noted for its fine Indonesian puppet collection. Open 9–1 Th–Su.

Sunda Kelapa, the old Dutch port north of Kota is a fascinating harbor area full of sailing ships, and the beautiful Makassar schooners. Visit the early morning fish market at Pasar Ikan, and the maritime museum (Museum Bahari).

Ancol Beach Resort (Taman Impian Jaya Ancol), a large amusement/recreation complex, off Jalan Laksamana Martadinata E of Sunda Kelapa. An oceanarium, art market (Pasar Seni), theater, marina, bowling alleys, and beachside picnic areas.

Useful Information

Directorate General of Tourism Office, Jalan Kramat Raya 81 (tel:348-480); *Visitor's Information Center,* Jalan Thamrin 9 (tel:354-094); *Taxi* (tel:325-607); *Police* (tel:110); *U.S. Embassy,* Jalan Medan Merdeka Selatan 5 (tel:360-360); *Voltage Guide:* 110/220 V, two round-pin outlets are used.

Special Trips/Tours

Taman Mini-Indonesia, near the Halim airport S of central Jakarta. An interesting open-air museum that depicts the various ethnic groups and cultures of Indonesia, including 27 traditional houses representing the 27 provinces of Indonesia. Open 9–5 daily.

The well-known *Bogar Botanical Gardens* (Kebun Raya), are in Bogar, some 37 miles S of Jakarta. Adjoining a fine Dutch-built palace, these beautifully landscaped gardens are noted for their herbarium and orchid house, and contain thousands of species of tropical plants.

Further afield, in central Java, is the beautiful city of *Yogyakarta,* steeped in Javanese culture and history. Known for its ancient Buddhist and Hindu temple sites, the city is also famous for its 18th-century *Sultan's Palace* (Kraton), a walled city noted for its magnificent pavilions and traditional architecture. Be sure to visit the *Museum Sono-Budoyo.* Jalan Malioboro is the street for the leather goods, silverware, and batik shops that the city is known for.

Weather

Jakarta has a tropical, monsoon climate, with warm to hot and humid summers, and winters with temperatures only a few degrees lower than those in the summer. Summer daytime high temperatures typically reach into the high 80s, falling to the mid 70s at night. Winter daytime highs are usually in the mid 80s, also dropping to the mid 70s at night. Rainfall, well distributed throughout the year, is normally heavy. The wet season is from November to March.

JAKARTA: TEMPERATURES AND PRECIPITATION

Month	J	F	M	A	M	J	J	A	S	O	N	D
Average Daily Temperature												
(Fahrenheit) Max.	84	84	86	87	87	87	87	87	88	87	86	85
Min.	74	74	74	75	75	74	73	73	74	74	74	74
Average Number of Days with Precipitation												
	18	17	15	11	9	7	5	4	5	8	12	14

Kyoto: Japan

Sights to See

Kyoto Imperial Palace, Imadegawa & Karasuma Sts. Residence of the Imperial family from 1331 to 1868. Repeatedly destroyed by fires, the present classically simple structure dates from 1855. The garden, Shishinden Hall, Seiryoden Hall, and Kogosho Palace are particularly noteworthy. NOTE: to visit the Imperial Palace, apply for a pass with your passport, 20 minutes before the 10 A.M. or 2 P.M. tour, at the Imperial Household Agency office (open 9–12, 1–4 M–F, 9–12 Sa) located in the NW corner of the outer palace grounds.
Nijo Castle, off Oike between Sembon & Horikawa Sts. A spacious Shogun residence built in 1603, noted for its interior decorations and architectural beauty. Do not miss the meticulous Ninomaru Garden. Open Tu–Su.
Heian Shrine, off Marutamachi St. at Higashioji St. Late-19th-century Shinto shrine with vermillion-lacquered buildings and a beautiful garden.
Higashi-Honganji Temple, Shichijo & Karasuma Sts., N of Kyoto Station. The city's largest wooden structure, this Jodo-Shinshu Buddhist temple was built in 1895. Open 9–5 daily.
Nishi-Honganji Temple, just W of the Higashi-Honganji Temple. The other main temple of the Judo-Shinshu sect of Japanese Buddhism, with fine architecture and wood sculpture. Apply at the temple office for admission to the inner buildings. Open 9–5 daily.
Toji Temple, across the railroad tracks, just south of the above two temples. Its pagoda is the highest (200 ft.) in Japan. Open 9–5 daily.
Kyoto National Museum, a few blocks E of Kyoto Station. Excellent collection of Japanese prehistoric, religious, and secular art. Open 9–4 daily.
Sanjusangendo Temple, near the National Museum. A 13th-century Buddhist temple known for its unique gilded sculptures. Open 9–5 daily.
Ryoanji Temple, NW of central Kyoto, in the Nishijin district of Kyoto. Noted for its rock and sand garden, a superb example of the dry landscape garden developed for Zen temples. Open daily.
Kinkakuji Temple (Golden Pavilion), just to the E of Ryoanji Temple, is famous for its gold-leaf pavilion, and its beautiful garden.

Useful Information

Tourist Information Center (TIC), Kyoto Tower Bldg., Higashi-Shiokojicho, Shimogyo-ku (tel:371-5649); *Home Visit Program* (visit a Japanese home and chat for a few hours—Tourist Section, Kyoto City Government, Kyoto Kaikan Bldg., Okazaki, Sakyo-ku, tel:752-0215); *Teletourist Service for Special Events* announcements in English (tel:361-2911); closest *U.S. Consulate* is in Osaka, at 11–15 Nishitenma 2-chome, Kita-ku (tel:06/315-5900); *Voltage Guide:* 110 V, two flat, parallel blade outlets are used.

Special Trips/Tours

Toei Uzumasa Movie Village, near the Uzumasa Station on the Keifuku Railway's Arashiyama Line, in the Ukyoku district of W Kyoto. A film studio, with large-scale open sets depicting feudal Japanese village life. Watch the filming and visit the Film Art Hall and the village's laboratory. Open 9–5 daily, March–Nov. 15, shorter hours the rest of the year.

Nara, Japan's capital from A.D. 710 to 784, and often called the cradle of Japan's arts, crafts, literature, and industries, is only 26 miles S of Kyoto. Principal sights in the area, include *Kasuga Grand Shrine; Todaiji Temple,* known for its "Daibutsu," the world's largest bronze statue of Buddha, itself housed in the world's largest wooden structure; *Nara National Museum; Kofuku-ji Temple;* and *Nara Park* (Deer Park), famous for its tame deer. About 45 minutes outside Nara, the world renowned *Horyuji Temple,* repository of some of the country's best architectural, sculptural, and pictorial art objects, is worth visiting.

Weather

Kyoto has a temperate climate, with changeable weather at all times of the year. Summer daytime high temperatures typically reach into the mid 80s, falling to the low 70s at night. Winter daytime highs are usually in the upper 40s or low 50s, dropping to the low 30s at night.

KYOTO: TEMPERATURES AND PRECIPITATION

Month	J	F	M	A	M	J	J	A	S	O	N	D
Average Daily Temperature												
(Fahrenheit) Max.	47	48	54	65	72	77	86	85	79	72	61	50
Min.	30	32	35	47	55	62	73	72	67	56	42	31
Average Number of Days with Precipitation												
	5	7	9	10	9	13	11	8	10	7	5	4

Osaka: Japan

Sights to See

Osaka Castle, across the Tosabori River from central Osaka, and a 15-minute walk from Tanimachi-Yon-chome subway station. The castle tower is a reproduction of the 16th-century original. Visit the historical museum inside the tower, and catch the view from the 7th floor. Open 9–8:30 in summer, 9–5 the rest of the year.

Temmangu Shrine, just to the E of City Hall, 3 minutes from Minamimorimachi subway station, was founded in the 10th century. The great 9th-century scholar Sugawara Michizane, God of Academics, is enshrined here and it is the site of the July "Tenjin Matsuri" Festival.

Museum of Oriental Ceramics, Nakanoshima Park, close to City Hall. Excellent collection of antique Chinese and Korean ceramics. Open 9:30–4:30 Tu–Su.

Ohatsu Tenjin Shrine, on the other side of City Hall, a 10-minute walk from Osaka Station, in the Sonazaki amusement district. Setting of the famous "Lovers' Suicide at Sonezaki" story.

Matchomachi-suji Ave., home of the toy, firework, and doll dealers that Osaka is well known for. Most are open to the public.

Shitennoji Temple, in S central Osaka, just N of the Tennoji Station. Founded in the 6th century, it is the oldest temple in Japan, although the pagoda, main hall, Deva Gate, and the Gate of Happiness are reconstructions of the originals. Known for its murals, sacred stone arch, paintings, and sculptures.

Tennoji Park, W of the Temple, contains a botanical garden, a zoo, and a library.

Osaka City Art Museum, Tennoji Park, has a fine collection of ancient and modern arts. Open 9:30–5 Tu–Su.

Tsutenkaku Tower, adjacent to Tennoji Park, a 5-minute walk from Ebisucho subway station. Fine view of the city from its 300-ft. observation dock.

Sumiyoshi Shrine, at the S edge of Osaka, near Sumiyoshi-Koen Station, founded in the 3rd century. The present 19th-century buildings are noted for their unique architectural style. Famous for the arched bridge in the Shrine's grounds.

Useful Information

Osaka Tourist Association, Osaka Municipal Government, Semba Center Bldg. (No. 2), Samba-ku (tel:261-3948); *Osaka City Tourist Information Office,* East Exit, JNR Osaka Station (tel:345-2189); *Japan Travel Phone,* a nationwide telephone service for those who need English-language assistance or travel information, toll-free outside Tokyo or Kyoto, dial 106 and tell the operator "Collect call, T.I.C. please," service available 9–5 daily; *U.S. Consulate,* Sankei Bldg., 11–15 Nishitema 2-chome, Kita-ku (tel:315-5900); *Voltage Guide:* 110 V, two flat, parallel blade outlets are used.

Kyoto, some 37 miles N of Osaka, and world-renowned for its temples, shrines and beautiful gardens, is one of the world's most attractive cities. Principal attractions, include *Kyoto Imperial Palace, Nijo Castle, Heian Shrine, Higashi and Nishi Shrines, Toji Temple, Kyoto National Museum,* and the *Sanjusangendo, Ryoanji,* and *Kinkakuji temples.*

Nara, Japan's capital in the 8th century, and often called the cradle of Japan's arts, crafts, literature, and industries, is about 19 miles E of Osaka. Sights to see include *Kasuga Grand Shrine, Todaiji Temple, Nara National Museum, Kofuku-ji Temple,* and *Nara Park.*

Takarazuka, a spa resort between Osaka and nearby Kobe to the west, is home to the *Takarazuka Family Land* (containing a zoo, botanical gardens, hot-spring baths, and amusement facilities), and the *Takarazuka Grand Theater.* The theater features the well-known "Takarazuka Revue," an all-female musical group. Open 9:30–5 Th–Tu.

Weather

Osaka has a temperate climate, with changeable weather at all times of the year. Summer daytime high temperatures typically reach into the mid 80s, falling to the low 70s at night. Winter daytime highs are usually in the upper 40s, dropping to the low 30s or high 20s at night. The wettest months are July, September, and October.

OSAKA: TEMPERATURES AND PRECIPITATION

Month	J	F	M	A	M	J	J	A	S	O	N	D
Average Daily Temperature												
(Fahrenheit) Max.	45	47	54	64	72	77	84	87	80	70	59	50
Min.	28	30	36	47	55	63	71	73	67	56	41	33
Average Number of Days with Precipitation												
	5	6	10	10	10	12	10	9	12	11	7	6

Tokyo: Japan

Sights to See

Imperial Palace. The roof of the Palace Hotel offers a good view of the palace and its grounds, which are only open to the general public twice a year (Jan. 2 & April 29). Outside the palace walls along the high-stoned moats are a group of parks, including the East Garden (Higashi Gyoen). Open 9–4 Tu–Su.
Kitanomaru Park, immediately N of the palace. A fine park with pleasure boating on Chidorigafuchi.
National Museum of Modern Art, Kitanomaru Park. Occasional exhibitions of Japanese and Western art. Also noted for its crafts gallery, which houses a unique contemporary collection. Open Tu–Su.
Korakuen Garden, N of the palace, just S of Kasuga-dori Ave. One of the great classical gardens.
Ginza, Japan's most famous shopping district, with giant department stores (depatos), and smaller specially shops. Centered on the intersection of Chuo-dori & Harumi-dori Sts., the Ginza district is full of boutiques, restaurants, bars, and nightclubs.
Tokyo Tower, SW of Ginza in Shiba Park, off Hibiya-dori Ave. On a smog-free day, it affords magnificent panoramas, including Mt. Fuji.
Meiji Shrine, to the W of the central city, near the Meiji-Jingumae subway station. One of the finest in Japan, located in serene, heavily wooded grounds. Visit the Treasure House, N of the main shrine building, and the iris garden.
Shinjuku Gyoen National Garden, across Koshu-Kaido Ave. from the Meiji Shrine, at the Shinjuku-Gyoenmae subway station. One of Tokyo's largest and most popular parks. Open 9–4 Tu–Su.
Ueno Park, NE of the city center, at the Ueno subway station. Site of some of

the best museums in Tokyo, including the *Tokyo National Museum* (one of the finest collections of Japanese and Asian art in the world), the *National Science Museum,* (international and Japanese scientific achievement exhibits).

Useful Information

Tourist Information Center (TIC), 6-6 Yurakucho 1-chome, Chiyodaku (tel:502-1461); NOTE: *Japan Travel Phone* is a nationwide telephone service for those in need of English language assistance. Toll-free outside Tokyo—dial 106 and tell the operator, "Collect call, T.I.C. please"; 9–5 daily. In Tokyo, call 502-1461; *U.S. Embassy,* 10–1 Akasaka 1-chome, Minato-ku (tel:224-5000); *Events Phone*—in English (tel:503-2911); *Voltage Guide:* 110 V, two flat, parallel blade outlets are used.

Special Trips/Tours

Nikko National Park, is situated in beautiful mountains just out side Nikko, some 93 miles N of Tokyo. It is noted for its lakes (particularly Lake Chuzenji), waterfalls (Kegon Waterfall and Dragon's Head Cascade), and forests. The area is also famous for its superb shrines and temples, including the *Toshogu Shrine, Rinnoji Temple,* and *Daiyuin Mausoleum.*
Fuji-Hakone-Izu National Park, SW of Tokyo is about 3 hours away by train, and is one of Japan's more popular tourist destinations. *Mt. Fuji* (Fuji-san) can be partially "scaled" by taking the bus up to the 8,250-ft. level (from Kawaguchi-ko). The panoramas are worth the trip. *Hakone* is a volcanic mountain area, known for its hot springs. The *Izu Peninsula* is known for its beautiful coastal and island scenery.

Weather

Tokyo has a temperate climate, with very changeable weather. Summer daytime high temperatures typically reach into the mid 80s, dropping to the low 70s or high 60s at night. Winter daytime highs usually are in the upper 40s or low 50s, falling to around 30 at night. September and October are the wettest months, with occasional heavy rains and strong winds.

TOKYO: TEMPERATURES AND PRECIPITATION

Month	J	F	M	A	M	J	J	A	S	O	N	D
Average Daily Temperature												
(Fahrenheit) Max.	47	48	54	63	71	76	83	86	79	69	60	52
Min.	29	31	36	46	54	63	70	72	66	55	43	33
Average Number of Days with Precipitation												
	5	6	10	10	10	12	10	9	12	11	7	5

Seoul: South Korea

Sights to See

Kyongbok (Great Happiness) Palace, located behind the Capitol Building in central Seoul. Dating from the 14th century, and rebuilt in the original style in 1867, it is noted for its grand Throne Room, and beautiful Kyongheru Banquet Hall. The grounds contain some extraordinarily fine buildings and ancient pagodas.

National Museum, Kyongbok Palace. Fine collection of Korean painting, sculpture, and pottery, along with stone and brass Buddhas. Open 9–6 Tu–Su.

National Folk Art Museum, Kyongbok Palace. Exhibits of traditional houses, clothing styles, and Korean festivals. Open 9–6 W–M.

Changdok (Illustrious Virtue) Palace, E of Kyongbok Palace, off Yulor-ro. Dating from the late 14th century, rebuilt in the 17th, it is the best preserved of Seoul's five palaces. The grounds contain the Tohnwa Mun (Gate of Mighty Transformation), the Kumchongyo (Forbidden Stream Bridge), and the Injongjon (Hall of Benevolent Government). NOTE: You must join a tour group to see the palace and the adjacent *Secret Garden (Piwon),* a 78-acre wooded parkland surrounding Changdok Palace. Ponds, springs, pleasure pavilions, and stone bridges in beautifully landscaped gardens. Tours start at 10:40, 1:10, and 3:40 during the summer.

Chong Myo Royal Shrine, just S of the Changdok Palace. The ancestral tablets of the Yi Dynasty kings and queens are housed in traditional Korean temples.

Toksu (Virtuous Longevity) Palace, immediately W of City Hall across Taepyeong-ro. Former seat of government in the 17th, late 19th and early 20th centuries. Be sure to visit the *Museum of Modern Art* in the Palace grounds.

Pagoda Park, at intersection of Chong-ro & Samil-ro. Noted for its finely sculptured 13-story pagoda.

Namdaemun (South Gate) Market, between Namdaemun-ro and Taege-ro, NE of Seoul Railway Station. A bustling, colorful market full of vendors plying their wares.

Seoul Tower, Namsan Park, in S central Seoul. A 445-ft. tower that affords magnificent views of the city from its observation platform.

Useful Information

Seoul Tourist Information (tel:756-4819); *Korea National Tourism Corp.,* Kukdong Bldg., Chung-gu, 3-ka (tel:261-7001/6); *American Express,* Daewoo Center, 541, 5-ka, Namdaemun-ro, Chung-ku (tel:753-2435); *U.S. Embassy,* 82 Sejong-ro, Chongro-ku (tel:732-2601); *Voltage Guide:* 110 V, two flat, parallel blade outlets are used.

Special Trips/Tours

The *Korean Folk Village* is near Suwon, some 25 miles S of Seoul off the Seoul-Pusan Expressway. An entire village of the Yi dynasty is re-created with the houses, crafts, occupations, and lifestyles of rural communities depicted. There are craft demonstrations, restaurants, and exhibitions of folk dancing, acrobatics, and puppet plays. The walled city of Suwon is worth seeing itself. The walls, dating from the late 18th century, and recently restored, offer good vantage points of the city. The beautiful *Rainbow Gate* is just E of the North Gate.

Kyongju, capital of the Silla Kingdom from 313 to 939 is definitely worth the $4\frac{1}{2}$-hour train trip if you have the time. Visit the branch of the National Museum, Tumuli Park and its Heavenly Horse Tomb (Chonma-chong), and the Punhwang-sa Pagoda.

Weather

Seoul has a continental type of climate, with warm to hot summers, and cold winters. Summer daytime high temperatures typically reach into the mid 80s, falling to the low 70s at night. Winter daytime highs are usually in the 30s, dropping to the low 20s at night. The rainy season is from June through September.

SEOUL: TEMPERATURES AND PRECIPITATION

Month	J	F	M	A	M	J	J	A	S	O	N	D
Average Daily Temperature												
(Fahrenheit) Max.	32	37	47	62	72	80	84	87	78	67	51	37
Min.	15	20	29	41	51	61	70	71	59	45	32	20
Average Number of Days with Precipitation												
	8	6	7	8	10	10	16	13	9	7	9	9

Kuala Lumpur: Malaysia

Sights to See

Jame Mosque (Masjid Jame), in K.L.'s center, where the Kelang and Gombak rivers meet. Beautifully situated in a grove of coconut palms, this fine old red and white mosque is built in the traditional Arabian style.
Chinatown, just S of the Masjid Jame. Centered on the busy Jalan Petaling. Visit the ornate Chan See Shu Yuen temple on Jalan Petaling.
Railway Station, on Jalan Damansara S of Chinatown. Beautiful early-19th-century Moorish-style building with domes, arches, pillars, and minarets.
National Art Gallery, next to the Malayan Railways headquarters, opposite the railway station. Collection of works by Malaysian artists. Open 10–6 daily.
National Mosque (Masjid Negara), NW of the railway station, off Jalan Venning. A modern mosque, built in the traditional decorative Muslim style, it is one of the largest in SE Asia.

National Museum (Muzium Negara), on Jalans Damansara at the entrance to the Lake Gardens W of the railway station. Fine collection of local and regional antiquities. Open 9–6 Sa–Th, 9–12, 2:45–6 F.

National Monument, off Jalan Parlimen in Lake Gardens. A bronze sculpture depicting soldiers holding up the national flag, it commemorates the successful conclusion of a struggle against terrorists in the 1950s.

Lake Gardens (Tasek Perdana). In addition to the National Museum and Monument, the gardens are also the site of Parliament House, and a lake for boating. The gardens also offer good views of K.L.

Sunday Market, on Jalan Raja Muda, NE of the city center. A very colorful Malay-style bazaar held on Saturday nights. Sample the many different Malay foods offered.

Useful Information

Tourist Development Corp. (TDC) Information Office, 17/F, Wisma MPI, Jalan Raja Chulan (tel:423-033); *Tourist Information* (tel:80-778); *American Express,* Jalan Raja Chulan (tel:289-911); *U.S. Embassy,* 376 Jalan Tun Razek (tel:248-9011); *Emergency* (tel:999 for fire, police, and ambulance); *Voltage Guide:* 220 V, two round-pin or three-prong rectangular blade outlets are used.

Special Trips/Tours

The famous *Batu Caves* are just 8 miles N of K.L. on the road to Ipoh. These huge natural caverns, containing a Hindu shrine, are illuminated to show off the stalagmites and stalactites. Another 6 miles farther N along the same road is *Templer Park,* a tropical forest preserve, with walking paths through the jungle, waterfalls, and limestone cliffs affording fine views.

The ancient port and former capital city, *Melaka* (Malacca), about midway between K.L. and Singapore, is Malaysia's most historic town, and is well worth a side trip. Founded in the early 15th century, this predominantly Chinese city has a number of sights, including the 17th century *Dutch Stadthuys* (town hall), now an interesting museum; *Cheng Hoon Tang Temple,* the oldest Chinese temple in the country; *Tranquerah Mosque;* and the *Porta de Santiago,* the one remaining relic of the 16th-century A'Famosa Portugese fortress.

Weather

Kuala Lumpur has a tropical equatorial climate with high temperatures that do not vary very much throughout the year. Summer daytime high temperatures are typically in the high 80s or low 90s, dropping to the mid to low 70s at night. Winter temperatures differ from those of the summer by only a degree or two. Humidity is high all year. There are two rainy seasons, one in March–May, and another in September–November, although all months receive quite a bit of rain.

KUALA LUMPUR: TEMPERATURES AND PRECIPITATION

Month	J	F	M	A	M	J	J	A	S	O	N	D
Average Daily Temperature												
(Fahrenheit) Max.	90	92	92	91	91	91	90	90	90	89	89	89
Min.	72	72	73	74	73	72	73	73	73	73	73	72
Average Number of Days with Precipitation												
	14	14	17	20	16	13	12	14	17	20	20	18

Singapore

Sights to See

Sri Mariamman Temple, South Bridge Rd. Singapore's oldest Hindu temple, noted for its towering entrance with multicolored gods, goddesses, soldiers, and cows.

Thian Hock Keng Temple (Tian Fu Gong), Telok Ayer St. A beautiful Taoist temple with pillars, stonework, and carvings from China.

National Museum and Art Gallery, Stamford Rd. A diverse collection with emphasis on items from SE Asia, but particularly noted for its Haw Par collection of priceless jade and other precious carved stone. Open 9–5:30 daily.

Arab Street. Originally set aside for Arabs and other Muslims, this colorful street and adjoining lanes are full of Muslim traders selling their diverse wares. Visit the nearby *Sultan Mosque,* on North Bridge Rd.

Siong Lim Temple (Shuang Lin Si), Jolan Toa Payoh. A huge and elaborate Buddhist temple complex noted for its landscaped gardens and fine wood carvings.

Botanic Gardens, at the intersection of Holland and Cluny Rds., NW of central Singapore. Tropical and subtropical plants in profusion, along with an orchid house.

Chinese Garden, Jurong. Based on those of Beijing's Summer Palace. Classical gardens, complete with curving bridges, a pagoda, stone lions, bamboo groves, and lotus-filled ponds. Open 9–6 M–Sa, 8:30–6 Su.

Japanese Garden, off Yuan Ching Road in Jurong near the Chinese Gardens. Splendid formal Seiwaen garden based on models of the 14th & 15th centuries. Open 9–6 M–Sa, 8:30–6 Su.

Jurong Bird Park, between Jalin Ahmad Ibrahim and Jalan Buroh, in W Singapore. A large park, with a huge walk-in aviary, with over 3,000 birds from all over the world. See the bird show at 10:30 and 3:30 daily, and the world's tallest human-made waterfall.

Tiger Balm Gardens (Haw Par Villa), Pasir Panjang Rd. Bizarre fantasyland of stone, where statues and tableaux depict Chinese myths and legends. Open 9–6 daily.

Sentosa Island, off the S tip of Singapore island. A resort island with a wide range of amusements and attractions. Accessible by ferry from the World Trade

Center, or by a cable-car ride from Mt. Faber via Jardine Steps cable station. Open 7:30–11 M–Th, 7:30–12 F–Su.

Useful Information

Singapore Tourist Promotion Board, Tudor Court, Tanglin Rd. (tel:235-6611); *U.S. Embassy,* 30 Hill Street (tel:338-0251); *Emergency* (tel:999 for police, fire, and ambulance); *Taxi* (tel:452-5555); *Voltage Guide:* 110/220 V, three-prong rectangular blade outlets are used.

Special Trips/Tours

A Harbor and Island cruise on a good day is an excellent way to see part of Singapore's bustling port, one of the busiest in the world. Passenger liners, supertankers, container ships, coastal fishing vessels, and Indonesian sailing boats make a very colorful scene. Boats stop at Kusu and St. John's Island, and leave from Clifford Pier on Collyer Quay. Junk cruises are also offered, as are dinner cruises.

Weather

Singapore has a hot, wet humid tropical climate, with little temperature variation from month to month. Summer daytime high temperatures typically reach into the high 80s, dropping to the mid 70s at night. The average high and low temperature in the winter months are perhaps a degree or so cooler. Rainfall is fairly well distributed, although November through January is the wettest period.

SINGAPORE: TEMPERATURES AND PRECIPITATION

Month	J	F	M	A	M	J	J	A	S	O	N	D
Average Daily Temperature												
(Fahrenheit) Max.	86	88	88	88	89	88	88	87	87	87	87	87
Min.	73	73	75	75	75	75	75	75	75	74	74	74
Average Number of Days with Precipitation												
	17	11	14	15	15	13	13	14	14	16	18	19

Manila: Philippines

Sights to See

Intramuros (Walled City), the ruins of the 16th-century Spanish settlement, in central Manila, S of the Pasig River. Many sections of the original walls are intact or under reconstruction.
San Augustine Church, Gen. Luna & Real Sts., Intramuros. The oldest stone church in the Philippines and the only church to survive the Battle of Manila during WW II. Noted for its wood carvings.

Manila Cathedral, N of San Augustine, off Gen. Luna St., Intramuros. Rebuilt after the Battle of Manila. Noted for its stained-glass windows. Excellent views of the city from its bell tower.

Fort Santiago remains, overlooking the Pasig River, off Bonifacio Dr., Intramuros. Infamous dungeons built by the Spanish and used as a prison by the Japanese during WW II. Visit the small museum.

Malacanang Palace, across the Pasig River, on J. P. Laurel overlooking the river. Former home of Spanish and American governors, and Filipino presidents, including Marcos. Now open to the public: 9–11:30 and 2–4 M, W, & Th.

Plaza Miranda, in Qulapo N of the Pasig, across the Quezon Bridge. The focal point of much of Manila, with the *Quiapo Church,* famous for its Shrine of the Black Nazarene, bordering the plaza.

Rizal Park (Luneta), immediately S of Intramuros. Dedicated to the national hero, with a monument and Rizal library. Enjoy the Chinese and Japanese gardens, and the world-famous sunsets over Manila Bay.

National Museum, Agrifina Circle, just NE of Rizal Park. Noted for its fine shell collection, as well as Philippine flora and fauna. Open 9–12, 1–5.

Cultural Center Complex, S of the Manila Yacht Club on Manila Bay. On 1,700 acres of reclaimed land, with the Cultural Center of the Philippines, the Folk Arts Theatre, the Philippines Center for International Trade exhibitions, and the national Design Center.

Nayong Pilipino (Philippine Village), S of downtown, right next to the airport. The traditions and handicrafts of each of the major regions of the Philippines are presented and demonstrated. Open daily.

Useful Information

Tourist Information Center, Ground Floor, Tourism Bldg. Agrifina Circle, Rizal Park (tel:501-703); *U.S. Consulate,* 1201 Roxas Blvd. (tel:521-7116); *Taxi* (tel:995-256, 922-3412, or 707-721); *Voltage Guide:* 110/220 V, two flat, parallel blades or two round-pin outlets are used.

Special Trips/Tours

The former summer capital and resort town of *Baguio,* 5,000 ft. up in the mountains, is some 150 miles N of Manila. Considered to be one of the most beautiful areas in the Philippines, it offers a wide range of recreational opportunities. It is also the stepping-off point for the famous, incredible *rice terraces of Banaue.* Carved out of the mountain sides over 2,000 years ago by tribesmen without metal tools, and up to 500 ft high, they are an engineering marvel. The daylong bus trip through remote mountain country is most worthwhile.

Weather

Manila has a tropical monsoon type of climate with a single season of heavy rain. Spring and summer daytime high temperatures typically reach into the high 80s or low 90s, falling to the mid 70s at night. Winter daytime highs are usually in the mid 80s, dropping to the low 60s at night. Rainfall is especially heavy between July and September.

MANILA: TEMPERATURES AND PRECIPITATION

Month	J	F	M	A	M	J	J	A	S	O	N	D
Average Daily Temperature												
(Fahrenheit) Max.	86	88	91	93	93	91	88	87	88	88	87	86
Min.	69	69	71	73	75	75	75	75	75	74	72	70
Average Number of Days with Precipitation												
	6	3	4	4	12	17	24	23	22	19	14	11

Taipei: Taiwan

Sights to See

National Palace Museum, in the Wai Shuang Hsi suburb across the Keelung River N of central Taipei. Has the world's largest and richest collection of Chinese art. Open 9–5 daily.
National Revolutionary Martyrs' Shrine, Peian Rd., en route to or from the National Palace Museum. A very impressive example of classical Chinese architecture.
Taipei Fine Arts Museum, Chungshan N. Rd., opposite the Zoo. The largest of its kind in SE Asia. Open 9–5 Tu–Su.
Confucian Temple, Chiuchuan Street, in the NW part of central Taipei. Dedicated to the Chinese philosopher Confucius, who is highly respected here.
Chiang Kai-shek Memorial Hall and Gardens, Hsinyi Rd., Section 1. An impressive white marble structure, with a huge blue-tiled traditional roof. Open 9–5 daily.
National Museum of History, 49 Nanhai Rd., just W of the C.K.S. Memorial Hall. Excellent collection of artifacts dating from 2,000 B.C. Open 9–5 daily. In the *Botanical Gardens* to the rear of the museum are the National Science Hall, the National Central Library, and the National Taiwan Arts Hall.
Lungshan (Dragon Mountain) Temple, Kuang Chou St. & Hsi Yuan Rd., NW of the Botanical Gardens. One of the most striking temples in Taiwan, it is the oldest Buddhist temple in Taipei, famous for its stone sculpture, woodcarving, and ornate roof.
Presidential Office Building Plaza, N of the National Museum of History, between Kueiyang Street & Paoching Rd. Dominated by the tall-spired, red brick Presidential Office Building, the plaza is the scene of sunrise and sunset national flag raising and lowering ceremonies. Facing the Presidential Building is the *East Gate,* one of Taipei's four remaining gates.
Taipei New Park, just E of the Presidential Building. A delightful park in the middle of the city, complete with a three-tiered pagoda, pavilions, and a lake.
Taiwan Provincial Museum, at the N end of New Park. Natural history and

anthropological exhibits. Noted for its collection of aboriginal pottery, wood carvings, textiles, and weapons. Open 9–5 daily.

Useful Information

The Tourism Bureau, 9/F, 280 Chunghsiao E. Rd., Sec. 4 (tel:721-8541); *Travel Information Service Center* (tel:712-1212); *English Speaking Telephone Directory Assistance* (tel:311-6796); *American Express,* 3/F, 214 Tunhua N. Rd. (tel:715-1581); *U.S. Embassy*—the *American Institute in Taiwan,* 7 Lane 134, Hsin Yi Rd., Section 3 (tel:709-2000) handles unofficial relations (Taiwan's lack of diplomatic recognition can create problems if you lose your passport, so don't!); *Voltage Guide:* 110/220 V, two flat, parallel blade outlets are used.

Special Trips/Tours

Taroko Gorge is a spectacular 12-mile-long limestone gorge on the island's E coast. The road that has been carved through it, part of the E-W Cross Island Highway, affords magnificent views of the region's rugged, thickly forested scenery.

Sun Moon Lake, in the island's central interior, is just over two hours' drive SE of Taichung, S of Taipei along the N-S Freeway. You can enjoy the mountain scenery, take a lake cruise, visit one or more of the Buddhist temples in the area, or see the nearby aboriginal village. Be sure to see the Tsu En pagoda.

Weather

Taipei has a tropical monsoon climate. Summer daytime high temperatures typically reach into the low 90s, dropping to the mid 70s at night. Winter daytime highs are usually in the mid 60s, falling to the mid 50s at night. The wet season is from May through Sept.

TAIPEI: TEMPERATURES AND PRECIPITATION

Month	J	F	M	A	M	J	J	A	S	O	N	D
Average Daily Temperature												
(Fahrenheit) Max.	66	65	70	77	83	89	92	91	88	81	75	69
Min.	54	53	57	63	69	73	76	75	73	67	62	57
Average Number of Days with Precipitation												
	9	13	12	14	12	13	10	12	10	9	7	8

Bangkok (Krung Thep): Thailand

Sights to See

Temple of the Emerald Buddha (Wat Phra Keo), compound of the Royal Palace, between Maharar and Sanam Chai Roads. A 31 inch figure carved out of translucent emerald-colored jasper, it is particularly venerated. The chapel con-

taining the Buddha is noted for its mother-of-pearl inlaid doors, and murals. Open 9:30–12, 2–4 daily.
Royal Palace compound itself, with the grand *Chakri Palace, Dust Hall,* a splendid example of Thai architecture, and the *Amarin,* especially noted for its gilded thrones. Open 9:30–noon, 2–4 daily.
Temple of the Reclining Buddha (Wat Po), one block S of the Royal Palace. A 160-ft. statue of the Reclining Buddha with the soles of its feet inlaid with mother-of-pearl. Open 8–5 daily.
Temple of the Dawn (Wat Arun), on the opposite bank of the Chao Phya River across from the Wat Po. Noted for its five tall spires. See the collection of *King's Barges* adjacent to Wat Arun.
National Museum, just N of the Royal Palace. One of the best in SE Asia, it is noted for its collection of Buddhist sculpture, and pieces illustrating Thai life and culture. Open 9–noon, 1–4 Tu–Th, S–Su.
Jim Thompson House, Rama & Phya Thai Rds. Beside a canal with a luxuriant garden. Noted for its superb collection of Asian objets d'art. Open 9:30–3:30 M–F.
Suan Pakkad Palace, Phya Thai & Sri Ayutthaya Rds. Known for its lacquer pavilion, which is decorated with 17th-century gold-leaf murals. Open 9–4 M–Sa.
Pasteur Institute's Snake Farm, Rama IV & Henri Dunant Rds. Poisonous snakes are fed daily and venom is "milked" from cobras and kraits to make serum.
Sunday or Weekend Market, opposite the North Bangkok Bus Terminus. Hundreds of stalls selling everything from antiques and gems to exotic foods and wild animals. Sa & Su.

Useful Information

Tourism Authority of Thailand (TAT), Rajadamnero Nok Ave. (tel:282-1143); *Tourist Police,* same address (tel:281-5051 or 281-0372); *U.S. Embassy,* 95 Wireless Rd. (tel:252-5040); *Emergency* (tel:191); *Voltage Guide:* 220 V, two flat, parallel blade outlets are used.

Special Trips/Tours

The Rose Garden, a riverside tropical park/country club about 56 miles W of Bangkok on the road to Nakhon Pathom. Noted for its Thai Village featuring traditional activities, such as Thai classical dancing, village handicrafts, a Thai wedding ceremony, a Buddhist ordination, sword fighting, and working elephants.
Nakhon Pathom, 37 miles W of Bangkok. Site of the tallest Buddhist monument in the world, the 3,809-ft.-high *Phra Pathom Chedi,* which marks the spot where Buddhism was introduced to the country over 2,000 years ago. Just S of Nakhon Pathom is *Damnoensaduak,* Thailand's most colorful and energetic floating farmers market.

Ayutthaya, some 43 miles N of Bangkok. The capital between 1350 and 1767, it is known for its magnificent ruins of palaces, temples, and fortifications. The principal ruins lie around the Royal Palace (Phra Raja Wang Luang). South of Ayutthaya is *Bang Pa-in,* former summer residence of the early Chakri monarchs.

Weather

Bangkok has a tropical monsoon climate, with uniform temperatures year-round, and a pronounced rainy season (monsoon) from May through October. Summer daytime high temperatures reach into the low 90s, falling to the high 70s at night. Winter daytime highs are usually in the high 80s dropping to the mid to low 70s at night.

BANGKOK: TEMPERATURES AND PRECIPITATION

Month	J	F	M	A	M	J	J	A	S	O	N	D
Average Daily Temperature												
(Fahrenheit) Max.	89	91	93	95	93	91	90	90	89	88	87	87
Min.	68	72	75	77	77	76	76	76	76	75	72	68
Average Number of Days with Precipitation												
	1	1	3	3	9	10	13	13	15	14	5	1

Africa and the Middle East
Alexandria (Al-Iskandariyah): Egypt

Sights to See

Greco-Roman Museum, Sharia el Mathaf, off Sharia Gamel Abdel Nasser. A fine, large collection of antiquities from Alexandria and the Nile delta from the Greco-Roman period. Open 9–4 daily, 9–11:30, 1:30–4 F.
Kom el Dikka Roman Amphitheater, near Masr Station, SW of the Greco-Roman Museum across Sharia Gamel Abdel Nasser. Dating from the 2nd century, this well preserved, white marble amphitheater is in an area still undergoing excavation. Open 9–4 daily.
Pompey's Pillar, Sharia el Amoud el Sawari, SW of the Roman Amphitheater. A single, 84-ft.-high granite victory column erected for emperor Diocletian as part of the Greco-Egyptian Temple of Serapeum (now in ruins). Erroneously connected with Pompey by the Crusaders, the name has persisted. Open 9–4 daily.
Catacombs of Kom el Shogafa, just S of Pompey's Pillar. Dating from the 1st and 2nd centuries, these Roman tombs are noted for the sculptures and reliefs depicting Egyptian gods with Roman bodies. Open 9–4 daily.
Abul Abbas Mosque, just W of the Corniche, between the W and E Harbors, N of Sharia Gamel Abdel Nasser. Fine example of Islamic architecture.

Fort Qait Bay, at the E tip of the peninsula between the W and E Harbors. An Islamic, 15th-century fort built on the ruins of the Pharos Lighthouse. Inside, a Naval Museum is noted for its scale model of the ancient lighthouse. Open 9–2 daily.
Ras el Tin Palace and Gardens, at the W tip of the same peninsula. Former royal palace, now used for visiting dignitaries. Closed to the public, but the gardens are open.
Montazah Palace, E of Alexandria on the shores of the Mediterranean. King Farouk's former summer palace. Closed to the public, but the palace is surrounded by beautifully landscaped gardens. Open 7–sunset daily.

Useful Information

Tourist Office, Shari Nabi Danial, off Midan Saad Zaghloul (tel:80-7611); *American Express,* 26 Sharia el Horriyya; *U.S. Consulate,* 110 Sharia el Horriyya (tel:82-1911); *Voltage Guide:* 110/220 V, two round-pin or three-prong rectangular blade outlets are used.

Special Trips/Tours

El-Alamein, site of one of the decisive battles of WW II when Montgomery's Allied forces halted the advance of Rommel's Afrika Corps, is some 64 miles W of Alexandria on the Mediterranean. On the E side of the village is the British War Cemetery, and on the W side are the German and Italian Cemeteries and the *War Museum.* The museum contains weaponry and military attire. Open 9–6 daily.

On the way to or from El-Alamein, some 7 miles S of Bahig, is *St. Menas.* Site of a once-prosperous town and pilgrimage center, the ruins include several churches, monastery buildings, sacred baths, cemetery, and what's left of the town itself. The *Basilica of Arcadius* is the oldest existing Christian structure in the country.

With one of the best Mediterranean beaches in Egypt, the resort area of *Sidi Abdel Rahman* is some 12 miles further W of El-Alamein. Dine at the El-Alamein Hotel (tel:80-6473).

Still further W along the Mediterranean coast, if you have the time, is *Marsa Matruuh.* Some 180 miles W of Alexandria, it is fast becoming Egypt's principal resort area. Particularly noted for its superb, white sand beaches, it also has a few sights worth seeing, including *Rommel's Cave Museum* (open 10–4 daily); and *Cleopatra's Bath.* Some 15 miles outside Marsa Matruuh is *Ageeba Beach,* considered by many to be one of the most beautiful beaches in the world.

Weather

Alexandria has a Mediterranean climate with hot and sunny summers and warm sunny winters. Summer daytime high temperatures typically reach into the mid to high 80s, dropping to the low 70s at night. Winter daytime highs are usually in the mid to upper 60s, falling to the 50s at night. Rainfall is low, with a short "rainy season" from November through January.

ALEXANDRIA: TEMPERATURES AND PRECIPITATION

Month	J	F	M	A	M	J	J	A	S	O	N	D
Average Daily Temperature												
(Fahrenheit) Max.	65	66	70	74	79	83	85	87	86	83	77	69
Min.	51	52	55	59	64	69	73	74	73	68	62	55
Average Number of Days with Precipitation												
	7	5	3	1	0	0	0	0	0	1	4	7

Cairo (Al-Qahirah): Egypt

Sights to See

Cairo panorama from the Cairo Tower (El Borg) just S of the 6 October Bridge, on El Gezira island in the Nile.

Egyptian Museum, Tahrir Square, next to the Nile Hilton, just S of the 6 October Bridge in downtown Cairo. The world's most important and largest collection of Egyptian antiquities, including 5,000-year-old Pharaonic treasures. Open 8–4 daily.

Mosque of El-Azhar, Shada al-Muizz, at the end of Sharia el-Azhar, E of the downtown area, in the center of the medieval walled city of Cairo. One of the best examples of Islamic architecture in the world. Dating from the 10th century, its university is a leading center of Moslem learning. Open 9–3 Sa–Th, 9–11, 1–3 F.

Museum of Islamic Art, Midan Ahmad Mahar, at Sharia Port Said and Sharia Muhammad Ali, W of the El-Azhar Mosque. One of the world's finest collections of Islamic art. Open 9–4 Sa–Th, 9–11, 1–4 F.

The Citadel, off Shada Salah Salem, S of El-Azhar Mosque. Dating from the 12th century, the Citadel complex is noted for its *Mosque of Muhammad Ali,* a 19th-century Baroque structure famous for its tall minarets and alabaster walls that also affords magnificent views of Cairo. Open 8–6 Sa–Th, 8–12, 1–6 F.

Mosque of Sultan Hassan, Midan Salah el Din, just to the W of, and below, the Citadel. Dating from the 14th century, this massive Mamluk mosque is noted for its interior decorations and inscriptions. Open 8–6 daily.

Mosque of Ibn Tulun, off Sharia Saliba, W of the citadel. Completed in 879, it is Cairo's oldest and largest mosque. It is also considered to be the best example of pure, classic, Islamic architecture. Open 8–6 daily.

Mausoleum of Qaitbay, in the N part of the City of the Dead (El Ashrafiyya), behind the Citadel. Noted for its elaborate stone dome and tall minaret.

Coptic Museum, next to the remains of the Roman Fort of Babylon, Old Cairo, SW of the Citadel toward the Nile. Superb collection of Coptic art and antiquities from A.D. 300–1,000. Open 9–4 Sa–Th, 9–11, 1–4 F.

El Mouallaqa Church, next to the Coptic Museum. Dating from the 4th century, it was constructed over the ruins of the old Roman fortress gateway. Considered to be the most attractive of Cairo's Coptic churches.

Useful Information

Main Tourist Office, 5 Sharia Ada (tel:92-3000); Giza Tourist Office (tel:85-0259); *American Express,* 15 Sharia Kasr el Nil (tel:75-3142); *U.S. Embassy,* 5 Sharia Latin America (tel:355-7371); *Ambulance* (tel:123); *Police* (tel:122); *Voltage Guide:* 110/220 V, two round-pin or three-prong rectangular blade outlets are used.

Special Trips/Tours

The very impressive, monumental *Pyramids of Giza* and the *Sphinx,* Egypt's main tourist attractions, are located just 10 miles W of Cairo. The great *Pyramid of Cheops* (450 ft.), estimated to contain over 2 million tons of stone, dates from about 2,690 B.C., and took some 100,000 laborers 20 years to complete. The *Pyramid of Chephren,* slightly smaller, dates from 2,650 B.C., and the smallest, the *Pyramid of Mykerinus,* dates from about 2,600 B.C. The *Sphinx,* dwarfed by the three pyramids, lies some 500 ft. SE of the Cheops Pyramid. There are six additional pyramids to the S of the Pyramid of Cheops, built to house the remains of the families of the Pharaohs. The Pyramids can be reached by taxi, or by the #8 or 900 bus that leaves from in front of the Mugamma Building on Midan Tahir.

Weather

Cairo has a hot, dry, desert climate. Summer daytime high temperatures typically reach into the mid 90s, dropping to around 70 at night. Winter daytime highs are usually in the upper 60s, falling to the low 50s or high 40s at night. Precipitation is very low year round, with virtually no rain at all from April through October.

CAIRO: TEMPERATURES AND PRECIPITATION

Month	J	F	M	A	M	J	J	A	S	O	N	D
Average Daily Temperature												
(Fahrenheit) Max.	65	69	75	83	91	95	96	95	90	86	78	68
Min.	47	48	52	57	63	68	70	71	68	65	58	50
Average Number of Days with Precipitation												
	1	1	1	0	0	0	0	0	0	0	1	1

Haifa: Israel

Sights to See

Baha'i Shrine and Gardens, Sderot HaZionut, halfway up Mount Carmel. The worldwide headquarters of the Baha'i faith, it is Haifa's best-known landmark.

The views from the formal gardens are magnificent. Open 9–noon daily; gardens from 8–5 daily.

Carmelite Monastery, Derekh Stella Maris, NW of the Baha'i Shrine. An impressive 19th-century church, and a small antiquities museum. Excellent panoramas of Haifa's coastline. Open 8:30–1:30, 3–6 M–Sa.

Elijah's Cave, off Derekh Allenby below the Carmelite Monastery (catch the new funicular down). Holy to Jews, Christians, and Moslems, the caves are believed to have sheltered Elijah the prophet from the wrath of King Ahab. Open 8–6 Su–Th, 8–1 F.

Clandestine Immigration and Naval Museum, 204 Rehov Allenby, opposite Elijah's Cave. Exhibits detailing the illegal immigration during the British blockade. Open 9–3, Su–Th, 9–1 F.

National Maritime Museum, 198 Rehov Allenby, adjacent to the Naval Museum. Jewish contribution to seafaring is highlighted. Open 10–4 Su–Th, 10–1 Sa.

Gan Ha'Em (Mother's Park), Central Carmel, off Rehove Hanassi. A beautiful park. At the NE edge of Gan Ha'Em park, on Rehove HaTishbi, are the Stekelis Museum of Prehistory, Natural History Museum, a Zoo, and the Biological Institute. All open 8–4 Su–Th, 8–1 F, 9–4 Sa.

Tikotin Museum of Japanese Art, 89 Sdero Hanassi, Central Carmel. Fine, small collection. Enjoy the Japanese rock garden. Open 10–5 Su–Th, 10–2 Sa.

Haifa Museum Complex, 26 Rehov Shabbetai Levi, in Ha-Dar. Comprised of the museums of ancient art (excellent Greco-Roman culture and Coptic art collections), modern art, and music and ethnology. Open 10–1 Su–Th, 10–2 Sa, 6–9 Tu, Th, & Sa.

Useful Information

Government Tourist Information Office 27 Sderot Herzl (tel:66-6521); *Post Office*, Rehov Shabbatai Levi & Rehov Hanevi'im; *U.S. Consulate*, 12 Yerushalayim (tel:67-0615); *What's On In Haifa* (tel:640840); *Police* (tel:100 in emergency); *Emergency* (tel:101 for ambulance); *Voltage Guide:* 220 V, two round-pin or two flat, angled blade outlets are used.

Special Trips/Tours

Across Haifa Bay lies *Acre* (Akko), some 15 miles by road. Noted for its 18th-century parapets and much older minarets, this ancient Phoenician port has seen Romans, Arabs, Crusaders, Turks, and, more recently, Jewish immigrants. Notable sights include: the *Mosque of El-Jazzar*, considered to be one of the most beautiful in the country; the subterranean *City of the Crusaders;* the *Citadel-Museum of Heroism;* the *Crypt of St. John;* and the *bazaar* in the narrow, winding medieval street of the Old City.

Nazareth (Nazaret) is only some 21 miles SE of Haifa via Hwy. 75. The road passes through some very scenic countryside, and the *Balfour Forest lookout* just past Migdal HaEmek, affords great vistas of the Jezreel Valley, and the Carmel, Gilboa, and Ephraim mountains. Nazareth's most important sight is the 20th-century *Basilica of the Annunciation,* the largest church in the Middle East, on Rehov Casa Nova. It is especially noted for the many wall murals, mosaics, stained-glass windows, and sculptures donated from countries and individuals around the world.

Tiberias (Teverya) and the *Sea of Galilee,* where the miracles of the New Testament occured, are only about another 20 miles or so NE of Nazareth (40 miles E of Haifa). Once a great center of learning, Tiberias today is Israel's water-sport capital, and a touring base for exploring the area around the Sea of Galilee. The *Kinnereth Sailing Co.* (tel:067-58-007), operates daily cruises from Tiberias to Ein Gev on the opposite shore of the Sea of Galilee.

Weather

Haifa enjoys a Mediterranean climate with hot, dry summers and mild, wetter winters. Summer daytime high temperatures are typically in the high 80s, dropping to the mid 70s at night. Winter daytime highs are usually in the mid 60s, falling to around 50 at night. The "rainy" season extends from November through February.

HAIFA: TEMPERATURES AND PRECIPITATION

Month	J	F	M	A	M	J	J	A	S	O	N	D
Average Daily Temperature												
(Fahrenheit) Max.	65	67	71	77	83	85	88	90	88	85	78	68
Min.	49	50	53	58	65	71	75	76	74	68	60	53
Average Number of Days with Precipitation												
	13	11	7	4	1	0	0	0	0	2	7	11

Jerusalem

Sights to See

Western (Wailing) Wall (HaKotel HaMa'aravi), in the Jewish Quarter of the Old City. A remnant of the Second Temple, it is the holiest of Jewish sites.

Dome of the Rock, Temple Mount, N of the Western Wall. Splendid mosque, known for its intricate mosaics under the golden dome. Open 8–11, 12:15–3, 4–5 Sa–Th.

El Aksa Mosque, at S end of Temple Mount. Noted for its stained-glass windows and Byzantine ceilings.

Via Dolorosa (Way of the Cross), N of Temple Mount in the Moslem Quarter, running SW to the Church of the Holy Sepulchre. The route believed to have been taken by Jesus carrying the cross, with the 14 stations commemorating incidents along the way.

Church of the Holy Sepulchre, in the Christian Quarter. Traditional site of Jesus' crucifixion, burial, and resurrection. Open 4 A.M.–8 P.M.

Mount of Olives (Har Ha-Zetim), NE of the Old City. Site of the world's oldest Jewish Cemetery, many churches, and the Catholic Garden of Gethsemane. Also provides great views of the Old City.

Rockefeller Museum, just N of the Old City on Rehov Sultan Suleiman, near Herod's Gate. Excellent archaeological collection. Open 10–5 Su–Th, 10–2 F, Sa.

Mount Zion (Har Ziyyon), at the SW corner of the Old City opposite Zion Gate. Site of the Coenaculum, Room of Christ's Last Supper, the traditional *Tomb of David,* below, and the *Chamber of the Holocaust* next door. The huge, 20th-century *Dormition Abbey* affords fine panoramas of the city.

Citadel (Tower of David), S of Jaffa Gate, N of Mount Zion. The views from this tower, the highest point in the Old City, are excellent. Catch the evening sound and light show (March 15–November 15), and the audiovisual slide shown in the Jerusalem City Museum in the Crusader Hall of the Western Tower.

Knesset (Parliament), Rehov Eliezer Kaplan, West Jerusalem. Noted for its giant Menorah outside and the Chagall tapestries inside. Guided tours 8:30–2:30 Su & Th.

Israel Museum, Rehov Ruppin on the Hill of Tranquility, S of the Knesset. A complex of several museums, including archaeological, Jewish ceremonial art, and ethnographical collections. Particularly noted for the sculptures in the Billy Rose Art Garden, and the Shrine of the Book, which houses the Dead Sea Scrolls. Open 10–5 Su, M, W, & Th, 4–10 Tu, 10–2 F & Sa.

Useful Information

Government Tourist Information Offices, 24 Rehov Hamelekh George (tel:24-1281); and Jaffa Gate, Old City (tel:28-2295); *Municipal Tourist Information Office,* 17 Rehov Yafo (tel:22-8844); *Main Post Office,* 23 Rehov Yafo; *U.S. Consulate,* 18 Rehov Agron (tel:23-4271) and 27 Rehov Nablus, East Jerusalem (tel:27-2681); *Police* (tel: 100 in emergency); *Ambulance* (tel:101); *Voltage Guide:* 220 V, two round-pin or two flat, angled blade outlets are used.

Special Trips/Tours

Bethlehem, birthplace of Christ, is just 5 miles S of Jerusalem, via Hwy. 60. A destination of pilgrims from all over the world for centuries, particularly around Christmas time, Bethlehem has a number of notable sights, including the *Church of the Nativity,* Manger Square; the *Well of David,* King David St., off Manger Square; the *Milk Grotto,* SE of the Church of Nativity on Milk Grotto St.; *Rachel's Tomb,* Jerusalem Rd.; and *Shepherd's Field* (where an angel appeared to shepherds to announce the birth of Christ), Shepherd's St.

The road W of Jerusalem (Hwy. 1) to the *Dead Sea* (1,300 ft. below sea level), and then S through the desert community of *Qumran* (where the Dead Sea Scrolls were found), and the nature preserve of *Ein Gedi,* to the massive clifftop fortress of *Massada,* makes a fascinating trip. *Massada,* about 70 miles from Jerusalem, is the site of the famous Roman siege of some 960 Jewish zealots in A.D. 70, and a national symbol. Catch the cable-car ride up to the fortress and enjoy the views of the Dead Sea.

Weather

Jerusalem has a Mediterranean climate with hot, dry summers, and mild, wetter winters. Summer daytime high temperatures typically reach into the mid to upper 80s, falling to the 60s at night. Winter daytime highs are usually in the high 50s or low 60s, dropping to the 40s at night. The wet season extends from November through February.

JERUSALEM: TEMPERATURES AND PRECIPITATION

Month	J	F	M	A	M	J	J	A	S	O	N	D
Average Daily Temperature												
(Fahrenheit) Max.	55	56	65	73	81	85	87	87	85	81	70	59
Min.	41	42	46	50	57	60	63	64	62	59	53	45
Average Number of Days with Precipitation												
	9	11	3	3	1	0	0	0	0	1	4	7

Tel Aviv-Jaffa: Israel

Sights to See

Tel Aviv and Jaffa panoramas from the observation deck of the *Shalom Mayer Tower* (Migdal Shalom), Rehov Ahad Ha'Am. Open 9–7 Su–Th, 9–1 F.

Great Synagogue, Rehov Ahad Ha'Am, N of the tower. Noted for its huge dome and stained-glass windows.

Carmel Market (Shuk HaCarmel), Rehov Allenby & Rehov HaCarmel, in the Neve Tzedek quarter NW of Shalom Tower. The city's largest open-air market. Colorful.

Museum of Antiquities (a.k.a. Jaffa Museum), 10 Rehov Mifratz Shlomo, Old Jaffa, SW of Shalom Mayer Tower. Exhibits of local archaeological finds. Open 9–1 Su–F, 6–9 M & Th.

Jaffa Old City itself is a delightful artists' colony, full of private and public galleries, studios, nightclubs, and cafes among restored ruins.

Flea Market (Shuk Hapishpishim), between Rehov Ziyyon & Rehov Me-Ragusa, Old Jaffa. The country's largest.

Helena Rubinstein Art Pavilion, 6 Sderot Tarsat, N of the Shalom Tower, at the N end of Sderot Rothschild. Continually changing art exhibits. Open 9–1, 5–9 Su–Th, 10–2 Sa.

Tel Aviv Museum, 27 Sderot Shaul Hamelekh, NE of the Rubinstein Pavilion. Fine collection of Israeli and international modern art. Open 10–2, 5–9 Su–Th, 11–2 Sa.

Ben Gurion's House, 17 Sderot Ben Gurion, W of Tel Aviv Museum near the Mediterranean shore. Memorabilia and exhibits in the home of Israel's first prime minister. Open 8–2 Su–Th, 5–7 M & Th, 8–1 F, 11–2 Sa.

Ha-Aretz Museum Complex, N of the Yarkon River, on Rehov Hauniversita. Several small museums with folklore, coin, ceramic, science, and technology exhibits, and a planetarium. It is especially noted for the superb *Glass Museum* with its collection of Bronze Age and Islamic glass. Open 9–4 Sa–Th, 9–1 F. *Nahumm Goldmann Museum of the Jewish Diaspora* (Beth Hatefutsoth), Tel Aviv University, Ramat Aviv suburb, NE of the Ha-Aretz Museums. Jewish history illustrated with dioramas, murals, slide and film shows, and models. Open 10–5 Su–Tu, & Th, 10–7 W.

Useful Information

Israeli Government Tourist Office, 7 Rehov Mendele, off Ben Yehuda (tel:22-3266); *American Express,* 16 Rehov Ben Yehuda (tel:29-4654); *U.S. Embassy,* 71 Rehov Hayarkon (tel:65-4338); *Main Post Office,* 132 Rehov Allenby; *Voltage Guide:* 220 V, two round-pin or two flat, angled blade outlets are used.

Special Trips/Tours

A drive down the Mediterranean coast to the excellent beach resort of *Ashkelon,* one of the original Philistine city-states, is well worth it. Apart from the fine beaches, the town offers a number of interesting sights, including a *Roman Tomb* N of Afridar Beach; two *Roman Sarcophagi* in the courtyard of the Afridar Tourist and Cultural Events Center; the ruins of a 5th-century *Byzantine Church;* and a *National Park* with Crusader ruins and sculptures, S of Afridar Beach.

On the way to or from Ashkelon, pass through the *Bat Yam* beach resort area, and, a little inland, *Rishon Le Zion,* the major center of Israel's wine industry.

Some 32 miles N of Tel Aviv lies the Roman capital of Judea, *Caesarea,* one of Israel's premier archaeological sites. The ruins, stretched out along a Mediterranean beach, include a *Roman Amphitheater;* a 12th-century *Crusader City;* a 5th-century Byzantine *Street of Statues;* a Roman *Hippodrome;* and a 2nd-century *Roman Aqueduct.*

Weather

Tel Aviv-Jaffa has a Mediterranean climate with hot, dry summers, and mild, wetter winters. Summer daytime high temperatures are typically in the high 80s, dropping to the mid 70s at night. Winter daytime highs are usually in the mid 60s, falling to around 50 at night. The "rainy" season lasts from November through February.

TEL AVIV: TEMPERATURES AND PRECIPITATION

Month	J	F	M	A	M	J	J	A	S	O	N	D
Average Daily Temperature												
(Fahrenheit) Max.	65	67	71	77	83	85	88	90	88	85	78	68
Min.	49	50	53	58	65	71	75	76	74	68	60	53
Average Number of Days with Precipitation												
	13	11	7	4	1	0	0	0	0	2	7	11

Mombasa: Kenya

Sights to See

Old Harbor, on the E side of Mombasa Island, S of the Nyali Bridge. Small coastal dhows, trading between E. Africa and Somalia, or even Arabia, are frequently in the harbor.

Fort Jesus, off Nkrumah Rd., Old Harbor. Late-16th-century Portugese fort, complete with old cannons. The museum inside illustrates the fort's Portugese, Arab, and British history. Open 9–6 daily.

Customs House and Fish Market off Nkrumah Rd., N of Fort Jesus, Old Harbor. The surrounding shops specialize in Persian Gulf carpets, brassware, and chests.

Old Town, behind the Old Harbor. A maze of narrow streets and passages, with overhanging balconies and carved doorways on the Arab-style houses.

Bazaar, centered along and off Biashara St., between Digo Rd. & Jomo Kenyatta Ave., just W of Old Town. Colorful bazaar full of items from Kenya and East Africa generally.

Elephant Tusks Arch, Moi Avenue. Four crossed steel elephant tusks built in the 1950s to commemorate a visit by British royalty. The city's main landmark.

Uhuru Park and Monument, Moi Ave., W of Mnazi Moia. Mombasa's national freedom monument, commemorating Kenya's independence in 1963.

Digo Road, intersecting Moi Ave., immediately to the W of Old Town. Lined with churches, mosques, Hindu temples, colonial buildings, and street markets.

Diana Beach, 17 miles S of Mombasa. With beautiful white sand and palm trees, and protected by a reef, it is considered to be the best beach among the many stretching for miles along the Indian Ocean S of Mombasa.

Nyali, Bamburi, & Shanzu beaches, N of Mombasa. Good beaches, but more developed, and crowded, than those south of Mombasa.

Useful Information

Visitor Information Bureau, Moi Avenue, near the Elephant Tusks arch (tel:24-173); *American Express,* c/o Express Kenya Ltd., Nkrumah Road (tel:24-461); *Emergency* (tel:999); *U.S. Consulate,* Palli House, Nyerere Ave. (tel:31-5101); *Voltage Guide:* 220 V, two round-pin or three-prong rectangular blade outlets are used.

Special Trips/Tours

Shimba Hills National Reserve, noted for its roan and sable antelope, is just S of Mombasa, inland from the Diani Beach area on a plateau overlooking the Indian Ocean. Buffalo, elephant, lion, and leopard can also be seen on the reserve, as well as much bird life. The entrance is near Kwale, SW of Ngombeni.

About 65 miles N of Mombasa up the coast is the beach resort of *Watamu,* with its water sports and deep-sea fishing. Offshore is the *Watamu Marine National Park,* with glass-bottom-boat rides over the coral gardens. Just NW of

Watamu, inland, are the *Gedi Ruins,* well-preserved remains of a 13th-century Arab-African port town.

Further N up the coast is the big-game fishing canter of Kenya, *Malindi,* about 80 miles N of Mombasa. With an international reputation for its barracuda, sailfish, kingfish, and marlin, it is fast becoming a major resort area in its own right. White sand beaches, coral reefs, golf, horseback riding, scuba diving and snorkeling, in addition to big-game fishing, enhance its allure.

If you have the time, the delightful Afro-Arab town of *Lamu,* some 212 miles N of Mombasa (134 miles N of Malindi), is well worth visiting. Located offshore on Lamu Island, it is almost medieval in character. Most of its buildings date from the late 18th century, although two structures, the *Friday Mosque* and *Pwani Mosque,* date from the early 16th and late 14th centuries, respectively. Known for its maze of narrow streets, overhanging houses and verandahs, shuttered windows, and carved doors, Lamu is a colorful piece of the past, where the inhabitants have changed very little. Noteworthy sights include the *Lamu Museum,* located on the waterfront, with its fine collection of local tribal crafts; the *Friday* and *Pwani mosques;* and the fort, off the main square. Excursions to the 14th- and 15th-century Arab ruins on *Pate* and *Manda island* nearby, are also worthwhile.

Weather

Mombasa has a hot, humid tropical climate. Summer (Dec.–Feb.) daytime high temperatures typically reach into the high 80s, falling to the mid 70s at night. Winter (June–Aug.) daytime highs are usually in the low 80s, falling to the low 70s at night. The rainy season extends from April through June.

MOMBASA: TEMPERATURES AND PRECIPITATION

Month	J	F	M	A	M	J	J	A	S	O	N	D
Average Daily Temperature												
(Fahrenheit) Max.	87	87	88	86	83	82	81	81	82	84	85	86
Min.	75	76	77	76	74	73	71	71	72	74	75	75
Average Number of Days with Precipitation												
	6	3	7	15	20	15	14	16	14	10	10	9

Nairobi: Kenya

Sights to See

National Museum of Nairobi, Museum Hill, off Uhuru Highway. Excellent collection of fossils of prehistoric man, together with displays of birds, mammals, and tribal crafts. Open 9:30–6 daily.

Snake Park, opposite the National Museum. Large collection of snakes and reptiles. Open 9:30–6 daily

City Park, between Forest & Limuru Rds., E of the National Museum. Noted for its flower gardens.

Nairobi Arboretum, Arboretum Rd., W of the National Museum, off State House Rd. Fine collection of over 270 species of trees. Open sunrise–sunset.
Kenyatta International Conference Center, Harambee Ave., between Parliament & Talfa Roads. The city's most famous landmark. The revolving restaurant at the top of the 27-story tower affords magnificent views.
Uhuru Park, across Uhuru Highway, E of the Conference Center. Neatly kept park with a small boating lake.
Municipal Market, just N of Kenyatta Ave., between Koinange & Muidi Mbingu Sts. Colorful produce market.

Useful Information

Nairobi Tourist Office, Moi Ave. & City Hall Way; *U.S. Embassy,* Haile Selassie & Moi Avenues (tel:33-4141); *American Express,* Consolidated House, Standard Street (tel:334-7277); *Voltage Guide:* 220 V, two round-pin or three-prong rectangular blade outlets are used.

Special Trips/Tours

Nairobi National Park, just outside the city, is the closest of Kenya's national parks and game reserves. Containing just about all of Kenya's game species except the elephant, it is noted for its animal orphanage at the park's Langata Rd. entrance.

Part of the *Great Rift Valley,* a deep trench in the earth's crust that stretches all the way from Mozambique to the Red Sea, can be seen from Ngong Hill, 10 miles E of Nairobi. Marked by steep escarpments, the valley floor contains large, shallow alkaline lakes noted for the thousands of colored flamingoes that feed on the algae. *Lake Nakuru,* and its surrounding national park, about 100 miles NW of Nairobi, is renowned for its varied and prolific bird life. *Lake Naivasha,* closer to Nairobi, off the Nairobi-Nakuru road, is also known for its fantastic bird life.

Aberdare National Park, one of the least known, but considered by many to be one of the most attractive parks in Kenya, is due N of Nairobi. The world famous Treetops lodge is located on its E side, just N of Nyeri. *Mount Kenya National Park* to the E of Aberdare, with 17,058-ft. Mt. Kenya as its centerpiece, is probably as famous for its scenery as its wildlife.

The country's best game reserve, the *Masal Mara Game Reserve,* is some 200 miles W of Nairobi across the border from Tanzania's Serengeti National Park. Noted for its large herds of grazing animals, it also has lions, leopards, elephants, buffalos, and rhinos. It is especially famous for the annual (July–Sept.) migration of wildebeest.

Located on the Kenya-Tanzania border 145 miles S of Nairobi, and below the impressive *Mount Kilimanjaro* (19,340 ft.), is *Amboseli National Park,* particularly known for its lions and cheetahs, as well as giraffes and elephants. It is also a Masai reserve.

The country's largest park, *Tsavo National Park,* divided in two by the Nairobi-Mombasa Highway, is about halfway between the capital and the coastal city of Mombasa, 315 miles to the SE. It is especially known for its large herds of elephants, and *Mzima Springs* in the W half of the park. The springs are inhabited by crocodiles and hippos, which can be observed from a glass-paneled tank.

One of the country's newest tourist attractions is *Lake Turkana,* in the Great Rift Valley, some 475 miles N of Nairobi. Put on the map by Richard Leakey's discovery of Australopithecus, this remote, wild corner of Kenya is particularly noted for its beautiful scenery and excellent fishing (famous for its giant Nile perch). The region is also home to the colorful, nomadic herdsmen, the Turkana. *Ferguson's Gulf* is the sport-fishing center on the lake's western shore. Launches out to the *Central Island National Park,* a notable breeding ground for the lake's infamous Nile crocodiles, leave from the Lake Turkana Fishing Lodge.

Weather

Although located just south of the equator, Nairobi has a pleasant climate due to its almost 6,000-ft. elevation above sea level. Summer (Dec.–Feb.) daytime high temperatures are typically in the high 70s, falling to the mid 50s at night. Winter (June–Aug.) daytime highs are usually in the high 60s or low 70s, dropping to the low 50s at night. There are two rainy seasons, extending from March to May, and from October through December.

NAIROBI: TEMPERATURES AND PRECIPITATION

Month	J	F	M	A	M	J	J	A	S	O	N	D
Average Daily Temperature												
(Fahrenheit) Max.	77	79	77	75	72	70	69	70	75	76	74	74
Min.	54	55	57	58	56	53	51	52	52	55	56	55
Average Number of Days with Precipitation												
	5	6	11	16	17	9	6	7	6	8	15	11

Fez (Fes): Morocco

Sights to See

Fez el Bali, the Old Quarter or Old City. Full of narrow winding alleys and covered bazaars, with all kinds of craft workshops; grocery, spice, pottery, tanning, and weaving markets; dye pits; tea shops; restaurants; and famous mosques. A guide is highly recommended. Check with your hotel.

Dar Batha Museum of Moroccan Arts, just inside the Bab Boujeloud gate, the medina (Old City). Noted for its Berber carpets, embroidery, jewelry, and leatherwork as well as its Moorish garden. Open 8–6 W–M.

Bou Inania Medersa, rue Talaa Kobira, the medina. Former 14th-century Qu'ranic college, known for its carved walls.

Attarine Medersa, rue de Souq el Attarine, the medina. Another 14th-century college, considered by many to be the medina's most attractive religious structure. Especially noted for its fine, intricate carvings, and bronze doors. The view of the nearby Karaouyine Mosque from the terrace is magnificent.

Karaouyine Mosque, rue Boutouil, the medina. Dating from the 9th century, it is Morocco's largest mosque, and known for its exquisite interior, which, unfortunately, is off-limits to non-Muslims, but can be glimpsed through the many doorways.

Fondouk Nejjarine (stable of the Carpenters), off Nejjarine Square near the Karaouyine Mosque, the medina. An 18th-century stable for pack animals.

Zawiya of Moulay Idriss, near the the Fondouk Nejjarine. Contains the tomb of Moulay Idress II, the founder of Fez in the early 9th century. Off limits.

Seffarin Medersa, off place Seffarine, the medina. Dating from the 13th century. Nearby are the coppersmiths plying their trade on place Seffarine.

Dar El Makhzen (Royal Palace), off rue Bou Ksisset, just off the place des Alaouites, Fez el Jedid (New Town). A huge, sprawling complex containing the beautiful sultan's palace.

Vieux (Old) Mechouar, between the Bab Dekaken and Bab Segma gateways, Fez el Jedid. Famous for its dancers, jugglers, and storytellers.

Borj Nord Weapons Museum, just N of Fez el Bali and E of Kasbah des Cherarda above the Old City. Diverse collection of weapons and armory from around the world, housed in a well-preserved medieval fortress. Open 8–12, 3:30–7:30 daily, closed Tu.

Useful Information

Moroccan National Tourism Office, place de la Resistance (tel:23-460); *Syndicat d'Initiative* (City Information Bureau), place Mohammed V (tel:24-769); the closest *U.S. Embassy or Consulate* is in Rabat, at 2 ave. de Marrakesh (tel:07/62-265); *CTM* (Buses), blvd. Mohammed V & rue Ksar el Kebir (tel:22-041); *Post Office,* ave. Hassan II & Blvd Mohammed V, Fez el Jedid; *Voltage Guide:* 110/220 V, two round-pin outlets are used.

Special Trips/Tours

About 37 miles W of Fez is *Meknes,* like Fez, one of Morocco's four Imperial Cities. Dating from the 10th century, it is known for its ramparts, gateways, mosques, and palaces, but particularly for the imposing *Dar el Kebira* (Imperial City) complex, now largely in ruins. One of the largest palaces in the world, it is entered through the impressive *Bab Mansour gate.* Inside, the *Tomb of Moulay Ismail's* mosque is the only one that can be entered by non-Muslims in Morocco. Other noteworthy sights include the *Christian Dungeon;* the *Darel Makhzen imperial palace;* and the *Sultan Gardens.* Meknes's medina, although interesting enough, is not as enthralling as the one in Fez. The *Dar Jamal Handcrafts Museum,* on Bab Djama En-Nouar square in the medina, is worth a look.

The Roman ruins of *Volubilis* are just 20 miles N of Meknes, located on an open plain. Dating from the 2nd century, the former capital of Mauritania Tingitan covers over 100 acres, and has many oil mills, the remains of a Roman bakery, a forum, a triumphal arch, impressive colonnades, and a few mosaics.

Weather

Fez enjoys a Mediterranean climate, with hot summers and mild, sunny winters. Summer daytime high temperatures typically reach the high 90s or low 100s, falling to the upper 60s at night. Winter daytime highs are usually in the mid 60s, dropping to the 40s at night. Rainfall is low year-round.

FEZ: TEMPERATURES AND PRECIPITATION

Month	J	F	M	A	M	J	J	A	S	O	N	D
Average Daily Temperature												
(Fahrenheit) Max.	65	68	74	79	84	92	101	100	92	83	73	66
Min.	40	43	48	52	57	62	67	68	63	57	49	42
Average Number of Days with Precipitation												
	7	5	6	6	2	1	1	1	3	4	3	7

Marrakesh: Morocco

Sights to See

Djemaa el Fna (Assembly of the Dead), a huge square in the center of the old town, Marrakesh's focal point, and the largest souk in Morocco. In the late afternoon the market activities give way to the acrobats, jugglers, fire-eaters, story-tellers, water-sellers, musicians, magicians, and snake charmers.

Koutoubia Mosque, overlooking the Djemaa el Fna. A 12th-century structure with a magnificent minaret noted for its exterior decorative work. Closed to non-Muslims.

The 12th-century walls of Marrakesh's medina, with their many gates, notably the Bab Agnaou.

Museum of Moroccan Arts, Dar Si Said Palace, off the Riad Zitoun Jedid quarter, E of Djemaa el Fna. Fine collection of Moroccan handicrafts. Open 9–noon, 4–7 W–M.

Bahia Palace and Gardens, S of the Museum of Moroccan Arts. This 19th-century structure is the only royal palace open to the visitor (assuming the royal family or its guests are not in residence). Famous for its fine decoration and its Moorish gardens, complete with fountains. Open 9–1, 4–7 W–M.

Ruins of El Badi Palace, SE of Bahia Palace. Dating from the late 16th century, it was believed to be the finest Moroccan palace before being dismantled in the late 17th century.

Dar El Makhzen (Royal Palace), in the S part of the medina, just S of pl. J. El Mansour, S of the El Badi ruins. Closed to visitors.

Saadian Tombs, just E of the Bab Agnaou gate in the Medina, W of the El Badi ruins. Modeled after the interior of Spain's Alhambra in Granada, they are noted for their very elaborate decorations, particularly the Chamber of the Twelve Columns, dating from the 16th century. Open daily.

Medersa Ben Youssef, at the N end of the medina. A former college dating from the 14th century, it was the largest Qur'anic school in North Africa. It is especially noted for its superb central courtyard. Open 8–noon, 3–7 Tu–Su. *Menara Gardens,* at the W end of Avenue de la Menara, outside the medina, in the new city. Laid out by the Almohads in the 12th century, it has a small pavilion built by Sultan Abd Er Rahman for his amorous escapades.

Useful Information

National Tourist Office, ave. Mohammed V, at pl. Abdel Moumen ben Ali (tel:30-258); *Syndicat d'Initiative* (City Information Bureau), 170 Ave. Mohammed V (tel:33-297); the closest *U.S. Embassy or Consulate,* is in Rabat, at 2 ave. de Marrakesh (tel:7/62-265); *Post Office,* pl. du XVI Novembre; *Voltage Guide:* 110/220 V, two round-pin outlets are used.

Special Trips/Tours

The *Ourika Valley,* SE of Marrakesh, in the foothills of the Atlas Mountains, is a popular side trip. More spectacular is the Atlas ski resort of *Oukaimeden,* located about 50 miles from Marrakesh. Situated at well over 7,000 ft. it offers a welcome respite from Marrakesh's heat in the summer.

Longer drives up and over the Atlas passes to the remote towns or villages of *Erfoud, Ksar el Souq, Ouarzazate, Tinghir,* and *Zagora,* each settled by a Berber tribe or clan with its unique style of clothing, and with its own kasbah (fortress), daily markets, and special crafts, make for fascinating trips. *Zagora,* situated between the Draa River and a ridge of mountains, is particularly dramatic, with its well-preserved kasbah just outside town.

For the more adventurous, a drive along the western fringes of the *Sahara Desert,* the world's largest, following the route of the Ksour (a series of fortified Saharan villages), is a rewarding experience. You will, of course, catch only a glimpse of this vast desert, largely comprised of hamadas (rocky plateaus) interrupted by wadis (dry valleys), but just this glimpse is a remarkable sight. One of the most spectacular natural attractions in Morocco is the Grand Canyon-like *Gorges du Dades,* N of Boulmane-Dades, E of Ouarzazate.

Weather

Marrakesh has a Mediterranean climate with hot summers, and mild sunny winters. Summer daytime highs typically reach into the high 90s or low 100s, dropping to the mid 60s at night. Winter daytime highs are usually in the mid to high 60s, falling to the 40s at night. Rainfall is low year-round.

MARRAKESH: TEMPERATURES AND PRECIPITATION

Month	J	F	M	A	M	J	J	A	S	O	N	D
Average Daily Temperature												
(Fahrenheit) Max.	65	68	74	79	84	92	101	100	92	83	73	66
Min.	40	43	48	52	57	62	67	68	63	57	49	42
Average Number of Days with Precipitation												
	7	5	6	6	2	1	1	1	3	4	3	7

Rabat: Morocco

Sights to See

Great Mosque, ave. Moulay Hassan & ave. Mohammed V. An 18th-century structure, noted for its fine carvings and tall minaret.

Museum of Antiquities (Musee Archeologique), Zankat al Brihi, just E of the Great Mosque. Fine collection of Roman bronzes from Volubilis. Open 9–6 W–M.

Gate of the Winds (Bab er Rouah), in the Almohad Walls, at the end of ave. Moulay Hassan, W of the Great Mosque. Considered to be the best of the five surviving city gates.

Royal Palace (Dar El Makhzen), SW of the Great Mosque, inside the Machouar. A sprawling, traditional Islamic complex. When the king is in residence, on certain Friday mornings there is an impressive ceremony, with great pageantry, marking his visit to the Great Mosque. Check with your hotel or the tourist office for dates and times.

Chella, just outside the city walls, through Bab El Zair, E of the Royal Palace. An Arab necropolis, now in ruins, known for its impressive 14th-century stone gate, mosque ruins, fine gardens, and royal tombs.

Hassan Tower, N of Chella, between ave. Al Alaouyne & blvd. Abi Regreg, overlooking the Bou Regreg Near the Pont Moulay Hassan to Sale. Rabat's major landmark, the unfinished 11th-century minaret is 144 ft. high. Do ask to climb the tower, it affords fine panoramas of Rabat and neighboring Sale across the Regreg River.

Mausoleum of Mohammed V, next to the Hassan Tower. The final resting place of the present King's father, who led Morocco to its present-day independence.

Museum of Moroccan Arts, Oudaia Kasbah, off blvd. el Alou, NE of the Hassan Tower. Fine collection of jewelry, ceramics, fabrics and brocades, and Moroccan costumes. Open 9–12, 1–6 W–M.

The Medina (Old Quarter), between blvd. el Alou & rue Souika, and rue des Consuls & rue Sidi Fatah, SW of the Oudaia Kasbah. Full of shops selling arts and crafts, particularly Rabat's famous carpets.

Useful Information

Moroccan National Tourist Office, 22 Charia Al-Jazair (tel:21-252); *Syndicat d'Initiative* (City Information Bureau), rue Patrice Lumumba (tel:23-272); *Main Post Office,* ave. Mohammed V & rue Soekarno; *CTM* (Buses), Pl. Mohammed Zerktouni (tel:75-124); *U.S. Embassy,* 2 Ave. de Marrakesh (tel:62-265); *Voltage Guide:* 110/220 V, two round-pin outlets are used.

Special Trips/Tours

Sale, Rabat's neighbor across the Bou Regreg River, is worth exploring. Very compact, with narrow, whitewashed streets lined with windowless houses, it is in many respects more traditional than Rabat. Its medina has many interesting *souks,* and is much less tourist-oriented than Rabat's. Notable sights include the 14th century *Medersa of Abou Al Hassan,* known for its richly detailed Moorish architecture; the 12th-century *Great Mosque;* and the 13th-century *Bob Mrisa gate.*

The coastal road from Rabat to Casablanca is scenic and passes a number of attractive beaches and beach resorts, notably *Mohammedia,* the principal ocean resort for Rabat and Casablanca.

Casablanca itself, Morocco's largest city, is about 90 minutes SW of Rabat. More European in appearnce than Fez or Rabat, it doesn't have their historical and cultural attraction. However, there are a number of notable sights, including *United Nations Square* (place des Nations Unies); *Arab League Park* (Parc de la Ligue Arabe), with its attractive lakes and promenades and *Cathedral of Sacre Coeur,* the *Notre Dame de Lourdes,* on blvd. Mohammed Zerktouni, noted for its stained glass; and the *Medina,* both old and new. Casablanca's *Old Medina,* just S of the harbor, contains a Great Mosque dating from the 18th century and the usual souks. King Hassan's *Royal Palace* is located in the New Medina, which lies SE of the Old Medina, and dates from the 1920s. It also contains a good handcrafts market.

Weather

Rabat has hot, dry summers and mild, wetter winters. Summer daytime high temperatures are typically in the low 80s, dropping to the low 60s at night. Winter daytime highs are usually in the mid 60s, falling to the upper 40s at night. Although relatively low all year, rainfall is concentrated in the late fall and winter months.

RABAT: TEMPERATURES AND PRECIPITATION

Month	J	F	M	A	M	J	J	A	S	O	N	D
Average Daily Temperature												
(Fahrenheit) Max.	63	65	68	71	74	78	82	83	81	77	70	65
Min.	46	47	49	52	55	60	63	64	62	58	53	48
Average Number of Days with Precipitation												
	9	8	10	7	6	2	0	0	2	6	9	10

Dar es Salaam: Tanzania

Sights to See

National Museum, Shaaban Robert St., in the Botanical Gardens. Fine ethnographical collection. However, the museum is internationally known for its "Hall of Man" exhibits of human fossils discovered by Dr. Leakey at Olduvai Gorge, including the 1.75-million-year-old skull of Zinjanthropus Bosei (Nutcracker Man). Open 9:30–7 M-Sa, 2–7 Su.

Dar es Salaam waterfront Beautiful, palm-fringed bay that is usually full of dhows and other exotic boats engaged in their maritime trade. Sunday sunset watching is a local tradition.

Kariakoo market, between Mkunguni & Mchikicha Sts. and Sikukuu & Msim-bazi Sts., S of Mnazi-Mmoja Park. The city's principal market. Very colorful and full of exotic fruit, spices, local handicrafts, and fresh fish.
Village Museum, Bagamoyo Rd., some 6 miles from downtown Dar es Salaam. A collection of authentic, traditional housing of various Tanzanian ethnic groups, with artisans demonstrating traditional handicrafts skills. Open 9:30–7 daily.
Msasani Village, just 5 miles N of the capital along the coast. A picturesque fishing village with local fishermen working on their nets or outrigger sailing boats ("ngalawa").

Useful Information

Tanzania Tourist Office, IPS Building, Samora Machel Ave. (tel:26-680); *U.S. Embassy,* 36 Laibon Rd. (tel:37-501); *Main Post Office,* City Dr. & Maktaba St.; *Voltage Guide:* 220 V, two round-pin or three-prong rectangular blade outlets are used.

Special Trips/Tours

The prime attractions of Tanzania, of course, are the great game reserves, such as world-famous *Serengeti National Park,* and the less-well-known *Selous Game Reserve,* along with the spectacular *Mt. Kilimanjaro,* Africa's highest mountain, and the *Ngorongoro Crater.* The popular northern circuit, accessible via Kilimanjaro International Airport between *Arusha* and Moshi, covers Arusha, *Lake Manyara, Serengeti,* and *Tarangire national parks, Ngorongoro Crater, Olduvai Gorge,* and *Mount Kilimanjaro.*
Arusha National Park, located 20 miles E of Arusha, is noted for its buffalo, rhino, giraffe, colobus monkey, warthog, bush pig, and elephant. The *Momella Lakes* have a profusion of birds. *Ngurdoto Crater* is a reserve within a reserve, where the wildlife can only be viewed from the crater rim.
Mount Kilimanjaro (19,340 ft.), straddling the border with Kenya, is accessible from Marangu, 75 miles E of Arusha. Located just below the equator, it is permanently snowcapped, and a magnificent sight, visible for several hundred miles. It is also relatively easy to climb (5 days minimum).
Lake Manyara National Park, 75 miles W of Arusha, is noted for bird life, particularly flamingoes, and for tree-loving lions.
Tarangire National Park, 67 miles W of Arusha and S of Lake Manyara, is famous for its black rhino, oryx, and lesser kudo, along with its buffalos, elephants, and lions.
Ngorongoro Crater, 112 miles W of Arusha, is an awe-inspiring natural wonder, one of Africa's most beautiful areas of wildlife in the world's largest intact caldera. Famous for its huge herds of plains game, the 100-square-mile caldera also supports elephant, lion, rhino, and hippo, together with 10,000 Masai.
Olduvai Gorge, 32 miles W of Ngorongoro Crater. The world-famous site of the renowned *Leakey excavations,* which turned up the skull of Zinjanthropus

Bosei (Nutcracker Man—now in Dar es Salaam's National Museum), and other fossils of early man.

Serengeti National Park, Tanzania's largest park, is some 150 miles W of Arusha. Probably Africa's most famous game reserve, it is best known for its lions, and the annual, spectacular migration of hundreds of thousands of plains game, followed by the predatory hyenas and lions. The migration starts in May or June.

Weather

Dar es Salaam has a hot, humid tropical climate. Temperatures are fairly uniform year-round, with summer (Dec.–Feb.) daytime highs typically reaching into the high 80s, failing to the upper 70s at night. Winter (June–Aug.) daytime highs are usually in the mid 80s, dropping to the high 60s at night. The rainy season extends from March through May.

DAR ES SALAAM: TEMPERATURES AND PRECIPITATION

Month	J	F	M	A	M	J	J	A	S	O	N	D
Average Daily Temperature												
(Fahrenheit) Max.	87	88	88	86	85	84	83	83	83	85	86	87
Min.	77	77	75	73	71	68	66	66	67	69	72	75
Average Number of Days with Precipitation												
	8	6	12	19	15	6	6	7	7	7	9	11

South and Central America
Buenos Aires: Argentina

Sights to See

May Plaza (Plaza de Mayo), the heart of Buenos Aires, surrounded by historic government buildings.

Pink House (Casa Rosada), on the E side of the Plaza de Mayo. The pink-hued Presidential Palace. Noted for its statuary and lavish interior. Currently closed to the public.

Council House (El Cabildo), on the W side of Plaza de Mayo. Former house of the Spanish viceroy's counselors, and site of the declaration of Argentina's independence. Now a museum devoted to the May 1810 revolotuion. Open 3–7 W–Su.

The Cathedral (La Catedral), on the N side of the Plaza de Mayo. Largest church in Argentina, noted for its huge central nave. It contains the tomb of revolutionary hero General Jose de San Martin.

Republic Plaza (Plaza de la Republica), Av. Corrientes & Av. 9 de Julio. Dominated by the city's famous landmark, the 220 ft. *Obelisk* (El Obelisco), commemorating the founding of Buenos Aires.

July Ninth Avenue (Avenida 9 de Julio), running NS through Plaza de la Republica, it is one of the widest avenues in the world. Catch the lighted fountains at night. Ideal for people watching from one of the many "confiterias."
Colon Theater (Teatro Colon), Tucuman 1161, just off Av. 9 de Julio N of Plaza de la Republica. One of the world's great opera houses, it is famous for its plush interior and huge stage. Tours daily.
San Martin Plaza (Plaza San Martin), Calle Florida & Av. Santa Fe, NE of Teatro Colon. At the center of the city's most fashionable district.
National Gallery of Fine Arts (Museo de Bellas Artes), Av. Libertador Gral. San Martin 1473, NW of Plaza San Martin. Argentina's best art gallery, with works of contemporary Argentinian and European artists, and domestic wooden carvings. Open 9–12:45, 3–6:45 Tu–Su.
Recoleta Cemetery (Cementerio Recoleta), Calla Junin, near the Museo de Bellas Artes. Burial place for the rich and famous, including Evita Peron. Open 7–6 daily.
National History Museum (Museo Historico Nacional), Defensa 1600. Trophies and mementoes of historical events. Open 2–6 Th–Su.
The Mouth, or Little Italy (La Boca), on the S edge of the city in the Old Port area. A colorful, Italian community famous for its nightlife.

Useful Information

Tourist Information Center, Av. Santa Fe 883 (tel:31-2232); *U.S. Embassy*, Av. Colombia 4300 (tel:774-7611); *Buenos Aires City Tourism Board Information Stand*, Calle Florida 800 & 100; *Voltage Guide:* 220 V, two round-pin or three-prong rectangular blade outlets are used.

Special Trips/Tours

The *Palermo Parks* (Parque Tres de Febrero), in the suburb of Palermo, some 10 minutes from Retiro Station are worthwhile. Noted for their rose garden, Andalusian Patio, and Japanese garden, they are a favorite of city residents. The *Hipodromo Argentino*, a world-famous horse racecourse, is also here. Opposite the parks are the *Botanical Gardens* and *Zoo*.

The attractive resort town of *San Isidro* on the River Plate shore is about 30 minutes from Buenos Aires. It is noted for its fine colonial buildings and plaza.

Some 250 miles E of Buenos Aires on the Atlantic coast is *Mar del Plata,* the country's major beach resort, with reputedly the largest casino in the world at *Bristol Beach.* The town's *Plaza San Martin* is very attractive, *Playa Grande* is perhaps the most fashionable beach, but the *Villa Gesell,* and *Pinamar* beaches N of Mar del Plata are also attractive, and much less crowded. Frequent daily trains leave the *Constitucion Railway Station* for the 5-hour trip.

Weather

Buenos Aires's summer (Dec.–March) daytime high temperatures typically reach into the low 80s, dropping to the low 60s at night. Winter daytime highs are usually in the high 50s or low 60s, falling to the 40s at night. September to January is the wet season.

BUENOS AIRES: TEMPERATURES AND PRECIPITATION

Month	J	F	M	A	M	J	J	A	S	O	N	D
Average Daily Temperature												
(Fahrenheit) Max.	85	83	79	72	64	57	57	60	64	69	76	82
Min.	63	63	60	53	47	41	42	43	46	50	56	61
Average Number of Days with Precipitation												
	7	6	7	8	7	7	8	9	8	9	9	8

La Paz: Bolivia

Sights to See

Plaza Murillo, the traditional center of La Paz, surrounded by the Italian Renaissance Presidential Palace, the National Congress and the cathedral.
La Paz Cathedral, Plaza Murillo. An impressive, huge, modern cathedral.
National Museum of Art (Museo Nacional del Arte), Calle Socabaya across from the cathedral. Fine collection of Latin American paintings, both modern and colonial. Open Tu–Su.
Murillo House and Museum (Museo y Casa de Murillo), Calle Jaen, 4 blocks NW of the cathedral. Originally the home of one of Bolivia's national heroes, it is noted for its fine colonial art and furniture collection. Open Tu–Su.
Church and Monastery of San Francisco (Iglesia y Monasterio de San Francisco), Plaza San Francisco, 3 blocks SW of the cathedral across the Prado. Dating from the 16th century, it is especially noted for its richly decorated interior.
Calle Sagarnaga, running SW from Plaza San Francisco. This narrow, ascending cobblestone street is lined with Indian shops specializing in handicrafts. The *Witchdoctor's Market* on Calle Linares, off Sagarnaga, is worth visiting. Av. Buenos Aires, W of Sagarnaga via Max Peredes, is the main Indian street market.
El Prado (Av. Mariscal Santa Cruz and Avenida 16 de Julio) between Plaza San Francisco and Plaza del Estudiante. La Paz's main avenue, with statues, fountains, cafes, and the city's most fashionable shops.
Camacho Market (Mercado Camacho), Av. Camacho & Calle Bueno, one block N of El Prado near the W end of Parque Central Roosevelt. A large, colorful outdoor market with Indian vendors selling just about everything. Especially busy on weekends.
National Museum of Archaeology (Museo Nacional Arqueologico de Tiahuanaco), Av. Tihuanaco 3 blocks E of the Camacho Market. Excellent pottery and textile collection from Tiahuanaco. Open Tu–Su.

Useful Information

Bolivian National Tourist Office, Calle Juan de la Riva, Edificio Ballivian (tel:36-7463); *Tourist Information Kiosk,* Av. 16 de Julio 1440 (Prado); *Post Office,* on Ayacucho near Potosi; *U.S. Embassy,* Edificio Banco Popular, Calle Colon 290 (tel:35-0251); *Police* (tel:110); *Voltage Guide:* 110/220 V, two flat, parallel blade or two round-pin outlets are used.

Special Trips/Tours

One of the world's great archaeological sites, the *pre-Inca ruins of Tiahuanaco,* are some 42 miles from La Paz near the S edge of Lake Titicaca (about a 3-hour bus trip). Dating from around A.D. 800, these impressive monoliths and monuments are being reconstructed. Particularly noteworthy are the *Temple of Kalasasaya,* the *Acapana pyramid,* and the *Gates of the Sun and the Moon.* Most of the best statues are in La Paz's *National Museum of Archaeology* (see above).

Copacabana, some 98 miles from La Paz on Lake Titicaca itself (the world's highest navigable lake), is a resort town dating from pre-Inca times. Be sure to see the local church, noted for its fine main chapel altar and famous 16th-century Dark Virgin of the Lake (Virgin of Candelaria) statue. If you have more time, the 6-hour return trip out to the *Island of the Sun,* legendary home of the first Inca, is worthwhile. The Pilko Calma ruins offer fine views.

A trip into the *Bolivian jungles* (yungas) is a worthwhile experience. The road running NE of La Paz to *Coroico* and *Chulumani* passes through some spectacular scenery, over La Cumbre Pass (15,500 ft.), and down into the verdant, tropical jungle around Caranavi. Do check on tours into the Yungas with your hotel.

Weather

Despite its location in the tropics, at 12,000 ft. La Paz has a cool, spring-like climate throughout the year. Summer (Dec.–Feb.) daytime high temperatures are typically in the mid to high 60s, dropping to the low 40s at night. Winter (June–Aug.) daytime highs are usually in the low 60s, falling to the lower 30s at night. The rainy season extends from December through March. NOTE: acclimatization to La Paz's 12,000-ft. altitude takes time and many visitors may suffer from mountain sickness on arrival. Sunburn is also a potential hazard, because of the thin atmosphere.

LA PAZ: TEMPERATURES AND PRECIPITATION

Month	J	F	M	A	M	J	J	A	S	O	N	D
Average Daily Temperature												
(Fahrenheit) Max.	63	63	64	65	64	62	62	63	64	66	67	65
Min.	43	43	42	40	37	34	33	35	38	40	42	42
Average Number of Days with Precipitation												
	21	18	16	9	5	2	2	4	9	9	11	18

Rio de Janeiro: Brazil

Sights to See

Rio itself from Sugarloaf Mountain (Pao de Acucar). The view from this world-famous peak overlooking Guanabara Bay is just magnificent. The 1,230-ft. mountain top is reached by two cable cars, the first of which leaves from the Praia Vermelha station at the end of Avenida Pasteur. Open 8–9 daily.

The view from Hunchback Mountain (Corcovado), is equally stunning. This 2,300-ft. peak, topped by the 130-ft. statue of Christ the Redeemer, is reached by train (8–dusk daily) from the Cosmo Velho station, or by road.
Avenida Rio Branco, in the city center. Lined with ornate buildings, it is Rio's main commercial street.
National Museum of Fine Arts (Museu Nacional de Belas Artes), Av. Rio Branco 199. Fine collection of original paintings and sculptures, together with reproductions. Open 12:30–6 Tu-F, 3–6 Sa–Su.
San Antonio Convent and Church (Convento e Igreja de Santo Antonio), off Largo da Carioca, just NW of the Museum of Fine Arts. Early-17th-century structure noted for its sacristy.
Church of St. Francis of the Penitence (Igreja de San Francisco da Penitencia), adjacent to San Antonio Convent on Rua Uruguiana & Carioca. Known for its interior carving and gilding, and ceiling painting by Jose de Oliveira.
Metropolitan Cathedral (Catedral Metropolitana), Av. Republica de Chile, near Largo da Carioca. A modern structure noted for its huge stained-glass windows.
Flamengo Park (Parque Flamengo), on the Flamengo waterfront. A popular landscaped park on reclaimed land.
Museum of Modern Art (Museu de Arte Moderna), Av. Infante dom Henrique 85, Flamengo Park. Constructed almost entirely of glass, this museum has an excellent modern art collection. Open 12–7 Tu–Sa, 2–7 Su.
Copacabana, S of Sugarloaf Mountain. At the core of Rio's beach resort area, the long, curved stretch of Copacabana and Leme beaches, backed by skycraper apartments, is world famous.
Botanical Garden (Jardim Botanico), Rua Jardim Botanico, Corcovado. Considered to be one of the world's best with over 7,000 varieties of plants. Especially noted for the transverse avenues of royal palms. Open 8–6 daily in summer, 8:30–5:30 rest of year.
National Museum (Museu Nacional), Quinta da Boa Vista, Sao Cristovao. Housed in the former principal palace of the Emperors of Brazil, this museum has outstanding natural science, archaeological, and anthropological collections. Open 10–5 Tu–Su.

Useful Information

Tourist Information, Sala do Turismo, Praca Maua 7, and Rua Mariz e Barros 13 (tel:293-1313); *Rio de Janeiro Tourism Office,* Rua da Asambleia 10, Room 814 (tel:242-8000); *Touring Club do Brasil,* Av. Gen. Severiano 201, Botafogo (tel:295-7440); *U.S. Consulate,* Av. Presidente Wilson 147 (tel:292-7117); *Police* (tel:243-6716); *Voltage Guide:* 110/220 V, two round-pin outlets are used.

Special Trips/Tours

The *Tijuca Forest,* W of Copacabana and Ipanema is an ideal spot to get away from the bustle of the city and take a relaxing walk through a tropical forest. Be sure to see the famous *Cascatinha waterfall*. *Paqueta island* in Guanabara Bay, is accessible via the frequent ferry service from Praca Quinze de Novembro. It is one of the most attractive of the bay's many islands.

Weather

Rio de Janeiro has a hot, humid tropical climate with frequent sea breezes tending to cool things off. Summer (Dec.–Feb.) daytime high temperatures typically reach into the mid 80s, falling to the low 70s at night. Winter (June–Aug.) daytime highs are usually in the mid 70s, dropping to the 60s at night. December through April is the wet season.

RIO DE JANEIRO: TEMPERATURES AND PRECIPITATION

Month	J	F	M	A	M	J	J	A	S	O	N	D
Average Daily Temperature												
(Fahrenheit) Max.	84	85	83	80	77	76	75	76	75	77	79	82
Min.	73	73	72	69	66	64	63	64	65	66	68	71
Average Number of Days with Precipitation												
	13	11	12	10	10	7	7	7	11	13	13	14

Sao Paulo: Brazil

Sights to See

Sao Paulo Itself from one of the revolving restaurants or the observation deck at the top of the 41-story *Edificio Italia*. South America's tallest building. Av. Ipiranga & Av. Sao Luis. Open daily.

Patriarch's Plaza (Praca da Patriaca), at the commercial center of the city. The Times Square of Sao Paulo.

Sao Paulo Cathedral, Praca de Se, just E of Praca da Patriarca on Rua Direita. A huge neo-Gothic structure, noted for its opulant crypt chapel.

Japantown (Liberdale), S of the Cathedral along Praca da Liberdade & Rua Galvao Bueno. The center of Sao Paulo's large Japanese immigrant population. Curio shops, restaurants, and neat rock gardens.

Museum of Sacred Art (Museu de Arte Sacra), Av. Tiradentes 676, near Luz Park. Fine collection of religious art. Open 1–5 Tu–Su.

Sao Paulo Art Museum (Museu de Arte de Sao Paulo), Av. Paulista 1578. Excellent collection of European paintings, together with contemporary Brazilian art. Open 2–6 Tu–Su.

Ibirapuera Park (Parque Ibirapuera), in the suburbs. One of the largest urban parks in the world, it is a well-tended oasis in Sao Paulo's concrete jungle. Be sure to visit the *Japanese Pavilion* and the *Planetarium*. Open daily.

Museum of Contemporary Art (Museu de Arte Contemporanea), Pereira Pavilion, Parque Ibirapuera. A fine collection of Western and South American modern art. Open 1–6 Tu–Su.

Butanta Institute (Institute Butanta), Av. Dr. Vital Brasil 1500, Pinheiros. World-famous snake farm where their venom is used as antitoxins. Interesting museum. Open 8–5 daily.

Pioneer House (Casa do Bandeirante), Praca Monteiro Lobato, near the Instituto Butanta. A reconstructed 17th-century home of Brazil's colonials, complete with authentic period pieces. Open 12–5 Tu–Sa, 9–5 Su.

Zoological Gardens (Jardim Zoologico), Av. Miguel Stefano, Agua Funda. Full of exotic tropical animals in a forest setting. Open 9–6 Tu–Su.

Useful Information

Tourist Office, Av. Sao Luiz 115 (tel:257-7248); *Sao Paulo Information Office,* Praca da Republica 154 (tel:259-2200); *U.S. Consulate,* Rua Padre Joao Manuel 933 (tel:881-6511); *Police* (tel:228-2276); *Voltage Guide:* 110/220 V, two round-pin outlets are used.

Special Trips/Tours

The Iguacu Falls, on the Brazil/Argentina border near Foz do Iguacu, and one of the main attractions in Brazil, if not South America, are a 2-hour flight from Sao Paulo via Vari, plus a 30-minute bus ride from the Foz do Iguacu airport. Higher and much wider than Niagara Falls, they are truly spectacular. Particularly the U-shaped *Devil's Throat (Garganbta do Diablo)* Falls, reached by a canoe trip. The magnificent natural setting is accentuated by the surrounding ferns, begonias, orchids, and parrots.

Between Sao Paulo and Rio de Janeiro is one of Sao Paulo's principal resort areas, *Campos de Jordao,* a 3-hour drive via the Presidente Dutra Hwy. through Sao Jose dos Campos. A delightful mountain resort, it has a definite European flavor.

Santos, the beach resort of *Bertioga,* and the islands of *Guaruja* and *Ilhabela* (Ilha de Sao Sebastiao), are just over two hours' drive from Sao Paulo via the Anchieta and Imigrantes Hwys. *Santos,* Brazil's largest port, is also a resort town with magnificent beaches. The island of *Guaruja,* reached by ferry from the Ponta da Praia on the Santos beachfront area, is a popular resort destination with palm-tree-lined beaches. The beaches N of Santos on the road to Bertioga are cleaner and much less crowded.

Weather

Sao Paulo has a moderate climate despite its location at the edge of the tropics, due to its 2,665-ft. altitude. Summer (Dec.–March) daytime high temperatures are typically in the low 80s, dropping to around 70 at night. Winter (June–Sept.) daytime highs are usually in the low 70s, falling to around 60 at night. The wet season extends from October through March.

SAO PAULO: TEMPERATURES AND PRECIPITATION

Month	J	F	M	A	M	J	J	A	S	O	N	D
Average Daily Temperature												
(Fahrenheit) Max.	81	82	80	76	73	71	70	71	71	73	76	79
Min.	70	70	69	65	62	59	58	59	61	62	65	68
Average Number of Days with Precipitation												
	14	12	13	11	10	7	7	8	11	13	14	15

Santiago: Chile

Sights to See

Santiago itself from San Cristobal Hill (Cerro San Cristobal), Parque Metropolitano. At just over 1,100 ft. above the city, the views are magnificent. Reached by the funicular at the end of Calle Pio Nono.

Armaments Plaza (Plaza de Armas), Calle Catedral & Paseo Ahumada, four blocks S of Mapocho Station. The heart of Santiago.

Cathedral (Catedral), on the W side of Plaza de Armas. Dating from the 16th century, it has been rebuilt several times. Noted for its wooden figure of Saint Francis Xavier, a 17th-century silver lamp, and a fine painting of the Last Supper. Open daily.

National Historical Museum (Museo Historico Nacional), Plaza de Armas 951. Fine exhibits illustrating Chile's history. Open Tu–Su.

Pre-Columbian Museum (Museo Precolombino), Bandera & Compania, 1 block W of Plaza de Armas. Superb collection of pre-Columbian art from all over Latin America. Open 10–8 Tu–Su.

Presidential Palace (Palacio de la Moneda), Calle Moneda & Calle Teatinos, 4 blocks SW of Plaza de Armas. Historic palace containing the presidential offices. Not open to the public.

San Francisco Church (Iglesia San Francisco), Av. Libertador O'Higgins & Calle San Francisco, 5 blocks E of the Presidential Palace. Dates from the 16th century.

Museum of Colonial Art (Museo del Arte Colonial), next to San Francisco Church. An excellent collection of religious paintings and sacred ornaments. Open Tu–Su.

Santa Lucia Hill (Cerro Santa Lucia), 4 blocks NE of San Francisco Church across Av. Libertador O'Higgins. Beautiful gardens and a castle overlooking Santiago.

Fine Arts Museum (Museo de Bellas Artes), Parque Forestal, across Av. Presidente Balmaceda N of Cerro Santa Lucia. Considered one of the best in S. America. Open 10–1:15, 2–6 Tu–Sa, 10–1:30 Su.

Natural History Museum (Museo de Historia Natural), in Parque Quinta Normal, W of the downtown area. Famous for the 500-year-old Mummy of Cerro El Plomo, and its dinosaur remains. Open 10–1, 2–6 Tu–Sa, 2–5:45 Su.

Useful Information

National Tourist Office, Catedral 1159 (tel:698-2151 or 696-0474); *American Express,* 1356–1360 Agustinas; *U.S. Embassy,* 1343 Agustinas (tel:71-0133 or 71-0326); *Voltage Guide:* 220 V, two round-pin outlets are used.

Special Trips/Tours

Vina del Mar, perhaps Chile's most fashionable beach resort, is some 85 miles NW of Santiago via Hwy. 68. This attractive community is famous not only for its beaches and beautiful gardens, but also for its gambling casinos, particularly the *Municipal Casino,* off Av. San Martin. Sights to see include the president's *Summer Palace* on Cerro Castillo, *Plaza Vergara,* the lighted fountains of *Plaza Mexico,* and *Quinta Vergara park* with its Museum of Fine Arts.

The world-famous ski resort of *Portillo,* site of the 1966 World Alpine Ski Championships, is about 4 hours NE of Santiago by car (some 5 hours by train). At over 9,000 ft., in the Chilean Andes, it is a world-class ski resort, surrounded by magnificent peaks, and enjoys ideal weather. Although primarily a winter ski area with a June–Sept. season, it is open all year and offers sailing and fishing in the beautiful *Laguna del Inca,* along with hiking. Don't miss the statue of *Christ the Redeemer,* perched on top of a 12,000-ft. mountain marking the border with Argentina, and seen from the road just beyond Portillo.

Weather

Santiago has a Mediterranean type of climate. Summer (Dec.–Feb.) daytime high temperatures typically reach into the mid 80s, falling to the 50s at night. Winter (June–Aug.) daytime highs reach into the upper 50s, dropping to the high 30s at night. Rainfall amounts are low throughout the year. May through August is the wettest time of year.

SANTIAGO: TEMPERATURES AND PRECIPITATION

Month	J	F	M	A	M	J	J	A	S	O	N	D
Average Daily Temperature												
(Fahrenheit) Max.	85	84	80	74	65	58	59	62	66	72	78	83
Min.	53	52	49	45	41	37	37	39	42	45	48	51
Average Number of Days with Precipitation												
	0	0	1	1	5	6	6	5	3	3	1	0

Bogota: Colombia

Sights to See

Bogota itself from the top of Monserrate, one of the two mountains immediately E of the city. Reached by funicular and cable car at the end of Av. Jimenez. The view is magnificent.

Quinta de Bolivar, Calle 20, No. 2–23, at the base of Monserrate. Once the home of Bolivar, it is a museum full of Bolivar memorabilia. Open 10–4:30 Tu–Su.
The Gold Museum (Museo del Oro), Calle 16, No. 5–41, downtown W of Quinta de Bolivar. A unique, superb collection of pre-Columbian Indian gold artifacts. Open 9–4 Tu–Sa, 9–12 Su.
San Francisco Church (Iglesia de San Francisco), opposite the Museo del Oro. Dating from the 16th century, it is noted for its high altar, choir stalls, paintings, and beautiful carved ceiling.
Church of La Veracruz (Iglesia de La Veracruz), also opposite the Museo del Oro next to the San Francisco Church. Known for its Rococo ornamentation.
Plaza de Bolivar, Calle 10, about 5 blocks S of San Francisco Church. The heart of Bogota, surrounded by the *Capitol* with its fine colonnades, the *Municipal Palace,* and the *cathedral.*
La Candelaria Colonial Quarter (Barrio La Candelaria), around the Plaza. Explore the narrow streets in this district, it has the best colonial buildings and most of the huge mansions in Bogota.
Cathedral (Catedral), Plaza de Bolivar. Dating from the 16th century, and rebuilt in classical style in the 19th, it is noted for the wrought silver on its altar and carved choir loft.
Sanctuary Chapel (Capilla del Sagrario), adjoining the cathedral. Beautiful interior with famous 17th-century paintings by Gregorio Vasquez Arce y Ceballos.
Museum of Colonial art (Museo de Arte Colonial), Carrera 6, No. 9–77, just S of the cathedral. Excellent collection in one of the finest colonial buildings in Bogota. Open 9:30–6:30 Tu–Sa, 10–5 Su.
San Carlos Palace (Palacio San Carlos), Carrera 6 & Calle 10, opposite the Museum of Colonial Art. See the Changing of the Guard ceremony at 5 P.M. daily.
Archaeological Museum (Museo Arqueologico), Carrera 6, No. 7–43. Noted for its superb pre-Columbian pottery collection. Open 10–5 Tu–Sa, 10–1 Su.
National Museum (Museo Nacional), Carrera 7, No. 28–66. Fine archaeological, ethnographic, historical, & fine arts collections. Open 9:3–6:30 Tu–Sa, 10–5 Su.

Useful Information

National Tourist Office, Calle 28, No. 13A–15 (tel:283-9466); *Bogota Tourist Office,* Carrera 7, No. 26–62 (tel:283-2053); *U.S. Embassy,* Carrera 10, No. 38–49 (tel:285-1300); *Post Office,* Carrera 7, No. 16–36; *Voltage Guide:* 110 V, two flat, parallel blade outlets are used.

Special Trips/Tours

The *underground Salt Cathedral of Zipaquira* is some 31 miles N of Bogota in a salt mine just outside Zipaquira. With a roof 75 ft. above the floor, and four aisles, this huge cathedral is noted for its main altar, carved out of solid salt rock (as is the whole cathedral). Open 9:30–12, 1–4:30 M–Sa, 10:30–4:30 Su.

If you have more time, *Cartagena* on the Caribbean Sea, and an hour from Bogota by air, is definitely worth visiting. Famous for its walled fortifications, narrow winding streets, and general colonial ambience, it has a number of notable sights, including the *plazas de Bolivar, de los Coches,* and *de las Bovedas,* the *cathedral,* the *Church of Santo Toribio de Mongrovrjo,* and the Baroque *Palace of the Inquisition.*

Weather

Bogota has a temperate climate due to its 8,678-ft. altitude. Temperatures are remarkably uniform year-round, with daytime highs in the mid to high 60s, falling to the low 50s or upper 40s at night. Rainfall is frequent. March–May and October–November are the wettest periods.

BOGOTA: TEMPERATURES AND PRECIPITATION

Month	J	F	M	A	M	J	J	A	S	O	N	D
Average Daily Temperature												
(Fahrenheit) Max.	67	68	67	67	66	65	64	65	66	66	66	66
Min.	48	49	50	51	51	51	50	50	49	50	50	49
Average Number of Days with Precipitation												
	6	7	13	20	17	16	18	16	13	20	16	15

Quito: Ecuador

Sights to See

Quito itself from Panecillo Hill (Cerro Panecillo), on the SW side of the colonial section of Quito. The views of the city and surrounding Andes are superb.

Independence Plaza (Plaza Independencia), at Calles Eugenio Espejo & Garcia Moreno. Surrounded by ecclesiastical and government buildings, this tree-lined plaza is the heart of the old city.

Cathedral (Catedral), on the S side of Plaza Independencia. With its green tile cupolas and gray stone porticos, it is noted for Caspicara's "The Descent from the Cross," and General Sucre's tomb. Open 6–10, 2–4 daily.

La Compania Church, Calle Sucre one block W of Plaza Independencia. Famous for its gold-plated high altar, it is the most ornate church in Quito, with a beautifully carved facade. Open 10–11, 1–5 daily.

San Francisco Church (Iglesia de San Francisco), on Plaza San Francisco, two blocks W of La Compania Church. The oldest church in South America (1535), it is famous for its ornate Baroque interior and exterior, and its excellent colonial art collection.

Santo Domingo Church and Monastery (Iglesia y Monasterio de Santo Domingo), Plaza Santo Domingo (Sucre), 6 blocks S of San Francisco Church. Noted for its fine wood carvings and Chapel of the Rosary.
Central Bank Museum (Museo del Banco Central), Av. 10 de Agosto near Alameda Park, several blocks E of the old colonial section of Quito. The 5th-floor archaeological museum is one of the best in S. America. The 6th-floor museum of colonial and religious art is also worth visiting. Open 9–5 Tu–F, 10–5 Sa. & Su.
National Museum of Colonial Art (Museo Nacional de Arte Colonial), Cuenca & Mejia. Fine collection of Ecuadorian paintings and sculptures. Open 9–12, 3–6 M–F, 9–noon Sa & Su.
Caamano Museum (Museo Jijon y Caamano), Av. 12 de Octubre & Calle Robles, Catholic University library building. Excellent archaeological and historical collection. Open 9–12, 3–5 M–F.

Useful Information

National Tourist Office, Reina Victoria 516 (tel:23-9044); *Quito Tourist Office,* Palacio Municipal, Plaza Independencia (tel:52-7002); *U.S. Embassy,* Av. Patria & Av. 12 de Octubre (tel:562-890); *American Express,* Av. Amazonas 339 (tel:560-488); *Post Office,* Benalcazar 688, near Plaza de la Independencia; *Voltage Guide:* 110/220 V, two flat, parallel blade outlets are used.

Special Trips/Tours

The equator and the *Equatorial line Monument,* just over 14 miles N of Quito, is a very popular side trip. There is a park, restaurants, gift shops (you can get a certificate authenticating your visit to the equator), a small museum, and a tourist center.
    A definite must is a trip to one of the many *Indian markets* in one or more of the towns and villages outside Quito. These markets provide an opportunity to appreciate Ecuadorian Indian life (which is very different from that of the Indians of Peru and Bolivia, despite their common origins), and experience some of the country's magnificent scenery. You can also pick up bargains in native handicrafts and textiles. Check with your hotel for information on tours offered to the markets mentioned below. Some 75 miles N of Quito is *Otavalo* with its colorful Indian market on Saturday. Especially noted for its woolen goods, the market (actually three separate ones) lasts from 6 A.M. to 1:30 P.M. About 45 miles S of Quito, the Indian market in *Saquisili* occupies all eight of the town's plazas on Thursdays (7–11 A.M.). Pottery and tablecloths are good buys here. Some 20 minutes from Saquisili is the village of *Latacunga* with a Saturday and Tuesday market. Leather goods and textiles are good buys here. The largest Indian market in Ecuador is held on Mondays in *Ambato,* some 75 miles S of Quito. It is noted for its rugs, woolen goods, and ponchos.

Weather

Despite its location straddling the equator, Quito has a delightful climate, due to its 9,500-ft. elevation above sea-level. Temperatures are remarkably uniform throughout the year, with daytime highs typically in the low 70s, falling to the mid 40s at night. The rainy season lasts from October to May.

QUITO: TEMPERATURES AND PRECIPITATION

Month	J	F	M	A	M	J	J	A	S	O	N	D
Average Daily Temperature												
(Fahrenheit) Max.	72	71	71	70	70	71	72	73	73	72	72	72
Min.	46	47	47	47	47	45	44	45	45	45	45	46
Average Number of Days with Precipitation												
	16	17	20	22	21	12	7	9	14	18	14	16

Panama City: Panama

Sights to See

France Plaza (Plaza de Francia), located in the heart of El Casco Viejo, the old fortified city, at Panama City's southern tip. A tree-lined plaza with several monuments and an obelisk dedicated to the French engineers who started work on the Panama Canal.

Promenade of the Dungeons (Paseo de las Bovedas), a walkway built on a massive stone seawall originally built to protect the city from pirates. Behind Plaza de Francia. Fine views of the bay.

Ruins of Santo Domingo Church (Iglesia de Santo Domingo), Av. A. near Paseo de las Bovedas. Noted for its 300-year-old flat arch, made of stone. Visit the *Museum of Colonial Religious Art* adjacent to the Santo Domingo ruins. Open 10–3:30 Tu–Sa, 3–5:30 Su.

Independence Plaza (Plaza de la Independencia), Av. Central. Colonial Panama City's principal square, surrounded by the cathedral, Archbishop's Palace, and the old Cabildo. Numerous busts of the Republic's founders.

Cathedral (Catedral), Plaza de la Independencia, a.k.a. Plaza Catedral. Dating from the late 17th century, its is noted for its mother-of-pearl-encased twin towers and domes.

Church of San Jose (Iglesia de San Jose), Calle 8a, just S of the cathedral. Famous for its golden Baroque altar, transferred from Panama Viejo.

Presidential Palace (La Presidencia), Av. Norte overlooking the bay. A magnificent white building, noted for its gardens and herons kept in a fountain area.

National Museum of the Panamanian Man (Museo Nacional del Hombre Panameno), Plaza 5 de Mayo, N of the Presidential Palace. One of the continent's finest anthropological museums. Open 10–3:30 Tu–Sa, 3–6 Su.

Old Panama (Panama Viejo), on the Pacific Ocean some 4 miles from downtown Panama City. Repeatedly ransacked by pirates, the original settlement stands in ruins, now partially restored. Notable ruins are the *cathedral*, the moss-covered government buildings, and the 350-year-old *King's Bridge* (Puenta del Rey) that linked the city to the historic Las Cruces trail.

Useful Information

Panama Institute of Tourism, Citibank Building, 5th Floor, Via Espana 124 (tel:64-4000); *U.S. Embassy,* Apartado 6959, Panama 5 (tel:27-1777); *Post Office,* Plaza Catedral, Calle 6 and Av. Central; *Voltage Guide:* 110 V, two flat, parallel blade outlets are used.

Special Trips/Tours

One of the great engineering wonders of the world, the *Panama Canal,* should definitely be on your list. Built between 1904 and 1914, it is some 50 miles long, and rises and descends 85 ft. through six sets of huge locks. The most accessible are the *Miraflores Locks,* where a visitors' area allows you to appreciate the mechanics of passage through the canal. See the film and commentary (open 9–5 daily). The scenery along the route of the canal is quite beautiful, and can be seen by package tour, boat, or a railroad trip. Check with your hotel for details.

The Pacific resort island of *Taboga,* about 12 miles offshore (boats leave from Pier 18 in Balboa) makes a nice trip. Covered in lush tropical vegetation, the island has magnificent beaches, a picturesque fishing village overlooking the harbor, offers fine snorkeling, and has no automobiles. A real delight.

The *Pacific beaches,* W of Panama City along the Pan-American Highway, are just superb. Noteworthy are those at Playa Coronado, San Carlos, Playa Rio Mar, Playa Nueva Gorgona, and Playa Santa Clara.

Weather

Panama has a hot and humid tropical climate with remarkably uniform temperatures year-round. Summer daytime high temperatures are typically in the high 80s, falling to the mid 70s at night. Winter daytime highs are just about the same, dropping to the low 70s at night. Panama's rainy season extends from March to November, with October and November being the wettest months.

PANAMA CITY: TEMPERATURES AND PRECIPITATION

Month	J	F	M	A	M	J	J	A	S	O	N	D
Average Daily Temperature												
(Fahrenheit) Max.	88	89	90	87	86	87	87	86	85	85	85	87
Min.	71	71	72	74	74	74	74	74	74	73	73	73
Average Number of Days with Precipitation												
			4	2	1	6	15	16	15	15	16	18	18	12

Cuzco: Peru

Sights to See

Armaments Plaza (Plaza de Armas), in the heart of the city. Surrounded by Colonial arcades and four of the town's many churches.
Cathedral (Catedral), on the N side of Plaza de Armas. Built on the site of the Palace of Viracocha, this fine, 17th-century Baroque structure is noted for its native wood carving and choir stalls. Open 10–12, 3–5 daily.
Church of El Triunfo, adjacent to the Cathedral. The first church built by the Spanish in Cuzco. Noted for its granite altar. Open daily.
Palace of the Admiral (Palacio del Almirante), between Ataud & Purgatorio, just N of the Cathedral. An imposing Renaissance building housing the Regional History Museum, with paintings by local artists. Open 9–12, 3–5 M–F, 9–12 Sa.
La Compania Jesuit Church (La Compania de Jesus), on the E side of the Plaza de Armas. Widely considered to be Cuzco's most beautiful church. Built on the site of the Inca Temple of the Serpents, and rebuilt in the 17th century, it is famous for its cloister, interior murals, and paintings. Open 12–6 daily.
Calle Loreto, running SE from Plaza de Armas past La Compania de Jesus. Narrow street with the Inca walls of the House of Women of the Sun on one side and the House of Serpents on the other.
Religious Art Museum (Museo de Arte Religioso), Calle Hatunrumiyoc & Herrajes, just E of Plaza de Armas. Occupying the former archbishop's residence, it is noted for its colonial furniture as well as its collection of paintings. Open 9:30–12, 5–5 M–S, 3–5 Su.
Museum of Archaeology, National University of Cuzco, Calle Tigre 165. A superb collection of pre-Columbian stonework, textiles, implements, keros, turquoise figures, and mummies. Open 7:45–12:15, 3–5:30 M–F.
Church of La Merced, between Av. Sol & Calle San Bernardo, S of Plaza de Armas. Fine colonial church, famous for its monastery's cloisters, choir stalls, and jeweled monstrance. Open 8:30–12, 2:30–5:30 daily.
Cuzco Indian Market, Calle Tupack Amaru, S of Plaza San Francisco. Colorful open-air Indian market.

Useful Information

Tourist Office, Plaza de Armas, and at Tecsecocha 474; closest *U.S. Consulate,* is in Lima, at Av. Inca Garcilaso de la Vega & Av. Espana (tel:14/338-000); *Tourist Police,* Portal de Belen, Plaza de Armas (tel:22-1961); *Post Office, Av. del Sol & Garcilaso: Voltage Guide:* 220 V, two flat, parallel blade or two round-pin outlets are used.

Special Trips/Tours

The village of *Pisac* is some 20 miles from Cuzco and has a colorful Indian market on Thursday and Sunday mornings that is definitely worth visiting (either by taxi or with a tour group). A trip to Pisac is made all the more rewarding by the Inca ruins along the way. Just outside Cuzco on the road to Pisac is the ruined fortress of **Sacsahuaman**. It is famous for three parallel walls, containing 21 bastions, that run for over 390 yards. The Incaic stone are larger (some are over 300 tons) than those at Machu Picchu, and fit together perfectly without cement or mortar. The Inca throne, from which the Inca reviewed his armies, is carved out of solid rock. A few miles further is the **Kenko (Quenco) Amphitheater and Temple,** with its large stone altar and underground network of tunnels. It has fine examples of Inca stone carving. The Inca fortress of **Puca-Pucara** is also in the immediate vicinity. The spring shrine and spa of **Tambo Machay** is a little further N and still in good working condition—the water continues to flow into the Inca bath.

Some 45 miles NW of Cuzco, beyond Pisac, is **Ollantaytambo**. Located in the Urubamba Valley, the center of the Inca Empire, and built on and out of the stones of an Inca town, it is one of the few Inca towns still inhabited and not rebuilt by the Spanish. The well-known *Bath of the Princess* (Bano de la Nusta) is located between the town and the temple fortress ruins known as Inca Misanca. Especially noteworthy are the terraces above the town.

The real Inca gem, of course, is **Machu Picchu**, "The Lost City of the Incas." Never found by the Spanish, and not discovered by outsiders until 1911, this remarkably well preserved city, over 8,000 ft. up on a mountain saddle, is some 75 miles N of Cuzco and should not be missed. Reached only by foot, or by the narrow-gauge railroad, Machu Picchu with its temples, terraces, altars, palaces, squares, towers, and fountains, all connected by staircases carved out of solid rock, is truly spectacular. Trains leave Cuzco's San Pedro Station daily for the 3-to-4-hour trip—an experience in itself (sit on the left-hand side going there, right-hand coming back). If possible, try and spend the night at Machu Picchu so that you will get a chance to see the ruins without the many day-trip tourists scattered all over.

Weather

Cuzco, at just over 10,500 ft., has a pleasantly moderate climate. Summer (Dec.–Feb.) daytime high temperatures reach into the high 60s, dropping to the mid 40s at night. Winter (June–Aug.) daytime highs are around 70, falling to the low 30s at night. November through March is the wet season.

CUZCO: TEMPERATURES AND PRECIPITATION

Month	J	F	M	A	M	J	J	A	S	O	N	D
Average Daily Temperature												
(Fahrenheit) Max.	68	69	70	71	70	69	70	70	71	72	73	71
Min.	45	45	44	40	35	33	31	34	40	43	43	44
Average Number of Days with Precipitation												
	18	13	11	8	3	2	2	2	7	8	12	16

Lima: Peru

Sights to See

Armaments Plaza (Plaza de Armas), at the center of Lima, one block S of the Rio Rimac. A beautiful plaza marking the site of Pizarro's founding of the city in 1535.

Changing of the Guard, Government Palace (Palacio de Gobierno), Plaza de Armas. Takes place 12:45–1 daily.

Cathedral (Catedral), Plaza de Armas. A huge structure noted for its silver-covered altars, wall mosaics, and glass coffin allegedly containing the remains of Francisco Pizarro. Open 8–noon daily.

Church of Santo Domingo (Iglesia de Santo Domingo), Jiron Camana 170, NW of Plaza de Armas. Dating from 1549, it is known for its two high towers, and an altar urn containing the remains of the New World's first saint, Santa Rosa de Lima. Open 7–1, 4–8 daily.

San Francisco Church (Iglesia de San Francisco), Jiron Ancash 300, NE of Plaza de Armas. Dating from the 16th century, this Baroque church is noted for its carved stalls, beautiful ceilings and cloisters, and three levels of catacombs. Open 10–1, 3–5 daily.

Church of San Pedro (Iglesia de San Pedro), Jiron Ucayali 300, 2 blocks SE of Plaza de Armas. An early-17th-century Baroque church, known for its gilded wood carvings, tilework, and altars. Open 7–1, 5:40–10:30 daily.

Torre Tagle Palace (Palacio Torre Tagle), Jiron Ucayali 363, down the block from San Pedro church. Considered to be Lima's best surviving example of secular colonial architecture. Only the patio is open.

National Museum of Art (Museo de Arte), Paseo Colon 125, some 10 blocks S of San Pedro church. Excellent collection illustrating the chronological history of Peruvian culture. Open 9–7 Tu–Su.

Gold Museum (Museo del Oro), Av. Primavera in suburb of Monterrico. Superb collection of worked gold from the Spanish colonial era and earlier. Open 12–7 daily.

Museum of Anthropology and Archaeology (Museo de Antropologia y Arqueologia), Plaza Bolivar in suburb of Pueblo Libre. The most interesting museum in Peru. Open 10–6:30 Tu–Sa, 10–6 Su.

Rafael Larco Herrera Museum (Museo Arqueologico Larco Herrera), Av. Bolivar 1515, Pueblo Libre. Famous collection of pre-Inca pottery, along with textiles and gold and silver objects. Don't miss the erotic art display. Open 9–1, 3–6 M–Sa.

Useful Information

Peruvian National Tourist Office, Avenida Belen 1066 (tel:72-1928); *Tourist Office* (Enturperu), Av. Javier Pradoeste 1358; *U.S. Embassy & Consulate,* Av. Garcilaso de la Vega 1400 (tel:33-8000); *American Express,* Lima Tours, Avenida Belen 1040 (tel:27-6624); *Voltage Guide:* 220 V, two flat, parallel blade or two round-pin outlets are used.

Special Trips/Tours

In the attractive suburb of San Isidro, at the corner of Av. Rosario & Nicolas de Rivera, are the *pre-Inca of Huallamarca*. Specimens found in the excavated pyramid are exhibited in the adjoining museum. Open 9–5 daily.

The pre-Inca *Pachacamac Ruins and Museum* are 20 miles S of Lima, off the Southern Panamerican Hwy. in the Lurin Valley. Dating from 900 B.C., these former pyramidal ruins were later built on by the Incas. Notable structures include the 14th-century *Temple of the Sun,* and the reconstructed Temple of the Virgins. Archaeological discoveries are displayed in the adjoining museum, which is open 10–5 daily.

Weather

Lima has a dry, desert-like climate. Summer (Dec.–Feb.) daytime high temperatures typically reach into the low 80s, dropping to the mid 60s at night. Winter (June–Aug.) daytime highs usually reach into the high 60s, falling to the upper 50s at night. Although Lima receives very little precipitation, it does experience frequent "garua," a light drizzle.

LIMA: TEMPERATURES AND PRECIPITATION

Month	J	F	M	A	M	J	J	A	S	O	N	D
Average Daily Temperature												
(Fahrenheit) Max.	82	83	83	80	74	68	67	66	68	71	74	78
Min.	66	67	66	63	60	58	57	56	57	58	60	62
Average Number of Days with Precipitation												
	1	0	0	0	0	1	1	2	1	0	0	0

Montevideo: Uruguay

Sights to See

Constitution Plaza (Plaza Constitucion or Matriz), in the center of the historic colonial part of town, with its narrow streets and 18th-century buildings.

Montevideo Cathedral (Catedral de Montevideo), on the W side of Plaza Constitucion. Large, ornate 18th-century structure. Open daily.

Town Hall (Cabildo), opposite the cathedral on Plaza Constitucion. The former town hall, it contains an excellent museum devoted to illustrating the city's history. Open 2–8 Tu–Su.

Independence Plaza (Plaza Independencia), 4 blocks E of Plaza Constitucion. The heart of Montevideo, it is surrounded by government buildings, hotels, theaters, and offices. In its center is an equestrian statue of Jose Gervasio Artigas, Uruguay's national hero, with his mausoleum underground.

Natural History Museum (Museo de Historia Natural), Buenos Aires 652, just off Plaza Independencia on the ground floor of the Solis Theater. Archaeological exhibits and native flora and fauna. Open 2–5 Tu, Th, & Su.

Legislative Palace (Palacio Legislativo), at the end of Av. Libertador Lavallejo, which starts 5 blocks E of Plaza Independencia. A huge, fine building constructed of multicolored marble, noted for its ornate interior and stained-glass windows. Open daily.

National Pre-Columbian and Colonial Art Museum (Museo Nacional), in the Municipal Building, Av. 18 de Julio & Ejido. Excellent collection of art. Open Tu–Su.

Prado Park (El Prado), off Av. Libertador Lavallejo, about 3 miles N of Av. 18 de Julio. A beautiful park, with lakes, immaculate lawns, and a rose garden.

Rodo Park (Parque Rodo), Rambla Pres. Wilson opposite Playa Ramirez, SE of Plaza Libertad. Montevideo's most popular park, with an amusement park and boating lake.

National Museum of Fine Arts (Museo Nacional de Bellas Artes), Rodo Park. Collection of contemporary works by Uruguayan artists. Open 1–5 Tu–Su.

Useful Information

National Tourist Office, Av. Libertador Lavallejo 1409, Fourth floor (tel:91-4340); *Tourist Information Center,* Plaza Libertad (tel:90-5216); *U.S. Embassy,* Calle Lauro Muller 1776 (tel:40-90-50); *American Express,* c/o Turispart Ltd., 924 Mercedes (tel:92-0852); *Police* (tel:890); *Voltage Guide:* 220 V, two round-pin or three-prong rectangular blade outlets are used.

Special Trips/Tours

The beach resorts of *Atlantida, La Floresta, Solis, Piriapolis, Portezuelo, Maldonado,* and *Punta Ballena* are strung out along the attractive Atlantic coastline E of Montevideo, Uruguay's Riviera. By far the best though, is *Punta del Este,* situated on a narrow peninsula, some 90 miles from Montevideo. It is famous throughout South America for its beautiful beaches (Playa Mansa is safer than the more dangerous Playa Brava), and casinos. There is also plenty of tennis, golf, fishing, and superb seafood to keep you busy. *Lobos Island,* a nature reserve with a huge sea-lion colony some 6 miles offshore, makes an interesting excursion.

To the west of Montevideo on the River Plate is the 17th-century Portugese settlement of *Colonia.* Its narrow cobblestone streets, rebuilt city walls, and Colonial buildings in the historic section are very attractive. Noteworthy sights to see include the *Parochial Church,* the *Plaza,* and the *Municipal Museum.*

Weather

Montevideo has a temperate climate, with warm to hot summers and mild winters. Summer (Dec.–Feb.) daytime high temperatures typically in the low 80s, dropping to around 60 degrees at night. Winter (June–Aug.) daytime highs are usually in the high 50s, falling to the 40s at night. Rainfall is well distributed throughout the year.

MONTEVIDEO: TEMPERATURES AND PRECIPITATION

Month	J	F	M	A	M	J	J	A	S	O	N	D
Average Daily Temperature												
(Fahrenheit) Max.	83	82	78	71	64	59	58	59	63	68	74	79
Min.	62	61	59	53	48	43	43	43	46	49	54	59
Average Number of Days with Precipitation												
	6	5	5	6	6	5	6	7	6	6	6	7

Caracas: Venezuela

Sights to See

Caracas itself from Mount Avila Peak. The view of the city on one side, and Venezuela's Caribbean coast on the other, from this 7,000-ft. peak, is just spectacular. Check to see if the cable car is running, otherwise use the road.
Plaza Bolivar, Av. Norte & Este. An attractive square surrounded by government buildings and the cathedral.
City Hall (Concejo Municipal), Plaza Bolivar. Houses three museums: one on the Criollo Way of Life; one devoted to E. Boggio's paintings; and one on ceramics. All open 9:30–12, 3–5 M–F, 9:30–5 Sa–Su.
Bolivar's Birthplace (Casa Natal del Libertador) on Calles Traosos & San Jacinto, just E of City Hall. Reproduction, with period furniture, personal effects, and paintings. Open 9–12, 2–5 Tu–Sa, 10–5 Su.
Bolivar Museum (Museo Bolivariano), adjacent to Casa Natal. Contains Bolivar's war relics. Open 9–12, 3–5 Tu–F, 10–1, 3–6 Sa–Su.
The Capitol (El Capitolo Nacional), Plaza Bolivar. Famous for its gilded dome, and paintings by Martin Tovary Tovar in its Elliptical Salon. Open Tu–Su.
Cathedral (La Catedral), just to the E of Plaza Bolivar. Noted for its beautiful facade and paintings by Rubens and Murillo. Open daily.
San Francisco Church (Iglesia de San Francisco), Av. Universidad & Calle San Francisco, 2 blocks S of Plaza Bolivar. Famous for its colonial altars. Open daily.
Santa Teresa Basilica (La Basilica de Santa Teresa), Centro Simon Bolivar, 3 blocks S of Plaza Bolivar. Noted for its image of the Nazareno de San Pueblo. Open daily.
Museum of Fine Arts (Museo de Bellas Artes), Plaza Morelos in Parque Los Cabos, about 2 miles E of Centro Simon Bolivar along Av. Bolivar. Fine collection. Open 9–12, 3–5:30 Tu–F, 10–5 Sa–Su.
Colonial Arts Museum (Museo de Arts Colonial), Quinta Anauco & Av. Panteon, in suburb of San Bernardino. Excellent collection devoted to the country's colonial past. Open 9–12, 2–5 Tu–Sa, 10–5 Su.
East Park (Parque del Este), between Autopista Francisco Fajardo & Av. Francisco de Miranda, in E part of Caracas. Lush tropical trees, lakes, a zoo, an aviary, and sports fields. Open Tu–Su.

Useful Information

Venezuelan Tourist Corp., Centro Capriles, Plaza Venezuela (tel:781-8311); *U.S. Embassy,* Avenida Francisco Miranda, La Floresta (tel:284-7111 or 284-6111); *Police* (tel:169); *Weather* (tel:41-0279); *Voltage Guide:* 110 V, two flat, parallel blade outlets are used.

Special Trips/Tours

The Venezuelan Riviera beach resorts of *Niaguata, Macuto,* and *Catia La Mar* are just north of Caracas, over Mount Avila, on the Caribbean. The beaches at *Niaguata* and *Macuto,* E of La Guaira are the best. The German immigrant village of *Colonia Tovar,* some 40 miles into the mountains between Caracas and Valencia, is worth a trip. Stop off in *El Junquito* on the way to or from Caracas.

If you have more time, the trip to the Sierra Nevada de Merida town of *Merida* (418 miles SW of Caracas and just over an hour's flight-time) is worthwhile. It is famous for its *cable car to Pico Espejo,* at 15,600 ft. the highest and longest cable car in the world. The panoramic views from top are magnificent. The cable car operates mornings from Wednesday to Sunday.

Weather

With its 3,400-ft. altitude, Caracas enjoys a moderate climate despite its location in the tropics. Daytime high temperatures in the summer typically reach into the high 70s, dropping to around 60 degrees at night. Winter daytime highs are also usually in the upper 70s, falling to the mid 50s at night. The rainy season lasts from June to November.

CARACAS: TEMPERATURES AND PRECIPITATION

Month	J	F	M	A	M	J	J	A	S	O	N	D
Average Daily Temperature												
(Fahrenheit) Max.	75	77	79	81	80	78	78	79	80	79	77	78
Min.	56	56	58	60	62	62	61	61	61	61	60	58
Average Number of Days with Precipitation												
	6	2	3	4	9	14	15	15	13	12	13	10

The Caribbean
Anguilla

Sights to See

The Valley, in the central part of Anguilla, just inland from the Crocus Bay on the island's N coast. The island's principal town and administrative center.
Wall Blake House Museum, The Valley. A traditional plantation house, converted to a handicraft center and museum, devoted to the island's history.

Warden's Place, The Valley. Restored 18th-century official government residence, now an art gallery.

Shoal Bay, NE of The Valley. Noted for its fine coral garden, and *The Fountain,* a large underground cave with an unfailing supply of fresh water, and Arawak artifacts and petroglyphs. Pirates and smugglers, it is said, used the underground cave.

Island Harbour, NE of The Valley on Anguilla's N coast. A picturesque fishing village populated by the descendants of Irish settlers, and center of the island's lobster fishing industry.

Navigation Hill (150 ft.), just E of Island Harbour. Affords fine views of the N part of the island.

Dutch Fort ruins, Sandy Hill, on Anguilla's S coast, S of Island Harbour. The scene of fighting during the second French invasion of Anguilla in 1796.

Rendezvous Bay, to the W of Blowing Point Harbour, SW of Sandy Hill, on the island's S coast. A beautiful, long, crescent-shaped beach with sand dunes.

Salt Ponds, West End, on Anguilla's W end. The picking and harvesting of salt from evaporation ponds is an island industry. Another large salt pond is E of Sandy Ground Village, to the W of The Valley.

Sports

Boating: many of the island's resort hotels have small sailboats or windsurfers for rental. Otherwise contact *Tamariain Water Sports* (tel:497-2020), Cul de Sac, Blowing Point; the *Malliouhana Water Sports Center* (tel:6741), at the Malliouhana Hotel, Meads Bay; or *Tropical Watersports* (tel:6779), Cape Juluca, at Sandy Ground. For larger yacht charters, contact the *Baccarat* (tel:2470), *Classic Yacht Charters* (tel:2367), or Suntastic Cruises Ltd., (tel:497-3400).

Fishing: *Tamariain Water Sports* (tel:497-2020), Cul de Sac, Blowing Point, offers fishing charters, as does *Tropical Watersports* (tel:6779), Cap Juluca. Otherwise, arrangements can be made through your hotel with local fishermen.

Golf: there are no golf courses on the island.

Horseback Riding: the *Coral Bay Resort* (tel:2151), The Valley, offers riding facilities.

Snorkeling and Scuba Diving: many of the hotels and resorts have snorkeling equipment available. Otherwise, contact *Island Water Sports* (no phone), Road Bay; or *Tamariain Water Sports* (tel:497-2020), Cul de Sac, Blowing Point, who also offer scuba equipment rentals, guided dives, and lessons. *Malliouhana Water Sports Center* (tel:6741), Malliouhana Hotel, Maids Bay, also offers scuba diving.

Swimming: *Rendezvous, Cove,* and *Shoal Bays,* on the island's SW coast, are all very popular. *Road Bay* and *Crocus Bay* on the N coast are also good swimming beaches, together with *Shoal Bay* to the W of Island Harbour.

Tennis: the *Cinnamon Reef* (tel:2727), Little Harbour; *Rendezvous Hotel* (tel:2549), Rendezvous Bay; and *Malliouhana* (tel:2741), Meads Bay, have tennis courts for guests.

Windsurfing: Tropical Watersports (tel:6779) at Cap Juluca offers rentals, as well as *Sandy Island Enterprises* (tel:6395).

Weather

Anguilla, in the British Leeward Islands, enjoys remarkably even temperatures year-round. Summer daytime highs are typically in the high 80s, dropping to the mid 70s at night. Winter daytime highs are usually in the low 80s, falling to the low 70s at night. The rainy season extends from July through November.

ANGUILLA: TEMPERATURES AND PRECIPITATION

Month	J	F	M	A	M	J	J	A	S	O	N	D
Average Daily Temperature												
(Fahrenheit) Max.	82	83	85	86	88	88	87	88	89	87	85	83
Min.	70	70	70	72	74	75	75	75	74	74	73	72
Average Number of Days with Precipitation												
	12	9	9	8	10	13	14	16	13	14	16	13

Antigua

Sights to See

Nelson's Dockyard. Restored 18th-century naval dockyard used by Horatio Nelson in the 1780s. Now has a museum (Admiral's House) and is one of the Caribbean's major yacht marinas.
Shirley Heights, above Nelson's Dockyards. Extensive fortifications, barracks, and powder magazines for the tropps that guarded the dockyard. Views, especially at sunset, are excellent.
St. John's Cathedral, between Long & Newgate Sts., St. John's. Dating from the 17th century and rebuilt twice. Noted for its pitch-pine interior.
The Market, at the S end of St. John's on Market Street. A busy, colorful outdoor farmers' market especially on Friday and Saturday mornings.
Seaview Farms. Pottery is a cottage industry on the island, and most of the craftspeople exhibit their wares on their front porches.
Fig Tree Drive, a 20-mile circular drive through the island's mountain range and fishing villages along the S coast. Start on the drive outside Liberta, north of Falmouth. Fig is Antiguan for bananas, so don't be surprised if you don't see any fig trees!
Rum Distillery (home of Cavalier and Old Mill rums), next to Deep Water Harbor (tel:2-1071 or 2-1012 to arrange a visit).
Devil's Bridge, at Indian Town near Long Bay on the E coast. A natural bridge with surf-spouting blowholes.

Sports

Boating: most hotels have small sailboats available. Nelson's Dockyard may have some charter yachts. Check *Nicholson Yacht Charters* (tel:463-1530), at

English Harbor for interisland cruises. *Buccaneer Cove* or *Code's Halcyon Cove Water Sports* rent boats. Day cruises on the *Jolly Roger,* a 108-ft. "pirate ship," with sightseeing, snorkeling, dancing, drinks, and a lunch, leave from Dickenson Bay (tel:2-2064).

Fishing: sport fish are abundant in the waters around Antigua. Many boats leave from Nelson's Dockyard at English Harbor. Contact *Caribbean Water Sports* (tel:2-0256); Hugh Bailey (tel:3-1036). *Catamaran Hotel,* Falmouth Harbor (tel:3-1036), and *Halcyon Cove Water Sports* at Dickenson Bay (tel:2-0256), also have fishing charters.

Golf: *Cedar Valley GC* (tel:462-0161), has an 18-hole course 3 miles outside St. John's. *Half Moon Bay Hotel GC* (tel:2-2726), has a 9-hole course.

Horseback Riding: *Reliable Stable* (tel:1-4086), *Wadadli Stables* (tel:1-2721), and a stand next to *Halcyon Cove Hotel* rent horses. Beach riding is discouraged by the government.

Water Skiing: offered by many hotels, particularly at *Dickenson, Hodges, Falmouth, Half Moon,* and *Marmora Bays,* and at *Galleon Beach* at English Harbour.

Snorkeling and Scuba Diving: *Dive Runaway* (tel:2-1318), *Dive Antigua* (tel:2-0256) and *Caribbean Water Sports* (tel:2-0258) offer instruction, along with *Blue Water Beach Hotel* (tel:2-0290) in Soldier Bay. The best spots are the reefs and wrecks off the NE, S, and W coasts, especially *Salt Fish Tail,* and *Horseshoe* reefs, and around a sunken square-rigger in *Deep Bay.*

Swimming: virtually all the beaches are very good and unspoiled, and most are protected by offshore reefs. The best ones are at *Pigeon Point,* near Falmouth Harbor, and at *Dickenson Bay.*

Tennis: most of the larger hotels have courts, allowing non-guests to play, although guests do have preference. The best courts are at the *Halcyon Cove Beach Resort* (tel:2-0256) and *Half Moon Bay* (tel:3-2101).

Windsurfing: contact *Patrick's Windsurfing School* (tel:2-3094), or *Blue Waters Beach Hotel* (tel:2-0290).

Weather

Antigua experiences fairly uniform temperatures year-round. Summers are hot, with daytime highs in the high 80s, dropping to the mid 70s at night. Winters are warm and sunny, with daytime highs in the upper 70s or low 80s, falling to the low 70s at night. The winter months are the driest, sunniest, and least humid.

ANTIGUA: TEMPERATURES AND PRECIPITATION

Month	J	F	M	A	M	J	J	A	S	O	N	D
Average Daily Temperature												
(Fahrenheit) Max.	82	83	85	86	88	88	87	88	89	87	85	83
Min.	70	70	70	72	74	75	75	75	74	74	73	72
Average Number of Days with Precipitation												
	12	9	9	8	10	13	14	16	13	14	16	13

Aruba

Sights to See

William III Tower (Willem III Toren), Oranjestraat, in Oranjestad, the island's capital. An old lighthouse that was part of Fort Zoutman, and is one of the major landmarks in Oranjestad.
Aruba Museum (Museo Arubano), in Fort Zoutman and the William III Tower. Collection of artifacts illustrating the island's history. Open 9–4 M–F, 9–12 Sa.
Wilhelmina Park, S of Fort Zoutman across L. G. Smith Blvd., along the waterfront. Beautiful gardens full of exotic tropical flora.
"Schooner Harbor," W of Wilhelmina Park on the waterfront. Colorful, floating market of Venezuelan fish, fruit, and vegetable sellers.
Nassaustraat, Oranjestad's main street. Lined with offices, banks, shops, and boutiques.
De Palm Island, entertainment village (restaurants, theater, shops, water-sport center), built on a coral reef. Reached only by boat (tel:2-4400).
Aruba's windward (northeast) coast. Spectacular scenery with huge rocks being pounded by waves, forming a natural bridge near Andicouri. Boca Mahos, just to the NW of Andicouri, is particularly attractive.
Boca Prins Dunes, on the NE coast, are especially rugged and beautiful. "Dune sliding" is a popular pastime.
Hooiberg (Mt. Haystack), a 541-ft. hill in the center of Aruba with great views of the island, and, on a clear day, Venezuela.
Casibari area, just W of Hooiberg. Noted for its huge rocks hollowed out by weathering.

Sports

Boating: most hotels have small sailboats for rent. *Aruba Nautical Club Marina* (tel:2-3022), in Spanish Lagoon, and the *Bucuti Yacht Club* (tel:2-3793) frequently have charter yachts. *De Palm Watersports* (tel:2-4400) offers sailing trips and charters, and glass-bottom-boat cruises. *Pelican Watersports* (tel:2-3888), 1 Rockerfellarstraat, also offers cruises.
Fishing: Aruba's coastal waters are rich in sport fish. *De Palm Watersports* (tel:2-4400) charters boats. The *Mahi-Mahi* (tel:2-4022/2-7014) offers full- or half-day charters, as does the *Macabi* (tel:2-2756).
Golf: the Aruba Golf Club (tel:9-3485) has an 11-hole course near St. Nicolaas at the E end of Aruba.
Horseback Riding: Rancho El Paso (tel:2-3310), at Washington 44, offers horseback riding.
Snorkeling and Scuba Diving: Aruba offers excellent snorkeling and scuba diving, especially along the island's NW coast at *Arashi, Malmok,* and *Palm Beach, Baby Beach* and *Bachelor's Beach,* off Colorado Point at the SE tip of Aruba, are also good snorkeling spots. *De Palm Watersports* (tel:2-4400), and *Pelican Watersports* (tel:2-4739), Oranjestad, offer instruction and guided trips, and also rent equipment, as does *Caribbean Sea Adventure* (tel:4-5804), L. G. Smith Blvd., Orangjestad.

Swimming: the best beaches on Aruba are on its W and S shores (the *"Turquoise Coast"*). *Palm Beach* and *Eagle Beach* on the island's NW shore are the best, particularly *Palm Beach*. *Malmok,* a little further N, also has a fine beach.
Tennis: most of the island's hotels have courts, and there are a number of private clubs where visitors can play. Check with your hotel.
Water Skiing: most oceanfront hotels on Aruba offer both tows and lessons. *De Palm Watersports* (tel:2-4400) offers water skiing instruction.

Weather

Summers in the Netherlands Antilles are hot, with daytime highs in the high 80s, "dropping" to the upper 70s at night. Winters are warm and sunny, with daytime high temperatures in the low 80s, falling to the mid 70s at night. Aruba is drier than most Caribbean islands; the "rainy season" extends from October to December.

ARUBA: TEMPERATURES AND PRECIPITATION

Month	J	F	M	A	M	J	J	A	S	O	N	D
Average Daily Temperature												
(Fahrenheit) Max.	83	84	84	86	86	87	87	88	89	88	86	84
Min.	75	74	74	76	77	78	77	78	78	78	76	75
Average Number of Days with Precipitation												
	14	8	7	4	4	7	9	8	6	9	15	16

Barbados

Sights to See

Trafalgar Square, Bridgetown. Complete with a statue of Admiral Nelson, built in 1813 (30 years before its London counterpart), this square is in the center of the capital.
Old Harbour (the Careenage), Bridgetown. Usually full of fishing boats and interisland shipping vessels.
St. Michael's Cathedral, Bridgetown. A rebuilt 17th-century structure, known for its antique memorial tablets.
Barbados Museum, Garrison Savannah, Bridgetown. A diverse collection illustrating the island's history, including Arawak artifacts.
The Platinum Coast, on the island's NW coast between Holetown and Speightstown. Site of the island's finest hotels and winter homes of the wealthy.
Bathsheba Coast. A spectacular, rugged section of the island's NE coast. Stop off in Bathsheba itself, a picturesque fishing village.
Andromeda Gardens, near Tent Bay on the Bathsheba coast. Excellent display of tropical plants and flowers in a beautiful setting, complete with waterfalls.
Speightstown. Former whaling town still functioning as a fishing port. Visit the main street market.
Farley Hill. A national park preserve, with picnic facilities and great views of the island.

East Coast Highway. A very scenic highway that follows the coast.
Sam Lord's Castle, on the island's SE coast. Former home of the legendary 19th-century Sam Lord. Now part of a luxury resort.
Harrison Caves, near Welchman Hill Gully. Ride the electric tram and enjoy the waterfalls.
Atlantis II (sightseeing submarine), off the W coast. Twelve dives per day (tel:436-8929), 9–9 daily.

Sports

Boating: most hotels either loan or rent small sailboats. Cruise yachts may be available through the *Barbados Cruising Club* (tel:426-4434) or the *Barbados Yacht Club* (tel:427-1125). For an interesting few hours on a "Pirate Ship," sign up for a 4-hour cruise on the *Jolly Roger* through your hotel, or call (tel:426-0767 or 422-2450). The *Vanessa Ann* (tel:414-2015) offers 5-hour cruises along the W coast.
Fishing: sport fish are abundant, particularly off the N and S coasts. *Jolly Roger* (tel:426-0767), *Sandy Beach* (tel:428-9033), and *Scuba Safari* (tel:426-9947) offer fishing trips.
Golf: an 18-hole course is at *Sandy Lane* (tel:422-1405). The *Rockley Resort* (tel:427-5890) and *Heywoods Resort* (tel:223-9815), both have 9-hole courses.
Horseback Riding: Brighton Riding Stables (tel:425-9381), St. Michael; *Sharon Hill Stables* (tel:425-0099), St. Thomas; *Sunbury Riding Stable* (tel:423-6780), St. Philip; and *Valley Hills Riding Stables* (tel:423-0033) offer riding facilities.
Water Skiing: many hotels have the equipment, otherwise contact *Willie's Water Sports* (tel:425-1060) at Paradise Beach, or *Scuba Safari* (tel:426-0621) at the Barbados Hilton.
Snorkeling and Scuba Diving: most W coast hotels either loan or rent the appropriate equipment. *Scuba Safari* (tel:426-0621) on Hilton Drive, *The Dive Shop Ltd.* (tel:426-9947) in St. Michael, and *Willie's Water Sports* (tel:425-1060) at Paradise Beach, offer instruction and diving trips. *Folkstone Park* and other W coast areas are very popular.
Swimming: the W coast is best for swimming, with most of the hotels having their own beaches, complete with chaises, umbrellas, and snack and drink bars. *Crane Beach,* on the SE coast, is also popular.
Tennis: the *Sandy Lane* (tel:432-1311) and *Paradise Beach* (tel:429-7151) hotels have the best tennis courts. Several other hotels/resorts have tennis courts, allowing non-guests to pay.

Weather

Barbados's summers are hot, with daytime highs in the mid to high 80s, dropping to the mid 70s at night. Winters are warm and sunny, with temperatures reaching the low 80s during the day and falling to around 70 at night. The rainy season is from June to December.

BRIDGETOWN: TEMPERATURES AND PRECIPITATION

Month	J	F	M	A	M	J	J	A	S	O	N	D
Average Daily Temperature												
(Fahrenheit) Max.	83	83	85	86	87	87	86	86	87	86	85	83
Min.	70	69	70	72	73	74	74	74	74	73	73	71
Average Number of Days with Precipitation												
	13	8	8	7	9	14	18	16	15	15	16	14

Bermuda

Sights to See

Front Street in Hamilton, the colony's capital, has Bermuda's best shops, many of them in Hamilton's oldest buildings. On the other side of Front Street are the carriage stand, the flagpole, and the city's piers.

Bermuda Historical Society Museum, Par-la-Ville Park, N of the Yacht Club, has a good collection on the history of Bermuda.

Session House, on the highest point in Hamilton, between Reid & Church Sts, is known for its Italian Renaissance facade and Jubilee Clock Tower.

Bermuda Cathedral, Church Street NW of Session House. An impressive neo-Gothic structure, with three beautiful stained-glass windows.

City Hall of Hamilton, Church Street, W of Bermuda Cathedral. Known for its modern wind-clock tower, and exhibits hosted by the Bermuda Society of Arts.

St. Theresa's Cathedral, Cedar Ave., NW of Bermuda Cathedral. Modern Spanish-style structure.

Fort Hamilton, Happy Valley Rd. on the E side of Hamilton. A restored 19th-century fort, which also affords beautiful views of Hamilton and the harbor.

Bermuda Aquarium, Museum, and Zoo, North Shore Road, Hamilton Parish. One of the best aquariums in the world. See the parrot theater.

Botanical Gardens, E of Hamilton, on Berry Hill Road. Full of native plants. Visit the Camden House museum of horticulture. The nearby Arboretum on Middle Rd., Devonshire Parish, is also worth visiting.

St. George's, at the E end of Bermuda. The island's first capital, founded in 1612, with a well-preserved historic core. Be sure to visit *Fort St. Catherine, King's Square, State House,* and the beautifully restored *Somers Wharf.*

Bermuda Maritime Museum, Ireland Island. Housed in an old Victorian fort, it has a fine collection illustrating Bermuda's maritime history. Especially noteworthy is the *Tucker Treasure,* a collection of relics and valuables taken from local shipwrecks.

Sports

Boating: one of the world's sailing capitals, Bermuda has every kind of boating/sailing available. Contact *Salt Kettle Boat Rentals* (tel:6-4863); *Bermuda Water Tours Ltd.* (tel:5-3727); *Harrington Sound Marina* (tel:2-5572); or *John Shirley*

Boat Rentals (tel:4-0914). Great Sound and Harrington Sound are the two best sailing/boating areas. *Bermuda Island Cruises, Ltd.* (tel:5-2525) and *BDA Water Tours, Ltd.* (tel:5-3727) offer sea cruises of varying duration.

Fishing: sport fish are abundant in Bermuda's waters. Contact the organizations just listed, *Bermuda Charter Booking Service* (tel:2-6246), or the *Bermuda Sports Fishing Associates* (tel:5-1986).

Golf: the island has three 18-hole, world-class golf courses open to the public and two private ones. The public courses are *Port Royal,* in Southampton; *Belmont Hotel, Golf & Beach Club* (tel:6-1301) in Warwick; and *Castle Harbour Hotel, Beach & Golf Club* (tel:3-8161) in Tucker's Town.

Horseback Riding: both beach and trail riding is available. Contact *Lee Bow Riding Centre* (tel:2-4181), Devonshire; or *Spiceland Riding Centre* (tel:8-8212), Warwick.

Snorkeling and Scuba Diving: the best spots are *Long, Horseshoe,* and *Church Bays,* and *Warwick Beach.* For either instruction, rental equipment or guided trips, contact *Skin Diving Adventures & Blue Water Divers* (tel:4-1034); *Grotto Bay Scuba School* (tel:3-8333); *Dave McLeod* (tel:6-4736); *South Side Scuba* (tel:8-1833); *Nautilus Diving Ltd.* (tel:8-2332). *Bermuda Water Sports* (tel:3-2640); *Pitman's Boat Tours* (tel:4-0700) and *Hayward's Explorer Snorkeling Cruises* (tel:2-8652) offer snorkeling trips.

Swimming: the beaches on the South Shore are the most popular, with the ones at *Church, Horseshoe,* and *Long bays* and *Warwick beach* being the best.

Tennis: most of the larger hotels have courts and allow non-guests to play, although guests do have preference. *Government Tennis Stadium,* Pembroke Parish (tel:2-0105), and the *Port Royal Tennis Courts* (tel:4-0974), Southampton Parish, are open to the public.

Water Skiing: Bermuda Water Sports/Ski Bermuda (tel:3-2640) at the Grotto Bay Hotel; *Bermuda Waterski Centre* (tel:4-3354), Somerset Bridge: and *Somerset Bridge Cruises* (tel:4-0234), Somerset, offer tows. *Great* and *Harrington Sounds* are the best areas.

Weather

Bermuda has a subtropical climate. Summers are hot with daytime highs in the mid 80s, dropping to the low 70s at night. Winters are mild to warm, with temperatures typically reaching the high 60s during the day, falling to around 60 at night.

HAMILTON: TEMPERATURES AND PRECIPITATION

Month	J	F	M	A	M	J	J	A	S	O	N	D
Average Daily Temperature												
(Fahrenheit) Max.	68	68	68	71	76	81	85	86	84	79	74	70
Min.	58	57	57	59	64	69	73	74	72	69	63	60
Average Number of Days with Precipitation												
	14	3	12	9	9	9	10	13	10	12	13	15

Bonaire

Sights to See

Breedestraat is the center of the duty-free shopping area in Kralendijk, the capital city. The capital, a small town of pastel-colored Dutch colonial houses, is located on the island's sheltered W coast.

The waterfront in Kralendijk, with its lighthouse and promenade. Just north of the North Pier is the busy Fish Market, best visited in the mornings. The town's two Piers (North and South), on Kralendijk's waterfront, are active spots with fishing boats, sailing yachts, and island sloops tied up alongside.

Folklore Institute Museum (Instituto Folklore), located in the Old Kralendijk Fort, between C. F. B. Hellmundweg and J. A. Abraham Blvd. opposite the Ro-Ro Pier. Collection of old utensils, artifacts, and musical instruments from Bonaire. Open 9–11:30, 1:30–3:30 M–F.

Goto Meer, an inland lake in the N part of the island. Famous for its flocks of pink flamingoes.

Washington-Slagbaai National Park, at the northernmost part of the island. Essentially a nature preserve (some 13,500 acres), it is known for the incredible variety of birds nesting there. A good bird-watching spot is the Poos di Mangel watering hole. An excellent place to picnic. Open 8–5 daily.

Rincon, just east of Goto Meer. The oldest settlement on Bonaire. Noted for its picturesque, pastel-colored houses.

Boca Onima, near the town of Rincon, on the N coast. Grottoes sculpted into the volcanic rock by the action of the waves and wind erosion. Some of the caves contain Indian petroglyphs.

Seroe Largo observation point, just N of Kralendijk. Great views of the W coast and Kralendijk, and (at night) the lights of Curaçao, some 40 miles away across the sea.

Lac Bay (Lac Baai), SE of Kralendijk on the E coast. A fine beach, fringed by mangroves. Take one of the glass-bottom-boat rides.

Sports

Boating: most hotels have small sailboats to use or rent. The Playa Lechi Marina, S of the Bonaire Beach Hotel, may have larger boats or yachts. *Bonaire Scuba Center* (tel:8448, ext. 300) at the *Bonaire Beach Hotel & Casino* has windsurfing boards for rent. *The Bonaire Trading Co.* (tel:8300) on Kerkweg, rents all kinds of boats. Kralendijk Bay is a popular sailing spot.

Fishing: there are several kinds of sport fish in the waters around Bonaire. Contact the Playa Lechi Marina. Otherwise, the *Flamingo Beach Hotel* (tel:8285) and the *Bonaire Beach Hotel* (tel:8448) feature fishing charters.

Golf: the *Bonaire Beach Hotel* (tel:8448) has a miniature golf course. There are no regular golf courses.

Horseback Riding: contact *Tinis Stables* (tel:8448), at the Bonaire Beach Hotel.

Snorkeling and Scuba Diving: the island's real sport. A coral reef itself, Bonaire is a divers' heaven, with the dive spots about 20 yards offshore all along the W side of the island and all around the small island of *Klein Bonaire. Pink Beach* is also an excellent spot for both snorkeling and scuba diving. For instruction, rental equipment, and diving trips, contact *Aquaventure* (tel:8290) at the Habitat Hotel; *Bonaire Scuba Center* (tel:8448, ext.300) at the Bonaire Beach Hotel; *Peter Hughes Dive Bonaire* (tel:277–3484) at the Divi Flamingo Beach Resort & Casino; or *Buddy Watersports* (tel:4266 or 8799). NOTE: it is strictly illegal to collect any coral or other marine life.

Swimming: the white sandy beaches around *Kralendijk* are very good, as well as those in *Lac Bay* and along the *coastline of Washington-Slagbaai Park.*
Tennis: the *Bonaire Beach Hotel* has two courts, allowing non-guests to play, although guests do have preference. *Kralendijk* has two public courts.
Water Skiing: make arrangements through your hotel. Otherwise contact *Bonaire Scuba Center* (tel:8448 ext. 300) at the *Bonaire Beach Hotel & Casino.*

Weather

Bonaire experiences remarkably uniform temperatures year-round. Summers are hot, with daytime highs typically in the mid to upper 80s, dropping to the upper 70s at night. Winters are warm and sunny, with daytime highs in the low 80s, falling to the mid 70s at night. Bonaire and the Netherlands Antilles generally are much drier than most other Caribbean islands. The wettest months are October, November, and December.

BONAIRE: TEMPERATURES AND PRECIPITATION

Month	J	F	M	A	M	J	J	A	S	O	N	D
Average Daily Temperature												
(Fahrenheit) Max.	83	84	84	86	86	87	87	88	89	88	86	84
Min.	75	74	74	76	77	78	77	78	78	78	76	75
Average Number of Days with Precipitation												
	14	8	7	4	4	7	9	8	6	9	15	16

British Virgin Islands

Sights to See

Road Town, on Tortola Island, and the capital of the British Virgin Islands (BVI), is the center of activity and home to most of the BVI's population.
Mt. Sage, Tortola Island. The vistas from this, the island's highest point at a little under 2,000 ft., are marvelous. A National Park, containing the remanants of the original tropical rain forest that once covered the island, surrounds Mt. Sage.
Long Bay beach on the N coast of Beef Island, across the Queen Elizabeth Bridge from the E end of Tortola.
Virgin Gorda Island. The second largest island in the group, it is virtually undeveloped. Speedy's Fantasy (tel:49-55240) operates the 30-minute ferry service from Road Town to Tortola.

The Baths, on Virgin Gorda Island. Huge rocks and boulders, caves and sea pools.
Cooper Island. A perfectly beautiful island that is easy to reach by sailboat or by arrangement through Treasure Isle Hotel (tel:49-42501).
Anegada Island. Best reached by air-taxi from Beef Island or Virgin Gorda. Noted for its superb beaches, particularly in a series of coves on the N coast. Also famous for the magnificent coral reefs that surround the island.
Good tours of Tortola Island are provided by *Travel Plan Tours* (tel:49-42347). Similarly, *Virgin Gorda Tours Association* (tel:49-55252) has a good reputation for tours of Virgin Gorda.

Sports

Boating: most hotels have small boats or sailboats available or to rent. To charter a larger boat or yacht, contact *The Mooring's Ltd.* (tel:49-42331); *Caribbean Sailing Yachts Ltd.* (tel:49-42741); *West Indies Yacht Charters* (tel:49-52363); *Trimarine Boat Co.* (tel:49-42490); or *Tortola Yacht Charters* (tel:49-42221), all on Tortola. On Virgin Gorda, contact *North South Yacht Charter Ltd.* (tel:49-55433); *Malcolm & Niki Precious* (tel:49-55555); and *Rainbow 2* (tel:49-55555). Sailing instruction is given by the *Offshore Sailing School,* through the *Treasure Isle Hotel* (tel:49-42501) outside Road Town, Tortola. Boardsailing or windsurfing instruction is offered by *Boardsailing B.V.I.* (tel:52447), Beef Island.
Fishing: deep-water sport fishing is not as developed as on other Caribbean islands. Nevertheless, *Charter Fishing Virgin Islands* (tel:49-43311), *Prospect Reef Harbour,* or the *Anagada Reefs Hotel* (tel:49-43425), Setting Point, Anagada, offer sport fishing. Otherwise, check through your hotel to see if there are any local fishermen willing to take you out.
Golf: there are no golf courses on the British Virgin Islands at present.
Horseback Riding: best arranged through your hotel or *Tamarind Country Club Hotel* (tel:49-52477). The horses and facilities at *Peter Island Hotel and Yacht Harbour* (tel:49-42561) on Peter Island have a good reputation.
Snorkeling and Scuba Diving: Marina Cay, Cooper Island, and *Anegada Island* are generally held to be the best spots. The *R.M.S. Rhone* wreck, on the W end of Salt Island, is a popular dive site. Contact the following dive organizations: *Aquatic Centres* (tel:49-42858/9); *Baskin in the Sun* (tel:49-42858); *Underwater Safaris* (tel:49-43235); or *Blue Water Divers* (tel:49-42847) in Road Town, Tortola. On Virgin Gorda, *Dive BVI Ltd.* (tel:49-55513); and *Kilbride's Underwater Tours* (tel:49-42746).
Swimming: Long Bay and *Cane Garden* have the best beaches on Tortola. *Devil's, Spring,* and *Trunk Bays,* all on Virgin Gorda, are also excellent. The N coast of *Anegada,* particularly *Bone Bay* and *Table Bay,* also offers good swimming beaches.
Tennis: the large hotels have courts and non-guests are usually allowed to play, although guests have preference. The best courts are at the *Prospect Reef Hotel* (tel:49-43311), Road Town, Tortola.

Water Skiing: *Prospect Reef Hotel* (tel:49-43311) on Tortola has skiing equipment and tows.

Weather

The British Virgin Islands enjoy remarkably uniform temperatures year-round. Summers are hot, but not excessively so. Daytime highs typically reach the mid to high 80s, dropping to the mid 70s at night. Winters are warm to hot and sunny, with daytime highs in the low 80s and temperatures in the 70s at night. Rainfall is distributed throughout the year, but July through November is the wet season.

TORTOLA: TEMPERATURES AND PRECIPITATION

Month	J	F	M	A	M	J	J	A	S	O	N	D
Average Daily Temperature												
(Fahrenheit) Max.	82	83	85	86	88	88	87	88	89	87	85	83
Min.	70	70	70	72	74	75	75	75	74	74	73	72
Average Number of Days with Precipitation												
	12	9	9	8	10	13	14	16	13	14	16	13

Cayman Islands

Sights to See

George Town, the capital on Grand Cayman Island, is a small town with small, neat houses, international banks, and tourist shops. See the Marine Building on the waterfront, the Government buildings on Fort St., and visit the General Post Office on Edward Street if you are a stamp collector.

Cayman Maritime and Treasure Museum, North Church St. Exhibits on boat building, turtling, and pirates.

Crowns and Sceptres Museum, on the waterfront, George Town. Exact replicas of the British Crown Jewels, along with replicas of robes worn by knights and ceremonial swords.

Seven Mile Beach, N of George Town. Regarded as one of the finest beaches in the Caribbean.

The Turtle Farm, at Northwest Point at the end of West Bay. The world's only sea-turtle nursery, with thousands of giant turtles.

Hell, near the Turtle Farms. Noted for its coral rock formations, and nearby tiny, thatched-roof post office, which cashes in on the name.

Botabano, a small fishing village at the NW end of North Sound opposite West Bay.

Coconut Walk Bay, on the SW tip of Grand Cayman. A beautiful beach and lighthouse.

Pedro's Castle, Old Jones Bay between Savannah and Bodden Town on the S coast. The oldest building in the Cayman Islands.

Bodden Town, the Cayman's first capital. Visit Gun Square with its cannon, and Pirates Cave.

South coast between Bodden Town and East End. Contains attractive Moon Bay, and a series of "blow holes" in the cliffs to the E of Moon Bay.
Atlantis Submarine underwater trip. Billed as the world's first professional recreational submarine, the 50-ft., 28-passenger Atlantis Submarine (tel:9-7700) offers several excursions daily out of George Town Harbour. Both day and night dives are offered.

Sports

Boating: several of the hotels/resorts have sailboats available for the use of guests. Rental boats are available from *Harbour House Marina* (tel:9-2007); *Bob Soto's Diving Ltd.* (tel:9-2483); *Aqua Delights Ltd.* (tel:7-4444, ext. 686); and *Surfside Water Sports* (tel:7-4224), who also offer sailing instruction and parasailing. For a short lunch or dinner cruise on the "pirate ship," *Queen Anne's Revenge,* contact *Blackbeard Fun Tours* (tel:9-5151) in George Town.
Fishing: the waters around the Caymans are abundant with sport fish. For charter fishing, contact the *Tortuga Club* (tel:7-7551), in East End.
Golf: the *Britannia Golf Course* (tel:9-7440), Seven Mile Beach, has a 9-hole championship course. It can also be played as an 18-hole Cayman course with the Cayman ball designed by Nicklaus.
Snorkeling and Scuba Diving: this is the sport, in one of the world's best diving areas. Most hotels have snorkeling equipment for rent, and the dive spots are typically close offshore. For diving instruction, rental equipment, and guided dive trips, contact *Bertmar Aqua Sports* (tel:9-2514); *Bob Soto's Diving Ltd.* (tel:9-2022); *Cayman Diving School* (tel:9-4729); *Cayman Kai* (tel:7-9491); *Dive Grand Cayman Ltd.* (tel:9-5679); *Surfside Water Sports* (tel:7-4224); *Seasports* (tel:9-3965); or the *Tortuga Club* (tel:7-7551). Good dive spots include *Bloody Bay* at the W end of Little Cayman island and off *Cayman Brac island.* For the adventurous, *Research Submersibles Ltd.* (tel:9-3870), offers 800-ft. wall dives on their PC-8 submersible, a 20-ft.-long, 5.5-ton observation/one atmosphere craft.
Swimming: the best beaches are along *Seven Mile Beach,* N of George Town. The *S coast of Little Cayman* is a series of unspoiled beaches, protected by an almost continuous offshore reef. *Coconut Walk Bay,* on the SW tip of Grand Cayman, also has a beautiful beach.
Tennis: most of the hotels/resorts have courts available for guests only. The *Grand Cayman Holiday Inn* (tel:7-4444) has the best courts. Anybody can play at the *Caribbean Club* (tel:7-4099), at *Le Club Cayman* (tel:7-4000), Seven Mile Beach, or at the *Tortuga Club* (tel:7-7551) in East End.
Water Skiing: offered at several hotels/resorts. Try the *Cayman Kai* (tel:7-9556), Rum Point, or *Aqua Delights Ltd.* (tel:7-4444, ext.686).

Weather

Summers are hot, with daytime highs typically around 90, falling to the mid 70s at night. Winters are very warm and sunny, with daytime highs usually in the mid 80s, dropping to the high 60s at night. The rainy season is from May through October.

CAYMAN ISLANDS: TEMPERATURES AND PRECIPITATION

Month	J	F	M	A	M	J	J	A	S	O	N	D
Average Daily Temperature												
(Fahrenheit) Max.	86	86	86	87	87	89	90	90	89	88	87	87
Min.	67	67	69	71	72	75	73	73	73	72	71	68
Average Number of Days with Precipitation												
	3	3	2	3	4	5	6	7	6	9	6	5

Curaçao

Sights to See

Willemstad, Curaçao's capital city. With its distinctive Dutch flavor, and 18th-century pastel houses, it is a delightful town to explore on foot.

The Waterfront area, starting at the Curaçao Plaza Hotel. The foundations of the hotel are part of the early-17th-century "Waterfort." Cannons can still be seen on the battlements.

Fort Amsterdam, just behind the Curaçao Plaza Hotel at the E end of the Queen Emma Bridge. Dating from the 18th century, the fort was the historic center of the old fortified town. Now it houses several government offices and the governor's residence.

Wilhelmina Plein, Curaçao's principal square, just to the E of Fort Amsterdam. The *Stadhuis,* the *Raadzaal* (Town Hall), and the *Statenzaal,* housing the parliament of the Netherlands Antilles, are all located on the square.

Queen Emma Bridge (Koningin Emma Brug), a pontoon bridge that connects one side of the city with the other across a shipping canal.

The Handelskade district N of Queen Emma Bridge along St. Anna Bay (St. Anna Baai). Lined with beautiful yellow and red brick houses.

Floating Market, right past the customs building on the corner of Handelskade and De Ruyterkade along Sha Caprileskade. A colorful floating market full of Venezuelan sailboats and schooners plying their vegetables, fruit, and fish.

Old Jewish Quarter (Scharloo), N of the Waaigat across the Zugbrucke from the Floating Market. Area of stately homes built by the early Jewish merchants.

Mikve Israel-Emanuel Synagogue and Museum, Columbusstraat and Kerkstraat, S of Sha Caprileskade. An early-17th-century colonial Dutch building, and the oldest synagogue in the western hemisphere.

Curaçao Museum, van Leeuwenhoekstraat in Otrobanda across the Queen Emma Bridge. Good collection of art, furniture, and general Curaçaoiana. Open 10–12, 2–5 Tu–Su.

Spanish Water (Spaanse Water), a few miles E of Willemstad. A beautiful sheltered natural harbor with many water-sport activities.

Mt. Christoffel, at the NE end of the island. The centerpiece of a wildlife park, this 1,239-ft. peak affords tremendous views of the island. Visit the Landhuis Savonet natural history museum at the entrance to the park.

Boca Tabla Grotto, on the N coast, just N of Christoffel Park. Most famous of the many grottoes on Curaçao.

Sports

Boating: boats can be rented from *Seascape Diving* (tel:62-5000). Windsurfing boards can also be rented from *Seascape Diving,* from *Sun Dive* (tel:62-4888) at the Holiday Beach Hotel, or from *Dive Curaçao & Watersports* (tel:61-4944) at the Princess Beach Hotel and Casino. The *Curaçao Yacht Club* (tel:3-8038) has reciprocal arrangements with members of most stateside yacht clubs.

Fishing: the waters off Curaçao have many species of sport fish. *Seascape Diving* (tel:62-5000) at the Concorde hotel arranges deep-sea fishing trips, as does *Dive Curaçao & Watersports* (tel:61-4944) at the Princess Beach Hotel & Casino.

Golf: the *Curaçao Golf & Squash Club* (tel:7-3590), Schottegatweg Noord, is the island's only course (9 holes).

Horseback Riding: rides are available at *Joe Pinedo's ranch* (tel:8-1616), and *Rancho Alegre* (tel:7-9160).

Snorkeling and Scuba Diving: most hotels have the basic snorkeling equipment available for guests. Scuba gear, instruction, and diving guides are available from *Peter Hughes Underwater Curaçao* (tel:61-6666); *Dive Curaçao & Watersports* (tel:61-4944); *Masterdive* (tel:5-4312); *Sun Dive* (tel:62-4888); *Piscadera Watersports* (tel:62-5000); and *Seascape Diving* (tel:62-5000).

Swimming: Westpunt and *Westpunt Bay,* at the W end of the island, are among the best beaches, along with the *Knipsbaai* and *Playa Jeremi* beaches on the W coast.

Tennis: most hotels have courts and allow non-guests to play, although guests do have preference.

Water Skiing: contact *Seascape Diving* (tel:62-5000).

Weather

Summers are hot, with daytime highs typically in the mid to high 80s, falling to the high 70s at night. Winters are warm to hot, with daytime highs usually in the low to mid 80s, dropping to the mid 70s at night. Curaçao is much drier than other Caribbean islands, although it does have a "rainy" season from October through December.

CURAÇAO: TEMPERATURES AND PRECIPITATION

Month	J	F	M	A	M	J	J	A	S	O	N	D
Average Daily Temperature												
(Fahrenheit) Max.	83	84	84	86	86	87	87	88	89	88	86	84
Min.	75	74	74	76	77	78	77	78	78	78	76	75
Average Number of Days with Precipitation												
	14	8	7	4	4	7	9	8	6	9	15	16

Dominica

Sights to See

Roseau, Dominica's capital on the SW coast. A jumble of wooden or concrete one- and two-story buildings, many with balconies and wooden shutters, typical of the colonial period. There are no duty-free shops.

Roseau's harbor-front area along Bay Street. Lined with commercial buildings and warehouses, it has two colorful markets at either end.

Cathedral of Our Lady of Fair Haven, corner of Queen Mary St. & Turkey La., Roseau. The island's main Roman Catholic church, dating from the 19th century.

Roseau's Botanical Gardens, above Roseau beyond Bath Rd. Full of Caribbean plants (from all over the islands, not just from Dominica).

Scott's Head, at the southernmost end of the island. Affords great views of the Atlantic on one side and the Caribbean on the other.

Grand Bay, some 10 miles SE of Roseau on the island's S coast, has an excellent beach with a fine view of Martinique in the distance.

Morne Trois Pitons National Park. A large rain-forest preserve in the S central part of the island. Noted for its exotic, lush tropical vegetation, and its *Emerald Pool,* a waterfall-filled grotto. Also in the park are *Freshwater Lake,* a deep lake filling the crater of an extinct volcano; *Trafalgar Falls,* a fine waterfall; *Sulphur Springs;* and *Boiling Lake,* nested in a volcanic crater.

Portsmouth, on the N end of Dominica, is the island's second town, surrounding the best anchorage on the island.

Ruins of Fort Shirley, just NW of Portsmouth, at the Cabrits. Dates from the 18th century.

Carib Indian Reservation, on the NE coast, the last bastion of the fiercely independent Carib Indians, some of whom still live in the traditional huts made of branches and leaves. The woodcarvings and basketwork are good buys.

Central Forest Reserve, E of Salisbury. Densely forested area with Morne Diablotin (4,748 ft.), the island's highest peak.

Dominica Tours (tel:8-2638), at Castle Comfort, has a good reputation for their tours of the island.

Sports

Boating: motorboat and sailboat trips are available from the *Anchorage Hotel* (tel:8-2638) at Castle Comfort near Roseau. Boat charters are also available through *Dive Dominica* (tel:9-2188).

Fishing: sport fishing charter boats are available at the *Anchorage Hotel* (tel:2638), or through *Castaways* (tel:9-6244), N of Roseau.

Golf: there are no golf courses on the island.

Hiking and Mountain Climbing: the *Morne Trois Pitons National Park* and the *Central Forest Reserve* provide excellent terrain for hiking, climbing, and birdwatching. *Dominica Tours* (tel:8-2638); and *Wilderness Adventure Tours* (tel:8-2198), offer guided tours into the island's interior.

Snorkeling and Scuba Diving: snorkeling equipment can be rented from the *Castaways* (tel:9-6244) and *Anchorage Hotel* (tel:448-2638). Instruction, rental equipment, and guided dives are provided by *Dive Dominica* (tel:448-2188) and the *Anchorage Hotel* (tel:448-2638). With their magnificent banks of coral, *Anse Noire, Hampstead Beach,* and *Hodges Beach* areas, on the N coast near *Calibishie,* are very popular with divers.

Swimming: there are few sand beaches, mostly in the N around Portsmouth, and some good black sand beaches, for example at *Pagua Bay,* near Marigot on the NE coast. Freshwater swimming in the many rivers is very popular on Dominica.

Water Skiing: equipment is available at the *Castaways* (tel:9-6244), north of Roseau.

Weather

Like most Caribbean islands, Dominica experiences remarkably even temperatures year round. Summers are hot, with daytime temperatures typically in the mid to high 80s, dropping off to the mid 70s at night. Winters are warm to hot and sunny. Winter daytime highs are usually in the low 80s, with lows in the high 60s or low 70s at night. July through December is the wet season, with August, September, and October being the wettest months.

DOMINICA: TEMPERATURES AND PRECIPITATION

Month	J	F	M	A	M	J	J	A	S	O	N	D
Average Daily Temperature												
(Fahrenheit) Max.	83	84	85	86	87	86	86	87	88	87	86	84
Min.	69	69	69	71	73	74	74	74	74	73	72	71
Average Number of Days with Precipitation												
	19	15	14	13	17	19	20	20	25	20	19	19

Dominican Republic

Sights to See

Columbus Square, Santo Domingo. At the heart of the colonial city, complete with a statue of Christopher Columbus, commemorating his discovery of the island.

Cathedral of Santa Maria la Menor, on the S side of Columbus Square, Santo Domingo. Built in the early 16th century, it is a beautiful example of the Spanish Renaissance architectural style, and the oldest cathedral in the western hemisphere.

The Alcazar, Santo Domingo. The restored 16th-century palace built for Columbus's son, Diego. Full of 16th-century antiques, paintings, and period tapestries. Visit the adjacent *Museo Virreinal.*

La Atarazana district, near the Alcazar, Santo Domingo. Renovated colonial arsenal, with boutiques, galleries, cafes, and restaurants.

National Pantheon, Calle las Damas, Santo Domingo. A former Jesuit monastery, it is noted for its huge chandelier and ceiling mural.

Museum of the Royal Houses (Museo de las Casas Reales), Calles las Damas, Santo Domingo. Fine collection of Santo Domingoania.

Casa del Cordon, Calles Emiliano Tejera & Isabel la Catolica, Santo Domingo. Oldest house in the New World, now occupied by a bank.

Museum of the Dominican Man (Museo del Hombre Dominicano), Plaza de la Cultura, Santo Domingo. Good pre-Columbian collection.

Plaza de la Cultura, Santo Domingo. A park with several worthwhile points of interest, including the *Gallery of Modern Art* and the National Theater, which hosts opera, jazz, ballet, and music concerts.

Altos de Chavon, a re-created 15th-century village near Casa de Campo, built by Gulf & Western. Watch artisans practice pre-Columbian handicrafts.

Puerto Plata, about 130 miles NW of Santo Domingo on the island's N Atlantic coast. Walk around the town and take the funicular to the top of Isabel de Torres peak for superb views.

Los Tres Ojos (the three eyes), on the E side of the Rio Ozama near the Autopista de las Americas, about 20 minutes from Santo Domingo. A famous cave, with three lakes, stalactites, and stalagmites.

Sports

Boating: small boats and sailboats are usually available at most hotels/resorts.

Fishing: the waters around the Dominican Republic are abundant in sport fish. Charter fishing boats are available from *Mundo Submarino* (tel:682-3466) in Santo Domingo and *Casa de Campo Yachting and Beach Club* (tel:687-6979) in La Romana. *Prieto Tours,* on Avenida 27 de Febrero, Santo Domingo, offers deep-sea fishing trips. Freshwater fishing is also good.

Golf: the island has two world-class courses, the 18-hole *Cajuiles I,* in La Romana along the Coast, and the 18-hole *Cajuiles II,* inland near La Romana; both are part of the *Casa de Campo* resort complex (tel:682-9656). The *Playa Dorado Hotel* (tel:586-3800), in Puerto Plata, and the *Santo Domingo Country Club* both have courses, but guests and members do have preference.

Horseback Riding: horses can be rented at the *International Riding Club* (tel:533-6321) and the *National Horseback Riding School* (tel:682-5482) in Santo Domingo. *Casa de Campo* (tel:682-9656), La Romana, also has riding facilities, as does *Villas Doradas* (tel:586-3000) in Puerto Plata.

Snorkeling and Scuba Diving: snorkeling equipment is available at most hotels/resorts. Guided scuba dives are offered by *Mundo Submarino,* 99 Gustavo Mejia Ricart (tel:566-0344). *La Caleta Reef,* near the Las Americas airport is one of the best dive spots. The *north coast* beaches around Puerto Plata are excellent snorkeling spots.

Swimming: the best *south coast* beaches are near *Boca Chica,* E of Santo Domingo. However, the really good beaches are on the *north coast* around Puerto Plata.

Tennis: most of the hotel/resort complexes have tennis courts, some of which allow non-guests to play, although guests do have preference. The *Hotel Santo Domingo* (tel:532-1511) and *Santo Domingo Sheraton* (tel:685-5151) have excellent courts.

Weather

Summers are hot, with daytime highs typically in the upper 80s, falling to the low 70s at night. Winter daytime highs are usually in the mid 80s, dropping to the mid 60s at night. The rainy period is from May through November.

SANTO DOMINGO: TEMPERATURES AND PRECIPITATION

Month	J	F	M	A	M	J	J	A	S	O	N	D
Average Daily Temperature												
(Fahrenheit) Max.	84	85	85	85	86	87	88	88	88	87	86	85
Min.	66	66	67	69	71	72	72	73	72	72	70	67
Average Number of Days with Precipitation												
	7	6	5	7	11	12	11	11	11	11	10	8

Grand Bahama Island

Sights to See

International Bazaar, Freeport. Ten acres of shops on twisting lanes, imitating those of the countries represented. Stop off at one of the many restaurants. Watch the artisans in the adjacent *Straw Market.*
Museum of Underwater Exploration, Underwater Explorers Club, Bell Channel Bay. Displays, movies, and multimedia exhibits featuring Bahamian waters.
Garden of the Groves, Lucaya. A beautiful botanical garden full of tropical and subtropical flora.
Rand Memorial Nature Center, on East Settlers Way, near Freeport. An unspoiled nature center, with exotic flora and fauna, including West Indian flamingoes, and a tropical bird aviary.
West End, 25 miles E of Freeport. A sleepy village, with old dilapidated warehouses and piers left over from its bootlegging days during prohibition. On your way to, or back from, West End, stop off at the *Hydro Flora Gardens,* between Seagrape and Bootle Bay, to witness this new farming method. The picturesque fishing villages of *Eight Mile Rock, Sea Grape,* and *Holmes Rock* are worth exploring to get a taste of Bahamian life outside the main centers.
Dolphin Experience, Port Lucaya Marketplace on the waterfront. Feed or swim with the dolphins (tel:373-1244).

Sports

Boating: most beach hotels have small sailboats available. The Bahamas are a major yacht chartering area, however, and yachts typically need to be reserved months in advance. Arrangements can be made through a travel agent or your hotel. Otherwise contact *Lucayan Harbour Inn Marina* (tel:373-1666); *Running Man Marina* (tel:352-6834); or *Xanadu Marina* (tel:352-8720). For a moonlight cruise on a glass-bottom boat with spectacular floodlight-illuminated views of underwater life, contact *Reef Tours Ltd.* (tel:373-5880).

Fishing: the waters around Grand Bahama abound in sport fish. Fishing charter arrangements can be made through your hotel, or you can contact the *Xanadu Marina* (tel:352-8720) or *Reef Tours Ltd.* (tel:373-5880) for sport fishing charters. *Bimini* is the big-game fishing capital of the world, and several daily flights leave via Nassau. On Bimini, contact the *Bimini Big Game Fishing Club* (tel:347-2391); *Bimini's Blue Water, Ltd.* (tel:347-2166); or the *Compleat Angler Hotel* (tel:347-2122).

Golf: Grand Bahama has six 18-hole golf courses. The *Bahamas Princess Golf Club* (tel:352-6721), the *Bahama Reef Golf and Country Club* (tel:373-1055), the *Fortune Hills Golf and Country Club* (tel:373-4500), and the *Lucayan Golf and Country Club* (tel:373-1066) in the Freeport/Lucaya area. The sixth course, the *Grand Bahama Hotel and Country Club* (tel:348-2030) is in West End.

Horseback Riding: Pinetree Stables (tel:373-3600) in Freeport offers rides.

Snorkeling and Scuba Diving: most beach hotels have snorkeling equipment available. For scuba instruction, equipment rental, and guided dives, contact the *Underwater Explorers Society* (tel:373-1244), next to the Lucayan Bay Hotel. NOTE: their museum is worth seeing. Good dive spots include *Treasure Reef, Zoo Hole, the Caves,* and *West End Point.*

Swimming: most of the hotels have their own stretch of beach, or have access arrangements to one. *Taino Beach* is very popular.

Tennis: the *Bahama Princess Country Club* and *Bahama Princess Tower* (tel:352-6721), the *Holiday Inn* (tel:373-1333), and the *Lucayan Bay Hotel* (tel:373-1555) all have good courts. Some allow non-guests to play, although guests do have preference.

Water Skiing: contact *Holiday Water Sports* (tel:373-1458), next to the Holiday Inn in Lucaya.

Weather

Summers are hot, with daytime highs typically in the upper 80s, falling to the mid 70s at night. Winters are warm and sunny, with daytime highs usually in the upper 70s, dropping to the mid 60s at night. The rainy season is from June through October.

BAHAMAS: TEMPERATURES AND PRECIPITATION

Month	J	F	M	A	M	J	J	A	S	O	N	D
Average Daily Temperature												
(Fahrenheit) Max.	77	77	79	81	84	87	88	89	88	85	81	79
Min.	65	64	66	69	71	74	75	76	75	73	70	67
Average Number of Days with Precipitation												
	6	5	5	6	9	12	14	14	15	13	9	6

Grenada

Sights to See

The Careenage (Inner Harbor) of St. George's, the capital city of Grenada. Ringed by many 18th- and 19th-century brightly colored buildings, and full of sailboats, yachts, and schooners.
Fort George (Fort Rupert), situated above the inner harbor. An 18th-century French fort, complete with walls, still-functioning cannons, dungeons, and a maze of underground passages. Now police headquarters.
Market Square, St. George's. Locals bring their wares on Saturday mornings to make a very colorful scene. This is the place to buy spices.
Anglican Church, at the lower end of Church St., St. George's. A late-17th-century structure, noted for its fine marble altar, frescoes, and stained glass.
Botanical Gardens and Zoo, at the S end of St. George's. A wide variety of tropical trees and flowers, and rare Caribbean animals and birds.
Fort Frederick on Richmond Hill. Constructed in the late 18th century, it affords excellent views of the city and harbor below.
Bay Gardens, NE of St. George's. Stroll along the walkways and admire the lush tropical plants, especially the fruits and spices.
Concord Falls, in the mountains NW of St. George's. A 50-ft. waterfall that is a favorite picnic spot.
Grand Etang Forest Reserve, NE of St. George's. An area of unspoiled tropical forest, home to many rare birds. See Grand Etang Lake, a spectacular lake in the crater of an extinct volcano.
Carriacou, one of Grenada's dependencies, just over 20 miles NE of Grenada. Known for its fine beaches.

Sports

Boating: most hotels have small boats and sailboats for rent. Jet skis, paddleboats, catamarans, and speedboat rides are available on the beach between the Holiday Inn and the Spice Island Inn on *Grand Anse Beach.* For yacht charters, contact *Grenada Yacht Services, Ltd.* (tel:2883) in St. George's; *Grenada Sailing School* (tel:4458); or *Spice Island Yacht Charters* (tel:4342), Prickly Bay, L'Anse aux Epines. Day charters and sunset cocktail cruises are offered by *Carin Travel* (tel:4363) at Grand Anse. The *Rhum Runner* (tel:4233), a glass-bottom catamaran, offers cruises off the S coast.
Fishing: the waters around Grenada are abundant in sport fish. Contact *Grenada Yacht Services* (tel:2883) or *Dodd Gorman* (tel:2508), or make arrangements through your hotel.
Golf: the *Grenada Golf & Country Club* (tel:4554) has a 9-hole course at Woodlands, outside St. George's.
Snorkeling and Scuba Diving: most beach hotels have snorkeling equipment available. Scuba equipment, instruction, and guided dives are offered by *Grenada Yacht Services* (tel:2883) and *Virgo Water Sports* (tel:4410). The submerged reef on the island's W coast is the most popular area for diving. *Hog* and *Calivigny islands* are two popular snorkeling spots.

Swimming: Grenada's best beaches include *Grand Anse* (one of the best in the Caribbean); L'Anse aux Epines; those at *Horseshoe, Musquetta, Grand, Cato,* and *Black bays* on the S coast; and *Levera* on the NE coast. *Sauteurs Bay,* also on the N coast, has a superb beach, too. The island dependency of *Carriacou* has excellent beaches, especially *Paradise Beach.*

Tennis: several hotels/resorts have courses, including *Calabash* (tel:4234); *Remada Renaissance* (tel:4371); *Secret Harbor* (tel:4548); and *Twelve Degrees North* (tel:4580). Most allow non-guests to play, although guests do have preference. There are several private tennis clubs in St. George's that will grant temporary memberships to visitors for a nominal fee. These include the *Richmond Hill Tennis Club* and the *Tanteen Tennis Club.*

Weather

Grenada's summers are hot, with daytime highs typically in the upper 80s. Temperatures drop off to the mid 70s at night. Winters are warm to hot, and sunny. Daytime highs are usually in the low 80s, falling to the high 60s at night. The wet season is from June through December, with August and September usually the wettest months.

GRENADA: TEMPERATURES AND PRECIPITATION

Month	J	F	M	A	M	J	J	A	S	O	N	D
Average Daily Temperature												
(Fahrenheit) Max.	82	83	84	87	88	88	87	88	88	87	85	83
Min.	69	69	70	72	73	74	74	74	73	72	71	70
Average Number of Days with Precipitation												
	18	13	13	10	16	20	22	23	21	19	20	19

Guadeloupe

Sights to See

Pointe-a-Pitre, Grand-Terre. Guadeloupe's largest city. A delightful French-Riviera-like community with white colonial buildings and modern high-rise condominiums and apartment buildings. Walk along *La Darse,* the old port full of schooners and yachts. Visit the very colorful open-air market on the quays in the morning.

Cathedrale de St. Pierre et St. Paul, Pointe-a-Pitre. Noted for its exterior ironwork skeleton.

Fort Fleur d'Epee, Grand-Terre. An 18th-century fort complete with dungeons and battlements.

Ste. Anne, Grand-Terre. A picturesque village, Pointe-des-Chateaux, Grand-Terre. Large cliffs where the Caribbean meets the Atlantic. A favorite picnic spot.

Parc Naturel of Guadeloupe, Basse-Terre. On your way to the capital, Basse-Terre, drive over *La Traversee* highway through these lush, tropical, forest-clad mountains straddling Basse-Terre. If you are so inclined, hike to the waterfalls at *Carbet,* or to the *Cascade aux Ecrevisses* (waterfalls), about 10 minutes from the first park pull-off from Pointe-a-Pitre.

Basse-Terre, Guadeloupe's capital city, on Basse-Terre. See the 17th-century *Fort St. Charles;* the 19th-century cathedral; the *Place du Champ d'Arbaud,* a charming square surrounded by colonial buildings; and the excellent *Botanical Garden* (Jardin Botanique).

La Soufriere, Basse-Terre. Take one of the color-coded (for degree of difficulty), marked trails to this dormant volcano's crater (4,813 ft.). See the waterfalls (Les Chutes du Carbet). Affords excellent views. NOTE: some sections of the marked paths are difficult, so care is required, particularly in the summit area.

Sports

Boating: most beach hotels/resorts rent small sailboats. To charter larger yachts, contact: *Locaraibes* (tel:90-8280); *Soleil et Voile* (tel:90-8181); *Basse-Terre Yachting* (tel:81-1145); or *Guadeloupe Yachting* (tel:82-2032).

Fishing: the waters around Guadeloupe are rich in sport fish, particularly off *Basse-Terre's West coast.* For deep-water fishing trips contact *Caraibes Fishing* (tel:84-4180) in St. François; *Fishing Club Antilles* (tel:84-1500) in Bouillante; or *Guadeloupe Chartaire* (tel:82-3447) in Pointe-a-Pitre.

Golf: Golf St. François (tel:88-4187), Grand-Terre, is an 18-hole course (considered one of the best in the Caribbean), that is open to everybody.

Horseback Riding: Le Relais du Moulin Hotel (tel:88-2396), at Chateaubrun near Ste. Anne, and *Le Criolo* (tel:84-3890), in St. Felix, both offer facilities.

Snorkeling and Scuba Diving: most hotels rent snorkeling gear and arrange both snorkeling and scuba trips. For instruction, rental equipment, and guided scuba dives, contact *Les Heures Saines* (tel:90-8272); *Aqua-Feri Club* (tel:84-2626); or *Karuketa Plongee* (tel:98-8663) in Gosier. The *Nautilus Club* (tel:98-704), and *Chez Guy* (tel:98-8172), operate in Malendure. The *western and southern coasts of Basse-Terre* are considered to have the best spots. In addition, there is excellent snorkeling on the coral reefs off the coast around *St. François,* as well as off *Gosier. Pigeon Island* is also popular.

Swimming: the S coast of Grand-Terre, particularly between *Bas-du-Fort* and *Gosier,* and around *Ste. Anne* and *St. François,* is considered to have the best beaches.

Tennis: the *Amical Tennis Club* (tel:82-1381) at Bas-du-Fort, *Club Tennis de Dugazon* (tel:82-0681) in Abymes, and the *Tennis Club du St. François* (tel:84-4001) all make arrangments for non-members to play. Many of the hotels/resorts with tennis courts allow non-guests to play, although guests have preference.

Water Skiing: most beach hotels offer water skiing equipment. Try *Frantel,* Bas-du-Fort (tel:83-6444); *La Toubana,* Ste. Anne (tel:88-2557); *Bois Joli Hotel,* Terre de Haut, Iles des Saintes (tel:99-5038).

Weather

Guadeloupe experiences remarkably even temperatures year round. Summers are hot, with daytime highs typically in the high 80s or low 90s, dropping to the low

70s at night. Winter daytime highs are usually in the low to mid 80s, falling to the upper 60s at night. The rainy season last from June to December.

GUADELOUPE: TEMPERATURES AND PRECIPITATION

Month	J	F	M	A	M	J	J	A	S	O	N	D
Average Daily Temperature												
(Fahrenheit) Max.	84	85	87	88	89	90	90	90	89	89	87	86
Min.	68	67	68	69	70	72	73	73	72	72	70	69
Average Number of Days with Precipitation												
	16	11	13	10	11	15	21	20	16	17	18	16

Haiti

Sights to See

The Iron Market, Port-au-Prince. A teeming indoor market where you have to jostle the crowds and bargain with the vendors, who seem to sell everything.
Palais National, between rue Jean-Marie Guilloux & rue Oswald Durand, Port-au-Prince. Modeled after the Capitol building in Washington, DC, this prominent white structure is best viewed from the *Place du Marron Inconnu,* with its statue.
Champ de Mars (Square of the Heroes of Independence). A statue of Haiti's first emperor, Dessalines, in a landscaped park.
Musee d'Art Haitien, S of the square of heroes, Port-au-Prince. Known for its Haitian primitives.
Musee du Peuple Haitien, Champs du Mars, Port-au-Prince. An excellent collection of voodoo ceremonial objects, pre-Columbian stone and pottery implements, and interesting pieces of Haitiana.
Cathedrale de la Sainte Trinite, rue Pavee, Port-au-Prince. Known for its naive biblical murals by famous Haitian painters.
Cathedrale Notre-Dame, rue du Dr. Aubry, Port-au-Prince. Noted for its famous rose windows.
Kenscoff. South of Port-au-Prince in the mountains. Visit the open-air market, the Baptist Mission craft shop, and Fort Jacques. The views from the road up to and down from the village are beautiful. Stop off at the *Jane Barbancourt Distillery* for a tour and free samples.
Cap-Haitien, on the N coast of Haiti. A charming old colonial capital with a rebuilt cathedral, it is now becoming an artists' colony. It is better known, however, as a base for exploring King Henri Christophe's *Palais de Sans Souci* ruins, and his very impressive *Citadelle La Ferriere* (sometimes billed by Haitians as the "eighth wonder of the world"). It was built over 3,000 ft. up in the mountains by 20,000 slaves to protect the King and his retinue from a feared attack by Napoleon.

Sports

Boating: a number of resorts have small sailboats to rent, including *Kyona Beach Club* (tel:2-4580), in Montrouis; *Kaliko Beach* (tel:2-5773); in Ouanga Bay; and *Taino Beach* (tel:2-7009), in Grand Goave. The *Ibo Beach marina* (tel:7-1200) on Cacique Island rents sailboats and windsurfers.
Fishing: deep-sea sport fishing is not well developed on Haiti. You might check on local fishermen through your hotel.
Golf: the Petionville Golf Club, above Port-au-Prince, has a 9-hole course.
Horseback Riding: beach riding is available at the *Ibo Beach* (tel:7-2100) and *Kaliko Beach* (tel:2-5773) resorts.
Snorkeling and Scuba Diving: most beach hotels and resorts have snorkeling gear available. *Sand Cay* and *Ounga Bay* are popular spots. For scuba diving instruction, rental equipment, and guided dives, contact *Georges Kenn* (tel:7-0479) in Petionville; or *Baskin-in-the-Sun* (tel:2-5773) at the Kaliko Beach Club.
Swimming: the beaches at Grand Goave W of Port-au-Prince and those N of the city are regarded as the best swimming beaches. Otherwise, try the hotel pools.
Tennis: several of the hotels have tennis courts, and although guests do have preference, some do allow non-guests to play. Try the *Royal Haitian* (tel:4-0485) in Port-au-Prince and *El Rancho* (tel:7-2080) and *Hotel Montana* (tel:7-1920) in Petionville.
Water Skiing: the *Ibo Beach* (tel:7-1200); *Kyona Beach Club* (tel:2-4580); and *Taino Beach* (tel:2-7009) resorts have skis and tows available.

Weather

Haitian summers are hot, with daytime highs typically in the low to middle 90s, dropping off to the mid to low 70's at night. Winters are warm to hot and sunny, with daytime high temperatures usually reaching the mid to high 80s, falling to the high 60s at night. The rainy season lasts from April to October.

HAITI: TEMPERATURES AND PRECIPITATION

Month	J	F	M	A	M	J	J	A	S	O	N	D
Average Daily Temperature												
(Fahrenheit) Max.	87	88	89	89	90	92	94	93	91	90	88	87
Min.	68	68	69	71	72	73	74	73	73	72	71	69
Average Number of Days with Precipitation												
	3	5	7	11	13	8	7	11	12	12	7	3

Jamaica

Sights to See

Crafts Market, Water Lane at the W end of the waterfront area, Kingston. One of the Caribbean's best.
National Gallery of Art, 12 Ocean Blvd., on Kingston's waterfront. Fine collection of works by contemporary artists.

Institute of Jamaica, East St., Kingston. Good art, natural history, and history museums.

Hope Botanical Gardens, Old Hope Rd., Kingston. Noted for its Orchid House and ornamental gardens.

Port Royal, across Kingston's harbor on the Palisades. Former headquarters of Henry Morgan's buccaneers.

Spanish Town, W of Kingston. Jamaica's old capital. Antique Sq., and King's House archaelogical museum.

Sam Sharpe Square (The Parade), Montego Bay. Surrounded by government buildings, a church, restored Georgian buildings, and tropical gardens.

Falmouth, an 18th-century port town, some 20 miles E of Montego. Stroll around the Albert George Market, and Olivier & Seaboard Sts.

North coast between Falmouth and Ocho Rios. Beautiful coastline with a really magnificent beach at *Runaway Bay.* Visit the Runaway Caves, and see the Spanish colonial ruins in Discovery Bay.

Dunn's River Falls, on the road between Montego and Ocho Rios. Well-known cascading waterfall with night feasts every Th.

Ocho Rios, almost 70 miles E of Montego Bay on the N coast. Sprawling resort area, known for its *"Fern Gully,"* a twisting road, and surrounding gardens.

Carinosa Gardens, Ochos Rios Bay. A 20-acre tropical garden overlooking the bay, with waterfalls, an aviary, a craft shop, a restaurant, and orchid and water gardens.

Port Antonio, further E along the N coast, about 130 miles from Montego Bay. A very picturesque fishing village surrounding two harbors. Known also for the nearby *Blue Hole lagoon, Somerset Falls,* and the *Nonsuch Caves* with their fossilized sealife.

The Blue Mountains, NE of Kingston, via Old Hope Rd. Over 7,000 ft. high, they afford magnificent vistas.

Sports

Boating: most beach hotels have small sailboats or windsurfers for rent. For larger yachts, contact *Jamaica Yacht Charters* (tel:952-2578) in Montego Bay; *Morgan's Harbour Marina* (tel:924-8464) in Port Royal; the *Royal Jamaica Yacht Club* (tel:928-6685) in Kingston and the *Montego Bay Y.C.* (tel:952-3028).

Fishing: the deep-sea fishing centers are Montego Bay and Port Antonio. Contact *Seaworld Resorts Ltd.* (tel:953-2180).

Golf: Montego Bay has four 18-hole courses, at *Half Moon* (tel:953-2560); *Ironside Golf Club* (tel:953-2800); *Wyndham Rose Hall Beach Hotel* (tel:953-2650); and *Tryall* (tel:952-5110). There is also an 18-hole course at the *Runaway Bay Hotel* (tel:973-3435) in Runaway Bay, and one at the *Upton Country Club* (tel:974-2528) in Ocho Rios. Kingston has two 18-hole courses, at the *Constant Spring Golf Club* (tel:924-1610) and the *Caymanas Country Club.*

Horseback Riding: contact *Good Hope Plantation* (tel:954-2289); *White Witch Stables* (tel:953-2746); or *Rocky Point Stables* (tel:952-1526) in Montego Bay;

contact *Chukka Cove* (tel:972-2506); *Prospect Plantation* (tel:974-2058) in Ocho Rios; and *Hedonism II* (tel:957-4200) in Negril.

Snorkeling and Scuba Diving: most beach hotels have snorkeling equipment available. For scuba instruction, equipment rental, and guided dives, contact *Poseidon Nimrod Club* (tel:952-1365), or *Water World* (tel:952-0865) in Montego Bay; *Tojo Watersports* (tel:954-2450) in Falmouth; *Hedonism II Water Sports* (tel:957-4200); or *Negril Scuba Center* (tel:957-4220) in Negril; and *Island Dive Shop* (tel:972-2519); *Caribbean Water Sports* (tel:973-3507); or *Sea* and *Dive Jamaica Ltd.* (tel:974-2552) in Ocho Rios.

Swimming: the best beaches are on the *north coast*. Try *Cornwall* and *Doctor's Cave* beaches in Montego Bay.

Tennis: try the courts at *Half Moon* (tel:953-2211); *Rose Hall Beach Hotel & Country Club* (tel:953-2650); and *Round Hill* (tel:952-5150) in Montego Bay; or *Jamaica Beach Resort* (tel:972-2382); *Jamaica Inn* (tel:974-2514); and the *Plantation Inn* (tel:974-2501) in Ocho Rios.

Weather

Summers are hot, with daytime highs normally around 90, dropping to the low 70s at night. Winters are warm to hot, with daytime highs usually in the mid 80s, falling to the high 60s at night. The rainy season extends from May through October.

KINGSTON: TEMPERATURES AND PRECIPITATION

Month	J	F	M	A	M	J	J	A	S	O	N	D
Average Daily Temperature												
(Fahrenheit) Max.	86	86	86	87	87	89	90	90	89	88	87	87
Min.	67	67	68	70	72	74	73	73	73	73	71	69
Average Number of Days with Precipitation												
	3	3	2	3	4	5	4	7	6	9	5	4

Martinique

Sights to See

La Savane, Fort-de-France. A large park in the center of town, with palm trees and mangoes, lined with shops and cafes on its sides and bordered by a crafts market, the ferry dock, and *Fort St. Louis* jutting out into the harbor.

Cathedrale St. Louis, a block away from the park, between rues Blenac & Antoine Siger, Fort-de-France. An impressive iron building, with fine stained glass.

Fruit and Vegetable Market (Marche), NW of the cathedral on rue Antoine Siger, Fort-de-France. A lively daily morning market, with a tremendous variety of tropical fruits and exotic spices.

Boulevard Alfassa, Fort-deFrance. Along the edge of the harbor. Visit the *Caribbean Arts Center,* which displays and sells the work of local artists.

Rue de la Liberte, Fort-de-France. The main street. Visit the *Musee Departmental de la Martinique,* with its Arawak and Carib collection.
Schoelcher Library, rue de la Liberte. A fine example of Romanesque-Byzantine architecture.
St. Pierre. Martinique's Pompeii. The eruption of the now dormant Mt. Pelee in 1902 destroyed this community on the NW coast.
Le Carbet. A small fishing village on the site of Columbus's landing in 1502, NW of Fort-de-France.
Route de la Trace. From Fort-de-France to Deux-Choux, a narrow road makes an excellent drive through the island's tropical rain forest.
Grand'Riviere, at the N tip of the island. A very picturesque fishing village in a magnificent setting.
Leyritz, Basse Pointe, just SE of Grand'Riviere. A restored plantation that now functions as an inn and restaurant and cultivates bananas.

Sports

Boating: most hotel beaches have small sailboats for rent. For yacht charters, contact *Shipshop* (tel:71-4340) in Fort-de-France; *Carib Charter* (tel:71-5896); *Dufour Antilles* (tel:76-3535) or *Voile et Vent Antilles* (tel:76-4340), Marina Pointe du Bout; or *Caraibes Nautique* (tel:66-0506), Hotel Bakoua. *Presentations Plus* (tel:66-0774), at the Marina Pointe du Bout, also rents boats.
Fishing: the waters around Martinique have a number of sport fish. Make charter arrangements through your hotel water-sports desk. The *PLM Azur Carayou* (tel:66-0404), in Pointe du Bout, has a fishing boat, as does the *Hotel Meridien Trois-Ilets* (tel:66-0000). Otherwise, it is not a well developed sport.
Golf: the 18-hole *Empress Josephine* (tel:76-3281) public course in *Les Trois-Ilets,* near Pointe du Bout, is the island's best.
Horseback Riding: Ranch de Galocha (tel:76-4397) near Anses d'Arlets, about 20 minutes from Pointe du Bout, provides horses for mountain rides. In Trois-Ilets contact *Black Horse Ranch* (tel:66-0004).
Snorkeling and Scuba Diving: snorkeling gear is available from most beach hotels. For scuba instruction, equipment rental, and guided dives, contact *Bathy's Club* (tel:66-0000) at the Meridien; or the *Latitude Scuba Club* (tel:73-6984) at the Latitude resort near Carbet. The *south coast beaches near Ste. Anne* are good snorkeling spots, as is the *Anses d'Arlets area.*
Swimming: The *Pointe du Bout beaches* are good. Those around Ste. Anne and *Le Diamant* on the S coast are excellent and uncrowded. The beaches at *Grand Anse* and *Petit Anse,* near the resort of Les Anses d'Arlets, are beautiful.
Tennis: most of the large hotels have courts and allow non-guests to play, although guests do have preference. Try those at the *PLM La Bateliere* (tel:71-9041), N of Fort-de-France.
Water Skiing: the *Bakoua Beach* (tel:66-0202) in Pointe du Bout and the *PLM La Bateliere* (tel:71-9041) N of Fort-de-France offer water skiing. Also available at most beaches near the big hotels.

Weather

Martinique's summers are hot, with daytime highs typically in the mid 80s, dropping to the mid 70s at night. Winters are warm to hot, with daytime highs in the low 80s, falling to the high 60s at night. The rainy season is from May through November.

MARTINIQUE: TEMPERATURES AND PRECIPITATION

Month	J	F	M	A	M	J	J	A	S	O	N	D
Average Daily Temperature												
(Fahrenheit) Max.	83	84	85	86	87	86	86	87	88	87	86	84
Min.	69	69	69	71	73	74	74	74	74	73	72	71
Average Number of Days with Precipitation												
	19	15	15	13	18	21	22	22	29	19	20	19

Montserrat

Sights to See

Saturday morning market, S end of Parliament St., Plymouth. Colorful market full of rural farmers with their produce. Visit the nearby *Handicraft Center,* which displays and sells local craft products.

Government House, above Sugar Bay just S of Plymouth. A large Victorian building with an ornate gable, surrounded by beautiful poinciana gardens and lawns.

St. Anthony's Church, outside Plymouth to the north. Dating from the mid-17th century, it is known for its two silver communion chalices, gifts of emancipated slaves.

Montserrat Historical Society Museum, NE of Plymouth on the lower slopes of Richmond Hill. Located in the tower of an old sugar mill, it has interesting exhibits on the island's history, together with a postage stamp collection.

Fox's Bay Bird Sanctuary, NW of Plymouth just beyond Bransby Point on the island's west coast. Home of the unique Montserrat oriole.

Soufriere Volcano. Due E of Plymouth in the Soufriere Hills, the youngest and most southerly of the island's volcanoes, with a number of separate peaks, including *Gage's Soufriere* and *Galway's Soufriere,* with impressive pools of molten lava and hot springs. The hike is strenuous.

Bransby Point Gun Battery, a restored six-gun battery on the W coast, dating from the 17th century.

Great Alps Waterfall. About 15 minutes S of the capital, near the settlement of Morris. A 70-ft. waterfall plunges into a picturesque pool. The climb to the pool is not easy and usually requires a guide, due to the fast-growing tropical vegetation.

Chance Peak. A 3,000-ft. mountain in the island's center that affords magnificent panoramas of Montserrat and the surrounding seas. For serious hikers.

Hell's Gate rock formation. An unusual rock formation on the island's N coast, just NE of Silver Hill, one of Montserrat's volcanoes.

Sports

Boating: contact the *Vue Pointe Hotel* (tel:5210), Olde Towne or Captain Martin (tel:491-4738). Check your hotel's activities desk for the names of individuals who rent their sailboats or other craft.

Fishing: local fishermen sometimes are willing to take people along for a fee. Your hotel is the best source of current information.

Golf: the island has one 9-hole course, the *Belham River Valley Golf Course* (tel:491-5220) at the Montserrat Golf Club.

Horseback Riding: contact *Sanford Farms* (tel:491-3301) for beach or mountain riding.

Snorkeling and Scuba Diving: contact the *Vue Pointe Hotel* (tel:5210) or *Captain Martin* (tel:491-4738). Experienced guides are available on the island, but you'd better bring your own snorkeling and scuba equipment, since none may be available for rent.

Swimming: the volcanic sand beaches all around the island are readily accessible and provide ideal, uncrowded conditions. *Carr's Bay,* on the NW coast N of St. Peters, is very popular, and has one of the few beaches on the island with regular sand.

Tennis: both *Montserrat Springs Hotel* (tel:2481) and the *Vue Pointe Hotel* (tel:5210) have courts that are available to non-guests, although guests do have preference.

Weather

Montserrat enjoys remarkably even temperatures year-round. Summers are hot, with daytime highs usually in the upper 80s, falling to the mid 70s at night. Winters are warm to hot, with daytime highs typically in the low 80s, dropping to the low 70s at night. The rainy season is from June through November, with October and November usually the wettest months.

PLYMOUTH: TEMPERATURES AND PRECIPITATION

Month	J	F	M	A	M	J	J	A	S	O	N	D
Average Daily Temperature												
(Fahrenheit) Max.	82	83	85	86	88	88	87	88	89	87	85	83
Min.	70	70	70	72	74	75	75	75	74	74	73	72
Average Number of Days with Precipitation												
	12	9	9	8	10	13	14	16	13	14	16	13

Nassau–New Providence Island

Sights to See

Rawson Square, focal point of Bay Street, the busy shopping center of Nassau, New Providence. Site of many governmental buildings.

Prince George Wharf, Nassau. Mooring place for the cruise ships. Stop off in the *Straw Market,* one of the region's largest.

Parliament Square, just S of Rawson Square, Nassau. The site of the much-photographed colonial-style Parliament Buildings and the Swordfish Fountain.

Fort Fincastle, Nassau. An 18th-century castle, built in the shape of a ship's bow. Below the fort is the 66-step *Queen's Staircase,* built by slave labor. Also adjacent to the fort is the *Water Tower,* a 126-ft. structure that affords marvelous views.

Government House, Mount Fitzwilliam, Nassau. Noted for its statue of Columbus on the long flight of stairs leading to its entrance, and the changing of the guard ceremony on alternate Saturdays at 10 A.M.

Fort Charlotte, at the W end of Nassau. Another imposing 18th-century British fort, complete with moat and dungeons.

The Botanical Gardens, below Fort Charlotte. Noted for their beautiful waterfalls, landscaped gardens and profusion of tropical plants.

Paradise Island, across Paradise Bridge from Nassau. See the daily feeding of the dolphins in the central lagoon, Versailles Gardens, the French cloister, Hurricane Hole yacht haven, and the famous beach.

Coral World, on Silver Cay, near Nassau. A reef tank and observation towers, plus shark, stingray, and turtle tanks. Accessible via shuttle from Cable Beach.

Sports

Boating: most beach hotels have small sailboats for rent. For short-notice charters, or day sails, contact *Nassau Yacht Haven* (tel:322-8173); *Bayshore Marina* (tel:322-8232); or the *Nassau Harbour Club* (tel:323-1771).

Fishing: fishing charter arrangements can be made through your hotel. Bimini is known as the big-game fishing capital of the world, and there are twice-daily flights from Nassau. On Bimini, contact the **Bimini Big Game Fishing Club** (tel:347-2391); *Bimini's Blue Water, Ltd.* (tel:347-2166); or the *Compleat Angler Hotel* (tel:347-2122).

Golf: the best golf course on New Providence is the 18-hole *South Ocean Beach Hotel & Golf Club* (tel:327-4117) at Lyford Cay. Other 18-hole courses include the *Ambassador Beach Hotel* and *Golf Club* (tel:327-8231); *Coral Harbour Club* (tel:327-7146); and *Paradise Island Golf Club* (tel:325-7431).

Horseback Riding: contact the *Harborside Riding Stables* (tel:326-3733), on Paradise Island, or *Happy Trails* (tel:323-5613) at Coral Harbour.

Snorkeling and Scuba Diving: most hotels have snorkeling equipment available, and can arrange for scuba instruction and guided dives. Otherwise, contact

Underwater Tours (tel:322-3285) or *Peter Hughes' Dive South Ocean* (tel:326-4391). Good dive spots include *Rose Island Reefs,* close to Nassau harbor; *Goulding Cay Reefs,* at the W end of New Providence; and *Gambier Deep Reef.*
Swimming: most hotels have their own stretches of beach, or have arrangements for guests to use a nearby beach. Paradise Beach on Paradise Island is very popular. Other good ones include *Love Beach* on the N shore of New Providence; *Adelaide Beach* on the S shore; and *Balmoral Island,* reached by boat from the Balmoral Hotel on Cable Beach.
Tennis: the best courts around Nassau are at the *Ambassador Beach* (tel:387-8231) on Cable Beach, and the *Nassau Beach Hotel,* (tel:327-7711). *Paradise Towers Hotel* (tel:326-2000), and *Holiday Inn* (tel:326-2101) on Paradise Island also have good setups.
Water Skiing: Nassau's *Cable Beach* and *Paradise Island* are the two popular water skiing spots. *Wyndham Cable Beach Hotel & Casino* (tel:327-7070) offers tows.

Weather

Summers in the Bahamas are hot, with daytime highs usually in the upper 80s, falling to the mid 70s at night. Winters are warm, with daytime highs usually in the upper 70s, dropping to the mid 60s at night. The rainy season extends from June through October.

BAHAMAS: TEMPERATURES AND PRECIPITATION

Month	J	F	M	A	M	J	J	A	S	O	N	D
Average Daily Temperature												
(Fahrenheit) Max.	77	77	79	81	84	87	88	89	88	85	81	79
Min.	65	64	66	69	71	74	75	76	75	73	70	67
Average Number of Days with Precipitation												
	6	5	5	6	9	12	14	14	15	13	9	6

Puerto Rico

Sights to See

Forts San Cristobal and El Morro (Castillos San Cristobal and de San Felipe del Morro), Old San Juan. Two well-preserved forts.
Museum of Colonial Architecture (Museo de la Arquitectura Colonial), W of the Plaza de Colon in Calle Fortaleza, Old San Juan. Housed in the Casa de Callejon. Noted for its fortification models.
Church of San Jose (Iglesia de San Jose), Plaza de San Jose, Old San Juan. A 16th-century Gothic structure noted for Ponce de Leon's coat of arms by the altar.
Pablo Casals Museum (Museo Pablo Casals), Plaza de San Jose, Old San Juan. The maestro's cello and memorabilia on display.

Casa Blanca, Calle San Sebastian, Old San Juan. Built for, but never occupied by, Ponce de Leon. Now an interesting museum featuring early Puerto Rican life.

San Juan Cathedral, Old San Juan. Noted for its 16th-century Gothic celings, and tomb of Ponce de Leon.

Museum of the Indian (Museo del Indio), NE of the cathedral, at corner of Calles Luna & San Jose. Good collection of Indian artifacts.

La Fortaleza, Calle Recinto Oueste, Ols San Juan. The residence of governors since the 16th century.

Caribbean National Forest (El Yunque). From San Juan take Rte. 3 E through Rio Grande to Mameyes Palmer, turning S on Rte. 191 up into the only tropical forest in the U.S. National Forest system. Full of exotic flora and fauna, including a number of rare species of parrot. The Visitors Center is open 9–5 M–Su.

Luquillo Beach, 4 miles from Mameyes Palmer. Probably the most famous beach on the island.

San German, just off Rte. 2 between Ponce and Mayaguez. Puerto Rico's second oldest city, after San Juan, with beautiful plazas, and a real colonial feeling. Visit the old church's, *Porta Coeli,* museum.

Rio Camuy Cave Park, inland from Mayaguez, known for its Empalme Cave with stalagmites, stalactites, and rock formations.

Sports

Boating: many of the larger beach hotels have small sailboats for rent. For larger yacht or boat rentals/charters, contact *Villa Marina Yacht Harbor* (tel:863-4051), in Fajardo, *Palmas del Mar's Sailing Center* (tel:852-6000) in Humacao, or *Playta Boat Rentals* (tel:722-1607) in Condado.

Fishing: for fishing charters, contact *San Juan Marina* (tel:725-0139), or *Torruella Fishing Center* (tel:725-1408) in Miramar: *Benitez Deep-Sea Fishing* (tel:723-2292/791-1015) in San Juan; or *Marina de Palmas Yacht Club* (tel:852-3450) in Humacao.

Golf: several of the island's larger resorts have world-class courses. The *Berwind Country Club* (tel:876-2230) in Rio Grande and the *Dorado del Mar* course (tel:724-4187) allow tourists to play. The *Club de Golf* (tel:852-3450), at Palmas del Mar in Humacao, has an excellent course.

Horseback Riding: horses can be rented at *Palmas del Mar Equestrian Center* (tel:852-4785) in Humacao, and at *Hacienda Carabali* (tel:726-0992) for beach riding.

Snorkeling and Scuba Diving: some of the major hotels have excellent programs through their water-sport centers. For scuba diving, contact the *Caribbean School of Aquatics* (tel:721-1000, ext. 1361) in San Juan; *Caribe Aquatic Adventure* (tel:721-0303, ext. 447) in San Juan; or the *Yaguez Diving School* (tel:832-9067) in Mayaguez.

Swimming: the best beaches include *Isla Verde,* close to San Juan, *Luquillo* to the E, and *Cerro Gordo, Sardinera,* and *Punta Salinas* W of San Juan.

Tennis: the best courts are at three of the islands resorts: *Dorado Beach* (tel:796-1600); and *Cerromar Beach* (tel:796-1010) in Dorado; and *Palmas del Mar* (tel:852-3450, ext. 2527) in Humacao. San Juan Central Park has public courts.

Water Skiing: San Juan's *Condado Lagoon* is the place.

Weather

Summer daytime high temperatures are typically in the mid 80s, dropping to the mid 70s at night. Winter daytime highs are usually in the low 80s, falling to around 70 at night. Rainfall is distributed evenly throughout the year, with frequent showers.

SAN JUAN: TEMPERATURES AND PRECIPITATION

Month	J	F	M	A	M	J	J	A	S	O	N	D
Average Daily Temperature												
(Fahrenheit) Max.	80	80	81	82	84	85	85	85	86	85	84	81
Min.	70	70	70	72	74	75	75	76	75	75	73	72
Average Number of Days with Precipitation												
	20	15	15	14	16	17	19	20	18	18	19	21

St. Barthelemy

Sights to See

Port de Plaisance harbor, Gustavia. Surrounded by shops, boutiques, and cafes, this picturesque yacht-filled harbor is the center of activity for much of the island.

Town Hall, Gustavia. Noted for the original records in Swedish of laws and town plans (Sweden owned the island between 1784 and 1877). Indeed, Gustavia, named for a Swedish king, has an interesting mixture of Swedish Colonial architecture.

Anse du Gouverneur, a delightful small cove accessible by foot only, below Morne Lurin just SE of Gustavia.

Corossol, on the S coast near Grand Pointe, is a delightful, picturesque fishing village famous for its straw hats, baskets, and place mats.

Baie de St. Jean, on the N coast, NE of Gustavia. Considered by some to be one of the best beaches in the whole Caribbean.

Montagne du Vitet, the island's highest peak (922 ft.), accessible by the road E of Baie de St. Jean that circles the mountain. Excellent views.

Sports

Boating: most beach hotels have small sailboats for rent. Some also arrange day sails to St. Bart's offshore islands. For larger yacht charters, contact *Loulou's Marine* (tel:27-6274); *Offshore Sailing* (tel:27-6238); *Yacht Charter Agency* (tel:27-6238); or *St. Barths Ship and Sail* (tel:27-6408). Windsurfing is popular, and boards can be rented from *Jack Windsurfing* (tel:27-6319), near Le Pelican, and the *Filao Beach Hotel* (tel:27-6484), both on St. Jean Baie. *El Sereno Beach* (tel:27-6480) and *St. Barth's Beach* (tel:27-6273) hotels, Grand Cul de Sac, also offer windsurfing rentals.

Fishing: *Pierrot Choisy* (tel:27-6122) offers fishing charters and has a good reputation. Otherwise, fishing charters can be arranged with local fishermen through your hotel.

Golf: there are no golf courses on St. Barthelemy.

Snorkeling and Scuba Diving: several of the beach hotels have snorkeling equipment available. For instruction, scuba equipment rental, and guided dives, contact *St. Barth's Water Sports* (tel:27-6616); *La Marine Service* (tel:27-6450); or *Loulou's Marine* (tel:27-6274). *Gouverneur, Cul de Sac,* and *St. Jean* beaches are all good snorkeling spots.

Swimming: most of the island's beaches are excellent. Among the most popular are *Baie de St. Jean* and *Anse du Grand Cul de Sac,* NE of the capital; and *Anse de la Grande Saline. Anse du Gouverneur,* SE of Gustavis, is a special cove, accessible only by foot. Other secluded coves are *Anse du Colombier* at the NE tip of the island, *Anse des Flamands,* and the *Petite Anse* just N of Gustavia. NOTE: topless bathing is considered quite normal and acceptable.

Tennis: there are only three courts on the islands, one at the *St. Barth's Beach Hotel* (tel:27-6273), Grand Cul de Sac; another, the only lighted court, at the *Hotel Manapany* (tel:27-6655) in Anse des Cayes; and one, the best bet, at the *Taiwana Club* (tel:27-6319) on the Baie des Flamands.

Water Skiing: for equipment and tows, contact *St. Barth's Water Sports* (tel:27-6616); or the *Association Sportive et Culturelle du Centre de Colombier* (tel:27-6107). Water skiing is authorized only between 8:30 A.M. and 3 P.M., and only in *Colombier Bay.*

Weather

St. Barthelemy enjoys remarkably even temperatures year-round. Summers are hot, with daytime highs typically in the mid to upper 80s, dropping to the mid 70s at night. Winters are warm to hot, and sunny. Winter daytime highs usually reach the low 80s, with temperatures falling off to around 70 degrees at night. The rainy season extends from July through November, with August, September, and October being the wettest.

St. BART'S: TEMPERATURES AND PRECIPITATION

Month	J	F	M	A	M	J	J	A	S	O	N	D
Average Daily Temperature												
(Fahrenheit) Max.	82	83	85	86	88	88	87	88	89	87	85	83
Min.	70	70	70	72	74	75	75	75	74	74	73	72
Average Number of Days with Precipitation												
	12	9	9	8	10	13	14	16	13	14	16	13

St. Croix

Sights to See

Fort Christiansvaern, Christiansted. An 18th-century fort built with red ballast bricks on the foundations of a 17th-century French fort.

Scalehouse, Christiansted waterfront near the fort, Christiansted. The restored former 19th-century Danish Customs House, now the local tourism office.

The Steeple Building, Company Street, Christiansted. Former Lutheran Church that now houses a museum, with exhibits on the history of St. Croix and the Virgin Islands.

Government House, King Street, Christiansted. Former residence of the Danish governor-general, noted for its crystal chandeliers.

Cruzan Rum Distillery, West Airport Rd., just outside Christiansted. Watch Virgin Islands rum in the making and enjoy a sample. Open 9–noon, 1–4 M–F.

Fort Frederik, Frederiksted. A restored 18th-century Danish fort that was considered the first to sound a foreign salute to the U.S. flag in 1776.

Market Place, Prince & Queen Sts., Frederiksted. A colorful and busy week-long market.

Customs House, Strand Street, Frederiksted. An 18th-century building, now housing the Visitor's Bureau.

Buck Island Reef, Buck Island, St. Croix. Catch the "Reef Queen," a glass-bottom boat that makes a half-day trip over the reef and surrounding coral beds. Boats leave from Christiansted daily.

St. George Village Botanical Garden, 3 miles E of Frederiksted in St. George. Full of native flora.

Whim Greathouse, Centerline Rd., 2 miles E of Frederiksted. A restored 18th-century plantation house, with a working sugar mill and small museum.

Sports

Boating: the beach hotels usually have small sailboats available. For larger yacht charters, contact *Caribbean Sea Adventures* (tel:773-5922); *Llewellyn's Charter Inc.* (tel:773-5037); *Mile-Mark Charters* (tel:773-2285); *Sun Sails* (tel:773-6015); or *Watersports Inc.* (tel:773-0754).

Fishing: you can make arrangements through your hotel, or contact *Caribbean Sea Adventures* (tel:773-5922); *Sun Sails* (tel:773-6015); or *Watersports Inc.* (tel.773-0754).

Golf: there are two 18-hole courses on St. Croix. One at the *Carambola Beach* (tel:778-0747), and the other at the *Buccaneer Beach Hotel* (tel:773-2100). The public can play at either one. There is also a 9-hole course at *The Reef* (tel:773-9250).

Horseback Riding: contact *Jill's Equestrian Stable* (tel:772-2880) at Sprat Hall Plantation, or *Hidden Valley Equestrian Stables* (tel:798-8670).

Snorkeling and Scuba Diving: many of the beach hotels have snorkeling equipment available. For scuba instruction, equipment rental, and guided dives,

contact *Caribbean Sea Adventures* (tel:773-5922) and *Dive Experience* (tel:773-3307), in Christiansted; *Sea Shadows* (tel:778-3850), in Cane Bay; and *Cruzan Divers* (tel:773-6011) in Frederiksted. *Buck Island* is the site of the nature trail of the *Underwater National Park*. Other popular diving spots include *Sugar Bay, Salt River,* and *Davis Bay* drop-offs, and *Pink Coral* and *North Cut*.
Swimming: the island's best beaches are at Davis Bay, N of Frederiksted, and Cane Bay, on St. Croix's N shore. Nude bathing is done at Isaac's Bay.
Tennis: the *Buccaneer Hotel* (tel:773-2100) has the best courts, and allows non-guests to play, although guests do have preference. Other courts are at the *Caribbean Tennis Club* (tel:773-7285); *Hotel on the Cay* (tel:773-2035); and *Grapetree Beach Hotel* (tel:773-0430).
Water Skiing: some of the island's hotels have equipment and tows available. Or contact *Above and Below* (tel:772-3701), in Frederiksted, or *Caribbean Sea Adventures* (tel:773-5922) in Christiansted.

Weather

St. Croix experiences remarkably even temperatures year-round. Summers are hot, with daytime highs usually in the high 80s, falling to the mid 70s at night. Winters are warm to hot, and sunny. Winter daytime high temperatures reach into the low 80s, dropping into the low 70s at night. The rainy season extends from July to November, with October normally being the wettest month.

U.S. VIRGIN ISLANDS: TEMPERATURES AND PRECIPITATION

Month	J	F	M	A	M	J	J	A	S	O	N	D
Average Daily Temperature												
(Fahrenheit) Max.	82	83	85	86	88	88	87	88	89	87	85	83
Min.	70	70	70	72	74	75	75	75	74	74	73	72
Average Number of Days with Precipitation												
	12	9	9	8	10	13	14	16	13	14	16	13

St. Kitts-Nevis

Sights to See

The Circus, the main square in Basseterre, St. Kitts. Noted for St. Kitts's version of "Big Ben," a large Victorian clock tower.
The Treasury Building, on the waterfront in Basseterre, St. Kitts. Noted for its architectural detail.
The Old Court House, Pall Mall, Basseterre, St. Kitts. Noted for its museum and first-floor library.
The Post Office, Basseterre, St. Kitts. Island stamps are much in demand among philatelists.
St. Kitts Sugar Factory, just outside Basseterre, St. Kitts. Take one of the daily tours.

Frigate Bay, on the "flank," or narrow peninsula, of land S of Basseterre, St. Kitts. Site of the island's most recent hotel and resort development.

Mt. Misery. St. Kitts's highest mountain (3,792 ft.). The hike to the top is not too difficult and will be rewarded with magnificent views.

Brimstone Hill Fortress, St. Kitts. The Gibraltar of the West Indies. A partially reconstructed and restored 18th-century fortress built on top of a 700-ft. cliff by the British, on the NW coast between Old Road and Sandy Point. Stop by the Visitors Center.

Alexander Hamilton House, Charlestown, Nevis. The site of Hamilton's birth in 1757. There is a small museum adjacent to the overgrown and fenced-off ruins of the house.

Montpelier Estate, Nevis. Site of the 1787 marriage between Horatio Nelson (Lord Nelson) and Frances Herbert Nisbet, whom Nelson courted on his frequent trips to the island to obtain water.

Sports

Boating: ST. KITTS: most beach hotels have small sailboats for rent, especially at *Frigate Bay. Beachcomber Sailboat Rental,* in Basseterre, rents sailboats and Sunfish. Larger yachts for day sails can be obtained through the *Ocean Terrace Inn* (tel:2380). NEVIS: contact *Golden Rock Estate* (tel:5346) or *Oualie Beach Pub* (tel:5329).

Fishing: ST. KITTS: contact *Colin Pereira* at the Ocean Terrace Inn (tel:2754); *Pelican Cove Marina* (tel:2754); or *Kenneth's Dive Center* (tel:2670) for fishing charters. NEVIS: *Golden Rock Estates* (tel:5346) arranges fishing trips.

Golf: ST. KITTS: there is an 18-hole championship course at Frigate Bay at the *Jack Tar Village Royal St. Kitts* (tel:8651), and there is a 9-hole course at *Golden Rock* on St. Kitts. NEVIS: there is no golf course on Nevis.

Horseback Riding: ST. KITTS: contact *The Stable* (tel:465-3226), or make arrangements through your hotel. NEVIS: the *Nisbet Plantation* (tel:5325), in Newcastle has facilities, allowing non-guests to ride when you make arrangements through your hotel.

Snorkeling and Scuba Diving: ST. KITTS: most beach hotels have snorkeling gear. *Caribbean Water Sports* (tel:8651) and *Kenneth's Dive Center* (tel:2670), offer instruction, rental equipment, and guided dives. NEVIS: *Oualie Beach Pub* (tel:5329), in Mosquito Bay, offers equipment and instruction. *Pinney's Beach* is a popular spot.

Swimming: ST. KITTS: the best beaches are at the island's S end, including those at *Friar's Bay* and *Banana Bay.* NEVIS: just about all of the island's beaches are excellent and uncrowded. The reef-protected *Pinney's Beach* is one of the best.

Tennis: ST. KITTS: *Jack Tar Village Royal St. Kitts* (tel:2651) has the island's best courts. *St. Kitts Lawn Tennis Club* (tel:2046) allows visitors to play. NEVIS: most hotels have courts. *Croney's Old Manor* (tel:5445) in Gingerland has the best.

Water Skiing: ST. KITTS: a number of hotels have equipment for their guests. *Caribbean Water Sports* (tel:8651), Pelican Cove, offers equipment and tows. NEVIS: *Oualie Beach Pub* (tel:5329), Mosquito Bay, has tows.

Weather

St. Kitts and Nevis enjoy remarkably even temperatures year-round. Summers are hot, with daytime highs typically in the upper 80s, dropping to the mid 70s at night. Winters are warm to hot, and sunny, with daytime highs usually in the low 80s, falling to the low 70s or upper 60s at night. The rainy season is from July through November.

ST. KITTS AND NEVIS: TEMPERATURES AND PRECIPITATION

Month	J	F	M	A	M	J	J	A	S	O	N	D
Average Daily Temperature												
(Fahrenheit) Max.	82	83	84	85	86	87	86	87	88	85	85	83
Min.	69	69	70	71	73	74	75	75	73	73	72	71
Average Number of Days with Precipitation												
	11	10	9	8	9	12	13	16	13	14	15	13

St. Lucia

Sights to See

Columbus Square, in Castries, the island's capital. With the *Cathedral of the Immaculate Conception* on one side and the famous restaurant, *Rain,* on another.
Saturday morning waterfront market, Jeremy St., Castries. Very colorful, with island women balancing baskets on their heads, farmers, and craftspeople plying their wares.
Fort Charlotte, on the Morne Fortune hill beind the capital. An 18th-century fortification with well-preserved military buildings, a small museum, and terrific views.
Pigeon Island, a national park connected to the N tip of St. Lucia by a causeway at Gros Islet.
Anse La Raye, about 5 miles S of Castries. A picturesque small fishing village, with fishermen working on the beach. On the way to Anse La Raye, stop off at *Marigot Bay,* considered by many to be one of the most beautiful in the Caribbean.
The Pitons. Two volcanic cones (each around 2,500 ft.) jutting out of the Caribbean along the coast, S of the small fishing village of Soufriere. Best viewed from the last range of hills before Soufriere.
Mt. Soufriere. The only drive-in volcano in the world, with natural sulfur baths and more fragrant baths at Diamond Falls.
Mouile-a-Chique, at the S tip of the island, where the Caribbean meets the Atlantic. The views along the shore and out to sea are magnificent.

Sports

Boating: most hotels have small sailboats available. For chartering larger yachts, contact *Stevens Yachts* (tel:2-8648) and *Trade Wind Yacht Charters* (tel:2-8424) in Rodney Bay; the *Moorings* (tel:3-4357), in Marigot Bay; or *Aquasail Yacht Charter* (tel:2-5754), in Castries. A good day trip is the *Buccaneer Day Cruise*, or on the 140-ft. square-rigger *Unicorn*, both of which sail from Castries down the W coast to Soufriere. Check with your hotel for details.

Fishing: the waters around St. Lucia are abundant in sport fish. Make arrangements through your hotel, or contact *Dive St. Lucia* (tel:2-4127) or *Mako Watersports* (tel:2-0412) for charters.

Golf: the 9-hole course at the *Hotel La Toc* (tel:2-3081) is open to non-guests. There is another 9-hole course at the *Cap Estate Golf Club* (tel:2-8523) at the N end of the island.

Horseback Riding: several of the island's hotels have riding facilities or access to them. *Trims Stables* (tel:2-8273), near Cap Estate rents horses, as does the *Cap Estate Stables* (tel:2-8626).

Snorkeling and Scuba Diving: most beach hotels have snorkeling equipment available. For scuba instruction, equipment rental, and guided dives, contact *Dive St. Lucia* (tel:2-4127) in Castries. *Scuba St. Lucia* (tel:4-7355) at the Anse Chastenet Hotel, offers instruction also.

Swimming: the W coast has the best beaches, including *Vigie Beach* and *Coc Bay,* N of the capital and *La Toc Bay,* to the south. *Pigeon Island* also has a long, sandy, artificial beach. *Vieux Fort,* near the airport, also has good, reef-protected beaches.

Tennis: most of the larger hotels have their own courts, and arrangements can usually be made to play even if your hotel does not. The best courts are at the *Hotel La Toc* (tel:2-3081) S of Castries, and at the *St. Lucian Hotel* (tel:2-8351), Reduit Beach.

Water Skiing: most hotels have equipment available.

Wndsurfing: most beach hotels will rent windsurfers, otherwise contact the *St. Lucian* (tel:2-8351), Castries Reduit Beach.

Weather

St. Lucia enjoys remarkably even temperatures year-round. Summers are hot, with daytime highs usually in the upper 80s, falling to the mid 70s at night. Winters are warm to hot, and sunny. Daytime high temperatures typically reach

ST. LUCIA: TEMPERATURES AND PRECIPITATION

Month	J	F	M	A	M	J	J	A	S	O	N	D
Average Daily Temperature												
(Fahrenheit) Max.	82	83	84	87	88	88	87	88	88	87	85	83
Min.	69	69	69	71	73	74	74	74	74	73	72	71
Average Number of Days with Precipitation												
	18	13	13	10	16	21	23	22	21	19	20	19

the low 80s, dropping to the high 60s at night. The rainy season is from May to December, with August being the wettest month.

St. Martin-St. Maarten

Sights to See

Marigot, capital of French St. Martin. Smaller and more subdued than Philipsburg, with a picturesque fishing and excursion boat harbor.
Grand-Case, St. Martin. On a strip of land between an old salt-pan and a magnificent beach. Known for its concentration of fine restaurants.
Peninsula des Terres-Basses, St. Martin. The most westerly part of the island, with beautiful beaches.
Mt. Flagstaff (1,286 ft.), straddling the border, W of the Quartier d'Orleans to Beneden Prinsen Road. A short hike will reward you with panoramic views.
Central Square (De Ruyterplein), Philipsburg, Sint Maarten. At the center of the Dutch capital, surrounded by the harbor, government buildings, and the shopping district along Front Street.
Courthouse, De Ruyterplein & Voorstraat, Philipsburg, Sint Maarten. Originally an 18th-century structure, it now houses the Town Hall.
Fort Amsterdam ruins, SW of Philipsburg between the Groot Baai and Klein Baai, Sint Maarten. A 17th-century Dutch fort, the first on the island. Enjoy the beautiful beach at *Klein Baai.*
Simsonbaai, to the west of Philipsburg, Sint Maarten. A picturesque Dutch-style fishing village.

Sports

Boating: most beach hotels have small sailboats available. ST. MARTIN: contact *Papagayo* (tel:87-5385) or *Patrick's Watersports* (tel:87-5177) for sailing excursions to offshore islands. SINT MAARTEN: contact *Sail-In* (tel:4386) at the Mullet Bay Marina for sailboat rentals and/or sailing instruction. Daily excursions around the island on ketches can be arranged through *Wathey Travel Service* (tel:2520), *Watersports Unlimited* (tel:52-3434), or *Red Ensign Watersports* (tel:2-2929).
Fishing: the waters around St. Martin/Sint Maarten have a number of sport fish. ST. MARTIN: contact *Le Pirate Hotel* (tel:87-7837) in Marigot, for deep-sea fishing. SINT MAARTEN: *Bobby's Marina* (tel:2-2366).
Golf: the *Mullet Bay Resort* (tel:4-2801) in Sint Maarten, has the island's only course (18 holes). Non-guests can play.
Horseback Riding: on St. Maarten contact *Crazy Acres Riding Center,* Cole Bay (tel:5-22061).
Snorkeling and Scuba Diving: most beach hotels have snorkeling equipment available. ST. MARTIN: for scuba instruction, equipment rental, and guided dives, contact *Under the Waves* (tel:87-5187); *Patrick's Watersports* (tel:87-5177), at Le Galion Hotel; or *Marigot Nautic Sports* (tel:87-5472). SINT MAARTEN: contact *Watersports Unlimited* (tel:52-3434), Philipsburg; *Beach*

Bums (tel:5252), in Simpson Bay; or *Maho Watersports* (tel:54-4387), Mullet Bay at the W end of Sint Maarten.

Swimming: most of the island's beaches are excellent, on both sides of the border. ST. MARTIN: *Rouge Bay,* and *Grand'Case* have excellent beaches. SINT MAARTEN: *Long Bay,* and *Maho Bay* and *Mullet Pond Bay* near Juliana Airport, have beautiful beaches; the latter two with excellent facilities for swimmers. A nudist beach is on the French side at Orient Bay.

Tennis: most of the large hotels have at least one court. The best facilities are at the *Mullet Bay Resort* (tel:4-2801), in Sint Maarten. Non-guests are usually allowed to play.

Water Skiing: most beach hotels on both sides of the island have gear and tows. On Sint Maarten, contact *Red Ensign Watersports* (tel:2-2929), Oyster Pond.

Weather

St. Martin/Sint Maarten summer daytime highs are typically in the high 80s, falling to the mid 70s at night. Winters are sunny, with daytime highs usually in the low 80s, falling to around 70 at night. The rainy season is from July through November.

ST. MARTIN/ST. MAARTEN: TEMPERATURES AND PRECIPITATION

Month	J	F	M	A	M	J	J	A	S	O	N	D
Average Daily Temperature												
(Fahrenheit) Max.	82	83	85	86	88	88	87	88	89	87	85	83
Min.	70	70	70	72	74	75	75	75	74	74	73	73
Average Number of Days with Precipitation												
	12	9	9	8	9	12	11	13	14	13	14	12

St. Thomas-St. John

Sights to See

Harbor and waterfront, Charlotte Amalie, St. Thomas. Seventeenth- and 18th-century warehouses full of duty-free shops, cruise ships, and yachts.

Fort Christian, at the E end of Charlotte Amalie, St. Thomas, near King's Wharf. A 17th-century Danish fort, it now houses a museum with Danish period memorabilia and Arawak and Carib Indian artifacts.

Government House, Kongens Gade, Charlotte Amalie, St. Thomas. The 19th-century seat of the Danish Colonial Council, now the U.S. Governor's residence. Noted for the Camille Pissarro paintings.

French Town ("Cha Cha Town"), just W of Charlotte Amalie, St. Thomas. A colorful little town, the residents of which speak a northern French dialect.

Coral World, Coki Beach on St. Thomas's N coast. An underwater observatory where visitors who don't snorkel or dive can observe underwater life.

Drake's Seat, Crown Mountain Rd., St. Thomas. Magnificent views of St. Thomas and many other islands.

Virgin Islands National Park, St. John. Crisscrossed with hiking trails so that you can explore its exotic flora and fauna up close. Trunk Bay, N of Cruz Bay, St. John. Widely considered to be one of the Caribbean's most beautiful. *Atlantis Submarine* view of local reefs, West Indies Dock, Charlotte Amalie (tel:776-5650).

Sports

Boating: most beach hotels have small sailboats available. The Virgin Islands are a major center of yacht chartering in the Caribbean; as a result, there are literally dozens of excellent chartering services on St. Thomas. However, most charters have to be booked months in advance. Possibilities for last-minute, day charters on ST. THOMAS include *Spur of the Moment Charters* (tel:774-5630); *Sea Adventures* (tel:774-9652); *Watersports Center* (tel:775-0755); and *VI Charter Yacht League* (tel:774-3944). Charters with skipper and crew are available from *Caribbean Yacht Charters* (tel:775-3604); *Watersports Center* (tel:775-6755); and *Avery's Boathouse* (tel:774-0111). Sea Vista Excursion's *Virgin Mermaid I,* billed as the world's largest glass-bottom boat, offers cruises, c/o *Mahogany Run* (tel:775-1957). On ST. JOHN contact *St. John Watersports* (tel:776-6256); *Cinnamon Bay Watersports Center* (tel:776-6458); or *Cruz Bay Watersports* (tel:776-6234).
Fishing: the waters around the U.S. Virgin Islands are abundant in sport fish. ST. THOMAS: for sport fishing charters, contact *American Yacht Harbor* (tel:775-6454); *Frenchman's Reef Sea Adventures* (tel:774-8500); or *Fish Hawke Marina* (tel:775-9058). ST. JOHN, contact *Cruz Bay Watersports* (tel:776-6234).
Golf: ST. THOMAS: *Mahogany Run* (tel:775-5000), next to Magen's Point Hotel, has an 18-hole course.
Horseback Riding: ST. JOHN: the *Pony Express Riding Stable* (tel:776-6922) offers both beach and mountain riding. There are no facilities on St. Thomas.
Snorkeling and Scuba Diving: most hotels and even the main tourist beaches will have snorkeling equipment available. ST. THOMAS: for scuba instruction, equipment rental, and guided dives, contact *Watersports Center* (tel:775-0755); *Virgin Island Diving School* (tel:774-8687); or *Joe Vogel Diving Company* (tel:775-7610). ST. JOHN: contact *St. John Watersports* (tel:776-6256) or *The Dock Dive Shop* (tel:776-6338).
Swimming: all beaches are public. ST. THOMAS: *Lindberg, Magens Bay,* and *Sapphire* are all excellent beaches. ST. JOHN: go to *Trunk* and *Reef Bays.*
Tennis: many of the hotels/resorts have courts, but cater only to guests. ST. THOMAS: tennis courts at *Frenchman's Reef* (tel:774-8500) are open to non-guests, as are those at *Bluebeard's Castle Hotel* (tel:774-1600). ST. JOHN: the *Caneel Bay Plantation* (tel:776-6111) has courts open to non-guests, although guests do have preference.
Water Skiing: ST. THOMAS: *Frenchman's Reef* resort (tel:774-8500) offers equipment and tows.

Weather

Summer in the U.S. Virgin Islands are hot, with daytime highs typically in the high 80s, dropping to the mid 70s at night. Winters are sunny, with daytime highs in the low 80s, falling to the low 70s at night. The rainy season is from July to December.

U.S. VIRGIN ISLANDS: TEMPERATURES AND PRECIPITATION

Month	J	F	M	A	M	J	J	A	S	O	N	D
Average Daily Temperature												
(Fahrenheit) Max.	82	83	85	86	88	88	87	88	89	87	85	83
Min.	70	70	70	72	74	75	75	75	74	74	73	72
Average Number of Days with Precipitation												
	12	9	9	8	10	13	14	16	13	14	16	13

St. Vincent

Sights to See

The waterfront in Kingstown, St. Vincent's capital. The port area is bustling with activity, with island schooners, cruise ships, yachts, and larger oceanic transports loading and unloading their cargoes.

The Market, opposite the Court House, between Bay & Halifax Sts., Kingstown. A particularly colorful scene on Saturday mornings, with farmers, fishermen, and merchants from all over the island playing their wares.

Fort Charlotte ruins just north of Kingstown, some 600 ft. above the Caribbean. The museum inside is worth a visit, but the view of Kingstown and the northernmost Grenadine islands is wonderful.

Botanic Garden and St. Vincent Museum, just N of Kingstown and E of Fort Charlotte. The garden, the oldest in the Americas, is full of lush tropical plants, and the museum is noted for its Arawak Indian artifacts.

St. Mary's Catholic Church, Grenville St., Kingstown. Dating from the early 19th century, it is a curious mix of architectural styles.

St. George's Cathedral, opposite St. Mary's. Noted for its Georgian architecture and stained-glass windows.

The Queen's Drive, E of Kingstown. Starting from Sion Hill, the road winds into the hills above Kingstown, affording magnificent panoramas.

Falls of Baleine, accessible by three-hour boat trip from Kingstown. Make arrangements through your hotel.

Barrouallie, a genuine, operating whaling village on St. Vincent's W coast between Layou and Chateaubelair. Fishermen set out in colorful small boats to hunt whale with harpoons, the old-fashioned way.

Carib Rock, Don't miss the rock engraving of a human face, one of the finest petroglyphs in the Caribbean, dating from about 600 A.D., on a side road just over a mile north of Layou.

Mt. Soufriere (4,049 ft.), one of the two most active volcanoes in the Caribbean (it last erupted in 1979), in the N central part of St. Vincent. A local guide is advisable, but the hike to the summit will be rewarded with superb views of St. Vincent and the Grenadines.

Marriqua Valley, NE of Kingstown on the island's interior. One of the Caribbean's most heavily cultivated areas.

Sports

Boating: most beach hotels have small sailboats for rent. For chartering larger yachts, contact *Caribbean Sailing Yachts, Ltd.* (tel:458-4308); or *Mariners Yacht Scuba Shop* (tel:458-4228).

Fishing: contact *Mariners Yacht Scuba Shop* (tel:458-4228) or make arrangements with local fishermen/skippers through your hotel.

Barrouallie, on the leeward coast, is the principal fishing center.

Golf: there is a 9-hole course at the *Aquaduct Golf Course* (tel:458-7421), near Layou. Arrangements to play are made through your hotel.

Horseback Riding: contact the *Ra-Wa-Cou Hotel* (tel:458-4459), in Mt. Pleasant, or *Cotton House* (tel:456-7777), which have riding facilities and trails.

Snorkeling and Scuba Diving: most beach hotels have snorkeling equipment available. For scuba instruction, equipment rental, and guided dives, contact *Dive St. Vincent* (tel:458-4714); *Dive Bequia* (tel:458-3504); or *Mariners Aquatic Sports* (tel:458-4228). *Indian Bay* on St. Vincent is a popular spot, along with the shallow water just off *Young Island,* in the Grenadines. *Canouan Island,* in the Grenadines, is thought by many to have some of the most beautiful snorkeling reefs in the Caribbean.

Swimming: all of St. Vincent's beaches are public and just about all are excellent. Beaches at the N end of the island are made of black volcanic sand, in the south they tend to be a golden coral. The *leeward or western side* of St. Vincent is the best for swimming.

Tennis: several of the hotels have courts, usually just one for guests. Anyone can play at the *Kingstown Tennis Club* (tel:456-1288), Murray Rd., by paying a nominal temporary membership fee. There are public courts just outside Kingstown.

Weather

St. Vincent experiences remarkably even temperatures year-round. Summers are hot, with daytime highs consistently in the upper 80s, falling into the mid 70s at

ST. VINCENT: TEMPERATURES AND PRECIPITATION

Month	J	F	M	A	M	J	J	A	S	O	N	D
Average Daily Temperature												
(Fahrenheit) Max.	82	83	84	87	88	88	87	88	88	87	85	83
Min.	69	69	69	71	73	74	74	74	73	72	71	70
Average Number of Days with Precipitation												
	18	13	13	10	16	21	23	22	21	19	20	19

night. Winters are warm to hot, and sunny. Daytime highs reach into the low 80s, dropping to the high 60s at night. The rainy season lasts from July through November.

Sint Eustatius-Saba

Sights to See

Fort Oranje, in the Upper Town part of Oranjestad, capital of Sint Eustatius. A restored 17th-century fortress with imposing bastions, it was built to protect the harbor and merchants of this formerly bustling entrepot. It now houses government offices, the local tourist office, and a museum. The views are good, too.
Oranjestad Museum, Fort Oranje, Sint Eustatius. A collection of mostly Victorian furniture and memorabilia from homes around the island.
De Graaf House, van Toningenweg, Upper Town, Oranjestad, Sint Eustatius. Admiral Rodney's headquarters after the British occupied the island in 1781.
Dutch Reformed Church, on the way to Fort de Windt, Sint Eustatius. A partially restored church noted for its stone-rubbing opportunities.
Honen Dalim, on the edge of Oranjestad, Sint Eustatius. The first Jewish synagogue in the western hemisphere.
Sugarloaf, White Wall, just outside Oranjestad, Sint Eustatius. A mini replica of the one in Rio, it offers panoramic views.
The northeast coast of Sint Eustatius, particularly the golden beaches, which are pounded by the Atlantic, is especially attractive.
Quill, a 1,949-ft. extinct volcano, surrounded by dense tropical forest, at the S central part of Sint Eustatius. You can either hike to its deep crater, or ride a burro.
The Bottom, Saba's capital, perched above the little harbor in Fort Bay, with the commissioner's official residence, and *Cranston's Antique Inn,* a popular island hangout.
Windwardside, Saba. The island's second largest settlement, almost 2,000 ft. up near Saba's center. It has most of the shops of interest to the tourist.
Harry L. Johnson Museum, Windwardside, Saba. Noted for its fine collection of antique furnishings in a former sea captain's house.

Sports

Boating: SINT EUSTATIUS: a few small sailboats are available for rent from the *Old Gin House* (tel:2319) in Lower Oranjestad. SABA: no commercial facilities exist at present, although *Saba Deep* (tel:4-3347) offers round-the-island cruises.
Donkey Riding: there is no horseback riding on either of the two islands, but it is possible to rent donkeys in Oranjestad, on St. Eustatius.
Fishing: not a well-developed sport on either island, but the *Old Gin House* (tel:2319) in Lower Oranjestad on Eustatius does organize deep-sea fishing trips.
Golf: there are no golf course on either island.

Snorkeling and Scuba Diving: SINT EUSTATIUS: underwater ruins of a part of old Oranjestad that tumbled into the sea in Oranje Bay is a favorite spot. Scuba equipment can be rented, and guided dives can be arranged, through the *Dive Statia* (tel:3-2348) in Lower Oranjestad. SABA: *Saba Deep* (tel:3347) and *Sea Saba Dive Center* (tel:4-2246), Windwardside, offer the island's only organized diving.

Swimming: SINT EUSTATIUS: the best swimming can be found on the island's *southwest beaches*. SABA: the island doesn't really have any proper beaches (it is a volcano sticking right out of the Caribbean with rather steep sides), although *Wells Bay* comes the closest.

Tennis: SINT EUSTATIUS: there is only one court, at the *Community Center,* in Oranjestad. SABA: only one court, a public one in The Bottom, and a concrete one at that!

Weather

Sint Eustatius and Saba enjoy remarkably even temperatures year-round. Summer daytime highs are typically in the mid to upper 80s, falling to the mid 70s at night. Winter daytime highs are typically in the low 80s, dropping to around 70 at night. The rainy season extends from July through November.

SINT EUSTATIUS/SABA: TEMPERATURES AND PRECIPITATION

Month	J	F	M	A	M	J	J	A	S	O	N	D
Average Daily Temperature												
(Fahrenheit) Max.	82	83	85	86	88	88	87	88	89	87	85	83
Min.	70	70	70	72	74	75	75	75	74	74	73	72
Average Number of Days with Precipitation												
	12	9	9	8	10	13	14	16	13	14	16	13

Trinidad and Tobago

Sights to See

Frederick Street, Port of Spain, Trinidad. The capital's chief shopping area, at the center of downtown.

National Museum and Art Gallery, Frederick & Gordon Sts., Port of Spain, Trinidad. Noted for its collection of Carnival costumes, and Amerindian artifacts.

Royal Botanic Gardens, near Queen's Park Savannah, Port of Spain, Trinidad, has 70 acres of tropical plants and flowers, together with an orchid house.

Central Market, Beetham Hwy., in the suburbs of Port of Spain, Trinidad. One of the island's most colorful sights, full of color and the smell of spices.

Asa Wright Nature Center, about an hour N of Port of Spain, Trinidad, at Spring Hill Estate in the mountains. A bird watcher's delight, full of exotic birds. Be sure to take binoculars, insect repellent, and rain gear.

Caroni Bird Sanctuary, about 30 miles S of Port of Spain. A large reserve on mangrove islands, toured by boat, and home to the magnificent Scarlet Ibis. Take your binoculars and insect repellent.
Blue Basin, in the Diego Martin Valley, 10 miles outside Port of Spain, Trinidad. A freshwater pool fed by a waterfall.
Fort George. The views from this early-19th-century fort on top of a 1,500-ft. hill are terrific.
Pitch Lake, near La Brea along the southern edge of the Gulf of Paria, Trinidad. The world's largest deposit of asphalt; it naturally replenishes itself.
Fort King George, an 18th-century British fort built above Scarborough, Tobago. Noted for the superb views of Rockly Bay and the island's south coast.
Charlotteville, Tobago. A picturesque fishing village set above Man O'War Bay.
Speyside, Tobago. A charming fishing village on the NE coast. It is the jumping-off point to the island of *Little Tobago,* habitat of Birds of Paradise.
Buccoo Reef, Tobago. Off the island's SW shore. All the equipment is supplied on this very popular snorkeling tour of a worn but still attractive reef.

Sports

Fishing: sport fish are fairly abundant in the waters around Trinidad and Tobago, and also Trinidad's *Caroni River.* TRINIDAD: for fishing charters, contact *Hub Travel* (tel:625-3011); *Caroni Tours* (tel:663-4115), or make arrangements through your hotel. TOBAGO: contact *Stanley Dillon* (tel:639-8765), Milford Bay.
Golf: TRINIDAD: the *Moka Golf Club's* (tel:629-2314) 18-hole course, in Maraval, is the best. TOBAGO: the famous *Tobago Golf Club* at Mount Irvine Bay Hotel (tel:639-8871) has an 18-hole course that is excellent. Guests do have preference.
Snorkeling and Scuba Diving: TOBAGO: has the better developed snorkeling facilities, with most beach hotels having equipment available. *Buccoo Reef,* about a mile offshore from Pigeon Point, is a popular snorkeling spot. For scuba instruction, equipment rental, and guided dives, contact *Dive Tobago* (tel:639-2266); *Adventures Unlimited* (tel:639-8871); or *Turtle Beach Hotel* (tel:639-2851). TOBAGO: contact *Tobago Scuba Ltd.* (tel:630-4327), Speyside, or *Dive Tobago* (tel:639-2266).
Swimming: TRINIDAD: some of the popular beaches include *Maracas* and *Balandra* in the N, and *Manzanilla* and *Mayaro* on the E part of the island. TOBAGO: *Back Bay, Englishman's Bay,* and *Bacolet Beach* are all just excellent.
Tennis: TRINIDAD: the *Trinidad Country Club* (tel:622-3470) allows visitors to play, as does the *Trinidad Hilton* (tel:624-3211); although guests do have preference. TOBAGO: the *Mount Irvine Bay Hotel* (tel:639-8871), has the best courts.

Weather

Trinidad and Tobago enjoy remarkably even temperatures year-round. Summer daytime highs are consistently in the upper 80s, dropping to the low 70s at night. Winter temperatures are only a degree or two lower than during the summer months. The rainy season lasts from June to November.

TRINIDAD & TOBAGO: TEMPERATURES AND PRECIPITATION

Month	J	F	M	A	M	J	J	A	S	O	N	D
Average Daily Temperature												
(Fahrenheit) Max.	87	88	89	90	90	89	88	88	89	89	89	88
Min.	69	68	68	69	71	71	71	71	71	71	71	69
Average Number of Days with Precipitation												
	14	10	9	9	12	19	22	23	19	18	18	17

Turks and Caicos

Sights to See

Front and Duke Streets in Cockburn Town, Grand Turk. Horse- and donkey-drawn vehicles are a common sight on these two streets at the heart of this picturesque little capital of the colony. Front Street has a number of colonial style buildings dating from the early 19th century.

Governor's Beach, at the S end of Grand Turk. The island's finest beach.

Cockburn Harbor, at the SW end of S. Caicos. The second largest settlement in the colony. Its excellent natural harbor is the site of the annual S. Caicos Regatta. Full of fishing boats and visiting yachts.

Conch Bar Caves, Middle Caicos. Beautiful pure white stalactites and stalagmites and underground salt lakes in limestone caves that have barely been explored.

Arawak and Lucayan Indian artifact site, between the villages of Bambarra and Lorimer on Middle Caicos. The site is currently being excavated by American archaeologists.

Three Mary Cays, near Whitby on N. Caicos. A delightful nature preserve.

Iguana Cay and Joe Grant's Cay nature reserves. In the NW part of E. Caicos. Some think that these cays are the finest in the area, with their rare plant and animal life and coral variety.

Southwest coast of Pine Cay. Believed by many to have one of the most beautiful beaches in the Caribbean, if not the world.

Fort George Cay National Park, off the N coast of Pine Cay. Ruins of a British fort.

Providenciales. A charming island undergoing development, with beautiful beaches, marinas, and the colony's greenest vegetation. See *Chalk Sound,* a land-locked lagoon with recent deposits of limestone, to the west of Five Cays settlement. The main tourist center on the island is around Turtle Cove and its yacht basin.

Salt Cay, Salt Islands just SW of Grant Turk. Balfour Town has some old whaling industry remnants, old salt sheds, salt ponds, and windmills. Otherwise, it is very quiet, although there is excellent snorkeling off Balfour Beach.

Sports

Boating: most of the hotels have small sailboats available. Turtle Cove Marina on the N shore of Providenciales is the only modern marina on the islands.
Fishing: sport fish are abundant off most of the islands. A number of local fishermen/skippers take individuals or groups out. Fishing charters are best handled through your hotel. *Third Turtle Inn* (tel:4230), on Providenciales, has good sport fishing facilities and *Executive Tours* (tel:946-4524), on Provo, offers charters.
Snorkeling and Scuba Diving: this is the real sport on the islands, which are considered by many to have some of the finest snorkeling and diving reefs in the world. Several of the hotels have diving packages, and/or dive shops. For example, *Kittina Hotel* (tel:2232) on Grand Turk; *Third Turtle Inn* (tel:4230), and *Island Princess* (tel:4260) on Providenciales; and *Meridian Club* (no phone) on Pine Cay. for scuba instruction, equipment rental, and guided dives, contact *Turk-Cai Watersports Ltd.* (tel:3223) on S. Caicos; or *Turks Island Divers Ltd.* (tel:2386) on Grand Turk. On Providenciales, contact *Provo Turtle Divers Ltd.* (tel:946-4232). On *Grand Turk* most diving is done on the leeward (west) side of the island. *South Caicos* offers wall diving, shallow reefs, and midrange sites. On Providenciales, the wall diving off *North West Point* is excellent. *West Caicos* offers dramatic scuba diving with its abrupt shoreline and deep water.
Swimming: virtually all of the beaches on all of the islands are ideal. On Grand Turk, *Governor's Beach* is very popular.
Tennis: several of the colony's hotels/resorts have tennis courts, but access to them is generally for their guests. Check through your hotel to see if arrangements can be made.

Weather

The Turks and Caicos enjoy the even temperatures that are characteristic of the Caribbean. Summers are hot, with daytime highs in the upper 80s, falling to the high 70s at night. Winters are warm to hot, and sunny. Daytime highs in the

TURKS & CAICOS: TEMPERATURES AND PRECIPITATION

Month	J	F	M	A	M	J	J	A	S	O	N	D
Average Daily Temperature												
(Fahrenheit) Max.	81	81	82	84	86	87	88	89	88	87	84	82
Min.	70	70	71	73	75	77	77	78	77	76	73	71
Average Number of Days with Precipitation												
	13	8	8	6	8	9	10	12	11	13	14	13

winter reach into the low 80s, dropping into the low 70s at night. Although drier than the Caribbean islands to the south, the Turks and Caicos do have a rainy season, extending from September through December, with November usually being the wettest month.

Australia and the Pacific

Brisbane: Australia

Sights to See

Panorama of Brisbane from City Hall's Tower Lookout, King George Square. The best vantage point for viewing the city. Brisbane's best known landmark, it also houses a library, museum, and art gallery.
The Observatory, Wickham Terrace, 2 blocks N of City Hall. Originally built as a windmill by convicts in 1829, it has been used as a treadmill, signal post, and meteorological station.
Treasury Building, Queen & George Sts., 2 blocks S of City Hall. Fine example of Italian Renaissance architecture.
Parliament House, Alice & George Sts., 7 blocks SE of City Hall. Fine example of French Renaissance architecture.
The Botanic Gardens, Alice St., just NW of Parliament House. A popular recreational area in Brisbane.
Queensland Art Gallery, Queensland Cultural Centre, South Brisbane, across the Victoria Bridge. Fine collection of modern Australian paintings. Open 10–5 daily.
Queensland Museum, also in the Queensland Cultural Centre. Natural history and technology exhibits. Open 9–5 daily.
Newstead House, Newstead Park, Breakfast Creek Rd. The city's oldest residence (1846). Now a museum. Open 11–3 M–Th, 2–5 Su.
Earlystreet Historical Village, 75 McIlwraith Ave., Norman Park, E of downtown Brisbane. A restored/recreated pioneer town, with many fine old Queensland buildings. Open 10:30–4:30 daily.

Useful Information

Queensland Government Tourist Bureau, Adelaide & Edward Sts. (tel:31-2211); *American Express,* 229 Queen St. (tel:229-2022); *Public Transportation* (tel:225-4444); *Taxi* (tel:391-0191, 229-1000, or 831-3000); *U.S. Consulate,* 383 Wickham Terr. (tel:839-8955); *Emergency* (tel:000 for ambulance, fire, or police); *Voltage Guide,* 220 V, two flat, angled blade outlets are used.

Special Trips/Tours

About 7 miles W of downtown Brisbane on Jesmond Road, Fig Tree Pocket, is the *Lone Pine Koala Sanctuary* where visitors can actually cuddle koalas. Kangaroos, wombats, emus, dingoes, and all kinds of other native animals populate the park. Open 9:30–5 daily. One of the best ways to get to Lone Pine is via the river cruise boat, which leaves at 1:15 P.M. from Hayles Wharf, Queens Wharf Road, North Quay (tel:229-7055).

On the way to or from Lone Pine, the *Mount Coot-tha Forest Park* is also worth visiting, with its magnificent views of Brisbane. The park also contains the *Mt. Coot-tha Botanic Gardens* (Open 7–5 daily), full of Australian native and tropical plants, and the *Sir Thomas Brisbane Planetarium* (open 12–7 W–Su), the country's largest.

Some 50 miles S of Brisbane, stretching from Southport to Coolangatta is the *Gold Coast,* Australia's Miami Beach. The superb white sandy beaches, warm water, and the MacPherson Ranges (mountains) inland, together with the *Dreamworld* amusement park and the Sea World marine park, among other attractions, make this the country's premier resort area.

Lamington National Park, inland from the Gold Coast, noted for its fine scenery, lush rain forest, and magnificent birds, is worth visiting, as is *Stradbroke Island* offshore across Moreton Bay. Contact *Jetaway Cruises* (tel:36-3367).

Weather

Brisbane has a subtropical climate. Daytime high temperatures in the summer (Dec.–Feb.) typically reach into the mid 80s, falling to the high 60s at night. Winter (June–Aug.) daytime highs are usually in the high 60s, dropping to around 50 at night. The rainy season extends from December through March.

BRISBANE: TEMPERATURES AND PRECIPITATION

Month	J	F	M	A	M	J	J	A	S	O	N	D
Average Daily Temperature												
(Fahrenheit) Max.	85	85	82	79	74	69	68	71	76	80	82	85
Min.	69	68	66	61	56	51	49	50	55	60	64	67
Average Number of Days with Precipitation												
	13	14	15	12	10	8	8	7	8	9	10	12

Canberra: Australia

Sights to See

Parliament House, King George Terrace, deliberately designed as the focal point of the city. An impressive, white building surrounded by beautiful gardens. Has a visitors gallery and items of national and historic interest in its King's Hall.

National Library of Australia, on the shore of Lake Burley Griffin, just N of Parliament House. Houses over 3 million volumes, plans, historic maps, photographs, and other items of national interest. Open 9–10 M–Th, 9–4:45 F–Su.

Australian National Gallery, just east of Parliament House on the shore of Lake Burley Griffin. Houses the national art collection. Open 10–5 daily.

The Carillon, in front of the National Gallery, on Aspen Island, Lake Burley Griffin. One of the world's biggest (53 bells), it was a gift from the U.K.

Australian-American War Memorial, at the NE end of King's Ave., across Kings Ave. Bridge. Commemorates U.S. aid to Australia during WW II.
Captain Cook Memorial, Lake Burley Griffin, near the Commonwealth Ave. Bridge, N of Parliament House. One of the world's highest water jets at 450 ft.
Regatta Point Planning Exhibition, Commonwealth Park, overlooking the Cook memorial. Models, audiovisual displays, and photographs illustrate Canberra's rapid development. Open 9–5 daily.
Lake Burley Griffin. Named after Canberra's American designer, Walter Burley Griffin. An artificial lake, it is a major recreational resource. Cruises leave from the ferry terminal in the West Basin.
Australian War Memorial, Anzac Parade, Limeston & Fairbairn Aves., NE of the Captain Cook Memorial. The capital's most popular attraction, it honors Australian war dead. A museum houses a fine, huge collection of war relics, aircraft, paintings, and exhibition galleries. Open 9–4:45 daily.
National Botanic Gardens, Clunies Ross St. on the lower slopes of Black Mountain, W of the city center. 100 acres full of native flora. Open 9–5 daily.
Telecom Tower, above the Botanic Gardens, at the top of Black Mountain (2,664 ft.). The panoramas of the national capital area from the viewing platforms of this 640-ft. tower are superb.

Useful Information

Canberra Tourist Bureau, Jolimont Centre, Northbourne Ave. (tel:49-7555); *U.S. Embassy,* Moonah Pl. (tel:70-5000); *Emergency* (tel:000 for police, ambulance, fire); *Public Transportation* (tel:95-0251); *Voltage Guide,* 220 V, two flat, angled blade outlets are used.

Special Trips/Tours

Tidbinbilla Nature Reserve, is some 25 miles SW of Canberra. A large reserve for Australian flora and fauna in a natural bush setting, it is worth visiting. Open 9–6 daily. Next to the Nature Preserve is the *Tidbinbilla Deep Space Tracking Station,* operated by the Australian Department of Science for NASA. The visitor center has radio telescopes, spacecraft and antenna models, and audiovisual displays. Open 9–5 daily.

On the same road to or from Tidbinbilla, stop off at the *Mt. Stromio Observatory's Visitor Center.* The large silver domes house the telescopes of the Australian National University. Open 9:30–4 daily.
Cooma, the gateway to Australia's Alps, *The Snowy Mountains,* and the beautiful *Kosciusko National Park,* is about 90 minutes from Canberra. Drop by the Visitors Center on Sharp St. for information on taking the very worthwhile tour of the huge *Snowy Mountains Hydro-Electric Scheme,* dubbed as one of the engineering wonders of the world.
Mt. Kosciusko (7,300 ft.), Australia's highest mountain, is the centerpiece of the national park's beautiful scenery, and the center of the country's ski country. The main ski resorts are the villages of *Thredbo, Perisher Valley,* and *Smiggin Holes.*

Weather

Canberra enjoys a warm, temperate climate moderated by its altitutde of 1,837 ft. Summer (Dec.–Feb.) daytime high temperatures typically reach into the low 80s, falling to the mid 50s at night. Winter (June–Aug.) daytime highs are usually in the mid 50s, dropping to the 30s at night. Rainfall is fairly evenly distributed throughout the year.

CANBERRA: TEMPERATURES AND PRECIPITATION

Month	J	F	M	A	M	J	J	A	S	O	N	D
Average Daily Temperature												
(Fahrenheit) Max.	82	82	76	67	60	53	52	55	61	68	75	80
Min.	55	55	51	44	37	34	33	35	38	43	48	53
Average Number of Days with Precipitation												
	7	7	7	7	7	9	10	11	9	11	8	8

Hobart: Australia

Sights to See

Panorama of Hobart from Mt. Wellington (5,005 ft.), some 12 miles W of downtown Hobart by road. Superb views of the city.

Battery Point, just E of the city center on the River Derwent. Historic area with early-19th-century colonial cottages and buildings.

Tasmanian Maritime Museum, Cromwell Street, Battery Point. Fine collection of models and exhibits on Tasmania's seafaring history. Open 2–4:30 daily.

Van Dieman's Land Folk Museum, 103 Hampden Rd., Battery Point, just W of the Maritime Museum. Fine folk museum devoted to Australia's pioneers. Open 10–5 M–F, 2–5 Sa–Su.

Anglesea Barracks, Davey St., W of the folk museum. Australia's oldest military barracks. Open 9–5 M–F.

Salamanca Palace, Castray Esplanade Row, N of the folk museum. Art and craft shops, galleries, and restaurants in restored, mid-19th-century warehouses.

Sullivans Cove waterfront area, between Princes and Macquarie Wharves, N of Salamanca Palace. Busy harbor area with yachts, fishing boats, and harbor cruises leaving from Franklin Wharf.

Tasmanian Museum and Art Gallery, 5 Argyle St. Fine collection noted for its exhibits on the now extinct Tasmanian Aborigines. Open 10–5 daily.

Model Tudor Village, 827 Sandy Bay Rd., S of central Hobart. Excellent miniature reproduction of an English Tudor village. Open 9–5 daily.

Shot Tower, Channel Highway, Taroona, some 6 miles S of Hobart. Historical tower that offers magnificent views of the Derwent Estuary. Open 9–5 daily.

Useful Information

Tasmanian Government Tourist Bureau, 80 Elizabeth St. (tel:34-6911); closest *U.S. Embassy or Consulate* is in Canberra, at Moonah Pl. (tel:62/70–5000); *Post*

Office, Elizabeth & Macquarie Sts; *Public Transportation* (tel:34-5670 and 44-1599); *Emergency* (tel:000 for ambulance, fire, and police); *Voltage Guide:* 220 V, two flat, angled blade outlets are used.

Special Trips/Tours

The ruins of an old, infamous, penal colony at *Port Arthur,* Australia's Alcatraz, are some 60 miles SE of Hobart on the Tasman Peninsula. Used as a penal settlement for thousands of people deported from England during the mid-19th century, it is a major tourist attraction, and in the process of restoration. Visit the old *Lunatic Asylum* building, housing a museum and an audiovisual theater, and take one of the guided tours.

Tasmania's *east coast* is very attractive, offering picturesque villages, excellent fishing, especially out of the old whaling town of *Bicheno,* and spectacular coastal scenery, particularly at *Coles Bay* and *Freycinet National Park.* *Launceston,* Tasmania's second city in the N part of the island, is noted for its gardens and colonial buildings. *Launceston's City Park,* N of Tamar Street, with its fine conservatory, and *Wildlife Sanctuary,* S of the downtown area, are well worth visiting. The *Queen Victoria Museum and Art Gallery,* on Wellington St. has a fine, eclectic collection devoted to the island's history. Just outside Launceston, a chairlift ride over *Cataract Gorge* and a picnic in the gardens of Cataract Cliff Grounds is a popular activity.

Tasmania's W coast is particularly attractive, with its densely forested mountains, beautiful lakes and rugged coastline. *Cradle Mountain–Lake St. Clair National Park, Wild Rivers National Park,* inland, and *South West National Park,* on the SW coast, all offer excellent hiking and other outdoor recreational activities among marvelous scenery. A half-day *cruise up the Gordon River,* through Macquarie Harbour, is really worthwhile. During the summer, boats leave daily from Strahan pier, on the W coast.

Weather

Hobart has a mild temperate climate, with changeable weather. Summer (Dec.–Feb.) daytime high temperatures typically reach into the high 60s or low 70s, dropping to the low 50s at night. Winter (June–Aug.) daytime highs are usually in the low 50s, falling to the low 40s at night. Precipitation is fairly evenly distributed throughout the year. The island's W coast gets much more rain than Hobart.

HOBART: TEMPERATURES AND PRECIPITATION

Month	J	F	M	A	M	J	J	A	S	O	N	D
Average Daily Temperature												
(Fahrenheit) Max.	71	71	68	63	58	53	52	55	59	63	66	69
Min.	53	53	51	48	44	41	40	41	43	46	48	51
Average Number of Days with Precipitation												
	13	10	13	14	14	16	17	18	17	18	16	14

Melbourne: Australia

Sights to See

Victorian Arts Centre, St. Kilda Rd., on the S side of the Yarra River. A complex composed of three main buildings: the Concert Hall; the spire-topped Theatres Building; and the National Gallery; together with bars, restaurants, shops, and an outdoor stage.

National Gallery of Victoria, Victorian Arts Centre. Excellent collection of Australian and European paintings and artifacts.

Royal Botanic Gardens, across St. Kilda Rd., E of the Victorian Arts Centre. Considered to be the most beautiful in Australia, and, indeed, one of the world's best examples of traditional lanscaping. See the *Shrine of Remembrance, LaTrobe's Cottage,* and the *flower clock* in the adjacent King's Domain.

City Square, in the heart of downtown Melbourne. An area of boutiques, sidewalk cafes, waterfalls, and flower gradens.

National Museum of Victoria, between Russell & Swanston Sts., N of the Yarra River. Fine collection of Australiana. Open 10–5 M–Sa, 2–5 Su.

Old Melbourne Gaol, Russell St., just N of the National Museum. Houses unique exhibits tracing the story of the transportation of convicts and the development of Victoria's penal system. Open 10–5 daily.

Captain Cook's Cottage, Fitzroy Gardens, East Melbourne. Especially shipped from England as a memorial of Cook's discovery of eastern Australia. Fitzroy Gardens is known for its spacious lawns, conservatory, and "The Fairy Tree."

Royal Zoological Gardens, Royal Park, N of central Melbourne, and reached by train from the Flinders Street Station. The unique animals of Australia (emus, koalas, wombats, kangaroos, etc.), are featured. Open 9–5 daily.

Polly Woodside, Normandy Rd. and Phayer St., South Melbourne. A restored square-rigged commercial sailing ship, the centerpiece of a fine display of Australia's maritime history. Open 10–4 M–F, 12–5 Sa–Su.

Useful Information

Melbourne Tourism Authority, 20th Level, Nauru House, 80 Collins Street (tel:654-2288); *Victoria Tourism Commission* (Victour), Victour Travel Centre, 230 Collins Street (tel:602-9444); *River Cruisers Melbourne,* 1 Princes Walk (tel:63-4694); pick up *This Week in Melbourne,* available at hotel lobbies or at Victour; *U.S. Consulate,* 24 Albert Rd., South Melbourne (tel:697-7900); *Voltage Guide,* 220 V, two flat, angled blade outlets are used.

Special Trips/Tours

Mount Dandenong Lookout, in the Dandenong Ranges some 22 miles from Melbourne, is a favorite vantage point for viewing the city and its suburbs. The hills are well known for their unique wildlife (Lyrebird, platypus, and the bell and whip birds). The *Puffing Billy Railroad,* a narrow-gauge steam train, runs through the ranges, leaving from Belgrave, off Old Monbulk Road.

Ballarat, a former 1850s gold-rush town, is 65 miles NW of Melbourne. A quiet, attractive provincial town, its main attraction is *Sovereign Hill,* a reconstructed gold-mining town and theme park.

Phillip Island, about 87 miles SE of Melbourne, is world famous for its *Penguin Parade,* which takes place every night of the year at dusk, as hundreds of small Fairy Penguins return to their nests after a day of fishing. Summerland Beach.

Weather

Melbourne has a warm temperate climate, with changeable weather. Summer (Nov.–March) daytime high temperatures typically reach into the upper 70s, dropping to the high 50s at night. Winter (June–Aug.) daytime highs are usually in the mid 50s, falling to the mid-40s at night. Rainfall is well distributed, although more frequent in winter.

MELBOURNE: TEMPERATURES AND PRECIPITATION

Month	J	F	M	A	M	J	J	A	S	O	N	D
Average Daily Temperature												
(Fahrenheit) Max.	78	78	75	68	62	57	56	59	63	67	71	75
Min.	57	57	55	51	47	44	42	43	46	48	51	54
Average Number of Days with Precipitation												
	9	8	9	13	14	16	17	17	15	14	13	11

Perth: Australia

Sights to See

Kings Park, immediately W of, and overlooking, downtown Perth. Over 1,200 acres of bushland, botanic gardens, and wildflowers. Affords panoramic views of Perth by day or night.

Old Mill, Mill Point, S of Kings Park just across the Narrows Bridge. Dating from 1830s, it now houses a folk museum with a fine collection of early colonial tools and artifacts. Open 1–5 M, W, Th, & Su, 1–4 Sa.

Perth Zoological Gardens, South Perth, just SE of Old Mill. Unique collection of Western Australian fauna.

The Cloisters, between Hay St. & St. Georges Terrace, opposite Mill St. Noted example of fine Perth architecture. Built in 1858, it is known for its particularly fine brickwork. Indeed, St. Georges Terrace itself has many fine 19th-century buildings.

Government House, Stirling Gardens, off St. Georges Terrace. Built in 1864 as the official residence of the State Governor.

Town Hall, Hay & Barrack Sts., one block N of Stirling Gardens. Convict labor was used to build this unusual building, a fine example of colonial architecture.

London Court Arcade, between Hat St. & St. Georges Terrace, a few blocks

NW of the Town Hall. A touch of Old England. A busy, Tudor-style shopping arcade.

Western Australian Museum, Francis and Beaufort Sts. Fine collection of Australian paintings, and an excellent collection on Aboriginal history and culture. Open 10:30–5 M–Th, 1–5 F–Su.

Art Gallery, 47 James St., close to the museum. Excellent collection of modern masters, contemporary Australian paintings, and Aboriginal art. Open 10–5 M–Sa, 1–5 Su.

Fremantle, Perth's port, 12 miles downstream, at the mouth of the Swan River. Best viewed from Memorial Park.

Fremantle Museum, 1 Finnerty St., in Fremantle, 12 miles SW of Perth. Excellent exhibits depicting the history of Western Australia. Open 9–5 daily.

America's Cup Museum, 43 Swan St., North Fremantle. Devoted to the famous yacht race with models of all the competing yachts. Open 9:30–5 daily.

Rottnest Island, some 12 miles offshore. A popular resort and wildlife sanctuary. Reached by hydroplane or ferry from Perth's Barrack Street Jetty.

Useful Information

West Australian Government Travel Centre, 772 Hay St. (tel:321–2471 or 322-2999); *Information for Travelers,* Shop 26, Merlin Centre, Adelaide Terrace (tel:325-3200); *U.S. Consulate,* 16 St. Georges Terr. (tel:9/221-1177); *Taxi* (tel:22-0111 or 25-5555); *Emergency* (for police, fire, or ambulance—tel:000); *Public Transportation Information* (tel:325-8511); *Voltage Guide,* 220 V, two flat, angled blade outlets are used.

Special Trips/Tours

A drive out to the *Darling Ranges,* E and SE of Perth, is a popular excursion. Known for their unspoiled scenery and beautiful panoramas, these hills are especially beautiful in the spring, when they are blanketed in wildflowers.

Yanchep National Park, 31 miles north of Perth along the coast, is a 6,000-acre parkland noted for spring wild flowers and limestone caves, and home to black swans and a koala colony. Visit the nearby *Atlantis Marine World* for the performances of dolphins and seals in the aquatic entertainment center.

If you have more time on your hands, the famous town of *Kalgoorlie* is in the old goldfields, some 372 miles W of Perth along the Great Eastern Highway (94). The "golden mile," as it was known, has many early-20th-century buildings and a mine for tourists to visit. The nearby gold-rush town of *Coolgardie,* has an interesting mining museum. Other old ghost towns from the gold-rush days include Boulder, Gwalia, and Broad Arrow.

Weather

Perth enjoys a Mediterranean-type climate with warm to hot summers (Dec.–March), and mild winters (June–Aug.). Summer daytime high temperatures typically reach into the mid 80s, falling to the low 60s at night. Winter daytime highes are usually in the mid 60s, dropping to around 50 at night. Winter is the rainy season.

PERTH: TEMPERATURES AND PRECIPITATION

Month	J	F	M	A	M	J	J	A	S	O	N	D
Average Daily Temperature												
(Fahrenheit) Max.	85	85	81	76	69	64	63	64	67	70	76	81
Min.	63	63	61	57	53	50	48	48	50	53	57	61
Average Number of Days with Precipitation												
	3	3	5	8	15	17	19	19	15	12	7	5

Sydney: Australia

Sights to See

Sydney from Sidney Tower, Centrepoint, Market & Pitt Sts. The panoramic views of the city are spectacular from the observation platform of this tower: at 1,073 ft. the tallest structure in Australia.

Sydney Opera House, one of the most famous buildings in the world, with its sharply curving roof shaped like sails, is a symbol of both the city and Australia. Tours are held between 9 and 4 daily.

The Rocks, Sydney's oldest neighborhood, between Circular Quay and Sydney Harbor Bridge. This area, Australia's birthplace, has undergone a complete restoration. See *Cadman's Cottage,* the city's oldest building, which now houses a museum and visitor center, and the *Argyle Center* (arts and crafts).

Circular Quay. Now the busy locale of ferry wharves and departure point for Harbor cruises, this horseshoe-shaped quay is the place where the original British immigrants established a colony in 1788.

Royal Botanic Gardens, on the shores of Farm Cove, E of the Opera House. Full of exotic Australian shrubs and trees, amid expansive lawns, fountains, and statues.

Art Gallery of New South Wales, S of the Botanic Gardens, in the Domain, between Art Gallery Rd. & Sir John Young Circle. An excellent collection of Australian art. Open 10–5 M–Sa, 12–5 Su.

Mitchell Library, housed in the State Library of New South Wales, Shakespeare Place, W of the Art Gallery. Excellent collection of historical documents.

Australian Museum, College & William Sts., opposite Hyde Park. Excellent collections of Aboriginal and South Seas art. Open 10–5 Tu–Sa, 12–5 S & M.

Paddington district, about 1½ miles SE of central Sydney, along Oxford St. Formerly a slum area, it is now full of chic restaurants, fashionable pubs, art galleries, shops, and Victorian terrace houses.

Useful Information

The Travel Centre of New South Wales, 16 Spring St., (tel:23-1444); *Sydney Tourist Information Service* (tel:669-5111); *Rocks Visitor Center,* 104 George

St. (tel:27-4972); *Sydney Convention and Visitors Bureau,* 100 Market St. (tel:232-1377); *Sydney Visitors Information Centre,* Martin Plaza (tel:235-2424); *Ferry Service Timetable* (tel:27-9251); *U.S. Consulate,* T & G Tower, Park & Elizabeth Sts. (tel:261-9200); *Voltage Guide,* 220 V, two flat, angled blade outlets are used.

Special Trips/Tours

A *Sydney Harbour tour* is a must. Several regular daily harbor cruises by ferries and hydrofoil leave from Circular Quay. Contact the *Tourist Information Service* (tel:669-5111); or *Captain Cook Cruises* (tel:27-9408). A ferry ride from Wharf 5 at Circular Quay to the *Taronga Zoo,* Bradleys Head Rd., Mosman, is a good way to appreciate Sydney's beautiful waterfront location on Port Jackson.
Ku-ring-gai Chase National Park, about 15 miles N of Sydney, has excellent examples of Australian flora and fauna, a koala sanctuary, and aboriginal rock paintings.
The *Blue Mountains National Park,* about 56 miles W of Sydney has some of the most spectacular scenery in E Australia, including deep gorges and ravines and dramatic cliffs. Visit the Tourist Information Centre, Echo Point, Katoomba. Be sure to see *Jenolan Caves* and *The Three Sisters* (rock formations), two of the most popular sites in the Blue Mountains.

Weather

Sydney has a warm temperate climate, with warm to hot summers (Nov.–March) and cool, not cold, winters (June–Aug.). The weather is changeable at all times of the year. Summer daytime high temperatures typically reach into the high 70s, falling to the mid 60s at night. Winter daytime highs are usually in the mid to low 60s, dropping to the upper to mid 40s at night. Rainfall is well distributed throughout the year.

SYDNEY: TEMPERATURES AND PRECIPITATION

Month	J	F	M	A	M	J	J	A	S	O	N	D
Average Daily Temperature												
(Fahrenheit) Max.	78	78	76	71	66	61	60	63	67	71	74	77
Min.	65	65	63	58	52	48	46	48	51	56	60	63
Average Number of Days with Precipitation												
	14	13	14	14	13	12	12	11	12	12	12	13

Fiji (Viti Levu)

Sights to See

Suva, capital of Fiji on Viti Levu island. The downtown shopping area along Thompson, Cumming, and Renwich Sts. has many duty-free shops.
Market, between King's Wharf and the bus station along Princes St. Busy daily morning market with vendors selling fruit, vegetables, and souvenirs.

Victoria Parade, along the waterfront S of the post office. Suva's main street, with many of the island's best shops, banks, and hotels.

Fiji Museum, in Thurston Gardens, off Victoria Parade. Excellent collection of Fijian artifacts. Open 8:30–4:30 M–F, Su.

Government House, adjacent to Thurston Gardens. Noted for its landscaped grounds and the Changing of the Guard ceremony (first Tu of the month at 11 A.M.).

Colo-I-Suva Forest Park, about 7 miles N of Suva on Princess Rd. Noted for its waterfalls, canyons, and beautiful tropical forest.

Orchid Island, some 6 miles W of Suva on the S coast road to Nadi. A combination cultural center/museum/zoo. Noted for its replica of an old Fijian village where villagers, in traditional clothing, demonstrate island handicrafts. Open daily.

Pacific Harbour, 30 miles W of Suva, beyond Orchid Island. Cultural exhibits illustrating and demonstrating the many crafts of the islands. Performances by the *Dance Theatre of Fiji* and the famed firewalkers from the island of Beqa are also featured. Open M–Sa.

Coral Coast along Viti Levu's S coast. Can be seen either from the Queen's Road that parallels the coast, or from the Coral Coast Railway that runs between the Fijian Hotel, on Yanuca Island, and Natadola Beach.

Sigatoka, small community on Viti Levu's S coast, noted for its *Nadroga Mosque.*

Slatoka Valley, Viti Levu's main agricultural area, inland from the town, Known for its fine scenery.

Nadi, duty-free shops are the only tourist attraction in Fiji's third largest city. Just outside town on Queen's Rd., is the *Waqadra Botanical Garden.*

Nausori Highlands, inland from Nadi, offer spectacular scenery and fine vistas of Viti Levu's coast.

North coast of Viti Levu. Notable points of interest include Navala, a picturesque village in the mountains above Ba, the "Black Christ" church mural in the village of Naiserelagi, and the fine waterfall between the village of Wailotua and Korovou.

Sports

Boating: contact the *Royal Suva Yacht Club* (tel:23-666), Suva. Several outfits offer coral viewing cruises, including: *Tropic Cruises,* and *Oolooloo Cruises Ltd.* in Suva. *South Sea Island Cruises Ltd.* (tel:7-1445), in Nadi; *Beachcomber Cruises Ltd., Stardust Cruises, Seafarer Cruises,* and *Blue Lagoon Cruises,* all in Lautoka, offer longer cruises to some of the outlying Fijian islands.

Fishing: contact *Deep Sea Fishing Ltd.,* Korolevu; *South Sea Island Cruises Ltd.* (tel:7-1445), or *Marau Gamefishing* (tel:1-5347), Pacific Harbour.

Golf: Pacific Harbour has the island's best course. The *Fijian Resort Hotel* has a 9-hole course, as do the *Naviti Beach* and *Korolevu Beach* resorts along the Coral Coast. There are public golf courses in Suva, Nadi, and Lautoka.

Horseback Riding: several of the resorts offer riding for their guests, including *Plantation Village.*

Snorkeling and Scuba Diving: many of the resorts offer snorkeling equipment. For scuba diving, contact *Scuba Hire* (tel:361-241), Suva; *Dive Centre Fiji* (tel:23-337) in Lami just outside Suva; *South Sea Island Cruises Ltd.* (tel:7-1445), Nadi; *Diver Services* (tel:60-496) in Lautoka; or *Sea Sports Ltd.* (tel:0-598), in Korolevu.

Swimming: the white sand beaches of Fiji's Coral Coast offer fine beaches. *Natandola Beach* is considered one of the best. The offshore island resorts off Nadi and Lautoka have ideal beaches for swimming.

Tennis: most of the larger resorts have tennis courts for guests. The best courts are at *John Newcombe's Tennis Ranch,* in Nadi.

Whitewater Rafting: contact *Pacific Crown Aviation* (tel:361-532) for trips on the Navua River, and *Wilderness Adventures Ltd.* in Suva, for trips down the Ba River.

Weather

Fiji has a tropical oceanic climate with fairly high temperatures and humidity year-round. Summer (Dec.–Feb.) daytime highs are typically in the mid 80s, dropping to the mid 70s at night. Winter (June–Aug.) daytime highs are usually around 80 degrees, falling to the high 60s at night. The rainy season extends from December through May.

FIJI: TEMPERATURES AND PRECIPITATION

Month	J	F	M	A	M	J	J	A	S	O	N	D
Average Daily Temperature												
(Fahrenheit) Max.	86	86	86	84	82	80	79	79	80	81	83	85
Min.	74	74	74	73	71	69	68	68	69	70	71	73
Average Number of Days with Precipitation												
	18	18	21	19	16	13	14	15	16	15	15	18

Island of Hawaii: Hawaii

Sights to See

Hawaii Volcanoes National Park. Cantered around the 13,680-ft. Mauna Loa Peak. Site of the world's most active volcano, Kilauea. Stop off at the Wahaula Visitor Center, at the Kalapana entrance, and at the Kilauea Visitor Center on Crater Rim Rd. Call the Volcano Hotline (967-7977) before you go: if Kilauea is too active, you can still see the magnificent eruptions from the air. Contact Lacy Helicoptors (885-7272), or Anuene Aviation (961-5591).

Mauna Kea Observatory is also worth a visit if you have access to a 4-wheel-drive vehicle. Stop by the U. of Hawaii visitors gallery.

Hilo, the island's largest city and county seat. Surrounded by orchid fields and nurseries. Visit the *Liliuokalani Park.*

Akaka Falls State Park, N of Hilo, off Hwy. 19. A beautiful waterfall in a magnificent tropical garden.

Hamakua Coast, on the NE of the island, N of Hilo. Known for its unusual scenery.

Kamuela Museum, in Waimea (Kamuela), at the junction of Hwys. 19, 250, and 190. Noted for its ancient and royal Hawaiian artifacts.

Kailua-Kona, on the island's W coast. Originally Hawaiian royalty's 19th-century retreat, it is now the resort center of the island. Be sure to drop by Kailua Pier, with its game fishing boats, and visit *Hulihee Palace* and *Mokuakuau Church.*

South Point, literally at the island's southernmost tip. Lava flows and formations, petroglyphs, and ancient temples (heiaus) make this spot interesting.

Sports

Boating: the opportunities to charter or rent a sailboat on Hawaii are limited. Boating seems to be limited to sport fishing, or sailboarding. For the latter, contact *West Hawaii Sailboards,* Kamuela (885-7744). *Captain Cook Cruises* (329-2955), offers glass-bottom-boat trips over the volcanic reefs of the Kona coast. *Captain Bean's Cruises* (329-2955), offers evening dinner cruises.

Fishing: the Kona coast has some of the best sport fishing in the world. For charters, contact: *Foxy Lady Sport Fishing* (325-5552); *Keene Charters* (329-4332); *Kona Coast Activities* (329-2971); *Kona Charter Skippers Association* (329-3600); or *Kona Seafari Center* (329-3008) all in Kailua-Kona.

Golf: the island of Hawaii has four golf resorts: the *Keauhou Golf Course,* Kona at Keauhou (322-3431); world-famous *Mauna Kea Beach Hotel and Golf Course* (228-3000); the *Mauna Lani Resort* (885-6655); the *Seamountain Golf Course* (928-6222); and the *Sheraton Royal Waikoloa Beach Golf Club* (885-6060). Public courses include *Hilo Municipal* (959-7711); and *Volcano Golf Club,* 29 miles S of Hilo (967-7331).

Horseback Riding: contact *Ironwood Outfitters,* Kahua Ranch (885-4941); *Mauna Kea Beach Stables,* Waimea (882-7222); and *Waikoloa Country Stables,* Waikoloa Village (883-9335).

Snorkeling and Scuba Diving: the Kona Coast has some excellent snorkeling spots, including *Anaehoomalu Beach, Mahukona Beach,* and *Hookena Beach Park.* The larger hotels have snorkeling gear available, otherwise contact *Fairwind* (322-2788) in Keauhou or *Big Island Marine* (329-3719). For scuba equipment rental, instruction, and guided trips, contact *Ala's Kona Divers* (325-7640); *Dive Makai Charters* (329-2025); *Gold Coast Divers* (329-1328); or *Hawaiian Divers* (329-3600), all in Kailua-Kona.

Swimming: the best beaches on the island are on the NW coast, particularly around Kawaihae. *Anaehoomalu Beach, Spencer Beach Park,* and *Hapuna Beach and Park,* are all excellent spots.

Tennis: most of the hotels in the Kailua-Kona area have courts, and there are some 50 public courts in the Kailua-Kona and Keauhou areas. The island has two tennis resorts: the *Keauhou Beach Summit Hotel,* 78-6740 Alii Dr., Kailua-Kona (322-3441); and the *Naniloa Surf,* 93 Banyon Dr., Hilo (935-0831).

Weather

Hawaii's summer daytime high temperatures typically reach into the low 80s, dropping to the low 70s at night. Winter daytime highs are usually in the mid to high 70s, falling to the upper 60s at night. December and January are normally the wettest months. The NE coast receives much more rain than the SW coast.

KAILUA-KONA: TEMPERATURES AND PRECIPITATION

Month	J	F	M	A	M	J	J	A	S	O	N	D
Average Daily Temperature												
(Fahrenheit) Max.	76	76	77	78	80	81	82	83	83	82	80	78
Min.	69	67	67	68	70	72	73	74	74	72	70	69
Average Number of Days with Precipitation												
	14	11	13	12	11	12	14	13	13	13	13	15

Honolulu

Sights to See

Waikiki Beach, along Kalakaua Ave. This 2½-mile-long beach is one of the most famous swimming and surfing beaches in the world.
Kapiolani Park, Kalakaua & Monsarrat Aves. Names after the wife of Hawaii's last King. See the Kodak Hula Show at 10 A.M. Tu–F just off Monsarrat Ave., and the *Queen Kapiolani Rose Garden,* Monsarrat & Paki Aves. Open 24 hours.
Diamond Head (Lae'ahi), at SE boundary of Waikiki. The views from the slopes of this 760-ft. volcanic crater are spectacular. There is a state park inside the crater.
Royal Hawaiian Shopping Center, 2201 Kalakaua Ave. Crafts, boutiques, and restaurants fill this outdoor mall.
Iolani Palace, King & Richards Sts. The final residence of Queen Liliuokalani (who was a famous songwriter as well as a monarch). Take the Palace tour, by appointment only (536-6185) 9–2:15 W–Sa.
Honolulu Academy of Arts, 900 S. Beretania St. Excellent Asian and Oriental collection. Open 10–4:30 T, W, F, Sa, 11–8 Th, 2–5 Su.
Kawaiahao Church, King & Punchbowl Sts. Noted for its building material—coral. Open daily.
Mission Houses Museum, 55 S. King St., opposite the Kawaiahao church. Restored homes of the first missionaries. Open Tu–Su.
Chinatown, bounded by Honolulu harbor, Bishop & Beretania Sts., has all the characteristics of other U.S. Chinatowns. It is also Honolulu's red-light district.
Bishop Museum, Likelike Highway in Kalihi. Fascinating collection of Hawaiiana; also artifacts from the Pacific area generally, and Polynesia specifically. Open 9–5 daily.
Lyon Arboretum, 3860 Manoa Rd. Noted for its tropical plants, shrubs, and trees. Open 8–4:30 daily.

Ala Moana Center, Ala Moana Blvd. Huge shopping center.
Pearl Harbor and the Arizona Memorial. Cruise boats leave from Kewalo Basin near Waikiki (471-3901). Free boat tours of the *Arizona Memorial,* honoring those who died when the *U.S.S. Arizona* was sunk during the Japanese bombing of Pearl Harbor, leave from the Halawa Landing, (422-0561) 8–3 Tu–Su.
Sea Life Park, Makapuu Point at the E tip of Oahu, about 7 miles outside Honolulu. Noted for its 300,000-gallon Hawaiian Reef Tank and the thousands of Hawaiian marine specimens. On your way there or back, stop off at the *Blow Hole,* near *Koko Head Natural Park.* Waves force water through a tiny hole in a lava ledge and blow miniature geysers high into the air.

Useful Informtion

Hawaii Visitors Bureau, 2270 Kalakaua Avenue (923-1811); *Volcano Hotline* (967-7977); *Taxi* (836-0011, 531-1333, or 847-3566); *Surf Report* (836-1952); *Helicopter Sightseeing Flights* (Royal Helicopters 836-2868, Hawaii Pacific Helicopters 836-1566).

Special Trips/Tours

Polynesian Cultural Center, on Oahu's north shore in Laie, is an hour and 15 minutes from Waikiki. It is made up of native villages representative of those in Fiji, Tonga, New Zealand, Tahiti, Samoa, the Marquesas, and Hawaii. Live entertainment. Open M–Sa (293-3333).
The drive to Kailua, on the NE side of Oahu, via Hwy. 61 is spectacular. Stop at the *Pali Lookout,* near the top of the highway before it descends into Kailua, and enjoy the view. Also see the Queen Emma Summer Palace (Hanaiakamalama), 2913 Pali Hwy. (Hwy. 61), the former royal summer retreat. Open 9–4 daily.
Waimea Falls Park, between Haleiwa and Kahuku on the island's NW shore. The 1,800-acre park is situated in a narrow canyon extending into the Koolau mountains, and is full of tropical plantlife, birds, hiking trails, and a beautiful waterfall. Open 10–5:30 daily.
If you have come this far, you should try to see the *other Hawaiian Islands,* particularly *Hawaii* or *Maui. Hawaii* is best known for its active volcanoes, Mauna Loa and Kilauea, centerpieces of the *Volcanoes National Park.* Stop by the Kilauea Visitors Center, Crater Rim Rd. (967-7311). *Maui,* the second largest island, has the *Haleakala National Park* (with the inactive Haleakala Crater) to offer, plus such delightful communities as the old whaling settlement of *Lahaina.* NOTE—interisland excursion fare tickets are the cheapest way to catch a flight out of Honolulu.

Weather

Honolulu has a tropical oceanic climate, with fairly uniform temperatures all year around. Daytime highs are typically in the low 80s during the summer, in the mid 70s during the winter. Temperatures usually don't fall below the high 60s or low 70s. The one noticeable seasonal difference is in rainfall, where the winter months are the wettest.

HONOLULU: TEMPERATURES AND PRECIPITATION

Month	J	F	M	A	M	J	J	A	S	O	N	D
Average Daily Temperature												
(Fahrenheit) Max.	76	76	77	78	80	81	82	83	83	82	80	78
Min.	69	67	67	68	70	72	73	74	74	72	70	69
Average Number of Days with Precipitation												
	14	11	13	12	11	12	14	13	13	13	13	15

Island of Kauai: Hawaii

Sights to See

Waimea Canyon, the "Grand Canyon of the Pacific," in W Kauai. Take Rte. 55 out of Waimea, just past the Captain Cook monument. Over 3,000 ft. deep and 12 miles long, the island is truly spectacular. Stop off at the Kokee Museum and see its nature exhibits.

Kalalau Lookout, past the Kokee tracking station at the end of Hwy. 55. The lush tropical forest drops 4,000 ft. to the blue Pacific below. One of the best panoramas in the Hawaiian islands.

Captain Cook's Landing, Waimea Bay. The place where the explorer first set foot on Hawaii in 1778.

Old Russian Fort (Ft. Elizabeth), just SE of Cook's Landing. Ruins of a fort built by an employee of the Russian Fur Co. of Alaska in 1817, hoping to claim Kauai for the Czar.

Pacific Botanical Gardens, Lawai. The world's leading tropical horticultural park. Tours at 9 and 10:15 A.M. on Tu. Tours are limited.

Kukui-o-Lono Gardens, S of Kalaheo off Hwy. 50. Centered around the ruins of two Hawaiian temples. Noted for its Oriental objets d'art, and Hawaiian rock symbols.

Kauai Museum, 4420 Rice St., Lihue. Noted for its dioramas, wood calabashes and quilt collections, and exhibits on local history.

Grove Form Homestead Museum, Nawilwili Rd., Lihue. An 80-acre working museum of plantation life.

Fern Grotto. A beautiful cave, filled with luxuriant ferns. Reached by boat from the Wailua Marina.

Waioli Mission House, Hanalei. Built in 1841, this building houses a museum containing artifacts and furniture of the missionary period. Open 9–3 Tu–Sa.

Sports

Boating: only one outfit rents sailboats on Kauai, the *Kalapaki Beach Club* (245-9290). Windsurfing is big. Contact *Aquatics Kauai* (822-9213), *Garden*

Island Windsurfing (826-9005), or *Pacific Ocean Activities* (822-3455). *Island Adventures* (245-9662) in Hanalei and Nawiliwili offers kayaking.
Fishing: the waters around Kauai are abundant in sport fish. For charters, contact *Paradise Charters* (245-3728) and *Lady Ann Charters* (245-8538) out of Nawiliwili Harbor; *SeaBreeze Sport Fishing* (828-1285); *Sea Fever Sport Fishing* (826-6815); and *Foxy Wahine* (826-6164) out of Hanalei.
Golf: Kauai has five excellent courses: the *Westin Kauai,* Lihue (245-5050); *Kiahuna Golf Village,* Kauai (742-9595); *Princeville Makai Golf Course,* Hanalei (826-9666); *Wailua Golf Course,* N of Lihue (245-2163); and the 9-hole *Kukuiolono Golf Course,* Kalaheo (332-9151).
Horseback Riding: trail riding in Kauai's interior and along the N coast is offered by *Highgates Ranch,* Wailua Homesteads (822-3182), and *Pooku Stables,* Princeville Ranch near Hanalei (826-6777).
Snorkeling and Scuba Diving: Most hotels/resorts have snorkeling equipment available, otherwise it can be rented at *South Shore Activities* at the Sheraton (742-6873). Popular beaches are *Anini* and *Kee* on the N coast, and *Koloa Landing* and *Palama* in the south. For scuba equipment rental, instruction, and guided dives, contact: *Kauai Divers* (742-1580) in Pooipu; *Ocean Odyssey* (822-9680) and *Get Wet* (822-4884) in Wailua. *Fathom Five* (742-6991) in Koloa also offers complete diving services and rentals.
Swimming: *Kalapaki Beach, Anahola Bay* and *Salt Pond Beach Park* are all excellent swimming beaches on the island's S coast. *Hanalei Bay,* on the N coast, is another excellent beach. As with all Hawaiian islands, caution is advised, especially in winter.
Tennis: almost all of the hotels and condos on Kauai have at least one tennis court. In addition, the island has a number of excellent tennis resorts, including the *Coco Palms Resort Hotel,* Lihue (822-4921); *Hanalei Bay Resort,* Hanalei (826-6522); *Kiahuna Plantation,* Kola (742-6411); *Westin Kauai,* Lihue (245-5050); and the *Waiohai Tennis Club,* Poipu Beach (742-9511).
Water Skiing: *Terheggen International Ski Club* (822-3574) offers tows on the Wailua River.

Weather

Kauai has a tropical oceanic climate with fairly uniform temperatures year-round. Summer daytime high temperatures typically reach into the low 80s, dropping to the low 70s at night. Winter daytime highs are usually in the mid to

KAUAI: TEMPERATURES AND PRECIPITATION

Month	J	F	M	A	M	J	J	A	S	O	N	D
Average Daily Temperature												
(Fahrenheit) Max.	76	76	77	78	80	81	82	83	83	82	80	78
Min.	69	67	67	68	70	72	73	74	74	72	70	69
Average Number of Days with Precipitation												
	14	11	13	12	11	12	14	13	13	13	13	15

high 70s, falling to the upper 60s at night. December and January receive the most rain. The NE part of the island gets much more rain than does the SW.

Island of Maui: Hawaii

Sights to See

Haleakala National Park, centered around the massive Haleakala Crater, the wood's largest dormant volcano. If you have the time, the drive up to the crater's rim, at 10,023 ft. (about 3 hours from Kaanapali), is truly spectacular. Try to catch the sunrise. Do check the crater hotline (572-7749) for weather and wind conditions. Maui Helicopter (871-7855) at Kahului Airport, offers helicopter rides into the crater.

Lahaina, former capital of Kamehameha the Great, and whaling anchorage in the early 19th century.

Carthaginian II, moored in Lahaina harbor in front of the Pioneer Inn. A restored replica of a 19th-century square-rigged brigantine, it is a floating whaling museum. Open 9–4:30 daily.

Baldwin House Museum, Front St., Lahaina, facing the harbor. Noted for its 19th-century furniture, medical equipment, and Oriental porcelain. Open 9:30–5 daily.

Sugar Cane Train (Lahaina-Kaanapali and Pacific Railroad). A narrow-gauge steam locomotive pulls passengers for 25 minutes through sugar cane fields, with views of the ocean on one side and Lanai on the other. Board at either Puukolii Boarding Platform, Lahaina Station, or the Kaanapali Station (661-0089).

Whalers Village Museum, Kaanapali Beach Resort. Illustrates every aspect of whaling. Open 9–9 daily.

Tedeschi Vineyards and Winery, on Hwy. 37, near the Ulupalakua Ranch. Hawaii's only vineyard and winery, complete with tasting room and gift shop. Open 10–5.

Hana and the HanaHighway (Hwy. 36). Starting in Wailuku, the highway skirts the N coast of E. Maui, noted for its fine scenery.

Sports

Boating: most beach hotels have small sailboats available. Otherwise, contact: *Seabern Yachts* (661-8110) in Lahaina or *Maui Sailing Center* (879-5935) in Maalasa Bay for yacht rentals or charters.

Fishing: for charters, contact *Aerial Sportfishing Charters* (667-9089); *Finest Kind Sport Fishing* (661-0338); *Lahaina Charter Boats* (667-6672); or *David Rockett Fishing Charters* (661-4511), all in Lahaina. In Maalaea: *Ocean Activities Center* (879-4485).

Golf: Maui has four golf resorts: *Kapalua Golf Club,* N of Lahaina (669-8044); *Makena Golf Course,* S of Wailea (879-3344); *Royal Kaanapali Golf Courses,* Kaanapali Beach at Lahaina (661-3691); and the *Wailea Golf Club,* Wailea (877-2966). *Waiehu Municipal Golf Course,* Waiehu, near Kahului, is open to the public.

Horseback Riding: in W. Maui, contact: *Kaanapali Kau Lio* (667-7896) in Kaanapali Beach; and *Pony Express Tours* (667-2202) and *Rainbow Ranch, Ltd.* (669-4991) in Lahaina. In E. Maui, contact *Pony Express Tours* (667-2202) in Haleakala; or *Thompson Riding Stables* (878-1910) in Kula, both of whom offer trail rides into Haleakala Crater. *Charley's Trail Rides and Pack Trips* (248-8209) and *Hotel Hana-Maui* (248-8211) operate trail rides out of Hana.

Snorkeling and Scuba Diving: Maui's W coast is excellent for diving and snorkeling. Most hotels have snorkeling gear for rent, otherwise contact *Alihilani Snorkel Sails* (661-3047) or *Scotch Mist Sail & Snorkel* (661-0386) in Lahaina. For scuba diving, contact *Central Pacific Divers* (661-8718), *Lahaina Divers* (661-4505), or *Maui Dive* (667-2080), all in Lahaina.

Swimming: the best beaches are on W. Maui, and on the SE coast of E. Maui. The finest include *Kapalua Beach, Honolua Beach* and *Napili Bay* on W. Maui; and *Keawakapu Beach, Makena Beach* and *Wailea Beach* in the Kihei and Wailea areas. NOTE: caution is advisable.

Tennis: Maui has a number of hotel/resorts with excellent tennis facilities, including *Kaanapali Shores* (667-2211), *Maui Marriott* (667-1200), and *Royal Lahaina Tennis Ranch* (661-3611)—all in Kaanapali Resort. Elsewhere on the island, are the *Kapalua Bay Hotel & Villas* (669-5656) in Kapalua and the *Maui Inter-Continental Wailea* (879-1922) and *Stauffer Wailea Beach Resort* (879-4900), both in Wailea. The *Lahaina Civic Center* has good public courts.

Weather

Maui has a tropical oceanic climate with fairly uniform temperatures year-round. Summer daytime highs typically reach into the low 80s, dropping to the low 70s at night. Winter daytime highs are usually in the mid to high 70s, falling to the upper 60s at night. Winter is the wet season. The NE coast receives the most rain.

LAHAINA: TEMPERATURES AND PRECIPITATION

Month	J	F	M	A	M	J	J	A	S	O	N	D
Average Daily Temperature												
(Fahrenheit) Max.	76	76	77	78	80	81	82	83	83	82	80	78
Min.	69	67	67	68	70	72	73	74	74	72	70	69
Average Number of Days with Precipitation												
	14	11	13	12	11	12	14	13	13	13	13	15

Island of Molokai: Hawaii

Sights to See

Kalaupapa Peninsula, on the island's N coast. Site of a former leper colony. Best reached by the famous *"Molokai Mule Ride,"* down a steep cliff and through a rain forest, with dramatic panoramic views along the way. Contact Molokai Mule Tours (567-6088).

Father Damien's Statue, Kalaupapa Peninsula. Built in memory of the Belgian priest who devoted his life to treating the lepers in the 19th century.
Palaau Park, off Hwy. 47, NE of Kualapuu, overlooking the Kalaupapa Peninsula. A beautiful wilderness area, with the famous Kalaupapa Lookout, an arboretum, and phallic rocks.
Puu Nana, off Hwy. 46 in the W central part of the island. A 1,381-ft. peak, affording spectacular sunset viewing. On a clear day you can see Oahu.
Maunaloa, near Puu Nana on Hwy. 46. A former company town, now an arts and crafts center.
Molokai Ranch Wildlife Park, near Kepuhi Beach, W. Molokai. An exotic wildlife preserve. The ranch offers a 90-minute camera safari. The tour office is outside the Sheraton Molokai in Kepuhi Beach (552-2555).
Halawa Valley, at the E and of the island. One-time center of the island's population, but cleared by a tsunami in 1946, this beautiful valley is noted for its ancient heiaus (temples), and two plunging waterfalls, *Moaula Falls* (a 250-ft. cascade), and Hipuapua Falls.
Kaunakakai, the island's principal town. Locale of the Hawaiian song "Cock-eyed Mayor of Kaunakakai."

Sports

Boating: there are no boats or yachts for rent or charter on the island, although Rodonis (533-3311) and Noio (558-8910), in Kaunakakai, both offer sailing cruises. *Moloakai Fish and Dive Co.* (553-5926), also arranges sailing charters.
Fishing: the waters around the island are abundant in sports fish, especially the SW coast. For charters contact *Alele II* (558-8190); *Molokai Fish and Dive* (563-5926); *Noio Fishing & Trading Co.* (558-8910); or *Welakahao Fishing* (558-8253), all in Kaunakakai.
Golf: the island has one superb golf resort, the *Kaluaki Hotel & Golf Club,* W. Molokai (Ted Robinson–designed course with spectacular ocean footage) (552-2555). The public has access to the *Ironwood Hills Golf Club* (9 holes) (567-6121) in Kualapuu.
Horseback Riding: contact *Hawaiian Horsemanship Unlimited* (552-0056) in Kualapuu, or, in E. Molakai, contact *Halawa Valley Horse Rides* (553-5071).
Snorkeling and Scuba Diving: the east end of the island is considered to be the best spot. Bring your own equipment, because the *Molokai Fish and Dive Co.* (553-5926) in Kaunakakai is the only outfit that rents scuba equipment or organizes dives. *Noio* (558-8910) in Kaunakakai, offers snorkeling cruises.
Swimming: the hard-to-reach beaches on the island's E end are considered the best for swimming. Caution is advisable at all beaches, particularly those at the W end of the island, due to coral formations and exposed rock just below the surface. Best check with your hotel.
Tennis: the best facilities are those at the *Kaluaki Hotel and Golf Club* (552-2555). Public courts are available in Kaunakakai.

Weather

Molokai has a tropical oceanic climate with fairly uniform termperatures year-round. Summer daytime high temperatures typically reach into the low 80s, dropping to the low 70s at night. Winter daytime highs are usually in the mid to high 70s, failing to the upper 60s at night. Although the frequency of rainfall is pretty uniform year-round, winter is the wet season, with December and January normally the wettest months. The eastern part of the island receives much more rain than the western part, however.

MOLOKAI: TEMPERATURES AND PRECIPITATION

Month	J	F	M	A	M	J	J	A	S	O	N	D
Average Daily Temperature												
(Fahrenheit) Max.	76	76	77	78	80	81	82	83	83	82	80	78
Min.	69	67	67	68	70	72	73	74	74	72	70	69
Average Number of Days with Precipitation												
	14	11	13	12	11	12	14	13	13	13	13	15

Island of Oahu: Hawaii

Sights to See

Pearl Harbor and the U.S.S. Arizona Memorial Cruise boats leave from Kewalo Basin near Waikiki (471-3901). Free boat tours of the *U.S.S. Arizona* Memorial, honoring those who died when Japan bombed Pearl Harbor, leave from the Halawa Landing, 8–3 Tu–Su.

Diamond Head (Lae'ahi), at the SE boundary of Waikiki. The views from the slopes of this 760-ft. volcanic crater are spectacular.

Iolani Palace, King & Richard Sts. The final home of Queen Liliuokalani (who was a famous song writer as well as a monarch). Take the Palace Tour, by appointment only (536-2474), 9–2:15 W–Sa.

Honolulu Academy of Arts, 900 S. Beretania St. Excellent collection of Asian and Oriental art. Open 10–4:30 T, W, F, Sa, 11–8 Th, 2–5 Su.

Bishop Museum, Likelike Hwy. in Kalihi. Fascinating collection of Hawaiiana; also artifacts from the Pacific area. Open 9–5 daily.

Polynesian Cultural Center, on Oahu's N shore of Laie. Made up of native villages representative of those in Fiji, Tonga, New Zealand, Tahiti, Samoa, the Marquesas, and Hawaii. Live entertainment.

Sea Life Park, Makapuu Point at the E tip of Oahu. Noted for its 300,000-gallon Hawaiian Reef Tank and the thousands of Hawaiian marine specimens.

Sports

Boating: Pier 12 Ocean Center, Kewalo Basin, Honolulu (521-6305) offers sailing yacht rentals. The *Froomes Sailing Company* Inc., 789 Kailua Rd.,

Kailua (261-2961) specializes in catamaran rentals, as does *U-Sail Rental* (946-0130), on Kalia Rd., Waikiki.

Fishing: the Kewalo Boat Basin, Ala Moana Boulevard, is one of Oahu's major sport fishing centers. Contact *Coreene C's Sport Fishing Charters* (536-7472); *Island Charters* (536-1555); *Kono* (531-0060); or *Sport Fishing Hawaii* (536-6577).

Golf: in the Honolulu area, the public places to play are the *Ala Wai Golf Course,* Honolulu (737-2414); *Mililani Golf Course,* Mililani Town (623-2254); *Olomana Golf Links,* N of Waimanola (259-7926); *Pali Golf Course,* Pali Lookout (261-9784); the *Pearl Country Club,* Aiea (487-3802); and the *Ted Makalena Golf Course,* Walpahu (671-6488). The island's two resort courses, are the *Sheraton Makaha Resort and Country Club,* Makaha (695-9511); and the *Turtle Bay Hilton and Country Club,* Kahuku (293-8811).

Horseback Riding: contact *Sheraton Makaha Resort,* Makaha (695-9511); *Koko Crater Stables* (395-2628); or the *Horseback Riding Tour Co.* (538-7636).

Snorkeling and Scuba Diving: Hanauma Bay is Oahu's best snorkeling spot. Most beach hotels in Waikiki rent snorkeling equipment to guests. Contact *Dan's Dive Shop,* 660 Ala Moana Blvd. (536-6181); or *Fort DeRussy Beach Services* on Waikiki Beach (949-3469). For scuba diving, contact *American Dive Hawaii,* 404 Piikoi St. (239-5733); *Dan's Dive Shop;* or South Sea Aquatics, 1050 Ala Moana Blvd. (538-3854).

Swimming: Waikiki Beach is the most popular, and one of the safest, beaches on Oahu. Other spots include *Kailua Beach Park* and *Kahana Bay Beach Park* on the E side of the island.

Tennis: many of Waikiki's larger hotels have tennis courts available for guests, and will sometimes allow non-guests to play. *Ala Moana Park,* 1201 Ala Moana Blvd.; *Diamond Head Tennis Center,* 3908 Paki Ave.; and the *Kapiolani Tennis Courts,* 2748 Kalakaua Ave., are all public courts in the Waikiki area. Excellent tennis resorts include: *The Ilikai,* 1777 Ala Moana Blvd., Honolulu (949-3811); the *Sheraton Makaha Resort and Country Club,* Makaha Valley Rd., Makaha (695-9511); and the *Turtle Bay Hilton and Country Club,* Kahuhu (293-8811).

Weather

Oahu enjoys a tropical oceanic climate, with fairly uniform temperatures all year round. Daily highs in the summer are typically in the low 80s, failing to the low to mid 70s at night. Winter daytime high temperatures are usually in the mid to

OAHU: TEMPERATURES AND PRECIPITATION

Month	J	F	M	A	M	J	J	A	S	O	N	D
Average Daily Temperature												
(Fahrenheit) Max.	76	76	77	78	80	81	82	83	83	82	80	78
Min.	69	67	67	68	70	72	73	74	74	72	70	69
Average Number of Days with Precipitation												
	14	11	13	12	11	12	14	13	13	13	13	15

upper 70s, dropping to the high 60s at night. Winter is the wet season. The northeastern coast is much wetter than the relatively dry southwest coast.

Auckland: New Zealand

Sights to See

The city of Auckland can best be seen from the summit of *Mount Eden,* one of the city's 14 extinct volcanoes, and the highest point in Auckland. The panoramic views from this former Maori stronghold are magnificent.

War Memorial Museum, Auckland Domain, just SE of downtown. Excellent collection of Maori and South Pacific artifacts, including a war canoe, weapons, and authentic Maori houses.

Winter Garden, adjacent to the War Memorial Museum. A fine collection of tropical and subtropical plants. Open 10–12, 1–4 daily.

Auckland City Art Gallery, Kitchener St., adjacent to Albert Park. An excellent, diverse collection of Old Masters and modern works, together with an extensive collection of New Zealand art. Open 10–4:30 M–Th, 10–8:30 F, 1–5:30 Sa–Su.

Auckland Zoo, Motions Road, Western Springs. Especially noted for its nocturnal house, holding its collection of kiwis, New Zealand's unique flightless birds. Open 9:30–5:30 daily.

Museum of Transport and Technology, Great North Road, Western Springs. A fine collection of antique equipment and machines. Also noted for its Pioneer Village, where 19th-century New Zealand is re-created. Open 9–5 daily.

Lion Safari Park, Redhills Road, in Massey, outside Auckland. You can drive through the park and admire not only the lions, but the water buffalo, camels, emus, and other animals as well.

Kelly Tarlton's Underwater World, opposite Orakei Wharf, just outside Auckland. Noted for its underwater tunnel ride, from which you can observe sea creatures in their natural environment. Don't miss the slide show on undersea wonders.

New Zealand Heritage Park, in the suburb of Mount Wellington. A unique showplace exhibiting New Zealand's way of life, featuring a nature world, a culture world, and an agriworld.

Useful Information

New Zealand Government Tourist Travel Board Office, 99 Queen Street (tel:798-180); *Taxi* (tel:792-792 or 328-991); *Emergency* (tel:111 for fire, police, or ambulance); *American Express,* 95 Queen St. (tel:798-243); the nearest *U.S. Embassy* is in Wellington, at 29 Fitzherbert Terr. (tel:04/722-068); *Voltage Guide:* 220 V, two flat, angled blade outlets are used; *Post Office,* Queen St., between Quay and Customs Sts. Check the *Great Time Guide to Auckland and Northland,* a monthly, as well as the weekly *Auckland Tourist Times* for information on what's going on in Auckland.

Special Trips/Tours

Be sure to catch the *harbor steam ferry* across to Devonport on the North Shore. The ferries leave from the Queens Wharf terminal on Quay Street. The *Old Ferry Arts and Crafts Market* is held on the Devonport Wharf every Saturday.

Waitomo Caves, with the world-famous **Glow Worm Grotto,** are just S of Hamilton near Otorohanga, some three hours from Auckland. Although many other caves have the beautiful stalactites and stalagmites, they do not have these unusual glow worms. Visit the nearby *Ohaki Maori Village.*

One of New Zealand's principal tourist attractions, **Rotorua,** is some 150 miles S of Auckland. Famous for its thermal activity and mineral waters, it is also a center of the Maori culture. Soak in a hot thermal pool, sample food from Maori earth ovens and thermal springs, and watch the Maori groups provide dance and song entertainment. Walk around the traditional village site, *Whakarewarewa,* where carved meeting houses and huts are surrounded by boiling mud pools and geysers. Visit the *Maori Arts and Crafts School* where master carvers and weavers teach their apprentices.

Weather

Auckland has a cool temperate climate. Summer (Dec.–March) daytime high temperatures typically reach into the low 70s, falling to the high 50s at night. Winter daytime highs are in the high 50s, dropping to the mid 40s at night. Rainfall is evenly spread.

AUCKLAND: TEMPERATURES AND PRECIPITATION

Month	J	F	M	A	M	J	J	A	S	O	N	D
Average Daily Temperature												
(Fahrenheit) Max.	73	73	71	67	62	58	56	58	60	63	66	70
Min.	60	60	59	56	51	48	46	46	49	52	54	57
Average Number of Days with Precipitation												
	10	10	11	14	19	19	21	19	17	16	15	12

Christchurch: New Zealand

Sights to See

Cathedral Square, at the center of Christchurch at the intersection of Worcester & Colombo Sts. The nucleus of the city, with the city's best known landmark, the cathedral, at its center. Listen in on the "speaker's corner."

Christchurch Cathedral, Cathedral Square. Neo-Gothic in design, the tower offers fine views of this very English city. Open 9–4 M–Sa, 12:30–4:30 Su.

Canterbury Museum, Rolleston Ave. & Worcester St. An excellent Antarctica exhibit, together with a fine ornithological section and a Maori collection. Open 10–4:30 M–Sa, 2–4:30 Su.

Botanic Gardens, Rolleston Ave. & Worcester St., behind the museum, and part of Hagley Park. One of the finest in the southern hemisphere, they are noted for the wide variety of native and exotic flora.

McDougall Art Gallery, in the Botanic Gardens. Fine collections of art, sculpture and pottery, in addition to the noted Maori paintings. Open 10–4:30 M–F, 1–5:30 Sa–Su.

Ferrymead Historic Park, Bridle Path Rd., Heathcote. Interesting early transport museum. Open 10–4 daily.

Willowbank Wildlife Reserve, 60 Hussey Road, some 20 minutes outside Christchurch. Contains a large collection of birds and animals in a fine natural park. Open 10–6 daily.

Lyttleton Harbor, Lyttleton, just S of the city. The busy and picturesque port of Christchurch, with old wooden cottages clinging to the surrounding hillsides. The harbor itself is the flooded crater of an extinct volcano. The *Summit Road to Lyttleton* offers spectacular views of the coast and the Southern Alps to the west.

Useful Information

Canterbury Information Centre, 75 Worcester St. (tel:99-629); *New Zealand Government Tourist Bureau,* Cathedral Square (tel:794-900); *Taxi* (tel:795-795 or 799-799); *Emergency* (tel:111 for fire, police, and ambulance); *American Express,* 226 High Street (tel:66-772); the nearest *U.S. Embassy* in in Wellington, at 29 Fitzherbert Terrace (tel:04/722-068); *Voltage Guide:* 220 V, two flat, angled blade outlets are used; *Post Office,* Cathedral Square.

Special Trips/Tours

The ***Banks Peninsula,*** just SE of Christchurch, is a scenic promontory with an interesting, originally French settlement, *Akaroa.* The French influence is evident in the architecture, street names, and shops of this quaint village.

The *Southern Alps,* New Zealand's alpine country, are certainly worth seeing. The *Arthur's Pass Road* (Hwy. 73), is the shortest route across the Southern Alps, and also the highest, affording magnificent mountain scenery. *Arthur's Pass National Park* is worth seeing. However, for the best alpine scenery, you should see ***Mount Cook National Park*** in the beautiful, spectacular snow-capped Southern Alps, 205 miles W of Christchurch, via Hwys. 1, 8, and 80. Centered around Mount Cook (12,530 ft.), New Zealand's highest mountain, the park contains 22 peaks over 10,000 ft. in addition to the *Tasman Glacier.* The glacier, the longest in the world outside the polar regions, is over 18 miles long, and up to 2 miles wide in places. For an exhilarating experience, catch the ski plane that operates regular flights to the head of the glacier. Be sure to stop by the Visitor Centre in Mount Cook Village.

If you have more time on your hands, the ***Fjordland National Park,*** at the SW end of South Island is definitely worth a visit. An extended cruise is the best way to see the beautiful sounds, notably *Milford Sound,* with its waterfalls cascading through densely forested valleys. *Lake Te Ana-au,* with its glowworm caves, is also worth seeing.

Weather

Christchurch enjoys a mild temperate climate. Daytime high temperatures in the summer (Dec.–March) typically reach into the high 60s or low 70s, falling to the low 50s at night. Winter daytime highs are usually in the low 50s, dropping to the mid 30s at night. Rainfall is spread fairly well throughout the year, although the winter months are the wettest.

CHRISTCHURCH: TEMPERATURES AND PRECIPITATION

Month	J	F	M	A	M	J	J	A	S	O	N	D
Average Daily Temperature												
(Fahrenheit) Max.	70	69	66	62	56	51	50	52	57	62	66	69
Min.	53	53	50	45	40	36	35	36	40	44	47	51
Average Number of Days with Precipitation												
	10	8	9	10	12	13	13	11	10	10	10	10

Wellington: New Zealand

Sights to See

Wellington itself from the Mount Victoria Lookout, at 648 ft., at the S end of the city, which offers the best overall panoramas; or from the *Kelburn Lookout* above the Botanical Gardens. The cable car to Kelburn leaves from Cable Car Lane, just off Lambton Quay, opposite Grey St., downtown.
Botanical Gardens, at the top of the cable-car ride. Full of native and exotic plants, the gardens are noted for their beautiful flower displays.
Parliament Buildings, to the NE of the Botanical Gardens off Bowen St. Three structures, including the Parliament House with its visitors' gallery, the General Assembly Library, and the Executive Wing of Parliament House, better known as the "Beehive."
Government Buildings, down Bowen St., just below the Parliament Buildings. One of the world's largest wooden structures.
Old St. Paul's Cathedral, Mulgrave St. Dating from 1866, this Gothic structure is one of the country's most beautiful wooden churches. It is especially noted for its interior. Open 10–4:30 M–Sa, 1:30–4:30 Su.
National Museum and Art Gallery, Buckle St., S of the central area of Wellington. The museum is noted for its Maori artifacts, and Captain Cook displays. The National Art Gallery, upstairs, has a fine collection of both national and international works. Both open 10–4:45 daily.
The Carillon Bell Tower, Buckle Street, next to the National Museum. New Zealand's national war memorial.
Wellington Zoo, Manchester St., Newtown S of downtown Wellington. Known for its nocturnal Kiwi House. Open 10–4 daily.

Useful Information

New Zealand Government Tourist Bureau, 26-31 Mercer St. (tel:739-269); *Visitors Centre,* Mercer & Victoria Sts. (tel:735-063); *Post Office,* Waterloo Quay; *Taxi* (tel:893-0232 or 859-900); *U.S. Embassy,* 29 Fitzherbert Terrace, Thorndon (tel:722-068); *Emergency* (tel:111 for ambulance, fire, or police); *Voltage Guide:* 220 V, two flat, angled blade outlets are used.

Special Trips/Tours

The *Kapiti Coast,* N of Wellington between Paekakariki and Waikane on the North Island's SW coast has excellent beaches and is a popular resort area. Just N of Paraparaumu is the *Southward Car Museum,* with a large collection of automobiles. In McKay's Crossing, Paekakariki, is the *Wellington Tramway Museum* and the *Memorial Gates to the U.S. Second Marine Division* commemorating the division's stationing here during WW II.

Inland, NE of Wellington, across the Rimutaka Range at the head of the Wairarapa Valley is *Masterton.* A growing arts and crafts community, it is home to the *Wairarapa Arts Centre* and beautiful *Queen Elizabeth Park.* North of Masterton is the *Mount Bruce Native Bird Reserve.*

Some 6 hours N of Wellington in the central part of North Island is the majestic *Tongariro National Park,* dominated by three active volcanoes. The highest is over 9,000 ft., and all three snow-capped peaks offer excellent skiing in winter, and fine hiking in the summer. Just N of the park is *Lake Taupo,* center of a world-renowned trout fishing area.

Weather

Wellington has a temperate, maritime climate with very changeable weather. Summer (Dec.–Feb.) daytime high temperatures typically reach into the high 60s, falling to the mid 50s at night. Winter (June–Aug.) daytime highs are usually in the mid 50s, dropping to the low 40s at night. Rainfall is frequent and well distributed throughout the year, although May through August is somewhat wetter than the rest of the year.

WELLINGTON: TEMPERATURES AND PRECIPITATION

Month	J	F	M	A	M	J	J	A	S	O	N	D
Average Daily Temperature												
(Fahrenheit) Max.	69	69	67	63	58	55	53	54	57	60	63	67
Min.	56	56	54	51	47	44	42	43	46	48	50	54
Average Number of Days with Precipitation												
	10	9	11	13	16	17	18	17	15	14	13	12

Tahiti

Sights to See

Bougainville Park, next to the Post Office, just off blvd. Pomare, Papeete, Tahiti's capital. Contains a statue of the navigator, flanked by two cannons.
Vaima Center (Centre Vaima), one block E of Bougainville Park, Papeete. Tahiti's largest shopping center, together with restaurants and theaters.
Catholic Cathedral, rue de Gen. de Gaulle, just one block SE of the Vaima Center. A late-19th-century structure, noted for its crucifixion paintings.
Papeete Market, across rue Gauguin, E of the Cathedral. Colorful market full of local produce. Best seen early in the morning, especially Sunday morning.
Catholic Archbishop's Palace, just E of downtown Papeete. Fine example of colonial architecture.
Museum of Tahiti and Islands (Musee de Tahiti et des Iles), Pointe des Pecheurs in Punaauia, 10 miles SW of Papeete. Excellent collection of Polynesian art and culture. The surrounding *Polynesian Botanical Garden* is worth spending time in. Open 9–5 Tu–Su.
Matae of Arahurahu (Temple of Ashes), a stone open-air altar, just S of Paea on Tahiti's W coast, some 6 miles S of the Museum of Tahiti. Once the most important pagan temple on Tahiti.
Gauguin Museum, Papeari, 30 miles SE of Papeete. Dedicated to the life and art of Paul Gauguin, with copies of the artist's paintings of Tahitian life. Open 9–5 daily.
Botanical Gardens, adjacent to the Gauguin Museum in Papeari. Many varieties of tropical plants, flowers, shrubs, and trees. Open 8–5 daily.
Tomb of Pomare V., Arue just NE of Papeete. A pyramid topped by a funeral urn, on the ancestral land of the royal Pomare family.
Museum of Discovery (Musee de la Decouverte), Mahina, Point Venus, some 8 miles NE of Papeete. Wax figures of Cook, de Bougainville, Wallis, and the Tahitian chief at the time of European discovery. Open 9–3 daily, 9–12 on weekends.
Moorea Island, 10 miles NW of Tahiti. Reached by air or by boat from Papeete's harbor—30 to 60 minutes depending on the boat—the KEKE III (tel:2-8060) is the fastest. Notable sights include *Cook's Bay* (Baie de Cook) on the island's N shore; *Paopao village* church; the *Polynesian temples* (Marae Titiroa, Marae Ahu O Mahine, and Marae Afareaito) in Opunohu valley in Moorea's center; and *Le Belvedere lookout* at the head of the Opunohu valley.

Sports

Boating: Tahiti Mer et Loisirs (tel:3-9799) offers charter cruises to most of Tahiti's islands, as well as sailboat and windsurfer rentals. *Tahiti Aquatique* (tel:2-8042), Hotel Maeva Beach, Faaa, offers glass-bottom-boat trips, cruises, and sailboat rentals.

Fishing: *Tahiti Mer et Loisirs* (tel:3-9799), Papeete, offers deep-sea fishing charters. Alternatively, contact Taniera (tel:2-7669 or 3-5344).
Golf: the 18-hole *Atimaono Golf Course* (tel:7-4241), just outside Mataiea on Tahiti's S coast is open to the public. Closed Tu.
Hiking: Mt. Aorai (6,780 ft.) is a favorite climb for many visitors; although lower than Mt. Orohena, it is more accessible and less dangerous. The strenuous hike will be rewarded with magnificent views.
Snorkeling and Scuba Diving: *Tahiti Aquatique* (tel:2-8042), Faaa, offers snorkeling cruises. Contact *Tahiti Plongee* (tel:3-6251), or *Tahiti Mer et Loisirs* (tel:3-9799), Papeete, for scuba diving.
Swimming: just about all the beaches are superb. Topless sunbathing is quite common.
Tennis: many of the hotels/resorts have courts.
Water Skiing: contact *Tahiti Mer et Loisirs* (tel:3-9799), Papeete, for equipment and tows.

Weather

Tahiti has a hot, humid tropical oceanic climate alleviated by frequent sea breezes. Summer (Dec.–Feb.) daytime high temperatures are typically in the high 80s, dropping to the low 70s at night. Winter (June–Aug.) daytime highs are normally in the mid 80s, falling to the high 60s at night. The rainy season extends from December through March.

TAHITI: TEMPERATURES AND PRECIPITATION

Month	J	F	M	A	M	J	J	A	S	O	N	D
Average Daily Temperature												
(Fahrenheit) Max.	89	89	89	89	87	86	86	86	86	87	88	88
Min.	72	72	72	72	70	69	68	68	69	70	71	72
Average Number of Days with Precipitation												
	16	16	17	10	10	8	5	6	6	9	13	14

Resources

Professional Associations

American Society of Travel Agents (ASTA), 1101 King St., Alexandria, VA 22314; (703)739-2782). The largest travel trade association, with some 23,000 members in 129 countries around the world. Offers educational seminars and workshops, and educational manuals and materials, in addition to its promotional functions. Publishes a magazine on travel agency management that regularly features articles on destinations around the world, including the "Business Trip Planner," which typically has more detail on individual cities around the world.

Association of Retail Travel Agents (ARTA), 1745 Jefferson Davis Hwy., Suite 300, Arlington, VA 22202; (703)553-7777. Mostly independent retail travel agents, some 2,000 strong. Offers a newsletter to members, as well as usual promotional activities.

National Tourist Offices

Virtually every country has one or more national tourist offices in the U.S., usually in New York and Los Angeles. Many have three or more, with offices in Chicago or Houston in addition to ones in New York and Los Angeles. If the country doesn't have a separate tourist office, either run by themselves or by a U.S. public relations firm, their embassy in Washington, D.C., will usually serve that function. Whether you can get any useful information from them is entirely another matter!

While they are ostensibly set up to promote tourism, it is really amazing that some are extremely lax, or negligent, in answering written requests, or even answering the phone. I have repeatedly written to several tourist offices requesting information and have yet to receive any acknowledgment. I have followed these letters with phone calls (checking beforehand to make sure that I have both the correct address and phone number), and just could not get through.

Either the national tourist offices in question have only one phone line that is besieged, or they are grossly understaffed or have incompetent and/or negligent staffs. So be prepared for some frustration when requesting information. It is also extremely important to be as specific as possible when asking for information. Asking for "some brochures" will get you just that—some glossy brochures that are not likely to be very informative.

This is not to say, by any means, that all national tourist offices are useless. Indeed, some are superb. Particularly helpful are those of the U.K., Canada, Japan, and W. Germany. If you have a need for really specific information, it is often a good idea (if you have the time), to write directly to the individual town or city's tourist office in the country you would like more information from. Addresses can be obtained from the better guide books, or from the national tourist offices in this country.

Some national tourist offices have a wealth of information and are very well operated by courteous and knowledgeable staffs. Others, unfortunately, are not. When you call better results can sometimes be obtained by asking for the press officer of the tourist office, if the receptionist is unable or unwilling to provide you with the information that you request. *Travel Weekly's World Travel Directory,* 1989 (New York: Ziff-Davis Publishing Co.), lists the national tourist offices with their addresses and phone numbers.

General Background Information

Apart from a good encyclopedia, such as the *Encyclopedia Brittanica, Collier's Encyclopedia*, 1985 (New York: Macmillan Educational Co.), or *The World Book Encyclopedia*, 1984 (Chicago: World Book, Inc.), your best bet is the 5-volume *Worldmark Encyclopedia of the Nations*, 1984 (New York: Worldmark Press, distributed by John Wiley & Sons, Inc.), with individual volumes on the United Nations, Africa, the Americas, Asia and Oceania, and Europe. These volumes constitute a practical guide to the geographic, historical, political, social, and economic system of all nations, their international relationships, and the U.N. system.

More condensed, and current, versions of essentially the same thing are given in:

The World Almanac and Book of Facts, 1990 (New York: Pharos Books).

The Universal Almanac, 1990 (Kansas City: Andrews and McMeel).

Rand McNally, 1986, *World Facts in Brief, 1986* (Chicago: Rand McNally).

Stonehouse, B., 1986, *Facts on File: Pocket Guide to the World* (New York: Facts on File Publications).

Kurian, G. T., 1983, *World Data: A Treasury of Geographical Knowledge* (New York: World Almanac Publications).

More specialized encyclopedias exist, such as *The International Geographic Encyclopedia and Atlas*, 1979 (Boston: Houghton Mifflin, Co.) or the *Larousse Encyclopedia of World Geography*, 1965 (New York: Odysey Press), but run the risk of being a little out of date in some matters.

If you need to know something about the world's oceans and islands, or the world's rivers and lakes, then the following two references can be consulted:

Huxley, A. ed., 1962, *Standard Encyclopedia of the World's Oceans and Islands* (New York: G. P. Putnam and Sons).

Gresswell, R. K. and A. Huxley, 1965, *Standard Encyclopedia of the World's Rivers and Lakes* (New York: G. P. Putnam and Sons).

On the more practical side two standard references are:

Travel Weekly's World Travel Directory, 1989 (New York: Ziff-Davis Publishing Co.), which lists wholesale tour operators, cruise lines, airlines, car rentals, railroads, holidays, travel agencies of the world, and destinations of the world (including tourist offices, weather, special attractions, calendar of events, ground operators, and, where applicable, entry regulations, holidays, embassies, and consulates).

Directory of International Business Travel and Relocation, 1980 (Detroit: Gale Research Co.).

On the light side, two amusing "reference" works, are:

McClintock, J. and D. Helgren, 1986, *Everything is Somewhere: A Geographic Quiz Book* (New York: Quill, William Morrow).

DeSola, R. 1975, *Worldwide What and Where: Geographic Glossary and Traveler's Guide* (New York: Avon Books).

Atlases

Several good atlases exist, including the *National Geographic Atlas of the World*. One of the best is *The Times Atlas of the World,* 1985, 7th edition. It contains 122 double-paged, 8-color maps, and a fully updated index-gazetteer with over 200,000 entries. Size 18″ × 12″; 520 pp.

A serviceable, much less expensive atlas, is *The World Atlas,* 1982, New York: Random House, 112 pp.

Geography Texts

An introductory overview of basic geographical concepts and an introduction to the regional geography of the world is provided by De Blij, H. J., 1978, *Geography: Regions and Concepts* (New York: John Wiley and Sons).

Each continent or major world region has its own set of standard geographical texts, dealing in more or less detail with such topics as the terrain, climate, population, languages, religions, political geography, agriculture, settlements, industry, transportation and trade. For Europe, good examples, although somewhat dated, include:

Jordan, T. G., 1973, *The European Culture Area: A Systematic Geography* (New York: Harper and Row).

Malmstrom, V. H., 1971, *Geography of Europe: A Regional Analysis* (Englewood Cliffs, NJ: Prentice-Hall).

Hoffman, G. W. ed., 1977, *A Geography of Europe: Problems and Prospects* (New York: John Wiley and Sons).

Weather Information

The best worldwide weather data book is:

Pearce, E. A. and C. G. Smith, 1984, *The Times Books World Weather Guide* (New York: Times Books).

The U.S. Department of Commerce also publishes *Climates of the World,* 1977 (Washington DC: U.S. Government Printing Office). The principal features of climates of all the continents are discussed. Worldwide temperature and precipitation maps are included. Monthly and annual temperatures and precipitation data for 800 stations throughout the world are included.

Weather Trak is a computerized phone service that tells the weather and the forecast for over 235 cities worldwide. Callers punch a code (usually the telephone area code for the city that interests them), and a computer gives the weather. Contact: *Cities,* Box 7000, Dallas, TX 75209, for a list of cities covered by the service, and their codes. *American Express* operates a 900-WEATHER line that provides temperatures and forecasts for 600 places around the world, and *Avis* also has a 900 number (1-900-884-AVIS) that gives average high and low temperatures and extended weather outlooks for an unspecified number of destinations. Callers have to provide the area code or first three letters of the city for which information is desired.

Many good newspapers, the *New York Times,* for example, not only give local weather forecasts, but a traveler's forecast for domestic cities. In addition they give temperatures and general weather conditions in foreign cities for the preceding day, which, of course, gives you some idea of what to expect if you are traveling there today or tomorrow.

Health Information

The Centers for Disease Control, U.S. Department of Health and Human Services, publishes an annual report, *Health Information for International Travel*, which is published as a supplement to the *Morbidity and Mortality Weekly Report* (Washington, DC: U.S. Government Printing Office). It provides reasonably up-to-date and comprehensive information on immunization requirements and recommendations for international travelers, along with health hints for travelers. The Centers for Disease Control also have two phone numbers (404)332-4559 and (404)332-4555 that provide health information.

Travel Alerts and Advisories

The State Department operates regional bureaus and individual "country desks" where the most up-to-date information on travel alerts and advisories can be obtained. Phone numbers are published in the *Federal Yellow Book*.

The State Department's *Citizen's Emergency Center* (202)647-5225 also gives callers the latest, up-to-date information on travel alerts or advisories, warnings and restrictions. On request, they will provide a printed rundown of travel advisories.

World Status Map, PO Box 466, Merrifield, VA 22116, gives a summary of global travel conditions in its monthly newsletter. Another newsletter, *Weekly Risk Assessment*, published by Risks International, Alexandria, VA (703)836-6126, provides reports on analysis of terrorist activities worldwide.

Travel Guides/Books

The principal travel guidebook series include the well-known *American Express, Let's Go, Frommer's, Fielding's, Fodor's, Birnbaum's*, and *Fisher's* series, along with the venerable *Michelin* and *Baedeker's* guides from Europe, with extensive coverage. Less-well-known guides, with less extensive or even limited coverage, include the *Lonely Planet, Insight, The World at Its Best, A to Z World Travel, Rand McNally, Berlitz Travel, Traveller's, Blue Book, Maverick, Kosey Travel*, and the *Michael Haag* guides.

The choice is very wide, some are published annually, others only every other year or less frequently. Some series, such as *Fodor's*, pretty much cover the world, while others are essentially limited to one small part of the world—for example, the *Maverick Guides*, which cover Australia, New Zealand, and Hawaii. Some are targeted to the budget traveler *(Lonely Planet, Let's Go)* emphasizing youth hostels, college dorms, inexpensive neighborhood cafes and cafeterias, while others *(Birnbaum's)* are aimed at the middle- to upper-income experienced traveler.

Some tend to focus on lodging and meals *(Frommer's* and *Fielding's)*, while others concentrate on historical and cultural information and noteworthy sights *(Baedeker's)*, and still others *(Birnbaum's)* spend more time on touring itineraries and other special-interest "diversions"—sporting activities, antique hunting, game hunting, music festivals, shopping, gastronomic tours, etc. Some of the guidebooks are very selective and very subjective in what they cover *(Fisher's)*, while others *(Fodor's)* are very dry in their descriptions.

Some areas of the world are very well covered. For instance, all the major series emphasize *Western Europe*, while *Africa*, particularly Africa south of the Sahara, is poorly covered. This, of course, reflects travel patterns to a great extent. Between 5 and 6 million Americans travel to Europe every year, while fewer than 100,000 per year visit Africa.

A growing trend is for the major guidebook series to cover more individual countries, regions within a particular country, and individual cities *(Access Guides, Fodor's, American Express, Berlitz)*. Special interest travel topics are also receiving more attention—for example: Frommer's *Dollarwise Guide to Skiing—East and West,* and their *A Shopper's Guide to Best Buys in England, Scotland, and Wales;* Fielding's *Selective Shopping Guide to Europe, Europe with Children, Motoring and Camping Europe, Havens and Hideways USA, African Safaris,* and *Worldwide Cruises;* and Fodor's *Views to Dine by Around the World.* If you want to plan a music festival holiday, then Carol P. Rabin's, 1984, *Music Festivals in Europe and Britain* (Stockbridge, MA: Berkshire Traveller Press) may be just the ticket.

Birnbaum's has a *USA For Business Travelers,* along with a *Europe for Business Travelers,* with information on where to obtain such business services as audiovisual equipment, limousines, messenger services, photocopying, secretaries/stenographers, and translators, in addition to the usual sights, hotels, and restaurants coverage. Berlitz also has a *Business Travel Guide: Europe,* as does the International Herald Tribune, with its *Guide to Business Travel and Entertainment in Europe.*

Another point to remember is that the quality of volumes within a particular series will vary, depending on the author or authors, and on the volumes' currency. Some are very good at giving detailed information (complete street addresses, phone numbers, hours of operation, good directions, and other helpful tips), while other guidebook series don't do as thorough a job.

The *Insight Guides* are well illustrated with full-color photographs, which can give the reader a good "feel" for the area covered, and others *(Baedeker's)* offer good maps. Some give star ratings for sights, hotels, and restaurants—*Fisher's, AAA,* and *Baedeker's* (sights only)—while others leave it to the reader to infer ratings from the descriptions, or just list sights, hotels, and restaurants, with no attempt to distinguish the really worthwhile from the more pedestrian.

Since no one guidebook can possibly cover everything, it is advisable to consult more than one. One extremely good resource that summarizes the better travel guides available today by regions and countries of the world is:

Hayes, G. and J. Wright, 1988, *Going Places: The Guide to Travel Guides* (Boston, MA: The Harvard Common Press).

NOTE: if you have trouble locating a particular guidebook, particularly those for out-of-the-way places, a number of bookstores specialize in stocking them. For instance, *Book Passage,* 57 Post St. (4th Floor), San Francisco, CA 94104; (800)321-9785 has a catalog listing 4,000 titles: and *Travel Books Unlimited,* 4931 Cordell Ave., Bethesda, MD 20814, (301)951-8533, has an excellent collection and also publishes an annual catalog.

Customs and Manners

If you need a guide to international behavior, so that you are conversant with each country's protocol, customs, etiquette, and so on, then two sources can be recommended:

Parker Pen Co., 1985, *Do's and Taboos Around the World* (Elmsford, NY: The Benjamin Co.).

Kennedy Center for International Studies, 1986, *Culturgrams* (Provo, UT: Brigham Young University). The culturgrams are four-page cultural orientations to some 90 countries around the world covering customs, manners, lifestyles, and other specialized information. They include maps, addresses of embassies, and national tourist offices.

While the two sources listed above cover the world, one source deals just with Europe.

N. L. Braganti & E. Devine, 1984, *The Travelers' Guide to European Customs and Manners* (New York: Meadowbrook, distributed by Simon and Schuster).

A witty book, giving insights into European manners and mores, and culture generally, is

L. Barzini, 1984, *The Europeans* (New York: Penguin Books).

A very amusing, irreverent guide to the subtle and not so subtle differences between Americans and the English is given in

J. Walmsley, 1987, *Brit-Think, Ameri-Think: A Transatlantic Survival Guide* (New York: Penguin Books).

Travel Magazines

The following is a list of the better known, widely available, travel magazines, listed alphabetically.

Business Traveller, monthly, published by Perry Publications, London, UK. Devoted to the interests of business travelers, with good feature articles on individual destinations, airports, and a regular cost of living index on 45 world cities.

Condé Nast Traveler, monthly, published by Condé Nast Publications, New York. An excellent upscale magazine with frequent features on exotic destinations, and a very good "Traveler's File" section.

Cruise Travel, bimonthly, published by World Publishing Co. Devoted to cruises, with port of the month, ship of the month, and cruise of the month feature articles. Again, lots of photos, but not a great deal of hard, useful information.

European Life and Leisure, bimonthly, published by Inabnit Publications. Upscale magazine for "the sophisticated American traveler" to Europe. Glossy articles on European royalty/celebrities, chateaus, mansions, and the "good life," plus features on individual regions, cities, shopping, hotels, and so on. Nice photographs.

Islands Magazine, bimonthly, published by Islands Publishing Co., Santa Barbara, CA. Glossy, color-photo-filled magazine devoted to islands. Good for background reading, but presents little useful, hard information.

National Geographic Traveler, quarterly, published by the National Geographic Society, has fine general articles with superb photos. The "Travel-Wise" sections that accompany each place-specific article are excellent, giving detailed information on how to get there, how to get around, things to see and do, nearby attractions, places to stay, and places to eat. Emphasis tends to be on the middle-income traveler.

Tours and Resorts, bimonthly, published by World Publishing Co. Emphasis on tours and resorts worldwide, with a tour-of-the-month feature. Lots of photos, not much in the way of useful, practical information.

Travel-Holiday, monthly, published by Travel Magazine, Inc., is a good general travel magazine with articles on places, regions, special interest features (shopping, time sharing, and bird watching, for example). Not as much detailed, specific information as given in *Travel and Leisure,* and *National Geographic Traveler,* however. The December issue has a comprehensive guide to fine dining in North America. Tends to aim at the middle-income traveler.

Travel and Leisure, monthly, published by American Express, is an excellent travel magazine, with insightful, detailed feature articles on individual places, destinations, and regions, along with articles on food/restaurants, hotels, travel trends, and special interest features. Emphasis is on the mid- to upper-income traveler.

Each major airline, of course, has its own inflight magazine, such as United's *United,* and American's *Ambassador,* which sometimes have good, interesting articles on individual destinations.

Geography Magazines
GEO Special, quarterly, published by Gruner and Jahr AG & Co., Hamburg. With each issue focusing on a particular geographic region (recent examples include the Himalayas and East Africa), this is a superb magazine providing some real in-depth reporting and a truly excellent "feel" for a place.

National Geographic, monthly, published by the National Geographic Society. Mixture of geographical articles (places, regions), with a historical, cultural, and socioeconomic content, plus "scientific" articles on such topics as "Glaciers on the Move," "California Deserts," etc. Excellent photos. Good for getting a feel for the place.

Special Interest Magazines With Useful Travel-Related Content
Almost every national magazine, and even many of the regional magazines, have either travel or travel-related sections as a regular or semi-regular feature, or have occasional travel articles with useful information. Even *Better Homes and Gardens* has occasional feature articles on the best buys in family vacation resorts. The magazines listed below are just an indication of the diversity and range of magazines available.

American West, bimonthly, published by American West Publishing Co. Devoted to the history and lore of the American West, but has occasional useful articles on fly fishing, river rafting, and so on, and a biannual travel calendar listing western festivals and events.

Americas, bimonthly, published by the Organization of American States. Devoted to the geography, history, and culture of the Americas. Has occasional travel sections— e.g., "Tourism off the Beaten Track" (Galapagos Islands, St. Lucia, Brazil's Sao Luis, Barbados's east coast, and Mexico's Sierra Madres).

Archaeology, bimonthly, published by the Archaeological Institute of America. Devoted to archaeological topics worldwide (books, new excavations, archaeological films, etc.), with an annual travel guide (March/April) to excavations in progress—where they are and how to get there.

Bon Appetit, monthly, published by Bon Appetit Publishing Co. An upscale food and entertainment magazine with a regular "Bon Voyage" section, and frequent articles on the cuisine and restaurants of a particular region of the world—e.g., Lower Mississippi, Bavaria, etc.

Changing Times, monthly, published by The Kiplinger Washington Editors, Inc. Essentially devoted to financial and consumer topics, it also has occasional travel-related articles, such as special reports on "different" vacations (yacht charters, archaeological digs, hideaways, cultural tours, wildlife projects).

Connoisseur, monthly, published by The Hearst Corp. Upscale high-fashion magazine with emphasis on the good things in life. Good travel related articles—e.g., shopping in Hong Kong, hotel dining, restaurants, etc.

Esquire, monthly, published by Esquire, Inc. Men's general/fashion magazine with occasional travel-related feature articles, and a regular spring guide to summer vacations, and fall guide to winter vacations.

Fortune, biweekly, published by Time Inc. Devoted to the business world and the economy, but has a useful, semi-regular "On the Road" section that features various city's nightclubs, restaurants, jazz radio-stations, and so on. The "On Your Own Time" section also occasionally has pertinent articles, e.g., on sailing schools.

Golf Digest, monthly, published by Golf Digest/Tennis, Inc. Devoted to golf instructional tips, pro tour information and golf records, along with such travel pertinent items as best new courses, places to play, and, in its February issue, an annual resort directory for vacationing golfers.

Gourmet, monthly, published by The Condé Nast Publications, Inc. Devoted to food, good cuisine, and the good life, with articles on food preparation, recipes, and restaurants, along with feature articles on the cuisine and restaurants of a particular region, city, or island.

Horse & Rider, monthly, published by Rich Publishing Co. Devoted to equestrian topics (training, breeding, health, equine events, etc.), but also has feature articles on horse-packing, an outfitters guide, and other travel pertinent topics.

In Britain, monthly, distributed in the U.S. by In Britain, Clifton, NJ. Devoted to travel in the United Kingdom. Excellent source of British destination information. Feature articles on individual towns, and regions, plus a fine "Forthcoming Events" calendar.

Money, monthly, published by Time, Inc. Devoted to financial topics, but occasionally has feature articles on good buys in travel—e.g., African Safaris, family resorts—or tax deductible adventures.

Outside, monthly, published by Mariah Publications, Co. Devoted to outdoor activities, with articles on mountaineering, kayaking, board-sailing, diving, cross-country skiing, etc. Has a useful nationwide expedition services directory of outfitters nationwide that provide access to these activities.

Sail, monthly, published by Sail Publications, Inc. Devoted to sailing (sailing tips, offshore voyaging, coastal cruising, design, new boats, etc.), it also has feature articles on cruising areas and a useful guide to bareboating fleets worldwide, including a list of brokers.

Ski, monthly September-April, published by Times Mirror Magazine, Inc. Devoted to skiing, with feature articles on where to ski, ski equipment, skiing tips, and so on.

Skiing, monthly Sept.–March, published by CBS Magazines, Los Angeles, CA. Devoted to skiing, with feature articles on skiing tips, instruction, equipment, resorts, the skiing scene, racing, cross-country skiing, places to ski, and so on. Also publishes a *Skier's Directory* in the fall, which is an excellent guide to over 400 ski areas in the U.S.

Skin Diver, monthly, published by Petersen Publishing Co. Feature articles on photography, dive boats, dive equipment, and so on, but also articles on foreign travel (Diving News from Down Under, Dive Bonair, etc.), and on local (U.S.) diving—e.g., the Florida Keys Dive Guide. Also has a useful worldwide diver's directory.

Smithsonian, monthly, published by the Smithsonian Associates. Magazine of the Smithsonian Institution, with diverse articles on all aspects of life, science, and nature. Many have relevance to travel, dealing with destinations. They tend to be of a general nature, however, with few hard facts. Good for background pieces—e.g., New York's garment district, Australia's outback, etc.

Sports Afield, monthly, published by The Hearst Corp. Devoted to angling, shooting, nature, camping, sport vehicles, hunting, and so on, it also has frequent feature articles on dude fishing ranches (April, 1985) and other travel-related topics.

Tennis, monthly, published by Golf Digest/Tennis, Inc. Devoted to tennis topics (playing tips, equipment, world tennis player rankings, tennis tours, etc.), it also has feature articles on new tennis resorts, and has a "Places to Play" guide to some 300 resorts in the U.S. and abroad.

Town & Country, monthly, published by The Hearst Corp. Upscale fashion magazine devoted to the good life, with regular features on fashion, health and beauty, architecture and design, and regular travel feature articles—e.g., "Best Bistros of Paris," "Royal Shopping," "The Spell of an Island Called Sicily," etc.

Yachting, monthly, published by Yachting, Inc. Devoted to sailing (cruising, racing, equipment, new boats, chartering tips, etc.), it also has a useful annual international chartering guide.

Travel Newsletters

A note of caution is warranted here, and that is that while *all* publications come and go, editorial policies may change, and editors leave, the newsletter business is notorious for the number of new entrants and its high mortality rate. All of the following newsletters existed at the time of writing, however.

The Business Flyer, Holcon, 21 Pleasant St., Newton Center, MA 02159; (617)782-9095; (800)343-0664. 8 pp., published monthly. Devoted to topics of interest to the frequent business flyer. Up-to-date information on bonuses for frequent fliers and frequent guests of hotels.

Consumer Reports Travel Letter, Consumer Union, 256 Washington St., Mount Vernon, NY 10553; (800)525-0643. Excellent, unbiased newsletter on all manner of travel and travel-related topics. Published monthly.

The Diabetic Traveler, PO Box 8223, Stamford, CT 06905. Devoted to issues concerning the diabetic traveler.

Directions, Travel Information Center, Cox Road, Woodstock, VT 05091. Travel tips for travelers in the eastern United States. No details on frequency of publication available.

Family Travel News, 109 Columbia Ave., Hartsdale, NY 10530. Devoted to family travel, "to make family trips more economical, educational, and enjoyable." Published six times a year.

Hideway Report, Harper Associates, Drawer 300, Fairfax Station, VA 22039. "A connoisseur's guide to peaceful and unspoiled places," it covers unusual and expensive accomodations around the world. Published monthly.

Island Properties Report, Box 58, Woodstock, VT 05091. Devoted to Caribbean real estate and business investments, as well as reports on current political and social conditions and economic development opportunities in the Caribbean. Published eight times a year.

The Itinerary, PO Box 1084, Bayonne, NJ 07002; (201)858-3400. Published six times a year. Tours of Europe for the disabled.

Inn Review, 105 East Court St., Kankakee, IL 60901; (815)939-3509. 8 pp., published 10 times a year. Personal reviews of country inns, small hotels, B & B's, etc.

International Railway Traveler, Box 35067-A, Louisville, KY 40232. Devoted to train travelers and train buffs.

International Travel News, PO Box 271309, Escondido, CA 92027; (619)487-3213. 60 pp., published monthly. Provides up-to-date news and reference material about the world of travel. Relies heavily on information, feedback from readership.

LTD Travel, 116 Harbor Seal Court, San Mateo, CA 94404; (415)573-7998. Published quarterly. Tips and general information for disabled travelers.

The Mature Traveler, Box 141, Pittman, NJ 08071. Devoted to travel tips for older Americans. Travel warnings, travel tips, travel bargains, and so on. Published monthly.

Off Beat, 1250 Vallejo St., San Francisco, CA 94109. Tips on where to go and where not to go. Quarterly.

Partners-In-Travel, Box 491145, Los Angeles, CA 90049, bimonthly. A highly abridged precis of the latest travel news gleaned from the Sunday travel sections of 24 major newspapers and major magazines.

The Privileged Traveler, 42 Usonia Rd., Pleasantville, NY 10570; (914)769-3883. 12 pp., published bimonthly. Provides "privileged information" about travel discoveries—e.g., shopping services in Hong Kong.

Tour de France, 931 Les Glaciers, 73210 La Plagne, France 79-09-08-18. 12 pp, published monthly. Devoted to travel in France.

Travel China Newsletter, 570 Windermere Ave., Toronto, Ont., Canada M6S 3L8, quarterly. Devoted to travel in China.

Travel Smart for Business, Communications House, Inc., Dobbs Ferry, NY; (914)693-8300. Travel consumer news, worldwide (cheap car rental services, airline discounts, tipping traditions, etc.). Published monthly.

Travel With Your Children (TWYCH), 80 8th Avenue, New York, NY 10011; (212)206-0688. Devoted to tips for, and issues surrounding, traveling with children.

Travel Woman Newsletter, Box 49520, Chicago, IL 60649. Devoted to travel tips for "pink-collar women" (teachers, nurses, secretaries, social workers) and housewives on a budget. Published monthly.

Unique & Exotic Travel Reporter, Box 98833, Tacoma, WA 98499. Devoted to tips on out-of-the-ordinary, unusual travel (jungle and mountain treks, Viennese opera trips, etc.).

World Status Map, Box 2533, Fairfax, VA 22031. Monthly updates on State Department travel advisories and warnings and other pertinent reports from around the globe. Plus visa requirements, inoculations, and length of stay details/restrictions. Published monthly.

Travel Videos

Among the latest entries into the travel information field are travel videos. These range in quality from slick professional productions imparting useful information in the form of a visual guide that can give you a real feel for an area to amateurish productions that are nothing better than a series of poor picture postcards.

Some are really nothing more than video ads for hotels and airlines, or self-congratulatory, chamber of commerce–produced ads for locals. Others are independently produced and quite good, for example: *International Video Network, Laura McKenzie's Travel Tips,* and *Travelvision International.*

Some companies that produce travel videos are

Gessler, 900 Broadway, New York, NY 10003; (212)673-3113.

International Adventure Video, 400 Webster, Suite 140, Palo Alto, CA 94301; (415)321-9943.

International Video Network, 3744 Mt. Diablo Blvd., Suite 102, Lafayette, CA 94549; (800)443-0100.

Journey to Adventure with Gunther Less, 430 W. 54th St., New York, NY 10019; (212)489-8130; (800)457-0056.

Kodak Video Exchange Club, 175 Humboldt St., Rochester, NY (800)237-8400, ext. 250.

Laura McKenzie's Travel Tips, 12636 Beatrice St., PO Box 66930, Los Angeles, CA 90066; (213)306-4040.

Shilo Productions, 14755 Ventura Blvd., Suite 1604, Sherman Oaks, CA 91403 (818)784-1146.

Travel Images, PO Box 1980, Laramie, WY 82070; (800)423-2820.

Travel Video Corp., 3320 E. Shea Blvd., Phoenix, AZ 85028 (800)826-5557; (602)996-5222.

Travelvision International, 5630 Beverly Hill, Houston, TX 77057; (713)975-7077; (800)325-3108.

World of Cruise Ships, 2611 Garden Rd., Monterey, CA 93940; (408)375-4474.

Cassettes: Tours on Tape

Although self-guided audiotape cassettes for museums, national parks, and national monuments or historic districts have been available for some time, their number and quality have increased. Firms prominent in the business and covering more than a single destination/area, include:

Comprehensive Communications, Inc. (Auto Tape Tours), Box 385, Scarsdale, NY 10583; (914)472-5133.

Travelcassettes Artours, Box 982, New Haven, CT 06504; (203)785-8687.

Tours by Tape, 6 E. 46th Street, New York, NY 10017; (212)986-5894.

Warner Audio Publishing, Box 718, New York, NY 10011; (800)528-6050.

Regional/City Magazines

Almost every large metropolitan area in the United States and Canada has its own regional magazine. These are gold mines of information on the current arts, entertainment, and restaurant scenes. Most have annual restaurant reviews, frequently with a compilation of the area's best restaurants, in the opinion of either the restaurant critic/food editor or readers.

In addition to the city/metropolitan area magazines, a number of good regional magazines offer the reader all kinds of travel information in addition to the usual fare. Among the best, are

California, monthly, published by California Magazine, Los Angeles. Concentrates on California culture, history, books, lively arts, movies, restaurants, places, and so on.

Ohio, monthly, published by Ohio Magazine, Columbus, OH. Devoted to Ohio's history, industry, arts and entertainment, restaurants, places, and so on.

Sunset: The Magazine of Western Living, monthly, published by Lane Publishing Co. Although principally devoted to building and crafts, food and entertaining, and gardening and landscaping, it is also an excellent source of travel information on the western United States, including Alaska and Hawaii. For example, a recent issue had feature articles on putting, riding, biking, and swimming in Palm Springs, hiking in Hawaii, and kayaking in Baja. It also had an interesting article on Sir John Soan's Architect's Museum in London, U.K.

Texas Monthly, monthly, published by Texas Monthly, Inc. Devoted to Texas politics, business, culture, and arts and entertainment. Very good monthly section on restaurants, theater, music, dance, sports, and nightlife in Texas cities.

Trade Publications

Tour & Travel News, biweekly, published by CMP Publications, Inc., Manhasset, NY. Concentrates on the leisure travel industry.

Travel Weekly, twice a week, published by Murdoch Magazines, New York, Covers all manner of topics pertinent to the travel industry (hotels, airlines, agencies, travel trends, travel personalities, new area attractions, etc.). Frequently has useful pull-out reference guides to particular regions, countries, cities, and other destinations.

The Travel Agent, twice a week, published by Fairchild Publications, New York. Covers all kinds of topics relevant to the travel industry. Has good regional sales guides, published periodically.

Sunday Newspaper Travel Supplements

Many of the nation's newspapers have good travel sections or supplements, providing the reader with useful, hard information, in addition to the normal "chatty" travel articles that may get you inspired to travel, but don't offer anything in the way of tangible, useful information. Among the better ones are the following newspapers, which have worthwhile travel sections/supplements in their Sunday editions: *Atlanta Journal & Con-*

stitution; Baltimore Sun, Boston Globe; Cleveland Plain Dealer; Denver Post, Chicago Tribune; Houston Post; Los Angeles Times; Miami Herald; New York Times; Philadelphia Inquirer; St. Louis Post-Dispatch; San Francisco Examiner; and the *Washington Post.*

By far the best is the *New York Times* with its regular "Shopper's World," "What's Doing In," "Travel Advisory," "Practical Traveler," and "Q/A" sections. Also good is the *Los Angeles Times,* with its "Jerry Hulse's Travel Tips," "Tours and Cruises," and "Savvy Traveler" sections.

Partners-In-Travel (Box 491145, Los Angeles, CA 90049), a bimonthly newsletter, gives highly abridged precis of the latest travel news scanned from Sunday Travel sections and major magazines.

The *Society of American Travel Writers* (1120 Connecticut Ave., NW, Suite 940, Washington, DC 20036; (202)785-5567), whose stated purpose is to serve the traveling public (readers, viewers, and listeners) with complete, accurate, and interesting information on travel destinations, facilities, and services, publishes an annual membership directory listing active members and their affiliations.

Index